T0331198

MACHINE LEARNING EVALUATION

As machine learning gains widespread adoption and integration in a variety of applications, including safety and mission-critical systems, the need for robust evaluation methods grows more urgent. This book compiles scattered information on the topic from research papers and blogs to provide a centralized resource that is accessible to students, practitioners, and researchers across the sciences. The book examines meaningful metrics for diverse types of learning paradigms and applications, unbiased estimation methods, rigorous statistical analysis, fair training sets, and meaningful explainability, all of which are essential for building robust and reliable machine learning products. In addition to standard classification, the book discusses unsupervised learning, regression, image segmentation, and anomaly detection. It also covers topics such as industry-strength evaluation, fairness, and responsible AI. Implementations using Python and scikit-learn are available on the book's website.

NATHALIE JAPKOWICZ is Professor and Chair of the Department of Computer Science at American University, Washington, DC. She previously taught at the University of Ottawa. Her current research focuses on lifelong anomaly detection and hate speech detection. She has also researched one-class learning and the class imbalance problem extensively. She has received numerous awards, including Test of Time and Distinguished Service awards.

ZOIS BOUKOUVALAS is Assistant Professor in the Department of Mathematics and Statistics at American University, Washington, DC. His research focuses on the development of interpretable multimodal machine learning algorithms, and he has been the lead principal investigator of several research grants. Through his research and teaching activities, he is creating environments that encourage and support the success of underrepresented students for entry into machine learning careers.

MACHINE LEARNING EVALUATION

Towards Reliable and Responsible AI

NATHALIE JAPKOWICZ
American University, Washington, DC

ZOIS BOUKOUVALAS
American University, Washington, DC

CAMBRIDGE
UNIVERSITY PRESS

Shaftesbury Road, Cambridge CB2 8EA, United Kingdom

One Liberty Plaza, 20th Floor, New York, NY 10006, USA

477 Williamstown Road, Port Melbourne, VIC 3207, Australia

314–321, 3rd Floor, Plot 3, Splendor Forum, Jasola District Centre, New Delhi – 110025, India

103 Penang Road, #05-06/07, Visioncrest Commercial, Singapore 238467

Cambridge University Press is part of Cambridge University Press & Assessment, a department of the University of Cambridge.

We share the University's mission to contribute to society through the pursuit of education, learning and research at the highest international levels of excellence.

www.cambridge.org
Information on this title: www.cambridge.org/9781316518861

DOI: 10.1017/9781009003872

When citing this work, please include a reference to the DOI 10.1017/9781009003872

First published 2025

A catalogue record for this publication is available from the British Library

A Cataloging-in-Publication data record for this book is available from the Library of Congress

ISBN 978-1-316-51886-1 Hardback

This book is dedicated to my mother, Suzanne. Maman, thank you encouragement and unshakable trust in my abilities. Although Nor about international history and politics are more approachable than m that you will, nonetheless, be happy to see it in print!

— Nathalie

To my beloved wife and colleague, Maria Barouti, and my dear Panagiotis Boukouvalas and Niki Iliopoulou. Each of you has played role in shaping my journey, and I dedicate this book to you as a toke and appreciation!

— Zois

Contents

Part II   Evaluation for Classification

Part III   Evaluation for Other Settings

Abbreviations

10-fold CV	10-fold cross-validation
5×2 CV test	5×2 cross-validation test
5-fold CV	5-fold cross-validation
AI	artificial intelligence
AIC	Akaike information criterion
ANOVA	analysis of variance
AUC	area under the ROC curve
AUROC	area under the ROC curve
BERT	bidirectional encoder representations from transformers
BIC	Bayesian information criterion
BLEU	bilingual evaluation understudy
CD	critical difference
CDF	cumulative distribution function
CI	confidence interval
CNN	convolutional neural network
CV	cross-validation
DBI	Davis–Bouldin index
DBSCAN	density-based spatial clustering of applications with noise
DEA	data envelopment analysis
DET	detection error tradeoff
EM	excess mass criterion
EM algorithm	expectation maximization algorithm
EMR	exact match ratio
ERM	empirical risk minimization
FN	false negative
FP	false positive
FPR	false positive rate
FWER	family wise error rate

GAN	generative adversarial networks
HDI	high density interval
HL	Hamming loss
HS	Hamming score
i.i.d.	independently and identically distributed
ICA	independent component analysis
k-fold CV	k-fold cross-validation
LC	loss comparison
LDA	linear discriminant analysis
LIME	local interpretable model-agnostic explanation
LOO	leave-one-out
MAE	mean absolute error
MAP	maximum a posteriori
MCMC	Markov chain Monte Carlo
MDS	multi-Dimensional scaling
MSE	mean squared error
MV	mass volume criterion
NEC	normalized expected cost
NHST	null hypothesis significance testing
NLP	natural language processing
NMF	nonnegative matrix factorization
NPV	negative predictive value
PCA	principal component analysis
PDD	partial dependence plots
PDF	probability density function
Pdf	probability distribution function
PPCA	probabilistic principal component analysis
PPV	positive predictive value
PU	positive-unlabeled
RBF	radial basis function
RMSE	root mean squared error
ROC	receiver operating characteristic
ROPE	region of practical equivalence
ROUGE	recall-oriented understudy for gisting evaluation
SCAR	selected completely at random
SCM	set covering machine
SHAP	Shapley additive explanations
SIM	simple and intuitive measure
SOM	self-organizing maps
SRM	structural risk minimization

SSE	sum of squares error
SST	sum of squares totals
SVM	support vector machine
TN	true negative
TP	true positive
TPR	true positive rate
t-SNE	t-distributed stochastic neighbor embedding
VAE	variational autoencoders
XAI	explainable AI
XGBoost	extreme gradient boosting
XML	explainable machine learning

Preface

This book was born a few months after the beginning of the pandemic, at 9:45pm on June 2, 2020, to be exact, when Zois responded positively by email to Nathalie's invitation to participate in its creation. Nathalie had believed, for several years by then, that her 2011 book on evaluation, coauthored with Mohak Shah, was not capturing enough of the new developments in machine learning, and she was interested in reviving the project. Mohak's industry career, characterized by many moves and increasing sets of responsibilities, had made it impossible for Mohak to commit to the project. Nathalie's move from the University of Ottawa to American University, along with a new role as department chair, had made it difficult for Nathalie to envision working on a project as demanding as a new book without a partner. Nevertheless, with the popularization of machine learning through advances in deep learning and the creation of the data science discipline, it became clear that writing a comprehensive book on machine learning evaluation was becoming an urgent matter. Zois' positive email reply was the long-awaited catalyst! Being forced to stay home because of the pandemic reinforced our decision, and armed with a contract from Cambridge University Press, we set out to work. It took time – a lot longer than expected – but, despite new courses to teach and new administrative tasks to attend to, we made it happen and are pleased with the result!

Fear might have been an important motivator for this book. As more and more products embedding machine learning components are hitting the market, and as their applications are increasing in impact, we believe that it is urgent to inform society of ways to make these products safe and reliable. We view it as crucial for everyone involved in the design, application, and release of machine learning products to understand how to conduct machine learning evaluation, and maybe more importantly, to be aware of its uncertainty and the risks it comes with. If products like self-driving cars and automated hiring systems are to be deployed, everyone involved in the process, even the consumer, should know about the risks associated with their use.

The book plays a number of important roles. Foremost, it is meant to educate machine learning practitioners about the need for a thorough evaluation and the fact that evaluation is intimately linked to the application at hand. There are many evaluation tools appropriate for different applications, and each focuses on the specific goals the application is trying to achieve. Is the goal to diagnose patients as accurately as possible, like in a medical screening device? Is it to balance resources and needs in the fairest possible way, like in a public health program? Is it to minimize financial risk to make a business viable? Whatever the purpose of the evaluation, a particular set of techniques will be most appropriate to handle it, and the central purpose of the book is to expose the reader to these different tools so that, when the time comes, he or she will be able to select those most appropriate for the purpose of the application.

The second goal of the book is to sensitize the reader to the fact that neither machine learning nor its evaluation should be approached with certainty. Machine learning can produce unexpected results and evaluation, while able to roughly assess the worth of a machine learning-based system, can miss some very important limitations of that system. Nevertheless, neither the learning algorithms nor their evaluation are the results of random calculations, and by considering the fascinating mechanisms used by both learning algorithms and evaluation mechanisms, we hope to give readers the tools necessary to either build sufficient trust in an algorithm or know when to reject one as not being reliable enough for deployment.

On the practical side, the third goal of the book is to provide tools that make the implementation of the evaluation process easier. Some of these tools already exist, and in such cases, we point the reader to them and illustrate their uses. Others are homemade and, likewise, shared at https://github.com/zoisboukouvalas/MachineLearningEvaluation_TowardsReliableResponsibleAI.

Finally, the fourth role filled by our book concerns the future. This is the beginning of machine learning deployment. The evaluation of machine learning systems is bound to evolve and improve as more and more approaches get deployed. For the time being, the certainty with which evaluation tools are assessed depends on statistical principles rather than customer reactions to deployed products. We hope that with our book as a basis, future machine learning evaluators will be ready to move to the next level of evaluation to integrate other considerations such as safety, ethics, and legality.

Acknowledgments

There are many people who made the writing of this book possible and to whom we are immensely grateful. First and foremost, we would like to thank Mohak Shah for generously allowing us to reuse some of the content he provided in the 2011 book. Mohak also took time out of his busy schedule to give us advice on the organization of various chapters and of the overall book. His discerning eye and swift analytical skills led to an improved framing of our discussion and to the correction or clarification of certain passages. We are very honored to have had him be the first reader of the complete draft. We would also like to thank all our colleagues and students for their support during this undertaking and the valuable discussions we held with them. They include Michael Baron, Colin Bellinger, Paula Branco, Nicolas Cloutier, Roberto Corizzo, Evan Crothers, Kamil Faber, Kushankur Ghosh, William Klement, Bartek Krawczyk, Zhen Liu, Caitlin Moroney, Sunday Okechukwu, Sabrina Ripsman, Myles Russell, Liam Spoletini, Herna Viktor, and Bei Xiao.

Roberto Corizzo and Colin Bellinger helped us think through the best evaluation practices for the many problems we collaborated on. Both, with their deep understanding of the field, attention to detail, and creativity, guided us in refining our thoughts on specific aspects of evaluation. Evan Crothers helped us truly understand the ethical issues that creep into most methodological decisions as well as the societal dangers of the methods we deploy. Liam Spoletini and Sunday Okechukwu are owed a huge thank you for all the effort they put into the creation of the GitHub site that accompanies the book. Without it, the book would not be as useful. Nicolas Cloutier, a high-school intern, impressed us greatly and deserves a big thank you as well for unearthing the Cochran Q test for use in the multi-classifier single-domain case, a situation that had eluded us for many years! We also thank Herna Viktor, Roberto Corizzo, Kamil Faber, and Sabrina Ripsman for suggesting the addition of material that enhanced the quality of the book.

Many thanks to our editor at Cambridge University Press, Lauren Cowles, for her encouragements throughout the project and her excellent advice. We would also like to thank Arman Chowdhury, our editorial assistant, Clare Dennison, our senior content manager, and Jasintha Jacob Srinivasan, our project manager. We are extremely grateful, as well, to Eleanor Bolton, our copyeditor, for her careful reading of our manuscript.

Nathalie would also like to thank her family for putting up with her throughout the writing of the book. This often translated into last-minute meals hastily put together (and usually cooked in the microwave), less-than-ideal orderliness in the house, and little attention to homework or other matters. I will try to amend for my failings during the writing of the book (unless I just dive into another project and keep this up for another few years!). Thank you to my husband, Norrin, for his constant encouragement and advice; juggling the chairing of our respective departments at the same time and throughout the pandemic, along with managing our academic, family, and other pursuits has been an interesting proposition! I couldn't have done it without his love and support! Thank you to Shira, now a fellow scientist and great sounding board, and to Dafna for patiently enduring my obsession with computer work; as everybody knows, you are a great kid! Thank you as well to my mother, Suzanne, in Paris, who is always excited to hear about my projects. I am sorry that my father, Michel, who passed away 15 years ago, could not enjoy this moment. I am also sorry that my father-in-law, Michael, who passed away during the writing of the book, is not with us today as we would have enjoyed discussing its content together. Thank you to my mother-in-law, Toba, for her constant care and support.

Zois would like to express his heartfelt gratitude to his wife, Maria Barouti, who is not only a dedicated researcher but also a passionate machine learning educator. Throughout numerous hours of discussion and collaboration, she has generously shared her expertise, insights, and enthusiasm for the field of machine learning. Her guidance has been invaluable in helping me understand what is important in machine learning and how it should be presented to better benefit newcomers to this field. Maria, your visionary outlook for academia's future has given it a profound sense of relevance and purpose. Your commitment to educating others and empowering them with the knowledge that will shape the future of machine learning advancements leaves me in awe. Lastly, I would like to extend my deepest thanks to my beloved parents, Panagiotis and Niki, who have been my unwavering guiding stars, illuminating my path through every challenge and triumph. Your boundless love, selfless sacrifices, and unwavering encouragement have played a pivotal role in shaping the person I am today. I am forever indebted to the values and principles you instilled in me, forming the very foundation of my character.

Part I

Preliminary Considerations

1
Introduction

Recent advances in deep learning have spearheaded impressive automated capabilities in visual and natural language processing and resulted in machine learning becoming a very popular discipline. While a decade or so ago only a handful of individuals – well read in matters of artificial intelligence (AI) and machine learning – perceived the inherent contributions that machine learning could bring to their field of expertise, today many people believe that machine learning will solve all of their problems: for better or for worse, machine learning has become ubiquitous. In such a climate, evaluating machine learning's performance is of paramount importance, especially when large-scale deployments of tools based on its foundations are under consideration.

Performance evaluation in machine learning and, more generally, artificial intelligence has always been an important aspect of the field. Back in 1950, Turing famously designed a test he called the "imitation game," now known as the "Turing test," to evaluate the "intelligence" of the machine. In truth, any computer system must be subjected to testing and evaluation, and the software engineering discipline, born in the mid to late 1980s, created strict guidelines on how to do so. The issue with AI and machine learning, however, is that their testing and evaluation are not easy feats. While in traditional computer systems the range of outcomes is narrow and often quantifiable, in AI and machine learning, it is neither. The goal here is to get the machine to behave "intelligently." Yet, what is intelligence? First, not every human being behaves the same way, and second, humans must function in unpredictable settings. These and many other considerations are what make the evaluation of AI and machine learning systems ill-defined. In fact, with the release of ChatGPT in 2022, the debate is on, once again, as it probably was when ELIZA, one of the first computer programs able to converse in English with people, was released in the 1960s. Though the book does not go into the more philosophical side of the problem, one thing is clear: in order to mimic humans adequately, the computer program needs to be able to *generalize* to unknown situations, and, as a result, it has to include nondeterministic "behavior." It is this lack of determinism, or the system's *inductive* behavior, that makes testing in the context of machine learning so complex, and this is one aspect of the problem into which our book takes a deep dive.

Another aspect relates to the fact that machine learning is now mature enough to be embedded in products designed to hit the market. Its evaluation is thus leaving the realm of philosophical questioning and becoming a practical matter. This shift from an inconsequential practice necessary to publish research papers, but not robust enough to truly assess the practical value of the resulting product, is a crucial one. Another essential function of this book is to bridge the gap between these two evaluation paradigms. It presents many different evaluation methods with the goal of covering the various situations that may arise when deploying a product: Is the product competitive? Robust? Safe? Fair? What is its expected benefit–cost ratio? While we cannot envision all the situations that could arise, the book gives the readers many tools that will allow them to determine what evaluation practice will serve their specific situation best. This is particularly transparent in the case of evaluation metrics discussed in Chapters 4, 5, 8, and 9, where different applications (e.g., medical, information retrieval, security) and learning paradigms (e.g., supervised, anomaly detection, time-series analysis, unsupervised) call for different types of measurements with overlaps occasionally occurring.

1.1 Motivation for This Book

The deep learning revolution is what motivated us most to write this book. Until deep learning started bearing fruit a few years ago, the technology was not mature enough to be considered for widespread use in sensitive applications such as self-driving cars, automatic screening of job applicants, and so on. As a result, we reasoned, the evaluation methods previously considered may not be robust enough for the types of applications machine learning is now encountering. This is not to say that machine learning tools were not evaluated and used in practical applications before, but instead, it is to emphasize that their uses are becoming more widespread now, and their domains of application more and more sensitive. This, we feel, requires further scrutiny. Moreover, while machine learning evaluation was a topic of conversation in the research community and within a circle of practitioners tightly linked to that research community, at this point, the need to understand how to evaluate machine learning algorithms adequately has spread to a much larger audience. It encompasses many scientific circles beyond the traditional machine learning community (e.g., chemists, biologists, physicists, environmental scientists, medical researchers), the business community with its various sectors, and even social studies and the arts.

The purpose of this book is to present a concise, yet complete, intuitive, yet formal, presentation of machine learning evaluation. The book has a predecessor, cowritten by one of the current coauthors, but although the new book builds upon the old one, it departs radically from it by increasing its coverage, updating its suggested methodologies, and, generally speaking, proposing a more robust approach. Not insignificantly, the new book also expands the reach of the discussion to the broader community.

An additional motivation for this book, which also ties together the reasons previously mentioned, is that although the situation has improved, evaluation of machine learning algorithms is often seen as an annoying and non-rewarding task. After all, creating new algorithms is a lot more exciting than testing them! More often than not, researchers or practitioners feel that they *need* to perform the task of evaluation to satisfy crusty conference or journal reviewers or bosses, but that the task is well below their skill levels. The view in this book, actually, is that, first, the evaluation of machine learning algorithms is a fascinating field of study in and of itself, and, second, the result of this evaluation has become of extreme practical importance now that the world embraces machine learning and embeds it in its products.

Indeed, the field has, at last, matured to the point where the safety of the technology must be considered in ways similar to the way in which the safety of other technological or medical advances have had to be assessed for many years. While such evaluation might have been seen as overkill, and perhaps rightly so, in the earlier years of machine learning, now that self-driving cars use the technology as well as medical diagnostic or hiring systems, the issue cannot be ignored any longer, and approaches similar to phased medical trials or other industrial-strength evaluation need to be put in place. In fact, the time might have come for teams of evaluators, independent from the developers, to test AI products. Perhaps, even, the equivalent of the CDC or FDA for AI needs to be put in place to approve or prevent AI-based products from reaching the market in order to protect the consumer from physical or psychological harm and ensure the fairness of the product.[1] The purpose of this book is to lay out the various tools available to conduct a rigorous performance evaluation for a variety of machine learning paradigms including those used in supervised learning, unsupervised learning, image processing applications, large language models, and so on. The tools presented should also help evaluate different aspects of practical uses that may differ from one area of application to the next. To make the task of evaluation easier, the book refers the reader to existing evaluation tools, or provides new ones, where they are lacking, on what is currently the most prevalent machine learning development platform, scikit-learn.

There are a variety of reasons why we believe that the time has come to write this book. As mentioned previously, in the 13 years since the publication of its predecessor, there has been an explosion of people using machine learning tools, and trying to make sense of how to evaluate their performance. This new audience is not as homogenous as it was 13 years ago since, in addition to computer scientists, it includes many statisticians, data scientists, and practitioners of various disciplines ranging from the core sciences to the social sciences, including the medical sciences, education, journalism, and even arts disciplines such as literature, visual arts, and music.

In addition to the explosion and diversity of new users, there has also been a data explosion, bringing into focus different types of data (e.g., images, text), much larger amounts (sometimes in the order of terabytes), and a true desire to leverage the data toward robust industrial products. This last change makes the issue of evaluation essential and raises questions that were not considered with the same urgency in the past, such as privacy, bias, and explainability matters, as well as domain and task-dependent considerations. These, along with the model's correctness, need to be properly assessed before a product can be deployed or commercialized. By the same token, new machine learning tasks have emerged or, at least, become more prevalent. This includes computer vision tasks such as image

---

[1] A practical advantage of this suggestion, by the way, would be to free developers from having to perform as rigorous an evaluation of their ideas since these could be pitted professionally at a later stage. More to the point, however, such a division of labor would lead to a less biased evaluation process since the evaluators would have no stake in the products they are testing.

segmentation, unsupervised learning, and data stream analysis. Each of these new tasks requires new analysis tools.

In summary, the different types of data and their amounts, the new tasks that have emerged, as well as the stricter evaluation imperatives that are – or should be – in effect, may, in certain cases, require the use of evaluation tools different from those discussed previously, and ready access to these tools is imperative.

1.2 Contents and Organization of the Book

Machine learning evaluation typically refers to the evaluation of classification. The scope of this book extends beyond the task of classification, although classification remains a predominant aspect of machine learning and is covered thoroughly.

The presentation of the book is designed to appeal to both machine learning researchers and practitioners. Specifically, we provide both an informal discussion and access to simple-to-use tools with clear guidelines on when to use them (when possible), as well as more formal, theoretical explanations to support some of these practical considerations. To reflect the current trend in the field, all of the code provided is written in Python and uses the scikit-learn package (though some of the tools exist, in a previous version, in R).

The book is organized into four parts. Part I reviews essential statistical and machine learning concepts that are needed to provide context for the remainder of the book. This includes random variables, distributions, confidence intervals, and hypothesis testing on the statistical side; as well as the concepts of loss function, risk, empirical and structural risk minimization, regularization, the bias–variance tradeoff, clustering, dimensionality reduction, latent variable modeling, and generative learning on the machine learning side. In addition, Part I presents the de facto way in which machine learning evaluation is conducted, reviewing, along the way, well-known concepts such as the confusion matrix, micro- and macro- averaging, as well as well-known classification, regression, and clustering metrics; error estimation methods such as the holdout and k-fold cross-validation, and basic statistical tests such as the t-test and the sign test. Many of the evaluation methods covered in this part are well known to most practitioners of machine learning. In addition to reviewing them, we explain why they are, oftentimes, not sufficient. This prompts a discussion of why it is necessary to go beyond the material covered in the first part of the book, thus motivating the need for its further three parts.

Part II discusses machine learning evaluation in the important classification setting. In particular, it discusses the metrics that have been proposed for that setting, paying particular attention to the issues of class imbalances, costs, uncertainty, and calibration; the error-estimation/resampling approaches that have been proposed and their relationship to the bias and variance of the error estimates; and the different approaches to statistical analysis, including null hypothesis statistical testing, confidence intervals, effect size, and power analysis, as well as newer Bayesian analysis approaches that have recently been proposed in the machine learning literature.

Part III then turns to machine learning tasks other than classification. Evaluation methods for many tasks are presented, including those for classical paradigms such as regression analysis, time-series analysis, outlier detection, and reinforcement learning, and also newer tasks such as positive-unlabeled classification, ordinal classification, multi-labeled classification, image segmentation, text generation, data stream mining, and lifelong learning. A full chapter is then devoted to the important unsupervised learning paradigm, and evaluation methods for tasks including clustering and hierarchical clustering, dimensionality reduction, latent variable models, and generative models are discussed.

Finally, Part IV turns to practical considerations related to evaluation and deployment. First, machine learning evaluation is presented in a software engineering light whose goal is to herald the future of machine learning's use in industrial applications. Topics include data, algorithms, and platform imperfections, online testing, along with a description of current industry practice, and suggestions for improvements. The next chapter turns to the question of how to practice machine learning in a responsible manner. In particular, it dives into the issues of data and algorithmic bias, fairness, explainability, privacy, and security among others, and advocates the need for human-centered machine learning.

The book concludes with a discussion of how the performance evaluation components discussed throughout the book unify into an overall framework for in-laboratory evaluation. This is followed by a discussion of how to move from a laboratory setting to a deployment setting based on the material covered in Part IV of the book. Associated with this deployment, we emphasize the potential social consequences of machine learning technology, together with their causes, and suggest that these potential social effects should be considered as part of the evaluation framework.

The book comes accompanied by the Github site https://github.com/zoisboukouvalas/ MachineLearningEvaluation_TowardsReliableResponsibleAI, which was written by American University graduate students Liam Spoletini and Sunday Okechukwu. The site provides Python code that illustrates how to implement the different evaluation methods discussed in the book. This, therefore, provides a quick way for machine learning designers and practitioners to apply evaluation techniques to their applications.

2

Statistics Overview

This chapter aims to introduce the basic elements of statistics necessary to understand the more advanced concepts and procedures that will be introduced in later chapters. Needless to say, rather than trying to be exhaustive, we will discuss the most relevant concepts. Furthermore, this overview will have more of a functional than an analytical bias, our goal being to encourage better practice in machine learning. In certain cases, this chapter will provide a brief introduction to a topic that will then be developed in more detail in later chapters.

The chapter is divided into four sections. In Section 2.1, we define the notion of random variables and their associated quantities. Section 2.2 then introduces the concept of probability distributions and discusses one of the extremely important results in statistics theory, the central limit theorem. Section 2.3 discusses the notion of confidence intervals. Finally, Section 2.4 briefly covers the basics behind hypothesis testing and discusses the concepts of type I and type II errors and the power of a test. If the reader is already acquainted with these concepts, they can confidently omit this chapter.

2.1 Random Variables

A random variable is a function that associates a unique numerical value with every outcome of an experiment. That is, a random variable can be seen as a measurable function that maps the points from a probability space to a measurable space. Here, by probability space we mean the space in which the actual experiments are done and the outcomes achieved. This need not be a measurable space, that is, the outcomes of an experiment need not be numeric. Consider the most standard example of a coin toss. The outcomes of a coin toss can be a "head" or a "tail." However, we often need to map such outcomes to numbers, that is, measurable space. Such a quantification allows us to study their behavior. We can precisely achieve this by using the notion of a random variable. Naturally, the range of values that a random variable can take would also depend on the nature of the experiment that it models. For a fixed set of outcomes of an experiment, such as the coin toss, a random variable results in discrete values. Such a random number is known as a discrete random variable. By contrast, a continuous random variable can model experiments with infinite possible outcomes.

The probabilities of the values that a random variable can take are also modeled accordingly. For a random variable x, these probabilities are modeled using a probability distribution, denoted $P(x)$ when x is discrete and using a probability density function, denoted by $p(x)$, when x is continuous. As such, a probability distribution associates a probability with each of the possible values that a discrete random variable can take. It can thus be seen as a list of these probability values.

In the case of a continuous random variable, which can take an infinite number of values, we need a function that can yield the probability of the variable taking on values in a given interval. That is, we need an integrable function. The PDF fulfills these requirements.

In order to look at this closely, we first take a look at the cumulative distribution function (CDF). With every random variable, there is an associated CDF that provides the probability of the variable taking a value less than or equal to a value x_i for every x_i. That is, the CDF $p_{cdf}(x)$ is

$$p_{cdf}(x) = P(x \le x_i), x \in \mathbb{R}.$$

Given a CDF, we can define the PDF $p(\cdot)$ associated with a continuous random variable x. The PDF $p(x)$ is the derivative of the CDF with respect to x:

$$p(x) = \frac{d}{dx} p_{cdf}(x).$$

If x_a and x_b are two of the possible values of x, then it follows that

$$\int_{x_a}^{x_b} p(x)dx = p_{cdf}(x_b) - p_{cdf}(x_a) = P(x_a < x < x_b),$$

where $\int(\cdot)$ denotes the integral operator. Hence, $p(x)$ can be a PDF of x if and only if for all $x \in \mathbb{R}$,

$$\int_{-\infty}^{\infty} p(x)dx = 1$$

and

$$p(x) > 0, x \in \mathbb{R}.$$

The expected value of a random variable x denotes its central value and is generally used as a summary value of the distribution of the random variable. The expected value generally denotes the average value of the random variable. For a discrete random variable x taking m possible values $x_i, i \in \{1, \ldots, m\}$, the expected value can be obtained as

$$\mathbf{E}[x] = \sum_{i=1}^{m} x_i P(x_i),$$

where $P(\cdot)$ denotes the probability distribution with $P(x_i)$ denoting the probability of x taking on the value x_i. Similarly, in the case when x is a continuous random variable with $p(x)$ as the associated PDF, the expected value is obtained as

$$\mathbf{E}[x] = \int_{-\infty}^{\infty} x p(x)dx.$$

In most practical scenarios, however, the associated probability distributions or PDFs are unknown. What is available is a set of values that the random variables take. In such cases

we can consider, when the size of this set is acceptably large, this sample as representative of
the true distribution. Under this assumption, the sample mean can then be used to estimate
the expected value of the random variable. Hence, if S_x is the set of values taken by the
variable x then the sample mean can be calculated as

$$\bar{x} = \frac{1}{|S_x|} \sum_{i=1}^{|S_x|} x_i,$$

where $|S_x|$ denotes the size of the set S_x.

The expected value of a random variable summarizes its central value. However, it does
not provide any indication about the distribution of the underlying variable by itself. That is,
two random variables with the same expected value can have entirely different underlying
distributions. A better sense of a distribution can be obtained by considering the statistics
of variance in conjunction with the expected value of the variable.

The variance is a measure of the spread of the values of the random variable around its
central value. More precisely, the variance of a random variable (probability distribution
or sample) measures the degree of the statistical dispersion (the spread of values). The
variance of a random variable is always nonnegative. Hence, the larger the variance, the
more scattered the values of the random variable with respect to its central value. The
variance of a random variable x is calculated as

$$\text{Var}(x) = \sigma^2(x) = \mathbf{E}[x - \mathbf{E}[x]]^2 = \mathbf{E}[x^2] - \mathbf{E}[x]^2.$$

In the continuous case, this means that

$$\sigma_2(x) = \int_{-\infty}^{\infty} (x - \mathbf{E}[x])^2 p(x) dx,$$

where $\mathbf{E}[x]$ denotes the expected value of the continuous random variable x and $p(x)$
denotes the associated PDF. Similarly, for the discrete case,

$$\sigma^2(x) = \sum_{i=1}^{m} P(x_i)(x_i - \mathbf{E}[x])^2,$$

where, as before, $P(\cdot)$ denotes the probability distribution associated with the discrete random variable x.

Given a sample of the values taken by x, we can calculate the sample variance by replacing the expected value of x by the sample mean:

$$\text{Var}_S(x) = \sigma_S^2 = \frac{1}{|S_x| - 1} \sum_{i=1}^{|S_x|} (x_i - \bar{x})^2.$$

Note that the denominator of the above equation is $|S_x| - 1$ instead of $|S_x|$.[1] The above
estimator is known as the unbiased estimator of the variance of a sample. For large $|S_x|$,
the difference between $|S_x|$ and $|S_x| - 1$ is rendered insignificant. The advantage of using

---

[1] This is known as Bessel's correction.

$|S_x| - 1$ is that in this case it can be shown that the expected value of the variance $\mathbf{E}[\sigma^2]$ is equal to the true variance of the sampled random variable.

The variance of a random variable is an important statistical indicator of the dispersion of the data. However, the unit of the variance measurement is not the same as the mean, as is clear from above. In some scenarios, it can be more helpful if a statistic is available that is comparable to the expected value directly. The standard deviation of a random variable fills this gap. The standard deviation of a random variable is simply the square root of the variance. When estimated from a population or sample of values, it is known as the sample standard deviation. It is generally denoted by $\sigma(x)$. This also makes it clear that using $\sigma^2(x)$ for variance denotes that the unit of the measured variance is the square of the expected value statistic. We calculate $\sigma(x)$ as

$$\sigma(x) = \sqrt{\text{Var}(x)}.$$

Similarly, the sample standard deviation can be obtained by considering the square root of the sample variance. One point should be noted. Even when using an unbiased estimator of the *sample* variance (with $|S_x| - 1$ in the denominator instead of $|S_x|$), the resulting estimator is still *not* an unbiased estimator of the *sample* standard deviation.[2] Furthermore, it underestimates the true sample standard deviation. A biased estimator of the sample variance can also be used without significant deterioration. An unbiased estimator of the sample standard deviation is not known except when the variable obeys a normal distribution.

Another significant use of the standard deviation will be seen in terms of providing confidence to some statistical measurements. One of the main such uses involves the use of the standard deviation to provide confidence intervals, or margin of error, around a measurement (mean) from samples.

2.1.1 Performance Measures as Random Variables

The insights into the random variables and the related statistics we just presented are quite significant in evaluation. For instance, the performance measure of a classifier on any given dataset can be modeled as a random variable, and much of the subsequent analysis follows, enabling us to understand the behavior of the performance measure in both absolute terms and in terms relative to other performance measures or even the same performance measure across different learning settings. Various learning strategies have varying degrees of assumptions on the underlying distribution of the data. Given a classifier f resulting from applying a learning algorithm A to some training data S_{train}, we can test f on previously unseen examples from test data. Learning from inductive inference does make the underlying assumption, here, that the data for both the training and the test set comes from the same distribution. The examples are assumed to be sampled in an independently and identically distributed (i.i.d.) manner. The most general assumption that can be made is that the data (and possibly their labels) are assumed to be generated from some arbitrary

---

[2] This can be seen by applying Jensen's inequality to the standard deviation, which is a concave function unlike its square, the variance. We do not discuss these issues in detail since they are beyond the scope of this book.

underlying distribution. That is, we have no knowledge of this true distribution whatsoever. This is indeed a reasonable assumption as far as learning is concerned since the main aim is to be able to model (or approximate) this distribution (or the label generation process) as closely as possible. As a result, each example in the test set can be seen as being drawn independently from some arbitrary but fixed data distribution. The performance of the classifier applied to each example can be measured for the criterion of interest using corresponding performance measures. The criteria of interest can be, say, how accurately the classifier predicts the label of the example, or how much the model depicted by the classifier errs in modeling the example. As a result, we can, in principle, also model these performance measures as random variables, again from an unknown distribution possibly different from the one that generates the data and the corresponding labels. This is one of the main strategies behind various approaches to classifier assessment as well as general evaluation.

2.1.2 Example

Consider the results of Table 2.1, which were obtained by running three learning algorithms on the Labor Relations dataset from the UCI machine learning repository.[3] The learning algorithms used were the decision tree, logistic regression, and support vector machine (SVM). All simulations were run using a 10-fold cross-validation scheme[4] over the Labor Relations dataset from the UCI repository and the cross-validation runs were repeated 10 times on different permutations of the data.[5] The dataset contained 57 examples. Accordingly, reported results of the classifier errors on the test folds pertain to the ones on six examples in the first seven folds in the table, while the reported errors are over five examples in the last three test folds. The training and test folds within each run of cross-validation and for each repetition were the same for all the algorithms. With these results in the background, let us move on to discussing the concept of random variables.

Now, a classifier run on each test example (in each fold of each run) for the respective learning algorithms provides an estimate of its empirical error via the indicator loss function. The classifier experiences a unit loss if the predicted label does not match the true label. The empirical risk of the classifier in each fold can be obtained by averaging this loss over the number of examples in the corresponding fold. Table 2.2 provides this empirical risk for all the classifiers.[6] The entries in Table 2.2 correspond to the entries in Table 2.1 but divided by the number of examples in the respective folds. We can then model the empirical risk of these classifiers as random variables with the estimates obtained over each test fold and in each trial run as their observed values. Hence, we have 100 observed values for each of the three random variables used to model the empirical risk of the three classifiers. Note that the random variable used for the purpose can have values in the [0, 1] range with 0 denoting

---

[3] The UC Irvine (UCI) Machine Learning Repository (https://archive.ics.uci.edu/) is a collection of data used by the machine learning community. The Labor Relations dataset is available at DOI: 10.24432/C5CP4Q.

[4] Cross-validation and its repetition is discussed in detail in Sections 4.3.2, 6.4.3, and 7.2.1.

[5] This practice is discussed in Bouckaert (2003).

[6] We provide a detailed discussion about the notions of empirical risk and loss in Chapter 3.

Table 2.1. *Results for the decision tree (DT), logistic regression (LR), and support vector machine (SVM) algorithms on Labor Relations dataset from the UCI repository. Each trial represents a run of 10-fold cross-validation on the data. Columns f1 to f10 represent the number of errors in each run (test fold) of a 10-fold cross-validation trial. Columns f1 to f7 in each trial report the errors on a test fold of six examples while f8 to f10 report those on test folds of five examples each. This is due to the impossibility of dividing the Labor Relations dataset containing 57 sample examples into 10 folds of equal size.*

Trial No.	Classifiers	f1	f2	f3	f4	f5	f6	f7	f8	f9	f10	Trial error (sum)
	DT	0	0	2	0	0	2	2	2	0	2	10
1	LR	0	0	0	0	0	0	1	1	0	1	3
	SVM	0	0	0	0	0	0	1	1	0	2	4
	DT	0	1	1	0	0	1	2	2	1	1	9
2	LR	0	0	2	0	0	2	1	0	1	1	7
	SVM	0	0	0	0	0	1	1	0	0	1	3
	DT	1	1	0	2	2	3	1	1	1	2	14
3	LR	0	1	0	1	1	0	0	1	1	0	5
	SVM	0	1	0	0	1	0	0	1	1	0	4
	DT	0	1	1	0	0	1	1	1	1	0	6
4	LR	0	1	1	0	1	1	1	3	1	1	10
	SVM	0	0	0	0	0	1	1	3	1	0	6
	DT	0	0	1	1	1	1	1	0	1	1	7
5	LR	0	0	0	1	2	0	0	0	0	0	3
	SVM	0	0	0	1	1	0	0	0	0	0	2
	DT	0	1	0	0	0	0	2	0	0	1	4
6	LR	0	0	0	0	0	0	2	0	0	1	3
	SVM	0	0	0	0	0	1	0	0	0	0	1
	DT	1	0	1	0	0	1	1	0	0	1	5
7	LR	1	0	1	0	0	0	0	0	0	0	2
	SVM	1	0	0	0	0	0	0	0	0	0	1
	DT	1	0	2	2	0	2	1	0	2	0	10
8	LR	1	0	2	1	0	1	0	0	0	0	5
	SVM	1	0	1	1	0	1	0	0	0	0	4
	DT	1	1	2	1	0	0	1	0	0	2	8
9	LR	2	1	2	1	0	1	0	0	0	1	8
	SVM	1	0	1	1	0	0	0	1	0	1	5
	DT	1	0	0	2	3	0	0	2	2	2	12
10	LR	1	0	1	0	2	0	0	1	1	1	7
	SVM	2	0	0	1	1	0	0	1	1	0	6

Table 2.2. *Results for the decision tree (DT), logistic regression (LR), and support vector machine (SVM) on Labor Relations dataset from the UCI repository. Each trial represent a run of 10-fold cross-validation on the data. Columns f1 to f10 represent the ratio of errors to the number of samples in each run (test fold) of a 10-fold cross-validation trial.*

Trial No.	Classifiers	f1	f2	f3	f4	f5	f6	f7	f8	f9	f10
1	DT	0	0	0.333	0	0	0.333	0.333	0.333	0	0.333
	LR	0	0	0	0	0	0	0.167	0.167	0	0.167
	SVM	0	0	0	0	0	0	0.167	0.167	0	0.333
2	DT	0	0.167	0.167	0	0	0.167	0.333	0.333	0.167	0.167
	LR	0	0	0.333	0	0	0.333	0.167	0	0.167	0.167
	SVM	0	0	0	0	0	0.167	0.167	0	0	0.167
3	DT	0.167	0.167	0	0.333	0.333	0.5	0.167	0.167	0.167	0.333
	LR	0	0.167	0	0.167	0.167	0	0	0.167	0.167	0
	SVM	0	0.167	0	0	0.167	0	0	0.167	0.167	0
4	DT	0	0.167	0.167	0	0	0.167	0.167	0.167	0.167	0
	LR	0	0.167	0.167	0	0.167	0.167	0.167	0.5	0.167	0.167
	SVM	0	0	0	0	0	0.167	0.167	0.5	0.167	0
5	DT	0	0	0.167	0.167	0.167	0.167	0.167	0	0.167	0.167
	LR	0	0	0	0.167	0.333	0	0	0	0	0
	SVM	0	0	0	0.167	0.167	0	0	0	0	0
6	DT	0	0.167	0	0	0	0	0.333	0	0	0.167
	LR	0	0	0	0	0	0	0	0.333	0	0.167
	SVM	0	0	0	0	0	0	0.167	0	0	0
7	DT	0.167	0	0.167	0	0	0.167	0.167	0	0	0.167
	LR	0.167	0	0.167	0	0	0	0	0	0	0
	SVM	0.167	0	0	0	0	0	0	0	0	0
8	DT	0.167	0	0.333	0.333	0	0.333	0.167	0	0.333	0
	LR	0.167	0	0.333	0.167	0	0.167	0	0	0	0
	SVM	0.167	0	0.167	0.167	0	0.167	0	0	0	0
9	DT	0.167	0.167	0.333	0.167	0	0	0.167	0	0	0.333
	LR	0.333	0.167	0.333	0.167	0	0.167	0	0	0	0.167
	SVM	0.167	0	0.167	0.167	0	0	0	0.167	0	0.167
10	DT	0.167	0	0	0.333	0.5	0	0	0.333	0.333	0.333
	LR	0.167	0	0.167	0	0.333	0	0	0.167	0.167	0.167
	SVM	0.333	0	0	0.167	0.167	0	0	0.167	0.167	0

no risk (all the examples classified correctly) and 1 denoting the case when all the examples are classified incorrectly.

Let us denote the empirical risk by $R(\cdot)$. Then the variables $R(DT)$, $R(LR)$, and $R(SVM)$ denote the random variables representing the empirical risks for the decision tree, logistic regression, and SVM algorithms, respectively. We can now calculate the sample means for the three cases from the population of 100 observations at hand, and the *sample mean* for these random variables would then indicate the overall average value taken by them over the folds and runs of the experiment.

We have modeled the empirical risk as a continuous random variable that can take values in the [0, 1] interval and obtained the statistic of interest. An alternative approach is to model the risk as a binary variable that can take values in {0, 1}. Applying the classifier on each test example in each of the test folds would then provide an observation. These values can then be averaged over to obtain the corresponding sample means. Hence, by adding the errors made in each test fold and then further over all the trials, we would end up with a population of size $10 \times 57 = 570$. The sample means can then be calculated as

$$\overline{R}(\text{DT}) = \frac{10+9+14+6+7+4+5+10+8+12}{570} = 0.149,$$

$$\overline{R}(\text{LR}) = \frac{3+7+5+10+3+3+2+5+8+7}{570} = 0.092,$$

$$\overline{R}(\text{SVM}) = \frac{4+3+4+6+2+1+1+4+5+6}{570} = 0.063.$$

We will use continuous random variables for modeling as in the first case above since this allows us to model the empirical risk (rather than the loss function). Given that these sample means represent the mean empirical risk of each classifier, this suggests that SVM classifies the domain better than logistic regression, which in turn classifies the domain better than the decision tree classifier. However, the knowledge of only the average performance, via the mean, of classifier performance is not enough to give us an idea of their relative performances. We are also interested in the spread or deviation of the risk from this mean. The standard deviation, by virtue of representation in the same units as the data, is easier to interpret. It basically tells us whether the elements of our distribution have a tendency to be similar or dissimilar to each other. For example, in the population made up of 22-year-old ballerinas, the degree of joint flexibility is much more tightly distributed around the mean than it is in the population made up of all the 22-year-old young ladies (ballerinas and non-ballerinas). Thus, the standard deviation in the first case will be smaller than in the second. This is because ballerinas have to be naturally flexible and must train in order to increase this natural flexibility further, whereas in the general population, we will find a large mixture of young ladies with various degrees of flexibility and different levels of training. The standard deviations with respect to the mean empirical risks in each classifier case are 0.136 for decision tree, 0.114 for logistic regression, and 0.096 for the SVM classifier.

So what do these values tell us in terms of how to compare the performance of the decision tree, logistic regression, and SVM classifiers on the Labor Relations dataset? The relatively high standard deviations exhibited by decision tree and logistic regression tell us that the distribution of values around the sample means of these two experiments varies a great deal. That is, over some folds these two classifiers make very few errors (lower risk) compared to SVM while on others this number is relatively very high (and hence higher risk). Indeed, this behavior can be seen in Table 2.2. In comparison, SVM appears to be relatively more stable.

2.2 Probability Distributions

We introduced the notions of probability distributions and density functions in Section 2.1. Let us now focus on some of the main distributions that have both significant impact and implications on the approaches currently used in assessing and evaluating learning algorithms. Although data can be modeled using a wide variety of distributions, we would like to focus on two important distributions most relevant to the evaluation of learning algorithms: the normal (Gaussian) distribution and the binomial distribution. Among these, the normal distribution is the most widely used distribution for modeling classifier performance due to a variety of reasons, including the analytical tractability of the results under this assumption, asymptotic analysis capability owing to the central limit theorem (discussed in Section 2.2.4), the asymptotic ability to model a wide variety of other distributions, and so on. As we will see in later chapters, many approaches impose a normal distribution assumption on the performance measures (or some function of the performance measures). For instance, the standard t-test assumes the difference in the performance measure of two algorithms to be normally distributed around the zero mean.

The binomial distribution has recently earned more significance. It models a discrete random variable and can aptly be applied to model the number of successes in a series of experiments. Hence, this is the model of choice when we wish to model how frequently an algorithm succeeds in classifying an instance from the test set correctly (modeling the empirical risk using the indicator loss, especially when this risk is, as is typically the case, closer to zero). Modeling of the classification error in terms of the binomial distribution enables us to obtain very tight guarantees on the generalization error of the learning algorithm. We will see some such results with regard to the empirical risk minimization algorithms in Chapter 3. For now, let us start with the normal distribution.

2.2.1 The Normal Distribution

The normal, or Gaussian, distribution is used to model a continuous random variable. A continuous random variable x taking any value in the interval $(-\infty, \infty)$ is said to be normally distributed with parameters μ and σ^2 if the PDF of x can be denoted by

$$p(x) = \frac{1}{\sqrt{2\pi\sigma^2}} \exp\left[-\frac{1}{2}\left(\frac{(x-\mu)^2}{\sigma^2}\right)\right]. \tag{2.1}$$

The parameter μ, called the mean, here refers to the expected value $\mathbf{E}[x]$, and σ^2 represents the variance of the random variable around the mean. Note that we avoid denoting μ and σ^2 as functions of x since it is clear from the context. A variable x that is normally distributed with mean μ and variance σ^2 can be denoted as $x \sim N(\mu, \sigma^2)$, which has the same meaning as Equation (2.1). One important type of normal distribution is called the standard normal distribution. A random variable x distributed according to a standard normal distribution has mean $\mu = 0$ and variance $\sigma^2 = 1$, and is denoted as $x \sim N(0, 1)$. The normal distribution, when plotted, results in the famous symmetric bell-shaped curve around the mean. The characteristics of this curve, especially the center and width, are decided by the two parameters μ and σ^2 defining the normal distribution. With increasing variance, one would obtain a wider bell curve.

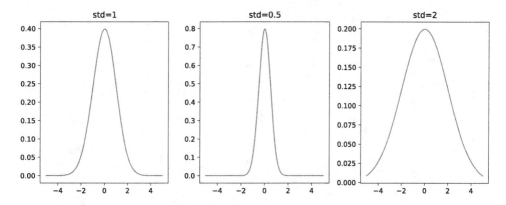

Figure 2.1 Normal distributions centered around 0 with standard deviations of 1 (the standard normal distribution), 0.5, and 2.

Figure 2.1 shows the shape of the standard normal distribution, along with two normal distributions also centered around 0, but with standard deviations of 0.5 and 2. Note the effect of increasing the variance (and hence the standard deviation).

2.2.2 The Binomial Distribution

The binomial distribution is used to model discrete random variables that generally take on binary values. Consider an hypothetical trial that can have two outcomes, success or failure. The probability of success in any given trial (or experiment) is denoted by p_s. Such trials are typically referred to as Bernoulli trials. Then the binomial distribution models the number of successes in a series of experiments with the probability of success in each experiment being p_s. An important assumption here is that the number of trials is fixed in advance. Furthermore, the probability of success in each trial is assumed to be the same. That is, p_s is fixed across various trials. Each trial is further assumed to be statistically independent of all other trials. That is, the outcome of any given trial does not depend on the outcome of any other trial.

Given this, a random variable x is said to be binomially distributed with parameters m and p_s, denoted by $x \sim \text{Bin}(m, p_s)$, if it obeys the probability distribution

$$P(x) = \binom{m}{k} p_s^k (1 - p_s)^{(m-k)},$$

which is simply the probability of exactly k successes in m trials.

Consider a classifier that maps each given example to one of a fixed number of labels. Each example also has an associated true label. We can model the event as a success when the label identified by the classifier matches the true label of the example. Then the behavior of the classifier prediction over a number of different examples in a test set can be modeled as a binomial distribution. The expected value $\mathbf{E}[x]$ of a binomial distribution can be shown to be the product mp_s, and its variance to be the product $mp_s(1 - p_s)$. In the extreme

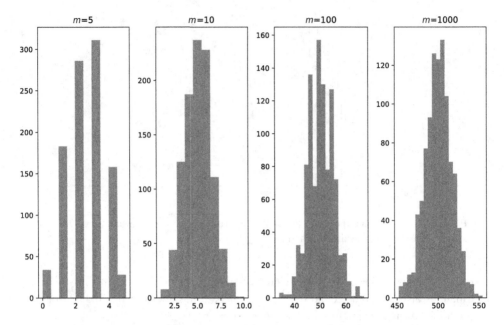

Figure 2.2 Binomial distributions with probability of 0.5 (unbiased) and trial size $m = 5$, $m = 10$, $m = 100$, and $m = 1000$, respectively. As the trial size increases, it is clear that the binomial distribution approaches the normal distribution.

case of $m = 1$, the binomial distribution becomes a Bernoulli distribution that models the probability of success in a single trial. In the case $m \longrightarrow \infty$, the binomial distribution approaches the Poisson distribution when the product mp_s remains fixed. The advantage of sometimes using a Poisson distribution to approximate a binomial distribution can come from the reduced computational complexity. However, we do not delve into these issues since these are beyond the scope of this book.

We now see the effect of m on the binomial distribution. Figure 2.2 shows four unbiased binomial distributions (an unbiased binomial distribution has $p_s = 0.5$) with increasing trial sizes. It can be seen that as the trial size increases, the binomial distribution approaches the normal distribution (for fixed p_s).[7] The probability of a success in a Bernoulli trial also affects the distribution. Figure 2.3 shows two biased binomial distributions with success probabilities of 0.3 and 0.8 over 10 trials. In these cases, the graph is asymmetrical.

2.2.3 Other Distributions

Many other distributions are widely used in practice for data modeling in various fields. Some of the main ones are the Poisson distribution, used to model the number of events occurring in a given time interval, the geometric distribution, generally used to model the

[7] Note that a continuity correction, such as one based on the de Moivre–Laplace theorem, is recommended in the case where a normal approximation from a binomial is used for large m.

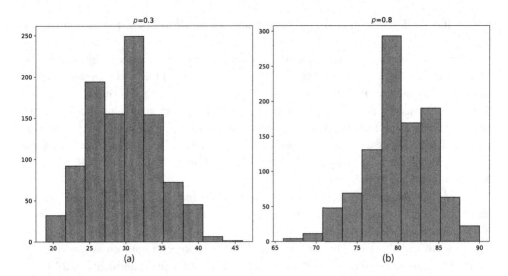

Figure 2.3 Binomial distributions with probability of success (a) $p_s = 0.3$ and (b) $p_s = 0.8$, respectively, with $m = 10$. For these biased distributions, the graph has become asymmetrical.

number of trials required before a first success (or failure) is obtained, and the uniform distribution, generally used to model random variables whose range of values is known and that can take any value in this range with equal probability. These, however, are not directly relevant to the subject of this book. Hence, we do not devote space to discussing these distributions in detail. Interested readers can find these details in any standard statistics book.

2.2.4 Central Limit Theorem

Let us now discuss a very important result known as the central limit theorem, or the second fundamental theorem of probability. We now state this theorem (without proof).

Theorem 2.1 The central limit theorem. *Let $x_1, x_2, \ldots, x_m$ be a sequence of m independent identically distributed random variables each with a finite expectation μ and variance σ^2. Then, as m increases, the distribution of the sample means of $x_1, x_2, \ldots, x_m$ approaches the normal distribution with a mean μ and variance $\frac{\sigma^2}{m}$ irrespective of the original distribution of $x_1, x_2, \ldots, x_m$.*

Let us denote by S_m the sum of m random variables. That is,

$$S_m = x_1 + x_2 + \cdots + x_m.$$

Then the random variable r_m defined as

$$r_m = \frac{S_m - m\mu}{\sigma \sqrt{m}}$$

is such that its distribution converges to a standard normal distribution as m approaches infinity.

The normal distribution assumption over certain variables of interest, or even statistics of interest (see the sampling distribution in Section 2.2.5), is one of the most common assumptions made to analyze the behavior of various aspects of learning algorithms, especially their performance on data. This assumption appears as an important consequence of the central limit theorem. The sample mean appears as a statistic of choice to investigate with the normal distribution assumption, as we will see later. We will also see how this assumption plays a central role in not only establishing a basis of analysis, but also in affecting the results obtained as a consequence.

The central limit theorem can be used to show that the sampling distribution of the sample mean can be approximated to be normal even if the distribution of the population from which the samples are obtained is not normal but is well behaved when the size of the sample is sufficiently large. This observation will have important implications especially in the case of statistical significance testing, where such results with the normality distribution assumption of the sample means are frequently put into practice, but the necessary factors for such assumption to hold, that is, the required sample size and the underlying population distribution, are often neglected.

2.2.5 Sampling Distribution

Consider a sample obtained from sampling data according to some given distribution. We can calculate various kinds of statistics on this sample (e.g., mean, variance, standard deviation). These are called sample statistics. The sampling distribution denotes the probability distribution or PDF associated with the sample statistic under repeated sampling of the population. This sampling distribution then depends on three factors: the size of the sample, the statistic itself, and the underlying distribution of the population. In other words, the *sampling distribution* of a statistic (example, the mean, the median, or any other description/summary of a dataset) is the distribution of values obtained for that statistic over all possible samplings of the same size from a given population.

For instance, we obtain m samples for a random variable x denoted $\{x_1, x_2, \ldots, x_m\}$ with known probability distribution, and calculate the sample mean $\overline{x} = \frac{1}{m} \sum_{i=1}^{m} x_i$. For instance, when using x to model the empirical risk, we can obtain the average empirical risk on a dataset of m examples by testing the classifier on each of these. Further, since this average empirical risk is a statistic, repeated sampling of the m data points and calculating the empirical risk in each case will enable us to obtain a sampling distribution of the empirical risk estimates. There can be a sampling distribution associated with any sample statistic estimated (although not always computable). For instance, in the example of Table 2.2, we use a random variable to model the empirical risk of each classifier and calculate the average (mean) empirical risk on each fold. Hence, the 10 runs with 10 folds each give us 100 observed values of $R(\cdot)$ for each classifier over which we calculate the mean. This, for instance, results in the corresponding sample mean of the empirical risk in the case of decision tree to be $\overline{R}(\text{DT}) = 0.149$.

Since the populations under study are usually finite, the true sampling distribution is usually unknown (e.g., note that the trials in the case of Table 2.2 are interdependent). Hence, it is important to understand the effect of using a single estimate of sampling distribution based on one sampling instead of repeated samplings. Typically, the mean of the statistic is used as an approximation of the actual mean obtained over multiple samplings. The central limit theorem plays an important role in allowing for this approximation. Let us see the reasoning behind this.

Denote a random variable x that is normally distributed with mean μ and variance σ^2 as $x \sim N(\mu, \sigma^2)$. Then, the sampling distribution of the sample mean $\bar{x}$ coming from m-sized samples is

$$\bar{x} \sim N\left(\mu, \frac{\sigma^2}{m}\right). \tag{2.2}$$

Moreover, if x is sampled from a population of (finite) size N, then the sampling distribution of the sample mean becomes

$$\bar{x} \sim N\left(\mu, \frac{N-m}{N-1} \times \frac{\sigma^2}{m}\right). \tag{2.3}$$

Note here the role of the central limit theorem described in Section 2.2.4. With increasing N, Equation (2.3) would approach Equation (2.2). Moreover, note how the sample mean in Equations (2.2) and (2.3) is basically the actual mean.

Another application of the sampling distribution is to obtain the sampling distribution of two means. We will see this in the case of hypothesis testing. Let x_1 and x_2 be two random variables that are normally distributed with means μ_1 and μ_2, respectively. Their corresponding variances are σ_1^2 and σ_2^2. That is, $x_1 \sim N(\mu_1, \sigma_1^2)$ and $x_2 \sim N(\mu_2, \sigma_2^2)$. We are now interested in the sampling distribution of the sample mean of x_1 over m_1 sized samples denoted $\bar{x_1}$ and the sample mean of x_2 over m_2 sized samples denoted $\bar{x_2}$. Then, it can be shown that the difference of the sampling means is distributed as

$$\bar{x_1} - \bar{x_2} \sim N\left(\mu_1 - \mu_2, \frac{\sigma_1^2}{m_1} + \frac{\sigma_2^2}{m_2}\right). \tag{2.4}$$

Finally, consider a variable x that is binomially distributed with parameter p. That is, $x \sim \text{Bin}(p)$. Then it can be shown that the sample proportion $\bar{p}$ also follows a binomial distribution parameterized by p. That is, $\bar{p} \sim \text{Bin}(p)$.

2.3 Confidence Intervals

Let us now discuss one of the important concepts where the sampling distribution of a population statistic plays a significant role. Consider a set of observations sampled according to some population distribution. This sample can serve to estimate a sample statistic of interest that can then be used to approximate the true statistic of the underlying distribution. The sample statistics discussed above, such as the sample mean, essentially give the point estimate of such statistics. Confidence intervals, on the other hand, give interval estimates in the form of a range of values in which the true statistic is likely to lie.

Hence, a confidence interval gives an estimated range of values that is likely to include an unknown population parameter, the estimated range being calculated from a given sample of data. This, in a sense, then associates reliability to the point estimates of the true statistic obtained from the sample. Accordingly, associated with this estimated range is a confidence level that determines how likely the true statistic is to lie in the confidence interval. This confidence level is generally denoted in the form $(1 - \alpha)$, where $\alpha \in [0, 1]$ is called the confidence parameter (or confidence coefficient). The most common value used for α is 0.05, referring to a confidence level of $1 - 0.05 = 0.95$, or 95%. Note that this is not the same as giving the probability with which the true statistic will lie in the interval. Rather, what this conveys is that if we were to obtain multiple samples repeatedly from the population according to the underlying distribution, then the true population statistic is likely to lie in the estimated confidence interval $(1-\alpha) \times 100\%$ of the time. As can be easily noted, reducing the value of α will have the effect of increasing the confidence level of the estimated range's likelihood of containing the true population statistic, and hence will widen the confidence interval. Similarly, increasing α would tighten the confidence interval. When computed over more than one statistic, the confidence interval becomes a confidence region.

Note that the above interpretation of the confidence interval is strictly a statistical interpretation and should not be confused with its Bayesian counterpart, known as the *credible interval*. The two can be identical in some cases; however, credible intervals can differ significantly when these are applied in a strong Bayesian sense with prior information integrated. We do not discuss Bayesian credible intervals in this chapter; however, we provide a detailed discussion of confidence intervals and Bayesian credible intervals in Sections 7.3 and 7.4, respectively.

Getting back to our ballerinas, if we compute, from our ballerina sample, the average degree of joint flexibility, we may not trust that this value is necessarily the true average for all ballerinas, but we can build a 95% confidence interval around this value and claim that the true average is likely to fall in this interval with 95% confidence. This confidence level is also related to the statistical hypothesis testing, as we will see later. However, the two notions do not necessarily have the same interpretation.

While the idea of providing interval estimates over the true statistic seems appealing, there are some caveats to this approach that should be taken into account. The most important of these is that the intervals are obtained based on strong parametric assumptions on the statistic of interest. In the most general form that we describe next, the statistic is assumed to be distributed according to a Gaussian distribution around the sample mean. Let us see this most common case.

As we have already seen, the sample mean can be relatively reliably used to compute the true mean. Hence, by making use of the standard error (sample standard deviation) obtained from the sample we can obtain a value Z_P that would determine the confidence limits (the end points of confidence intervals). Consider a random variable x distributed according to a normal distribution with true mean μ and variance σ^2. Let S_x be the sample of a set of values for x. We denote the sample mean by $\overline{x}$ calculated as

$$\overline{x} = \frac{1}{|S_x|} \sum_{i=1}^{|S_x|} x_i,$$

with each x_i denoting an observed value of x in the sample S_x, and $|S_x|$ denoting the size of the set S_x. Similarly, we can calculate the standard error (sample standard deviation), which according to our assumption will approximate $\sigma/\sqrt{|S_x|}$ (see Section 2.2.4). Next, we can standardize the statistic to obtain the random variable

$$Z = \frac{\overline{x} - \mu}{\frac{\sigma}{\sqrt{|S_x|}}}.$$

Now, we wish to find, at probability $1 - \alpha$, the lower and upper bound on the values of Z. That is, we wish to find Z_P such that

$$Pr(Z_P \le Z \le Z_P) = 1 - \alpha.$$

The value of Z_P can be obtained from the CDF of Z. Once Z_P is obtained, the confidence interval around $\overline{x}$ can be given as $(\overline{x} - Z_P \times \sigma/\sqrt{|S_x|}, \overline{x} + Z_P \times \sigma/\sqrt{|S_x|})$. Note that we do not know the true standard deviation σ. In this case, we use the sample standard deviation or standard error $\sigma(x)$ for the purpose. That is, at confidence level $1 - \alpha$ the value of the true mean μ lies between the lower and upper bounds of the confidence intervals (also known as confidence limits) denoted CI_{lower} and CI_{upper} such that

$$CI_{Lower} = \overline{x} - Z_P \times \frac{\sigma(x)}{\sqrt{|S_x|}},$$

$$CI_{Upper} = \overline{x} + Z_P \times \frac{\sigma(x)}{\sqrt{|S_x|}}.$$

Note that this is essentially the two-sided confidence interval, and hence we have considered a confidence parameter of $\alpha/2$ to account for the upper and the lower bounds of each while considering the CDF. This will have important implications in statistical hypothesis testing, as we will see in Section 2.4. The discussion up to now on the manner of calculating the confidence intervals was aimed at elucidating the process. However, tables with Z_P values corresponding to the desired level of significance are available (see Table A.1). Hence, for desired levels of confidence, these values can be readily be made use of to give the confidence intervals.

Let us go back to our example from Table 2.2. We calculated the mean empirical risk of the three classifiers on the Labor Relations dataset. Using the sample standard deviation, we can then obtain the confidence intervals for the true risk. The value of Z_P corresponding to $\alpha = 0.05$ (95% confidence level) is found to be 1.96 from Table A.1. Hence, for the decision tree,

$$CI_{Lower}^{R(DT)} = \overline{R}(DT) - Z_P \times \frac{\sigma(x)}{\sqrt{|S_x|}}$$

$$= 0.149 - 1.96 \times \frac{0.136}{\sqrt{100}}.$$

Similarly,

$$CI_{Upper}^{R(\text{DT})} = \overline{R}(\text{DT}) + Z_P \times \frac{\sigma(x)}{\sqrt{|S_x|}}$$

$$= 0.149 + 1.96 \times \frac{0.136}{\sqrt{100}}.$$

The confidence limits for the other two classifiers can be obtained in an analogous manner.

As already discussed, the confidence interval approach has also been important in statistical hypothesis testing. One of the most immediate applications of this approach employing the assumption of a normal distribution on the statistic can be found in the commonly used significance test, the *t*-test. The confidence interval calculation is implicit in the *t*-test that can be used to verify if the statistic differs from the one assumed by the null hypothesis. There are many variations to the *t*-test.

Figure 2.4 illustrates the result where the 95% confidence intervals for the three classifiers are shown around the mean. The figure shows that the true means of the error rates of these classifiers are probably quite distinct from one another, given the little overlap displayed by the graphs (an effect enhanced by the scale on the vertical axis too). It is worth noting that, although our conclusions may seem quite clear and straightforward, the situation is certainly not as simple as it appears. For starters, recall that these results have a 95% confidence level, indicating that there still is some likelihood of the true mean not falling in the intervals obtained around the sample mean empirical risk. Moreover, the results and

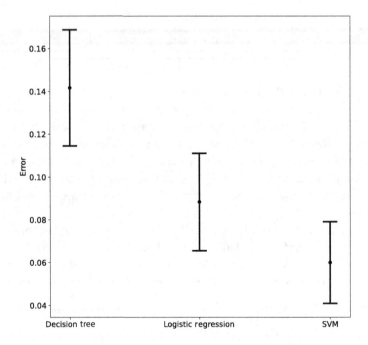

Figure 2.4 The confidence intervals for the decision tree, logistic regression, and support vector machine (SVM) classifiers.

subsequent interpretations obtained here rely on an important assumption that the sampling distribution of the empirical risk can be approximated by a normal distribution. Finally, there is another inherent assumption, which we did not state explicitly earlier and indeed is more often than not taken for granted, that of the i.i.d. nature of the estimates of risk in the sample. This final assumption is obviously violated given that the repeated runs of the 10-fold cross-validation are done by sampling from the same dataset. Indeed, these assumptions can have important implications. The normality assumption in particular, when violated, can yield inaccurate or even uninterpretable estimates of the confidence intervals as we will see in Chapter 7. We will also discuss the effects of such repeated sampling from the same set of instances.

Another issue has to do with the importance that confidence intervals have started gaining in the past decade, vis-à-vis the hypothesis testing approach discussed in Section 2.4. Indeed, in recent years, arguments in favor of using confidence intervals over hypothesis testing have appeared (e.g., Armstrong (2007)). The reasoning behind the recommendation goes along the following two lines:

- The meaning of the significance value used in hypothesis testing has come under scrutiny and has become increasingly contested. By contrast, confidence intervals have a simple and straightforward interpretation.
- Significance values allow us to accept or reject a hypothesis (as we will see in Section 2.4), but cannot help us decide by how much to accept or reject it. That is, the significance testing approach does not allow quantification of the extent to which a hypothesis can be accepted or rejected. Conversely, confidence intervals provide a means by which we can consider such degrees of acceptance or rejection.

Even though there is some merit to the above arguments with regard to the limitations of hypothesis testing, these shortcomings do not, by themselves, make confidence intervals a de facto method of choice. It suffices to state, here, that the confidence intervals approach also makes a normal assumption on the empirical error that is often violated. The confidence intervals approach, owing to this inherent assumption, can result in unrealistic estimates too. Moreover, statistical hypothesis testing, when applied taking into account the underlying assumptions and constraints, can indeed be helpful. To make this discussion clearer, let us now discuss the basics of statistical hypothesis testing.

2.4 Hypothesis Testing

Our discussion so far has focused on modeling and estimating the statistic of interest on any given sample and mapping these ideas to the problem of evaluating learning algorithms. Essentially, we can model the performance of the classifier, commonly its empirical risk, as a random variable and study its behavior. Just as in Sections 2.2.5 and 2.3, a typical approach would be to study the average performance of the classifier by obtaining the mean empirical risk (or any other monotonic performance measure). Given an estimate of the mean performance, the next question is, how reliable is this estimate? That is, how representative of the true statistic is this estimate of the expected value of the random variable? When put in the context of comparing two classifiers, the natural question to ask would be: Given the difference between the mean performances of two classifiers on a given dataset, how representative is this empirical difference of the difference in their true values? Statistical hypothesis testing aims to address these questions.

Statistical hypothesis testing, sometimes referred to as just hypothesis testing, plays a very important role in statistical inference. It is part of the branch of statistics known as *confirmatory data analysis*. Hence, as the name suggests, the main concern of their application is to *confirm* whether the observed behavior is representative of the true behavior. As soon as we interpret the confirmatory data analysis in this manner, it becomes clear that there is, indeed, an assumption on the true behavior (however weak) of the data at hand. Such analysis is essentially a deductive approach where we assume existence of a hypothesis (called the "null hypothesis") and then proceed to reject or accept (more appropriately "fail to reject") this hypothesis. Further, as a result of this null hypothesis existence requirement, we make (sometimes strong) assumptions on the behavior of the data at hand that might not be verifiable. For instance, recall how, as we discussed briefly in Section 2.3, the t-test assumes the empirical risk to be distributed according to a normal distribution in our example. Such assumptions are a source of considerably opposing viewpoints on the use of hypothesis testing. Indeed, there can be significant disadvantages to such an approach. Since assumptions on hypothesis are made a priori, this could lead to performing statistical testing in a preconceived framework. An immediate consequence of such assumptions is that conditions and results that might not be explained by the assumed models are left unaccounted for (in fact, even neglected). Finally, the outcomes of such testing can become uninterpretable, and in many cases even misleading, if the initial assumptions are violated. What, then, are the advantages of using such approaches? The first and foremost is the existence of strong, well-established and analytically tractable techniques for testing as a result of the modeling assumptions. This results in statistical testing methods that are theoretically justified. Consequently, this yields strong verifiable results when the underlying assumptions are satisfied.

This is different from the inductive nature of exploratory data analysis approaches where the observations and calculations on the data are used to obtain insights without any a priori assumptions. However, the downside of this approach, naturally, is that it may not yield concrete results, especially in the wake of limited data to support strong conclusions.

As already mentioned, much of the hypothesis testing, especially that relevant to our context, is centered around the idea of null hypothesis testing. Let us look at the null hypothesis testing in its general form. A null hypothesis characterizes, generally quantitatively, an a priori assumption on the behavior of the data at hand. For instance, this can be some statistic of interest such as the empirical mean of the data. By an a priori assumption on behavior, we mean that the behavior of the data (or a statistic on this data) is assumed to always hold, unless the observed statistic from the data contradicts it, in which case we have to reject this assumption (possibly in favor of an alternate explanation). The goal of this hypothesis testing is, then, to find the probability with which the data statistic of interest is at least as extreme as the one measured from the data (observed).

A typical statistical hypothesis testing procedure can be summarized as follows:

1. State the a priori hypothesis, the null hypothesis H_0, and possibly an alternate research hypothesis. This is an extremely important step since it has implications for the rest of the hypothesis testing procedure.
2. The null hypothesis that one typically wishes to refute is the opposite of the research hypothesis in which one is interested. Consider the assumptions made by this hypothesis on the data.
3. Decide on the suitable statistical test and the corresponding statistic (the one used to reject the null hypothesis).
4. Calculate the observed test statistic from the data and compare against the value expected according to the null hypothesis assumptions.
5. Decide on a critical region needed for the observed test statistic to lie in under the null hypothesis for it to be considered sufficiently extreme (that is, has extremely low probability) to be able to reject the null hypothesis.
6. If the observed test statistic lies in the critical region (has extremely low probability of being observed under the null hypothesis assumption), reject the null hypothesis H_0. However, note that when this is not the case, one would "fail to reject" the null hypothesis. This does not lead to the conclusion that one can accept the null hypothesis.

The final step makes an important point. In the case where the null hypothesis cannot be rejected based on the observed value of the test statistic, the conclusion that must be accepted does not necessarily hold. Recall that the null hypothesis was *assumed*. Hence, not being able to disprove its existence does not necessarily confirm it.

We are interested in comparing the performance of two learning algorithms. In our case then, the null hypothesis can, for instance, assume that the difference between the empirical risks of the two classifiers is (statistically) insignificant. That is, the two estimates come from a similar population. Since the errors are estimated on the same population, with the only difference being the two classifiers, this then translates to meaning that the two classifiers behave in a more or less similar manner. Rejecting this hypothesis would then mean that the observed difference between the classifiers' performances is, indeed, statistically significant (technically, this would lead us to conclude that the difference is not statistically insignificant; however our null hypothesis definition allows us draw this conclusion).

2.4.1 One- and Two-Tailed Tests

In the statistics literature, the one-tailed and two-tailed tests are also referred to as one-sided and two-sided tests, respectively. A statistical hypothesis test is called one sided if the values that can reject the null hypothesis are contained wholly in one tail of the probability distribution. That is, these values are all either lower than the threshold of the test (also known as the critical value of the test) or higher than the threshold, but not both. On the other hand, a two-tailed test enables rejecting the null hypothesis taking into account both tails of the probability distribution.

In other words, an H_0 expressed as an equality can be rejected in two ways. For instance, when we formulate H_0 to say that the difference between two sample means is equal to zero, then one can reject this hypothesis in two ways: first, if the difference is less than zero, and second, when the difference is greater than zero. If we are concerned only about either the lower or the higher statistic, a one-tailed test would suffice. However, when both ways of hypothesis rejection are significant, a two-tailed test is used.

For example, let us assume that we are comparing the results between decision tree and SVM from Table 2.2 and let us assume that we already know that SVM is never a worse classifier than decision tree on data similar to the Labour Relations dataset that we are using here. The hypothesis that we want to test is that on this particular domain, decision tree is, once again, not as accurate as SVM. In such a case, we hypothesize that the difference between the true risk of decision tree ($R(DT)$) and that of SVM ($R(SVM)$) has a mean of 0. Note that our assumption says that SVM is never worse than decision tree, and hence this difference is never considered to be less than zero. Under these assumptions, we can obtain the observed difference in the mean empirical risk of the two classifiers, $\overline{R}(DT) - \overline{R}(SVM)$, and apply a one-tailed test to verify if the observed difference is significantly greater than 0. We may not have any a priori assumption over the classifiers' performance difference, for example, in the case of decision tree and logistic regression in the above example. In such cases, we might only be interested in knowing, for instance, whether the observed difference between their performance is, indeed, significant. That is, this difference (irrespective of which classifier is better) would hold if their true distribution were available. We leave the details of how such testing is performed in practice and under what assumptions to a more elaborate treatment in Sections 7.2.1. and 7.3.1.

2.4.2 Parametric and Nonparametric Approaches to Hypothesis Testing

There are two main approaches to the statistical hypothesis testing, parametric and non-parametric, that come from the type of assumptions made to establish the null hypothesis. The parametric approach assumes a well-defined underlying distribution over the statistic of interest under this null hypothesis. Hence, it is assumed that the sample statistic is representative of the true statistic according to a well-defined distribution model such that its true defining statistic can be characterized systematically. The hypothesis test then aims at confirming, or more appropriately, rejecting the assumption that the behavior of the observed statistic of interest resembles that of the true statistic. A common example would be the student's t-test over the difference of true empirical risks of two classifiers. The test, as a null hypothesis, assumes that the two classifiers perform in a similar manner (that is, the two estimates of the observed empirical risks come from the same population). As a result, the difference between them is assumed to be distributed according to a normal distribution centered at zero (the mean of the normal distribution). As can again be noted, there is a correlation between the confidence interval approach and the normal distribution assuming hypothesis tests over the mean empirical error, in that confidence intervals can be obtained over the means simply by reversing the hypothesis testing criterion.

In contrast to parametric hypothesis testing, the nonparametric approaches do not rely on any fixed model assumption over the statistic of interest. Such tests often take the form of ranking-based approaches since this enables the characterization of two competing hypotheses in terms of their comparative ability to explain the sample at hand. An example would be the sign test for the comparison of two populations, which we will detail in Section 4.4.2 along with other statistical testing methods in the context of evaluating learning algorithms.

Of course, there are advantages and limitations with both the parametric and the nonparametric approaches. The nonparametric tests, as a result of independence from any modeling assumption, are quite useful in populations for which outliers skew the distribution significantly (not to mention, in addition, the case where no distribution underlies the statistics). However, the consequence of this advantage of model independence is the limited power (see the discussion on type II error in Section 2.4.3) of these tests since limited generalizations can be made over the behavior or comparison of the sample statistic in the absence of any concrete behavior model. Parametric approaches, on the other hand, are useful when the distributional assumptions are (even approximately) met since then strong conclusions can be reached. However, in case the assumptions are violated, parametric tests can be grossly misleading.

Let us now see how we can characterize the hypothesis tests themselves in terms of their ability to reject the null hypothesis. This is generally quantified by specifying two quantities of interest with regard to the hypothesis test, its type I error and its type II error, the latter of which also affects the power of the test.

2.4.3 Type I and Type II Error: Power of a Test

The type I and type II errors, and the associated power of a statistical test are now defined.

Definition 2.2 A type I error (α) corresponds to the error of rejecting the null hypothesis H_0 when it is, in fact, true (false positive). A type II error (β) corresponds to the error of failing to reject H_0 when it is false (false negative).

Note that the type II error above basically quantifies the extent to which a test validates the null hypothesis when it in fact does not hold. Hence, we can define the power of test by taking into account the complement of the type II error.

Definition 2.3 The power of a test is the probability of rejecting H_0 given that it is false:

$$Power = 1 - \beta.$$

These two types of errors are generally traded-off. That is, reducing the type I error makes the hypothesis test more sensitive in that it does not reject H_0 too easily. As a result of this tendency, the type II error of the test, that of failing to reject H_0, even when it does not hold, increases. This, then, gives us a test with low power. A low power test may be insufficient, for instance, for finding the difference in classifier performance as significant, even when it is so. The parametric tests can have more power than their nonparametric counterparts since they can characterize the sample statistic in a well-defined manner. However, this is true only when the modeling assumption on the distribution of the sample statistics holds. The α parameter is the confidence parameter in the sense that it specifies how unlikely the result must be if one is to reject the null hypothesis. A typical value of α is 0.05, or 5%. Reducing α then amounts to making the test more rigorous. In Chapter 5, we will see how this α parameter also affects the sample size requirement for the test in the context of analysing the hold-out method of evaluation.

In addition to these characteristics arising from the inherent nature of the test, the power of tests can also be increased in other manners (although with corresponding costs) as follows:

- **Increasing the size of the type I error** As already discussed, the first and simplest way to increase power, or lower the type II error, is to do so at the expense of the type I error. While we usually set α to 0.05, if we increased it to 0.10 or 0.20, then β would be decreased. An important question, however, is whether we are ready to take a greater chance at a type I error; that is, whether we are ready to take the chance of claiming that a result is significant when it is not, to increase our chance of finding a significant result when one exists. Often, this is not a good alternative, and it would be preferable to increase power without having to increase α.

- **Using a one-tailed rather than a two-tailed test** One-tailed tests are more powerful than two-tailed tests for a given α-level. Indeed, running a two-tailed test for $\alpha_2 = 0.05$ is equivalent to running two one-tailed tests for $\alpha_1 = 0.025$. Since α_1 is very small in this case, its corresponding β_1 is large, and, thus, its power is small. Hence, in moving from a two-tailed $\alpha_2 = .05$ test to a one-tailed $\alpha_1' = .05$ test, we are doubling the value of α_1, and thus decreasing the value of β_1', and in turn, increasing the power of the test. Of course, this can be done only if we know which of the two distribution means considered in the test is expected to be higher. If this information is not available, then a two-tailed test is necessary and no power can be gained in this manner.

- **Choosing a more sensitive evaluation measure** One way to separate two samples, or increase power, is to increase the difference between the means of the two samples. This can be done when setting up our experiments by selecting an evaluation measure that emphasizes the effect we are testing. For example, let us assume that we are using the balanced F-measure (also called the F_1-measure) to compare the performance of two classifiers, but let us say that precision is the aspect of the performance that we care about the most. (Both these performance measures will be discussed in Chapter 3.) Let us assume that, of the two classifiers tested, one was specifically designed to improve on precision at the expense of recall (complementary measure of precision used to compute the F-measure, also discussed in Chapter 3). If F_1 is the measure used, then the gains in precision of the more precise algorithm would be overshadowed by its losses in recall, given that both measures are weighed equally. If, however, we used the $F_{0.5}$ measure that weighs precision more than recall, the expected gains in precision would be more noticeable.[8] This would also have the effect of increasing the power of the statistical test.

---

[8] We assume, here, that we do not wish to disregard recall altogether since otherwise we would use the precision measure directly.

- **Increasing the sample size** Another way to separate two samples is to decrease their spread, or standard deviation. This is feasible by increasing the size of the sample. One way of doing so would be to use resampling methods such as a 10-fold cross-validation or its repeated runs. Of course, this is generally accompanied by additional computational costs, not to mention the bias in the resulting performance estimates as a result of relaxation of the data independence assumption and reuse of data in various runs.

The procedure for determining the power of a test will be discussed in Section 7.3. Before wrapping up this review of statistical concepts, let us see one final notion, that of the effect size of a statistical test.

2.4.4 Effect Size

The idea of separating the two samples in order to increase power comes from the fact that power is inextricably linked to the amount of overlap that occurs between two distributions. Let us see what we mean by this in the context of comparing classifier performance. If we are interested in characterizing the difference in risk of two classifiers, then, in the parametric case, our null hypothesis can assume this difference to be distributed according to a normal distribution centered at zero. Let us call this the standard distribution. We would then calculate the parameters of the distribution of the statistics of interest from the data. Let us denote this as the empirical distribution. Then, the farther the empirical distribution is from the standard distribution, the more confidence we would have in rejecting the null hypothesis. The strength with which we can reject the null hypothesis is basically the effect size of the test. Figure 2.5 illustrates this notion graphically. The distribution on the left is the standard distribution, while the one on the right is the empirical distribution with the straight vertical line denoting the threshold of the hypothesis test beyond which the null hypothesis (H0) is rejected. The overlap on the right of the threshold basically signifies the probability that we reject the null hypothesis (H0) even when it holds (type I error). The tail of the standard distribution is simply α. Similarly, the overlap on the left of the threshold denotes the probability that we do not reject the alternative hypothesis (H1) even though it does not hold (type II error, β). It is clear that moving the separating line to the left increases α while decreasing β. In fact, choosing any significance level α implicitly defines a trade-off in terms of increasing β. Note, however, that in the event of very large samples, these trade-offs can be deemed relatively unnecessary. Note, here, that we assumed in Figure 2.5 that the standard distribution lies on the left of the empirical distribution. This need not always be the case. If such a direction of the effect is known, we can use a one-tailed test. However, if we do not know this directionality, a two-tailed test should be employed. Finally, it can be seen that the two types of errors depend on the overlap on either side of the test threshold between the two distributions. Hence, if one were to reduce the standard deviations of (one of) the two distributions, this would lead to a reduction in the corresponding overlaps, thereby reducing the respective errors. This would in turn result in increased power.

Hence, we can see that a parametric modeling on the two distributions would rely on their overlap. Reporting the amount of overlap between two distributions would, thus, be

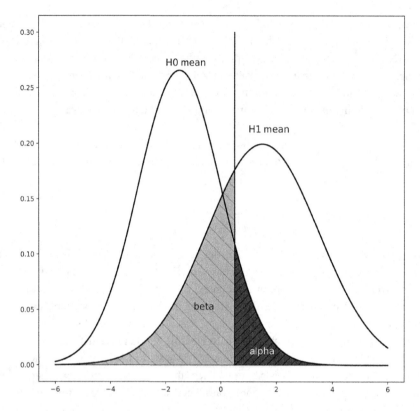

Figure 2.5 Type I and type II errors.

a good indicator of how powerful a test would be for two populations. Quantifying this overlap would then be an indicator of the test's *effect size*. Naturally, a large effect size indicates a small overlap while a small effect size indicates a large overlap. Several measures have been proposed to quantify the effect size of a test depending upon the hypothesis test settings. With regard to the more common case of comparing two means over the difference of classifier performance, Cohen's d statistic has been suggested as a suitable measure of the effect size. Effect size will be discussed in more detail in Section 7.3.

3

Machine Learning Preliminaries

This chapter aims to establish the conceptual foundation of the relevant aspects of machine learning on which the book rests. This very brief overview is in no way exhaustive. Rather, our main aim is to elucidate the relationship of these concepts to the performance evaluation of learning algorithms.

The chapter is divided into five sections. In Section 3.1, we briefly present the differences between human and machine learning. In Section 3.2, we go through supervised learning, the notion of risk and loss function, generalization error, and different learning algorithms. In Section 3.3, we provide a discussion on unsupervised learning and briefly present the basic ideas of clustering, dimensionality reduction, latent variable modeling, and generative learning. In Section 3.4, we go through the challenges of learning and provide a detailed discussion on the bias–variance trade-off. To conclude, Section 3.5 puts all the machine learning components that we discussed in previous sections into perspective and discusses them in the context of evaluation for machine learning.

3.1 Human Learning versus Machine Learning

Human learning is the process that allows us to acquire the skills necessary to adapt to the multitude of situations that we encounter throughout our lives. As human beings, we rely on many different kinds of learning processes at different stages to acquire different functionalities. We learn a variety of different skills, e.g., motor, verbal, mathematical, and so on. Moreover, the learning process differs with the situations and time, e.g., learning how to speak as a toddler is different from learning similar skill sets in a given profession. Variations in learning are also visible in terms of contexts and the related tools, e.g., classroom learning may differ from social contexts, rote learning may be more suitable for memorizing facts but differs from learning how to reason.

By contrast, machine learning aims at analogizing this learning process for computers. Efforts to automate learning have largely focused on perfecting the process of *inductive inference*. Inductive inference refers to observing a phenomenon and generalizing over it. Essentially, this is done by characterizing the observed phenomenon and then using this model to make predictions over future phenomena. Let us start by defining the more general learning problem.

3.2 Supervised Learning

The general model of learning can be described using the following three components:

1. An instance space $\mathcal{X}$ from which random vectors $\mathbf{x} \in \mathbb{R}^p$ can be drawn independently according to some fixed but unknown distribution.[1]
2. An output $y \in \mathcal{Y}$ for every vector $\mathbf{x}$ according to some fixed but unknown conditional distribution. In the more general setting, y need not be scalar but can annotate the example $\mathbf{x}$ with a set of values in the form of a vector $\mathbf{y}$.
3. A learning algorithm[2] A that can implement a set of functions f from some function class $\mathcal{F}$ over the instance space.

Given our three components, the problem of learning is that of choosing the best predictor from the given set of functions that can most closely predict the outcomes of the vectors. This predictor is generally selected based on a training set S of m training examples, drawn according to $\mathcal{X}$ with their respective outcomes. Each tuple of a vector x and its measurement y can be represented by $z = (\mathcal{X}, y)$, which can be assumed to be drawn independently from a joint distribution D.

Different configurations of the above setting yield different learning problems. When the learning algorithm has access to the outputs y for each example x in the training set, the learning is referred to as *supervised learning*. It is worth mentioning that the distinction in output type (class labels, quantitative measurements, or qualitative variables), has led to a naming for the prediction tasks: *regression* when we predict quantitative outputs and *classification* for when we predict qualitative outputs. The term *unsupervised learning* is used when the learning algorithm has no access to the outputs y for each example x in the training set. The availability of the outputs for input examples also dictates the goals of these two learning methods. The first aims to obtain a model that can provide an output based on the observed inputs, such as to provide a diagnosis based on a set of symptoms. The latter, on the other hand, tries to model the inputs themselves. This can be thought of as grouping together (or clustering) instances that are similar to each other, for example, patients with similar sets of symptoms.

Note that the above formulation for learning, although quite general, is constrained by the type of information that the learning algorithm A can get. That is, we consider this information in terms of training examples that are vectors in the n-dimensional Euclidean space. Providing information in terms of examples is arguably the most widely practised methodology. However, other approaches exist such as providing learning information via relations, constraints, functions, and even models. Moreover, there have recently been attempts to learn from examples with and without outputs together, an approach largely known as semi-supervised learning.

In addition, the mode of providing the learning information also plays an important role giving rise to two main models of learning: *active learning*, where a learner can interact with the environment and impact the data generation process, and *passive learning*,

---

[1] Note that random vectors are denoted as $\mathbf{x} \in \mathbb{R}^p$, while observed values or training examples are denoted as $x \in \mathbb{R}^p$.

[2] In Section 2.1.2 we saw learning algorithms based on decision trees, logistic regression, and support vector machines (SVM).

where the algorithm is given a fixed set of examples as a way of observing its environment, but lacks the ability to interact with it. It should be noted that active learning is different from online learning where a master algorithm uses the prediction of competing hypotheses to predict the label of a new example and then learns from its actual output. In this book, the focus is on passive learning algorithms. To familiarize the reader with important concepts of supervised learning, we demonstrate the learning problem with a classification task.

3.2.1 A Classification Example

The aim of a classification algorithm A is to obtain a mapping from the examples x to their respective labels y in the form of a predictor f that can also predict the labels for future unseen examples. When y takes on only two values as labels, the problem is referred to as a binary classification problem. While restricting our discussions to this problem makes it easier to explain various evaluation concepts, in addition to the fact that these algorithms are most familiar to the researchers, enabling them to put the discussion in perspective, this choice in no way limits the broader understanding of the message of the book in more general contexts. Needless to say, many of the proposed approaches extend to the multi-class case as well as other learning scenarios such as regression, and our focus on binary algorithms in no way undermines the importance and contribution of these paradigms in our ability to learn from data.

Consider the following toy example of concept learning aimed at providing a flu diagnosis of patients with given symptoms. Assume that we are given the database of imaginary patients shown in Table 3.1.

Here, the aim of the learning algorithm is to find a function that is consistent with the above database and can also be used to provide a flu or no-flu diagnosis for future patients, based on their symptoms. Note that by consistent we mean that the function should agree with the diagnosis, given the symptoms in the database provided. As we will see later, this constraint generally needs to be relaxed to avoid overspecializing the function that, despite agreeing on every patient in the database, might not be as effective in diagnosing future unseen patients.

Table 3.1. *Table of imaginary patients.*

Patient	Temperature ($^\circ$ C)	Cough	Sore throat	Sinus pain	Diagnosis
1	37.0	yes	no	no	No Flu
2	39.0	no	yes	yes	Flu
3	38.8	no	no	no	No Flu
4	36.8	no	yes	no	No Flu
5	38.5	yes	no	yes	Flu
6	39.2	no	no	yes	Flu

From the data in Table 3.1, the program could infer that *anyone with a body temperature above 38^3 and sinus pain has the flu*. Such a formula can then be applied to any new patient whose symptoms are described according to the same five parameters used to describe the patients from the database (i.e., temperature, cough, sore throat, and sinus pain) and a diagnosis issued.[4]

Several observations are worth making at this point. First, many formulae could be inferred from the given database. For example, the machine learning algorithm could have learned that *anyone with a body temperature of 38.5 or more and cough, a sore throat, or sinus pain has the flu*, or it could have learned that *anyone with sinus pain has the flu*. Second, as suggested by our example, there is no guarantee that any of the formulae inferred by the machine learning algorithm is correct. Since the formulae are inferred from the data, they can be as good as the data (in the best case), but not better. If the data is misleading, so will the result of the learning system. Third, what learning algorithms do is different from what a human being would do. A real (human) doctor would start with a theoretical basis (a kind of rule of thumb) learned from medical school that he would then refine based on his subsequent observations. He would not, thankfully, acquire all his knowledge based only on a very limited set of observations.

In terms of the components of learning described in the above formulation, we can look at this illustration as follows. The first component corresponds to the set of all potential patients that could be represented by the four parameters that we listed (temperature, cough, sore throat, and sinus pain). The example database we use only lists six patients with varying symptoms, but many more could have been (and typically are) presented. The second component, in our example, refers to the diagnosis, flu or no-flu, associated with the symptoms of each patient. A classification learning algorithm's task is to find a way to infer the diagnosis from the data. Naturally, this can be done in various ways. The third component corresponds to this choice of the classification learning algorithm. Different algorithms tend to learn under different learning paradigms to obtain an optimal predictor and have their own respective learning biases. Before we look at different learning strategies, let us define some necessary notions.

3.2.2 The Loss Function and the Notion of Risk

The choice of the best predictor is often based on the measure of *risk*, which is simply the degree of disagreement between the true output y of an observation vector x and the one assigned by the predictor $f : \mathcal{X} \rightarrow \mathcal{Y}$ that we denote by $f(x)$. Before defining the *risk* of a predictor, let us define the *loss function*. A loss function is a quantitative measure of the loss when the output y of the vector x is different from the output assigned by the predictor. We denote the generic loss function by $L(y, f(x))$ that outputs the loss incurred when y differs from $f(x)$. We can now define "the *risk* of the predictor f" as

---

[3] in degrees Celsius
[4] In fact, choosing such a formula would obviate the need to measure symptoms other than temperature and sinus pain.

$$R(f) = \int L(y, f(x)) dD(x, y), \tag{3.1}$$

where the probability measure $D(z) = D(x, y)$ is unknown. This risk is often referred to as the *true risk* of the predictor f. Under a classification task and for the zero-one loss, that is, $L(y, f(x)) = 1$ when $y \neq f(x)$ and 0 otherwise, we can write the *expected risk* as

$$R(f) \overset{\text{def}}{=} \Pr_{(x, y) \sim D} (f(x) \neq y). \tag{3.2}$$

Note that the predictor f in Equation (3.2) is defined given a training set. This makes the loss function a training-set dependent quantity. This fact can have important implications in studying the behavior of a learning algorithm as well as making inferences on the true risk of the predictor.

Empirical Risk

In general, it is not possible to estimate the true or expected risk of the predictor without knowledge of the true underlying distribution of the data and possibly their outputs. As a result, the expected risk takes the form of a measurable quantity known as the empirical risk. Hence, the learner often computes the *empirical risk* $R_S(f)$ of any given predictor $f = A(S)$ induced by the algorithm A on a training set S of size m according to

$$R_S(f) \overset{\text{def}}{=} \frac{1}{m} \sum_{i=1}^{m} L(y_i, f(x_i)), \tag{3.3}$$

which is the risk of the predictor with respect to the training data. Here, $L(y, f(x))$ is the specific loss function that can be a binary function (outputting only 1 or 0), or a continuous function, depending upon the class of machine learning tasks.

Illustration of the Notion of Empirical Risk under a Classification Task

Let us now concretely characterize the binary classification problem that we illustrated in Section 3.2.1. In a binary classification problem the label y corresponding to each example x is binary, that is, $y \in \{0, 1\}$. Hence, the aim of a binary classification algorithm is to identify a classifier that maps the examples to either of the two classes. That is, $f : \mathcal{X} \longrightarrow \{0, 1\}$. The risk of misclassifying each example by assigning a wrong class label is typically modeled as a zero-one loss. That is, the classifier incurs a loss of 0 whenever the output of the classifier matches the true label y of the observation vector x and 1 otherwise (i.e., when the classifier makes an error).

Hence, the classification problem is to minimize the probability of the misclassification error over the set S of training examples while making a promising case of good generalization. The true error in the case of a zero-one loss can be represented as shown in Equation 3.4:

$$R(f) \overset{\text{def}}{=} \Pr_{(x, y) \sim D} (f(x) \neq y) = \mathbb{E}_{(x, y) \sim D} I(f(x) \neq y), \tag{3.4}$$

where the indicator function $I(a)$ represents the zero-one loss such that $I(a) = 1$ if predicate a is true and 0 otherwise.

Similarly, the empirical risk $R_S(f)$ can be shown to be

$$R_S(f) \overset{\text{def}}{=} \frac{1}{m} \sum_{i=1}^{m} I(f(x_i) \neq y_i) \overset{\text{def}}{=} \mathbf{E}_{(\mathbf{x}, y) \sim S} I(f(\mathbf{x}) \neq y). \tag{3.5}$$

Note that the loss function $L(\cdot, \cdot)$ in Equation 3.3 is replaced by the indicator function in the case of Equation 3.5 for the classification problem. Given this definition of *risk*, the aim of the classification algorithm is to find a classifier f with low risk as close to the optimal classifier $f' \in \mathcal{F}$ given the training data. Note that f' is such that it exhibits the minimum risk among all the classifiers in $\mathcal{F}$ over the domain of application as discussed in Section 3.2.3. That is, the aim of the learning algorithms is to minimize the generalization error. This problem of selecting the best classifier from the classifier space given the training data is sometimes referred to as *model selection*.

3.2.3 Generalization Error

The *generalization error* is a measure of the deviation of the expected risk of the predictor $f = A(S)$ learned from the overall minimum expected risk. Hence, the generalization error of algorithm A over a sample S is

$$R(A, S) \overset{\text{def}}{=} R(f) - \inf_{f' \in \mathcal{F}} R(f'),$$

where inf denotes the infimum.

In other words, it is understood that the data on which the predictor is trained, while representative of the true distribution, may not lead the algorithm to learn the predictor f' with minimum possible risk. This can be mainly due to two reasons. First, there might not be enough data for the algorithm to make inference on the full underlying distribution. And second, the limited data that is available can further be affected by noise occurring from various sources such as errors in measurement of various values, data entry, or even label assignment. As a result, the best predictor output by the algorithm given the training data is generally not the best overall predictor possible. The additional risk that the predictor f output by the algorithm has over and above that of the best predictor in the predictor space f' is referred to as the generalization error. Note that the predictor f can have a zero training error and still might not be the best possible predictor since the true risk of f would still be greater than that of f'.

Hence, a learning algorithm basically aims at minimizing this generalization error. Given a training set $S = (x_1, \ldots, x_m)$ of m examples, the task of a learning algorithm is to construct a predictor with the smallest possible risk without any information about D, the underlying distribution. However, computing the true risk of a predictor as given above can be quite difficult. In our toy domain, for example, it is possible that the true formula for the flu concept is *anyone with a sore throat or sinus pain and a body temperature above 37.5 has the flu*. Of course, this formula could not necessarily be inferred from the given dataset, and, thus, the predictor output by the algorithm based on the training data would not perform as the desired ideal predictor since some instances of patients with the flu, in the true population, necessarily include patients with high body temperature and sore throats only.

Obtaining a predictor with minimum generalization error from the training data is a difficult task. There are some results in learning theory that, for a given formulation of the learning algorithm, can demonstrate that this can be achieved by minimizing the empirical risk, and, in some cases, additional quantities calculated from the data. For instance, the uniform risk bounds tie the minimization of generalization error to studying the convergence of empirical risk to the true risk uniformly over all predictors for the class of empirical risk minimization (ERM) algorithms discussed in Section 3.2.4.

3.2.4 Learning Algorithms

The issue of modeling the data by choosing the best predictor that not only describes the observed data but can also generalize well is at the core of the learning process. In order to explore the predictor space and choose the best possible predictor given some training data, various learning approaches have been designed. These vary in both the predictor space that they explore and the manner in which they select the most suitable predictor with respect to the training data. This optimization problem is the problem of *model selection*. This optimization is generally based on finding minimum empirical risk on the training data or the best trade-off of the empirical risk and the complexity of the predictor chosen. The model selection criterion of a learning algorithm is an essential part of the algorithm design. There are three main categories in which most of the learning algorithms can be categorized with regard to the model selection criterion that they utilize. These are the algorithms that learn by ERM, structural risk minimization (SRM), and regularization. These approaches, by themselves, have been proven to be quite effective and have also paved the way for other approaches that exploit these to yield better ones. Note, however, that unlike SRM, the ERM approaches focus on one predictor space and hence are relatively restrictive. Let us briefly look at these categories individually.

Empirical Risk Minimization (ERM)

The class of learning algorithms that learn by ERM makes the most direct use of the notion of risk as their optimization criterion to select the best predictor from the predictor space being explored. Given some training set S, the ERM algorithm A_{erm} basically outputs the predictor that minimizes the empirical risk on the training set. That is,

$$A_{\text{erm}}(S) = h' \stackrel{\text{def}}{=} \underset{h \in \mathcal{H}}{\text{argmin}} \; R_S(h).$$

Structural Risk Minimization (SRM)

This class of learning algorithms goes beyond the use of merely the empirical risk as the optimization criterion. Here, the underlying intuition is that more complex predictors generalize poorly (possibly because of overfitting). Hence, the idea is to discover predictors that not only have acceptable empirical risk but are also not unreasonably complex. Notice that by definition the class of SRM algorithms explores predictor spaces of increasing complexities and might not be restricted to one predictor space. However, it should be noted that these pre-dictor spaces of increasing complexity nevertheless belong to the same class. For instance, a learning algorithm that learns linear predictors will learn only linear predictors of increasing complexity (sometimes imposed implicitly using kernels, for instance, in the case of an SVM) but not other classes such as the decision trees.

An SRM algorithm aims at selecting a predictor (or model) with the least complexity (also referred to as *size* or *capacity*) that achieves a small empirical risk. For this, $\mathcal{H}$ is represented using a sequence of predictors of increasing sizes $\{\mathcal{H}_d : d = 1, 2, \ldots\}$ and the SRM algorithm A_{srm} is such that

$$A_{\text{srm}}(S) = h' \overset{\text{def}}{=} \underset{h \in \mathcal{H}_d, d \in \mathbb{N}}{\text{argmin}} \ (R_S(h) + p(d, |S|)),$$

where $p(d, |S|)$ is a function that penalizes the algorithm for predictor spaces of increasing complexity.

Let cm be some complexity measure on predictor space. We would have a set of predictor spaces $\mathcal{H} = \{\mathcal{H}_1, \ldots, \mathcal{H}_k\}$ such that the complexity of predictor space $\mathcal{H}_i$, denoted as $cm_{\mathcal{H}_i}$, is greater than or equal to $cm_{\mathcal{H}_{i-1}}$. Then the SRM algorithm would be to compute a set of predictors minimizing the empirical risk over the predictor spaces $\mathcal{H} = \{\mathcal{H}_1, \ldots, \mathcal{H}_k\}$ and then to select the predictor space that gives the best trade-off between its complexity and the minimum empirical risk obtained over it on the training data.

Regularization

There are other approaches that extend the above algorithms such as regularization where one tries to minimize the regularized empirical risk. This is done by defining a *regularizing term* or a *regularizer* (typically a norm on the predictor $||h||$) over the predictor space $\mathcal{H}$ such that the algorithm outputs a predictor h':

$$h' = \underset{h \in \mathcal{H}}{\text{argmin}} \ R_S(h) + \lambda ||h||^2.$$

The regularization in this case can also be seen in terms of the complexity of the predictor. Hence, a regularized risk criterion restricts the predictor space complexity. Here it is done by restricting the norm of the predictor. Other variants of this approach also exist such as normalized regularization. The details on these and other approaches can be found in Hastie et al. (2001), Herbrich (2002), and Bousquet et al. (2004), among others.

Learning Bias and Algorithm Formulation

Many early machine learning algorithms and even some novel ones have adopted the ERM principle. Among them are approaches such as decision tree learning, naive Bayes, set cov-ering machine (SCM; see for example Marchand and Shawe-Taylor (2002); Shah (2006)). However, further modifications and refinements of algorithms exploring the same predic-tor space have since appeared that incorporate other considerations accounted for by the SRM and regularization frameworks. That is, the underlying learning bias that an algorithm explores need not depend on the principle that it utilizes to learn. A linear discriminant function, for instance, can work purely in an ERM manner if it does not take into account any constraints on the weight vector that it learns (e.g., the norm of this vector) and focuses solely on the empirical risk on the training data. Perceptron learning algorithms are an example of such an approach. However, learning linear discriminant can also take on the form of SVMs in the SRM framework. Even on top of these, there have been regularized versions of linear discriminants available that take into account some regularization of the predictor space. For instance, attempts have been made to incorporate such regularization in the case of SVMs to obtain sparse predictors (SVMs with a small number of support vectors). Similarly, in deep learning, regularization actually penalizes the weight matrices of the nodes to bypass the issue of overfitting. Hence, it might not be a good idea to tie particular learning biases to learning strategies in definitive form. A learning bias such as a linear discriminant, decision tree, or neural network can be learned using more than one strategy.

3.3 Unsupervised Learning

In this chapter we have so far focused on supervised learning tasks. However, there is another type of learning called unsupervised learning. Unlike supervised learning, unsupervised learning lacks associated outputs for each training sample. This absence of output makes it impossible to train a regression or classification model since there are no targets to predict. Instead, unsupervised learning aims to explore the relationships among observations/variables or discover patterns within the input space. Throughout this book, we will explore various popular unsupervised learning tasks from an evaluation perspective. These tasks include clustering, dimensionality reduction, latent variable modeling, and generative learning. Now, let's take a brief look at each of these unsupervised tasks individually. We discuss each of them in much greater detail in Chapter 9.

3.3.1 Clustering

Clustering is the task of grouping a set of observations in a way that observations in the same group are more similar to each other than to those in other groups. To formalize this, one has to define the similarity between observations and means to measure that similarity. There is no uniform answer to this question as it is often a domain-specific question that needs to be addressed by an expert in the subject matter. It is worth mentioning that one can either cluster observations with respect to their variables/features or cluster variables/features with respect to their observations. There are many clustering methods, but two popular ones are K-means clustering (MacQueen 1967) and hierarchical clustering (Johnson 1967). In K-means clustering, we seek to group the observations into a preselected number of groups according to a particular distance metric such as the Euclidean distance. By contrast, hierarchical clustering outputs a tree-based structure of the observations called a dendogram, and through this dendogram it enables one to visualize all possible clusters. Clustering can be used in a wide range of applications, including anomaly detection, semi-supervised learning, image segmentation, and data visualization.

3.3.2 Dimensionality Reduction

Dimensionality reduction is the process by which we transform the data from a high-dimensional space into a low-dimensional space, where most of the information of the data is stored so that the low-dimensional representation reveals some meaningful properties of the original data. To mathematically formulate dimensionality reduction, we denote by x_i, $1 \leq i \leq N$, the ith p-dimensional real-valued observation, and by P we denote the projection mapping that is generated by a particular dimensionality reduction technique. Projection mapping P can be viewed as a transformation that maps a p-dimensional observation to a new space of dimension $q < p$. Popular dimensionality reduction techniques include principal component analysis (PCA), random projections, multi-dimensional scaling, isomap, linear discriminant analysis (LDA), and t-distributed neighbor embedding. Learning the lower-dimensional structure associated with a given set of data is gaining a lot of attention in the disciplines of computer vision, robotics, medical imaging, natural language processing, computational neuroscience, among others.

3.3.3 Latent Variable Modeling

Latent variable modeling refers to a family of methods that use one or more latent variables to explain and explore relationships between a larger set of observed variables. Based on the general linear latent variable modeling approach, the p variables comprising $\mathbf{x}$ are modeled according to

$$\mathbf{x} = \mathbf{A}\mathbf{z}, \tag{3.6}$$

where $\mathbf{A}$ is an $l \times p$ and $\mathbf{z} \in \mathbb{R}^p$ is the corresponding set of latent variables. Traditionally, in latent variable modeling we can assume that the latent variables can be recovered by a linear model from the original random variables as

$$\mathbf{z} = \mathbf{W}\mathbf{x}, \tag{3.7}$$

where $\mathbf{W}$ is an approximation of $\mathbf{A}^{-1}$. Different methods provide different ways for estimating the matrix $\mathbf{W}$. Such methods include LDA, singular value decomposition, nonnegative vector factorization, PCA, independent component analysis (Adali et al. 2014), dictionary learning, as well as multivariate latent variable modeling approaches such as canonical correlation analysis, independent vector analysis (Adali et al. 2014; Kim et al. 2006; Damasceno et al. 2021), and tensor factorization, among others.

3.3.4 Generative Learning

Generative learning refers to models that enable one to generate new data that look very similar to a given set of training data. For example, one can train a model on a set of training pictures of faces, and the trained model would be then able to generate new pictures of faces. Popular models include probabilistic latent variable generative models and generative adversarial neural networks. In summary, latent variable generative models aim to learn the joint probability distribution of $\mathbf{x}$ and the latent variables $\mathbf{z}$, given by the product of $p(\mathbf{x}|\mathbf{z})$, that defines how to map latent variables to the training points and the prior distribution $p(z)$. Learning the joint distribution $p(x, z)$ enables us to generate new samples x by following a sampling strategy. What makes this challenging is that the mapping from the latent variables to the training points becomes a problem of estimating the parameters of $p_\theta(x|z)$, where θ represents the parameters of the probabilistic model. Probabilistic PCA (Tipping and Bishop 1999) and variational autoencoders (VAEs) (Kingma and Welling 2013) are latent variable generative methods that have shown superior performance for many generative learning applications. In comparison, generative adversarial networks (GANs) can also generate realistic data but they work very differently compared to probabilistic PCA and VAEs. GANs are composed of two neural networks, the generator that tries to generate data very similar to the training data and the discriminator that tries to identify if generated data are fake or real. The idea behind GANs has been characterized by deep learning experts as "the most interesting idea in the last ten years in machine learning."

3.4 The Challenges of Learning

There are always certain challenges involved in selecting the best method for your machine learning task. Let us take a look at the issues involved from a model-fitting perspective also known as the problem of *regression*.[5] A model f that fits the data too closely might lead to *overfitting*. Overfitting refers to the problem of making a solution (function) too specific to generalize well in the future. Such a solution is, hence, not generally preferred. Similar is the problem where f underfits the data, that is, f is too general. See Figure 3.1 for an example.

3.4.1 Generalization and Specialization

Adopting a model, such as the straight line above, leads to a model that describes the data through its common behavior and does not focus on explaining individual or clusters of data points. This is a more general model. On the other hand, the dotted curve, for instance, aims at describing each and every data point. That is, it yields a highly specialized model. The more general the model, the higher the chances that it can underfit. That is, it can lead to too general a description of the data. The more specialized the model, the higher the chances that it can overfit. This is because it aims at explaining each individual data point leading to poor generalization. A successful learning strategy would aim at finding a solution that lies somewhere between the two, trading off some specialization so as to obtain better generalization. We will look into another intuitive take on this in the next section on bias and variance analysis.

3.4.2 Bias–Variance Trade-Off

The bias–variance analysis of the predictor risk has become a major source for understanding the behavior of learning algorithms. There have been various attempts to characterize

---

[5] This problem, however, also occurs in classification and other kinds of learning regimens.

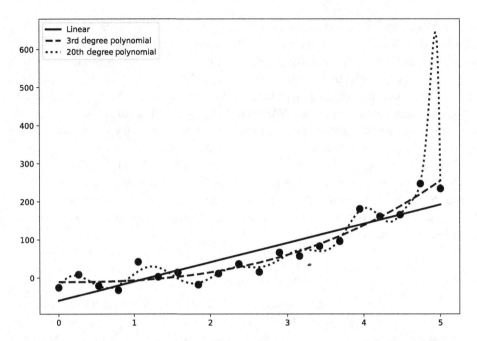

Figure 3.1 A simple example of overfitting and underfitting problems. Consider the problem of fitting a function to a set of data points in a 2-dimensional plane, known as the *regression problem*. Fitting a curve passing through every data point leads to overfitting. The other extreme, approximation by a line, might be a misleading approximation that underfits if the data is sparse. The issue of overfitting is generally addressed using approaches such as pruning or boosting. Approaches such as *regularization* and Bayesian formulations have also shown promise in tackling this problem. In case of sparse datasets we use some kind of smoothing or back-off strategy. A solution in between the two extremes, such as that shown by the dashed curve (3rd degree polynomial), might be desirable.

the bias–variance behavior of a predictor's risk given a fixed loss function. Even though the underlying principle relies on the idea that a nontrivial trade-off between the bias and the variance behavior of a loss function (and hence classifier risk) is desirable so as to obtain classifiers with better generalization performance, a unified framework that can bring together a formulation for understanding such behavior over a variety of loss functions is not yet available. One of the commendable attempts in proposing such a framework that incorporates prominent loss functions is due to Domingos (2000); this is the approach we follow here.

Bias–Variance Decomposition

In this section, we will describe the notion of bias and variance of arbitrary loss functions in a similar way to that of Domingos (2000). More precisely, given an arbitrary loss function we are concerned with its bias–variance decomposition. As we will see, studying the bias–variance decomposition of a loss function provides important insights into both the behavior of the learning algorithm and the model selection dilemma. Moreover, as we will see in later chapters, this analysis also has implications for the evaluation since the error estimation methods (e.g., resampling) can have significant effects on the bias–variance behavior of the loss function and, hence, different estimations can lead to widely varying estimates of the empirical risk of the classifier.

We described the notion of the loss function in Section 3.2.2. Let L be an arbitrary loss function that gives an estimate of the loss that a classifier incurs as a result of disagreement between the assigned label $f(x)$ and the true label y of an example x. Then, we can define the notion of *main prediction*.

Definition 3.1 Given an arbitrary loss function L and a collection of training sets $\mathbf{S}$, the *main prediction* is the one that minimizes the expectation of this loss function over the training sets. That is,

$$\overline{y} = \operatorname*{argmin}_{y'} \mathbf{E_S}[L(f(x), y')].$$

That is, the main prediction is the one that minimizes the expected loss of the predictor on training sets $\mathbf{S}$. In the binary classification scenario, this will be the most frequently predicted label over the examples in the training sets $S \in \mathbf{S}$. That is, the main prediction characterizes the label predicted by the predictor that minimizes the average loss relative to the true labels over all the training sets. This, hence, can be seen as the most likely prediction of the algorithm A given training sets $\mathbf{S}$.

Note here the importance of a collection of training sets $\mathbf{S}$ recalling the observation that we made in Section 3.2.2 on the nature of the loss function. The fact that a predictor is defined given a training set establishes a dependency of the loss function behavior on a specific training set. Averaging over a number of training sets can alleviate this problem to a significant extent. Another factor is the size of the training set since this has an effect on the loss function behavior too. Consequently, what we are interested in is averaging the loss function estimate over several training sets of the same size. However, such an averaging is easier said than done. In practice, we generally do not have access to large amounts of data that can enable us to have several training sets. A solution to this problem can come in the form of data resampling. We will explore some of the prominent techniques of data resampling in Chapter 6 and will also study the related issues.

Let us next define the optimal output $y^\dagger$ of an example x such that $y^\dagger = \operatorname*{argmin}_{y'} \mathbf{E}_y$ $[L(y, y')]$. That is, if an example x is sampled repeatedly then the associated output y need not be the same since y is also sampled from a conditional distribution $\mathcal{Y}|\mathcal{X}$.[6] The optimal prediction $y^\dagger$ denotes the output that is closest to the sampled output over these repeated samplings. This essentially suggests that, since there is a nondeterministic association between the examples and their respective output (in an ideal world this should not be the case), the sampled examples are essentially noisy, with their noise given by the difference between the optimal output and the sampled output. This gives us our next definition.

---

[6] Recall that the examples and the respective outputs are sampled from a joint distribution $\mathcal{X} \times \mathcal{Y}$.

Definition 3.2 The noise of an example x is defined as

$$N(x) = \mathbf{E}_y[L(y, y^\dagger)].$$

Hence, the noise of the example can basically be seen as a measure of misleading labels. The more noisy an example is, the higher the divergence, as measured by the loss function, of its label from the optimal label.

An optimal model would hence be the one that has $f(x) = y^\dagger$ for all x. This is simply the Bayes classifier in the case of classification with zero-one loss function. The associated risk is called the Bayes risk. We can now define the bias of a learning algorithm A.

Definition 3.3 Given a predictor f, for any example $z = (x, y)$, let $y^\dagger$ be the optimal output of x, then the bias of an algorithm A is defined as

$$B_A(x) = L(y^\dagger, \overline{y}).$$

As a consequence, the average bias is

$$\overline{B}_A = \mathbf{E}_x[B_A(x)].$$

The bias of algorithm A can hence be seen as a measure of the overall behavior of the algorithm, dependent of course on the chosen loss function, on example x. That is, this gives a quantification over the difference between the average prediction of the algorithm and the optimal output of the example x. This is basically a measure of the systematic loss of algorithm A and is independent of the training set. If an algorithm can always predict the optimal output, then the bias reduces to zero. Hence, in the classification case, the expected bias of an algorithm can be seen as the difference in the most frequent prediction of the algorithm and the optimal label of the examples.

Accordingly, we can also define the variance of an algorithm.

Definition 3.4 The variance of an algorithm A on an example x is defined as

$$V_A(x) = \mathbf{E}_S[L(\overline{y}, f(x))],$$

and hence the average variance is denoted as

$$\overline{V}_A = \mathbf{E}_x[V_A(x)].$$

Unlike the bias of the algorithm, the variance is not independent of the training set even though it is independent of the true output of each x. The variance of the algorithm can be seen as a measure of the stability, or lack thereof, of the algorithm from the average prediction in response to the variation in the training sets. Hence, when averaged, this variance gives an estimate of how much the algorithm diverges from its most probable estimate (the average prediction). Finally, the bias and variance are nonnegative if the loss function is nonnegative.

With these definitions in place, we can decompose an arbitrary loss function in its bias and variance components as follows: given an example x with true output y and given a learning algorithm that predicts $f(x)$ over a training set $S \in \mathbf{S}$, then, for an arbitrary loss function L, the expected loss over the training sets $\mathbf{S}$ and the true label y can be decomposed as

$$\mathbf{E}_{\mathbf{S},y}[L(y, f(\mathbf{x}))] = \lambda_1 N(\mathbf{x}) + B_A(\mathbf{x}) + \lambda_2 V_A(\mathbf{x}),$$

where λ_1 and λ_2 are loss function-based factors and the other quantities are as defined above.

Let us now look at the application of this decomposition on two specific loss functions in the context of regression and classification, respectively. We start with the regression case, that is, the squared loss. The squared loss is defined as

$$L_{sqr}(y, f(\mathbf{x})) = (y - f(\mathbf{x}))^2,$$

with both y and $f(\mathbf{x})$ being real valued. It can be shown that, for squared loss, $y^\dagger = \mathbf{E}_y[y]$ and $\overline{y} = \mathbf{E}_{\mathbf{S}}[f(\mathbf{x})]$ and, further, that $\lambda_1 = \lambda_2 = 1$.

Hence, in the case of squared loss the following decomposition holds, with $\lambda_1 = \lambda_2 = 1$,

$$\begin{aligned}
\mathbf{E}_{\mathbf{S},y}[(y - f(\mathbf{x}))^2] &= N(\mathbf{x}) + B_A(\mathbf{x}) + V_A(\mathbf{x}) \\
&= \mathbf{E}_y[L(y, y^\dagger)] + L(y^\dagger, \overline{y}) + \mathbf{E}_{\mathbf{S}}[L(\overline{y}, f(\mathbf{x}))] \\
&= \mathbf{E}_y[(y - \mathbf{E}_y[y])^2] + (\mathbf{E}_y[y] - \mathbf{E}_{\mathbf{S}}[f(\mathbf{x})])^2 + \mathbf{E}_{\mathbf{S}}[(\mathbf{E}_{\mathbf{S}}[f(\mathbf{x})] - f(\mathbf{x}))^2].
\end{aligned}$$

Coming to the focus of the book, the binary classification scenario, we can define the bias–variance decomposition for both the asymmetric loss (unequal loss in misclassifying an instance of class 0 to class 1 and vice versa) and symmetric loss (equal loss of misclassification of both classes) scenarios as in Theorem 3.5.

Theorem 3.5 *Given any real-valued asymmetric loss function L such that for labels y_1 and y_2, $L(y_1, y_2) \neq 0, \forall\, y_1 \neq y_2$, then, for a two-class classification algorithm A giving a classifier f,*

$$\mathbf{E}_{\mathbf{S},y}[L(y, f(\mathbf{x}))] = \left[P_{\mathbf{S}}(f(\mathbf{x}) = y^\dagger) - \frac{L(y^\dagger, f(\mathbf{x}))}{L(f(\mathbf{x}), y^\dagger)} P_{\mathbf{S}}(y \neq y^\dagger) \right] \cdot N(\mathbf{x})$$
$$+ B_A(\mathbf{x}) + \lambda_2 V_A(\mathbf{x}), \quad (3.8)$$

with $\lambda_2 = 1$ if $\overline{y} = y^\dagger$, and $\lambda_2 = -\frac{L(y^\dagger, \overline{y})}{L(\overline{y}, y^\dagger)}$ if $\overline{y} \neq y^\dagger$. Moreover, for a symmetric loss function we have

$$\mathbf{E}_{\mathbf{S},y}[L(y, f(\mathbf{x}))] = \left[2 \cdot P_{\mathbf{S}}(f(\mathbf{x}) = y^\dagger) - 1 \right] \cdot N(\mathbf{x}) + B_A(\mathbf{x}) + \lambda_2 V_A(\mathbf{x}),$$

with $\lambda_2 = 1$ if $L(\overline{y}, y^\dagger) = 0$, and $\lambda_2 = -1$ if $L(\overline{y}, y^\dagger) = 1$.

In the multi-class case, we can obtain a bias–variance decomposition for zero-one loss using the following theorem.

Theorem 3.6 *For a zero-one loss function (that is, the indicator loss function) in the multi-class classification scenario, the bias–variance decomposition can be shown to be*

$$\mathbf{E}_{S,y}[L(y, f(x))] = \left[P_S(f(x) = y^\dagger) - P_S(f(x) \neq y^\dagger)P_y(f(x) = y|y^\dagger \neq y) \right] \cdot N(x)$$
$$+ B_A(x) + \lambda_2 V_A(x), \tag{3.9}$$

with $\lambda_2 = 1$ if $\overline{y} = y^\dagger$, and $\lambda_2 = -P_S(f(x) = y^\dagger | f(x) \neq \overline{y})$ otherwise.

The bias–variance decomposition leads to some interesting observations about the behavior of the learning algorithm. With regard to the classification scenario, there are two main observations that warrant elaboration in the current context:

- When the algorithm is not biased on an example, the variance is additive. For biased examples the variance is subtractive. This can be noticed by looking at the bias–variance decomposition of Theorem 3.5. Note that when $B_A(x) = 0$, λ_1 reduces to zero and $\lambda_2 = 1$. Similarly, λ_2 is negative when $B_A(x) \neq 0$, that is, $L(\overline{y}, y^\dagger) = 1$. The above behavior suggests that the loss of an algorithm is reduced by increasing the variance in the case when the learner is biased on an example. That is, in this case, it is advisable to specialize the learner more. In an analogous manner, it pays to generalize the algorithm in response to an unbiased learner by reducing the variance, since in this case the parameter λ_2 becomes positive resulting in the variance being additive. These observations give a useful guide to model selection. A nontrivial trade-off between the bias and variance components can yield a classifier that can avoid overfitting and underfitting as a result. We discuss this in greater detail on a more qualitative level next.
- The first parameter λ_1 plays an important role. As defined in the case of zero-one loss, it suggests that when the prediction $f(x)$ of the classifier is not the same as the optimal prediction $y^\dagger$ (which minimizes the overall loss), then increasing the noise of the example can have the effect of reducing the average error of the algorithm. This is indeed an interesting property and can help explain the good performance of complex classification algorithms in the limited and/or noisy data scenarios. In summary, the zero-one loss is relatively robust to the variance of the algorithm, and in some cases can even benefit as a result of increased variance. However, in the case of multi-class classification scenarios, it can be shown that the tolerance to variance reduces as the number of classes increases.[7]

Note that this behavior holds in the case of zero-one loss, that is, the classification case. However the above decomposition of the error also gives appropriate behavior traits (and hence a guide to optimizing the model) of the algorithm in the regression case when the zero-one loss is replaced by a squared loss.

Model Selection and Bias–Variance Trade-Off

Let us now look at the issue of model selection as well as the issues of generalization (underfitting) and specialization (overfitting) of the algorithm from a bias–variance perspective. Recall our discussion of Section 3.4 on the challenges of learning. More specifically, recall Figure 3.1. Let us again consider the two extreme models that can be fit to the data. First is the case of a straight line. This is generally done in the case of linear regression. As can be seen, fitting a line can result in too simple a model. The error of this model is mainly

---

[7] This can be seen by analyzing the behavior of the bias and variance in Theorem 3.6 in an analogous manner.

attributable to its intrinsic simplicity rather than the dependence on the training data on which the model is obtained. As a result, the predominant factor in the resulting error of the predictor is its bias with respect to the examples. The other extreme in our case is the curve that aims at fitting each and every individual data point. This model too might not generalize well since it has extremely high dependence on the training data. As a result, the model will have a very high variance and will be very sensitive to changes in the training data. Hence, in this case the main source of the error of the model is its variance. Moreover, the problem of a high error due to high variance of the model can further be aggravated if the data is sparse. This explains why too complex a model can result in a very high error in the regression case (squared loss) when the data is sparse.

Note, with respect to the above discussion, that it does not mean that the contribution of the variance term in the case of too simple a model and the bias term in the case of too complex a model is zero. However, in the two cases the bias and the variance terms, respectively, are dominant in their contribution of the error, rendering the contribution of the other terms relatively negligible. As should be clear by now, a model that can both fit the training data well and generalize successfully at the same time can essentially be obtained by a nontrivial trade-off of the bias and variance of the model. A model with a very high bias can result in underfitting while a model with a very high variance results in overfitting. The best model would depend on an optimal bias–variance trade-off and the nature of the training data (mainly sparsity and size).

3.5 Evaluation: Putting Components in Perspective

We have shown how the issues of model selection and parameter settings, the loss function, and the bias–variance trade-off of the error of the learning algorithm are all intimately related. Let us briefly put these elements in perspective by looking at the overall learning process. Given a learning problem, we select a function class from which we hope to discover a model that can best describe the training data as well as generalize well on future unseen data obtained from the same distribution as the training data.[8] The learning algorithm is then applied to the training data and a model that best describes the training data is obtained.

The algorithm selects this model based on some quantitative measure taking into account the error of the model on the training data and possibly trading this accuracy off in favor of a better measure over model complexity. This process of obtaining the best model, given the training data and an optimization criterion, is called model selection. The behavior of the error of the learning algorithm can be analyzed by decomposing it into its components, mainly, bias and variance. The study of bias and variance trade-off also gives insight into the learning process and preferences of a learning algorithm. However, explicit characterization of the bias and variance decomposition behavior of the learning algorithm is difficult owing to two main factors: the lack of knowledge of the actual data generating distribution, and a limited availability of data. The first limitation is indeed the final goal of the learning process itself and hence cannot be addressed in this regard. The second limitation is important in

---

[8] It should be noted that there have also been recent attempts to design algorithms where this restriction on both the training and the test data coming from the same distribution is not imposed.

light of the first. In the absence of the knowledge of the actual data generating distribution, the quantities of interest need to be estimated empirically using the data at hand. Naturally, the more data available, the closer the estimate will be to the actual value. A smaller dataset size can significantly hamper reliable estimates. Limited data availability plays a very significant role both in model selection and in assessing the performance of the learning algorithm on test data. However, this issue can, to some extent, be ameliorated using what are known as data resampling techniques. We will discuss various resampling techniques, their use and implications, and their effect on the performance estimates of the learning algorithm in detail in Chapter 6 and Chapter 7. Even though our main focus is not on the effect of resampling on model selection, we will briefly discuss the issue of model selection, where pertinent, while discussing some of the resampling approaches.

In this book, we assume that given a choice of the model space we have at hand the means to discover a model that is best at describing the given training data and a guarantee on future generalization over such data.[9] Now, every learning algorithm basically explores a different model space. Consider another problem then. What if the model space that we chose does not contain such a model? That is, what if there is another model space that can better explain the data at hand? Let us go a step further. Assume that we have k candidate model spaces each available with an associated learning algorithm that can discover the model in each case that best describe the data. How do we choose the best model space among all these. Implicitly, how do we choose the best learning algorithm given our domain of learning? Looked at in another way, how can we decide which of the k algorithms is the best on a set of given tasks? *This problem, known as the evaluation of the learning algorithm, is the problem that we explore in this book.*

We can look at evaluating learning algorithms from a different perspective. Instead of having a domain of interest on which to find the best suited approach to learning, let us say that we have designed a generic learning algorithm. We now wish to evaluate how good our learning algorithm is. We can measure this "goodness" in various respects. For instance, what are the domains that are most suitable for our learning algorithm to apply to? How good is our learning algorithm compared to other such generic learning algorithms? On what domains? And so on. Some of the main issues underlying such evaluations are those of evaluation metrics and dataset selection and the concerns surrounding it.

We discuss traditional evaluation techniques in Chapter 4 and explain why these techniques are not sufficient in all cases. Chapters 5, 6, and 7 delve into more sophisticated approaches to evaluation metrics selection, error estimation/resampling, and statistical testing, respectively. These chapters are mostly concerned with the classification paradigm. In Chapters 8 and 9 we turn to evaluation methods for other supervised machine learning settings and unsupervised machine learning tasks, respectively. Finally, in Chapter 10 we discuss evaluation from an industrial perspective, and in Chapter 11 we discuss the ingredients necessary for the pursuit of responsible machine learning.

---

[9] We use the term guarantee loosely here. Indeed there are learning algorithms that can give a theoretical guarantee over the performance of the model on future data. Such guarantees, known as risk bounds or generalization error bounds, have even been used to guide the model selection process. However, in the present case, we also refer to implicit guarantees obtained as a result of optimizing the model selection criterion such as the ERM or SRM.

4

Traditional Machine Learning Evaluation

When first introduced to the field of machine learning, students and practitioners are typically informed about the importance of evaluating their models. They are also introduced
to some standard ways to proceed with that evaluation. This chapter presents a review of
these standard techniques and discusses why, while these procedures are very useful as a
starting point, they are not sufficient in all cases. Section 4.1 discusses why it is important
to evaluate machine learning systems, presents the main tenets of evaluation, and discusses
the evaluation process for different types of common machine learning problems (binary
and multi-class classification, regression analysis, and clustering). Section 4.2 looks at the
well-known metrics in use for these problems, including metrics derived from the confusion
matrix, as well as several distance and similarity metrics. Section 4.3 reviews the best
known error-estimation procedures, including the hold-out method and cross-validation,
while Section 4.4 reviews two common statistical tests: the t-test and the sign test. Finally,
Section 4.5 discusses why the evaluation methods presented in the chapter are a good start
but are not sufficient in many cases.

4.1 Overview of Machine Learning Evaluation

In this section, we motivate the need for machine learning evaluation, discuss its main
aspects, and describe the overall approach taken to evaluate models.

4.1.1 The Need for Machine Learning Evaluation

In order to answer the question of why machine learning evaluation is so important, we
should first contemplate what makes machine learning-based programming different from
other software engineering tasks. The main aspect, as far as evaluation is concerned, is that
while other programming tasks are typically deterministic, machine learning is *nondeterministic*. As discussed in Chapter 3, machine learning is governed by the data input to the
system as well as the biases of the learner, but at the end of the day, neither the characteristics
of the data nor these biases are sufficiently understood for a developer to predict what the
system will do. This is what is so fascinating about machine learning, but also what makes
it so difficult to harness and, possibly, so dangerous to rely on, at least in certain types of
sensitive practical applications.

While evaluation is, indeed, part of the answer, the problem does not stop there. If evaluation is not performed properly, then the situation is even more dangerous since the designer of the system may develop a false sense of security, thinking that the system was shown, through evaluation, to be functioning properly when it is, in fact, not. In truth, even if evaluation is performed properly, there will remain questions about the performance of the system, since we are, in effect, trying to predict the future and no one knows what the future may bring. Nonetheless, proper evaluation brings us closer to the answers we seek.

There are many ways in which evaluation can be done "wrong." Using the entire dataset for both training and testing a learning system, for example, is a common rookie mistake. In such cases, the designer will have an overly optimistic view of the system's predictive ability since it will have only been tested on data it has seen before. Whether or not the approach is generalizable to cases not found in the data remains unknown. Another issue concerns the metric used to estimate the system's capability. Accuracy (the percent of correctly classified instances), for example, used on extremely skewed or imbalanced datasets, yields misleading results, as demonstrated by the following example: assuming that a testing set contains 95 "negative" instances and 5 "positive" instances and that a classifier automatically outputs "negative" in all cases, then that extremely simplistic classifier would obtain a respectable 95% accuracy score when, in fact, it has not learned anything other than to predict the majority class. As it turns out, this is an extremely common problem given that many datasets are imbalanced and many classifiers – even sophisticated ones – revert to predicting the majority class when faced with high imbalances. There are many other, less obvious, pitfalls to evaluation that will be discussed throughout the book, but we hope that these two examples illustrate the kind of thing that can go wrong during the evaluation process and motivate the need for further investigation of the issue.

4.1.2 The Main Tenets of Machine Learning Evaluation

The evaluation of learning algorithms both in absolute terms and in relation to other algorithms involves addressing four main components:

- performance measures;
- error estimation;
- statistical significance testing;
- test benchmark selection.

We introduce each of these components in turn.

Performance measures In the realm of all the issues related to machine learning evaluation, those concerning evaluation metrics have, by far, received the most attention, both in terms of discussions and following. The purpose of an evaluation metric is to assess the learning system's performance quantitatively. While we discuss some of the most popular metrics in this chapter, it is important to keep in mind that all metrics have limitations. These limitations will be discussed in Chapter 5, which will also introduce other measures of performance that each emphasize different characteristics of the performance.

Error estimation Limited data availability or, perhaps more specifically, limited availability of relevant data in practical scenarios necessitates the use of resampling methods for the purpose of error estimation. The questions that arise then are: What data should be used for training the system and what data should be used for testing it? As discussed earlier, using all the data for both tasks is unacceptable as it yields an optimistically biased estimate of the system's predictive ability. There are a number of error estimation techniques starting with the well-known hold-out and cross-validation methods, which will be covered in Section 4.3. More complex, however, are questions of how to sample the data appropriately to deal with parameter optimization when a learner is highly dependent on the parameters it uses, how to address the loss of independence of the samples so important in statistical calculations, and what to do when the dataset is either very small or very large. These intricate questions will be considered in Chapter 6.

Statistical significance testing When comparing the predictive capability of different learning systems, it may be useful to assess whether the differences observed in the systems are statistically significant or not. This is a common procedure used in a variety of scientific fields that also applies to machine learning. One of the best-known statistical significance test is the t-test. An even simpler one is the sign test. We will describe these two tests in Section 4.4, but while these tests may apply in some cases, it turns out that they are, typically, not the most appropriate ones to use in machine learning experiments. Chapter 7 will dig into the question of statistical analysis in great detail, presenting both frequentist and Bayesian approaches for conducting statistical analysis in complex settings that involve multiple domains and multiple datasets, and discussing their advantages and limitations.

Test benchmark selection An additional component of machine learning evaluation is the selection of benchmark data. The experimental framework used by the machine learning community often consists of running large numbers of simulations on community-shared domains such as the domains from the UCI machine learning repository, OpenML, or Kaggle. There are many advantages to working in such settings. In particular, new algorithms can easily be tested in conditions resembling real-world conditions; problems arising in real-world settings can, thus, be promptly identified and focused on; and comparisons between new and old algorithms are easy since researchers share the same datasets. Unfortunately, coupled with these advantages, are a number of disadvantages, such as the multiplicity effect and community experiments discussed in Salzberg (1997), as well as issues of data quality since the repositories may not contain the kinds of data challenges that occur in real life. The multiplicity effect and community experiment phenomena are related to the discussion in Chapter 7 about the comparison of multiple classifiers on a single or multiple domains. Questions of data quality are discussed in Chapters 10 and 11.

4.2 Common Evaluation Metrics

4.2.1 Classification

The Confusion Matrix

The performance measures that we discuss in this section pertain to the problem of classification, and draw information solely from the confusion matrix. Let us start by discussing what the confusion matrix is, in the general case, for a classifier f. We begin with a formal definition and follow with a simple illustration of the concept in the binary case. An illustration of the concept in the multi-class case is given in Section 4.2.3.

Let us denote the confusion matrix by $\mathbf{C}$. Then $\mathbf{C} = \{c_{ij}\}, i, j \in \{1, 2, \ldots, l\}$, where i is the row index, j is the column index, and l denotes the number of labels. Generally, $\mathbf{C}$ is defined with respect to some fixed learning algorithm. An aspect worth noting is that given a training dataset and a test dataset, an algorithm learns on the training set, outputting a fixed classifier f. The test set performance of f is, then, typically recorded in the confusion matrix. This is why we define our confusion matrix entries as well as the measures derived from these with respect to a fixed classifier f. However, in the cases where the size of the overall data at hand is limited, resampling approaches are utilized that divide the data into training and test sets and perform runs over these divisions multiple times. In this case, the confusion matrix entries would be the averaged performance of the learning algorithm over all such runs (and, hence, represent the average performance of classifiers in each run). Of course, there are concerns with regard to the reliability of these estimates in the resampling scenario, but we postpone the discussion of resampling techniques and their associated issues to Section 4.3 and Chapter 6.

For the present case, assuming a fixed classifier f, let us denote the confusion matrix with respect to f as $\mathbf{C}(f)$. Then $\mathbf{C}(f)$ is a square $l \times l$ matrix for a dataset with l classes. Each element $c_{ij}(f)$ of the confusion matrix denotes the number of examples with a class i label that the classifier f assigns to class j. For instance, the entry $c_{13}(f)$ denotes the number of examples belonging to class 1 that are assigned to class 3 by classifier f.

Hence, for a test set T of examples and a classifier f, the confusion matrix $\mathbf{C}(f)$ can be defined as

$$\mathbf{C}(f) = \left\{ c_{ij}(f) = \sum_{x \in T} [(y = i) \text{ and } (f(x) = j)] \right\},$$

where x is a test example and y is its corresponding label such that $y \in \{1, 2, \ldots, l\}$.

We can easily make the following observations:

- $\sum_{j=1}^{l} c_{ij}(f) = c_{i.}(f)$ denotes the total number of examples of class i in the test set.
- $\sum_{i=1}^{l} c_{ij}(f) = c_{.j}(f)$ denotes the total number of examples assigned to class j by classifier f.
- All the diagonal entries c_{ii} denote the correctly classified examples for class i. Hence, $\sum_{i=1}^{l} c_{ii}(f)$ denotes the total number of examples classified correctly by classifier f.
- All the nondiagonal entries denote misclassifications. Hence, $\sum_{i, j: i \neq j} c_{ij}(f)$ denotes the total number of examples assigned to wrong classes by classifier f.

Table 4.1. *Confusion matrix for the binary classification case.*

Classifier f	Pred_Negative	Pred_Positive
Act_Negative	$c_{11}(f)$	$c_{12}(f)$
Act_Positive	$c_{21}(f)$	$c_{22}(f)$

Table 4.2. *Alternate representation of the confusion matrix.*

	Pred_Negative	Pred_Positive	
Act_Negative	True negative (TN)	False positive (FP)	N = TN + FP
Act_Positive	False negative (FN)	True positive (TP)	P = FN + TP

As can be seen in the above case, the entries of **C** deal with a deterministic classification scenario for the symmetric loss case. That is, f deterministically assigns a label on each instance with unit probability instead of making a probabilistic statement on its membership for different classes. Moreover, the cost associated with classifying an instance x to class $j, j \in \{1, \dots, l\}$ is the same as classifying it to class k such that $k \in \{1, \dots, l\}, k \neq j$. We will see in Section 5.6 how we can incorporate these considerations into the resulting performance measures.

The Binary Classification Case

The binary classification case is the most common setting in which the performance of a classifier is measured. Additionally, this setting serves well for illustration purposes with regard to the strengths and limitations of the various performance measures that will be discussed in Chapter 5. For $l = 2$ classes, the confusion matrix is obviously a 2×2 matrix and is generally of the form given in Table 4.1, which, calling the two classes "negative" and "positive," respectively, gives $\mathbf{C}(f)$ for the binary classification case.

Here, the rows represent the actual class of the test examples while the columns represent the class assigned (or predicted) by the classifier f. Hence, c_{11} denotes the element in the first row and first column and is equal to the total number of examples whose actual labels are negative and that are also assigned a negative label by the classifier f.

We can describe the binary confusion matrix in the more intuitive form shown in Table 4.2. This confusion matrix contains four characteristic values: the numbers of true positives (TP), false positives (FP), false negatives (FN), and true negatives (TN). Thus, TP and TN stand for the number of examples from the testing set that were correctly classified as positive and negative, respectively. Conversely, FN and FP stand for the positive and negative examples that were erroneously classified as negative and positive, respectively.

Let us illustrate this by an example. Consider applying a naive Bayes classifier to the Breast Cancer dataset in the UCI database[1] (we will discuss this and some other experiments

---

[1] See DOI:10.24432/C5DW2B.

Table 4.3. *Confusion matrix for naive Bayes applied to the breast cancer domain.*

Naive Bayes	Pred_Negative	Pred_Positive
Act_Negative	44	2
Act_Positive	4	93

in Section 5.3). The domain refers to the application of the classifier to predict, on a set of patients, whether a recurrence would occur. Hence, the two class labels refer to "positive" (recurrence occurred) and "negative" (recurrence did not occur). In this particular experiment, we divided the dataset randomly into a training set (containing 75% of the data) and a testing set (containing 25% of the data). After training the naive Bayes classifier on the training set and applying it to the testing set, we obtained the confusion matrix of Table 4.3.

Let us now interpret the meaning of the values contained in the confusion matrix. Relating the matrix of Table 4.3 to that of Table 4.2, we see that: $TP = 93$, $TN = 44$, $FP = 2$, and $FN = 4$. The confusion matrix shows that out of the $93 + 44 + 2 + 4 = 143$ patients in our test set who previously had breast cancer, $TP + FN = 93 + 4 = 97$ suffered a new episode of the disease while $FP + TN = 2 + 44 = 46$ had remained disease-free at the time the data was collected. Our particular naive Bayes classifier[2] predicts results that slightly differ from the truth both in terms of numbers of predictions and predicted class distributions. It predicts that $TP + FP = 93 + 2 = 95$ patients suffered a new episode of the disease and that $FN + TN = 4 + 44 = 48$ did not suffer from any new episode. This shows that this particular naive Bayes classifier predicts recurrence and lack thereof almost perfectly. It is slightly optimistic where "optimistic" refers to a smaller number of predicted recurrences (95) than the actual number of recurrences (97) and a larger number of predicted nonrecurrences (48) than the actual number of nonrecurrences (46). The confusion matrix further breaks these results up into their correctly predicted and incorrectly predicted components for the two prediction classes. That is, it reports how many times the classifier predicts a recurrence wrongly and how many times it predicts nonrecurrence wrongly. As can be seen, of the 95 recurrence cases predicted overall by naive Bayes, 93 were actual recurrence cases, while 2 were not. Similarly, out of the 48 cases for which naive Bayes predicted no recurrence, 44 cases were actual nonrecurrence cases, while 4 were recurrence cases.[3]

The code showing the matrix in Table 4.3 is available in the GitHub repository that accompanies the book.

---

[2] Note that nothing can be said about naive Bayes in general or even naive Bayes on this particular problem. Different partitions of the data into training and testing sets may yield different results. Here, we are only illustrating the meaning of the confusion matrix.

[3] Note, however, that the data was collected at a particular time. At that time, the people wrongly diagnosed by naive Bayes did not have the disease again. However, this does not imply that they did not develop it at any time after the data was collected, in which case naive Bayes would not be that wrong. We restrain ourselves from delving into this issue further for now. But this highlights an inherent limitation of our evaluation strategy and warns the reader that there may be more variables in play when a learning algorithm is applied in practice. Such application-specific considerations should always be kept in mind.

4.2.2 Important Metrics in the Binary Case

We now review some well-known, important metrics in the binary case.

Error Rate and Accuracy

We first present a formal definition of error rate and accuracy, relating them to the notions of risk discussed in Chapter 3. We then express them in terms of the TP, TN, FP, and FN measurements discussed in Section 4.2.1. This reflects the presentation style followed throughout this section.

Recall from Chapter 3 our definition of the empirical risk $R_T(f)$ of classifier f on test set T defined as

$$R_T(f) \overset{\text{def}}{=} \frac{1}{|T|} \sum_{i=1}^{|T|} I(f(x_i) \neq y_i), \tag{4.1}$$

where $I(a)$ is the indicator function that outputs 1 if the predicate a is true and zero otherwise, $f(x_i)$ is the label assigned to example x_i by classifier f, y_i is the true label of example x_i, and $|T|$ is the size of the test set.

In terms of the entries of the confusion matrix, the empirical error rate of Equation (4.1) can be computed as

$$R_T(f) = \frac{\sum_{i,j:i \neq j} c_{ij}(f)}{\sum_{i,j=1}^{l} c_{ij}(f)} = \frac{\sum_{i,j=1}^{l} c_{ij}(f) - \sum_{i=1}^{l} c_{ii}(f)}{\sum_{i,j=1}^{l} c_{ij}(f)}.$$

The error rate, thus, measures the fraction of the instances from the test set that are misclassified by the classifier. A complement to the error rate measurement, naturally, would measure the fraction of correctly classified instances in the test set. This measure is referred to as *accuracy*. Reversing the criterion in the indicator function of Equation (4.1) leads to the accuracy measurement $Acc_T(f)$ of classifier f on test set T, that is,

$$Acc_T(f) \overset{\text{def}}{=} \frac{1}{|T|} \sum_{i=1}^{|T|} I(f(x_i) = y_i).$$

This can be computed in terms of the entries of the confusion matrix as

$$Acc_T(f) = \frac{\sum_{i=1}^{l} c_{ii}(f)}{\sum_{i,j=1}^{l} c_{ij}(f)}.$$

For the binary classification case, our representations of the confusion matrix of Table 4.1 and, subsequently, Table 4.2 yields

$$Acc_T(f) = \frac{c_{11}(f) + c_{22}(f)}{c_{11}(f) + c_{12}(f) + c_{21}(f) + c_{22}(f)} = \frac{TP + TN}{P + N}$$

and

$$R_T(f) = 1 - Acc_T(f) = \frac{c_{12}(f) + c_{21}(f)}{c_{11}(f) + c_{12}(f) + c_{21}(f) + c_{22}(f)} = \frac{FN + FP}{P + N}.$$

Example In the example of naive Bayes applied to the breast cancer domain, the accuracy and error rates are calculated as

$$Acc_T(f) = \frac{93 + 44}{93 + 4 + 44 + 2} = 0.958,$$

$$R_T(f) = 1 - 0.958 = 0.042.$$

These results tell us that naive Bayes made a correct prediction in 95.8% of the cases or, equivalently, made prediction errors in 4.2% of the cases in this particular instance of the problem. How should such a result be interpreted? Well, it suggests that naive Bayes gets the correct diagnostic in over 9 out of 10 cases on average, and gets it wrong in fewer than 1 out of 10 cases. This seems pretty reliable.[4] What the accuracy and error rates do not tell us, however, is whether naive Bayes is overly pessimistic, overly optimistic, or a mixture of the two, in terms of telling people who should have no fear of recurrence that they will incur a new episode of cancer, or in telling people who should worry about it, not to do so. This is the typical context in which accuracy and error rates can result in misleading evaluation as discussed next.

True and False Positive Rates

The most natural metric aimed at measuring the performance of a classifier on instances of a single class is arguably its true positive rate. Although the nomenclature can be a bit misleading in the multi-class scenario (indeed, what class can be considered "positive" among the many classes), it is relatively more intuitive in the binary classification scenario where typical references to the instances of the two classes are made as "positive" and "negative." In its general form, this measure refers to the proportion of the examples of some class i of interest actually assigned to class i by the learning algorithm. In terms of the entries of the general confusion matrix $\mathbf{C}(f)$ described in Section 4.2.1, the true positive rate of a classifier f with regard to class i (that is, when the class of interest, the "positive" class, is class i) is defined as

$$TPR_i(f) = \frac{c_{ii}(f)}{\sum_{j=1}^{l} c_{ij}(f)}.$$

In an analogous manner, one can also be interested in the instances assigned to class i of interest that actually do not belong to this class. The false positive rate of a classifier quantifies this proportion. The false positive rate of classifier f with respect to class i is defined in terms of $\mathbf{C}$'s entries as

$$FPR_i(f) = \frac{\sum_{j:j\neq i} c_{ji}(f)}{\sum_{j,k:j\neq i} c_{jk}(f)}.$$

Hence, $FPR_i(f)$ measures the proportion of examples not belonging to class i that are, nonetheless, erroneously classified as belonging to class i.

---

[4] Please note, however, that using a training and testing regimen as we have done here with such a small dataset is not recommended. This example is used for illustration purposes. We will discuss appropriate resampling strategies in Section 4.3 and Chapter 6.

In the binary classification case, the above metrics, for the class of interest termed positive in accordance with the confusion matrix representations of Tables 4.1 and 4.2, simplify to

$$TPR(f) = \frac{c_{22}(f)}{c_{21}(f) + c_{22}(f)} = \frac{TP}{TP + FN}$$

and

$$FPR(f) = \frac{c_{12}(f)}{c_{11}(f) + c_{12}(f)} = \frac{FP}{FP + TN}.$$

True and false positive rates generally form a complement pair of reported performance measures when the performance is measured over the positive class in the binary classification scenario. In the binary classification scenario, we can obtain the same measures on the "negative" class (the class other than the "positive" class) in the form of true negative rate $TNR(f)$ and false negative rate $FNR(f)$ respectively. Our representations of Tables 4.1 and 4.2 yield

$$TNR(f) = \frac{c_{11}(f)}{c_{11}(f) + c_{12}(f)} = \frac{TN}{TN + FP},$$

$$FNR(f) = \frac{c_{21}(f)}{c_{21}(f) + c_{22}(f)} = \frac{FN}{FN + TP}.$$

In signal detection theory, the true positive rate is also known as the *hit rate*, while the false positive rate is referred to as the *false alarm rate* or the *fall-out*.

In the naive Bayes examples, the values are

$$TPR(f) = \frac{93}{93 + 4} = 0.9588,$$

$$FPR(f) = \frac{2}{2 + 44} = 0.0435,$$

$$TNR(f) = \frac{44}{44 + 2} = 0.9565,$$

$$FNR(f) = \frac{4}{4 + 93} = 0.0412.$$

Next, we discuss another complement metric that generally accompanies the true positive rate to form an important pair of metrics.

Sensitivity and Specificity

The true positive rate of a classifier is also referred to as the *sensitivity* of the classifier. The term has its origin in the medical domain where the metric is typically used to study the effectiveness of a clinical test in detecting a disease. The process of evaluating the test in the context of detecting a disease is equivalent to investigating how sensitive the test is to the presence of the disease. That is, how many of the positive instances (e.g., actual disease cases) can the test successfully detect? The complement metric to this, in the case of the two-class scenario, the true negative rate, would focus on the proportion of negative instances (e.g., control cases, or healthy subjects) that are detected. This metric is also called the *specificity* of the classifier. Hence, specificity is the true negative rate in the case of the binary classification scenario. That is, sensitivity is generally considered in terms of the positive class while the same quantity when measured over the negative class is referred to as specificity. Again, based on the binary classification confusion matrix of Table 4.2, we can define the two metrics as

$$Sensitivity = \frac{TP}{TP + FN}$$

and

$$Specificity = \frac{TN}{FP + TN}.$$

As can be seen, sensitivity is simply $1 - FNR(f)$ while specificity is the true negative rate $TNR(f)$.

In the example of naive Bayes applied to the breast cancer domain (Table 4.3), the sensitivity and specificity we obtain are $Sensitivity = \frac{93}{93+4} = 0.959$ and $Specificity = \frac{44}{2+44} = 0.957$. The 0.959 sensitivity value obtained tells us that naive Bayes rightly predicted 95.9% of the actual recurrence cases. Additionally, the specificity of 0.957 shows that in 95.7% of all cases of actual nonrecurrence, naive Bayes made the right prediction.

So what does this mean? To answer this question, we considered the situation of a patient who wants to put all the chances of survival on her side. A sensitivity of 0.959 tells us that naive Bayes missed only $100 - 95.9 = 4.1\%$ of the actual recurrence cases, meaning that if a physician chose not to administer the treatment reserved for patients with the greatest chances of recurrence, based on the naive Bayes' results we obtained, there is a 4.1% chance that the physician denied a potentially life-saving treatment to a patient who needed it. The specificity of 0.957, on the other hand, tells the patient that she may receive unnecessary treatment in $100 - 95.7 = 4.3\%$ of the cases.

Positive and Negative Predictive Values

Another aspect of assessment is the question of what the proportion of examples that truly belong to class i is from among all the examples assigned to (classified as) class i. The positive predictive value (PPV) measures this statistic over the classifier's performance on a test set (considering the class of interest i to be the "positive" class). This metric therefore measures how "precise" the classifier is when identifying the examples of a given class. PPV, therefore, is also referred to as *precision*. PPV has its origin in medical evaluation. The usage of the term "precision" for the metric is more common in the information retrieval domain.

In the context of the example of clinical test efficacy on patients used to introduce the concepts of sensitivity and specificity, we can imagine that a clinician would also be interested in learning the proportion of positive tests that detected the genuine presence of some pathology or condition of interest. Being typically applied in the binary class scenario, the PPV can be measured with respect to both classes of the test domain. By convention, PPV measures the proportion of correctly assigned positive examples. The complement of PPV in this context appears in the form of negative predictive value (NPV), which measures the proportion of correctly assigned negative examples. For example, when distinguishing two clinical conditions based on a test, it is desired that the test be highly effective in detecting both conditions, that is, it has high PPV and NPV values.

The *precision* or PPV of a classifier f on a given class of interest i (the positive class), in terms of the entries of $\mathbf{C}$, is defined as

$$PPV_i(f) = Prec_i(f) = \frac{c_{ii}(f)}{\sum_{j=1}^{l} c_{ji}(f)} = \frac{c_{ii}(f)}{c_{.i}(f)}.$$

In terms of the binary classification confusion matrix of Table 4.2, we can define the two metrics as

$$Prec(f) = PPV(f) = \frac{TP}{TP + FP},$$

$$NPV(f) = \frac{TN}{TN + FN}.$$

For the breast cancer prediction domain as predicted by naive Bayes, we obtain $PPV(NB) = \frac{93}{93+2} = 0.979$ and $NPV(NB) = \frac{44}{44+4} = 0.917$, which can be interpreted in the following way.

The 0.979 PPV value suggests that a positive prediction by naive Bayes is pretty reliable since it will be true in 97.9% of the cases, while the NPV value of 0.917 suggests that a negative prediction by naive Bayes is less reliable since such predictions were shown to be true in only 91.7% of the cases. Therefore, Bayes can function as a preliminary screening tool to look relatively reliably for positive conformance. It is less reliable when it comes to negative predictions.

Precision, Recall, and the F-Measure

Finally, one can focus on both the PPV over a class of interest in conjunction with the sensitivity of the classifier over this class. These are typical statistics of interest in domains such as information retrieval where one is interested, not only in the proportion of relevant information identified, but also in investigating the actually relevant information from the information tagged as relevant. As we have seen earlier, the first of these two statistics is simply the PPV, while the second statistic is the sensitivity or the true positive rate (TPR). In the information retrieval domain, these are generally referred to as *recall* and *precision*, respectively. At the risk of repeating ourselves, we restate the two metrics for the binary classification scenario:

$$Prec(f) = PPV(f) = \frac{TP}{TP + FP},$$

$$Rec(f) = TPR(f) = \frac{TP}{TP + FN}.$$

In the case of naive Bayes applied to the breast cancer recurrence prediction problem, we have, as calculated earlier $Prec(f) = \frac{TP}{TP+FP} = \frac{93}{93+2} = 0.979$ and $Rec(f) = \frac{TP}{TP+FN} = \frac{93}{93+4} = 0.959$. This means that of all the patients that were classified as recurrence cases, as many as 97.9% had lived through a recurrence of their breast cancer. This tells us that this naive Bayes model is quite precise when establishing a positive diagnostic. It also means that of all the patients it should have identified as recurrence cases, it identified 95.9% of them as such, that is, naive Bayes recalled 95.9% of all the patients it should have recalled as recurrence cases.

F-Measure The F-measure attempts to address the issue of convenience brought upon by a single metric versus a pair of metrics. It combines precision and recall in a single metric. More specifically, the F-measure is a weighted harmonic mean of precision and recall. For any $\alpha \in \mathbb{R}, \alpha > 0$, a general formulation of the F-measure can be given as[5]

$$F_\alpha = \frac{(1+\alpha) \cdot (Prec(f) \cdot Rec(f))}{((\alpha \cdot Prec(f)) + Rec(f))}.$$

There are several variations of the F-measure. For instance, the *balanced F-measure* weighs the recall and precision of the classifier evenly, that is, $\alpha = 1$:

$$F_1 = \frac{2 \cdot (Prec(f) \cdot Rec(f))}{(Prec(f) + Rec(f))}.$$

Similarly, F_2 weighs recall twice as much as precision and $F_{0.5}$ weighs precision twice as much as recall. The weights are generally decided based on the acceptable trade-off of precision and recall.

In our naive Bayes classified breast cancer domain, we obtain

$$F_1 = \frac{2 \cdot (0.979 \cdot 0.959)}{(0.979 + 0.959)} = \frac{1.878}{1.938} = 0.969,$$

$$F_2 = \frac{5 \cdot (0.979 \cdot 0.959)}{(4 \cdot 0.979 + 0.959)} = \frac{4.694}{4.875} = 0.963,$$

$$F_{0.5} = \frac{1.5 \cdot (0.979 \cdot 0.959)}{(0.5 \cdot 0.979 + 0.959)} = \frac{1.408}{1.449} = 0.972.$$

This suggests that the results obtained on both classes are pretty good and that this model of naive Bayes favors precision slightly more than recall.

The metrics discussed in this section are not demonstrated in the GitHub site that accompanies this book because scikit-learn provides excellent documentation on this subject. It is available at: https://scikit-learn.org/stable/modules/model_evaluation.html. The section discussing classification metrics specifically can be found at https://scikit-learn.org/stable/modules/model_evaluation.html#classification-metrics.

ROC Analysis and Area under the ROC Curve

We now turn our attention to receiver operating characteristic (ROC) analysis. ROC analysis provides quite a different performance evaluation method compared with the metrics discussed so far in that rather than comparing well-formed classifiers, it allows us to compare the learning algorithms from which classifiers can be derived. We will give a short

---

[5] Note that this α is different from the one used in statistical significance testing. However, since it is a conventional symbol in the case of F-measure, we retain it here. The different context of the two usages of α will disambiguate the two, helping avoid confusion.

introduction to this method in this section and discuss it in greater depth in Section 5.7. ROC analysis has its origin in signal detection theory as a means to set a threshold or an operating point for the receiver to detect the presence or absence of a signal. The signal is assumed to be corrupted by noise that, in turn, is assumed to be distributed according to a normal distribution. The choice of the best operating point depends on factors such as the variance of the noise that corrupts the signal, the strength of the signal itself, and the desired hit (detecting the signal when the signal is actually present) or false alarm (detecting a signal when the signal is actually absent) rate. The selection of the best operating point is typically a trade-off between the hit rate and the false alarm rate of a receiver.

In the context of learning algorithms, ROC graphs have been used in a variety of ways. ROC analysis is a very powerful graphical tool for visualizing the performance of a learning algorithm over varying decision criteria, typically in a binary classification scenario. The ROCs have been utilized, not only to study the behavior of algorithms, but also to identify optimal behavior regions, perform model selection, and, perhaps most relevant to our context, for the comparative evaluation of learning algorithms. However, before we proceed with the evaluation aspect, it would be quite helpful to understand the meaning of the ROC curve and its relation to other performance measures.

A ROC curve is a plot where the horizontal axis (the x-axis) denotes the false positive rate FPR and the vertical axis (the y-axis) denotes the true positive rate TPR of a classifier. As just discussed, the TPR is simply the sensitivity of the classifier while the FPR is $1 - TNR$ (TNR being the true negative rate) or equivalently $1 - Specificity$ of the classifier. Hence, in this sense, ROC analysis studies the relationship between the sensitivity and the specificity of each classifier that can be formed from a learning algorithm by changing the value of the threshold from which the classification can be derived. The higher the sensitivity and specificity of these classifiers, that is, the faster and the closer the curve gets to the topmost left corner (where sensitivity and specificity are both 1) prior to continuing on to the top right corner, the better its performance.

Figure 4.1 shows the ROC curves of the decision tree and support vector machine (SVM) algorithms applied to the UCI Labor Relations dataset[6] (the example from Table 2.2). The graph shows that, in this domain, the SVM algorithm is superior to the decision tree algorithm throughout the ROC space, that is, no matter what threshold is chosen to form classifiers from these algorithms. Although this represents one kind of situation, in others it is possible for one classifier to dominate some parts of the ROC space and the other classifier to dominate other parts (in such cases, the two ROC curves will cross). Chapter 5 will discuss ROC analysis in greater detail, and explain how the ROC curves are constructed.

Summary statistics and the AUC While ROC analysis affords the advantage of being able to visualize the performance of classifiers over their operating ranges, it does not allow us to quantify this comparative analysis that can facilitate decision making with regard to the suitability or preference of one classifier over others in the form of an objective scalar metric. Various summary statistics have been proposed to address this shortcoming. We discuss briefly the area under the ROC curve here (AUC or AUROC) and will discuss it in more detail along with a couple of other statistics in Chapter 5.

---

[6] See DOI: 10.24432/C5CP4Q.

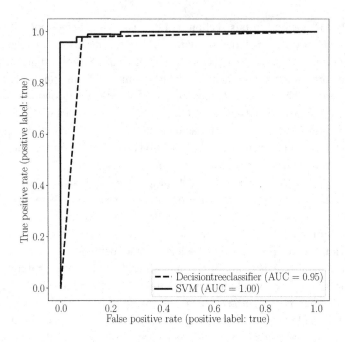

Figure 4.1 The ROC curves for two hypothetical scoring classifiers, f_1 and f_2.

   The AUC represents the performance of the classifier averaged over all the possible cost ratios. The AUC for a classifier f is such that $AUC(f) \in [0, 1]$, with the upper bound attained for a perfect classifier (one with $TPR = 1$ and $FPR = 0$). Moreover, the random classifier represented by the diagonal cuts the ROC space in half and, hence, $AUC(f_{random}) = 0.5$. For a classifier with a somewhat better performance than random guessing, we would expect it to have an AUC greater than 0.5.

ROC Analysis is discussed in the scikit-learn manual along with other evaluation metrics and methods. The discussion can be found at https://scikit-learn.org/stable/modules/model_ evaluation.html and, more specifically, https://scikit-learn.org/stable/modules/model_evaluation .html#classification-metrics. The accompanying GitHub repository provides code for displaying the ROC curve for one and two classifiers for comparison purposes.
The metrics discussed in this section are not demonstrated in the GitHub that accompanies this book because scikit-learn provides excellent documentation on this subject. It is available at: https://scikit-learn.org/stable/modules/model_evaluation.html. The section discussing classification metrics specifically can be found at https://scikit-learn.org/stable/modules/ model_evaluation.html#classification-metrics.

4.2.3 Important Metrics in the Multi-class Case

The confusion matrix defined in Section 4.2.1 was defined for multiple classes although until now, we only illustrated its use on binary classification. Table 4.4 illustrates the case

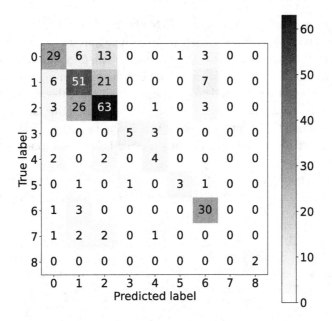

Figure 4.2 Sklearn-generated confusion matrix for SVM with radial basis function kernel applied to the UCI Yeast dataset.

of multi-class classification on the UCI Yeast dataset.[7] The nine different classes represent the cellular localization sites of proteins, and the confusion matrix indicates whether SVM with default radial basis function kernel classified it correctly.

As discussed in Sokolova and Lapalme (2009), there are two general approaches to evaluating the performance of classifiers on multi-class problems: *macro-averaging* and *micro-averaging*. A macro-average treats each class equally no matter how large or small that class is. A micro-average, on the other hand, does not take the size of the classes into consideration; each error counts for the same amount, whether it occurred in a large or a small class.

Accuracy, as defined at the beginning of Section 4.2.2, is a micro-average metric. For the confusion matrix shown in Figure 4.2, accuracy is

$$Acc = \frac{29 + 51 + 63 + 5 + 4 + 3 + 30 + 0 + 2}{52 + 85 + 96 + 8 + 8 + 6 + 34 + 6 + 2} = 62.96\%.$$

Balanced accuracy, by contrast, is defined as

$$Balanced_{Acc}(f) = \frac{\sum_{i,j=i}^{l} \frac{c_{ij}(f)}{\sum_{k=1}^{l} c_{i,k}(f)}}{l}.$$

The balanced accuracy for the confusion matrix of Figure 4.2 is thus

$$Balanced_{Acc} = \frac{\frac{29}{52} + \frac{51}{85} + \frac{63}{96} + \frac{5}{8} + \frac{4}{8} + \frac{3}{6} + \frac{30}{34} + \frac{0}{6} + \frac{2}{2}}{9} = 59.13\%.$$

[7] See DOI: 10.24432/C5KG68.

We note that on class 8 of the yeast dataset, SVM obtains 100% accuracy, while on classes 4 and 5 it only obtains 50% accuracy, and on class 7 it obtains 0%. Since classes 4, 5, and 7, where the classifier's performance is low, are quite small, they were not given the same importance in the micro-average case as they were in the macro-average case. As a result, the overall results obtained with standard accuracy are higher, and thus more optimistic than those reported by balanced accuracy. This is mitigated, however, by the fact that the excellent accuracy obtained on class 9 pertains to only two testing instances, yielding accuracy to, more or less, ignore this excellent performance while balanced accuracy gives it undue consideration.

It is also worth noting that, in addition to balanced accuracy, sklearn, also provides a weighted average solution where the different classes can be weighed with values provided by the user.

> Metrics for multi-class classification are discussed in the scikit-learn manual at https://scikit-learn.org/stable/modules/model_evaluation.html. The GitHub site accompanying this book illustrates its use for SVM trained and tested on five classes of the mnist digit dataset.

4.2.4 *Important Metrics in the Regression Case*

Regression is an important supervised learning paradigm that differs from classification in that rather than predicting a discrete class, the regressor derived from the learning algorithm outputs a real value. Regression can be used in two ways. The first way is the straightforward prediction of a quantity of interest at a later date, such as the value of a stock, the temperature of an ocean, and so on. The second way is the analysis of the relationship between the dependent variable (the output of the regressor) and the independent variables (the input to the regressor) either on a one-on-one basis or as the relationship between a subset of the independent variables and the dependent variable. Regression and its evaluation will be discussed in greater depth in Section 8.6, but we now present some of the well-known metrics typically used to evaluate the performance of regressors.

There are two well-known families of evaluation metrics for regression analysis: the mean square, root mean square, and mean absolute errors, in one family, and the R-square and adjusted R-square measure, in the other.

Mean Family of Measures

We present four metrics belonging to the same family of very intuitive metrics since they aggregate the prediction error made on every instance of the dataset and transform this aggregation into more interpretable measures:

- The sum of squares error (SSE) is defined as follows:

$$SSE = \sum_{i=1}^{n}(y_i - \hat{y}_i)^2.$$

- The mean squared error (MSE):

$$MSE = \frac{1}{n}\sum_{i=1}^{n}(y_i - \hat{y}_i)^2.$$

- The root mean squared error (RMSE), which is the square root of the MSE:

$$RMSE = \sqrt{MSE} = \sqrt{\frac{1}{n}\sum_{i=1}^{n}(y_i - \hat{y}_i)^2}.$$

- The mean absolute error (MAE), which sums the absolute errors made by the model:

$$MAE = \frac{1}{n}\sum_{i=1}^{n}|y_i - \hat{y}_i|.$$

In these definitions, n is the number of instances in the testing set, y_i is the ith observed value, and $\hat{y}_i$ is the value of the ith testing instance predicted by the regressor. SSE indicates the squared error made over all the testing instances and MSE shows the average squared error made per instance. In both cases, the error is squared so that underestimating and overestimating errors are treated the same way. Since squared errors are not necessarily intuitive, the RMSE corrects the issue by taking the square root of the MSE. The RMSE, thus, provides an average error per instance that indicates the amplitude of the average error per instance. MAE is similar to MSE and RMSE. However, instead of squaring the differences like in MSE, MAE takes its absolute value. Like RMSE, the MAE indicates the amplitude of the error. The lower the values of SSE, MSE, RMSE, and MAE, the better since a low value indicates only a small deviation from the true value.

R-Square Family of Measures

The R-square family of measures aims to assess the goodness of fit of a regression model. A model is said to fit the data well if the differences between the observed values and the model's predicted values are small. The R-square measure assesses how much of the variability in the dependent variable can be explained by the model. In other words, it measures the ratio of the total variance explained by the model by the total variance. In certain cases, it is also the square of the correlation coefficient (R) and can take values between 0 and 100%. In other cases, it can take negative values. The formula for the R-squared measure is

$$R^2 = 1 - \frac{\sum_{i=1}^{n}(y_i - \hat{y}_i)^2}{\sum_{i=1}^{n}(y_i - \bar{y}_i)^2},$$

where n is the number of instances in the testing set, y_i is the ith observed value, $\hat{y}_i$ is the value of the ith testing instance predicted by the regressor, and $\bar{y}_i$ is the mean of all y_i's. The R-square measure is a relative measure of goodness of fit, which looks at how well the model fits dependent variables, while the MSE, RMSE, and MAE are absolute measures. However, while R-square does a good job of evaluating how well the model fits the dependent variable, it does not look at the issue of overfitting. This actually implies that adding more variables to the regression model can only increase R^2 and never reduce it. This issue is addressed with the adjusted R-square measure shown here:

$$R^2_\alpha = 1 - \frac{(1 - R^2)(n - 1)}{n - p - 1},$$

where p is the number of independent variables in the data.

These metrics will be discussed and analyzed in more detail in Chapter 8, though in the meantime, we show an example on hypothetical regression results.

Example Table 4.4 lists the results obtained by four hypothetical regression algorithms on a testing set of nine data points. The first line in the table indicates the instance number, the second line, its true expected value, and the next four lines show the results of the four hypothetical regressors. Regress0 is the perfect regressor that gets all the results right. Regress1 is close to perfect in that it gets the right results +/- .08. Regress2 gets perfect results except in two cases where it makes extremely large errors of .6 and .9, respectively. Regress3 is similar to Regress2, but its errors are on the two cases are of .2 and .3, respectively. These errors are still large, but more manageable. We calculated the results obtained by SSE, MSE, RMSE, MAE, and R^2 for each case. These results are shown in Table 4.5.

The results tell us that, according to the R^2 results, Regress0 is perfect, and Regress1 close to perfect. Regress 3 could be considered acceptable, though it performs relatively badly, but Regress2 is unacceptable, obtaining a negative value for R^2. MSE, RMSE, and MAE show us a similar pattern, but do not make any statement about the acceptability of the results or not, the way R^2 does. It is left to the user and his or her knowledge of the

Table 4.4. *Results of four hypothetical regressors.*

Instance number	1	2	3	4	5	6	7	8	9
True value	.1	.6	.3	.4	.6	.9	.8	.7	.2
Regress0 (perfect)	.1	.6	.3	.4	.6	.9	.8	.7	.2
Regress1 (close)	.15	.52	.31	.48	.58	.87	.8	.65	.23
Regress2 (flagrant outliers)	.1	0	.3	.4	.6	0	.8	.7	.2
Regress3 (milder outliers)	.1	.4	.3	.4	.6	.6	.8	.7	.2

Table 4.5. *SSE, MSE, RMSE, MAE and R^2 Results obtained by the four hypothetical regressors.*

Regressor	SSE	MSE	RMSE	MAE	R^2 (%)
Regress0	0	0	0	0	0
Regress1	.0201	.00223	.047	.029	95.87
Regress2	1.17	.13	.36	.17	−62
Regress3	.13	.014	.12	.056	70.6

Table 4.6. R_α^2 *results obtained by two of the hypothetical regressors for number of independent variables* $p = 1, \dots, 4$.

Regressor	No. of independent variables			
	1	2	3	4
Regress1	95.28%	94.5%	93.4%	91.75%
Regress3	66.4%	60.8%	52.96%	41.2%

domain to decide what error is acceptable. Please also note that the pattern of errors (many small errors versus a few larger errors) is not detected by these metrics, since with slightly larger errors, a regressor such as Regress1 could obtain results similar to Regress3, despite the fact that the patterns of errors in these two regressors are very different.

Table 4.6 lists the results obtained using the R_α^2 metric with 1, 2, 3, or 4 dependent variables, by Regress1 and Regress3. These results show that the adjustment for overfitting decreases the original R^2 values of 95.87% and 70.6% for Regress1 and Regress3, respectively. The adjustment becomes more drastic as the number of independent variables increases, and it is greater for lower initial values of R^2. Given that many modern regression problems use a large number of independent variables (though possibly few latent ones), it is unclear how this adjusted value would help, except if p represented latent rather than actual independent variables.

> The metrics discussed in this section are not demonstrated in the GitHub site that accompanies this book because scikit-learn provides excellent documentation on this subject. It is available at: https://scikit-learn.org/stable/modules/model_evaluation.html. The section discussing regression metrics specifically can be found at https://scikit-learn.org/stable/modules/model_evaluation .html#regression-metrics.

4.2.5 An Important Metric in the Clustering Case

Clustering was briefly introduced in Section 3.3.1 and will be discussed in great detail in Section 9.1. In this section, we present one of the best-known metrics used to assess the performance of clustering algorithms.

In clustering problems, two cases are considered: the case where labels are available in the test set and the case where they are not. When labels are available, we refer to the situation as a situation of external validation and the metrics discussed in the context of classification can be used. When labels are not available, however, internal evaluation must be used. Internal evaluation consists of judging whether the clustering approach does a good job of grouping together the data that is similar and separating the clusters that are different. An important metric typically used in these cases is the Davies–Bouldin Index (DBI), which

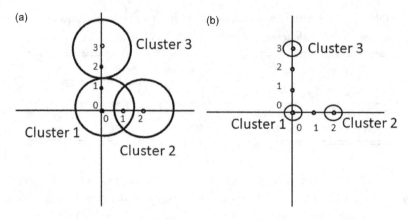

Figure 4.3 (a) Three large overlapping clusters; (b) Three small nonoverlapping clusters.

can be expressed as

$$DBI = \frac{1}{l} \sum_{i=1}^{l} max_{j \neq i} \frac{s_i + s_j}{d(c_i, c_j)},$$

where l is the number of clusters, c_i is the center of cluster i, s_i is the average distance of all points in cluster i from the cluster centroid c_i, and $d(c_i, c_j)$ is the distance of centroid c_i to centroid c_j. The smaller the value of the index, the better the clustering.

We illustrate DBI on the two situations shown in Figure 4.3. In both parts of the figure, $c_1 = (0,0); c_2 = (2,0); c_3 = (0,3)$, and thus, $d(c_1, c_2) = 2; d(c_1, c_3) = 3; d(c_2, c_3) = \sqrt{2^2 + 3^2} = 3.6$. We further assume that, in part (a), $s_1 = s_2 = s_3 = 1.5$, while in part (b), $s_1 = s_2 = s_3 = 0.5$. When applied to these cases of three clusters, we have

$$DBI = \frac{1}{3} \left[max \left(\frac{s_1 + s_2}{d(c_1, c_2)}, \frac{s_1 + s_3}{d(c_1, c_3)} \right) + max \left(\frac{s_2 + s_1}{d(c_1, c_2)}, \frac{s_2 + s_3}{d(c_2, c_3)} \right) + max \left(\frac{s_3 + s_1}{d(c_3, c_1)}, \frac{s_3 + s_2}{d(c_3, c_2)} \right) \right].$$

Using this formula in the large cluster case of Figure 4.3, we get

$$DBI = \frac{1}{3} \left[max \left(\frac{3}{2}, \frac{3}{3} \right) + max \left(\frac{3}{2}, \frac{3}{3.6} \right) + max \left(\frac{3}{3}, \frac{3}{3.6} \right) \right]$$

$$= \frac{1}{3} \left(\frac{3}{2} + \frac{3}{2} + \frac{3}{3} \right) = \frac{4}{3} = 1.33.$$

Using this formula in the small cluster case of Figure 4.3, we get

$$DBI = \frac{1}{3} \left[max \left(\frac{1}{2}, \frac{1}{3} \right) + max \left(\frac{1}{2}, \frac{1}{3.6} \right) + max \left(\frac{1}{3}, \frac{1}{3.6} \right) \right]$$

$$= \frac{1}{3} \left(\frac{1}{2} + \frac{1}{2} + \frac{1}{3} \right) = \frac{4}{9} = 0.44.$$

As discussed before, the smaller DBI value, the better the clustering. It is clear from Figure 4.3 that the situation with the small clusters (part (b)) is better than that with the large clusters (part (a)) since the small clusters are very compact and well separated from each other, whereas the large clusters overlap with each other and are not that compact. The DBI values we obtained reflect these observations as the DBI for the large clusters is much larger than the DBI for the small clusters.

Other metrics are available for clustering including Dunn's index and the sillouhette coefficient. These and other metrics will be discussed in Chapter 9.

The metrics discussed in this section are not demonstrated in the GitHub site that accompanies this book because scikit-learn provides excellent documentation on this subject. It is available at https://scikit-learn.org/stable/modules/model_evaluation.html. The section discussing clustering metrics specifically can be found at https://scikit-learn.org/stable/modules/model_evaluation .html#clustering-metrics.

4.3 Common Error Estimation Procedures

As mentioned in Section 4.1, when presented with a dataset, deciding how much data should be used for training and how much data should be used for testing is a difficult question. On the one hand, the more data is used for training, the better the learned model. On the other hand, the less data is used for testing the less reliable that model is since the user cannot satisfactorily assess how well it performs on previously unseen data. Error estimation consists of making the best use of the data at hand to both train and test learning algorithms. The two approaches discussed here are the famous hold-out and cross-validation approaches, but a full chapter, Chapter 6, is devoted to this issue where these approaches will be analyzed, and additional ones discussed.

4.3.1 Hold-Out Approach

In this method, a separate set of instances is reserved to assess the learning system's performance. This set is different from the training set used by the learning algorithm. The learning algorithm takes as input a labeled set of instances from the training set and outputs f, where f is a classifier, regressor, clustering system, etc.; f is then fed the unlabeled set of instances from the testing set and outputs results for each of these instances, and the estimate of the empirical error is obtained. In the case of a discrete binary classifier, this is basically the fraction of test instances that the classifier misclassifies. Conversely, the accuracy of the classifier is the fraction of the test instances that the classifier classifies correctly.

To illustrate the hold-out method, assume that we have a dataset containing 10 instances[8] as shown in Table 4.7.

The hold-out method consists of randomly selecting a number of instances for training (say two-thirds of the dataset) and using the rest for testing. Table 4.8 shows an example

---

[8] That is never enough to apply a learning algorithm to, but we wanted to illustrate the sampling concepts on a small enough example.

Table 4.7. *A hypothetical dataset with ten instances d1 to d10.*

d1	d2	d3	d4	d5	d6	d7	d8	d9	d10

Table 4.8. *Possible training and testing sets for the holdout method.*

Training:	d7	d4	d1	d3	d9	d5	d10		Testing:	d2	d6	d8

Table 4.9. *The shuffled dataset separated into five folds.*

d6	d9	d4	d1	d3	d5	d2	d7	d10	d8

of what that kind of sampling would result in. The learning system would be trained on the instances on the left of Table 4.8 and tested on the instances on the right.

Performance of the classifier on a separate test set is generally a good indicator of its generalization performance. Formal guarantees over the test set performance in terms of theoretical confidence intervals can be provided in this case, as will be shown in Chapter 6.

4.3.2 k-Fold Cross-Validation

The most popular error estimation approach in machine learning is k-fold cross-validation, which proceeds by dividing the dataset S containing m samples into k subsets of roughly equal sizes. Each subset is called a fold (hence the name of the method). The learning algorithm is then trained on $k - 1$ of these subsets taken together and tested on the kth subset. This is repeated k times with a different subset used for testing. Hence, each of the k folds becomes a test set once. The experiment thus returns k estimates of the resulting learning system's error rate (or other performance metric result) in each iteration. These estimates are then averaged together and constitute the error estimate.

We illustrate k-fold cross-validation on the dataset from Table 4.7. After randomly shuffling the initial dataset, let us assume we end up with the permutation shown in Table 4.9. If we assume $k = 5$, the five different folds are successively used as the testing fold while the other four folds represent the training set. At iteration 1, in this example, Table 4.10 shows the training (left) and testing (right) sets that will be used by the classifier. Similarly, Tables 4.11, 4.12, 4.13, and 4.14 represent the training and testing sets for folds 2, 3, 4, and 5, respectively. Once each fold has been evaluated, the results are averaged. Though we illustrated the process for $k = 5$, it is common to run the procedure with $k = 10$.

The most common value used in the case of machine learning algorithms is $k = 10$ with many empirical arguments in support of this number, especially in large size samples, owing mainly to the obtention of relatively less biased estimates as well as the observation of an acceptable computational complexity in calculating these error estimates.

Table 4.10. *Fold 1: Training and testing sets.*

Training:	d4	d1	d3	d5	d2	d7	d10	d8		Testing:	d6	d9

Table 4.11. *Fold 2: Training and testing sets.*

Training:	d6	d9	d3	d5	d2	d7	d10	d8		Testing:	d4	d1

Table 4.12. *Fold 3: Training and testing sets.*

Training:	d6	d9	d4	d1	d2	d7	d10	d8		Testing:	d3	d5

Table 4.13. *Fold 4: Training and testing sets.*

Training:	d6	d9	d4	d1	d3	d5	d10	d8		Testing:	d2	d7

Table 4.14. *Fold 5: Training and testing sets.*

Training:	d6	d9 4 d3	d4	d1	d5	d2	d7		Testing:	d10	d8

Table 4.15. *The shuffled dataset not separated into folds.*

d6	d9	d4	d1	d3	d5	d2	d7	d10	d8

4.3.3 Leave-One-Out Cross-Validation

Leave-one-out (or the *Jackknife*) is an extreme case of k-fold cross-validation. Leave-one-out is basically a k-fold cross-validation performed with $k = m$. The procedure is the same as that of k-fold cross-validation, but k is replaced by m.

We illustrate leave-one-out on the shuffled data from Table 4.15. This time, there are as many "folds" as there are instances; that is, 10 in this case. Table 4.16 represents the training and testing sets at iteration 1. Table 4.17 represents the training and test sets at iteration 2. This goes on until iteration 10 where the last iteration's training and testing sets are represented by Table 4.18. As for regular cross-validation, once each fold has been evaluated, the results are averaged.

Chapter 6 will discuss these resampling schemes in more depth and present additional ones.

Table 4.16. *Leave-one-out, first iteration: Training and testing sets.*

Training:	d9	d4	d1	d3	d5	d2	d7	d10	d8		Testing:	d6

Table 4.17. *Leave-one-out, second iteration: Training and testing sets.*

Training:	d6	d4	d1	d3	d5	d2	d7	d10	d8		Testing:	d9

Table 4.18. *Leave-one-out, last iteration: Training and testing sets.*

Training:	d6	d9	d4	d1	d3	d5	d2	d7	d10		Testing:	d8

> The holdout method is implemented in scikit-learn and its discussion can be found at https://scikit-learn.org/stable/modules/generated/sklearn.model_selection.train_test_split.html. Cross-validation is also discussed in depth in the scikit-learn manual at https://scikit-learn.org/stable/modules/cross_validation.html.

4.4 Common Statistical Tests

We now turn our attention to the statistical analysis of the results obtained by the metrics presented in Section 4.2 on the resampling regimens discussed in Section 4.3. We review two popular tests here, the t-test and the sign test. We present many more in Chapter 7.

4.4.1 Two Matched Samples t-Test

The t-test is an important and familiar approach in the statistical toolbox. It comes in various flavors. The most relevant variation in the machine learning context is the two-matched-sample version with unknown variances. This test can be considered to be a specific case of the more general t-test known as Welch's t-test, which is applicable in the case of two independent samples. For a more complete description of the entire family of t-tests, please, refer to statistical textbooks such as Howell (2020) and StatSoft (2006).

The two-matched-samples t-test can be useful for finding out whether the difference between two means obtained by applying two learning systems on the exact same partitions of the data is meaningful (statistically significant), that is, whether the two samples come from the same population. It does so by looking at the difference in observed means and standard deviations (i.e., the first and the second moments of the samples) between the two samples. As discussed in Chapter 2, hypothesis testing consists of assuming a null hypothesis, H_0, the opposite of what we are interested in showing by confirming whether the null hypothesis can be rejected based on our evidence.

In machine learning experiments, we hope to find a significant difference between the sample distributions from which the means were calculated. We are, thus, going to assume that, on the contrary, the two samples come from the same distribution. Therefore, we will assume that the difference between these means is zero, and see whether this null hypothesis, H_0 can be rejected. In order to see whether the hypothesis can be rejected, we need to find out what kind of differences between two samples can be expected due to chance alone. This can be done by considering the distribution of differences between sample means. Such a distribution is a sampling distribution (see Chapter 2) and will tend to *normality* (a normal distribution) as the sample size increases.

Given this normality assumption, we would expect the mean difference to deviate from zero according to the normal distribution centered around zero. We now check if the obtained difference (along with its variance) indeed displays this behavior. This is done with the following t-statistic:[9]

$$t = \frac{\bar{d} - 0}{\frac{\bar{s}_d}{\sqrt{n}}},$$

$$(4.2)$$

or equivalently,

$$t = \frac{\overline{pm}(f_1) - \overline{pm}(f_2)}{\frac{\bar{s}_d}{\sqrt{n}}},$$

$$(4.3)$$

where pm is a performance metric such as accuracy, F-measure, AUC, or MSE; $\overline{pm}(f)$ represents the mean value of pm obtained by f over the entire testing set; $\bar{d} = \overline{pm}(f_1) - \overline{pm}(f_2)$ represents the difference in the means of pm performance measures obtained by applying classifiers/regressors/clustering systems/etc. f_1 and f_2; and $\bar{s}_d$ denotes the sample standard deviation of this mean difference and can be defined as

$$\bar{s}_d = \sqrt{\frac{\sum_{i=1}^{n} (d_i - \bar{d})^2}{n - 1}},$$

$$(4.4)$$

where d_i is the difference between the performance measures of f_1 and f_2 for testing instance i, that is, $d_i = pm_i(f_1) - pm_i(f_2)$.

Note that $\overline{pm}(f)$ is the average performance measure of classifier/regressor/clustering system/etc. f,

---

[9] We know that the distribution of differences between sample means is zero, but we do not know what its standard deviation σ is. Therefore, we need to estimate it. We do so using our sample variance. This leads to an overestimate of the value that would have been obtained if σ had been known. This is why the distribution of z, perhaps familiar to some readers, cannot be used to accept or reject the null hypothesis. Instead, we use the Student's t-distribution, which corrects for this problem, and compare t to the t-table with degree of freedom $n - 1$.

$$\overline{pm}(f) = \frac{1}{n} \sum_{i=1}^{n} pm_i(f),$$

where n is the number of instances in the testing set.

Following the calculation of t (also called the t-statistics) in Equation (4.3), we use the t-table in Appendix A.2 to find the probability with which t, the computed t-statistics, is as large as or larger than the values listed in the table (also called critical values). The t-table lists the probabilities with which different mean differences are observable assuming that the two means come from samples emanating from the same distribution. The user, thus, needs to look for the largest critical value in the table (on the degree of freedom $n - 1$ line) that is smaller than t, the t-statistic we computed. The value associated with that critical value represents the significance level at which one can reject the null hypothesis.[10]

As discussed in Chapter 2, the user outputs this probability if he or she is solely interested in a one-tailed test and multiplies it by two before outputting it if he or she is interested in a two-tailed test. If this output probability, the p-value, is small (by convention, we use the threshold of .05 or .01), the user would reject H_0 at the .05 or .01 significance level. Otherwise, he or she would state that there is not enough evidence to conclude that H_0 does not hold or, in other words, that there is failure to reject the null hypothesis. The following example illustrates the use of the t-test as currently done in many cases.

Example In this example, we analyze the differences in performance of the decision tree and SVM classifiers on the Labor Relations dataset using the t-test. The results of the experiments were presented in Table 2.2 and represent the raw number of errors made by the classifier on each testing fold. The results were obtained by performing multiple trials by random resampling of the data, and running 10-fold cross-validation on each resampled set (or trial). Since each cell in Table 2.2 represents the error rate obtained by a given classifier on onefold, within one trial of the evaluation procedure, to compute the average error rate of this classifier for that trial, we simply average the results obtained by each classifier at each fold of one trial. This yields the average error obtained for that classifier in that trial. For example, consider the first row of Table 2.2, which corresponds to the first cross-validation run of the decision tree classifier on the Labor Relations dataset. The values in this row are 0, 0, 0.3333, 0, 0, 0.3333, 0.3333, 0.3333, 0, 0.333. We take the average of these values, which yields .167. This represents the value of $pm_1(DT)$ in our t-test setting. The same calculation is repeated for all the runs of the decision tree and SVM classifiers to yield the other $pm_i(DT)$ and $pm_i(SVM)$ values. Table 4.19 lists all the pm_i values for decision trees and SVM.

Our overall average performance measures are the average of the cross-validated error rates of the respective classifiers in each trial. From Table 4.19, we get

$$\overline{pm}(DT) = 0.14167,$$

---

[10] While this roughly follows the discussions surrounding Equation (2.4), it is not fully identical. That is because this section describes the two-matched-sample test, whereas Chapter 2 discussed the more general Welch's t-test.

Table 4.19. *pm_i values for DT and SVM.*

$pm_i(DT)$	.167	.15	.233	.1	.117	.067	.083	.167	.133	.2
$pm_i(SVM)$	.067	.05	.067	.1	.033	.017	.017	.067	.083	.1

$$\overline{pm}(SVM) = 0.06.$$

For $n = 10$, we thus, get

$$\bar{d} = 0.14167 - 0.06 = 0.08167,$$

and from Table 4.19 we can compute the various d_i values as:

$$d_1 = pm_1(DT) - pm_1(SVM) = 0.167 - 0.067 = 0.1,$$
$$d_2 = pm_2(DT) - pm_2(SVM) = 0.15 - 0.05 = 0.1,$$
$$d_3 = pm_3(DT) - pm_3(SVM) = 0.233 - 0.067 = 0.166,$$

$$\vdots \qquad \vdots \qquad \vdots \qquad \vdots \qquad \vdots$$

$$d_{10} = pm_{10}(DT) - pm_{10}(SVM) = 0.2 - 0.1 = 0.1,$$

and, thus,

$$\bar{s}_d = \sqrt{\frac{\sum_{i=1}^{n}(d_i - \bar{d})^2}{n-1}} = \sqrt{\frac{0.01747}{10-1}} = 0.04406,$$

so that

$$t = \frac{\bar{d} - 0}{\frac{\bar{s}_d}{\sqrt{n}}} = \frac{0.08167 - 0}{\frac{0.04406}{\sqrt{10}}} = 5.862.$$

The degree of freedom is $n - 1 = 9$. A look at the t-table in Appendix A.2 reveals that $t = 5.862$ is larger than the value shown for a degree of freedom of 9 and $p = 0.005$ (a value of 3.25), $p = 0.001$ (a value of 4.297), or $p = 0.0005$ (a value of 4.781). Since the one-sided test should be sufficient here, given that SVM performs consistently better than the decision tree classifier, we could safely reject the null hypothesis which states that the two classifiers' performances come from the same distribution. If, however, the user would prefer using a two-tailed test for more safety, the null hypothesis would be rejected with $p = 0.01$, $p = 0.002$, or $p = 0.001$ (the above p-values multiplied by 2). If all the assumptions of the t-test are met (this will be discussed in detail in Section 7.2.1), whether we use the one-tailed or two-tailed version, we could then conclude that the evidence from our experiments strongly suggests that SVM performs better than decision trees on the Labor Relations dataset (one-tailed test), or more generally, that SVM and decision trees show a statistically significant performance difference on the Labor Relations dataset (two-tailed test).

As previously mentioned, a more general version of the t-test called Welch's t-test is also available and applies to the case of two unmatched samples of size n_1 and n_2. In this case, the t-statistic is calculated as

$$t = \frac{\overline{pm}(f_1) - \overline{pm}(f_2)}{\sqrt{\frac{s_1^2}{n_1} + \frac{s_2^2}{n_2}}},$$

where s_1^2 and s_2^2 are the sample variances of the performance measures of the two classifiers, respectively, and n_1 and n_2 are their respective numbers of trials.

> Implementations of the t-test and other statistical tests are described in https://docs.scipy.org/ doc/scipy/tutorial/stats.html. Furthermore, the accompanying GitHub repository shows an example of the use of the t-test in the comparison of a decision tree with SVM on the UCI Labor Relations dataset.

4.4.2 The Sign Test (Wins, Losses, and Ties)

The sign test is perhaps the simplest of all statistical tests and has the added advantage of being nonparametric. The sign test is an estimate of the number of trials on which a classifier/regressor/clustering system/etc. f outperforms the other based on some performance metric. While the t-test can be applied to the case of several trials within the same experiment as shown in section 4.4.1, it cannot be used for comparing two learned functions f_1 and f_2 on different domains due to the commensurability assumption that will be discussed in Section 7.2.1. Given the nonparametric nature of the sign test, which relies on rankings instead of actual performance differences, however, the sign test can be used on both different trials on the same domains and different domains. Hence, if we have n datasets or trials and two functions f_1 and f_2, we calculate the number of datasets or trials on which f_1 outperforms f_2 (call this n_{f_1}) and the number of datasets or trials on which f_2 outperforms f_1 (call this n_{f_2}). Hence, we have $n_{f_1} + n_{f_2} \leq n$. The inequality holds in case we have an odd number of ties, as we see next.

The null hypothesis states that the functions being compared are equivalent and, hence, on average, win $n/2$ times over all the trials. Note that the number of trials on which the functions perform equally well is split between the two counts evenly (except when this number is odd in which case one count can be ignored). Hence, if the null hypothesis were to hold, then the number of wins should follow a binomial distribution. A lookup in the table of critical values (See the Table A.4) shows the critical number of datasets or trials for which one function should outperform another to be considered statistically significantly better at the α significance level. More specifically, a function should perform better on at least w_α datasets relative to the total number of datasets used in the experiment in order to be considered statistically better at the α significance level.

When scaled to a greater number of trials than the 100 shown in the Table A.4, the null hypothesis assumes them to be normally distributed with mean $n/2$ and variance $\sqrt{n}/2$.

In this case a z-statistic[11] (for classifier f_1) can be computed whereby an algorithm is significantly better with $p < \alpha$ if the number of wins for this algorithm n_{f_1} is such that

$$n_{f_1} \geq \frac{n}{2} + z_\alpha \frac{\sqrt{n}}{2}.$$

The values of z_α are found in Appendix A.1.

Finally, for each dataset or trial we can summarize the function's performance using any linear performance measure, for example, the average 10-fold cross-validation error or accuracy.

Example We use Table 2.2 once again, as we analyze, using the sign test, the results obtained by the decision tree algorithm and SVM on the Labor Relations data, as we previously did using the t-test. Table 4.19 lists all the pm_i's for both decision trees and SVM. From this table, we see that SVM wins nine times over decision trees and ties once. Since the table of critical values in Appendix A.4 shows that, for 10 datasets, a classifier needs to win at least eight times for the null hypothesis to be rejected with significance level $\alpha = 0.025$ (or $\alpha = 0.05$ in the two-tailed test), we can, therefore, reject the null hypothesis with the sign test and declare that our experimental results suggest that SVM performs better than decision trees on the Labor Relations data. In this case, therefore, both the t-test and the sign test can be successfully used. It is important to note, however, that the sign test is less powerful than the t-test, and there are cases where the t-test can reject null hypotheses that the sign test cannot reject.

4.5 The Importance of Studying Machine Learning Evaluation beyond This Chapter

This chapter presented many of the common evaluation strategies used in machine learning. One question the reader may ask is: Why go beyond this chapter? There are several reasons why we need to go beyond this chapter.

First, the chapter, especially the discussions of metrics, covered mostly evaluation for the task of classification. While classification certainly is central to the field of machine learning, it is by no means the only modality. Part III of the book will discuss other settings, including not only the other well-known settings such as regression and clustering, but also evaluation for newer settings such as positive unlabeled classification, multi-labeled classification, image segmentation, text generation, time-series analysis, lifelong-learning, and others.

Second, the evaluation methods covered in this chapter are methods geared at validating research and exploration outcomes, but may not be robust enough if used alone for the deployment of machine learning-based commercial products. Part IV of the book takes on the question of industrial-strength evaluation and responsible machine learning, which are both essential in making machine learning more reliable.

---

[11] A z statistic corresponds to the standard (or unit) normal distribution assumption.

Finally, even if the focus of the evaluation is only classification, and even if the purpose of the experiments is only research and exploration, the discussion of this chapter is very functional and covers only a portion of the tools available without explaining the context in which they were designed, or their proper use. Part II of the book will take a deep look at the classification context and discuss all the evaluation tools currently available, together with their advantages and limitations. In particular, the metrics introduced in this chapter will be explained in more detail and complemented by those that were not discussed. Error estimation methods will be cast in their theoretical framework and additional methods such as bootstrapping will be introduced. Finally, the statistical tests presented in this chapter will be analyzed in depth and supplemented by a variety of others that apply to many more situations. The purpose of Part II of the book is to give readers a solid understanding of the issues at hand when evaluating classifiers so that when the time comes for them to make decisions with respect to their specific caseload, they can make an informed decision that will help strengthen their conclusion. Furthermore, a good understanding of the evaluation tools pertinent to classification may prove useful for other settings as well, either because they could be reused directly or because they could be modified accordingly.

An Important Note An important remark worth making here is that machine learning evaluation should not be viewed as a static field. As new issues arise, new ways of assessing the algorithms provided must be designed. In certain cases, as the history of machine evaluation attests, approaches can be borrowed from other fields. This is what happened with precision and recall metrics, which were borrowed from information retrieval, ROC analysis, which was borrowed from signal processing, and sensitivity and specificity, which were borrowed from the medical field. At other times, metrics need to be created to deal with particular aspects of the data or the algorithms. This was the case, for example, with the G-mean, which was created to deal with the class imbalance problem. Error estimation methods as well as statistical tests have also been borrowed and adapted for machine learning situations. In order for machine learning evaluation to continue to evolve, it is important for its practitioners to be well versed in its current state of the art. One of this book's goals is to describe this current state of the art thoroughly.

Along with the above remark comes a warning: while researchers are invited to create new evaluation procedures to deal with new issues, two things are important to note. First, the new approaches must be principled and must follow an acceptable underlying theory. Second, while we recognize the need for new evaluation methods when a thorough review of the literature in our field and others does not produce a method that highlights the desired aspect of the methods that are being tested, we should warn against the creation of too many of these methods. If every researcher creates a new evaluation method to assess an approach, there will be no way to compare different approaches meant to address the same problem. The birth of a new evaluation approach, therefore, needs careful consideration.[12]

---

[12] An example of a careful approach to creating a sound evaluation approach is that taken by the L2M DARPA program, where a large group of researchers met regularly to create a standard set of metrics that capture all aspects of lifelong learning (New et al. 2022).

Part II

Evaluation for Classification

5

Metrics

Chapter 4 took a practical view of evaluation and, in the case of evaluation metrics, explained their purpose in a functional way. In this chapter, we take a step back to reflect upon the issue of choosing evaluation measures in a broader and more theoretical context.[1] Nonetheless, the chapter does not focus on theory alone. Practical questions related to evaluation measures are also discussed and their uses are illustrated on intuitive examples. This chapter focuses on metrics for classification. Metrics for other learning paradigms will be discussed at length in Chapters 8 and 9.

5.1 Overview of the Problem

5.1.1 Choosing an Evaluation Method

When considering the issue of choosing an appropriate performance evaluation method for an experimental study on classification, several questions come into play: the type of learning algorithm being evaluated, the type of information used in this evaluation, the types of practical problems that arise in the application domain, and the type of information output by the performance method.

Type of Learning Algorithm

The first issue, naturally, concerns the type of learning algorithm to be evaluated. With regard to the performance on the training or test instances, the algorithms can essentially be categorized into deterministic, scoring, and probabilistic algorithms.

Deterministic algorithms Deterministic algorithms output a fixed class label for each instance and, hence, can be better measured in terms of the zero-one loss. That is, the loss of misclassifying an example (assigning a wrong class label to the instance) is one or zero.

Scoring algorithms Another class of learning algorithms yields a score (typically continuous) on each test instance. These scoring classifiers are generally thresholded so as to

---

[1] The terms "evaluation measure" and "evaluation metric" or simply "measure" and "metric" are used more or less interchangeably in this book. The term "metric" is used when the measurement outputs one or two scalar values while the term "measure" is used in a more general context.

obtain deterministic labels for test examples. Examples of such algorithms can include neural networks and decision trees. In a binary classification scenario, a classifier that outputs scores on each test instance in a fixed interval $[a,b]$ can be thresholded at some point $s_t \in [a,b]$ such that examples with a score greater than s_t are classified as positive while examples scoring less than s_t are labeled as negative.[2] The scoring algorithms make an interesting case in terms of performance measurement since the resulting labeling depends on choosing an appropriate threshold. This can be considered similar to parameter selection (model selection) in other algorithms. However, scoring algorithms typically operate in a continuous space and, hence, their behavior can be tracked over the space of all possible thresholds using evaluation procedures such as ROC analysis, which was described in Section 4.2.2 and will be discussed in greater detail in Section 5.7.

Probabilistic algorithms The third class of algorithms, probabilistic classifiers, issue a probability estimate on the class membership of the example for various classes. In order to obtain deterministic class assignments from probabilistic classifiers, typically either a maximum a posteriori (MAP) or a Bayesian estimate is considered. Typically, the classifiers are tested once a deterministic labeling of the test instances is obtained. As a result, this can be organized in the form of a confusion matrix.

Type of Information Used

The second issue to consider is the kind of information the performance measure uses. We distinguish between two categories.

Information from the confusion matrix alone First, we have metrics that take information solely from the confusion matrix resulting from the application of the classifier obtained from a learning algorithm on the training data. These metrics are typically applied in the case of deterministic classification algorithms. Many of them were discussed in Chapter 4; we will add a few more specialized ones here, including those that apply chance correction to their calculations.

Information from the confusion matrix and more Second, we discuss the measures that take into account, in addition to the confusion matrix, information about the class distribution priors, and classifier uncertainty. Such measures are useful with regard to the scoring classifiers discussed above. ROC analysis falls into this category of approaches and was discussed, albeit partially, in Chapter 4. We will complete the discussion of such approaches in this chapter. We will also briefly discuss some Bayesian measures to account for probabilistic classifiers.[3]

---

[2] In this sense of continuous scores, these classifiers are also referred to as ranking classifiers. However, we avoid this term so as to avoid confusion with ranking algorithms (that obtain the ordering of a given set of instances). Note that scoring algorithms can be treated as ranking algorithms but the opposite does not necessarily hold.

[3] Please note that experimental measures have been proposed that take inputs additional to the confusion matrix, class distribution priors, and classifier uncertainty. For example, information such as time complexity and understandability has been integrated in performance evaluation. Such measures, however, do not fall in the mainstream, so their discussion is relegated to Appendix B.

Type of Practical Issues Considered

Other issues that arise while measuring algorithm performance, which are very often of great importance in practical applications of machine learning, are: the possible **asymmetric costs of misclassification** (when a classifier's error on examples of a certain class is deemed more serious than that on examples of other classes), taking into consideration **prior class distributions** to account for class imbalances, and **robustness in the presence of concept drift or noise**. We will briefly discuss these challenges. In addition, we will discuss the question of **calibration**, which is very important in domains where it is necessary for the probability associated with an outcome to be correct. This is important for prediction systems that issue probabilities.

Type of Performance Method's Output

Finally, we will look at how the representation of the output of the various performance measures affects the type and amount of information they convey, as well as their interpretability and understandability. For instance, we will see how **graphical measures** such as those used for scoring algorithms result in the visualization of the algorithm performance over different settings. The **scalar metrics**, by contrast, have the advantage of being concise and allowing for clear comparisons of different learning methods. However, because of their conciseness, they lack informativeness since they summarize a great deal of information into a scalar metric. The disadvantages of the graphical measures appear in the form of a difficult implementation and a possibly increased time complexity. In addition, results expressed in this form may be more difficult to interpret than those reported in a single metric.

Note: Monotonic and Nonmonotonic Metrics

While discussing performance metrics in this chapter, unless otherwise specified, we will discuss only monotonic metrics of performance. A monotonic performance metric $pm(\cdot)$ is such that, over the range of $pm(\cdot)$, either the relationship "$pm(f_1) > pm(f_2)$ implies that f_1 is 'better' than f_2, and vice versa" or "$pm(f_1) > pm(f_2)$ implies that f_2 is 'better' than f_1, and vice versa" holds. That is, a strict increase (or decrease) in the value of $pm(\cdot)$ indicates a better (or worse) classifier throughout the range of the function $pm(\cdot)$, or vice versa. Some metrics that are not strictly monotonic can be thought of, for example, using ideas such as Kologomorov complexity, which is a nonmonotonic metric over strings (Li and Vitanyi 1997), such as the class conditional probability estimate discussed in Kukar et al. (2002) in the context of a multi-class problem.

5.1.2 Organization of the Chapter

The remainder of the chapter is divided into eight sections. Section 5.2 presents an organization and ontology of performance measures used in supervised settings. Section 5.3 follows up with an example showing the diverse and, sometimes, contradictory nature of the information conveyed by different evaluation metrics. Section 5.4 then moves to the discussion of specific issues occuring with metrics with a multi-class focus that were not discussed in Chapter 4, including the important issue of agreement statistics. Section 5.5

discusses performance metrics with a single-class focus by contrasting them to metrics with a multi-class focus, and further describing metrics that were not discussed in Chapter 4. Section 5.6 then takes on the important issues of skew, costs, uncertainty and calibration that must be taken into consideration when evaluating classifiers. The discussion of visual analytic performance measures started in Chapter 4 is then continued in Section 5.7 by providing additional information about ROC analysis, and other methods such as cost curves, PR curves and so on in Section 5.8. The chapter concludes in Section 5.9 with a brief discussion of advanced topics in the area of evaluation measures that will be expanded upon in Appendix B. That information, for the most part, first appeared in Japkowicz and Shah (2011).

The implementation of evaluation metrics is discussed in length in the scikit-learn manual at https://scikit-learn.org/stable/modules/model_evaluation.html. The practical examples presented in this section are illustrated in the accompanying GitHub repository.

5.2 An Ontology of Performance Measures

Based on the above discussion and the information a performance measure is expected to take into account, we can design an ontology of these measures. We mostly cover the measures in current use with regard to classifier evaluation. Novel measures can certainly arise and either fit in appropriate places in the proposed ontology or even extend its design. Some of the measures presented in this ontology were discussed in Chapter 4, while others will be discussed in Sections 5.4–5.8. As discussed previously, measures used in machine learning settings other than classification will be discussed in Chapters 8 and 9, and are not included in this ontology. Figure 5.1 presents our ontology. It includes various performance measures widely used in the field and relevant to our context. Our discussion of the performance measures in this and the previous chapter follows this conceptual framework. Where relevant, we also discuss some other measures of performance, albeit briefly.

The ontology was built according to three dimensions. The first dimension concerns the type of information taken into consideration: the confusion matrix alone, the confusion matrix in conjunction with additional information, and information in forms other than the confusion matrix altogether.

The second dimension is dependent upon the category of classifier considered, a piece of information that has implications on the choice of measure. It distinguishes between the evaluation of deterministic classifiers, scoring classifiers, and continuous or probabilistic classifiers. For measures that consider the confusion matrix alone and focus on deterministic classifiers,[4] the ontology considers whether the metric focuses on all the classes in the domain, or whether it focuses on a single class of interest. The metrics corresponding to these two categories are covered in Chapter 4 and this chapter. In the case of measures that

---

[4] The confusion matrix alone can also be used for classifiers other than deterministic ones (e.g., by thresholding the decision function) or can, at least in theory, incorporate partial loss information. However, it is conventionally used for deterministic classifiers, which is why we focus on this use here.

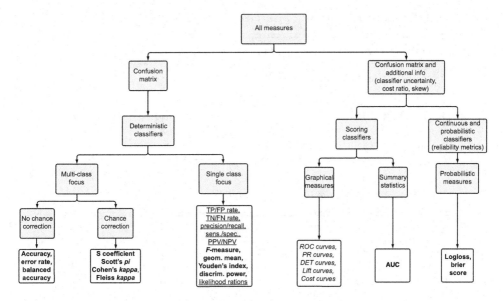

Figure 5.1 An ontology of performance metrics. Performance methods that return a scalar value are in bold type; underline indicates two-valued output metrics; italics indicate that the methods are graphical.

consider the confusion matrix together with extra information, the ontology differentiates between the scoring and the continuous or probabilistic classification algorithms. These measures are discussed in this chapter, although Chapter 4 discussed certain aspects of ROC analysis, which belongs to this category. Note that there exist measures that use information of types other than those represented in our ontology. This includes metrics that attempt to capture "interestingness," comprehensibility, or whether it is a multi-criteria metric. These types of metrics are more experimental and seldom used in machine-learning. Their discussion is, thus, relegated to Appendix B, which surveys research directions.

The third dimension, indicated by the font type of the characters describing the measure, concerns the format returned by the evaluation measure, or its output. In particular, we interest ourselves in how compressed the returned information is. Performance methods that return a scalar value are those that compress their information the most. They are, thus, practical metrics that make comparisons between learning methods quick and easy, but at the same time, they are the least informative because of their high compression rate. They are represented in bold format in the ontology. Methods that return two values, like precision/recall or sensitivity/specificity, are more informative because of their lower compression rate, but can make comparisons between algorithms more difficult. Indeed, what if one metric ranks one classifier better than the other, and the other metric does the opposite? In fact, combination measures such as the F-measure were created exactly for this reason, but, as single scalars, they fall back into the less informative category of metrics. The two-valued output metrics shown in the ontology are all underlined. Finally, we consider methods that return a graph such as ROC analysis or cost curves as the most informative

Table 5.1. *A study on the UCI breast cancer domain.*

Algorithm	Acc	TPR	FPR	Prec	Rec	F	AUC
NB	.94	.87	.02	.98	.87	.92	.99
SVM	.91	.85	.04	.93	.85	.89	.97
DTree	.94	.91	.04	.93	.91	.92	.93
RandFor	.94	.91	.04	.93	.91	.92	.99
XGBoost	.98	.96	0	1	.96	.92	1
Bagging	.92	.80	0	1	.80	.89	.98

Table 5.2. *A study on the UCI liver domain.*

Algorithm	Acc	TPR	FPR	Prec	Rec	F	AUC
NB	.71	.49	.08	.84	.49	.62	.75
SVM	.64	.88	.58	.58	.88	.70	.71
DTree	.68	.76	.39	.64	.76	.69	.68
RandFor	.75	.79	.28	.72	.79	.75	.79
XGBoost	.78	.79	.22	.77	.79	.78	.81
Bagging	.71	.67	.25	.71	.67	.69	.70

format of all, but also the most complex to handle practically. And in fact, like in the case of the F-measure, the AUC is used to summarize the ROC graph (and thus, once again, falls back into the category of least informative metrics). The graphical methods are represented in italics in the ontology.

5.3 Illustrative Example

Before proceeding to the discussion of the different performance measures one by one, let us illustrate how these measures each focus on different aspects of the effectiveness of the learning process and, thus, how they differ in their comparative assessments of the algorithms. In many practical applications, there is an inevitable trade-off between these performance measures. That is, making a classifier "better" in terms of a particular measure can result in a relatively "inferior" classifier in terms of another.

Tables 5.1 and 5.2 present the results of applying six different learning algorithms to two UCI domains: the Breast Cancer and Liver datasets.[5] Both domains are binary classification problems. The breast cancer dataset is comprised of 286 instances (201 negative, i.e., non-recurrence events; and 85 positive, i.e., recurrence events), with each instance containing nine nominal valued attributes. The liver dataset consists of 345 instances (145 positive and 200 negative) with six nominal valued attributes. The six learning algorithms considered, all

---

[5] For the Breast Cancer dataset see DOI: 10.24432/C5DW2B; for the Liver dataset see DOI: 10.24432/C54G67.

from the scikit-learn toolkit, are naive Bayes, support vector machines (SVM), decision tree (DT), random forest, extreme gradient boosting (XGBoost), and bagging. This represents a diverse set of well-known learning strategies and is illustrative of the diverse features of different performance metrics. We used the default parameter values in each case since our main aim here is to highlight the differences between performance metrics and not classifier optimization.

The results are reported using the following performance metrics: accuracy (Acc), the true and false positive rates (TPR/FPR), precision (Prec), recall (Rec), the F-metric (F), and the area under the ROC curve (AUC). The reported results use a train/test regimen with 80% of the instances used for training and 20% for testing. The same partition is used by all classifiers. For the time being, we do not focus on what each of these metrics means and how they were calculated. Our aim, instead, is to emphasize that different performance metrics, as a result of assessing different aspects of algorithm performance, yield different comparative results. We do not delve into the appropriateness of the train/test regimen either. We will discuss this and other error estimation methods in detail in Chapter 6.

Let us look into the results. All the metrics agree on certain points. In both domains, XGBoost is ranked as the top classifier by all metrics, and random forest as the second best. The metrics do not necessarily agree, however, as to which are the next best classifiers. For example, in the breast cancer domain, decision tree and naive Bayes get the same score as random forest according to accuracy, whereas the F-measure gives decision tree the same score as random forest, but gives a lower score to naive Bayes, while the AUC ranks naive Bayes higher than decision trees, though lower than random forest. In the liver domain, accuracy ties bagging and naive Bayes in third place, followed by decision tree, and SVM much lower. For the F-measure, it is naive Bayes that gets a much lower score than the other classifiers, and SVM that gets third place. Yet with the AUC, naive Bayes is in third place, followed by SVM, bagging, and decision tree. Please note that precision and recall as well as TPR and FPR can also be in disagreement with each other, but that should be considered separately as they are part of metric pairs that often trade off of each other. For example, according to precision, naive Bayes on the liver domain is the top classifier. However, it is ranked as the worst classifier in terms of recall. Keeping the two metrics in the pair high is the challenge. The F-measure that combines both shows how successful the classifier is at both precision and recall. In this particular case, recall is so low that the F-measure actually ranks naive Bayes as the worst classifier.

Of course, metric disagreement is a serious problem since a user is left with the questions of which evaluation metric to use and what their results mean. However, it should be understood that such disagreements do not suggest any inherent flaw in the performance metrics themselves. This, rather, highlights two main aspects of such an evaluation undertaking: i) different performance metrics focus on different aspects of classifier performance on the data and assess these specific aspects; ii) learning algorithms vary in their performance on more than one count. Taken together, these two points suggest something very important:

The algorithm's performance needs to be measured on the most relevant aspects of the domain, and the performance metrics considered should be the ones that focus on these aspects.

Such varying conclusions can be partly attributed to the lack of comprehensive performance metrics that take into account most or all of the relevant aspects of algorithm performance. However, perhaps a more important aspect is that of the relevance of the performance criterion. For instance, consider a scenario where a learning algorithm is deployed in a combat vehicle for the critical and sensitive task of assessing the possibility that land mines are present, based on certain measurements. Obviously, the most critical performance criterion here is the detection of *all* the mines even if this comes at the cost of some false alarms. Hence, a criterion that assesses performance on such comprehensive detection is more important than the overall accuracy of prediction. In an analogous manner, different learning tasks or domains impose different performance requirements on the learning algorithms which, in turn, requires performance metrics capable of assessing the algorithm performance on these criteria of interest.

In order to utilize an appropriate performance measure, it is, hence, necessary to learn its purpose, strengths, and limitations. The rest of the chapter focuses on studying these aspects of the performance measures that rely on the information conveyed solely by the confusion matrix as well as those that take into account additional information such as classifier uncertainty. The various performance measures that we study concern the binary classification scenario. However, the observations and findings with regard to their strengths and limitations also extend to the multi-class classification settings. The discussion starts with confusion matrix based–metrics that have a multiple-class focus and those that have a single-class focus, in Sections 5.4 and 5.5, respectively.

5.4 Performance Metrics with a Multi-class Focus

The metrics described in this section focus on the overall performance of learning algorithms on all the classes in a dataset. In particular, this refers to accuracy (or, equivalently, error rate) and balanced accuracy that were both defined in Chapter 4. This section introduces additional metrics that, unlike accuracy, error rate, and balanced accuracy, correct for chance. These are Scott's π and Cohen's κ metrics. We begin by discussing the strengths and limitations of accuracy (or error rate) illustrating the discussion with an example, and showing how balanced accuracy addresses some of these concerns; we then introduce the kappa metrics.

5.4.1 Strengths and Limitations

Accuracy and *error rate* effectively summarize the overall performance of a classifier taking into account all data classes. In addition to their practical usefulness, they are of great relevance to the subfield of machine learning theory as they give insights into the generalization performance of classifiers through the study of their convergence behaviors, as discussed in Appendix B. As a result of trying to summarize the information in a scalar metric, however, there are inevitably limitations to both the information that these metrics can convey and their effectiveness in different settings. In particular, the strength in summarizing can result in significant limitations when either the performance on different classes is of varying importance, or the distribution of instances in the different classes of the test data is skewed. The first limitation results in the lack of information conveyed by these metrics on the varying degree of importance on the performance on different classes. This limitation and the interest in class-specific performance estimates is addressed with the single-class focus metrics that we will discuss in Section 5.5. The second limitation regards the inability of these metrics to convey meaningful information in the case of skewed class distribution. Accuracy and error rates can be effective metrics when the proportion of instances belonging to different classes in the test set is more or less balanced (i.e., similar for different classes). As soon as this distribution begins to skew in the direction of a particular class, the more prevalent class dominates the measurement information in these metrics, thereby making them biased. This limitation is addressed to some extent by the balanced accuracy introduced in Chapter 4 and illustrated in the example in Section 5.4.2, and the scoring and reliability methods and metrics discussed in Section 5.6.

Another limitation of these metrics appears in the form of different misclassification costs. This is in line with the first limitation we discussed in this section but addresses a slightly different concern. Differing misclassification costs can be relevant in the case of both balanced and skewed class distributions. The problems in the case of skewed class distributions are related to the fact that accuracy (or error rate) does not distinguish between the *types* of errors the classifier makes (on one class as opposed to the other classes). The problems in the case of unequal misclassification costs relate to the fact that accuracy (or error rate) does not distinguish between the *importance* of errors the classifier makes over instances of one class in comparison to those of other classes. Let us illustrate the problems more specifically with the following hypothetical example.

5.4.2 Example

Consider two classifiers represented by the two confusion matrices of Tables 5.3 and 5.4. These two classifiers, H_A and H_B, behave quite differently from one another. The one symbolized by the confusion matrix of Table 5.3, H_A, does not classify positive examples very well, getting only 200 out of 500 right. However, it does not do a terrible job on the negative data, getting 400 out of 500 classified correctly. The classifier represented by the confusion matrix of Table 5.4, H_B, does the exact opposite, classifying the positive class better than the negative class with 400 out of 500 versus 200 out of 500 correct classifications. It is clear that these classifiers exhibit quite different strengths and weaknesses and should not be used blindly on a dataset such as the medical domain we previously used.[6] Yet, both classifiers exhibit the same accuracy:

$$Accuracy = \frac{400 + 200}{100 + 200 + 300 + 400} = \frac{200 + 400}{100 + 200 + 300 + 400} = .6 = 60\%.$$

---

[6] Of course, one can think of reversing the class labels in such cases. However, this may not exactly invert the problem mapping. Also, this trick can become ineffective in the multi-class case.

Table 5.3. *Hypothetical confusion matrix I for hypothetical classifier H_A.*

H_A	Pred_Negative	Pred_Positive	
Act_Negative	400	100	N = 500
Act_Positive	300	200	P = 500

Table 5.4. *Hypothetical confusion matrix II for hypothetical classifier H_B.*

H_B	Pred_Negative	Pred_Positive	
Act_Negative	200	300	N = 500
Act_Positive	100	400	P = 500

Table 5.5. *Hypothetical confusion matrix III for hypothetical classifier H_C.*

H_C	Pred_Negative	Pred_Positive	
Act_Negative	950	0	N = 950
Act_Positive	50	0	P = 50

While this lack of discrimination is concerning, another problem arises in the case of class imbalance and differing costs. Let us assume an extreme case where the positive class contains 50 examples and the negative class contains 950 examples. In this case, a trivial classifier would be incapable of discriminating between the positive and the negative class, but would blindly choose to return a "negative" class label on all the instances. The confusion matrix for such a hypothetical classifier H_C is shown in Table 5.5. Such a classifier would obtain a 95% accuracy:

$$Accuracy = \frac{0 + 950}{0 + 0 + 50 + 950} = .95 = 95\%.$$

This, however, is not representative of the classifier's performance at all: the classifier is very limited, whereas a 95% accuracy suggests strong performance! Since many classifiers, even nontrivial ones, take the prior class distributions into consideration for the learning process, the preference for the more dominant class would prevail, resulting in them behaving the way our trivial classifier does. Accuracy results may, thus, not convey meaningful information in such cases.

Chapter 4 introduced the balanced accuracy metric. Though it was introduced in the context of multi-class classification, it can also be used in binary classification problems. One may wonder whether it addresses the problems just discussed. To answer this question, we calculate the balanced accuracy of the two confusion metrics of Tables 5.3 and 5.4, as well as that of the highly imbalanced problem of Table 5.5. For the confusion metrics of

Tables 5.3 and 5.4, the balanced accuracy is the same in both cases and, in fact, returns the same result as traditional accuracy:

$$\frac{\frac{400}{500} + \frac{200}{500}}{2} = \frac{\frac{200}{500} + \frac{400}{500}}{2} = 0.6 = 60\%.$$

This suggests that balanced accuracy presents no advantage over traditional accuracy in these cases. On the other hand, the balanced accuracy for the extremely imbalanced problem is helpful as it returns a 50% result:

$$\frac{\frac{950}{950} + \frac{0}{50}}{2} = .5 = 50\%.$$

This result is much more realistic and informative than the 95% accuracy obtained by traditional accuracy. It suggests that in the case of skewed distributions or class imbalances, balanced accuracy is useful as it can detect issues that traditional accuracy or error rate do not detect.

Let us now consider the related question of how important it is to correctly classify the examples from the two classes in relation to each other. That is, how much cost do we incur by making the classifier more sensitive to the less dominant class while incurring misclassification of the more dominant class? In fact, such costs can move either way depending upon the importance of (mis)classifying instances of either class. This is the issue of misclassification costs. However, the issues of misclassification costs can also be closely related to, although definitely not limited to, those of class distribution. Consider the case where the classes are fully balanced like in the two confusion matrices of Tables 5.3 and 5.4. Assume, however, that we are dealing with a problem for which the misclassification costs differ greatly. In the critical example of breast cancer recurrence (the positive class) and nonrecurrence (the negative class), it is clear, at least from the patient's point of view, that false positive errors have a lower cost since these errors consist of diagnosing recurrence when the patient is, in fact, not likely to get the disease again; whereas false negative errors are very costly, since they correspond to the case where recurrence is not recognized by the system (and, thus, not consequently treated the way it should). In such circumstances, it is clear that the system represented by the confidence matrix of Table 5.3 is much less appropriate for this problem since it issues 300 nonrecurrence diagnostics in cases where the patient will suffer a new bout of cancer, whereas the system represented by the confidence matrix of Table 5.4 makes fewer (100) mistakes (needless to say that in practical scenarios, even this many mistakes will be unacceptable).

Clearly, accuracy (or the error rate metrics) and balanced accuracy do not convey the full picture. Hence, these metrics do not suffice *in their classical form*, in domains with differing classification costs. Nonetheless, these metrics do remain simple and intuitive ways to assess classifier performance, especially when the user is aware of the issues discussed above. These metrics serve as quite informative metrics when evaluating generic classifiers for their overall performance-based comparative evaluation. We will come back to the issue of dealing with misclassification costs (also referred to as asymmetric loss) as well as skewed distributions in Section 5.6.

There is an additional issue worth noting with respect to the metrics discussed so far: they all made the implicit assumption that the ground truth labels of the instances are unbiased and correct. That is, these labels do not occur by chance. While such a consideration is relatively less relevant when we assume a perfect process that generates the true labels (e.g., when the true labeling can be definitively and unquestionably established), it is quite important when this is not the case (in most practical scenarios). This can be the case, for instance, when the results from the learning algorithm are compared against some silver standard (e.g., labels generated from an approximate process, or a human rater). An arguable fix in such cases is the correction of chance, first proposed by Cohen (1960) for the two-class scenario with two different processes generating the labels. We now discuss some such chance correction statistics.

5.4.3 Correcting for Chance: Agreement Statistics

It has been widely argued that the conventional performance metrics, especially the accuracy estimate, do not take into account the correct classification as a result of a mere coincidental concordance between the classifier output and the "true" label generation process. Typically, at least in the case of classifier assessment, it is assumed that the true class labels of the data examples are deterministically known, even though they are the result of an arbitrary unknown distribution that the algorithm aims to approximate. These true labels are some-times referred to as ground truth. However, this assumption makes it impossible to take into account the inherent bias of the label generation process. Consider, for instance, a dataset, with 75% positive examples and the rest negative. Clearly, this is a case of imbalanced data and the high number of positive instances can be an indicator of the bias of the label generation process in labeling instances as positive with a higher frequency. Hence, if we have a classifier that assigns a positive label with half the frequency (an unbiased coin toss), then, even without learning on the training data, one would expect its positive label assignment to agree with the true labels in $0.5 \times 0.75 = 0.375$ proportion of the cases. Conventional measurements such as accuracy do not take such accurate classifications into consideration that can be the result of merely chance agreement between the classifier and the label generation process. This concern is all the more relevant in applications such as medical image segmentation where the true class labels (i.e., the ground truth) are not known at all. Experts assign labels to various segments of images (typically pixels) against which the learning algorithm output is evaluated. Not correcting for chance, then, ignores the bias inherent in both the manual labeling and the learned classifier, thereby confusing the accurate segmentation achieved merely by chance for an indication of the efficiency of the learning algorithm.

It has, hence, been argued that this chance concordance between the labels assigned to the instances should be taken into account when assessing the accuracy of the classifier against the true label generation process. Having their roots in statistics, such metrics have been used, although not widely, in machine learning and related applications. These metrics are popularly known as agreement statistics.[7] We will very briefly discuss some of the main variations with regard to the binary classification scenario. Most of these agreement

---

[7] The statistics literature refers to these as inter-class correlation statistics or inter-rater agreement metrics.

Table 5.6. *The two class confusion matrix.*

	Pred_Negative	Pred_Positive	
Act_Negative	True negative (TN)	False positive (FP)	$Y_N = TN + FP$
Act_Positive	False negative (FN)	True positive (TP)	$Y_P = FN + TP$
	$f_N = TN + FN$	$f_P = FP + TP$	

statistics were originally proposed in an analogous case of measuring agreement on class assignment (over two classes) to the samples in a population by two raters (akin to label assignment to instances of the test set in our case by the learning algorithm and the actual underlying distribution). These metrics were subsequently generalized to the multi-class multi-rater scenario under different settings.

As a result of not accounting for such chance agreements over the labels, it has been argued that accuracy tends to provide an overly optimistic estimate of correct classifications when the labels assigned by the classifier are compared to the true labels of the examples. The agreement metrics are offered as a possible, although imperfect, fix. We will come to these imperfections shortly. We discuss two main metrics of agreement between the two label generation processes that aim to obtain a chance-corrected agreement: Scott's π statistic (Scott 1955) and Cohen's κ statistic (Cohen 1960). The two metrics essentially differ in the manner that they account for chance agreements.

Let the actual process of label generation (the true label assigning process) be denoted as Y. Let Y_P and Y_N denote the number of examples to which this process assigns a positive and a negative label, respectively. Similarly, let us denote the classifier by f and accordingly denote by f_P and f_N the number of examples to which f assigns a positive and a negative label, respectively. The empirical estimates of these quantities can be obtained from the confusion matrix, as shown in Table 5.6.

Similarly, we can denote the probability of overall agreement over the label assignments between the classifier and the true process by P_o. The empirical estimate of P_o can also be obtained from the confusion matrix of Table 5.6 as

$$P_o = \frac{TN + TP}{m},$$

where $m = TN + FP + FN + TP$. Therefore, P_o represents the accuracy of the classifier.

Given these empirical estimates of probabilities, Scott's π and Cohen's κ have a common formulation in that they take the ratio of the difference between the observed and chance agreements, and the maximum possible agreement that can be achieved over and beyond chance. However, the two metrics treat the chance agreement in different manners. While Scott's π estimates the chance that a label (positive or negative) is assigned given a random instance *irrespective* of the label assigning process, Cohen's κ considers this chance agreement by considering the two processes to be fixed.

Accordingly, Scott's π is defined as

$$\pi = \frac{P_o - P_e^S}{1 - P_e^S},$$

where the chance agreement over the labels, denoted as P_e^S is defined as

$$P_e^S = P_P^2 + P_N^2 \tag{5.1}$$

$$= \left[\frac{(f_P + Y_P)/2}{m}\right]^2 + \left[\frac{(f_N + Y_N)/2}{m}\right]^2. \tag{5.2}$$

Cohen's κ, on the other hand, is defined as

$$\kappa = \frac{P_o - P_e^C}{1 - P_e^C},$$

where the chance agreement over the labels in the case of Cohen's κ, denoted as P_e^C is defined as

$$P_e^S = P_P^Y \cdot P_P^f + P_N^Y \cdot P_P^f$$

$$= \frac{Y_P}{m} \cdot \frac{f_P}{m} + \frac{Y_N}{m} \cdot \frac{f_N}{m}.$$

As can be seen, unlike Cohen's κ, Scott's π is concerned with the overall propensity of a random instance being assigned a positive or negative label and, hence, it marginalizes *over the processes*. Hence, in the case of assessing a classifier's chance corrected accuracy against a "true" label generating process (whether unknown or by, say, an expert), Cohen's κ is a more relevant statistic than Scott's π. We therefore illustrate Cohen's κ in the following example.

Illustration of Cohen's κ calculation Consider the confusion matrix of Table 5.7 representing the output of a hypothetical classifier H_k on a three-class classification problem. The rows represent the actual classes while the columns represent the output of the classifier. Now, just looking at the diagonal entries will give us an estimate of the accuracy of the classifier $Acc(H_k)$. As mentioned earlier with regard to the agreement statistics framework above, $Acc(H_k)$ is the observed agreement P_o. Hence,

$$P_o = \frac{60 + 90 + 80}{400} = 0.575.$$

Let us see how we can generalize Cohen's κ to this case. For this we need to obtain a metric of chance agreement. Recall that we computed the chance agreement in the case of Cohen's κ above as the sum of chance agreement on the individual classes. Let us extend that analysis to the current case of three classes. The chance that both the classifier and the actual label assignment agree on the label of any given class is the product of their proportions of the examples assigned to this class. In the case of Table 5.7, we see that the classifier H_k assigns a proportion $\frac{120}{400}$ of examples to class a (sum of the first column). Similarly, the proportion of true labels of class a in the dataset is also $\frac{120}{400}$ (sum of first row). Hence, given a random example, both the classifier and the true label of the example will come out to

Table 5.7. *Hypothetical confusion matrix to illustrate the calculation of Cohen's κ.*

H_k	Pred-a	Pred-b	Pred-c	Total
Act-a	60	50	10	120
Act-b	20	90	40	150
Act-c	40	10	80	130
Total	120	150	130	

be a, with probability $\frac{120}{400} \cdot \frac{120}{400}$. We can calculate the chance agreement probabilities for classes b and c in a similar fashion. Adding these chance agreement probabilities for the three classes will give us the required P_e^C. That is,

$$P_e^C = \frac{120}{400} \cdot \frac{120}{400} + \frac{150}{400} \cdot \frac{150}{400} + \frac{130}{400} \cdot \frac{130}{400}$$
$$= 0.33625.$$

Hence, we get Cohen's κ agreement statistic for classifier H_k with the above calculated values as

$$\kappa(H_k) = \frac{P_o - P_e^C}{1 - P_e^C}$$
$$= \frac{0.575 - 0.33625}{1 - 0.33625}$$
$$= 0.3597.$$

We can see that the accuracy estimate of 57.5% for classifier H_k may be overly optimistic since it ignores the coincidental concordance of the classifier with the true labels. Indeed, it can be seen that the classifier mimics the class distribution of the actual labels when assigning labels to the instances (even though the overlap on the instances assigned the correct labels is smaller). Hence, for a random instance, the classifier will assign a class label with the same proportion as the true class distribution (empirically over the dataset). This will result in the classifier being right, merely by chance, in about 33.6% cases as calculated above, over all the classes (the P_e^C value). A more realistic estimate of classifier effectiveness is, then, the proportion of labels that the classifier gets right over and above this chance agreement, which is what Cohen's κ represents.

In summary, the agreement metrics take the marginal probability of label assignments into account to correct the estimated accuracy for chance. There have been arguments against the metrics, mainly with regard to the imperfect accounting for chance as a result of the lack of knowledge of the true marginals. Moreover, the limitations with respect to the sensitivity of these metrics to issues such as class imbalance (generally referred to as bias), prevalence, and misclassification costs still appear in the case of these chance-corrected metrics. There are metrics that address these issues to some extent by proposing modified agreement metrics that account for bias and prevalence as well as other metrics that generalize the ones discussed here to the multi-class scenarios (though we show how this can be done in a simple case in the above example). One of the most popular generalizations has appeared in the form of Fleiss' κ statistic (Fleiss 1971), which generalizes the Scott's π metric. Even though the critiques with regard to the bias and prevalence behaviors of the above agreement metrics are well justified and should be taken note of, it should also be kept in mind that these agreement metrics are proposed as summary metrics and, hence, can provide, within the proper context (generally the same that applies to reliable accuracy estimation), acceptable and reasonable performance assessment.

Let us now shift our attention to metrics that aim to assess the effectiveness of the classifier on a single class of interest.

5.5 Performance Metrics with a Single-Class Focus

The metrics discussed in Section 5.4 generally aim at characterizing the overall performance of the classifier on instances of all classes. These metrics can be effective when the user is interested in observing the general behavior of classifiers and when other constraints regarding the effectiveness of these metrics are met (e.g., when the class distributions are balanced, the performance on different classes are equally important and so on). Depending on the application domain of the learning algorithm, however, there could be other concerns at play that may not be addressed by the metrics discussed previously. One of the leading concerns relates to the greater relevance of the algorithms' performance on a single class of interest. The performance on the single class can be relevant either with regard to the instances of this class itself or with regard to the instances of other classes in the training data. It can also serve the purpose of measuring the overall performance of the classifier with an emphasis on the instances of each individual class as opposed to an all-encompassing measurement resulting from metrics such as accuracy, error rate, or balanced accuracy. Of course, this requires reporting the statistics over all the classes of interest. This section focuses on some of the most prominent metrics that address these concerns. We will focus on the binary classification scenario, where such metrics are mostly applied and also appear in conjunction with their complement measurements.

A number of the metrics in the category of interest here were discussed in Chapter 4. These include the true and false positive rates, sensitivity and specificity, and positive and negative predictive values (PPV/NPV), as well as precision, recall, and the F-metric. We will explore some of the characteristics of these metrics and introduce a few others, such as the G-mean, Youden's index, the discriminant power, and likelihood ratios.

5.5.1 Characterization of the One-Sided Metrics

Using the same hypothetical matrices used in Section 5.4.2, Tables 5.3, 5.4, and 5.5, we discuss the way sensitivity, specificity, PPV, NPV, precision, recall, the F-metric, and the G-mean, which we introduce here, "interpret" the information conveyed in these matrices and compare it to accuracy's interpretations.

Sensitivity/Specificity vs Accuracy

In the following example, we compare accuracy to sensitivity and specificity. Recall our hypothetical example of Tables 5.3 and 5.4, which yielded the same accuracy in both cases. For the confusion matrix in the first case, H_A, we have

$$Sensitivity(H_A) = \frac{200}{200 + 300} = 0.4$$

and

$$Specificity(H_A) = \frac{400}{400 + 100} = 0.8.$$

However, for the second case, H_B, we get

$$Sensitivity(H_B) = \frac{400}{400 + 100} = 0.8$$

and

$$Specificity(H_B) = \frac{200}{200 + 300} = 0.4.$$

Unlike for accuracy, sensitivity and specificity show that there is a difference between the two matrices and that, in fact, the two matrices are diametrical opposites. In essence, the tests, taken together, identify the proportion of the two classes correctly classified. However, unlike accuracy, they do this separately in the context of each individual class of instances, thus catching both the difference and the relationship between the two matrices.

As a result of the class-wise treatment, it turns out that the metrics are able to reduce the dependency on uneven class distribution in the test data as well. This is very clear in the extreme case of class imbalance described in the hypothetical example of Table 5.5. In that situation, we get

$$Sensitivity(H_C) = \frac{0}{0 + 50} = 0$$

and

$$Specificity(H_C) = \frac{950}{950 + 0} = 1,$$

which suggests that the pair of metrics, unlike accuracy, has recognized the nature of the problem. Although the example is extreme in that no instance of the positive class is correctly classified and no instances of the negative class are misclassified as positive, in a more realistic case where some of these two situations could occur, sensitivity would remain close to 0, and specificity close to 1. For example, assuming that two instances of the positive class were correctly classified and five instances of the negative class were incorrectly classified, we would have

$$Sensitivity(H_C) = \frac{2}{2 + 48} = .04$$

and

$$Specificity(H_C) = \frac{945}{945 + 5} = .995.$$

Sensitivity and specificity thus have a number of advantages that accuracy or even balanced accuracy do not have. However, these advantages come at the cost of needing a metric for every class, instead of having a single global metric. In the case of a multi-class classification problem, this would lead to as many metrics as there are classes, making it difficult to interpret. There are also other aspects that one might be interested in but that are missed by the sensitivity/specificity pair. One such aspect is the study of the proportion of examples assigned to a certain class by the classifier that actually belong to this class. This value is captured by the PPV/NPV pair as we now show.

PPV/NPV vs Accuracy

PPV and NPV, defined in Chapter 4, tell us how much we can trust the classifications we observe. In other words, they tell us what proportion of examples classified as positive truly is positive, and what proportion of examples classified as negative truly is negative. In this section, we question what the PPV/NPV pair tells us in the three hypothetical situations we created. For the confusion matrix in Table 5.3, the PPV/NPV metrics return

$$PPV(H_A) = \frac{200}{200 + 100} = .6667 = 66.7\%,$$

and

$$NPV(H_A) = \frac{400}{400 + 300} = .5714 = 57.14\%.$$

For the confusion matrix in Table 5.4, the PPV/NPV metrics return

$$PPV(H_B) = \frac{400}{400 + 300} = .5714 = 57.14\%,$$

and

$$NPV(H_B) = \frac{200}{200 + 100} = .6667 = 66.7\%.$$

The results show us that the symmetry of the situation has been caught by the PPV/NPV pair. We can also see that, unlike sensitivity and specificity, which gave a .8 score to the class that was better classified in each of the first two hypothetical examples, PPV and NPV give less "enthusiastic" scores to the better-classified class (.67 instead of .8) and, in fact, less dismal scores to the lesser-classified class (.57 instead of .4) As a result, a definite judgment call on the superiority of the classifier in one case or the other cannot be made[8] based on the PPV/NPV metric pair which appears more cautious than sensitivity and specificity.

From a reliability perspective in the case of the extreme imbalance situation reflected in the confusion matrix of Table 5.5, PPV and NPV may give some insight into how reliable

---

[8] Perhaps that is a good thing as neither classifier is very good and such a judgment shouldn't be made. But this depends on the application domain and will not be discussed further.

the class-wise predictions of a classifier are, although the result needs to be considered carefully. In the Table 5.5 situation, PPV/NPV return

$$PPV(H_C) = \frac{0}{0+0} = undefined$$

and

$$NPV(H_C) = \frac{950}{950+50} = .95 = 95\%.$$

Though this may suggest that the PPV/NPV pair is appropriate for extreme cases of imbalance, one must be careful with this assessment. As previously mentioned, the case of classifier H_C defined in Section 5.4.2 is rather extreme. If, like in our discussion of sensitivity and specificity, we made the problem more realistic by allowing two true positive classifications and five false positive ones, we would have

$$PPV(H_C) = \frac{2}{2+5} = 28.6\%$$

and

$$NPV(H_C) = \frac{945}{945+48} = .952 = 95.2\%.$$

Those values are still somewhat indicative of the disparity in the confusion matrix, but note that if a classifier allowed two true positive classifications but no false positive ones (in a situation where, say, two positive instances were so "positive" that the classifier couldn't miss them, even if it were a classifier strongly biased toward the negative class, meaning that all the other instances, positive or negative, were uniformly classified as negative), then we would have

$$PPV(H_C) = \frac{2}{2+0} = 100\%$$

and

$$NPV(H_C) = \frac{950}{950+48} = .952 = 95.2\%.$$

The fact that the PPV value can fluctuate so easily based on very small changes to the confusion matrix, and can, in fact, give stellar scores to a very bad classifier (such as the last one considered) is quite concerning and suggests that the PPV/NPV pair may, in fact, not be the most adequate metric pair in the case of class imbalances.

This analysis together with that of sensitivity/specificity reinforces the observation already made in Section 5.3 that there is an information tradeoff carried through the different metrics. What this boils down to is that a practitioner has to choose, quite carefully, the quantity he or she is interested in monitoring while keeping in mind that other values matter as well, and that classifiers may rank differently depending on the metrics along which they are getting compared.

Precision/Recall vs Accuracy

We now investigate the way in which precision and recall "interpret" our two hypothetical matrices of Tables 5.3 and 5.4. We obtain

$$Prec(H_A) = \frac{200}{200 + 100} = 0.667$$

and

$$Rec(H_A) = \frac{200}{200 + 300} = 0.4$$

in the first case, and

$$Prec(H_B) = \frac{400}{400 + 300} = 0.572$$

and

$$Rec(H_B) = \frac{400}{400 + 100} = 0.8$$

in the second. The first observation is that these results are not completely new. Indeed, precision corresponds to PPV, and recall to sensitivity, two metrics previously discussed. What is new, however, is their combination in a pair, and that is what we comment on in this section. The logic of using precision and recall together, as discussed in Chapter 4, is that together they give us information on how well the classifier fares on the positive class. In particular, precision indicates the proportion of instances predicted as positive that truly are positive, while recall indicates the proportion of true positive instances present in the dataset correctly labeled as positive. Precision and recall are easy to understand when considered in the context of information retrieval, the field that proposed their use as a pair. Assuming that an algorithm looking for all science fiction features in a database of movies returns a set of S movies. Assuming, further that the entire database contains D movies, including SF science fiction movies. If we assume that X out of S movies retrieved by the algorithms are science fiction movies, then precision corresponds to the proportion of science fiction movies in the set of movies retrieved by the algorithm (i.e., $\frac{X}{S}$) while recall indicates the proportion of science fiction movies returned by the algorithm out of all the science fiction movies present in the database (i.e., $\frac{X}{SF}$).

The results on our hypothetical confusion matrices suggest that the first classifier is slightly more precise than the second on the positive class, but has low recall. The second classifier, on the other hand, has very high recall. This is useful information, though it is important to note that the precision and recall metrics do not focus on the performance of the classifier on any class other than the class of interest (the positive class). It is possible, therefore, for a classifier trained on a medical domain such as the breast cancer recurrence dataset introduced at the beginning of the chapter, to have respectable precision and recall values even if it does very poorly at recognizing that a patient who did not suffer a recurrence of her cancer is, indeed, healthy. This is disturbing since the same values of precision and recall can be obtained no matter what the proportion of patients labeled as healthy is actually healthy, as in the example confusion matrix of Table 5.8, which is similar to the confusion

Table 5.8. *Hypothetical confusion matrix IV over hypothetical classifier H_D.*

H_D	pos	neg
Yes	200	100
No	300	0
	P = 500	N = 100

matrix in Table 5.3 except for the TN value, which was set to zero (and the number of negative examples, N, which was consequently decreased to 100). Indeed, for that matrix, we get identical results to those obtained for H_A, despite the flagrant disparity between the two matrices:

$$Prec(H_D) = \frac{200}{200 + 100} = 0.667$$

and

$$Rec(H_D) = \frac{200}{200 + 300} = 0.4.$$

This disturbing phenomenon is caused by the fact that precision and recall have a one-class focus only. Yet, it is clear that the matrix for classifier H_D presents a much more severe shortcoming than the matrix for classifier H_A since it is incapable of classifying true negative examples as negative (it can, however, wrongly classify positive examples as negative!). Such behavior, by the way, is reflected by the accuracy metric, which assesses that classifier H_D is only accurate in 33% of the cases while H_A is accurate in 60% of the cases. Specificity, it turns out, also catches the deficiency of precision and recall. In fact, it does so in a much more direct way since it obtains 0 for H_D.

Turning now to the situation of extreme imbalance captured by the matrix of Table 5.5 that caused a classifier to classify all instances as negative, we have

$$Prec(H_C) = \frac{0}{0 + 0} = undefined$$

and

$$Rec(H_C) = \frac{0}{0 + 50} = 0.$$

Recall, as discussed in the context of sensitivity, captures the situation and is robust to small fluctuations in the number of positive examples recognized as positive. Precision, on the other hand, as discussed in the context of PPV, is not that reliable as it can take any value. In the particular example we chose here, where not a single positive instance is classified as positive, it is undefined. However, if we had allowed one positive instance to be well classified, it would take a value of 1. If there were one negative example mistakenly classified as positive and no positive example classified as positive, it would obtain a value of 0.

Combining Metric Pairs: F-measure and G-Mean vs Accuracy

We now discuss two combination metrics well known and commonly used by the machine learning community: the F-measure and the G-mean.

F-measure As discussed in Chapter 4, precision and recall can be combined using the F-measure. For our hypothetical example from Tables 5.3 and 5.4, we have

$$F(H_A) = \frac{2 * 0.67 * 0.4}{(2 * 0.67) + 0.4} = 0.31$$

and

$$F(H_B) = \frac{2 * 0.572 * 0.8}{(2 * 0.572) + 0.8} = 0.47.$$

This shows that with precision and recall weighed equally, H_B does a better job on the positive class than H_A. This is an advantage over accuracy, which does not distinguish between the two confusion matrices. Like accuracy, both F-measure results are relatively low, reflecting the fact that neither algorithm performs particularly well on the positive class. $F(H_C)$, the F-measure obtained in the extreme imbalance situation depicted in the confusion matrix of Table 5.5 is undefined since $Prec(H_C)$ is undefined. In general, given that precision is unreliable in extreme cases of imbalance, the use of the F-measure for such cases is not recommended.

Several variations of the F-measure were discussed in Chapter 4. If we use the F_2 rather than the F_1 measure, we get $F_2(H_A) = 0.46$ and $F_2(H_B) = 0.7$ on the matrices of Tables 5.3 and 5.4, respectively, which emphasize that recall is a greater factor in assessing the quality of H_B than precision. Similarly, the use of the $F_{0.5}$ measure results in $F_{0.5}(H_A) = 0.55$ and $F_{0.5}(H_B) = 0.632$, indicating that recall is very important in the case of H_B. Indeed, when precision counts for twice as much as recall, the two matrices obtain results that are very close to one another.

This goes to show that choosing the relative weight for combining precision and recall is very important in the F-measure calculations. However, in most practical cases, appropriate weights are not known, resulting in a significant limitation with regard to the use of such combinations of metrics. Another limitation of the F-measure results from the limitation of its components. Indeed, just as for the precision-recall metric pair, the F-measure leaves out the true negative performance of the classifier.

Geometric mean (G-mean) As discussed previously, the informativeness of accuracy generally decreases with increasing class imbalances. It is, hence, desirable to look at the classifier's performance on instances of individual classes. One way of addressing this concern is to use the sensitivity and specificity metrics in combination to report the performance of the classifier on the two classes (PPV/NPV and precision/recall do offer insights on the issue, but each pair of metrics has its shortcomings in the extreme class imbalance problem, as was discussed previously).

In this section we present the geometric mean, which proposes another view of the problem by combining the two metrics. The original formulation for classifier f was proposed by Kubat et al. (1998) and is defined as

$$Gmean(f) = \sqrt{TPR(f) * TNR(f)} = \sqrt{Sensitivity(f) * Specificity(f)}.$$

As can be seen, this metric takes into account the relative balance of the classifier's performance on both the positive and negative classes. $Gmean(f)$ becomes 1 only when $TPR(f) = TNR(f) = 1$. For all other combinations of the classifier's $TPR(f)$ and $TNR(f)$, the metrics weigh the resulting statistic by the relative balance between the two. In this sense, this metric is closer to the multi-class focus category of metrics discussed previously.

Using the two hypothetical matrices, H_A and H_B of Tables 5.3 and 5.4, respectively, the G-mean gives us the following (same) result for each matrix:

$$Gmean(H_A) = \sqrt{0.4 * 0.8} = Gmean(H_B) = \sqrt{0.8 * 0.4} = 0.5657.$$

This means that the distinction between the two situations that was recorded when considering sensitivity and specificity separately is now lost. For the case of the extreme class imbalance problem shown in Table 5.5, on the other hand, the G-mean is

$$Gmean(H_C) = \sqrt{0 * 1} = 0,$$

properly guarding us against using the classifier. The metric is robust to small deviations in sensitivity and specificity as well.

Another version of the G-mean, focusing on a single class of interest, can take the precision of the classifier $Prec(f)$ into account instead of its specificity. In the two-class scenario, with the class of interest being the positive class, this yields

$$Gmean_2 = \sqrt{TPR(f) * Prec(f)}.$$

Hence, $Gmean_2$ takes into account the proportion of the actual positive examples labeled as positive by the classifier as well as the proportion of the examples labeled by the classifier as positive that are, indeed, positive. Using the two hypothetical matrices, H_A and H_B, $Gmean_2$ gives us

$$Gmean_2(H_A) = \sqrt{0.4 * 0.667} = 0.5165,$$

$$Gmean_2(H_B) = \sqrt{0.8 * 0.572} = 0.6765,$$

thus correctly indicating that matrix B is more favorable to the positive class than matrix A. In the case of extreme imbalance, we have

$$Gmean_2(H_C) = \sqrt{0 * undefined} = undefined.$$

Please note, however, that, as discussed earlier, the situation we chose is unlikely to take place in real life and, in most cases, precision will be defined and, as a result, $Gmean_2$ will return 0 in the case of extreme imbalance (or a very small value).

5.5.2 Additional One-Sided Metrics

We now present a few additional one-sided metrics borrowed from the medical field. In particular, we present Youden's index, discriminant power and likelihood ratios. These metrics were introduced to the machine learning community by Sokolova et al. (2006).

Youden's Index

Youden's index is another metric that combines sensitivity and specificity, but it does so in a way different from the G-mean. Specifically, Youden's index was designed to test how well a classification system is able to avoid failure. It gives equal weight to the system's performance on the positive and negative classes. It is defined as

$$YoudenIndex = Sensitivity - (1 - Specificity).$$

We calculated the results obtained by Youden's index on our running example on the matrices of Tables 5.3 and 5.4, as well as on the extreme imbalance problem. For the confusion matrix in Table 5.3, we obtained

$$YoudensIndex(H_A) = .4 - (1 - .8) = .2,$$

while for the confusion matrix in Table 5.4, we obtained

$$YoudenIndex(H_B) = .8 - (1 - .4) = .2.$$

For the extreme imbalance problem in Table 5.5, we obtain

$$YoudenIndex(H_C) = 0 - (1 - 1) = 0.$$

This shows that combining the results according to Youden's index leads to identical values for both the scenarios of Tables 5.3 and 5.4, thus suggesting that Youden's index gives equal weight to each class. The result is also quite low, suggesting that a high score in one of the combined metrics (specificity, in the first case, and sensitivity in the second) is not sufficient to boost the index's score. In fact, it is interesting to see that the score issued by Youden's index is lower than that obtained on either one of the two compounds. What Youden's index does is compound the misgivings of one metric with those of the other, instead of allowing the success on one metric to compensate for the failure on another. This is well reflected in the extreme class imbalance scenario of Table 5.5, where despite obtaining perfect specificity, Youden's index is 0 due to the sensitivity being 0.

Discriminant Power

Discriminant power differs from Youden's index as it focuses on how well an algorithm discriminates between positive and negative instances. The formula is[9]

$$DiscriminantPower = \frac{\sqrt{3}}{\pi} \left(Log\left(\frac{Sensitivity}{(1 - Sensitivity)}\right) + Log\left(\frac{Specificity}{(1 - Specificity)}\right) \right).$$

---

[9] where Log corresponds to Log_{10}

The value obtained by discriminant power is interpreted as follows: the algorithm discriminates poorly if $DP < 1$; it is a limited discriminator if $1 < DP < 2$; a fair one if $DP < 3$; and does a good job in all other cases.

The results obtained on the scenarios of Tables 5.3 and 5.4 and the extreme class imbalance problem of Table 5.5 are given below:

$$Discriminant\ Power(H_A) = \frac{\sqrt{3}}{\pi} \left(Log \left(\frac{.4}{.6} \right) + Log \left(\frac{.8}{.2} \right) \right) = .234,$$

$$Discriminant\ Power(H_B) = \frac{\sqrt{3}}{\pi} \left(Log \left(\frac{.8}{.2} \right) + Log \left(\frac{.4}{.6} \right) \right) = .234,$$

$$Discriminant\ Power(H_C) = \frac{\sqrt{3}}{\pi} Log \left(\frac{0}{(1-0)} \right) + Log \left(\frac{1}{(1-1)} \right) = undefined.$$

Once again, combining sensitivity and specificity, this time according to the discriminant power, leads to identical values for both the scenarios of Tables 5.3 and 5.4. Furthermore, the value obtained is less than 1, which suggests that the hypothetical algorithms that generated the confusion matrices of Tables 5.3 and 5.4 are poor. It is interesting to note that while sensitivity and specificity were able to discern the differences between the two confusion metrics, both Youden's index and discriminant power, that combine these metrics, are as blind as accuracy to their differences.

For the extreme class imbalance scenario we created, the discriminant power is undefined. As previously discussed, that situation is extreme. In more realistic situations, the results would be more telling. By allowing two positive examples to be properly classified as positive and five negative ones to be wrongly classified as positive as we suggested before, the discriminant power obtains a value around 0.5, suggesting that the classifier that produced the confusion metric is poor.

Next, we discuss a pair of metrics also based on sensitivity and specificity that, this time, is able to capture the difference between the two confusion matrices of Tables 5.3 and 5.4.

Likelihood Ratio

An important pair of metrics related to the sensitivity and specificity of the classifier, known as the likelihood ratios, aims to combine these two notions to assess the extent to which the classifier is effective in predicting the two classes (Sokolova et al. 2006). Even though the metric combines sensitivity and specificity, there are two versions. Each version makes the assessment for an individual class. For the positive class, we have

$$LR_+ = \frac{Sensitivity}{1 - Specificity},$$

while for the negative class, we have

$$LR_- = \frac{1 - Sensitivity}{Specificity}.$$

Since these ratios are geared at a medical application, we first illustrate their use in our breast cancer domain, where LR_+ summarizes how many times *more* likely patients whose cancer did recur are to have a positive prediction than patients without recurrence; while LR_- summarizes how many times *less* likely patients whose cancer did recur are to have a negative prediction than patients without recurrence. In terms of probabilities, LR_+ is the ratio of the probability of a positive result in people who do encounter a recurrence to the probability of a positive result in people who do not. Similarly, LR_- is the ratio of the probability of a negative result in people who do encounter a recurrence to the probability of a negative result in people who do not.

A higher positive likelihood and a lower negative likelihood mean better performance on positive and negative classes, respectively, so we want to maximize LR_+ and minimize LR_-. A likelihood ratio higher than 1 indicates that the test result is associated with the presence of the recurrence (in our example) whereas a likelihood ratio lower than 1 indicates that the test result is associated with the absence of this recurrence. The further likelihood ratios are from 1, the stronger the evidence for the presence or absence of the recurrence, respectively. Likelihood ratios reaching values higher than 10 and lower than 0.1 provide acceptably strong evidence (Deeks and Altman 2004).

When comparing two algorithms, A and B, the relationships between the positive and negative likelihood ratios of both classifiers can be interpreted in terms of comparative performance as follows, for $LR_+ \geq 1$:[10]

- $LR_+^A > LR_+^B$ and $LR_-^A < LR_-^B$ implies that A is superior overall;
- $LR_+^A < LR_+^B$ and $LR_-^A < LR_-^B$ implies that A is superior for confirmation of negative examples;
- $LR_+^A > LR_+^B$ and $LR_-^A > LR_-^B$ implies that A is superior for confirmation of positive examples.

Example Applying this evaluation method to the confusion matrix that was obtained from applying naive Bayes to the breast cancer domain and shown in Table 4.1, we obtain the following values for the likelihood ratios of a positive and a negative test, respectively:

$$LR_+ = \frac{.53}{1 - .78} = 2.41,$$

$$LR_- = \frac{1 - .53}{.78} = 0.6.$$

This tells us that patients whose cancer recurred are 2.41 times more likely to be predicted as positive by naive Bayes than patients whose cancer did not recur; and that patients whose cancer did recur are 0.6 times less likely to be predicted as negative by naive Bayes than patients whose cancer did not recur. This is not a bad result, but the classifier would be more impressive if its positive likelihood ratio were higher and its negative likelihood ratio lower.

---

[10] If an algorithm does not satisfy this condition, then "positive" and "negative" likelihood values should be swapped

Following our previously discussed hypothetical example, we find that the classifier represented by Table 5.3, denoted H_A, yields

$$LR_+(H_A) = \frac{0.4}{1 - 0.8} = 2$$

and

$$LR_-(H_A) = \frac{1 - 0.4}{0.8} = 0.75,$$

while the classifier represented by Table 5.4, denoted H_B, yields

$$LR_+(H_B) = \frac{0.8}{1 - 0.4} = 1.33$$

and

$$LR_-(H_B) = \frac{1 - 0.8}{0.4} = 0.5.$$

We thus have $LR_+(H_A) > LR_+(H_B)$ and $LR_-(H_A) > LR_-(H_B)$, meaning that classifier H_A is superior at predicting positive if the instance is truly positive than classifier H_B; but that classifier H_B is better at ensuring that a positive instance does not get classified as negative than classifier H_A.

In the extreme class imbalance scenario of Table 5.5, the likelihood ratios take the values

$$LR_+(H_C) = \frac{0}{1 - 1} = undefined$$

and

$$LR_-(H_C) = \frac{1 - 0}{1} = 1.$$

As already discussed, in the slightly less extreme case where two positive instances are well classified and five negative ones wrongly classified as positive, L_+ will be close to 0 (0.0417) and L_- will be close to 1 (0.965).

Note that when interpreted in a probabilistic sense, the likelihood ratios used together give the likelihood in the Bayesian sense, which, along with a prior over the data, can then give a posterior on the instances' class memberships. The above discrete version has found wide use in clinical diagnostic test assessment. In the Bayesian or probabilistic sense, however, the likelihood ratios are used in the context of nested hypotheses. That is, on hypotheses that belong to the same class of functions but vary in their respective complexity this is basically model selection with regard to choosing a more (or less) complex classifier depending upon their respective likelihoods given the data at hand.

This concludes the discussion of the metrics listed in the leftmost side of the ontology of Figure 5.1, under the "confusion matrix" rubric. We now turn to the next branch of the ontology entitled "confusion matrix and additional info." Section 5.6 considers the metrics listed under the "continuous and probabilistic classifiers" rubric, while Section 5.7 continues the discussion on "scoring classifiers" started in Chapter 4 with a discussion of ROC analysis, and Section 5.8 introduces other graphical evaluation methods.

5.6 Skew/Imbalances, Cost, Uncertainty, and Calibration

This part of the chapter considers ways to add information to the entries of the confusion matrix so as to combine skew or imbalances, cost, uncertainty, and calibration considerations to the performance results. The part of Figure 5.1 discussed here pertains to the "continuous and probabilistic classifiers" rubric. In particular, we will discuss how to add class ratios and costs to our metrics and move on to discussing classifier uncertainty and calibration metrics such as log loss and Brier's score under the probabilistic metrics.

5.6.1 Skew and Cost Considerations

The entries of the confusion matrix are quite informative. However, each entry by itself can be misleading and, hence, an attempt is generally made to take into account the information conveyed by these entries in relation to other relevant entries of the matrix. As discussed in the previous sections, different performance metrics aim at addressing these relationships in different ways. For instance, while considering accuracy or error rates, the metrics combine the diagonal entries to obtain an overall evaluation on all classes (and not just on one particular class). Conversely, metrics such as sensitivity are typically studied in relation to their respective complements (e.g., specificity in the binary classification scenario) to present a relatively unbiased picture. This is important since partial information can be quite misleading.

However, even when such care is taken, there can be other confounding issues. These issues may need to be addressed at different stages of learning. In particular, the distinction between the solutions that can be offered *during* learning and the ones that can be applied *after* learning is important. We will briefly ponder upon this shortly. But before that, let us talk about the two issues that can be important in interpreting the results of the classifier on the test data as conveyed by the confusion matrix: class imbalances and misclassification costs.

Skew, Class Imbalances, and Long Tail Distributions

The first issue we consider pertains to the class distributions in the dataset. By class distribution, we mean the distribution of instances belonging to various classes in the test set. Alternatively, this is referred to as class imbalance (Japkowicz and Stephen 2002; Branco et al. 2016) or long tail distributions in the deep learning context with multiple classes (Zhang et al. 2023). We confronted this issue earlier in the chapter as well as in Chapter 4 while studying different performance metrics and also saw some attempts to take it into consideration while interpreting the results. One solution to evaluating classifiers under the class imbalance problem has been proposed that takes into account *class ratios* instead of fixing the measurements with regard to the class size of a particular class. *Class ratio* for a given class i refers to the number of instances of class i as opposed to those of other classes in the dataset.[11] Hence, in the two class scenario, the class ratio of the positive class as opposed to the negative class, denoted $ratio_+$, can be obtained as

$$ratio_+ = \frac{(TP + FN)}{(FP + TN)}.$$

In the multi-class scenario, for the class of interest being i, we get

$$ratio_i = \frac{\sum_j c_{ij}}{\sum_{j, j \neq i} c_{ji} + \sum_{j, j \neq i} c_{jj}}.$$

The entries can then be weighted by their respective class ratios. Balanced accuracy is one example of a metric that takes such ratios into consideration, but any other metric could be adapted to do so. For instance, in the binary case the *TPR* can be weighted by $ratio_+$ while the *TNR* can be weighted by $ratio_-$, the class ratio of the negative class. Such evaluation that takes into account the differing class distributions is referred to as skew-sensitive assessment. Other metrics for dealing with class imbalances in the multi-class classification case are presented in Branco et al. (2017) and Stapor et al. (2021) and include average accuracy, class balance accuracy, multi-class G-metric, and confusion entropy. Recent work by Bellinger et al. (n.d.), however, suggests that these metrics may not be sufficient as they do not take into consideration potential class imbalances within the minority class subconcepts. They recommend, instead, applying instance-weighting to the metrics.

Misclassification Costs

The second issue that confounds the interpretation of the entries of the confusion matrix that we wish to discuss here is that of asymmetric misclassification costs. There are two dimensions to this. Misclassifying instances of a class i can have a different cost than misclassifying the instances of class $j, j \neq i$. Moreover, the cost associated with the misclassification of class i instances to class $j, j \neq i$, can differ from the misclassification of class i instances to class $j', j' \neq j$.

For instance, consider a learning algorithm applied to the tasks of differentiating patients with acute lymphoblastic leukaemia (ALL) or acute myloid leukaemia (AML), and normal subjects based on their respective gene expression analysis (see Golub et al. (1999) for an example of this). In such a scenario, predicting one of the pathologies for a normal subject might be less costly than missing some patients (with ALL or AML) by predicting them as normal subjects (of course, contingent upon the fact that further validation can identify the normal subjects as such). On the other hand, missing patients can be very expensive since the disease can go unnoticed, resulting in devastating consequences. Further, classifying ALL patients as AML patients and *vice versa* can also have differing costs.

Asymmetric (mis)classification costs almost always exist in real-world problems. However, in the absence of information to definitively establish such costs, a comforting assumption, that of symmetric costs, is made. As a result, the confusion matrix, by default, considers

---

[11] Not to be confused with the likelihood ratios discussed in Section 5.5.2.

all errors to be equally important. The question then becomes: How can we effectively integrate cost considerations when such knowledge exists? Incorporating such asymmetric costs can be quite important for both effective learning on the data and sensible evaluation.

This brings us to a discussion on the distinction of solutions applied *during* the learning process and *after* the learning is done. The asymmetric cost of misclassification can be integrated into the learning process itself so as to make the learning algorithm sensitive to such costs. This would require the incorporation of an asymmetric loss function that would replace, for instance, the zero-one loss function in the classification case. This is easier said than done. Such asymmetric loss incorporation introduces its own set of challenges to the underlying learning theoretic model. However, we concern ourselves with the more relevant aspect, in the context of this book, of incorporating these costs in the assessment phase.

Accounting for misclassification costs during the evaluation phase is useful for many reasons. First, incorporating the costs in the learning process is difficult. Moreover, different learning algorithms may deal with such asymmetric loss in different ways (and with differing efficiency). Second, and perhaps a more important reason, is that such costs might not be available during learning. Also, these costs can be time sensitive; that is, the misclassification costs can change over time.

The most direct approach for incorporating misclassification costs is to weigh the nondiagonal entries of the confusion matrix accordingly. These cost estimates can either be known a priori or come from domain experts. Weighing the entries in this way results in the weighted variants of different performance metrics. For instance, the empirical error refers to the proportion of examples in the test set that appear in the nondiagonal entries of the confusion matrix. In the weighted estimate, each of the nondiagonal entries $c_{ij}, i \neq j$, of $\mathbf{C}$ is weighted by a respective cost, say, w_{ij}. The empirical error estimate is, then, obtained as a combination of these weighted proportions of the misclassified entries.

Note that cost considerations in the evaluation need not be the same as the skew or class distribution considerations discussed above. The cost of misclassification may or may not overlap with the presence or absence of class imbalance. Although attempts have been made to integrate the two by way of introduction of *cost ratios*, we do not discuss these here.[12]

5.6.2 Classification Uncertainty and Calibration

In addition to the skew and cost issues just discussed, the question of classification uncertainty and its alignment with reality is quite important to consider prior to deploying a classifier. In this section, we address this question and introduce two metrics that assess that alignment.

Classification Uncertainty

When looking at a classifier's output, we could look at classification errors, as we have done so far, using a confusion matrix, but we can also question how certain or uncertain the

---

[12] An introduction to cost-sensitive learning and the related issue of evaluation in such a setting can be found at https:// machinelearningmastery.com/cost-sensitive-learning-for-imbalanced-classification/.

Table 5.9. *The output of a probabilistic classifier on a hypothetical test set with two classes, "P" and "N."*

instance no.	Actual class	Predicted class	Probability
1	P	P	0.80
2	P	N	0.55
3	P	P	0.70
4	P	P	0.90
5	N	N	0.85
6	N	P	0.90
7	N	N	0.60
8	N	N	0.80
9	N	P	0.75
10	N	N	0.95

classifier was in making these classifications. Let us see this with an illustration. Consider the output of a probabilistic classifier on a hypothetical test set of 10 instances with two classes (too small and never recommended in practice), as shown in Table 5.9. The classifier outputs the class labels for each instance with associated probabilities. The table shows the predicted class as the one with a higher probability.

This is in contrast to a deterministic classifier that outputs a fixed class label on a test instance without making any implicit certainty statements. When considered in this sense – considering the output labels without (un)certainty information – the classifier of Table 5.9 makes three classification errors. However, this deterministic consideration, as done by the confusion matrix, loses the uncertainty information of the classifier. That is, it suggests that we should be equally confident in all the class labels predicted by the classifier or, alternatively, that the labels output by the classifier are all perfectly certain. Nonetheless, when looked at closely, the information in the table gives us a more detailed picture. In particular, instances that are misclassified with little certainty (e.g., instance no. 2) can quite likely correspond to instances often called boundary examples. By contrast, when misclassifications are made with high certainty (e.g., instance no. 6), then either the classifier or the examples need to be studied more carefully since such a behavior can be due to a lack of proper learning or to the presence of noise or outliers, among other reasons. There can also be other cases where uncertainty is introduced in the performance estimates (e.g., stochastic learning algorithms) and where it is not trivial to measure the performance of the learning algorithm on the test data. Altogether, the point we wish to make here, is that information about a classifier's certainty or uncertainty can be very important. As can be clearly seen, the confusion matrix, at least in its classical form, does not incorporate this information. Consequently, the lack of classifier uncertainty information is also reflected in all the performance metrics that rely solely on the confusion matrix.

Although classifier uncertainty adds information that may be useful in assessing performance, in certain types of situations the nature of the uncertainty is important. In particular, it is sometimes necessary to know whether the classifier's uncertainty aligns with reality. The category of metrics that assess whether a classifier's confidence reflects reality is called calibration. We discuss calibration next, and introduce two metrics that measure how well-calibrated a model is.

Calibration

A model is said to be well calibrated if, when it predicts a class with confidence p, it is correct $100 \times p\%$ of the time. Calibrating a model is important when the application domain requires all the information it can get from the classifier. For example, a predictor could be tasked with issuing information about the probability that trains arrive late at a particular station. If such a predictor were to state that the probability of trains arriving late at the station is low and if, in fact, that probability is high (e.g., most trains are late), then the system is badly calibrated and needs some sort of reset. While some models, such as logistic regression, automatically learn calibrated scores, many others, such as decision trees, SVMs and neural networks do not do so systematically. These learners often learn a score, but that score does not represent the probability of the classification being correct. For these cases, post-processing methods have been suggested including Platt's scaling (Platt 1999) and isotonic regression (Zadrozny and Elkan 2001). The two approaches have also been contrasted in Niculescu-Mizil and Caruana (2005), Caruana and Niculescu-Mizil (2006), and Fawcett and Niculescu-Mizil (2007a). We do not study these methods here. Instead, our focus is on the metrics that have been proposed to assess whether the scores obtained by classifiers are well calibrated or not. In particular, we present the log loss, also known as the cross-entropy metric and Brier's score. Newer approaches have also been proposed specifically for deep learning such as Vaicenavicius et al. (2019) and Nixon et al. (2019), but these will not be covered here.

Logarithmic loss The logarithmic loss (or log loss) assesses the difference between the predicted probability and the actual class (Dembla 2020). The log loss for one example in a binary classification setting is calculated as[13]

$$LogLoss(i) = -[y_i \times Ln(\hat{y}_i) + (1 - y_i) \times Ln(1 - \hat{y}_i)],$$

where y_i represents the class of the instance and $\hat{y}_i$ its prediction probability. The log loss value is indicative of how close the prediction probability is to the corresponding actual/true value (0 or 1 in the case of binary classification). The more the predicted probability diverges from the actual value, the higher the log loss value. For example, the log loss for instance no. 3 in Table 5.9 where the example's actual class is P(ositive) or 1 and the classifier predicts 1 with probability 0.7, is

$$LogLoss(3) = -[1 \times Ln(0.7) + 0] = 0.357.$$

---

[13] *Ln* is the natural logarithm.

For instance no. 4, which is also positive and predicted as such with probability 0.9, the log loss is smaller at

$$LogLoss(4) = -[1 \times Ln(0.9) + 0] = 0.105.$$

In the case of a negative instance wrongly classified as positive with probability 0.55, such as in instance no. 2, we obtain a large score as shown here:

$$LogLoss(2) = -[0 + 1 \times Ln(.45)] = 0.799.$$

To calculate the log loss of the entire model, we calculate the average log loss on each instance,

$$LogLoss = \frac{1}{N} \sum_{i=1}^{N} Logloss(i) = \sum_{i=1}^{N} -[y_i \times Ln(\hat{y}_i) + (1 - y_i) \times Ln(1 - \hat{y}_i)],$$

where N represents the total number of instances. We demonstrate its calculation on the example of Table 5.9:

$$LogLoss = \frac{1}{10} \times (-(Ln.8 + Ln.45 + Ln.7 + Ln.9 + Ln.85 + Ln.1 + Ln.6 + Ln.8 + Ln.25 + Ln.95))$$

$$= \frac{1}{10} \times (.223 + .799 + .357 + .105 + .163 + 2.303 + .511 + .223 + 1.386 + .051) = 0.6121.$$

With log loss, for a fully balanced binary classification problem the value 0.693 represents chance. It is worth noting that different thresholds apply to different situations of class balance and multi-class problems. For an imbalance on a binary problem such as the one seen in our table (four positive and six negative instances), the value is 0.67, rather than .693, is what represents chance.[14] The result we obtained of 0.6121 is, thus, slightly lower than chance but not very far from it and, therefore, not very good. This was somewhat expected, due to some misclassification made with high confidence in the dataset.

For multiclass classifiers, the log loss for a single example can be computed by adding a term for each class as follows:

$$LogLoss_i^C = -\sum_{c=1}^{C}[y_i^c \times Ln(\hat{y}_i^c)],$$

where C represents the number of classes in the problem. The log loss for the entire model is calculated by taking the average log loss for each example as in the binary case. Please note that the generalization to a multi-class problem is also known as the cross-entropy.

Brier's score Brier's score computes the mean squared error between the prediction probability for each example and its corresponding actual/true value. It is computed according to the formula

$$Brier\,Score = \frac{1}{N} \times \sum_{i=1}^{N}(\hat{y}_i - y_i)^2,$$

[14] For a good discussion of this issue, see https://stats.stackexchange.com/questions/276067/whats-considered-a-good-log-loss.

where y_i represents the class of the instance, $\hat{y}_i$ its prediction probability, and N the total number of instances. The Brier score for instance nos. 3 and 4, respectively, in Table 5.9 are

$$(\hat{y}_3 - y_3)^2 = (0.7 - 1)^2 = 0.09$$

and

$$(\hat{y}_4 - y_4)^2 = (0.9 - 1)^2 = 0.01.$$

For instance no. 2, it is

$$(\hat{y}_2 - y_2)^2 = (0.45 - 1)^2 = 0.303.$$

The values obtained on these three instances follow the same pattern as that shown by log loss.[15] Indeed, the classifier is more confident in the positivity of instance no. 4 (confidence: .9) than it is of instance no. 3 (confidence: .7), despite both instances being positive, which is why instance no. 4 obtains a lower (better) score than instance no. 3. On the other hand, the classifier wrongly classifies instance no. 2 as negative although it should have been positive. This is reflected by the large score obtained. Had the classifier been even more confident despite being wrong, as for instance no. 6, for example, then the score would have been even higher.

To calculate Brier's score for the entire model, the Brier score for each instance is calculated and the results for all the instances are averaged. We demonstrate its calculation on the example of Table 5.9, but we first rewrite the table by replacing P and N by 1 and 0, respectively, and flipping the probabilities from p to $1 - p$ in cases where the predicted class is 0, since the formula used for Brier's score assumes that $\hat{y}_i$ is the probability of the event occurring ($P(y_i = 1)$), whereas in the original table, the probability corresponds to that of the predicted class, whatever its value is (i.e., $P(y_i)$, whether the event occurred or not ($y_i = 1$ or $y_i = 0$)). The new table is shown in Table 5.10.

Using Table 5.10, we calculate Brier's score for the hypothetical classifier that produced it as

$$BrierScore = \frac{1}{10} \times \left((1 - .8)^2 + (1 - .45)^2 + (1 - .7)^2 + (1 - .9)^2 + (0 - .15)^2 + \cdots\right)$$

$$= \frac{1}{10} \times \left(.2^2 + .55^2 + .3^2 + .1^2 + (-.15)^2 + (-.9)^2 + (-.4)^2 + (-.2)^2 + (-.75)^2 + (-.05)^2\right)$$

$$= 0.204.$$

As expected, again Brier's score obtains a pretty bad score since the results is quite far from 0. That being said, Brier's score does not penalize the classifier as much as log loss since chance with Brier's score is 0.5 and 0.204 is quite far from it.

Both log loss and Brier's score are appropriate for checking how well calibrated a classifier is, though Merkle and Steyvers (2013) discuss which one is preferable for different

---

[15] Please note that for instance no. 2, the probability in Table 5.9 was reversed. The reason why that was done is explained later in this section.

Table 5.10. *The output of a probabilistic classifier on a hypothetical test set with two classes "P" and "N."*

instance#	Actual class	Predicted class	Probability
1	1	1	0.80
2	1	0	0.45
3	1	1	0.70
4	1	1	0.90
5	0	0	0.15
6	0	1	0.90
7	0	0	0.40
8	0	0	0.20
9	0	1	0.75
10	0	0	0.05

problems in the forecasting domain. In addition, and as previously mentioned, new metrics have recently been devised to evaluate calibration, such as in Nixon et al. (2019) and Vaicenavicius et al. (2019).[16]

We now return to another area of the ontology of Figure 5.1 that requires deeper discussions than those already held in Chapter 4: the graphical metrics falling in the "scoring classifier" rubric. They will be covered in the next two sections. In particular, Section 5.7 presents a deeper exploration of the very important ROC analysis method, while Section 5.8 discusses other kinds of graphical evaluation methods.

5.7 More Details on ROC Analysis

In Chapter 4 we described ROC analysis and the AUC, which summarizes the ROC curve. In this section, we continue our discussion of ROC analysis. In particular, we illustrate important aspects of the ROC space and explain in great detail how ROC curves are constructed in both the simple and resampling regimens. The section concludes with a discussion of ROC calibration and reviews attempts that have been made to extend ROC analysis to multiple classes.

5.7.1 ROC Space

Since, for both the *TPR* and *FPR*, it holds that $0 \leq TPR \leq 1$ and $0 \leq FPR \leq 1$, the ROC space is a unit square, as shown in Figure 5.2. The output of a deterministic classifier results in a single point in this ROC space. The point $(0,0)$ denotes a trivial classifier that classifies all the instances as negative and, hence, results in both the *TPR* and *FPR* being

[16] For more detail, please see the discussions in https://neptune.ai/blog/brier-score-and-model-calibration, https://towardsdatascience.com/classifier-calibration-7d0be1e05452, www.machinelearningplus.com/statistics/brier-score/, and the papers cited in the text of both the cited blogs and the chapter.

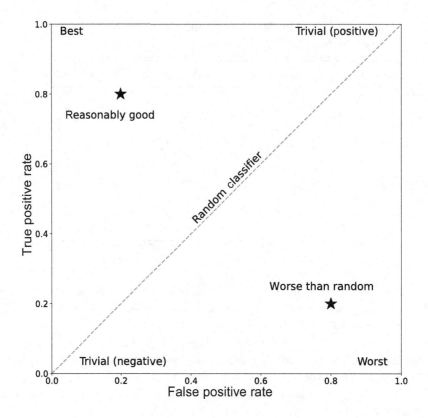

Figure 5.2 The ROC space.

zero. At the opposite corner of the square, the point $(1, 1)$ corresponds to the trivial classifier that labels all the instances as positive and, hence, has both the *TPR* and *FPR* values of unity. The diagonal connecting these two points $((0,0)$ and $(1, 1))$ has *TPR=FPR* at all the points. The classifiers falling along this diagonal can, therefore, be considered to be random classifiers (that is, they assign positive and negative labels to the instances randomly). It follows naturally that the classifiers lying above this diagonal perform better than random, while the ones below perform worse than random. This is illustrated in Figure 5.2. As a rule of thumb, for two points f_1 and f_2 in the ROC space, f_1 represents a better classifier than f_2 if f_1 is on the left of f_2 *and* higher than f_2.

The points $(1, 0)$ and $(0, 1)$ give the other two extremes of the ROC space. The point $(1, 0)$ has $FPR = 1$ while $TPR = 0$, meaning that the classifier denoted by this point gets all its predictions wrong. On the other hand, the point $(0, 1)$ denotes the ideal classifier, one that gets all the positives right and makes no errors on the negatives. The diagonal connecting these two points can be expressed as $TPR = 1 - FPR$ for all (TPR, FPR) pairs. Note that $1 - FPR$ is simply *TNR* (the true negative rate), as discussed earlier. This goes to show that the classifiers along this diagonal perform equally well on the positive and the negative classes.

An *operating point* in the ROC space corresponds to a particular decision threshold of the classifier that is used to assign discrete labels to the examples. The instances achieving a score above the threshold are labeled positive while the ones below are labeled negative. Hence, what the classifier effectively does is establish a threshold that discriminates between the instances from the two classes coming from two unknown, and possibly arbitrary, distributions. The separation between the two classes decides the classifier's performance for this particular decision threshold. Hence, each point on the ROC space denotes a particular *TPR* and *FPR* for a classifier. Now, each such point will have an associated confusion matrix summarizing the classifier performance. Consequently, an ROC curve is a collection of various confusion matrices over different varying decision thresholds for a classifier.

Theoretically, by tuning the decision threshold over the continuous interval between the minimum and maximum scores received by the instances in the dataset, we can obtain a different *TPR* and *FPR* for each value of the scoring threshold, which should result in a continuous curve in the ROC space (such as the ones shown in Figure 4.1 for two hypothetical classifiers f_1 and f_2). However, this is not necessarily the case in most practical scenarios. The reason for this are twofold. First, the limited size of the dataset limits the number of values on the ROC curves that can be realized. That is, when the instances are sorted in terms of the scores achieved as a result of the application of the classifier, then all the decision thresholds in the interval of scores of any two consecutive instances will, essentially, give the same *TPR* and *FPR* on the dataset, resulting in a single point. Hence, in this case, the maximum number of points that can be obtained are upper bounded by the number of examples in the dataset. Second, this argument assumes that a continuous tuning of the decision threshold is indeed possible. This is not necessarily the case for all the scoring classifiers, let alone the discrete ones where such tuning cannot be done at all. Classifiers such as decision trees, for instance, allow only for a finite number of thresholds (upper bounded by the number of possible labels over the leafs of the decision tree).

Hence, in the typical scenario of a scoring classifier, varying the decision threshold results in a step function at each point in the ROC space. A ROC curve can, then, be obtained by extrapolating over this set of finite points. Discrete classifiers, the ones for which such a tuning of the decision threshold is not possible, yield discrete points in the ROC space. That is, for a given test set T, a discrete classifier f will generate one pair $(FPR(f), TPR(f))$ corresponding to one point in the two dimensional ROC space (for instance, the *'s in Figure 5.2 represents two such discrete classifiers).

Figure 5.3 shows some examples of points given by six classifiers in the ROC space on some hypothetical dataset. The classifiers appearing on the left-hand side on a ROC graph can be thought of as more *conservative* in their classification of positive examples, in the sense that they have small false positive rates, preferring failure to recognize positive examples to risking the misclassification of negative examples. The classifiers on the right, on the other hand, are more *liberal* in their classification of positive examples, meaning that they prefer misclassifying negative examples than failing to recognize a positive example as such. This can be seen as quite a useful feature of ROC graphs since different operating points might be desired in the context of different application settings. For instance, in the classical case of cancer detection, labeling a benign growth as cancer leads to fewer negative

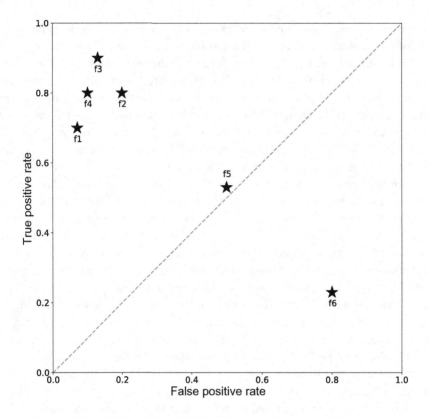

Figure 5.3 An example of a ROC plot for discrete classifiers.

consequences than failing to recognize a cancerous growth as such, while false negatives are not as serious in applications such as information retrieval.

Let us illustrate this more specifically in the plot of Figure 5.3. We see that the "best" overall classifier is f_3 since it is closest to point $(0, 1)$. Nevertheless, if retaining a small false positive rate is the highest priority, it is possible that, in certain circumstances, f_4 or even f_1 might be preferred. There is no reason why f_2 should be preferred to f_3 or f_4, however, since both its false positive and true positive rates are worse than those of f_3 or f_4. The classifier f_5 is very weak, barely better than random guessing. As for f_6, it can be made (roughly) equivalent to f_2 once its decisions are reversed in an analogous manner as the two classifiers symbolized by *s in Figure 5.2 are mirror images of each other along the center of the graph.

It should be noted that it is not trivial to characterize the performance of classifiers that are just slightly better than the random classifier (points just above the diagonal). A statistical significance analysis is required, in such cases, to ascertain whether the marginally superior performance of such classifiers, as compared to a random classifier, is indeed statistically significant. Finally, each point on the ROC curve represents a different trade-off between the false positives and false negatives (also known as the *cost ratio*). The *cost ratio* is defined by the slope of the line tangent to the ROC curve at a given point.

Having learned how to interpret the location of points in the ROC space, we now turn to the important question of how ROC curves are constructed. For more details about ROC analysis, including skew considerations and isometrics, please refer to Japkowicz and Shah (2011).

5.7.2 Constructing a ROC Curve on a Simple Test Domain

Let us now discuss the way in which ROC curves can be generated. We begin by describing the process used in the construction of a curve on a simple test domain, followed by the construction of curves in a resampling regimen.

Fawcett (2004, algorithm 1, p. 8) describes ROC curve generation as in the next paragraph. Note that the version we present below is not the most efficient ROC curve generation procedure but it is the simplest. We chose it because of its intuitive appeal, which is helpful in elucidating the underlying rationale of ROC curves. For more efficient methods, the reader is encouraged to refer to Fawcett (2004, 2006). The efficient implementations of ROC curve generation processes can also be found as a standard package in many machine learning toolkits such as scikit-learn and can be used off the shelf as illustrated in our accompanying examples.

Let T be the set of test instances; f be a scoring classifier; $f(i)$ be the continuous outcome of f for data point i; *min* and *max* be the smallest and largest values returned by f, respectively; and *incr* be the smallest difference between any two f values. Then, the simple procedure of Algorithm 5.1 can be used to generate a ROC curve over the classifier's (limited) empirical operating range.

Algorithm 5.1 Simple (but inefficient) algorithm for building a ROC curve

```
for t = min to max by incr do
    FP = 0
    TP = 0
    for i ∈ T do
        if f(i) ≥ t then
            if i is a positive example then
                TP = TP + 1
            else
                FP = FP + 1
            endif
        endif
    endfor
    add point (FP/N, TP/P) to ROC curve
endfor
```

Let us now apply this in the following example.

Example Table 5.11 shows the scores that a hypothetical classifier assigns to instances of a test set along with their true class labels. According to Algorithm 5.1, the threshold will

Table 5.11. *Points used to generate a ROC curve.*

Instance no.	1	2	3	4	5	6	7	8	9	10
Scores	.95	.9	.8	.85	.68	.66	.65	.64	.5	.48
True class	p	n	p	p	n	p	n	p	n	n

first be set at 0.48. At that threshold, we obtain $TPR = FPR = 1$, since every positive example has a score above or equal to 0.48, meaning that all the positive examples are well classified, but all the negative ones, with scores also above 0.48, are misclassified. Point $(1, 1)$ thus represents the first point on our curve. All the thresholds issued by increments of 0.05 until 0.5 yield the same results. At threshold 0.5, however, we obtain $TPR = 1$ and $FPR = 0.8$. Point $(.8, 1)$, therefore, represents the second point on our curve. The next relevant threshold is 0.64, which yields $TPR = 1$ and $FPR = 0.6$, yielding the third point, $(.6, 1)$, on the curve. Next comes the threshold 0.65, which yields $TPR = 0.8$ and $FPR = 0.6$, which represents the fourth point, $(.6, .8)$, on the curve. Please note that, for the first time, the TPR decreased and the FPR remained the same. We obtain the rest of the points in a similar fashion to obtain the graph of Figure 5.4.[17]

Now that the basics of ROC analysis have been explained, the remainder of the section discusses a number of more advanced issues including their use in a resampling regimen, their calibration, and their extensions to multi-class classification.

5.7.3 ROC Curves in a Resampling Regimen

Performance evaluation is typically estimated over several resampled versions of the dataset. This issue will be covered thoroughly in Chapter 6, but in the meantime, we question how error estimation using resampling can be achieved in the context of ROC analysis. For instance, when the commonly used k-fold cross-validation method is used for resampling, one question that comes up is how to combine the results of several cross-validation runs. As we have already briefly touched upon, the question of statistical validity is an important one when evaluating classifiers. Yet, the ROC curve building procedure discussed above only involves a single testing set. How do we, thus, combine the results obtained on k testing sets in the case of cross-validation? With regard to the k-fold cross-validation, three main approaches were proposed by Fawcett (2006): merging, vertical averaging, and threshold averaging.

Merging Merging consists of merging the results obtained on the test sets of each fold, and using this combined set as basis for deriving the ROC curve. The main advantage of this

---

[17] Note that the plots obtained by varying the thresholds of *continuous* or *scoring* classifiers output a step function on finite number of points that would approximate the true curve of the form of Figure 4.1 in the limit of an infinite number of points since, in principle, the thresholds can be varied in the interval $(-\infty, +\infty)$.

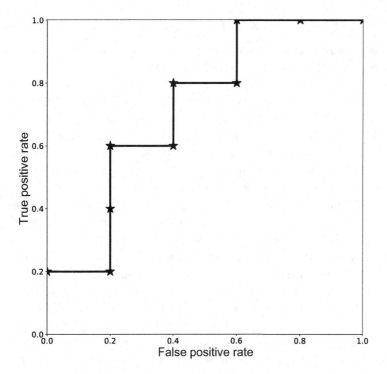

Figure 5.4 ROC analysis for the data of Table 5.11.

solution is that it is easy to implement. However, the approach does not average the results and as a consequence, it yields no metric of variance to be used in further statistical analysis.

Vertical averaging Vertical averaging consists of considering different false-positive rates, that is, different individual positions on the horizontal axis, finding the corresponding true-positive rates in each test fold, and averaging them. The false-positive rate/averaged true-positive rate combination yields as many points as the number of false-positive rates used. A ROC curve is then drawn from these points and the standard deviations of each true-positive rate average can be calculated and added to the curve. The advantage of this method is that confidence intervals can be built around the various true-positive rates, but the disadvantage is that the user does not control the values of the false-positive rates.

Threshold averaging In threshold averaging, a set of thresholds is chosen for which a point is calculated for each of the folds. These points are averaged (in this case, both the false-positive and the true-positive rates are averaged), and used to construct the combined ROC curve. The advantage of this method is that the user has control over the number of thresholds used as well as their values. Its disadvantage is that the interpretation of the confidence intervals that can be built is not as straightforward as in the case of vertical averaging, since each point has a horizontal and a vertical confidence interval.

The next section introduces yet another issue regarding the ROC thesholds.

5.7.4 ROC Calibration

Classifier thresholds based on the training set may or may not reflect the empirical realizations of labelings in the test set. That is, if the possible score interval is $[-\infty, +\infty]$, and if no example obtains a score in the interval $[t_1, t_2] \subset [-\infty, +\infty]$, then no threshold in the interval $[t_1, t_2]$ will yield a different point in the ROC space. The extrapolation between two meaningful threshold values (that is, ones that result in at least one different label over the examples in the test set) may not be very sensible. One solution to deal with this problem is *calibration*. All the scores in the interval $[t_1, t_2]$ can be mapped to the fraction of the positive instances obtained as a result of assigning any score in this interval. That is, for any threshold in the interval $[t_1, t_2]$, the fraction of instances labeled as positive remains the same and, hence, all the threshold scores in the interval can be mapped to this particular fraction.

This is a workable solution as long as there are no concavities in the ROC curve. Concavity in the curve means that there are skew ratios for which the classifier is suboptimal. This essentially means that better classifier performance can be obtained for the skew ratios lying in the concave region of the curve, although the empirical estimates do not suggest this. In case of concavities, the behavior of the calibrated scores do not mimic the desired behavior of the slope of the threshold interval. The classifier obtained over calibrated scores can overfit the data resulting in poor generalization. A solution for dealing with the issue of score calibration in the case of nonconvex ROCs has been proposed in the form of isotonic regression over the scores. The main idea behind the isotonic regression approach is to map the scores corresponding to the concave interval, say $[t_1^c, t_2^c]$ to an unbiased estimate of the slope of the line segment connecting the two points corresponding to the thresholds t_1^c and t_2^c. This in effect bypasses the concave segments by extrapolating a convex segment in the interval. We do not discuss calibration in depth here but more detail can be found in Zadrozny and Elkan (2002) and Fawcett and Niculescu-Mizil (2007a).

We now turn to the issue of extending ROC curves to multi-class datasets.

5.7.5 Extending the ROCs

Attempts have been made to extend ROC analysis to multi-class problems. However, ROC analysis in the multi-class case is much more complex than in the two-class case. In case of more classes, say l, the confusion matrix becomes an $l \times l$ matrix with the l diagonal elements representing correct classification while the $l^2 - l$ nondiagonal elements represent classification errors. The next natural question that arises, then, is how to generalize the AUC statistic to the multi-class scenario. Attempts to generate multi-class ROCs have resulted in various formulations for obtaining the area under the multi-class ROC curves. Among the different proposed methods of generating multi-class ROCs and, then, obtaining their AUCs, the following formulation for obtaining the AUC proposed by Hand and Till (2001) is the most noteworthy:

$$AUC_{multiclass}(f) = \frac{2}{l(l-1)} \sum_{l_i, l_j \in \mathcal{L}} AUC_{l_i, l_j}(f),$$

where $AUC_{multiclass}(f)$ is the total AUC of the multi-class ROC for the classifier f, $\mathcal{L}$ is the set of classes such that $|\mathcal{L}| = l$, and $AUC_{l_i, l_j}(f)$ is the AUC of the two-class ROC curve of f for the classes l_i and l_j. For more details on multi-class ROCs, some basic references include Fawcett (2006), Lachiche and Flach (2003), and Flach (2003).

5.8 Other Visual Analysis Methods

We now discuss some other visualization techniques that can be beneficial in some specific scenarios and also explore, where relevant, their relation to the ROC curves.

> Many of the visual analysis methods reviewed in this section are available from the model selection package of sklearn and the scikit-plot package: https://scikit-learn.org/stable/auto_examples/model_selection/ and https://scikit-plot.readthedocs.io/en/stable/metrics.html.

5.8.1 Lift Charts

Lift charts are a performance visualization technique closely related to ROC curves. Lift charts plot the true positives against the dataset size required to achieve this number of true positives. That is, the vertical axis of the lift charts plots the true positives (and not the *TPR*) while the horizontal axis denotes the number of examples in the dataset considered for the specific true positives on the vertical axis. In other words, the ROC curve counts the number of negative examples that have slipped into the data sample for which the classifier issued a particular true positive rate, while the lift chart counts both the positive and the negative examples in that set. In highly imbalanced datasets where, typically, the number of positive examples is much smaller than that of negative examples, the horizontal axes of lift charts and ROC curves look very similar as do the curves.

The use of lift charts is more common in the business domains. A typical example where lift charts are used in practice is in direct mail advertising. Typically, very few people respond to this kind of advertising; yet, the costs of mailing information to a large population can be high. The idea is to evaluate different classifiers whose goal is to identify the people most likely to respond to this kind of advertising. Lift charts allow a user to do so by expressing the result of classifiers in terms of curves similar to ROC curves that indicate which classifiers can identify actual respondents using the smallest sample size (i.e., the smallest number of people to whom the information should be mailed, and thus, the smallest cost for the best response).

5.8.2 Precision-Recall (PR) Curves

Precision-recall curves, sometimes abbreviated as PR curves, are similar to ROC curves and lift charts, in that they explore the tradeoff between the well-classified positive examples and the number of misclassified negative examples. As the name suggests, PR curves plot the precision of the classifier as a function of its recall. In other words, it measures the amount of precision that can be obtained as various degrees of recall are considered. For instance, in the domain of document retrieval systems, PR curves would plot the percentage of relevant documents identified as relevant against the percentage of relevant documents deemed as such with respect to all the documents in the sample. The curves, thus, look different from ROC Curves and lift curves since they have a negative slope. This is because precision decreases as recall increases. PR curves are a popular visualization technique in the information retrieval field, as illustrated by our earlier examples that discussed the notions of precision and recall. PR curves can sometimes be more appropriate than ROC curves in the events of highly imbalanced data (Davis and Goadrich 2006).

5.8.3 Cost Curves

Cost curves aim at plotting the relative costs directly, instead of making use of ROC isometrics to do so in a surrogate fashion, in order to determine the best classifier. In a sense, the information displayed by the cost curves is similar to that displayed by ROC curves. What makes cost curves attractive is their ease of use in determining the best classifier to use in situations where the error costs or class distribution, or more generally the skew, are known.

In more detail, cost curves plot the relative expected misclassification costs as a function of the proportion of positive instances in the dataset.

When considering different costs per class, a very simple modification of the cost curves can be applied. This modification only affects the identity of the axes. The meaning of the curves and the reading of the graph remain the same. In this context, rather than representing the error rate, the y-axis represents the normalized expected cost (NEC) or relative expected misclassification cost defined as

$$NEC = FNR \times p_C[+] + FPR \times (1 - p_C[+]),$$

where FNR and FPR are the false negative and false positive rates, respectively, and $p_C[+]$, the probability cost function, is a modified version of p[+] that takes costs into consideration.

5.8.4 Relative Superiority Graphs

Another method proposed to take cost into consideration while evaluating classifier performance has appeared in the form of relative superiority graphs that plot the ratio of costs, mapping them into the [0, 1] interval. The ratio of costs here refers to the relative expense of one type of error against another. That is, it refers to the relationship between the cost of making a false positive error against a false negative error. The rationale behind the relative superiority curve is that, while the precise costs of each type of error might either not be available or impossible to quantify, it may be the case that their relative costs are known. Mapping such relative costs, then, transforms the ROC curves into a set of parallel lines from which the superiority of classifiers in the regions of interest (of relative cost ratios) can be inferred. To replace the associated AUC, a loss comparison (LC) index is used in the case of relative superiority curves. In this context, sometimes interpreted as a binary version of the ROC curves, relative superiority curves can be used to identify whether one classifier is superior to another, with the LC index measuring the confidence in the inferred superiority.

5.8.5 DET Curves

Detection error tradeoff (DET) curves can be interpreted as an alternate representation of ROC curves in that instead of plotting the *TPR* on the vertical axis, DET curves plot the *FNR*. The DET curves are typically log-scaled so that the area corresponding to the classifiers performing better than the random classifier is expanded. Note that due to the change of vertical axis, this area is represented by the bottom left region of the DET space. This is in contrast to the ROC space, where this area is represented by the upper left region. As a consequence of log-scaling, the surface area pertaining to these better performing classifiers is expanded, enabling the user to obtain a better insight into their relative performances.

5.9 Advanced Topics

In this chapter, we presented the principal elements of the vast field of performance metrics for classification. However, there are many more advanced topics that have been left off from the main discussion for clarity's sake. These include the consideration of additional criteria such as training and/or testing time complexity, memory consumption, and the study of qualitative metrics accounting for questions such as understandability and conciseness. Furthermore, there have been both theoretical and experimental frameworks proposed to compare and contrast the different metrics and related research has been conducted on meaningful ways to combine the different metrics, going beyond those already discussed such as the F-metric, and G-mean. Finally, the question of performance metrics for classification can also be considered from a machine learning theory viewpoint, but this discussion has been left out of the chapter as well. In order for the reader to get a glimpse at such advanced topics, we have provided a summary of some of these approaches in Appendix B. The reader is welcome to consult this appendix, but it can also be skipped without consequences for the rest of the book.

6

Resampling

In Chapter 5, we discussed some of the concerns associated with choosing an appropriate performance metric for evaluation. Once a performance metric is decided upon, the next concern relates to finding an appropriate method for obtaining as unbiased an estimate of that performance metric as possible. Also of interest is how effective the method is in guaranteeing optimal proximity of that estimate to the true metric value.

Ideally, we would have access to the entire population and test our classifiers on it. Even if the entire population were not available, if a lot of representative data from that population could be obtained, error estimation would be quite simple. It would consist of testing the algorithms on the data it was trained on. While such an estimate, commonly known as the *resubstitution error*, is usually optimistically biased, as the number of instances in the dataset increases it tends towards the true error rate. Realistically, however, we are given a significantly limited-sized sample of the population and the resubstitution error cannot be used.

A reliable alternative consists of testing the algorithm on a large set of unseen data points. This approach is commonly known as the *holdout* method. Unfortunately, the holdout method still requires quite a lot of data for testing the algorithm's performance, and such an abundance of data is relatively rare in most practical situations. As a result, the holdout method is not always applicable. Instead, the limited amount of available data needs to be used and reused ingeniously in order to obtain sufficiently large numbers of samples for training and testing. This kind of data reuse is called *resampling*. Proper resampling is difficult to achieve since in order to be meaningful, it must be conducted in a way that guarantees that the data on which the estimates are obtained is representative of the actual distribution. In addition, it must ensure that the algorithms under scrutiny have reached a stable state so that they exhibit predictable performance.

Broadly, the resampling techniques used in machine learning can be divided into two categories: *simple resampling* and *multiple resampling*. The simple resampling techniques tend to use each data point for testing only once. Techniques such as *k-fold cross-validation* and *leave-one-out* are examples of simple resampling techniques (we may also include resubstitution in this category; however, we tend to use simple resampling to refer to the techniques that apply the algorithm multiple times, making the most use of the data). Multiple resampling techniques, on the other hand, do not refrain from testing data points more than once. Examples of such techniques include *random subsampling*, *bootstrapping*, *randomization*, and *repeated k-fold cross-validation*. In this chapter, we discuss different *error estimation* techniques based on different resampling regimens that might be suitable in offering better assurances with regard to the estimation of an algorithm's performance metric, especially in a limited data scenario.

While both simple and multiple resampling address the problems caused by the dearth of data, care needs to be taken with regard to the effect of using such approaches on the assumptions made by subsequent steps in the evaluation, specifically, the statistical significance tests already mentioned in Section 4.4, and that will be discussed in greater depth in Chapter 7. Recall that independence of the data used to obtain sample statistics is a fundamental assumption made by these tests. This chapter aims at highlighting this, other basic assumptions, and the conditions under which the different resampling approaches are appropriate. In particular, we will study the impact of using different resampling techniques on the resulting estimates in the context of their respective bias and variance behaviors. We will also discuss model selection considerations that come into play when applying these resampling techniques. The integration of resampling techniques with statistical tests will be covered in Chapter 7.

Figure 6.1 shows an ontology of the various error estimation methods discussed in this chapter. The discussion of these techniques will be presented using the error rate (risk) of the learning algorithm on the dataset as the performance metric. The main reason for adopting this performance metric is that it provides a concrete bias–variance analysis for classification, allowing us to explain the different aspects of the techniques more clearly. However, similar arguments would hold for other performance metrics as well.

The roadmap for the chapter is as follows. Section 6.1 presents the theoretical framework used to describe the error estimation methods discussed in this chapter formally. Section 6.2 presents the holdout method, and demonstrates how theoretically sound guarantees on

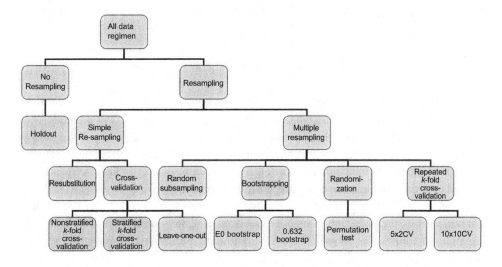

Figure 6.1 An ontology of error estimation methods.

the true risk can be obtained in this setting. The section also highlights the sample size requirements for applying the holdout method, and uses this requirement to motivate the use of resampling techniques instead, since only limited data instances are available in most practical scenarios. Before moving on to discussing the resampling techniques, Section 6.3 introduces the bias–variance framework that is subsequently used to qualitatively analyze the different error estimation methods, and also develop an understanding of their comparative advantages and limitations. Section 6.4 then discusses simple resampling methods. Section 6.5 looks at the issue of model selection in the resampling regimen. Section 6.6 presents multiple resampling methods. This is followed by a summary of the various resampling approaches and their pros and cons in Section 6.7 along with a short overview of advanced topics.

The implementation of the error estimation methods presented in this chapter is discussed in the scikit-learn manual.[1]

6.1 Theoretical Framework

Recall our definition of the *true or expected risk* of classifier f from Section 3.2.2:

$$R(f) = \int L(y, f(\boldsymbol{x})) dD(\mathbf{x}, y), \tag{6.1}$$

where $L(y, f(\boldsymbol{x}))$ denotes the loss incurred on the label $f(\boldsymbol{x})$ assigned to the example $\boldsymbol{x}$ by f and where the true label of $\boldsymbol{x}$ is y; the probability metric $D(\mathbf{z}) = D(\mathbf{x}, y)$ here is unknown.

For the zero-one loss, that is, $L(y, f(\boldsymbol{x})) = 1$ when $y \neq f(\boldsymbol{x})$ and 0 otherwise, we can write the expected risk as

$$R(f) \stackrel{\text{def}}{=} \Pr_{(\mathbf{x}, y) \sim D} (f(\boldsymbol{x}) \neq y). \tag{6.2}$$

However, in the absence of knowledge of the true distribution, the learner often computes the *empirical risk* $R_S(f)$ of any given classifier f on some training data S with m examples according to

$$R_S(f) \stackrel{\text{def}}{=} \frac{1}{m} \sum_{i=1}^{m} L(y_i, f(\boldsymbol{x}_i)). \tag{6.3}$$

Given that the classifier's empirical risk approximates its true risk, the aim of error estimation is clear-cut: to obtain as unbiased an estimate of empirical risk as possible. This empirical risk on the training set can be measured in a variety of ways, as we will see shortly. Naturally, the simplest approach to risk estimation would be to measure the empirical risk of a classifier f_S trained on the full training data S, on the same dataset S. This metric is often referred to as the resubstitution risk (or resubstitution error rate). We denote it as $R_S^{resub}(f_S)$. As can easily be seen, this results in judging the performance of a classifier on the data that was used by the algorithm to induce that classifier. Consequently, such an estimate is essentially optimistically biased. The best way to obtain a minimum resubstitution error

---

[1] The website for the implementations can be found here: https://scikit-learn.org/stable/modules/cross_validation.html.

estimate is to overfit the classifier to each and every training point. However, this would essentially lead to poor generalization as we saw in Section 3.2.3.

Before we look into other ways of obtaining empirical risk estimates, we would need to consider various factors that should be taken into account in this regard. The effect that the learning settings can have on the empirical risk estimate can arise from the following main sources:

- Random variation in the testing sets
- Random variation in the training sets
- Random variation within the learning algorithm
- Random variation with respect to class noise in the database.

An effective error estimation method should take into consideration these different sources of random fluctuations. In the simplest case, if we have enough training data we can consider a separate set of examples to test the classifier performance. This test set is not used in any way while training the learning algorithm. Hence, assuming that the test set is representative of the domain in which the classifier is to be applied, we can obtain a reliable risk estimate given enough training data. However, the question of whether we have enough training data is serious. We will discuss this in Section 6.2.2. But first, let us go ahead and look at the method of estimating risk on a separate testing set. This method has some very important advantages since concrete guarantees on the risk estimate can be obtained in this case.

6.2 Holdout Approach

In this method, as explained in Section 6.1 and in Section 4.3.1, a separate set of instances is reserved to assess the classifier's performance. This set is different from the training set used by the learning algorithm. The learning algorithm takes as input a labeled set of instances from the training set and outputs a classifier. This classifier is then given the unlabeled set of instances from the testing set. The classifier outputs labels for each of these instances and the estimate of the empirical error is obtained. In the case of a discrete binary classifier, the empirical error is basically the fraction of test instances that the classifier misclassifies. Conversely, the accuracy of the classifier is the fraction of the test instances that the classifier classifies correctly. The performance of the classifier on a separate test set is generally a good indicator of its generalization performance. Formal guarantees over the test set performance in terms of theoretical confidence intervals can be provided in this case as will be shown below.

More formally, if we have a test set T with examples drawn i.i.d. from $D(\mathbf{z})$, then the empirical risk takes the form

$$R_T(f) = \int L(y, f_S(\boldsymbol{x}))dD(\mathbf{x}, y), \tag{6.4}$$

where $f_S(\cdot)$ denotes the classifier output by the learning algorithm when given a training set S and with the underlying assumption that the test set T is representative of the distribution generating the data.

One of the biggest advantages of a holdout error estimate lies in its independence from the training set. Since the estimate is obtained on a separate test set, some concrete generalizations on this estimate can be obtained. Moreover, there is another crucial difference between a holdout error estimate and a resampled estimate. A holdout estimate pertains to the classifier output by the learning algorithm given the training data. Hence, any generalizations made over this estimate will essentially apply to any classifier with the given test set performance. We will see in Section 6.3.2 that this is not the case for the resampled error estimate. Let us now discuss the general behavior of the test set error estimate.

6.2.1 Confidence Intervals

We saw one approach to determine the confidence intervals around the empirical risk estimate in Section 2.3. That approach relied on the assumption that the empirical risk of the classifier on the test data can be modeled, in the limit, as a Gaussian. Based on this assumption, the mean empirical risk and the corresponding variance on the test examples were obtained. A confidence interval was then provided in terms of a Gaussian around the mean empirical risk with its tails removed at Z_P multiples of standard deviation σ on either sides with Z_P defining the critical region for a given confidence level α. However, this did not allow us to make any probabilistic statements on the true risk (recall the discussion in Section 2.3).

It turns out that an asymptotic Gaussian assumption might not be the best way to provide confidence intervals, especially when modeling empirical risks closer to zero. This issue is discussed at greater length in Japkowicz and Shah (2011). For now, it suffices to say that instead, a binomial distribution can be used more effectively to model the empirical risk in the case of discrete binary classifiers, leading us to make probabilistic statements on the upper and lower bounds for the true risk. Below is an example of such bounds obtained by modeling the error as a Bernoulli variable. Using this observation, and by applying Hoeffding's bound, we can get the following guarantee (the proof is given in Section 6.8).

For any classifier f, the true risk $R(f)$, with probability $1 - \delta$ and test error $R_T(f)$ on some test set T of m' examples, satisfies

$$|R_T(f) - R(f)| \leq t_{1-\delta} = \epsilon = \sqrt{\frac{1}{2m'} \ln\left(\frac{2}{\delta}\right)}. \tag{6.5}$$

Therefore, with probability $1 - \delta$,

$$R(f) \approx R_T(f) \pm t_{1-\delta}.$$

This bound basically gives the confidence interval within which we expect the true risk to fall with confidence $1 - \delta$ for some $\delta \in (0, 1]$. For example, fixing δ at 0.05, we can obtain a 95% confidence interval. Note the similarity between the parameter δ and the confidence parameter α of Section 2.3. However, the two are not essentially the same in terms of their interpretation, as should be clear from the earlier discussion of α and the proof of the bound in Equation (6.5) given in Section 6.8. A discussion of this issue along with a tighter version of the above bound can be found in Japkowicz and Shah (2011). In the present context, let us see how this observation affects the sample size requirement.

6.2.2 The Need for Resampling

It can be seen from Equation (6.5) that the convergence of the empirical risk to the true risk depends on the sample size m' and the true risk $R(f)$. This highlights the most prominent limitation of this method, which is its dependence on the size of the training data. A holdout estimate, to generalize well, requires a large sample size. This can be readily seen from the above analysis. Rearranging Equation (6.5) and solving for sample size m' gives us the bound on the required sample complexity as

$$m' \geq \frac{1}{2\epsilon^2} \ln\left(\frac{2}{\delta}\right).$$

This bound gives the minimum number of examples required for a given ϵ and δ. The sample size bound grows very quickly for small ϵ and δ. That is, for the confidence intervals to be any indicator of the classifier's performance, the required number of training examples is too large. With a single train and test partition, too few cases in the training group can lead to learning a poor classifier while too few test cases can lead to erroneous error estimates.

Ironically, one of the most common difficulties in machine learning problems is the dearth of data. Hence, as already discussed, if we use all the available data for training, it is not possible to have a reliable performance metric estimate about the future performance of the classifier. Second, if we divide this already small dataset into a training and a testing set, then reliable learning is not possible. Moreover, the sample size requirement grows exponentially with falling ϵ and δ limiting the utility of this approach in most learning scenarios where the overall availability of examples is limited. In such cases, researchers often make use of what are called *resampling* methods.

As the name suggests, these methods are based upon the idea of being able to reuse the data for training and testing. Resampling has some advantages over the single partition holdout method discussed above. Resampling allows for more accurate estimates of the error rates while allowing the learning algorithms to train on most data samples. We will discuss these methods in detail in Sections 6.4 and 6.6 from both an applied and a theoretical point of view. However, before proceeding to these, let us understand the bias–variance analysis, that we introduced in Section 3.4.2 in the context of error estimation. This will be instrumental in helping us analyze various error estimation methods with regard to their strengths, limitations, and applicability in practical scenarios. While the discussion in the next section may seem a bit too theoretical, it will enable the reader to put the subsequent discussion in perspective and obtain practical insights about various resampling techniques.

6.3 What Implicitly Guides Resampling?

Of course there are many types of resampling schemes, possibly leading to a variety of error estimates on the training error of the algorithm. What distinguishes one from the other?

More importantly: What should we care about when choosing one resampling method over another? When should we prefer one resampling method over others? These are the types of questions that we will be concerned with eventually. But it is probably better to see these issues in light of the resulting error estimate itself. What is it about the error estimate that is affected by resampling? Recall that we discussed in Section 3.4.2 how we can decompose the empirical error of a learning algorithm on the training data into its bias and variance components. We also discussed how this bias–variance decomposition affects the model selection problem. That is, how can trading-off bias and variance help us avoid overfitting and underfitting. Let us now see the interrelationship between the empirical error estimate and the amount of training data on which (and the manner in which) these estimates are obtained. It is necessary to understand this interplay in order to achieve an appreciation for various resampling schemes and to understand how one might be more suitable in some scenarios than some others. We have already seen the notion of the bias–variance decomposition of the empirical error of the algorithm. Let us now focus on its estimation, using an example to illustrate the process.

6.3.1 Estimating Bias and Variance

We have already seen how the error of an algorithm can be decomposed into bias and variance (and the noise component). Such a bias–variance decomposition enables us to understand the behavior of the algorithm as well as its model selection process. The bias and variance behavior of the algorithm's performance can be very useful to evaluate the algorithm both in absolute terms (how good the algorithm is, given the training sets, in terms of the chosen loss function) and in relative terms, with respect to other competing algorithms. However, as we have seen, the bias–variance decomposition of the algorithm's error necessitates knowing the true distribution of the data. That is, it require an a priori knowledge of the data generation process. However, modeling or approximating this data generation behavior is indeed the goal of designing the learning algorithm itself. As a result, it is impossible in practice to know the true values of the bias and variance in the absence of the knowledge of the data distribution. Hence, we would need to approximate these values using some empirical estimates that can be obtained from the data at hand rather than having them depend explicitly on the true underlying data distribution.

Let us, very briefly, look at how this can be done for some given training data with an example. Recall the bias–variance analysis of the empirical error of a classifier from Section 3.4.2. The first quantity that needs to be estimated so as to be able to study the bias–variance decomposition of the algorithm's error is the average prediction $\bar{y}$ of algorithm A. Note, however, that this should be done independently of the data on which the algorithm is to be subsequently tested. To achieve this, we can resort to resampling within the training examples when the data to train an algorithm is limited.

One way to perform such a division would be to divide the available training dataset S into two sets, as in the holdout method discussed in Section 6.2. One set is used to perform the training of the algorithm, call it S_{train} (say two-thirds of S), while the other is used to test the algorithm on examples not used in the training process (that is, previously unseen examples) denoted by S_{test}. The manner in which such a division is obtained leads to a variety of resampling techniques that further applies this partitioning repeatedly (with or without overlap), hence reusing these partitions for training and testing purposes as we will see later. However, in order to keep the current discussion simple, we stick to a single partition.

To achieve the effect of multiple datasets we can sample a collection **S** of n_{bs} training sets of some predefined size m from S_{train}. Training the algorithm on each training set yields a classifier whose loss on all examples can then be averaged, leading to an empirical estimate of the average prediction $\bar{y}$. Let f_i denote the classifier resulting from training algorithm A on a training set S_i sampled from S_{train}. When such sampling is done with replacement, the process is known as bootstrap sampling (Efron and Tibshirani 1993). We will describe bootstrap resampling in detail in Section 6.6.2, but for our purpose now it suffices to assume that we have some resampling of data that gives us a group of training sets. Then, the average prediction can be estimated as

$$\bar{y} = \frac{1}{n_{bs}} \sum_{i=1}^{n_{bs}} \sum_{j=1}^{m} f_i(\boldsymbol{x}_j).$$

Then, the error and the corresponding bias and variance terms can be estimated from the evaluation of the final classifier f (chosen after model selection; that is, generally, with optimized parameters) on the test set S_{test}. The test error of the classifier is just the average loss of the classifier on each example,

$$R_{S_{test}}(f) = \mathbf{E}_{(\mathbf{x},y) \sim S_{test}}[L(f(\boldsymbol{x}),y)] \cong \frac{1}{|S_{test}|} \sum_{i=1}^{|S_{test}|} L(f(\boldsymbol{x}_i),y_i),$$

where $(\mathbf{x},y) \sim S_{|S_{test}|}$ denotes that $(\mathbf{x},y)$ is drawn from $S_{|S_{test}|}$.

Note that in the case of a zero-one loss, the above equation reduces to the empirical error of Equation (6.5). However, we again run into the problem of estimating the decomposition terms in the absence of knowledge of the true data distribution. A common trick applied in such cases is the assumption of noiseless data. That is, we assume that the data has no noise and hence the noise term on the decomposition is zero. With this assumption, we can approximate the empirical estimates of the average bias as

$$\bar{B}_A = \mathbf{E}_{\mathbf{x}}[B_A(\boldsymbol{x})]$$
$$= \mathbf{E}_{\mathbf{x}}[L(y*,\bar{y})]$$
$$\cong \frac{1}{|S_{test}|} \sum_{i=1}^{|S_{test}|} L(y_i,\bar{y}),$$

and the net variance as

$$V_A(\boldsymbol{x}) = \mathbf{E}_{\mathbf{S}}[L(\bar{y},f(\boldsymbol{x}))]$$
$$\cong \frac{1}{|S_{test}|} \sum_{i=1}^{|S_{test}|} L(f(\boldsymbol{x}_i),\bar{y}).$$

The zero-noise assumption made above can be deemed acceptable since the main interest in studying the bias–variance behavior of the algorithm's error is in their variation in response to various factors that affect the learning process. Hence, we are interested in their relative values as opposed to the absolute values. However, in case the zero-noise assumption is violated, the bias term estimated above approximates the sum of the noise term and the bias term since we approximate the error of the average model.

6.3.2 Effect of Bias–Variance Trade-Off on Resampling-Based Error Estimation

The above method of (re)sampling the data is one of the many options. Indeed, what we did in Section 6.3.1 is basically a variation of the holdout method to measure the empirical error rate to illustrate our point. Resampling typically performs such partitioning of the data multiple times, which further affects the estimates. We will see these specific issues in conjunction with the associated resampling methods. However, there are a few points worth noting here. The choice of a particular resampling method also affects the bias–variance characteristic of the algorithm's error. This, then, can have important implications on both the error estimation and subsequent evaluation of classifiers (both absolute evaluation and with respect to other algorithms) and its future generalization, as a result of the impact of this choice on the process of model selection. As the approximations of the various terms in the bias–variance decomposition suggest, the size and the method of obtaining the training and test sets can have important implications. Most prominently, note that the approximations are averaged over all samples. Moreover, in the case of average prediction, they are also sampled over different training sets. As soon as the sample size is limited, these approximations encounter variability in their estimates. Further, if we have a small number of training sets, the average prediction estimate cannot be reliably obtained. This, then, affects the bias behavior of the algorithm. On the other hand, having too few examples to test would result in high variance.

In practical scenarios, we invariably encounter the situation of a very limited dataset, let alone insufficient training and test sets individually. Resampling methods further aim at using the available data in a "smart" manner so as to obtain these estimates relatively reliably. However, various modes of resampling the data can introduce different limitations on the estimates for the bias and variance and, hence, on the reliability of the error estimates obtained as a result.

For instance, when resampling is done with replacement, such as in our example above, we run the risk of seeing the same examples again (and missing some altogether). In such cases, the estimates can be highly variable (especially in the case of small datasets) since the examples in the training set might not be representative of the actual distribution. Another concern would arise when the partitioning of the data is done multiple times, since in this cases the error estimates are not truly independent if the different test set partitions overlap. Similarly, the bias may be underestimated for cases where the training sets overlap over multiple partitions. Although we will not focus on quantifying such effects for the various resampling methods we discuss here, we will highlight the limitations and the effects of sample sizes on the reliability of the error estimate thus obtained.

While discussing the resampling methods, we frequently refer to their behavior in the case of small, moderate, or large dataset sizes. However, mapping a concrete number to the sample size in these categories is nontrivial. The sample size bound in the case of a holdout test set gives us an idea of how the sample size is affected by the two parameters ϵ and δ. The δ term is fixed (to a desired confidence level). However, the ϵ takes into account, implicitly, the generalization error of the algorithm, which, in turn, depends on a multitude of factors including data dimensionality, classifier complexity, data distribution, and so on. Throughout our discussion we assume that we do not have the required number of samples that would justify a holdout-based approach. Hence, our reference to small, moderate or medium, and large size datasets are all bounded by this constraint. These terms respectively denote ranges over the number of instances in the data farther from the sample size bound on the left in descending order.

With the backdrop of different factors that play significant roles in the resulting reliability of the error estimates, let us now move on to the specific resampling methods starting with the simple resampling techniques.

6.4 Simple Resampling

By simple resampling, we refer to the methods that test each and every point in the dataset and do so exactly once. We will relate this notion back to the resubstitution method introduced earlier too. The two methods that we discuss next in this category, the k-fold cross-validation and leave-one-out are some of the most utilized methods for error estimation and for good reasons, as we will see later. Prior to that, however, we design a formalization that allows us to unify the various approaches that we discuss in a common framework.

6.4.1 A Resampling Framework

Consider a weight vector $\mathbf{w}$, each entry of which assigns a weight to each of the m examples $\mathbf{z}_i \in S$, $i \in \{1, \ldots, m\}$ in the training set S. In this section, we consider an ordered training set. Let $\mathbf{w} \in \{0, 1\}^m$. That is, $\mathbf{w}$ is a binary vector. The entries in $\mathbf{w}$ characterize the training set. That is, a value of 1 at w_i, the ith position in the weight vector $\mathbf{w}$, denotes the presence of the corresponding example $\mathbf{z}_i$ in the resampled training set partition.

Without loss of generality, let us say that there are k partitions. Then, we can consider a distribution P_W on the sets W of $\mathbf{w}$'s such that each distribution would define a possible resampling over the training set. Each such resampling would consist of partitioning the training data into k partitions such that $1 \leq k \leq m$, with a weight vector $\mathbf{w}_k$ denoting the examples belonging to the kth partition. The number of possible sets of valid weight vectors would then give a possible partitioning of the data.

We can, then, based on the proportion of examples in a partition S_k of the training set S, characterize the resampled performance estimate of the classifier on the set S. Define the set $S_{\overline{k}}$ to contain the examples in S that are not in S_k.

Given a set of weight vectors $W = \{\mathbf{w}_i\}, i \in \{1, 2, \ldots, k\}$ representing a valid partition over S, the resampled risk of the learning algorithm is denoted as (that is, the risk is defined once a partition is decided)[2]

$$R_S^{resamp}(f) = \mathbf{E}_W \int L(y, f_S^k(\mathbf{x})) d D^k(\mathbf{x}, y),$$

where $D^k(\mathbf{z}) = D^k(\mathbf{x}, y)$ denote the distribution of the partition S_k. That is,

$$R_S^{resamp}(f) = \frac{1}{k} \sum_{i=1}^{k} \left[\frac{1}{|S_k|} \sum_{j=1}^{|S_k|} L(y_j, f_S^k(\mathbf{x}_j)) \right],$$

where f_S^k denotes the classifier learned from the set $S_{\overline{k}}$.

We now discuss some of the simple resampling schemes under this framework. In all cases, we present a more functional description followed by analytical description under the above framework.

6.4.2 Resubstitution

As discussed earlier, resubstitution trains the classifier on the training set S and subsequently tests it over the same set S of examples. That is, we have the full mass of P_W on the weight vector $\mathbf{w} = \mathbf{1}$. Under our formalization, the case of $k = 1$ is the resubstitution case. We already discussed the fact that, as the classifier usually overfits the data it was trained on, the error estimate provided by this method is optimistically biased. This is why this approach is never recommended in practice for error estimation purposes. We will see how more reliable estimates can be obtained that are less biased and, hence, better approximators of the true risk.

6.4.3 k-Fold Cross-Validation and Its Variants

The most popular error estimation approach in machine learning is k-fold cross-validation. This was described in Section 4.3.2, but we now give a more formal description of the process. We also present a modified version called *stratified k-fold cross-validation* and discuss the special case where the dataset is divided into as many folds as there are samples, *leave-one-out*.

Traditional k-Fold Cross-Validation

We proceed with *k-fold cross-validation* by dividing the dataset S containing m samples into k subsets of roughly equal size. Each subset is called a fold (hence the name of the method). The learning algorithm is then trained on $k - 1$ of these subsets taken together and tested on the kth subset. This is repeated k times, with a different subset used for testing. Hence, each of the k-folds becomes a test set once. The experiment thus returns k estimates of the

---

[2] We will see that the expectation of resampling risk over all possible partitions estimates the risk of multiple trial resamplings.

resulting classifier's error rate in each iteration. These estimates are then averaged together and constitute the error estimate. Algorithm 6.1 shows the method in algorithmic form for better understandability.

Algorithm 6.1 k-fold cross-validation

−Divide the available training set S of size m in k nonoverlapping subsets S_i, $i = 1, \ldots, k$, of size (approximately) $\frac{m}{k}$
−Initialize $i = 1$
−Repeat while $i \leq k$
    − Mark the ith subset S_i as test set
    − For the test set S_i, generate the complement training dataset $S_{\bar{i}}$ containing all the examples from S except those in S_i
    − Train and test the learning algorithm on $S_{\bar{i}}$ and S_i, respectively
    −Obtain the empirical risk $R_{S_i}(f_j)$ (or any other performance metric of interest) of classifier f_j, trained on $S_{\bar{i}}$, and tested on S_i
        −Increment i by 1
−Average the $R_{S_i}(f_i)$ over all i's to obtain $R_S(f)$, the mean empirical risk of the k-fold cross-validation.
−Report $R_S(f)$

Note that, in the above, even though we stick to the notation $R_S(f)$ to denote the empirical risk of the k-fold cross-validation, we refer to the averaged empirical risk over the classifiers obtained in each of the k-folds. It is important to note that the k testing sets do not overlap. Each example is therefore used only once for testing, and $k - 1$ times for training.

Let us formalize this technique. In the k-fold cross-validation, we will consider the case of $k \geq 2$. The case of $k = 1$ is a special case called leave-one-out, and has achieved prominence in error estimation especially for small dataset sizes. We will discuss this later in this section. Getting back to $k \geq 2$, in the case where m is even, we can easily characterize the distribution P_W. For a given even m, the number of possible sets of binary weight vectors defining a valid partition of m examples in k subsets can be obtained with the formula

$$n_k^{\mathbf{w}} = \sum_{i=0}^{k-2} \binom{(m - \frac{im}{k})}{\frac{m}{k}}.$$

Then, P_W would have $\frac{1}{n_k^{\mathbf{w}}}$ mass on each of the possible $n_k^{\mathbf{w}}$ valid partitions and zero mass elsewhere. This is basically resampling the set S into k partitions without replacement.

More involved schemes can be thought of in the case of an odd m. However, we can easily find an acceptable solution by subtracting 1 from m in the case where m is odd and utilize the above formulation to resample the set S.

The most common value used in the case of machine learning algorithms is $k = 10$, with many empirical arguments in support of this number, especially in large size samples, owing mainly to the obtention of relatively less-biased estimates as well as the observation of an acceptable computational complexity in calculating these error estimates.

Stratified k-Fold Cross-Validation

Even if using a careful resampling method such as k-fold cross-validation, the split into a training and testing set may be uneven. That is, the split may not take into account the distribution of the examples of various classes while generating the training and test subsets. This can result in scenarios in which examples of the kind present in the testing set are either underrepresented in, or entirely absent from, the training set. This can yield an even more pessimistic performance estimate. A simple and effective solution to this problem lies in *stratifying* the data. Stratification consists of taking note of the representation of each class in the overall dataset and making sure that this representation is respected in both the training set and the test set in the resulting partitions of data. For example, consider a three-class problem with the dataset consisting of classes $C1, C2$, and $C3$. Let us assume, for illustration's sake, that the dataset is composed of 30% examples of class $C1$, 60% examples of class $C2$, and 10% examples of class $C3$. A random split of the data into a training and a testing set may very well ignore the data of class $C3$ in either the training or the testing set. This would lead to an unfair evaluation. Stratification does not allow such a situation to occur as it ensures that the training and testing sets in every fold or every resampling event maintain the relative distribution with 30% of class $C1$ examples, 60% of class $C2$ examples, and 10% of class $C3$ examples.

Informally, in the case of binary data, a straight-forward method to achieving stratification is shown in Algorithm 6.2.

Algorithm 6.2 Stratified k-fold cross-validation

- Divide the training data into two sets (one for each class)
- Generate k subsets in each of the two sets
- Combine one subset from each of the two sets to obtain k subsets that would maintain the original class distribution
- Perform the classical k-fold cross-validation over these k subsets

---

In the case of multi-class classification with l classes, the above method can easily be extended. Instead of dividing the data into two classes, divide the training set into l sets, one for each class, and proceed as above. Stratification for use with cross-validation has become a standard practice.[3]

Formalizing stratification in the case of binary classification, we would then sample from two distributions. Let the training set S of m examples be such that $m = m_p + m_n$, where m_p is the number of positive examples in the training set S and m_n is the number of negative examples. Hence, we can have $\mathbf{w} = \{w_1^p, w_2^p, \ldots, w_{m_p}^p, w_1^n, w_2^n, \ldots, w_{m_n}^n\}$. Then, for even m_p and m_n, we can characterize the distribution P_W as follows. The number of possible sets W of vectors $\mathbf{w}$ that partition the training set S in k stratified subsets can be calculated as

$$n_k^{\mathbf{w}} = \left[\sum_{i=0}^{k-2} \binom{(m_p - \frac{im_p}{k})}{\frac{m_p}{k}} \right] \cdot \left[\sum_{i=0}^{k-2} \binom{(m_n - \frac{im_n}{k})}{\frac{m_n}{k}} \right].$$

---

[3] See, for example, https://scikit-learn.org/stable/modules/generated/sklearn.model_selection.StratifiedKFold.html.

This distribution can be adapted to odd m_p and/or m_n analogous to the case of classical k-fold cross-validation above. Also, P_W will have equal mass on all the possible valid stratifications and zero mass elsewhere.

Leave-One-Out Cross-Validation

Leave-one-out (or the *jackknife*) is an extreme case of k-fold cross-validation. Leave-one-out is basically a k-fold cross-validation performed with $k = m$. The procedure is the same as that in Algorithm 6.1, but with $k = m$. Further, our formalization of the k-fold cross-validation from the last section applies to the case of the leave one out estimate as well with $k = m$. Leave-one-out was also explained in Section 4.3.3.

Discussion

There are a number of advantages to the practical approach of k-fold cross-validation. First, it is very simple to apply, and in fact, is available in machine learning packages such as scikit-learn, WEKA, and so on; it is not as computer intensive as leave-one-out or the repeated resampling techniques that will be discussed later; it is not a repeated approach, thus guaranteeing that the estimates obtained from each fold are obtained on nonoverlapping subsets of the testing set.

On the other hand, while the testing sets used in k-fold cross-validation are independent from each other, the classifiers built on the $k - 1$ folds in each iteration are not necessarily independent since the algorithm in each case is trained on a highly overlapping set of training examples. This can, then, also affect the bias of the error estimates. However, in the case of moderate to large datasets, this limitation is mitigated, to some extent, as a result of large-sized subsets. Another point worth noting here, is that unlike the holdout case that reports the error rate of a single classifier trained on the training set, the k-fold cross-validation is an averaged estimate over the error rates of k different classifiers (trained and tested in each fold).

For leave-one-out, as can be seen easily, the error estimates obtained at each iteration of the scheme refer to the lone testing example. As a result, this can yield estimates with high variances, especially in case of limited data. However, the advantage of leave-one-out lies in its ability to utilize almost the full dataset for training, resulting in a relatively unbiased classifier. Naturally, in the case of severely limited dataset size, the cost of highly varying risk estimates on test examples trumps the benefit of being able to use almost the whole dataset for training. This is because in the case of a very small dataset size, using even the whole set for training might not guarantee a relatively unbiased classifier. Almost analogically the risk estimates would also not account for mitigating the high variance when averaged. However, as the dataset size increases, leave-one-out can be quite advantageous except for its computational complexity. Hence, leave-one-out can be quite effective for moderate dataset sizes. Indeed, for large datasets, leave-one-out may be computationally too expensive to be worth applying, especially since a k-fold cross-validation can also yield reliable estimates. Independently of the sample size, there are a couple of special cases, however, where leave-one-out can be particularly effective. Leave-one-out can be quite beneficial when there is wide dispersion of the data distribution or when the dataset contains extreme values. In such cases, the estimate produced by leave-one-out is expected to be better than the one produced by k-fold cross-validation.

6.4.4 Limitations of Simple Resampling Methods

Simple resampling methods can serve as good evaluation approaches when the available data is limited. However, these methods also have some limitations. Resampling methods do not estimate the risk of a classifier but, rather, estimate the expected risk, $E_S(A(S))$, of a learning algorithm A over samples S of the size of the partitions used for training. This is, for example, $m(1 - 1/k)$ for k-fold cross-validation. Although, as mentioned above, these methods do try to make the most out of data by training on most cases, they suffer from the fact that no formal confidence intervals are known.[4] It is, thus, currently impossible to provide rigorous formal guarantees over the risk of the classifier. This is in contrast with holdout methods where such guarantees and confidence intervals can be precisely stated. Even under the normality assumption, the sample standard deviation of the k-fold cross-validation risk R_{CV}^k over the k different groups serves, at best, to give a rough idea of the uncertainty of the estimate. By contrast, the training set bounds, an approach discussed in Japkowicz and Shah (2011), have been shown to provide acceptably good guarantees over the generalization behavior of the classifier in terms of its empirical performance on the training set in some cases.

Finally, as we noted above, resampling provides the estimate of the average of the performances of (generally different) classifiers learned in various partitions. This is not the same as the estimate obtained in the case of the holdout case. This has both advantages and disadvantages. The main advantage is that one can test the robustness of the algorithm by studying the stability of the estimates across various partitions (for the respective learned classifiers). The main disadvantage is that when reporting the results and comparing them against those of other algorithms, we tend to compare the average of the performance estimates rather than the estimate of a fixed classifier f, unlike in the case of the holdout approach.

In the context of applying resampling techniques, one must guard against the risk of confusing or intertwining model selection with error estimation. This can have potentially undesirable implications. We now look at this issue in a bit more detail.

6.5 A Note on Model Selection

Recall that model selection essentially refers to choosing the best parameters for the learning algorithm so as to obtain a classifier having minimum training error. Once a classifier has reached the optimal criterion (e.g., a low training error), this classifier is then tested on the test set and its performance on that set is reported. In order to report as unbiased an estimate of classifier performance as possible, it is imperative that the model selection be carried out

---

[4] Approximate confidence intervals, however, will be derived as will be discussed in Chapter 7.

independently of the test instances. This is especially true for the resampling approaches since, in the wake of limited size datasets, the idea is to use as many examples for training as possible. However, if the instances put aside for testing in any given resampling run are used, even for validation, this would yield a classifier fine-tuned to obtain the best performance on this validation set, and hence result in an overly optimistic estimate of the classifier's performance.

6.5.1 Model Selection in Holdout

In the holdout scenario, a general approach to selecting the best hypothesis is to divide the data into three disjoint subsets (instead of two subsets as mentioned before): a training set, a validation set, and a test set. The learning algorithm is trained on the training set, yielding a set of candidate hypotheses (depending on, say, different parameter values that the algorithm takes as input). Each of these hypotheses is then tested on the validation set, and the one that performs best (e.g., makes the least number of errors) on this validation set is then selected. Testing of this *selected* hypothesis is done in the same manner; that is via the testing of its performance on the test set.

6.5.2 Model Selection in Resampling

In the resampling scenario, it is necessary to hold the test partition independent of the learning bias. That is, any model selection necessary to tune the learning algorithm should be done independently of the test partition, so as to obtain a relatively unbiased estimate of the classifier's performance on this test partition.

Consider, for instance, the case of k-fold cross-validation. When trying to perform error estimation using cross-validation, the algorithm builds a classifier using the $k - 1$ folds for training and tests it on the kth fold. However, if the algorithm also needs to perform model selection (i.e., find the best parameters for the classifier such as the kernel width for an SVM with radial basis function kernel) then this should be done independently of the test fold as well since, otherwise, for each fold, the algorithm would have a positive bias towards obtaining the classifier performing best on the test fold. One solution is to use a *nested k-fold cross-validation*. The idea behind the nested k-fold cross-validation is to divide the dataset into k disjoint subsets, just as in the k-fold cross-validation method described in Section 6.4.3. But now, in addition we perform a separate k-fold cross-validation *within* the $k - 1$ folds during training in order to compare the different parameter instantiations of the algorithm. Once the best model is identified for that training fold, testing is, as usual, performed on the kth testing fold. The rationale behind this approach is to make the algorithm totally unbiased in parameter selection.

The simple resampling methods discussed so far may not yield the desired estimates in some scenarios, such as extremely limited sample sizes, and more robust estimation methods are desired. Multiple resampling methods aim to do so (of course with some inherent costs). Let us then discuss some prominent multiple resampling methods.

6.6 Multiple Resampling

Multiple resampling refers to tests that potentially generate risk estimates based either on multiple samplings from the training set (e.g., bootstrap) or performing simple resampling multiple times (e.g., multiple k-fold cross-validation). The advantage of multiple resampling over simple resampling is in the additional stability of the estimates resulting from a large numbers of repetitions of sampling. However, it should be kept in mind that this can also lead to other estimation problems due to the extreme reuse, and thus loss, of independence of the data used in various multiple resampling runs.

Let us very briefly look at the intuition behind multiple resampling in view of our resampling framework, which would make this intuition over stability clearer. Recall that when we partition the data into k subsets, the resampled risk is basically an expectation over various $\mathbf{w} \in W$, where W is fixed. It is then natural to be interested in a relatively stable estimate of this resampled risk. A stable estimate is one with minimal (ideally none) dependency on any specific set of weight vectors W. We can obtain this by taking an expectation of the resampled risk over all possible sets of weight vectors. Hence, the multiple trial risk estimate of a resampling scheme, denoted $R_S^{MT}(f)$, is

$$R_S^{MT}(f) = \mathbf{E}_W \mathbf{E_w} \int L\left(y, f_S^k(\mathbf{x})\right) dD^k(\mathbf{x}, y),$$

where $D^k(\mathbf{z}) = D^k(\mathbf{x}, y)$ denotes the distribution of the partition S_k, and the expectation with respect to $\mathbf{w}$ denotes the expectation over all the fixed partitioning defined by W, with each $\mathbf{w}$ defining a particular partition.

An empirical way to estimate this expectation is, then, to perform multiple trials over each resampling scheme. This observation gives rise to various multiple trial versions of the simple resampling schemes, as well as the introduction of some new ones. Let us look at some prominent multiple resampling techniques.

6.6.1 Random Subsampling

The first, and probably the simplest, multiple resampling technique is random subsampling. The technique can be summarized as shown in Algorithm 6.3.

Algorithm 6.3 Random subsampling

- Initialize $i = 1$
- Repeat while $i \leq n$ (typically $n \geq 30$)
    - Randomly divide the data set into a training set S_{train}^i, usually containing 2/3rd of the data, and a testing set $S_{test}^i = S_{train}^i$ containing the examples from S not included in S_{train}^i
    - Train the algorithm on S_{train}^i and obtain a classifier f_i
    - Test f_i on S_{test}^i to obtain an estimate of the empirical risk $R(f_i)$
    - Increment i by 1
- Average the estimates $R(f_i)$ over the n repetitions to obtain the overall risk estimate $R(f)$
- Report $R(f)$

Random subsampling has an intuitive appeal. In the holdout framework, typically, the data was divided into two subsets with one used for training (and validation) and the other for testing purposes. Random subsampling, in the manner described in Algorithm 6.3, basically extends this notion to the multiple resampling scenario. Moreover, it carries the advantage of being able to use a larger amount of data for training purposes, resulting in less biased classifiers. However, in the limited data scenario the variance in the estimates can still be significant, due to the small test sets in each repetition. The problem is further aggravated for very small dataset sizes since, in this case, every iteration of the multiple runs would yield very similar classifiers.

6.6.2 Bootstrapping Approaches: The $\epsilon 0$, .632, and Balanced Bootstraps

The idea of bootstrapping comes from the question of what can be done when too little is known about the data. Bootstrapping works by assuming that the available sample is representative of the original distribution, and creates a large number of new samples – the bootstrapped samples – by drawing, with replacement, from that population. Different variations of bootstrap have been proposed (see Chernik (2007) for a review). We focus, in particular, on the $\epsilon 0$ and the .632 bootstraps, the two most common bootstrap techniques.

Let us first summarize the simpler $\epsilon 0$ bootstrap (also referred to as the $e0$ bootstrap) estimate. The resampling technique consists of drawing with replacement large numbers of datasets, bootstraps, of the same size as the original dataset. Each bootstrap may contain several copies of specific instances, and each of them may miss a number of instances from the original dataset. The missing instances are used as the testing set for the corresponding bootstrap, while the bootstrap itself is used as the training set. Then $\epsilon 0$ represents the average error rate obtained on each bootstrap/testing pair. The procedure is shown in more detail in Algorithm 6.4.

Algorithm 6.4 $\epsilon 0$ bootstrap

- Given a data set S with m examples
- Initialize $\epsilon 0 = 0$
- Initialize $i = 1$
- Repeat while $i \leq k$ (typically $k \geq 200$)
    - Draw, with replacement, m samples from S to obtain a training set S^i_{boot}
    - Define $T^i_{boot} = S \backslash S^i_{boot}$, i.e., the test set contains the examples from S not included in S^i_{boot}
    - Train the algorithm on S^i_{boot} to obtain a classifier f^i_{boot}
    - Test f^i_{boot} on T^i_{boot} to obtain the empirical risk estimate $\epsilon 0_i$
    - $\epsilon 0 = \epsilon 0 + \epsilon 0_i$
    - Increment i by 1
- Calculate $\epsilon 0 = \frac{\epsilon 0}{k}$
- Report $\epsilon 0$

Bootstrapping can be quite useful, in practice, in the cases where the sample is too small for cross-validation or leave-one-out approaches to yield a good estimate. In such cases, a bootstrap estimate can be more reliable.

Let us formalize the $\epsilon 0$ bootstrap to understand better the behavior and the associated intuition of not only the $\epsilon 0$ estimate but also the .632 bootstrap technique that it leads to. Going back to our resampling framework, let $\mathbf{w}$, in the case of a bootstrap resampling, be such that

$$\mathbf{w}_{boot} \in \mathbb{N}^m,$$

where

$$\forall\, i, 0 \le w_i \le m,$$

and

$$\|\mathbf{w}\|_1 = \sum_{i=1}^{m} w_i = m.$$

In this case, a weight vector, $\mathbf{w}_{boot} = \{w_1, w_2, \ldots, w_m\}$, and its complement, $\mathbf{w}_{boot}^c = \{w_1^c, w_2^c, \ldots, w_m^c\}$, are formed such that $w_i^c = 1$ if $w_i = 0$, and $w_i^c = 0$ otherwise. That is, the set $\mathbf{w}_{boot}^c$ is defined as soon as $\mathbf{w}_{boot}$ is known. In order to find all possible bootstrap sets, it suffices to identify the number of possible $\mathbf{w}_{boot}$. Hence, a distribution on W containing the vectors $\mathbf{w}_{boot}$ and $\mathbf{w}_{boot}^c$ is basically a distribution on $\mathbf{w}_{boot}$, which is what we do next.

For bootstrap sampling, $P_{\mathbf{w}}$ has equal mass on each of the possible $\mathbf{w}_{boot}$ in this new distribution. This is basically sampling with replacement and, under our original definition of $\mathbf{w}$, can be seen as in the following.

Recall that we have $\mathbf{w} \in \{0, 1\}^m$. Let $\mathbf{w}_1, \mathbf{w}_2, \ldots, \mathbf{w}_m$ be the m basis vectors such that each vector $\mathbf{w}_i$ has entry $w_i = 1$ and $w_j = 0, \forall\, j \neq i$. Now, let us consider a uniform distribution on this set of basis vectors. That is, the probability of sampling each $\mathbf{w}_i$ is equal. Then, we sample $\mathbf{w}_i$ from this distribution m times, with each sampling resulting in a weight vector $\mathbf{w}^i$ for $i = 1, 2, \ldots, m$. We can then obtain

$$\mathbf{w}_{boot} = \sum_{i} \mathbf{w}^i.$$

Bootstrap sampling relies on the assumption that the estimator obtained on a subsample (the sample obtained by bootstrapping) can approximate the estimate on the full sample. Let the size of our training sample S be m; that is, $|S| = m$. Then, as already mentioned, the bootstrap sampling method consists of sampling, *with replacement*, m examples *uniformly* from S. Let us call this resulting sample S_{boot}.

Since we sample the dataset with replacement, the probability of every example being chosen is uniform and is equal to $\frac{1}{m}$. Subsequently, the probability of an example not being chosen is $1 - \frac{1}{m}$. For any given example, the probability of it being not chosen after m samples therefore is $(1 - \frac{1}{m})^m$. Now,

$$\left(1 - \frac{1}{m}\right)^m \approx \frac{1}{e} \approx 0.368.$$

Hence, the expected number of distinct examples in the resulting sample of m instances is $0.632 \times m$. The test set T_{boot} is then formed from all the examples from S not present in S_{boot}. A classifier f_{boot} is then obtained on S_{boot} and tested on T_{boot}. The empirical risk estimate of f_{boot} is obtained on T_{boot}. This process is repeated k times and the respective risk estimates are averaged to obtain the $\epsilon0$ estimate as

$$\epsilon0 = \frac{1}{k} \sum_{i=1}^{k} \frac{1}{|T_{boot}^i|} \sum_{j=1}^{|T_{boot}^i|} I\left(f_{boot}^i(x_j) \neq y_j \right),$$

where f_{boot}^i denotes the classifier obtained by training the algorithm on S_{boot}^i, the training sample obtained in ith run with T_{boot}^i being the corresponding test set.

The $\epsilon0$ estimate obtained in the above manner can be pessimistic since the classifier is typically trained only over 63.2% of data in each run. The next metric, the .632 estimate, aims to correct for this pessimistic bias by taking into account the optimistic bias of the resubstitution error over the remaining fraction of $1 - 0.632 = 0.368$. The .632 bootstrap method is summarized in Algorithm 6.5.

Algorithm 6.5 .632 bootstrap

- Given a data set S with m examples
- Train the learning algorithm on S to obtain a classifier f_S
- Test f_S on S to obtain the resubstitution error rate
  $err(f) = R_S^{resub}(f_S)$
- Initialize the .632 risk estimate $e632 = 0$
- Initialize $i = 1$
- Repeat while $i \leq k$ (typically $k \geq 200$)
    - Draw, with replacement, m samples from S to obtain a
      training set S_{boot}^i
    - Define $T_{boot}^i = S_{boot}^i$, i.e., the test set contains the examples
      from S not included in S_{boot}^i
    - Train the algorithm on S_{boot}^i to obtain a classifier f_{boot}^i
    - Test f_{boot}^i on T_{boot}^i to obtain the empirical risk estimate $\epsilon0_i$
    - $e632 = e632 + 0.632 \cdot \epsilon0_i$
    - Increment i by 1
- Calculate $e632 = \frac{e632}{k}$
- Approximate the remaining proportion of the risk using $err(f)$ to
  give $e632 = e632 + 0.368 \cdot err(f)$
- Return $e632$

More formally, let the number of bootstrap samples generated be k. For each sample $i \in \{1, 2, \ldots, k\}$, we obtain a bootstrap sample S_{boot}^i and a corresponding bootstrap test set T_{boot}^i. Moreover, a classifier f_{boot}^i is obtained on each S_{boot}^i and tested on T_{boot}^i to yield a corresponding estimate $\epsilon0_i$. These estimates can, together, be used to obtain what is called the .632 bootstrap estimate, defined as

$$e632 = \frac{1}{k} \sum_{i=1}^{k} 0.632 \cdot \epsilon0_i + 0.368 err(f)$$

$$= 0.632 \cdot \epsilon0 + 0.368 \cdot err(f),$$

where $err(f)$ is the misclassification error of classifier f learned on the whole training set, on the training set; that is, $err(f)$ is the resubstitution error rate $R_S^{resub}(f_S)$ with f being the classifier f_S obtained by training the algorithm on the whole training set S.

Balanced Bootstrap Sampling

In balanced bootstrap sampling, the bootstrap samples are generated such that each example is present for a fixed number of times in all the samples altogether. Consider the case where we wish to generate balanced bootstrap samples from m examples in S such that each element is present exactly m_b times. This will result in m_b bootstrap samples. An easy way to generate this is to first obtain a vector of $m \cdot m_b$ indices with m_b entries for each element of $\{1, 2, \ldots, m\}$. The next step is to scramble this vector randomly and then divide the resulting vector into m_b vectors of m indices, each sequentially. This procedure draws a parallel with stratified cross-validation.

Discussion

In empirical studies, the relationship between bootstrap and the cross-validation estimates have received special attention. Bootstrapping can be a method of choice when more conventional resampling, such as k-fold cross-validation, cannot be applied owing to small dataset sizes. Moreover, the bootstrap also, in such cases, results in estimates with low variance as a result of an (artificially) increased dataset size. Further, the $\epsilon 0$ bootstrap has been empirically shown to be a good error estimator in cases of a very high true error rate while the .632 bootstrap estimator has been shown to be a good error estimator on small datasets, especially if the true error rate is small (i.e., when the algorithm is extremely accurate).

An interesting, though perhaps at first surprising, result that emanates from various empirical studies is that the relative appropriateness of one sampling scheme over the other is classifier dependent. Indeed, it was found that bootstrapping is a poor error estimator for classifiers such as the nearest neighbor that do not benefit from (or simply make use of) duplicate instances. In light of the fact that bootstrapping resamples with replacement, this result is not as surprising as it first appeared to be.

6.6.3 Randomization

The term randomization has been used with regard to multiple resampling methods in two contexts. The first one is what is referred to as randomization over samples. That is, estimating the effect of different reorderings of the data on the algorithm's performance estimate. We will refer to such randomization on training samples as permutation sampling or permutation testing. The second context in which randomization is used refers to the randomization over labels of the training examples. The purpose of this testing is to assess the dependence of the learning algorithm on the actual label assignment as opposed to obtaining the same or similar classifiers on chance label assignments. Like bootstrapping, randomization makes the assumption that the sample is representative of the original distribution. However, instead of drawing samples with replacement, like bootstrapping does, randomization reorders (shuffles) the data systematically, or randomly, a number of times. It calculates the quantity of interest on each reordering. Since shuffling the data amounts to sampling without replacement, it is one difference between bootstrapping and randomization.

Permutation Testing

In permutation testing, we basically look at the number of possible reorderings of the training set S to assess their effect on classifier performance. As we can easily see, there are a total of $m!$ possible reorderings of the entries of the vector $\mathbf{w}$ and hence those of the examples $\mathbf{z}$ in the training set S. We would then consider a distribution over these $m!$ orderings on unit vectors $\mathbf{w}$ and $P_{\mathbf{w}}$ that would have an equal probability ($= \frac{1}{m!}$) on each of the weight vectors.

Permutation testing can provide a sense of robustness of the algorithm to the ordering of the data samples and hence a sense of the stability of the performance estimate thus obtained. However, when it comes to comparing such estimates for two or more robust algorithms, permutation testing might not be very effective since the stability of estimates over different permutations is not the prominent criterion of difference between these approaches. Hence, we are more interested in the randomization over labels.

Randomization over Labels

We give an informal description of this technique for the binary label scenario, although extending it to the multi-label scenario is relatively trivial. The idea is to find out whether the error estimate obtained on the given data presents specific characteristics or whether it could have been obtained on similar but "bogus" data and, thus, does not stand out as particularly significant. The "bogus" data is created by taking the genuine sample and randomly choosing to either leave its label intact or switch it. Once such a "bogus" dataset is created, the classifier is run on this data and its error estimated. This process is repeated a very large number of times in an attempt to establish whether the error estimate obtained on the true data is truly different from those obtained on large numbers of "bogus" datasets. In this sense, this overlaps to some extent with the hypothesis testing methodology that we introduced in Section 4.4 and will discuss further in Chapter 7. We summarize the basic technique in Algorithm 6.6.

Algorithm 6.6 Randomization over labels

- Given a dataset S with m examples
- Decide on a performance metric pm
- Calculate pm on the data (denoted as pm_{obt})
- Repeat the following N times, where $N \in \mathbb{N}$ such that $N > 1000$
    - Shuffle the data
    - Assign the first n_1 samples to class 1 and the remaining n_2 samples to class 2
    - Calculate pm (here denoted pm_i^*) for the reshuffled data
    - If $pm_i^* > pm_{obt}$, increment a counter by 1
- Divide the value in the counter by N to get the proportion of times the pm on the randomized data exceeded the pm_{obt} on the data we actually obtained
- This is the probability of a result such as pm_{obt} under the null hypothesis
- Reject or retain the hypothesis stating that pm_{obt} is meaningful on the basis of this probability

Note that this can be applied not only to validate a given classifier's performance against a random set of labelings, but also to characterize the difference of two classifiers in a comparative setting. In this regard, this resampling is generally used as a sanity check test to compare the classifiers' performance over random assignments of labels to the examples in S. Hence, keeping the ordering of the examples in the training set constant, that is, keeping ordering over x constant, we can randomize the labels while maintaining the label distribution. Alternatively, we can randomize the examples while keeping the label assignment constant as shown in Algorithm 6.6. However, obtaining estimates over a large number of randomization of labels can be significantly computationally intensive.

6.6.4 Multiple Trials of Simple Resampling Methods

As we discussed in the context of bootstrapping, one of the more straightforward ways to obtain relatively stable estimates of the algorithm's performance to discount the dependence on the chosen set of weight vectors W (i.e., a particular partitioning) is to perform multiple runs over the simple resampling schemes. This may also help in another way: single runs of simple resampling methods suffer from the limitation of low replicability since they depend upon factors such as the data permutation used when performing the original trials, as well as not having precisely the same training and testing sets when trying to replicate the results. *Replicability*, in this context, quantifies the probability of obtaining the same error estimate when running a learning algorithm on a given training data twice.

One solution to remedy the replicability problem is to report the exact setting of the trial with the data. This is not often, if at all, done, nor is it practical to do in most cases. Multiple resamplings mitigate the variability effect over estimates to a certain extent in an indirect manner. Instead of trying to replicate the result over a single run of simple resampling, it averages the results over multiple runs (trials) in an attempt to obtain more stable estimates.

This, then, brings us to the question of how many runs of simple resampling methods to perform. Currently, there is no convincing theoretical model to guide this choice. As a result, this is largely determined empirically. A couple of suggestions have been proposed. The most prominent ones include the 5×2CV (Dietterich 1998) and 10×10CV (Bouckaert 2003), performing 5 repetitions of 2-fold cross-validation and 10 repetitions of 10-fold cross-validation, respectively. The main motivation for proposing these approaches, however, lies in their subsequent role when using the resulting error estimates to compare two learning algorithms on a given dataset. Hence, we will discuss the details and significance of these proposals in Chapter 7, in their proper context.

6.7 Important Considerations for Choosing a Resampling Method

Choosing the best resampling method for a given task should be done carefully if an objective performance estimate is to be obtained. As already seen, the bias–variance behavior of the associated loss is largely dependent on such choices and, in fact, also helps us guide this selection. For instance, it can be seen that increasing the number of folds in a k-fold cross-validation approach would result in estimates that are less biased since a larger subset of the data is used for training. However, doing so would result in decreasing the size of the test partitions, thereby resulting in an increase in the variance of the estimates.

In addition to their effects on the bias–variance behavior of the resulting error estimate, selecting a resampling method also relies on some other factors. One such factor is the nature of the classifiers to be evaluated. For instance, more stable classifiers would not need a permutation test. The less robust a classifier is, the more training data it would need to reach a stable behavior. In fact, it would also take multiple runs to approximate its average behavior. There are some dataset-dependent factors affecting the choice of resampling methods too. These include the size of the dataset and its spread (that is, the representative capability of the data) and the complexity of the domain that we wish to learn. A highly complex domain, for instance, in the presence of a limited dataset size, would invariably lead to a biased classifier. Hence, the aim would be to use a resampling scheme that would allow it to use as much data for learning as possible. A multiple resampling scheme can also be useful in such scenarios.

Precisely quantifying various parameters involved in the choice of a resampling method is extremely difficult. Let us take an indirect approach in discussing some important observations by looking at them in a relative sense. The points below should be viewed bearing in mind that the terms unbiased or almost unbiased are strictly relative with respect to the optimal classifier that can be obtained *given* the training data:

- The leave-one-out cross-validation error estimate is almost unbiased due to the fact that the training takes place on virtually all (all but one case) the available data and due to the fact that the testing sets are completely independent. This estimate, however, suffers from high variance due to the extreme behavior of the tested classifiers on the one-case test sets. The problem is further aggravated in the binary classification zero-one loss scenario for discrete classifiers (that do not give probabilistic labels). Leave-one-out has a particularly high variance on small samples.
- Bootstrapping has been shown to perform well in the cases where the sample is too small for cross-validation or leave-one-out approaches to yield a good estimate. In such cases, a bootstrap estimate shows less variance than simple resampling techniques (k-fold cross-validation for instance).
- In particular, the advantage of the $\epsilon 0$ bootstrap is its low variance, especially as compared to 10-fold cross-validation or leave-one-out. However, it is more biased than the 10-fold cross-validation estimator. It is however, pessimistically biased on moderately sized samples. Nonetheless, it gives good results in case of a high true error rate (Weiss and Kulikowski 1991).
- Like the $\epsilon 0$ bootstrap, the .632 bootstrap is also a low variance estimator. Unlike the $\epsilon 0$ estimator though, the .632 becomes too optimistic as the sample size grows. However, it is a very good estimator on small datasets, especially if the true error rate is small (Weiss and Kulikowski 1991).
- Though in cases of extremely small datasets, the k-fold cross-validation often does not perform as well as bootstrapping (and using more folds does not help), it does not suffer from drastic problems the way bootstrapping does in terms of increased bias or when the true error expectations are not met.

Other concerns that should be taken into account while opting for a resampling method include the computational complexity involved in employing the resampling method of choice and the resulting gain in terms of more objective and representative estimates. For instance, increasing the folds in a k-fold cross-validation all the way to leave-one-out resampling would mean increasing the number of runs over the learning algorithm in each fold. Further, if model selection is involved, this would require nested runs to optimize the learning parameters, thereby further increasing the computational complexity. Bootstrapping, on the other hand, can also be quite expensive computationally.

As we noted earlier, the relative appropriateness of one sampling scheme over the other has also been found to be classifier-dependent empirically. Kohavi (1995) further extends this observation to show that not only are the resampling techniques sensitive to the classifiers under scrutiny, but they are also sensitive to the domains on which they are applied. In light of these observations, it would only be appropriate to end this discussion with the take home message from the above observations echoed by Reich and Barai (1999, p. 11):

> The relations between the evaluation methods, whether statistically significantly different or not, varies with data quality. Therefore, one cannot replace one test with another, and only evaluation methods appropriate for the context may be used.

6.8 Advanced Topics

One of the main directions that the field of statistical learning theory has contributed to, in relation to classifier evaluation, is the study of the behavior of learning algorithms in terms not only of their empirical performance, but also of other information available from the data and the learning algorithms' predisposition to select one classifier over another; that is, the classical problems of model selection and learning bias. Some of the main quantities of interest in the learning theory context include the algorithms' future performance guarantees, the nature of the classifier space explored, and the complexity of the final classifier output by the learning algorithm on a given dataset, along with the corresponding trade-offs involved. In particular, attempts have been made at characterizing the performance of the classifier as well as the guarantees over its future performance. Such results have, generally, appeared in the form of generalization error bounds. These guarantees basically provide upper (and sometimes lower) bounds on the deviation of the true error of the classifier from its empirical error and take into account the precise quantities that a classifier learns from the data. Japkowicz and Shah (2011) discuss this parallel approach to error estimation and show a concrete example of such bounds.

We conclude this chapter with the proof of Equation (6.5) from Section 6.2.1.

Proof of Equation (6.5) Consider an algorithm A that, given some training set S, outputs a classifier $f = A(S)$. We wish to estimate the true risk $R(f)$ in terms of the risk on a distinct test sample T (disjoint from training set S). We can define the empirical risk of f on test set T as

$$R_T(f) \overset{\text{def}}{=} \frac{1}{m'} \sum_{i=1}^{m'} L(f(\boldsymbol{x}_i), y_i),$$

where $m' \overset{\text{def}}{=} |T|$ is the number of examples in the testing set. Note that the test set $T = z_1, \ldots, z_{m'}$ of m' samples is formed from the instantiation of the variables $\mathbf{Z}^{m'} \overset{\text{def}}{=} \mathbf{Z}_1, \ldots, \mathbf{Z}_{m'}$. Every $\mathbf{Z}_i$ is distributed according to some distribution D that generates the sample S. Each z_i consists of an example x_i and its label y_i. Each example x_i can hence be considered an instantiation of a variable $\mathbf{X}_i$, and its label y_i as an instantiation of variable Y_i.

Hence, over all the test sets generated from the instantiations of variables $\mathbf{Z}^{m'}$, the risk of some classifier f can be represented as

$$R(\mathbf{Z}^{m'}, f) \overset{\text{def}}{=} \frac{1}{m'} \sum_{i=1}^{m'} L(f(\mathbf{X}_i), Y_i),$$

where $L()$ is again the loss function over the misclassification. Now, consider the loss function $L = L_z$ such that L_z is a Bernoulli variable. Then the true risk can be expressed as

$$R(f) = \{\Pr(L_z(f(\mathbf{X}), Y)) = 1\} \overset{\text{def}}{=} p.$$

In order to bound the true risk $R(f)$ we make use of the Hoeffding inequality as stated in Theorem 6.1.

Theorem 6.1 *(Hoeffding–Bernoulli case) For any sequence $Y_1, Y_2, \ldots, Y_{m'}$ of variables obeying a Bernoulli distribution with $\Pr(Y_i = 1) = p \;\; \forall \, i$, we have*

$$\Pr\left[\left|\frac{1}{m'} \sum_{i=1}^{m'} Y_i - p\right| > \epsilon\right] \leq 2 \exp(-2m'\epsilon^2).$$

This implies that

$$\Pr\left[\left|\frac{1}{m'} \sum_{i=1}^{m'} Y_i - p\right| \leq \epsilon\right] \geq 1 - 2 \exp(-2m'\epsilon^2).$$

Now, since $L_z(f(\mathbf{X}), Y)$ is a Bernoulli variable, we have

$$\Pr\left[\left|R(\mathbf{Z}^{m'}, f) - R(f)\right| \leq \epsilon\right] \geq 1 - 2 \exp(-2m'\epsilon^2).$$

Equating the right-hand side of the above equation to $1 - \delta$, we get

$$t_{1-\delta} = \epsilon = \sqrt{\frac{1}{2m'} \ln\left(\frac{2}{\delta}\right)}.$$

Hence, for any classifier f, the true risk $R(f)$, with probability $1 - \delta$ and test error $R_T(f)$ on some test set T, satisfies

$$\left|R_T(f) - R(f)\right| \leq t_{1-\delta} = \sqrt{\frac{1}{2m'} \ln\left(\frac{2}{\delta}\right)}. \tag{6.6}$$

Therefore, with probability $1 - \delta$,

$$R(f) \approx R_T(f) \pm t_{1-\delta}.$$

Hence, it can be seen that the convergence of the empirical risk to the true risk depends on the sample size m' and the true risk $R(f)$.

7

Statistical Analysis

In this chapter, we ask whether the results observed using the performance metrics of Chapter 5 and the resampling methods of Chapter 6 are meaningful. In other words, do the differences observed between the compared algorithms reflect a true difference in performance, or are they obtained by mere chance? More specifically, still:

Can the observed results be attributed to real characteristics of the classifiers under scrutiny, or were they obtained by a combination of chance and the mix of data used to train the classifiers?

Statistical analysis provides tools that allow us to address these questions. The tools are particularly useful in detecting when the amount and type of observations are not sufficient to warrant the conclusions they led to. In such cases, more evidence must be sought. When the tools indicate that the amount and type of observations are sufficient, though, it is important to remember that while there is a good chance that the observed results are meaningful, this is not guaranteed. As a result, we should think of statistical analysis methods as methods that allow us to *gather useful support* for our observations.

Although it will almost never lead to fully conclusive answers, statistical analysis should nonetheless be recognized as very important for both the pursuit of knowledge and decision-making. In the latter situation, it is worth noting that critical decision-making is usually needed in uncertain settings. In such settings, an indicator, however small, can help the decision-maker make a slightly more informed decision, which is better than making that decision with no information whatsoever. A statistically significant difference can be that indicator. Let us now look, in more detail, at the specific questions on which statistical analysis is able to shed light.

Example 1 Consider the results of running logistic regression (LR) and support vector machine (SVM) algorithms on the UCI Labor Relations dataset and using the error rate (or empirical risk) as our performance evaluation metric; Table 2.1 presented these results. We saw that the (binary) empirical risk calculated from the table amounted to .092 for LR and .063 for SVM. These results were obtained over a 10-fold cross-validation regimen and are averages over different trials. A simple approach for deciding which of the two classifiers performs better is to observe that SVM obtains a lower error rate than LR on these experiments, and conclude that SVM is *consistently* superior to LR on the labor relations domain. This can be misleading, however, because averages, while extremely practical, can hide information that it is crucial to uncover in order to understand the difference in performance of two processes. Statistical analysis offers tools that allow us to unwrap the information conveyed by averages and inform us on the extent to which specific averages are reliable. Informally stated, statistical analysis works by observing the consistency of the difference in classifier performance, implicitly or explicitly. Such consistency estimates can either be obtained over multiple test cases (generally, test sets) or by performing multiple trials over a given test set. Such consistency would then indicate that the performance difference between two or more classifiers was not merely a chance result. We explain this more specifically with the following hypothetical example.

Example 2 Assume that classifiers A and B were tested in a 5-fold cross-validation regimen using the error rate as their performance metric, and that classifiers A and B obtained the following results on each fold, respectively. Classifier A: .012, .015, .02, .26, .009; and classifier B: .061, .054, .055, .062, .050. The average error rate for classifier A is thus 0.0632; and the average error rate for classifier B is thus 0.0564. A simple look at the average error rates of the two classifiers would therefore suggest that classifier B, the one with the lowest error rate, exhibits better performance than classifier A. Would you agree with this conclusion? Well, it's complicated! Classifier A usually performs much better than classifier B, since on typical folds it obtains error rates in the $[0.009, 0.02]$ interval while classifier B obtains error rates in the $[0.050, 0.062]$ interval. There was only onefold, however, on which classifier A performed miserably and obtained an error rate of 0.26. Given that the classifiers of the above example were tested on so few folds, can we really conclude what the average error rate results suggest? That is, are the above five folds sufficient to make any conjectures about the consistency of the classifier performances? It would, perhaps, be warranted if classifier A was shown on a large number of folds to obtain such bad results relatively often while classifier B was shown to remain more stable. However, it is also possible that on a large number of folds, classifier B would also have obtained bad results once in a while. Perhaps it is only by chance that our 5-fold sample did not contain a fold on which classifier B did not fail miserably. Perhaps the fold on which classifier A failed is the only fold where classifier A would ever fail, and it happened, quite by chance, to show up in our sample. Either way, one can see the problems caused by the sole display of average error rate results. Whatever they show is not the whole story.[1] It is necessary to use additional information to understand what averages may hide.

Statistical Analysis The purpose of statistical analysis is to help gather evidence of the extent to which the results returned by an evaluation metric averaged over different trials are representative of the general behavior of our classifiers. The tools it provides help us summarize this information. These tools fall into three categories:

---

[1] The example may not seem realistic, but here is a situation where it might be: let's assume that A is a binary classifier and B, a one-class classifier. Let's further assume that the domain is highly imbalanced and, by chance, fold 4 contained only instances of the larger class in the training set, whereas the other fold had a representative enough training sample of both classes. In such a case classifier A, which under normal conditions is more accurate than classifier B, would not be able to learn anything in fold 4, and thus do a bad job on that fold's testing set, whereas classifier B would perform in the same range as it normally does.

• Null hypothesis significance testing (NHST)
• Estimation statistics
• Bayesian analysis

The first category is the best known and most relied upon. It is taught in introductory courses in statistics and is considered staple knowledge for all science or social science practitioners and researchers. Its attractiveness, which resulted in its wide adoption, derives from the clear conclusions it yields. Indeed, after applying a statistical significance test, one gets a binary answer: yes, the results are statistically significant at some accepted significance level, or no, they are not. Aspects of the second category are also taught quite broadly, especially the notion of confidence intervals. That approach, though, has not traditionally been as popular because it does not yield such clear conclusions as the first one. This is changing, however, as will be discussed in Section 7.1. The third category relies on a different philosophy altogether: while the first two belong to the *frequentist* school of thought, the third belongs to the *Bayesian* school of thought. The difference between the two schools of thought is that in the frequentist approach, the analysis only relies on the observed data whereas in the Bayesian approach, prior information about the experiment under consideration is also used. The adoption of Bayesian statistics is a new development in many fields that rely on statistical analysis as will also be discussed in the next section.

Prior to diving fully into the description of these approaches, it is important to make two observations. First, the field of statistical analysis is evolving and has been so for over two decades. Second, up to until a few years ago, machine learning was a field focused on the development of tools that perform inferences rather than on the use of these tools for practical applications. Being, therefore, a cross between an engineering discipline and a scientific discipline, machine learning never fully established its need for and use of statistical validation. In the early 1990s, Weiss and Kulikowski (1991) suggested the use of statistical tests for machine learning, and Mitchell (1997) suggested the use of confidence intervals in his book on machine learning. Dieterich (1998) then reviewed five statistical tests and proposed a new one along with a resampling technique. A little later, Demšar (2006) suggested that the parametric tests used by the machine learning community to date were not appropriate and suggested new nonparametric ones, each appropriate for different scenarios. In addition, he pointed out issues with statistical testing in machine learning in general (Demšar 2008) as did Drummond (2006). More recently, Berrar and Lozano (2013) advocated for the use of confidence intervals and later proposed confidence curves (Berrar 2016). More recently still, Benavoli et al. (2017) suggested the use of Bayesian analysis, a suggestion that is starting to gain traction in the field.

The precursor to this book, Japkowicz and Shah (2011), presented traditional parametric statistical tests along with the nonparametric ones suggested by Demšar (2006), while also discussing some of the issues associated with the statistical testing paradigm. In this current book, we take a new and more thorough look at the problem and attempt to disentangle the complex issues surrounding the question of how to verify the significance of our experimental findings. This chapter first presents a general discussion of statistical analysis, underlining that there is no silver bullet in the landscape of methods available. It then presents the three different paradigms mentioned above, along with their advantages and pitfalls. In more detail, the remainder of the chapter is divided into five sections. Section 7.1 presents a general overview of the current lay of the land regarding trust that can be bestowed on results obtained through experimental research or testing. It also presents the two approaches to statistical testing we consider most appropriate for machine learning – NHST used in combination with estimation statistics and Bayesian testing – while also warning of each of their shortcomings. Section 7.2 then discusses, in detail, the NHST techniques deemed most useful for machine learning. Section 7.3 presents the aspects of estimation statistics most relevant to machine learning, focusing specifically on effect size, confidence intervals, and power analysis. These haven't been used broadly in machine learning yet, but they are gaining visibility in other disciplines and we believe that it is important to bring these new practices to light in the machine learning community as well. Section 7.4 discusses the Bayesian analysis recently suggested in Benavoli et al. (2017) within machine learning, and that is also gaining notice in other scientific disciplines. Section 7.5 concludes the chapter.

7.1 The Statistical Analysis Landscape for Machine Learning

Prior to getting into the details of which statistical analysis method to use when and each of their shortcomings, it is important to contemplate the purpose of statistical analysis from both a philosophical and practical analysis. Perhaps, the Covid pandemic gave us a better appreciation for issues regarding statistical analysis, and a greater understanding of what is at their core. What Covid emphasized for us is that at the core is the unknown: statistical analysis is applied in the context of a research program or the deployment of a new tool or product (e.g., drugs, vaccines) for which answers to fundamental questions are, at the outset, unknown. The research or marketing program asks a question and attempts to establish whether the answer it obtained in its limited experimental setting applies to all situations. However, the true answer to the question is unknown. Therefore, it is impossible to establish with 100% certainty that the answer obtained on the sample tested in the experiments is the answer to the question in general. Statistical analysis may help assess how much credence can be given to the answer, but it is not always correct, as illustrated in Section 7.1.1.

7.1.1 Illustration

On June 25, 2020, three months after Covid made its appearance on the international scene and while most of the world was under lockdown orders, a French doctor, Didier Raoult, and his team published a paper discussing the results of a retrospective study on the use of hydroxychloroquine for the treatment of Covid (Gautret et al. 2020).

Here is a reproduction of the article's abstract

Abstract

Background

Chloroquine and hydroxychloroquine have been found to be efficient on SARS-CoV-2, and reported to be efficient in Chinese COV-19 patients. We evaluate the effect of hydroxychloroquine on respiratory viral loads.

Patients and methods

French Confirmed COVID-19 patients were included in a single arm protocol from early March to March 16th, to receive 600mg of hydroxychloroquine daily and their viral load in nasopharyngeal swabs was tested daily in a hospital setting. Depending on their clinical presentation, azithromycin was added to the treatment. Untreated patients from another center and cases refusing the protocol were included as negative controls. Presence and absence of virus at Day6-post inclusion was considered the end point.

Results

Six patients were asymptomatic, 22 had upper respiratory tract infection symptoms and eight had lower respiratory tract infection symptoms.

Twenty cases were treated in this study and showed a significant reduction of the viral carriage at D6-post inclusion compared to controls, and much lower average carrying duration than reported in the litterature for untreated patients. Azithromycin added to hydroxychloroquine was significantly more efficient for virus elimination.

Conclusion

Despite its small sample size, our survey shows that hydroxychloroquine treatment is significantly associated with viral load reduction/disappearance in COVID-19 patients and its effect is reinforced by azithromycin.

As we know, despite the fact that the statistical analysis was done and the observed effect was considered significant enough to be published, hydroxychloroquine did not turn out to be the miracle cure we were all hoping for. Where does that leave us? Is statistical analysis not meaningful and, therefore, not to be relied upon? Was the study conducted badly? It turned out that, once scrutinized, critics found that the experimental design was flawed as the trial was not run as a double-blinded, randomized controlled trial, and therefore biases crept into the way in which cohort participants were chosen. The journal didn't originally notice the flaw, but they published a statement a few weeks after the article was published stating that: "the article does not meet the Society's expected standard."[2] Did the scientists realize this? Was it an honest mistake? Or were they, instead, manipulating the statistical tools to their advantage? Where does that leave statistical analysis altogether? The anecdote, we feel, illustrates three important issues associated with statistical analysis:

---

[2] www.isac.world/news-and-publications/official-isac-statement

- Statistical analysis is complex, and errors in its application or its interpretation are extremely common.
- Noticing such errors is not an easy feat.
- The context in which the analysis is done may matter. For example if the above study were about the role of hydroxychloroquine on some obscure disease rather than Covid, no one would have worried much about its results and the statistical analysis that went with it.

Other issues associated with statistical analysis can be summarized as follows (see Demšar (2008) and Drummond (2006) for more detail):

- Statistical analysis, even if done properly, does not guarantee that the results of a study will generalize to all cases.
- Statistical analysis can be purposely manipulated to enhance the results of a study (to get papers published and/or gain publicity).
- Statistical analysis is not an exact science: statisticians disagree on how to conduct it (e.g., frequentists versus Bayesianists; Fisher, on the one hand, and Neyman and Pearson, on the other; the use of *p*-values or not).
- If too much importance is given to statistical analysis, interesting results may never see the light of day while others are overblown.

In view of these observations, one may wonder why it is necessary to bother with statistical analysis in the first place. Without getting into any details, our stance in this book is that there is value to statistical analysis in that it can provide additional support to our observations. Indeed, we believe that much scientific progress, including the development of the Covid vaccines and their deployment, owes much to statistics, even if some of that trust is sometimes risky. Indeed, our belief comes with the understanding that statistical analysis is not sufficient to either make or break a claim. Its results are just there to provide additional information, such as to reinforce a conclusion. Consequently, we present the statistical tools that we feel are both reasonable and simple enough to use. In particular, we present three methodologies discussed in the machine learning evaluation literature, and advocate the use of two alternative approaches based on these methodologies: NHST tools enhanced by estimation statistics, and Bayesian statistics. The remainder of the section reviews the history of statistical analysis, discusses the two suggested approaches, and presents the relationship between the questions an experimenter may ask and the tools available to answer these questions.

> All the tools presented in this section are illustrated in the GitHub repository accompanying this book.

7.1.2 The History of Statistical Testing

As per Gill and Meir (1999), Cumming (2013), Nuzzo (2014), and Perezgonzalez (2015), the statistical method came into being in the following fashion. In the 1920s, Fisher (1925) introduced the operationalization of significance testing and the p-value as an informal tool to assess whether a research question was worth asking. Only if it were, would the real search for confirmation commence, and this search would use other tools. This procedure is the well-known hypothesis-testing procedure discussed in Section 4.4, where the scientist or practitioner sets up a null hypothesis (which s/he expects not be true and that is the opposite of what s/he is trying to assess). By showing that the probability of confirming the null hypothesis is low (a low p-value), Fisher suggested that the research question had passed the first test and was worth investigating further. The smaller the p-value, the higher the probability that the hypothesis is rejected. Fisher thought that $p < 0.01$ clearly showed the result to be significant and discussed follow-up experiments for p-values between 0.01 and 0.20. He emphasized that $p > 0.20$ should not be taken as evidence that the null hypothesis was true. An important aspect of Fisher's setting is that every aspect of the analysis can be done a posteriori, after the data has been collected and is ready to be analyzed.

Neyman and Pearson (1928) disagreed with Fisher's approach and proposed a different, more complex framework altogether in their search for an improvement to Fisher's framework. Instead of a hypothesis and its opposite, they considered two competing hypotheses, separated from one another to some degree recorded through the effect-size metric, which also indicates how relevant the difference between the two hypotheses is in the real world. In the Neyman–Pearson framework, however, only one hypothesis, the main hypothesis H_M, is truly estimated in the sense that only a portion of the alternative hypothesis is considered. A second big difference between Neyman–Pearson's and Fisher's frameworks is that while Fisher's analysis can be done completely a posteriori, the Neyman–Pearson framework requires that the experiment be set up ahead of time. This makes the procedure much less flexible than Fisher's, but, it is usually more powerful and better suited to industrial-level analysis. Fisher's method, on the other hand, allows for a more exploratory analysis.

Despite the differences between the two frameworks, they have been confused and combined into a new framework called *null hypothesis significance testing* (NHST), first introduced by Lindquist (1940). NHST is the procedure most often taught and used in the scientific community despite the debate surrounding it. Opposition to its use is rooted in the fact that the two approaches are incompatible and should not have been conflated. Though the tools used by both approaches may be similar, the two approaches start from different research philosophies and their results should be interpreted differently. Although teaching Fisher and Neyman–Pearson's approaches separately and advocating for the use of one or the other would be the optimal solution, Perezgonzalez (2015) recognizes that the predominance reached by NHST would be difficult to withstand. Instead, he proposes two ways to improve NHST. Depending on the person teaching or using it, NHST takes more of a Fisherian or a Neyman-Pearsonian flavor. Perezgonzalez (2015) proposes that each flavor be considered separately so then we can improve on each of them. Because the NHST's philosophy is closer to the Fisher philosophy, it is easier to improve that framework. For this reason, as well as the fact that this book is more geared toward laboratory exploratory machine learning than industry-strength machine learning deployment (although Chapter 10 does discuss industry-strength evaluation), we follow his advice on improving Fisher-leaning NHST. His suggestions for improving Neyman–Pearson-leaning NHST, however, are highly recommended for practitioners interested in testing their machine learning systems under more robust settings.

7.1.3 The Main Tenets of Improved Fisher-Flavored NHST

As already mentioned, Perezgonzalez (2015) argues that NHST is closer to Fisher's philosophy than to Neyman–Pearson's. It is therefore easiest to improve the Fisher-leaning version of NHST by adding a few useful Neyman–Pearson features than the other way around. The two recommendations he makes are:

• To add effect size calculations so that practical as well as statistical significance be considered.
• To add an estimation of the sample size expected to yield high enough power for the research to be sensitive enough to reach the expected effect size.

To these suggestions, we add that of Cumming (2013):

• To use confidence intervals that allow us to move from a dichotomous way of thinking (is there an effect or not?) to an estimation way of thinking (how much of an effect is there?).

We now describe briefly what each of these additions refer to. They will be discussed in greater detail in Section 7.3.

As previously mentioned, an important difference between the Fisher and Neyman–Pearson methods is the fact that Fisher considers only one hypothesis, the *null hypothesis*, whereas Neyman–Pearson considers two: the *main hypothesis* and the *alternative hypothesis*. The alternative hypothesis can be thought of as a second population, and the difference between the two populations (e.g., the difference between the means of the two populations, as in Cohen's *d* value) is known as the *effect size*. Also related to the alternative distribution are the notions of *type I* and *type II* errors in Neyman–Pearson's method. A type I error corresponds to the main hypothesis being wrongly rejected. A type II error corresponds to the alternative hypothesis being wrongly rejected. We denote α to be the probability of committing a type I error, and β to be the probability of committing a type II error. *Power* is related to β in that it is the probability that the main hypothesis is correctly rejected and the alternative hypothesis accepted. Given the statistical test selected, the expected effect size and the values of α and β, the sample size can be chosen a priori to ensure that the desired amount of power is attained. It is important to emphasize that power can be enhanced by increasing the sample size of a testing set. In industrial settings or other practical settings where data collection is part of the evaluation process, that is possible. In typical academic settings, however, the machine learning researcher does not control the collection of data. Instead, he or she uses preexisting datasets with a fixed sample size. Power, in such settings, is not a quantity that can be meaningfully manipulated without risking a decrease in performance due to the transfer of training samples to the testing sets. A *confidence interval*, the statistical feature suggested by Cumming (2013), indicates the range of plausible values for the estimated quantity. Any value outside that range is implausible. Any value inside the range could be the true value. The smaller the range, the more accurate the estimate. There is a clear relationship between confidence intervals and NHST. It can be described as follows (assuming that the null hypothesis stipulates that the difference of means of the two populations is zero). If the confidence interval of the null hypothesis includes 0, then 0 is a plausible value and the null hypothesis cannot be rejected. If, however, 0 lies outside the confidence interval, it is an implausible value and the null hypothesis can be rejected. This shows that confidence intervals subsume NHST since NHST can be performed using confidence intervals. Conversely, the additional information conveyed by confidence intervals gives us a greater understanding of our results than NHST alone.

There is a serious shortcoming of the frequentist approach, however, that must be mentioned. This shortcoming is present even when NHST is supplemented by estimation statistics. Specifically, a question that many machine learning researchers and practitioners would like to see answered, but that cannot be answered by the frequentist approach is: "With what probability can the null hypothesis be rejected?" This question cannot be answered because confidence and probability are different from one another and while the frequentist methodology can produce degrees of confidence, it cannot produce probabilities. Perhaps it would be useful to pause here in order to discuss the difference between confidence and probability more specifically.

Confidence versus Probability The easiest way to describe the difference between confidence and probability is to illustrate it through an example. Given a confidence interval for the mean difference in performance obtained between two classifiers and a degree of confidence for that interval (say, 95%), one can say that if one runs the same experiment 100 times, 95 times out of 100, the mean difference will fall within the confidence interval. Confidence, thus, tells us how often the experiment will return a value in a given range, but it tells us nothing about the frequency with which one will get this or that result within the range. Probability, on the other hand, is much more precise as it relates to the frequency with which each value can be obtained. In other words, the response to the question: "With what probability can one reject the null hypothesis?" requires more information than the question "With what confidence can one reject the null hypothesis?" Again, that's because the question surrounding probability requires knowledge of the actual value obtained every time one of the 100 experiments is run, instead of simply "yes" or "no," the value fell or didn't fall in the interval. As a result, one cannot estimate probabilities from NHST and Estimation Statistics alone.

An important advantage of Bayesian Analysis is that it provides probabilities and not merely confidence values. This and other features that will be discussed later are what makes Bayesian Analysis very attractive now that computers have enough power to run its analyses efficiently. That being said, the probabilities issued by Bayesian Analysis are dependent upon the choice of priors, and there is no guarantee that the priors used in the methods that will be described below are adequate.

Section 7.2 provides an extensive review of NHST-based statistical tests in all settings considered in Machine Learning. Subsequently, Section 7.3 discusses estimation statistics including effect size, confidence intervals, and power. Section 7.4, then, discusses Bayesian

Analysis. Prior to that, however, we conclude this section with a brief introduction to Bayesian analysis reasoning in Section 7.1.4 and a summary of all the tools and techniques discussed in the remainder of the chapter, along with the specific questions they answer in Section 7.1.5.

7.1.4 Bayesian Analysis

An alternative route for statistical analysis is to use Bayesian analysis. Bayesian analysis is described in simple intuitive terms in Hackenberger (2019) and is suggested as an approach for statistical analysis for machine learning by Benavoli et al. (2017).

While Bayesian statistics came into being earlier than the frequentist statistics from which NHST stems, it could not be applied rigorously until recently when efficient computer technologies and Markov chain Monte Carlo (MCMC) methods that allow the random sampling of data from probability distributions became available.

Bayesian analysis is simpler to interpret than frequentist statistics and, as Benavoli et al. (2017) argue, NHST does not answer the questions that machine learning is interested in answering while Bayesian analysis does. Indeed, what we are interested in is the probability with which we can rely on the observed difference between the classifiers that our tests show on our tasks. Benavoli et al. (2017) argue that frequentist statistics cannot answer this type of question and that the p-value does not represent this probability (see the discussion in Section 7.1.3). In Bayesian analysis, on the other hand, Benavoli et al. (2017) continue, the results we obtain are true probabilities and thus match our questions better. However, Bayesian analysis relies on the use of priors that, if unknown or not chosen carefully, could bias our results and issue unreliable probabilities. Bayesian analysis for machine learning is discussed in Section 7.4.

7.1.5 Overview of the Statistical Tools Available

We conclude this section with an overview of the tools discussed in the remainder of the chapter and the way in which these tools help answer the two essential questions (or series of related questions) experimenters seek to answer with regard to their observed results:

- **Question 1** Is the observed result representative of the truth? To what extent? How far from the truth is it?
- **Question 2** Are the observed results, if credible, of any practical value?

The first question is essential if we remember that our experiments were run on a single sample of all the possible samples that could have been extracted from the entire population. The question is thus asking: "Given that one could only use a small subset of the population, was that subset a good proxy for the truth? How confident can one be that it was? How far from the truth did we get?" It can also be thought of as asking: "If one could run the experiments on the whole population, would the same results be obtained as those obtained on the sample? How likely would it be to be so? How different would these results be from those observed on the sample?" The second question goes beyond the first one, once

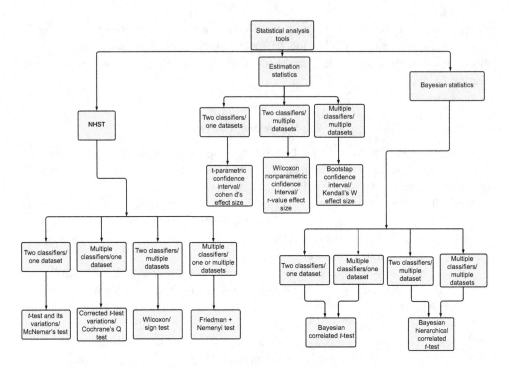

Figure 7.1 Overview of the statistical tools considered in this chapter.

it assumes that the first one was answered in the affirmative. It basically asks: "OK, so we know that what was observed is akin to what would have been observed on the entire population. Is that observation of practical significance?" For example, in the context of two classifiers, SVM and naive Bayes, tested with respect to precision, where, say, SVM performed better than naive Bayes, it asks: "Will deploying SVM on this population truly lead to more precise results, or would deploying naive Bayes be good enough given the sensitivity of the situation?"

Figure 7.1 presents an ontology of the statistical tools relevant to answer these two questions in each of the four experimental situations encountered in machine learning settings: the comparison of two classifiers on a single domain; the comparison of two classifiers on multiple domains; the comparison of multiple classifiers on one domain; and the comparison of multiple classifiers on multiple domains.

Two Classifiers/Single Domain

Question 1 Estimating whether the results are representative of the truth Question 1 can be answered partially using either a frequentist or a Bayesian approach.

Frequentist approach The first part of the question elicits a binary answer, yes or no (the results are or are not representative of the truth), and can be answered using the regular *parametric paired t-test*, or, preferably, a corrected t-test such as the 5×2 *CV t-test* (Dieterich 1998), the 5×2 *F-test* (Alpaydn 1999) test, or *corrected random subsampling*

(Nadeau and Bengio 2003). What cannot be answered using NHST is the second part of this first question: To what extent can we trust that the results are representative of the truth (or, what is the probability that the results are representative of the truth)? That subquestion cannot be answered using NHST because NHST only issues p-values, and p-values are not probabilities. NHST alone cannot answer the third subquestion either (how far the observed quantity is from the truth). The good news, though, is that that subquestion can be answered using estimation statistics. In the particular case of two classifiers compared on one domain, we can calculate the *parametric confidence interval* surrounding the difference between the classifiers used in the t-test or its variations. In addition to getting visual confirmation – if the null hypothesis was rejected – that zero lies outside the interval, we can observe the size of the interval. The smaller it is, the more confident we are that the observed difference is accurate; indeed, maybe the true difference is not the one we found, but it can't be that far from the truth, since the confidence interval is small. On the other hand, the larger the confidence interval is, the less confident we can be about the value we observed since the truth could be anywhere in that large interval.

Bayesian approach Question 1 can be answered using the *Bayesian correlated t-test*. This test has several advantages. First, it takes into consideration the correlation caused by the overlapping nature of the training sets in cross-validation or other resampling schemes, something the frequentist t-test doesn't do unless corrections such as the 5×2 CV or corrected random subsampling versions are used. Second, the Bayesian correlated t-test estimates the probability distribution function (pdf) of the posterior probability of the difference between two classifiers. This means two things: first, unlike in the frequentist method, it estimates probabilities rather than confidences; and second, it estimates *posterior* probabilities; that is, probabilities found after the experiments were run. This is also an important difference, given that the frequentist method depends on a sampling assumption made prior to running the experiments. This assumption is usually not met since usually the experimenter did not collect the data or have any say about its collection. This suggests that Bayesian analysis allows the direct answering of the first two subquestions in Question 1: "Is the observed result representative of the truth? To what extent?" Like the frequentist approach, the Bayesian approach is also able to answer the third subquestion, "How far from the truth is it?" as it provides a tool similar, in practice, to frequentist confidence intervals. That tool is called *high density intervals (HDIs)* and it summarizes the uncertainty of the estimate. However, despite all the advantages of the Bayesian method, it has one serious disadvantage, which we already mentioned in Section 7.1.4 but is worth reiterating: it requires knowledge of or an estimate of the priors on which all the calculations are based. In cases where this estimate is biased, so will the results of the statistical test.

Question 2 Estimating the practical value of the results Question 2 can also be answered using either a frequentist or a Bayesian approach.

Frequentist approach This question can be answered by calculating the effect size, once an effect has been discovered (i.e., the null hypothesis has been rejected). In the case of two classifiers compared on a single domain, the recommended effect size is *Cohen's d statistic*.

Bayesian approach Bayesian analysis comes with another tool discussed in Benavoli et al. (2017): the *region of practical equivalence (ROPE)*, which is similar to an effect size in practice. Indeed, the ROPE represents the region on the probability density function where the difference between the classifiers can be deemed irrelevant. For example, one can decide that a difference of 1% in accuracy is irrelevant and place the ROPE in the area where the difference is smaller than or equal to 1%.

Multiple Classifiers/Single Domains

The case of multiple classifiers compared on a single domain, although quite frequent in practice, is not a case that has been much discussed in the frequentist approach. Instead, the user is encouraged to use corrected or adapted versions of the tests recommended in the case of two classifiers on a single domain in the frequentist approach, and exact versions of the tests in the Bayesian approach.

Question 1 Estimating whether the results are representative of the truth Question 1 can again be answered partially using either a frequentist or a Bayesian approach:

Frequentist approach There are two approaches to answering Question 1 following the frequentist paradigm. Either the parametric tests used for the two classifiers/one domain case can be used together with a correction such as the Bonferroni correction or others. These corrections discount the type I error that accumulates as the number of comparisons (and therefore tests) grows. The idea is to make each test more stringent to decrease the chance of a type I error at each comparison. The second approach is nonparametric and consists of extending McNemar's test into the Cochran's Q test.

Bayesian approach The procedure is easier in the Bayesian case since the *Bayesian correlated t-test* can be repeated multiple times without needing any correction for multiple comparisons the way the frequentist *t*-tests do. Therefore, repetitions of the *Bayesian correlated t-test* is the recommended solution in the multiple classifier single domain case.

Question 2 Estimating the practical value of the results To answer Question 2, the procedure consists of following the steps suggested along with the frequentist or Bayesian approach chosen to answer Question 1.

Two Classifiers/Multiple Domains

Question 1 Estimating whether the results are representative of the truth Similarly to the case of two classifiers on a single domain, in the case of two classifiers on multiple domains, Question 1 can be partially answered using either a frequentist or a Bayesian approach.

Frequentist approach Using the frequentist approach, the recommended tests when multiple domains are involved are nonparametric tests. The particular nonparametric tests recommended for this setting are the *sign test* and *Wilcoxon's signed-rank test*. The sign test is a very simple test that was discussed in Chapter 4. However, it is not a very powerful test. Wilcoxon's signed-rank test is more powerful, but as with all nonparametric tests, it remains less powerful than a parametric test would be if it could be applied (which it cannot in this setting). As discussed in the two classifiers/one domain case, it is recommended to use an NHST test along with a confidence interval. Since Wilcoxon's is a nonparametric test, a nonparametric confidence interval that uses the *signed-ranks median confidence intervals* technique is recommended. Alternatively, the experimenter could also use a *bootstrap confidence interval* process to build the confidence interval.

Bayesian approach In the Bayesian approach, the recommended test is the *Bayesian hierarchical correlated t-test*, although Benavoli et al. (2017) also discuss the Bayesian sign and signed-tank test. As in the discussion in the case of two classifiers compared on one domain, the initial mean of the difference between both learners, its variance, and degree of freedom all need to be estimated based on prior information, which is an issue that is not encountered in the frequentist paradigm. The tools used to interpret the results of the test are visual or count-based. The quantities calculated are probabilities that the first classifier is better than the second, that the second is better than the first, or that the two classifiers fall in the ROPE.

Question 2 Estimating the practical value of the results As in the first setting, Question 2 can also be answered using either a frequentist or a Bayesian approach.

Frequentist approach This question can be answered by calculating the effect size, once an effect has been discovered (i.e., the null hypothesis has been rejected). In the case of two classifiers compared on multiple domains, the recommended effect size is the *rank biserial correlation coefficient (or r-value)*.

Bayesian approach As before, the **ROPE** is similar to an effect size in practice since it represents the region on the probability density function where the difference between the classifiers can be deemed irrelevant.

Multiple Classifiers/Multiple Domains

Question 1 Estimating whether the results are representative of the truth Question 1 can be partially answered using either a frequentist or a Bayesian approach.

Frequentist approach Once again, since multiple domains and multiple classifiers are involved, it is recommended to use a frequentist nonparametric test. Since in this situation multiple classifiers are involved, Wilcoxon's signed-ranked test does not apply. The recommended test is instead *Friedman's omnibus test* followed by *Nemenyi's post hoc* test.

Bayesian approach Once again, Benavoli et al. (2017) recommend the *Bayesian hierarchical correlated t-test* for this setting. (But once again, the initial mean of the difference between both learners, its variance, and degree of freedom all need to be estimated based on prior information.)

Question 2 Estimating the practical value of the results Question 2 can be partially answered using either a frequentist or a Bayesian approach.

Frequentist approach This question can be answered by calculating the effect size, once an effect has been discovered (i.e., the null hypothesis has been rejected). In the case of two classifiers compared on multiple domains, the recommended effect size is *Kendall's W test value*.

Bayesian approach As before, the **ROPE** is similar to an effect size in practice since the ROPE represents the region on the probability density function where the difference between the classifiers can be deemed irrelevant.

This concludes our introductory presentation of the chapter. The remaining sections discuss each of the tools just mentioned in great detail and provide computational implementations and illustrations in scikit-learn to accompany our discussion.

7.2 Null Hypothesis Statistical Testing

The majority of statistical tests available have been designed in the NHST framework. The number of statistical tests and their variation within this framework abounds. In this section, we will restrict ourselves to the discussion of the most appropriate such tests in the context of machine learning. In particular, we will continue our discussion of the t-test and the sign test from where we left them in Chapter 4, noting the machine learning scenarios in which they are appropriate, and introduce a number of other statistical tests appropriate for other types of situations. Matching scenarios to specific statistical tests is of the utmost importance in machine learning, especially since repeating experiments in that field is very easy. Such repetitions have the disadvantage of introducing elements of chance that, if not corrected, make it more likely than it should to reject the null hypothesis. As a result, differences may be deemed significant when they should, in fact, not. Assumptions regarding the shape of the distribution are also problematic and have led the field toward nonparametric tests for which the user does not need to make assumptions of normality in the distribution of their experimental results.

The specific NHST tests discussed in this section include the t-test, the most famous statistical test, which is a parametric test that is appropriate in the case of the comparison of two classifiers on a single domain. In particular, the version of the t-test used for that purpose is the two-matched-sample t-test and it is the version considered here. The sign test, a nonparametric test that was also discussed in Chapter 4, can be used in the context of the comparison of two classifiers on multiple domains or that of multiple classifiers on a single domain. Because the sign test is not very powerful, however, we will introduce the more powerful nonparametric Wilcoxon's signed-rank test for matched pairs. Like the sign test, it is applicable to the comparison of two classifiers on multiple domains or that of multiple classifiers on a single domain. Another nonparametric test appropriate for the case of multiple classifiers on a single domain is Cochran's Q test. Finally, we will introduce the Friedman test as well as its associated post-hoc test, Nemenyi, for the purpose of comparing multiple classifiers on multiple domains. Additionally, variants of the t-test that take resampling issues from Chapter 6 into consideration and McNemar's test, a nonparametric test, will be described in the context of comparing two classifiers on a single domain.

Note that in order to interpret the meaning of all these tests, tables must be consulted. All the tables associated with the tests discussed in this chapter have been included in Appendix A. In most cases, these tables are reproductions of Lindley and Scott (1984), though in a few cases we had to go to a different source; this will be indicated on the page containing the table. We would like to note that all the tables obtained from Lindley and Scott (1984) list values corresponding to the one-sided test (meaning that for a two-sided test, the p-values corresponding to these values need to be multiplied by two). Also, it is important to note that the p-values shown are the actual p-values multiplied by 100 (this was done to make the connection to the confidence level in percentages clear). So, when looking in the column corresponding to $p = 5$, for example, one is actually looking at the case of a p-value of 0.05.

Lastly, the list that we present along with the tests we discuss in this chapter is not exhaustive, but is representative of what can be employed in a given scenario. Moreover, with regard to comparing two classifiers on a single domain, a dependency on the error estimation technique used has been discovered by Dietterich (1998), among others, who propose modified versions of some tests that can be applied over multiple runs of simple resampling schemes for error estimation. We haven't included these methods explicitly in Figure 7.1, but they will be discussed in Section 7.2.1. They differ from the parametric tests used for comparing two classifiers on a single domain although their basic principle is similar. The main difference between these two families of methods lies in the manner in which the estimates of classifier performance are obtained.

7.2.1 Comparing Two Classifiers on a Single Domain

This section presents statistical hypothesis tests that are useful for the case where two classifiers are tested on a single domain. The main test used in this case is the well-known two-matched-samples t-test already discussed in Chapter 4. Following the resampling constraints discussed in Chapter 6, the t-test has been extended to take these constraints into consideration. This led to a number of variants that we discuss in this section. The t-test and its variants are parametric tests. For the case where parametric assumptions do not hold, we introduce a nonparametric alternative applicable to the two-classifier/one-domain situation: McNemar's test. Though McNemar's test has not been used very often in the machine learning literature, it is a powerful tool worth considering.

Since Chapter 4 already discussed the t-test, this section focuses on its major shortcomings and what has been done to address them. There are two categories of shortcomings. The first category pertains to the fact that a number of assumptions needs to be verified prior to applying the t-test. That is true no matter what scientific field the t-test is applied in. The second category pertains to issues specific to machine learning. In particular, it relates to the fact that the training sets used in each repetition of our experiments typically overlap. We begin by discussing the first category of issues and then move to the second, where we present variations of the t-test that are useful in machine learning.

Prior to delving into these considerations, we recall that the t-test comes in various flavors. However, the most relevant version in the machine learning context is the two-matched-sample version with unknown variances that we focused on in Chapter 4. The two-matched-sample version with unknown variances is the most relevant because machine learning experiments typically consist of comparing the performance of different algorithms on datasets and that the datasets are fully available to the experimenters who are able to design their experiments so that each algorithm is trained and tested on the same subsamples. This intuitively fairer comparison scheme allows machine learning practitioners to use the two-matched-sample version of the more general Welch's t-test that is also applicable in the case of two independent samples. For a more complete description of the t-test family, please refer to statistical textbooks such as Howell (2020) and StatSoft (2006). Since Section 4.4 discussed the t-test in detail and illustrated it with an example, there is no need to repeat the discussion here. Instead, we focus on how to use this powerful tool or its variations appropriately.

The Three Basic Assumptions of the t-Test

As illustrated in the example of Section 4.4, the t-test is quite easy to use. However, an important, though often overlooked, issue is that it relies on three basic assumptions that must all be verified for the test's results to be valid. Unfortunately, these do not automatically hold. The assumptions are:

- **Normality or pseudonormality** The t-test requires that the data on which the t-test is applied be a normally distributed population. The t-test is, fortunately enough, quite robust to this assumption when k-fold cross-validation is used and the size of each testing fold is large enough.[3]
- **Randomness of the samples** The t-test assumes that the samples from which the means are estimated are representative of the underlying population. Since the samples are obtained from the application of a classifier to data instances, this assumption implicitly makes it imperative that the instances in the testing set be randomly chosen from their underlying, even though arbitrary, distribution. This is necessary since the t-test relies on sample statistics such as the mean and standard deviation with the assumption that these are unbiased estimates of the population parameters. When using k-fold cross-validation, the subdivision into k folds is done randomly, so this condition is usually verified.
- **Equal variances of the populations** The paired t-test assumes that the two samples come from populations with equal variance. This is necessary since we use the sample information to estimate the entire population's standard deviation.

As just discussed, the pseudonormality of the means obtained by k-fold cross-validation can be assumed if the folds contain at least 30 samples. This is very easy to verify. For example, if using 10-fold cross-validation, the training set should contain at least 300 instances in order for each testing fold to contain 30 instances. Datasets, especially more recent ones, often contain many more than 300 instances, so this requirement is often easy to satisfy.

---

[3] The central limit theorem guarantees a normal distribution of the sample means when the samples are sufficiently large. The sample size requirement of 30 is widely found in the literature as a minimum required for this sample size. This number comes from a wide number of simulation studies that show how various distributions can converge to a normal distribution with increasing sample sizes and is used as an empirical guide.

The second assumption is usually difficult for machine learning researchers to verify for the simple reason that they are typically not the people who gathered the data used for learning and testing. They must, thus, trust that the people responsible for this task built truly random and representative datasets, and try to gather enough information about the dataset construction process to pass their own judgement. There are cases, however, when true randomness is difficult to achieve, and this trust can be problematic. Note that, by randomness, we mean choosing the samples in an independently and identically distributed (i.i.d.) manner. This does not mean making an assumption about the data distribution. The data can come from any arbitrary distribution. However, the assumption is based on the notion of i.i.d. sampling from this distribution, which is indeed hard to verify. What can be said, on the other hand, is that once the dataset is created, if k-fold cross-validation is applied, then since the creation of folds is random, from there on the process is random. Therefore, as long as the construction of the dataset followed appropriate rules, the second assumption should be verified.

The third assumption could be verified either by observing the calculated variances or by plotting the two populations (the measures on which the t-test is to be applied) and visually deciding whether they do indeed have (almost) equal variance. Alternatively, the similarity of variances can be tested using the F-test, Bartlett's test, Levene's test, or the Brown–Forsythe test. Again, these can be found in many statistics texts.

Overlapping Training Sets

As previously mentioned, new versions of the t-test focused on machine learning practice have been designed to take into consideration further aspects of the distributional assumption. In particular, these t-test versions take into consideration the overlap in training data that necessarily takes place in k-fold cross-validation, unless $k = 2$. These t-test versions include the *2-fold resampled matched pair t-test* proposed by Dietterich (1998), its improvement known as the *5 × 2 CV F-test* by Alpaydn (1999), and the *corrected resampled t-test* by Nadeau and Bengio (2003), as well as 10×10-fold cross-validation variations proposed by Bouckaert (2003, 2004). These are discussed next.

A discussion of the issues Dietterich (1998) was the first to discuss the specific machine learning shortcomings of the t-test that go beyond the classical considerations already discussed. While he considers that McNemar's test may be a good alternative to the t-test, he notes that, first, McNemar's test applies only under the condition where the number of disagreements between the two classifiers is large, and second, there are other subtle design issues involved that affect the distributional assumptions. The *resampled matched pair t-test* that was illustrated in Chapter 4 used cross-validated runs to create each testing set subsequently used in the t-test. As required by the t-test, each (cross-validated) testing set is independent of the other. However, it is important to note that while the testing sets are independent, the training sets are not since each cross-validated run involves the use overlapping training sets. Hence, even though cross-validation has an advantage in the sense that in each fold a high number of examples relative to the dataset size are available for training, the overlapping training sets bias the resulting classifiers. This effect, popularly known as correlated measurements (since each classifier is obtained on correlated sets instead of independent ones) is further aggravated when multiple trials are performed over these cross-validated runs. As a result, the version of the t-test discussed thus far is likely to show a very high type I error probability. Another version, known as the 2-*fold resampled matched pair t-test*, divides the dataset into a training set and a test set. At each trial, the algorithms to be compared are first trained on the training set and then tested on the test set. The roles of the two sets are reversed in the second fold. As a result of a single training and testing (and hence no overlaps) in *individual trials*, this method results in relatively less bias and type I error probabilities. However, the issues of overlapping datasets for both training and testing across trials combined with difficulties in estimating the variances across overlapping sets still figure in this design since, in order to be effective, the 2-fold test is typically repeated multiple times. The main issue in any cross-validated experiment is the problem of estimating the variance of the performance across folds. The overlapping training sets in such cases generally result in an underestimation of this variance. This consequently results in a high probability of type I error. This problem becomes more serious when multiple trials are involved. On the other hand, cross-validation results in larger training sets, rendering the tests more powerful. This is quite beneficial in case of limited training data availability. In the limit, a t-test design over a single trial, known as the *cross-validated t-test* (the version used in the Labor Relations dataset example of Chapter 2), is considered the most powerful as a result of high training set sizes. Here, a trial is replaced by a performance measure calculation over each individual fold in the cross-validation. The rest of the calculation follows accordingly. However, this also suffers with a high type I error probability. A tradeoff between the number of trials and the number of folds in each trial has been proposed empirically by Dietterich (1998), who limits the number of trials to five and uses a 2-fold cross-validation in each trial, resulting in the 5×2 CV t-test. The 5×2 CV t-test was further improved by Alpaydn (1999) who proposes a 5×2 CV F-test that has still higher power and a lower type I error probability. In order to deal with the underestimation of variance even better in the cross-validation experiments, Nadeau and Bengio (2003) proposed a corrected resampled t-test, a version of the 2-fold resampled matched pair t-test that incorporates the overlap into the variance estimation. In an interesting recent study, Stapor et al. (2021) found out that the way in which the folds were created could affect the outcome of the statistical test, especially in the presence of class imbalances, and that there were many chances for the outcome of the test to be wrong. This phenomenon seemed to be mitigated, at least to a certain extent, by the use of corrected t-tests over the use of the traditional t-test.

We now discuss these tests starting with those based on repetitions of random subsampling and moving on to those that use repeated k-fold cross-validation schemes.

Random subsampling   Dietterich (1998) describes the resampled paired t-test as a test in which several trials n (usually, $n = 30$) are conducted that each randomly divide the dataset into a training set, usually containing two-thirds of the data and a testing set containing the remaining cases. He devised a hypothesis test following this resampling technique, as follows.[4]

---

[4]   The random subsampling scheme was discussed in Chapter 6. Here, we focus on the ensuing t-test.

This test consists of performing n trials by splitting the dataset S into a training set S_{train} and S_{test}. Each time a classifier is obtained on S_{train} and tested on S_{test}. Let the performance of the two learning algorithms A_1 and A_2 to be compared on the set S_{test}^i, the test set on the ith of the N trials, be $pm_{f_{1_i}}^i$ and $pm_{f_{2_i}}^i$, where f_{1_i} and f_{2_i} are the classifiers obtained from algorithms A_1 and A_2, respectively, by learning on S_{train}^i during trial i. Hence, the difference in the average performance of the learning algorithms is

$$d_i = pm_{f_{1_i}}^i - pm_{f_{2_i}}^i.$$

The average difference is

$$\bar{d} = \frac{1}{n} \sum_{i=1}^{n} d_i,$$

and the t-statistic to be computed is the same as before,

$$t = \frac{\bar{d} \cdot \sqrt{n}}{s},$$

with

$$s = \sqrt{\frac{\sum_{i=1}^{n} (d_i - \bar{d})^2}{n-1}}.$$

The degree of freedom is $n-1$, so for a significance level $s = 0.025$, the null hypothesis can be rejected if $|t| > t_{n-1,0.975}$. For a typical $n = 30$, the threshold is $t_{29,0.975} = 2.04523$.

Dietterich (1998) notes that there are two issues with this approach: first the d_i's do not have a normal distribution, and second, they are not independent. The first issue relates to the fact that the training sets overlap, thus leading to $pm_{f_{1_i}}^i$'s and $pm_{f_{2_i}}^i$'s that are not independent; and the second issue relates to the fact that the testing sets overlap. As a result, this test shows a high probability of type I error, which actually increases as the number of trials increases.

We do not illustrate this test in the GitHub repository since it is not a reliable test.

Corrected random subsampling In order to address the shortcomings of random subsampling, Nadeau and Bengio (2003) proposed the corrected version of this test with reasoning that the high type I error observed in the original version is caused as a consequence of an underestimation of the variance due to overlapping samples. This was also noted by Bouckaert (2003). They correct the variance estimate by multiplying it by $\frac{1}{n} + \frac{|S_{train}|}{|S_{test}|}$ instead of $\frac{1}{n-1}$ (the quantity used to get an unbiased estimate of variance) with n being the number of trials, and $|S_{train}| = |S_{train}^i|$ and $|S_{test}| = |S_{test}^i|$ for all $i \in \{1, \ldots, n\}$.

Hence, the corrected version of the t-statistic becomes

$$t = \frac{\bar{d}.\sqrt{n}}{\sqrt{\left(\frac{1}{n} + \frac{|S_{train}|}{|S_{test}|}\right) \sum_{i=1}^{n} (d_i - \bar{d})^2}}.$$

174 *Statistical Analysis*

In their experiments, Nadeau and Bengio (2003) show that the corrected resampled t-test has an acceptable probability of type I error and has much better power than the cross-validated t-test, simple resampled t-test, and Dietterich's 5×2 CV, described next.

We illustrate this test in the GitHub repository using an implementation called corrected_dependent_ttest.[5]

The 5×2 CV test for comparing two classifiers In addition to the underestimation of the variance caused by training set overlaps, it has been observed that the k-fold cross-validated resampling scheme does not always estimate the mean of the difference between two learning algorithms properly. Dietterich's (1998) investigations led him to conclude that the difference between the two algorithms at a single fold of the process behaves better than the mean of these differences at each fold. He thus proposed a new estimate that makes use of this observation: the 5×2 CV estimate. The test consists of five repetitions of 2-fold cross-validation. As previously explained, in 2-fold cross-validation, the data is split at random into two sets of approximately the same size. A learning algorithm is trained on one set and tested on the other, and the process is repeated after exchanging the roles of each subset. The two estimates obtained from this procedure are averaged together.

In this method, five runs are conducted, dividing the dataset S randomly into S_{train} and S_{test} each time. Let the sets obtained in trial i be denoted by S_{train}^i and S_{test}^i. Moreover, two sets of estimates are obtained for each learning algorithm's performance. A classifier, say, $f_{1_{i1}}$, is obtained by training the algorithm A_1 on the set S_{train}^i of trial i. This yields a performance measure $pm(f_{1_{i1}})$ when tested on S_{test}^i. Similarly, the performance estimate $pm(f_{1_{i2}})$ is obtained when the algorithm A_1 is trained on S_{test}^i to yield the classifier $f_{1_{i2}}$, which is then tested on the set S_{train}^i. Similarly, for algorithm A_2, the performance measures $pm(f_{2_{i1}})$ and $pm(f_{2_{i2}})$ are obtained. Thus, in each of the five trials, a 2-fold cross-validation is performed.

Next, for each trial the two differences are calculated as

$$d_i^{(1)} = pm(f_{1_{i1}}) - pm(f_{2_{i1}}),$$
$$d_i^{(2)} = pm(f_{1_{i2}}) - pm(f_{2_{i2}}).$$

Next, an estimate of the variance is obtained as

$$s_i^2 = \left(d_i^{(1)} - \bar{d}_i\right)^2 + \left(d_i^{(2)} - \bar{d}_i\right)^2,$$

where

$$\bar{d}_i = \frac{d_i^{(1)} + d_i^{(2)}}{2}.$$

Finally, the following statistic is estimated:

$$\tilde{t} = \frac{d_1^{(1)}}{\sqrt{\frac{1}{5}\sum_{i=1}^{5} s_i^2}}.$$

[5] See https://gist.github.com/jensdebruijn/13e8eeda85eb8644ac2a4ac4c3b8e732.

Dietterich (1998) shows that under the null hypothesis, $\tilde{t}$ follows a t-distribution with five degrees of freedom. The null hypothesis is, hence, rejected by a t-table lookup (Appendix A.2) when $\tilde{t} > t$ for the desired level of significance.

Dietterich's (1998) experiments with this new test showed that its probability of issuing a type I error is lower than the k-fold CV paired t-tests, but the 5×2 CV t-test has less power than the k-fold CV paired t-test.

We illustrate this test in the GitHub repository using an implementation called Paired_ttest_5x2cv.

The 5×2 CV F-test Alpaydn (1999) noticed that the 5×2 CV test proposed by Dietterich (1998) has one deficiency: it is dependent on the $d_1^{(1)}$ chosen for the test. In fact, he ran experiments using other differences and showed that the test did not behave uniformly in such cases. In other words, the hypothesis was sometimes accepted and sometimes rejected. He surmised that a test should not depend on a random choice, and proposed a more robust version of Dietterich's test. His test is defined as

$$f = \frac{\sum_{i=1}^{5} \sum_{j=1}^{2} \left(d_i^{(j)}\right)^2}{2 \sum_{i=1}^{5} s_i^2}.$$

This test is approximately F-distributed with 10 and 5 degrees of freedom (use the tables in Appendix A.6).

Experimental results suggest that the 5×2 CV F-test has a lower chance of making a type I error than the 5×2 CV t-test and is more powerful. The test, however, was not compared to the k-fold cross-validated paired t-test.

We illustrate this test in the GitHub repository using an implementation called combined_ftest_5x2cv.

The $r \times k$ CV test The 5×2 CV t-test is a special case of the general $r \times k$ cross-validation approach. In such an approach, r runs of a k-fold cross-validation are performed on a given dataset for the two algorithms, and the empirical difference of their performance, along with its statistical significance are studied. Increasing the number of runs as well as folds, depending upon the dataset size, can help in addressing issues such as replicability. Indeed, Bouckaert (2003, 2004) studied the 5×2 CV test with an emphasis on replicability and found the method wanting. He proposed a version with $r = k = 10$. We first describe the method in its general form and then focus on the specific strengths and limitations of different versions of 10×10 cross-validated tests.

Let d_{ij} represent the difference in performance of the classifiers obtained from algorithms A_1 and A_2 on the test set represented by the ith fold in the jth run such that $1 \leq i \leq 10$ and $1 \leq j \leq 10$. Note that although we are only discussing the case of 10 runs and 10 folds, this strategy could be applied to any number of runs and folds, and r and k do not need to be equal. The technique is, hence, described in the general setting.

For r runs of k-fold cross-validation, we can obtain the average difference of the empirical error estimates as

$$\overline{d} = \frac{1}{k} \sum_{i=1}^{k} \frac{1}{r} \sum_{j=1}^{r} d_{ij}.$$

Note that the average difference $\overline{d}$ is basically an extension of the 5×2 CV version. However, estimating the variance is not straightforward since its estimate can be affected by the different manners in which the averages over fold and over runs can be obtained. Four main ways, among others, have been suggested to be relevant in obtaining variance estimates in these settings:

1. *Use all the data* This scheme obtains a variance estimate over all the folds and all the runs as

$$\hat{\sigma}^2 = \frac{\sum_{i=1}^{k} \sum_{j=1}^{r} (d_{ij} - \overline{d})^2}{k\dot{r} - 1}.$$

2. *Average over folds* In this scheme, the overall performance of the two algorithms averaged over the folds of a single k-fold cross-validation run is taken into account:

$$\hat{\sigma}^2 = \frac{\sum_{j=1}^{r} (d_{.j} - \overline{d})^2}{r - 1},$$

   where $d_{.j}$ is marginalized over the folds; that is, $d_{.j} = \frac{1}{k} \sum_{i=1}^{k} d_{ij}$.

3. *Average over runs* This scheme is analogous to *average over folds* except that the estimates over the same folds across all the runs are obtained:

$$\hat{\sigma}^2 = \frac{\sum_{i=1}^{k} (d_{i.} - \overline{d})^2}{k - 1},$$

   where $d_{i.}$ is defined as $\frac{1}{r} \sum_{j=1}^{r} d_{ij}$.

4. *Average over sorted runs* This scheme is similar to *average over runs* except for the fact that before averaging on each fold over all the runs, the estimates of k-folds in every single run are sorted in ascending order. Let $d_{o(i).}$ denote the averaged difference over all the runs for the ith fold after the ordering has been obtained by sorting the folds in each run. Hence, this averages the fold with the ith lowest performance in each run. Then, the variance is obtained as

$$\hat{\sigma}^2 = \frac{\sum_{i=1}^{k} (d_{o(i).} - \overline{d})^2}{k - 1}.$$

Based on the variance obtained from any of the above methods, a Z-score can be computed as

$$Z = \frac{\overline{d} \cdot \sqrt{f_d + 1}}{\sigma},$$

where f_d denotes the degrees of freedom, which is $k \cdot r - 1$ for the *use all data* scheme, $r - 1$ for *average over folds*, and $k - 1$ for both the *average over runs* and *average over sorted runs* schemes.

The 10×10 CV test Bouckaert (2003) investigated the above-mentioned four variations in the context of variance estimation in the case where $r = k = 10$ in an attempt to establish its reliability. Other variations were also considered but turned out to be either similar or less appropriate, in practice, than these four.

In the *use all data scheme* a degree of freedom $k \cdot r - 1$ would give $f_d = 99$. However, Bouckaert (2004) suggests the use of a calibrated paired t-test with $f_d = 10$ instead of 99 due to the fact that this choice shows excellent replicability. All the versions of the 10×10 CV tests typically do not yield a higher expected probability of type I errors than predicted for the experiments, although their type I error is higher than that of simple 10-fold cross-validation. However, the 10×10 CV scheme was shown to have as much, and often more power. Based on the empirical observations, a 10×10 CV method with the *use all data* scheme for variance estimation with $f_d = 10$ seems more appropriate when the aim is to have a test with high power rather than a low type I error. When replicability is important though, a 10×10 CV with the *average over sorted runs* scheme for variance estimation seems more suitable.

We illustrate the 10×10 test (use all data scheme) in the GitHub repository using our own implementation.

McNemar's Test

The t-test and its variations, as described in this section, are *parametric* tests because they make assumptions about the distribution over the performance measures. In particular, they assume that the distribution of the performance measures are normal or pseudo-normal. Let us now discuss a *nonparametric* alternative, McNemar's test, that does not make such assumptions. This test is generally applied to compare the classification errors of two classifiers. However, it can be customized to any monotonic measure of performance of classifiers.

We first divide the sample into a training set S and a test set T (just as in the case of the holdout method). Consider two learning algorithms A_1 and A_2 that yield the classifiers f_1 and f_2, respectively, on a training set S. We then test these classifiers on T and compute the McNemar contingency matrix $\mathcal{C}_{Mc}(f_1, f_2)$ as shown in Table 7.1, where

$$c_{00}^{Mc} = \sum_{i=1}^{|T|} [I(f_1(\mathbf{x}_i) \neq y_i) \wedge I(f_2(\mathbf{x}_i) \neq y_i)],$$

$$c_{01}^{Mc} = \sum_{i=1}^{|T|} [I(f_1(\mathbf{x}_i) \neq y_i) \wedge I(f_2(\mathbf{x}_i) = y_i)],$$

Table 7.1. *McNemar's contingency matrix of classifiers f_1 and f_2.*

		Classifier f_2	
		0	1
Classifier f_1	0	c_{00}^{MC}	c_{01}^{MC}
	1	c_{10}^{MC}	c_{11}^{MC}

$$c_{10}^{Mc} = \sum_{i=1}^{|T|} [I(f_1(\mathbf{x}_i) = y_i) \wedge I(f_2(\mathbf{x}_i) \neq y_i)],$$

and

$$c_{11}^{Mc} = \sum_{i=1}^{|T|} [I(f_1(\mathbf{x}_i) = y_i) \wedge I(f_2(\mathbf{x}_i) = y_i)],$$

with the rest of the notations as before.

That is, c_{00}^{Mc} denotes the number of examples in T misclassified by both f_1 and f_2; c_{01}^{Mc} denotes the number of examples in T that are misclassified by f_1 but correctly classified by f_2; c_{10}^{Mc} denotes the number of examples in T that are misclassified by f_2 but correctly classified by f_1; and c_{11}^{Mc} denotes the number of examples in T that are classified correctly by both f_1 and f_2.

The null hypothesis assumes that both f_1 and f_2 have the same performance and, hence, the same error rates. That is, $c_{01}^{Mc} = c_{10}^{Mc} = c_{null}^{Mc}$. The next step is to compute the following statistic that is approximately distributed as χ^2:

$$\chi_{McNemar}^2 = \frac{(|c_{01}^{Mc} - c_{10}^{Mc}| - 1)^2}{c_{01}^{Mc} + c_{10}^{Mc}}.$$

The $\chi_{McNemar}^2$ is then looked up against the table of χ^2 distribution values (see Appendix A.3) and the null hypothesis is rejected if the obtained χ^2 value exceeds the one in the table for the desired level of significance.

The $\chi_{McNemar}^2$ basically tests the goodness of fit that compares the observed counts to the expected distribution of counts if the null hypothesis holds. If this statistic is larger than $\chi_{1,1-\alpha}^2$, then we reject the null hypothesis with α significance level, or $1-\alpha$ confidence. For example, if the observed $\chi_{McNemar}^2$ is larger than $\chi_{1,0.05}^2 = 3.841$ (see the table in Appendix A.3) then we can reject the null hypothesis with 95% confidence, or .05 significance level, and thus conclude that the classifiers f_1 and f_2 have error rates that are statistically significantly different.

Note that if c_{01}^{Mc} and/or c_{10}^{Mc} are small ($c_{01}^{Mc} + c_{10}^{Mc} < 20$) then McNemar's statistic is not approximated by the chi-square distribution but should rather be approximated using a binomial distribution. Specialized χ^2 tables are available for McNemar's test that use this approximation when the size of $c_{01}^{Mc} + c_{10}^{Mc}$ diagonal in the contingency matrix is small.

We illustrate McNemar's test in the GitHub repository using mlxtend.evaluate.mcnemar_table and mlxtend.evaluate.mcnemar.

7.2.2 Comparing Multiple Classifiers on a Single Domain

The question of how to compare multiple classifiers on a single domain is not often raised in the literature despite the fact that the problem comes back often and the researcher or practitioner is left resourceless. In this section, we consider two ways to approach the problem: a parametric and a nonparametric approach. The parametric approach consists of using one of the t-test variations discussed in Section 7.2.1 on all possible pairs of classifiers, but to correct the test to account for the multiplicity of comparisons. The nonparametric approach consists of using an extension of McNemar's test, Cochran's Q test for comparing multiple classifiers (Kuncheva 2014).[6]

A Parametric Approach: Correction for the FWER

It is well known that performing pairwise comparisons has a drawback: as the number of comparisons increases, so does the probability of making a type I error; that is, of erroneously rejecting the null hypothesis of one of these tests. Since the number of pairwise comparisons increases quickly as the number of classifiers are added, even if only a single domain is being considered, the chance of committing a type I error does too. For example, if you decided to use the traditional α level of 0.05 and wanted to test 10 different classifiers on a given domain, the number of pairwise comparisons ($n \times (n-1)/2$), and therefore statistical tests, would be 45, and all of a sudden, $.05 \times 45 = 2.25$ of the rejected null hypotheses on these 45 tests would be expected to be unwarranted. Moving to a comparison of 15 classifiers would raise the number of wrongly rejected null hypotheses to $\frac{15 \times 14}{2} \times 0.05 = 5.25$, and the number would keep on increasing as the number of classifiers (or classifiers tuned in different ways) were added to the comparison. The increase in the probability of making a type I error is commonly known as the family wise error rate (FWER).

The simplest method proposed to correct for the FWER is Bonferroni's correction for multiple comparisons (Salzberg 1997). The correction attempts to address the issue by using a tighter scaling of the t-statistic. In particular, instead of rejecting the null hypothesis if $t \leq \alpha$, we reject it if $t \leq \frac{\alpha}{m}$, where m represents the number of tests. For example, in the situation where 10 classifiers are compared on a single domain, 45 pairwise statistical tests are needed, so instead of rejecting the hypothesis for each test at α level 0.05, we would need to do so at level $\frac{0.05}{45} = 0.0011$. Bonferroni's correction is known to be extremely conservative and, therefore, other methods have been proposed including the Bonferroni–Dunn test, Holm's method, Tukey's test, and many more. García and Herrera (2008) discuss some of these methods and present a study in the context of machine learning experiments. A study and comparison of the different approaches for dealing with multiple pairwise comparisons in the broader context (i.e., not machine learning) is presented in Midway et al. (2020).

---

[6] We thank Nicolas Cloutier for pointing this test out to us.

We discuss the Bonferroni correction in the GitHub repository with an example where four
classifiers (decision tree, logistic regression, random forest and SVM) are compared on the Labor
Relations dataset.

A Nonparametric Approach: Cochran's Q Test

Cochran's Q test is a nonparametric test that can be thought of as an extension of McNemar's test (discussed in Section 7.2.1). In Cochran's Q test, the Q-statistics for L classifiers
compared on a single domain, Q_C, is computed as

$$Q_C = (L - 1) \times \frac{L \times \sum_{i=1}^{L}(G_i)^2 - T^2}{L \times T - \sum_{j=1}^{N}(L_j)^2},$$

where G_i is the number of instances out of N testing instances correctly classified by one
classifier ($i = 1$), two classifiers ($i = 2$), ..., L classifiers ($i = L$); L_j is the number of
classifiers that classified instance z_j correctly (where $j = 1$ to N, with N representing the
size of the testing set); and T represents the total number of correct votes by the L classifiers.
In other words,

$$T = \sum_{i=1}^{L}(G_i) = \sum_{j=1}^{N}(L_j).$$

We reject the hypothesis, at significance level α, that all the classifiers compared perform
similarly if Q_C is larger than the critical value listed in the χ^2 table of Appendix A.3 for
degree of freedom $L - 1$ and significance α. If the null hypothesis is rejected, pairwise
McNemar tests with a Bonferroni correction can subsequently be used to determine which
pairs perform differently. Rashka (2014) provides a practical example of the application of
this test.[7]

We illustrate Cochran's Q test in the GitHub repository using mlxtend.evaluate.cochrans_q. We
also show, through an example, that Cochran's Q test is a generalization of McNemar's test.

7.2.3 Comparing Two Classifiers on Multiple Domains

The simplest approach to comparing two classifiers on multiple domains is to use the sign
test that was introduced in Section 4.4.2 or Wilcoxon's signed-rank test.

The Sign Test

The sign test is appropriate for the comparison of two classifiers and multiple domains;
however, it is generally too weak to be helpful. Therefore, we present the Wilcoxon signed-
rank test, which is the most appropriate alternative within the NHST context. It is important

---

[7] See http://rasbt.github.io/mlxtend/user_guide/evaluate/cochrans_q/.

to note that although Wilcoxon's signed-rank test is very easy to apply and quite practical, it is not as powerful a test as those that apply corrected p-values as discussed in García and Herrera (2008) that should be considered as an alternative to the procedure described in the next section.

Wilcoxon's Signed-Rank Test

The Wilcoxon's signed-rank test for matched pairs (for paired scores) abides by the following logic:

Given the same population tested under different circumstances $C1$ and $C2$, if there is improvement in $C2$, then most of the results recorded in $C2$ will be greater (better) than those recorded in $C1$ and those that are not greater will be smaller by only a small amount.

Also known as Wilcoxon's T test, this test is useful when a comparison is to be made between two circumstances $C1$ and $C2$ under which a common population is tested.[8] We will denote the T statistic for Wilcoxon's test as T_{wilcox} to avoid ambiguity with the usage of T for a test set.

We describe Wilcoxon's T test using the same convention as we used in the t-test. Let us consider two classifiers, f_1 and f_2, and the two conditions corresponding to their performance measures, $pm(f_1)$ and $pm(f_2)$, respectively. The procedure is as follows:

- For each trial $i, i \in \{1, 2, \ldots, n\}$, we calculate the difference in performance measures of the two classifiers $d_i = pm_i(f_2) - pm_i(f_1)$, where the subscript i denotes the corresponding quantity for the ith trial.
- We rank all the absolute values of d_i. That is, we rank $|d_i|$. In case of ties, we assign average ranks to each tied d_i.
- Next, we calculate the sums of ranks

$$W_{s1} = \sum_{i=1}^{n} I(d_i > 0) rank(d_i)$$

and

$$W_{s2} = \sum_{i=1}^{n} I(d_i < 0) rank(d_i).$$

- Assuming that there are r differences whose values are zero, there are two approaches to dealing with this issue. The first is to ignore these differences, in which case n takes on the new value of $n - r$. And all the further calculations follow in the same manner, as previously stated. Another approach is to split the ranks of these r zero-valued differences between W_{s1} and W_{s2} equally. In case r is odd, we just ignore one of the zero-valued differences. Hence, in this case, n retains its original value (except when r is odd where $n = n - 1$). The W_{s1} and W_{s2} are defined as

---

[8] In the machine learning context, the two circumstances tested over a common population correspond to testing the performance of two classifiers over a common population of datasets.

$$W_{s1} = \sum_{i=1}^{n} I(d_i > 0)rank(d_i) + \frac{1}{2}\sum_{i=1}^{n} I(d_i = 0)rank(d_i)$$

and

$$W_{s2} = \sum_{i=1}^{n} I(d_i < 0)rank(d_i) + \frac{1}{2}\sum_{i=1}^{n} I(d_i = 0)rank(d_i).$$

- Next, a T_{wilcox} statistic is calculated as $T_{wilcox} = min(W_{s1}, W_{s2})$.
- In case of smaller n ($n \leq 25$), exact critical values of T can be looked up from the tabulated critical values of T_{wilcox} to verify if the null hypothesis can be rejected.
- In case of larger n, the T_{wilcox} distribution can be approximated normally. We compute the following z-statistic as

$$z_{wilcox} = \frac{T_{wilcox} - \mu_{T_{wilcox}}}{\sigma_{T_{wilcox}}},$$

where $\mu_{T_{wilcox}}$ is the mean of the normal approximation of the distribution of T_{wilcox} when the null hypothesis holds,

$$\mu_{T_{wilcox}} = \frac{n(n+1)}{4},$$

and $\sigma_{T_{wilcox}}$ is the standard deviation of normally approximated T_{wilcox} when the null hypothesis holds,

$$\sigma_{T_{wilcox}} = \sqrt{\frac{n(n+1)(2n+1)}{24}}.$$

- Next, we look up the table for normal distribution to assess if the null hypothesis can be rejected for the desired significance level.
- In both cases (small and large n), the null hypothesis is rejected if T_{wilcox} is smaller than the critical values listed for n and the appropriate significance test considered in the respective tables.

Let us now illustrate this test with a hypothetical example that assumes that classifiers A, B, and C obtain the accuracy results shown in Table 7.2 on domains 1 to 10 (we assume further that each entry in the table is the result of 10-fold cross-validation). The table contains more results than needed to illustrate Wilcoxon's signed-rank test, but the extra results are needed to illustrate the tests in Section 7.2.4. For the Wilcoxon's signed-rank test, since the test can only compare two classifiers on multiple domains, we choose two classifiers from Table 7.2, namely classifiers A and C. The details of the test are illustrated in Table 7.3, where the first two columns represent the accuracy obtained by classifiers A and C, respectively, but divided by 100 in order to obtain accuracy rates in the [0, 1] interval. The next column represents their difference and the column after that represents the absolute value of their difference. These absolute values are ranked in increasing order in the next column

Table 7.2. *Sample accuracy results for Classifiers A, B,*
and C on 10 domains.

Domain	Classifier A	Classifier B	Classifier C
1	85.83	75.86	84.19
2	85.91	73.18	85.90
3	86.12	69.08	83.83
4	85.82	74.05	85.11
5	86.28	74.71	86.38
6	86.42	65.90	81.20
7	85.91	76.25	86.38
8	86.10	75.10	86.75
9	85.95	70.50	88.03
10	86.12	73.95	87.18

Table 7.3. *Illustration of Wilcoxon's signed-rank test on a hypothetical example.*

Domain No.	A Accuracy	C Accuracy	A−C	|A−C|	Ranks(|A−C|)	± Ranks(|A−C|)
1	.858	.842	+.016	.016	6	+6
2	.859	.859	0	0	remove	remove
3	.861	.838	+.023	.023	8	+8
4	.858	.851	+.007	.007	3.5	+3.5
5	.863	.864	−.002	.002	1	−1
6	.864	.812	+.052	.052	9	+9
7	.859	.864	−.005	.005	2	−2
8	.861	.868	−.007	.007	3.5	−3.5
9	.860	.880	−.02	.02	7	−7
10	.861	.872	−.011	.011	5	−5

and the sign of the difference is grafted onto the rank in the last column. The sum of signed-ranks is then computed, yielding the values of $W_{S1} = 26.5$ and $W_{S2} = 18.5$. According to the algorithm for T_{wilcox},

$$T_{wilcox} = min(W_{S1}, W_{S2}) = 18.5.$$

We look through the Wilcoxon table in Appendix A.5 for $n = 10 - 1 = 9$ degrees of freedom and find that the critical value, V, which must be larger than T_{wilcox} in order for the null hypothesis, which states that the two classifiers are not significantly different, to be rejected at the 0.05 level is $V = 8$ for the one-sided test, and $V = 5$ for the two-sided test. In both cases, we thus conclude that the hypothesis cannot be rejected at significance level $p = 0.05$ since $18.5 > 8 > 5$.

Wilcoxon's signed-rank test is implemented in the scipy.stats package and was used to compare the performance of naive Bayes and SVM on 10 different real-world domains (breast cancer, liver, balance scale, contact lenses, glass, hepatitis, hypothyroid, tic-tac-toe, diabetes, anneal), as described in the accompanying GitHub file.

7.2.4 Comparing Multiple Classifiers on Multiple Domains

We now move to an even more common situation in classifier evaluation, in which large studies pit multiple classifiers against each other on multiple domains. As already discussed, the *t*-test can be appropriate for the comparison of two classifiers on a single domain, but it should not be used in simultaneous comparisons of two or more classifiers on multiple domains. The problems that would arise as a result of this usage have been pointed out (see Salzberg 1997; Demšar 2006) and already arose in the case of multiple classifiers tested on a single domain. These problems can be traced to two main reasons. The first reason is quite practical in the sense that performing such pairwise testing requires too many paired tests to be performed in order to conduct all the pairwise comparisons possible in these experiments. Furthermore, analyzing the results in a unified manner would be rendered impractical. However, of even graver concern is the second reason, which would be implied by performing such pairwise comparisons. The more the pairwise tests are performed, the greater the chance of committing a type I error. For example, if one test gives us a 5% probability of making a type I error, then two tests will give us a 10% chance of doing so. Ten tests give us a 40% chance of doing so (see, for instance, Hinton (1995, p. 105)).

Statistics offers solutions so as to avoid performing such pairwise testing and subsequently dealing with the issues such testing causes. In particular, there is a family of statistical tests specifically designed for multiple hypothesis testing. Both parametric and nonparametric alternatives to perform multiple hypothesis testing are available with their respective strengths and limitations within this family. The general methodology for performing such tests is two fold.[9] The first step is to use multiple hypothesis tests, also known as omnibus tests. These are designed to confirm whether the observed differences between various classifier performances are statistically significantly different. That is, omnibus tests, by rejecting the null hypothesis, convey whether there exists at least one pair of classifiers with significantly different performances. This confirmation, if obtained, is then followed by what is known as post-hoc tests, tests that enable the identification of these significantly different pairs of classifiers while controlling for the experiment-wise error rate that takes the number of comparisons into consideration.[10]

In this section, we look at the principal omnibus test deemed most appropriate for the multiple classifier evaluation: the nonparametric test called the Friedman test. The famous

---

[9] Sometimes three fold when some preanalysis is performed using the so-called pre-hoc tests.

[10] Salzberg (1997) suggests another approach to deal with the problem of multiple comparisons: the binomial test with the Bonferroni correction for multiple comparisons. However, he himself remarks that such a test does not have sufficient power and that the Bonferroni correction is too drastic. Demšar (2006) agrees that the field of statistics produced more powerful tests to deal with these conditions, though, once again, García and Herrera (2008) maintain that these alternatives should be considered as they are more powerful.

parametric alternative for multiple hypothesis testing: the analysis of variance (ANOVA) makes assumptions that are generally too strong for machine learning settings and it is seldom used in the field. It will therefore not be discussed here, though a discussion can be found in Japkowicz and Shah (2011). This section will also describe the appropriate post-hoc test available if the Friedman test rejects the null hypothesis.

The Friedman Test

Generally, given enough samples, repeated measures ANOVA is robust to the violations of its normality assumptions to a significant extent. However, the difficulty in ascertaining the sphericity assumption, the assumption of equal variance between pairs of tests, has prompted some researchers to discourage the use of ANOVA to perform classifier evaluation (see, for instance, Demšar (2006)). There can also be other scenarios when the underlying assumptions made by ANOVA can be violated. One of the most obvious scenarios would be the case of ranking classifiers. Another is the case when the performance measure is only categorical (and not continuous). Further, ANOVA's assumptions do not hold in cases where the performance measures, unlike conventional measures such as accuracy, are not monotonic (hence potentially violating the equal interval assumption and quite possibly also the normality assumption). In such cases, an alternative worth considering would be a non-parametric method of comparing classifier performances. One of the better nonparametric tests available is the Friedman test; we describe this next.

Friedman Test Description

The Friedman test is the nonparametric counterpart of the repeated measure one-way ANOVA test. As in the case of Wilcoxon's test, the analysis is based on the ranks of each classifier on each dataset and not on the explicit performance measures. Consider n datasets and k classifiers to evaluate. The evaluation proceeds as follows:

- Each algorithm is ranked, for each dataset separately, according to the performance measure pm, in ascending order, from the best performing classifier to the worst performing classifier. Hence, for dataset i, the classifier j such that $pm_{ij} > pm_{ij'}$, for all $j', j, j' \in \{1, 2, \ldots, k\}, j \neq j'$, is ranked 1.[11] In case of a d-way tie just after the rank r, assign a rank of $((r+1) + (r+2) + \cdots + (r+d))/d$ to each of the tied classifiers.
- Let R_{ij} be the rank of classifier j on dataset i.
- We compute the following quantities:

  - The mean rank of classifier j on all datasets,

$$\overline{R}_{\cdot j} = \frac{1}{n} \sum_{i=1}^{n} R_{ij}.$$

---

[11] Note that, here, we make an implicit assumption that a higher value of the performance measure (e.g. accuracy) is always preferred. However, there are other performance measures, such as classification error $Err(f)$ of classifier f where a lower value is an indicator of better performance. In this respect, the statement $pm_{ij} > pm_{ij'}$ should be interpreted as a representation of this criterion. That is, the classifier j will be considered to outperform j' when j *performs better*. In case of a measure such as accuracy, this would hold when $Acc(j) > Acc(j')$ while in case of a measure such as classification error, this would hold when $Err(j) < Err(j')$. In this sense, a better representation would be $pm_{ij} \succ pm_{ij'}$.

– The overall mean rank,

$$\overline{R} = \frac{1}{nk} \sum_{i=1}^{n} \sum_{j=1}^{k} R_{ij}.$$

– The "sum of squares total" denoting the variation in the ranks,

$$SS_{Total} = n \sum_{j=1}^{k} (\overline{R}_{.j} - \overline{R})^2.$$

– The "sum of squares error" denoting the error variation,

$$SS_{Error} = \frac{1}{n(k-1)} \sum_{i=1}^{n} \sum_{j=1}^{k} (R_{ij} - \overline{R})^2.$$

- The test statistic, also called the Friedman statistic, is calculated as

$$\chi_F^2 = \frac{SS_{Total}}{SS_{Error}}.$$

- According to the null hypothesis stating that all the classifiers are equivalent in their performance and, hence, their average ranks $R_{.j}$ should be equal, the χ_F^2 follows a χ^2 distribution with $k-1$ degrees of freedom, for large n (usually > 15) and k (usually > 5).
- Hence, in case of large n and k, χ_F^2 can be looked up in the table for χ^2 distribution (Appendix A.3). A p-value, signifying, $P(\chi_{k-1}^2 \geq \chi_F^2)$ is obtained and, if found to be less than the critical value for the desired significance level, the null hypothesis can be rejected.
- In case of smaller n and k, the χ^2 approximation is imprecise and a table look-up is advised from tables of χ_F^2 values approximated specifically for the Friedman test (Appendix A.7).

Note that the above χ_F^2 statistic can be simplified to

$$\chi_F^2 = \left[\frac{12}{n \times k \times (k+1)} \times \sum_{j=1}^{k} (R_{.j})^2 \right] - 3 \times n \times (k+1).$$

It is important to note, however, that Stapor et al. (2021) has uncovered an important shortcoming of Friedman's test. Namely, depending on which other classifiers the two classifiers under scrutiny are being tested with, the results may be different. This suggests that Friedman's test cannot always be trusted and Stapor et al. (2021) propose to handle the multiple classifier multiple domain case, using repeated Wilcoxon's signed-rank tests corrected for multiple hypothesis testing, such as Bonferroni's correction or others (Midway et al. 2020). This is also supported by García and Herrera (2008).

An Illustration

To better explain Friedman's test, we illustrate our discussion with the hypothetical example from Table 7.2 that was presented in Section 7.2.3. Recall that in that section, we only compared classifiers A and C given that Wilcoxon's signed-rank test only applies to two classifiers. In this section, we will compare all three classifiers A, B, and C since the Friedman test applies to multiple classifiers on multiple domains.

We rewrite Table 7.2 in terms of the rank obtained by each classifier on each domain to produce Table 7.4; that is, we look across each row and assign attribute values 1, 2, or 3 to the largest, the second largest, and the third largest accuracies, respectively, that we find. We use average ranks for ties. If there are no differences between the algorithms, we would expect the ranks to be evenly spread amongst the datasets. That is, on some datasets, algorithm A would win; on others, algorithm B or C would win, so we would not notice any patterns. Yet, in our example, we see a pattern: Classifier B is always ranked third, whereas Classifiers A and C share the first and second place more or less equally (there may not be any difference between A and C, but this is not what is getting tested here; this question will be considered later in this section where we discuss post-hoc tests).

We then compute the following statistics for the Friedman test:

$$\chi_F^2 = \left[\frac{12}{n \times k \times (k+1)} \times \sum_{j=1}^{k} (R_{.j})^2 \right] - 3 \times n \times (k+1),$$

with $k - 1$ degrees of freedom, where k is the number of algorithms, and n the number of domains. In our example, this gives

$$\chi_F^2 = \left[\frac{12}{10 \times 3 \times (3+1)} \times \sum_{j=1}^{3} (R_{.j})^2 \right] - 3 \times 10 \times (3+1)$$

$$= \left[\frac{1}{10} \times ((15.5)^2 + (30)^2 + (14.5)^2) \right] - 120$$

$$= 15.05,$$

with two degrees of freedom.

Table 7.4. *Rewriting Table 7.2 as ranks.*

Domain	Classifier A	Classifier B	Classifier C
1	1	3	2
2	1.5	3	1.5
3	1	3	2
4	1	3	2
5	2	3	1
6	1	3	2
7	2	3	1
8	2	3	1
9	2	3	1
10	2	3	1
Rank sums $(R_{.j})$	15.5	30	14.5

The critical values for the χ_F^2 distribution for $k = 3$ and $n = 10$ are: 6.2 for a 0.05 level of significance and 9.6 at the 0.01 level of significance for a single-tailed test; and 7.8 for a 0.05 level of significance and 12.60 for a 0.002 level of significance for a two-tailed test. Since 15.05 is larger than all these values, we can confidently conclude that there is a significant difference between the three algorithms on these datasets.

> Friedman's test is implemented in the scipy.stats package and was used to compare the performance of four classifiers (decision trees, logistic regression, random forests, and SVM) on the 10 real-world domains already used in the Wilcoxon signed-rank test experiments as described in the accompanying GitHub file.

Post-Hoc Tests

We just described the most appropriate NHST "omnibus" statistical test for comparing multiple classifiers. As previously discussed, this test gives an assessment of whether the differences in the classifiers' performances on the datasets are statistically significant. However, to have a zoomed-in view of what these differences correspond to precisely, we need to perform a deeper analysis to pinpoint the specific differences.

Post-hoc tests are performed when a statistical test comparing multiple classifiers rejects the null hypothesis that the classifiers being compared are alike. These tests help in finding which classifiers actually differ. We describe, here, one of the post-hoc tests that can be used to identify these classifiers after the application of the Friedman test: the Nemenyi test.

The Nemenyi Test

The Nemenyi test works by discovering whether the rank differences obtained as a result of the Friedman test are, indeed, significant. To do so, it computes a q-statistic over the difference in average mean ranks of the classifier as follows:

- Following the way in which the ranking is done in the Friedman test, each algorithm is ranked for each dataset separately, according to the performance measure pm, in ascending order from the best performing classifier to the worst performing classifier. Hence, for dataset i, classifier j such that $pm_{ij} > pm_{ij'}$, for all $j', j, j' \in \{1, 2, \ldots, k\}, j \neq j'$ is ranked 1.[12] In case of a d-way tie just after rank r, assign a rank of $((r + 1) + (r + 2) + \cdots + (r + d))/d$ to each of the tied classifiers.
- Let R_{ij} be the rank of classifier j on dataset i.
- We compute the mean rank of classifier j on all datasets,

$$\overline{R}_{.j} = \frac{1}{n} \sum_{i=1}^{n} R_{ij}.$$

---

[12] See footnote 11.

- For any two classifiers j_1 and j_2, we compute the q-statistic as

$$q = \frac{\overline{R}_{.j_1} - \overline{R}_{.j_2}}{\sqrt{\frac{k(k+1)}{6n}}}.$$

- The null hypothesis is rejected after a comparison of the obtained q-value with the q-value for the desired significance table for critical q_α values where α refers to the significance level.[13] Reject the null hypothesis if the obtained q value exceeds q_α.

It can be said that the Nemenyi test works by computing the average rank of each classifier and taking their difference. In the cases where these average rank differences are larger than or equal to the critical q_α value, we can say, with the appropriate amount of certainty, that the performance of the two classifiers corresponding to these differences is significantly different from one another.

Example of the Nemenyi test In order to illustrate the process of the Nemenyi test, we go back to the comparison of three classifiers A, B, and C over 10 domains. However, rather than computing the average performance of each classifier on the 10 domains, we compute their mean ranks by dividing the rank sums at the bottom of Table 7.4 by 10, the number of datasets. This yields $\overline{R}_A = 1.55$, $\overline{R}_B = 3$, and $\overline{R}_C = 1.45$. The mean ranks between A and B is thus 1.45, that between B and C is of 1.55, and that between A and C is of 0.1.[14] To answer the question of which of these differences are significant in the context of the Friedman and Nemenyi tests, we compute the q values using the q-statistic formula. We get the following three q values:

$$q_{12} = \frac{\overline{R}_{.1} - \overline{R}_{.2}}{\sqrt{\frac{3\times(3+1)}{6\times 10}}} = \frac{|1.55 - 3|}{\sqrt{\frac{3\times(3+1)}{6\times 10}}} = \frac{1.45}{0.45} = 3.22,$$

$$q_{13} = \frac{\overline{R}_{.1} - \overline{R}_{.3}}{\sqrt{\frac{3\times(3+1)}{6\times 10}}} = \frac{|1.55 - 1.45|}{\sqrt{\frac{3\times(3+1)}{6\times 10}}} = \frac{.1}{0.45} = .22,$$

$$q_{23} = \frac{\overline{R}_{.2} - \overline{R}_{.3}}{\sqrt{\frac{3\times(3+1)}{6\times 10}}} = \frac{|3 - 1.45|}{\sqrt{\frac{3\times(3+1)}{6\times 10}}} = \frac{1.55}{0.45} = 3.44.$$

From the table in Appendix A.8, we see that $q_\alpha = 3.61$ for $\alpha = 0.05$, number of groups $= 3$, and $df = (n - 1)(k - 1) = 9 \times 2 = 18$. For the Nemenyi test, we divide this value by $\sqrt{2}$. This yields $q_\alpha = 2.55$. So we conclude that the null hypothesis can be rejected in both the cases of q_{12}, the comparison of classifiers A and B and q_{23}, the comparison of classifiers B and C, since the absolute values of these q-statistics are greater than 2.55, but that it cannot be rejected in the case of q_{13}, the comparison of classifiers A and C, since .22 < 2.55.

---

[13] The critical values of q basically are a studentized range statistic scaled by a division factor of $\sqrt{2}$.
[14] We only considered the absolute value of these differences in all cases.

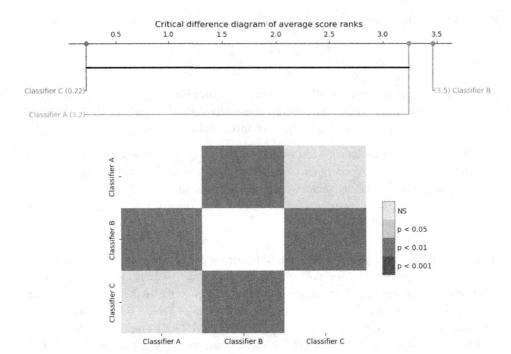

Figure 7.2 Critical differences diagrams for the Nemenyi test example. The α and p-value are related but different. While α, the significance value mentioned in the text, refers to a probability chosen in advance of running NHST, the p-values shown in this figure are computed a posteriori and refer to the probabilities of observing the given data when the null hypothesis holds.

Demšar (2006) proposed convenient ways to visualize the results of Nemenyi's test. These visualizations and implementations are discussed on various websites.[15] For our artificial example, this visualization yields the graphs of Figure 7.2 where part (a) shows the q values, also called critical differences, obtained along with the minimum difference necessary for these critical differences to be significant; and part (b) shows another visualization of whether the critical difference between two classifiers are significant or not, and if they are, what the degree of significance is.

Nemenyi's test is implemented in the scipy.stats package and was used to compare the performance of four classifiers on 10 different real-world domains following Friedman's test, as described in the accompanying GitHub file.

---

[15] For example, see https://medium.com/@catur.supriyanto/how-to-visualize-the-nemenyi-and-bonferroni-dunn-diagrams-in-python-aa6a311f1cee

7.3 Estimation Statistics: Confidence Intervals, Effect Size, and Power Analysis

As already mentioned, despite its common use NHST used alone is not the preferred statistical testing approach as it fails to answer crucial questions, and the use of estimation statistics on top of NHST is highly recommended when available (Perezgonzalez 2015). Estimation statistics is very well known, though sometimes under a different name such as estimation or new statistics, and in fact, the main aspects that are relevant to experiments in machine learning were already discussed in Chapter 2, but in a formal and limited way that did not necessarily make their application to the comparison of classifiers clear. The purpose of this section is to revisit these notions of estimation statistics in a way relevant to machine learning evaluation. In particular, it presents, once again, the concepts of confidence intervals, effect size, and power analysis.

7.3.1 Confidence Intervals

As already discussed, confidence intervals provide us with the opportunity to answer more informative questions about our results than null hypothesis testing alone (Cumming 2013). In particular, the size of the interval suggests a degree of precision in the estimate, and that information together with the overlap observed between different intervals can help give us some context as to why a null hypothesis was or was not rejected. For these reasons, we agree with the general opinion that confidence intervals are important tools of the statistical toolbox and that they should be used in machine learning experiments.

Parametric confidence intervals for the case of two classifiers compared over a single domain were discussed in Section 2.3; this will not be repeated here. However, we have not yet discussed how to construct confidence intervals for other kinds of experimental settings. The purpose of this section is to do just that. In particular, we present two different types of confidence intervals not previously mentioned: a nonparametric type associated with Wilcoxon's signed-rank test and for use in the case of two classifiers and multiple domains; and a bootstrap type, which can be used in place of either parametric or nonparametric methods no matter what the experimental setting. It is worth noting that these are only two confidence interval construction methods and that, especially in the case of bootstrap methods, more refined methods exist that could be useful for machine learning researchers and practitioners.[16]

Nonparametric Confidence Intervals

We now present the signed-rank median confidence intervals technique associated with Wilcoxon's signed-rank test and for use in the case of two classifiers compared over multiple domains. Our description follows the description found in Zaiontz (2023).[17] We recall that in the Wilcoxon's signed-rank context, the differences in performance of two classifiers are calculated over all the domains included in the experiment and these differences are converted into signed-ranks (see Section 7.2.3). In creating a confidence interval, we go

---

[16] See for example, https://influentialpoints.com/Training/nonparametric-or-parametric_bootstrap.htm.
[17] See https://real-statistics.com/non-parametric-tests/wilcoxon-signed-ranks-test/signed-ranks-median-confidence-interval/.

back to the differences in performances prior to their conversion into signed-ranks. The procedure works by proceeding through three steps.

Step 1 Find all the Walsh averages associated with the list of differences in mean performance obtained by the two classifiers under scrutiny on each domain. Walsh averages are defined as follows: for any $1 \leq i \leq j \leq n$, the Walsh averages are calculated as

$$w_{ij} = \frac{z_i + z_j}{2}.$$

By definition, there are $\frac{n \times (n+1)}{2}$ such Walsh averages.

Step 2 Once all the Walsh averages are calculated, the signed-rank table of critical values is consulted and the critical value, C, of interest for the sample size n and desired confidence level $(1 - \alpha) \times 100\%$ is identified.

Step 3 The confidence interval is formed by using the Cth smallest Walsh average as the lower bound and the Cth largest Walsh average as the upper bound.

We illustrate the calculation on our comparison of classifiers A and C on 10 domains, using the same hypothetical example as the one used to illustrate Wilcoxon's signed-rank test. The calculation of the differences in performance between classifiers A and C on the 10 domains were reported in Table 7.3. We recall that the difference between the two classifiers on domain 2 was 0, and that that difference was, thus, removed from our calculation. We therefore now have $n = 9$. The 45 Walsh averages for the nine differences listed in Table 7.3 in sorted order are

```
-0.0200 -0.0155 -0.0135 -0.0125 -0.0110 -0.0110 -0.0090 -0.0080 -0.0070
-0.0065 -0.0065 -0.0060 -0.0050 -0.0045 -0.0035 -0.0020 -0.0020 -0.0020
 0.0000  0.0010  0.0015  0.0025  0.0025  0.0045  0.0055  0.0060  0.0070
 0.0070  0.0080  0.0090  0.0105  0.0115  0.0150  0.0160  0.0160  0.0195
 0.0205  0.0225  0.0230  0.0235  0.0250  0.0295  0.0340  0.0375  0.0520
```

From the Wilcoxon table in Appendix A.5 for $n = 10 - 1 = 9$ degrees of freedom, we find that the critical value for a two-tailed 95% confidence interval is 5. We therefore look for the 5th smallest and the 5th largest Walsh average values, -0.011 and 0.025, and form our confidence interval around the median $-.002$.

We repeat the same procedure for classifiers A and B, which leads to the following 55 Walsh averages (since this time, no difference amounts to 9 so no comparison is removed and $n = 10$):

```
0.0960 0.0975 0.0990 0.1030 0.1045 0.1060 0.1065 0.1075 0.1080 0.1085
0.1100 0.1100 0.1115 0.1130 0.1130 0.1135 0.1155 0.1160 0.1165 0.1170
0.1185 0.1185 0.1190 0.1210 0.1215 0.1220 0.1240 0.1255 0.1270 0.1270
0.1325 0.1330 0.1345 0.1355 0.1360 0.1380 0.1400 0.1410 0.1430 0.1435
0.1455 0.1485 0.1505 0.1520 0.1550 0.1575 0.1605 0.1610 0.1625 0.1630
0.1660 0.1700 0.1800 0.1875 0.2050
```

Since for $n = 10$, the critical value for a two-tailed 95% confidence interval is 8, we look for the 8th smallest and largest Walsh averages, 0.1075 and 0.1610, respectively, and the median is $(.858 + .861)/2 = .8595$.

It is important to remember that the confidence intervals in this section are different in nature from those shown in Section 2.3, where the parametric confidence interval building procedure is shown for the case of two classifiers compared over a single domain. In that section, the confidence intervals were constructed for the sample means of classifier performance for each classifier A, B, and C. Here, instead the confidence intervals were constructed for the difference in performance between pairs of classifiers. We could, likewise, have constructed a confidence interval for the difference in performance in the case of two classifiers on a single domain. Since, for that purpose, we are relying on nonparametric statistics, and since these statistics rely on ranks, we calculated the confidence interval within which the medians of these differences (rather than their means) are likely to lie.

The accompanying GitHub repository shows the implementation of the calculation of the signed-ranks median confidence intervals technique on three classifiers: decision trees, SVMs, and linear regression over the 10 real domains used in the Wilcoxon's signed-rank test experiments (breast cancer, liver, balance-scale, etc.). The bounds of the confidence intervals are computed and plotted in Figure 7.3, which shows the differences between decision trees and linear regression, and between decision trees and SVM.

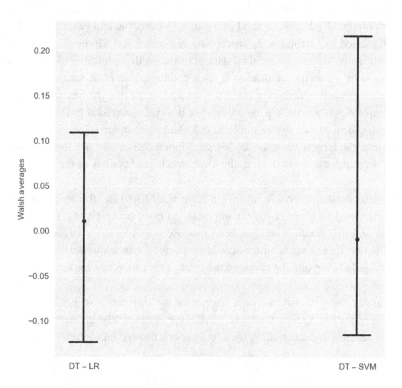

Figure 7.3 Wilcoxon confidence intervals for comparison between decision tree and logistic regression (left vertical bar) and decision tree and SVM (right vertical bar) on 10 domains.

Despite the difference between the confidence intervals of Section 2.3 and those of this section, their interpretation remains the same. Looking at the results in Figure 7.3, we conclude that the estimate of one difference is more likely to be accurate than the other based on the size of the confidence interval. In particular, we have more confidence in the reliability of the estimate of differences in performances between the decision tree and linear regression classifiers than between the decision tree and SVM classifiers because the 95% confidence interval for the difference between decision trees and linear regression is smaller than the 95% confidence interval for the difference between decision trees and SVM. This suggests that our estimate of a median for the first difference is most likely more precise than that for the second.

Bootstrap Confidence Intervals

Having talked about standard parametric and nonparametric confidence intervals for the specific experimental settings considered in machine learning, we now turn to a more general category of confidence interval construction methods that encompass both the parametric and nonparametric approaches previously considered. This family of approaches belongs to the bootstrap method of calculating a confidence interval (Wood 2005). This approach is extremely versatile and can be applied in all settings considered in machine learning experiments. It can be used in conjunction with the t-test and its proposed variations, Wilcoxon's signed-rank Test, and the Friedman/Nemenyi test combination. It is a fairly straightforward, though computationally heavy, method of escaping parametric and other types of assumptions. As discussed in Chapter 6, bootstrapping is a simulated Monte Carlo method with samples of the same size as the original dataset drawn with replacement from that dataset. The estimation of a statistic of interest is then conducted on each sample and averaged. We can then compute the median of the statistic and assume that the median represents the 50th percentile. We then calculate the confidence interval centered at the median according to a chosen confidence level. For example, to calculate a two-tailed 95% confidence interval, we can retrieve the largest value of the lowest 2.5 percentiles and the lowest value of the highest 2.5 percentiles and use them as the lower and higher bounds of the 95% confidence interval.

We now describe the procedure following Brownlee (2016) and the bootstrap estimation procedure discussed in Chapter 6. It is important to note, however, that this procedure is the simplest and that much work has been proposed to enhance it beyond this simplest form.[18] Although these enhancements could be useful for machine learning experiments, their discussion falls beyond the scope of the book. This procedure requires four steps:

Step 1 Evaluate the performance of a learner or the difference in performance of two learners with respect to a given metric (e.g., AUC, F-measure) by creating a large number of bootstrap samples and calculating the average performance on each sample.

Step 2 Calculate the median of these results.

---

[18] See, once again, https://influentialpoints.com/Training/nonparametric-or-parametric_bootstrap.htm.

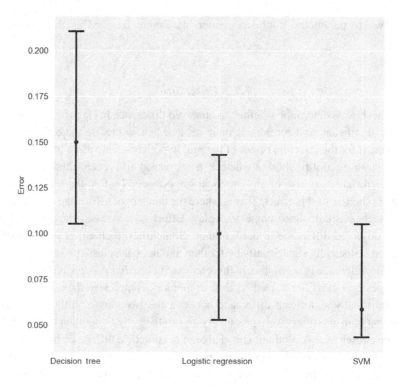

Figure 7.4 Bootstrapped confidence intervals for decision tree, logistic regression, and SVM tested on the Labor Relations dataset.

Step 3 Choose the desired confidence level and calculate the lower and upper percentiles associated with that level.

Step 4 Calculate the lower and upper boundary of the interval, based on the percentiles.

The computation is illustrated in the GitHub repository accompanying the book. In particular, we repeat the calculation and display of the confidence intervals computed in Section 2.3 for the decision tree, logistic regression, and SVM on the Labor Relations dataset, but instead of using the parametric approach detailed in that section, we use the bootstrapping approach just described. The picture is shown in Figure 7.4.

Comparing that figure with Figure 2.4, we see that the parametric confidence intervals of Section 2.3 are tighter than those of Figure 7.4. Furthermore, while the parametric version shows no overlap between the confidence interval of the decision tree and those of logistic regression and SVM, the confidence interval for logistic regression overlaps with those of both decision tree and SVM in the bootstrapped version. Based on this example, it therefore seems that parametric confidence intervals are more useful than bootstrapped ones, although, like in the parametric version, a clear difference between decision tree and SVM can be seen in the bootstrap intervals, suggesting their usefulness in this particular case. Furthermore, it is important to keep in mind that there are cases where parametric confidence intervals cannot be used as they violate their assumptions.

7.3.2 Effect Size

Null hypothesis tests determine whether an observed difference in classifier performance is statistically significant, and confidence intervals assess how precise the estimates are and provide context for the rejection or not of the null hypothesis. One thing these tools cannot convey, however, is confirmation of whether the observed difference, although statistically significantly different, is also of any practical importance. That is, the tools measure the *effect* but not the *size* of this effect. This is where the concept of effect size and the different ways in which it is calculated come into play. Effect size assesses the practical useful-ness of an observed difference in performance. Sometimes, a classifier (say classifier A) may perform statistically significantly better than another (say, classifier B), but practically speaking, the difference is negligible. In this context, if classifier A happened to have certain disadvantages over classifier B, such as time or memory complexity, then, if it were known that the statistically significant difference between the two was of little practical value, assuming that both classifiers were practically and statistically better than other candidates, B should be chosen over A. Without knowledge of the practical difference between A and B, however, costly accommodations could be made to use A rather than B, even though these costs would not be justified. Effect size was discussed in Section 2.4.4, but we now look at it in a more applied fashion.

So, practically speaking, what is an effect and what is an effect size? As discussed in Cumming (2013) and following Cohen (1992), an effect is a phenomenon of interest such as a measurement of a change in a population's attitude toward a product after viewing an advert for that product. The effect size is the magnitude of that change. For example, 20% of people becoming more favorable about a product after seeing the advert is an effect size. Effect sizes can be measured in the original units of the experiments (e.g., a difference in means), in unit-free measures (e.g., a percentage), or can be standardized (e.g., Cohen's d, which will be discussed below). In this section, we discuss three different effect size measures, each associated with the main families of frequentist statistical tests commonly used in machine learning.

Effect Size Associated with the t-Test: Cohen's d Statistic

In the context of comparing two algorithms on a single dataset, the effect size we are inter-ested in measuring is the difference in performance obtained by the two different algorithms. As previously mentioned, it is important to note that if the effect size is small, then even if the result is statistically significant, it is not of great interest. Measuring effect sizes thus allows us to go beyond NHST to find out not only whether the difference between the two algorithms is statistically significant, but also how significant its effect is, or in other words, how practically relevant the result is.

Many methods of assessing effect sizes can be found in the statistics literature such as Pearson's correlation coefficient, Hedges' G, the coefficient of determination, and so on, though the effect size in the case of the *t*-test, the statistical test used when comparing two classifiers on a single domain, is generally determined using Cohen's *d* statistic. Cohen's *d* statistic in case of two matched samples was briefly mentioned in Chapter 2. Here we describe it in greater detail. More specifically, given classifiers f_1 and f_2, Cohen's *d* statistic can be calculated as follows (we denote the Cohen's *d* statistic with the notation d_{cohen} to avoid ambiguity with *d*, the difference in means):

$$d_{cohen} = \frac{\overline{pm}(f_1) - \overline{pm}(f_2)}{\sigma_p},$$

where σ_p, the pooled standard deviation estimate, is defined as

$$\sigma_p = \sqrt{\frac{\sigma_1^2 + \sigma_2^2}{2}},$$

where σ_1^2 and σ_2^2 represent the variances of distributions 1 and 2, respectively.

As can be seen from its definition, Cohen's *d* statistic is a kind of *z*-score expressed in standard deviation units. Therefore, the *d* statistics can be interpreted in a "standard" way without knowing the details of the experiment. A typical interpretation proposed by Cohen for this effect size statistic is the following discretized scale:

- **[0.2 to 0.3]** A value in that range denotes a small effect, but is probably meaningful;
- **[Around 0.5]** A d_{cohen} value of about 0.5 signifies a medium effect that is noticeable;
- **[0.8 or more]** A d_{cohen} value of 0.8 or higher signifies a large effect size.

Please note that d_{cohen} need not lie in the [0, 1] interval and can indeed be even greater than 1 as we see below.

We illustrate Cohen's *d* statistic by applying its formula to the values obtained in the example of Table 2.2. After reducing the problem to a 10-fold problem where each fold for each algorithm takes the following values:[19]

$$dt : [0.1667, 0.15, 0.2333, 0.1, 0.1167, 0.06667, 0.0833, 0.1667, 0.1333, 0.2],$$

$$svm : [0.0667, 0.05, 0.0667, 0.1, 0.0333, 0.0167, 0.0167, 0.0667, 0.0833, 0.1].$$

We obtain the following means and variances for the decision tree and SVM algorithms, respectively:

$$mean(\text{DT}) = 0.142,$$
$$mean(\text{SVM}) = 0.060,$$
$$var(\text{DT}) = 0.00273,$$
$$var(\text{SVM}) = 0.00094.$$

---

[19] Note that we cannot use the variance obtained in Chapter 2 since these were based on a sample size of 100, while here we made the problem more manageable by averaging the results obtained on the 10-folds of each run, reducing the problem to a sample size of 10.

We thus have:

$$d_{cohen} = \frac{0.142 - 0.06}{\sqrt{\frac{0.00273 + 0.0009}{2}}} = 1.914.$$

From Cohen's guidelines, we conclude that since $d_{cohen} > 0.8$, the effect size is large. That is, the difference in the means of the two populations, and hence the performances of the two classifiers, do differ in a practically important way.

Cohen's d statistic is implemented in the GitHub repository and illustrated on the comparison of decision trees and SVM on the Labor Relations dataset.

Effect Size Associated with Wilcoxon's Signed-Rank Test

Cohen's d statistic is appropriate in the context of two classifiers compared on a single domain, but not under other circumstances. For the case of two classifiers compared on multiple domains, as already seen, Wilcoxon's signed-rank test rather than the t-test can be used. Two approaches have been proposed for calculating the effect size for Wilcoxon's signed-rank test. The first uses the standardized Z-score with the assumption that the sample size is large enough for the Wilcoxon statistics to approach the normal distribution, while the second uses the sum of ranks derived during the computation of the Wilcoxon's signed-rank test. In order to be able to ignore the sample size assumption, we decided to present the second estimate, though both calculations are described in Tomczak and Tomczak (2014). The sum-of-ranks based estimate, also known as the rank biserial correlation coefficient or r-value, is calculated using the following formula (Tomczak and Tomczak 2014):

$$r = \frac{4 \times \left| T - \left(\frac{R_1 + R_2}{2} \right) \right|}{n + (n + 1)},$$

where R_1 corresponds to the sum of ranks with positive signs (sum of ranks of positive values), R_2 corresponds to the sum of ranks with negative signs (sum of ranks of negative values), T corresponds to the smaller of the two values (R_1 or R_2), n corresponds to the total sample size (the number of domains on which the two classifiers are being compared), and r corresponds to the correlation coefficient.

This effect size can be interpreted in the same way as Pearson's correlation coefficient (r). Specifically, if $|r| \in [.1, 3)$, then the effect is small. If $|r| \in [.3, .5)$ then the effect is medium. If $|r| \geq .5$ then the effect is large.[20]

For illustration, we return to the hypothetical example used in the context of Wilcoxon's signed-rank test. The calculation of the differences in performance between classifiers A and C on the 10 domains were reported in Table 7.3. Despite the fact that the null hypothesis was not rejected, we compute the effect size just for practice. By doing so, we obtain

$$r = \frac{4 \times \left| 18.5 - \left(\frac{26.5 + 18.5}{2} \right) \right|}{9 + (9 + 1)} = 0.84,$$

---

[20] See https://rcompanion.org/handbook/F_04.html.

which suggests a large effect size. This effect size, however, should not be taken too seriously given that we do not have enough evidence that the values with which it was calculated can be relied upon, given that the null hypothesis was not rejected.

> The r-value is implemented in the GitHub repository and illustrated on the comparison of naive Bayes and SVM on the 10 domains that had been used to illustrate Wilcoxon's signed-rank test.

Effect Size Associated with Friedman's Test

Neither Cohen's d nor the rank biserial are appropriate for Friedman's test. Instead, the approach that has been proposed for calculating the effect size associated with Friedman's test is the Kendall's W test value, which uses the formula (Tomczak and Tomczak 2014)

$$W = \frac{\chi_W^2}{N \times (k-1)},$$

where W corresponds to the Kendall's W test value, χ_W^2 corresponds to the Friedman test statistic value, N corresponds to the sample size (the number of domains on which the comparison is being carried out), and k corresponds to the number of measurements per subject (the number of learning algorithms being compared in this experiment).

Kendall's W coefficient takes values between 0 and 1, where 0 corresponds to no relationship and 1 indicates a perfect relationship. Applying the formula to the case of comparing A, B, and C in our hypothetical example of Table 7.2, we get the value

$$W = \frac{15.05}{10 \times (3-1)} = .75.$$

This suggests a pretty large effect. That being said, because until a posthoc test is applied the relationship that caused the effect is unknown, it is not clear which effect this size actually relates to and whether we are seeing a cumulative effect of different phenomena. A different effect size measure can be applied once the location of the significant difference has been uncovered with Nemenyi's test.

> Kendall's W coefficient is implemented in the GitHub repository and illustrated on the comparison of the four classifiers on the 10 domains that had been used to illustrate Friedman's test.

7.3.3 Power Analysis

The third element of estimation statistics recommended to enhance NHST is the assessment of statistical power. However, while power analysis is important in assessing the probability that a study would yield a rejection of the null hypothesis given an expected or desired effect size, its calculation a posteriori, once the effect size and p-value are known, is flawed and does not add any information (Lydersen 2019). As a result, the utility of power analysis in the context of machine learning is limited to the cases where the researcher or practitioner is either creating a dataset and wonders how many samples are necessary to ensure high enough power given a desired outcome, or to save time by not performing experiments on existing datasets, given that it is likely that the null hypothesis would not be rejected at a significant enough level. Given how simple it is to run machine learning experiments, however, the latter consideration is not that important, and the main value of power analysis lies in the former situation.

Informally, power indicates the chance that the null hypothesis can be rejected by our experiment if a real effect is present. Power analysis depends upon four different variables related to the particular statistical test chosen for the experiment:

- Effect size;
- Sample size;
- Significance level;
- Statistical power.

We recall that the statistical significance of a test can be thought of as the probability of rejecting the null hypothesis when it is true. That is also known as the probability of making a type I error or a false positive. Statistical power, on the other hand, is the probability that a test will correctly reject the null hypothesis when it is false.

In other words, the higher the statistical significance of a test the higher the chance of committing a type I error; that is, of rejecting the null hypothesis when it is true. In the context of comparing classifiers, this means that a high significance level corresponds to a higher chance of saying that, say, classifier A performs better than classifier B, when in fact it doesn't. Statistical significance, therefore, needs to be kept low. However, at the same time, the effect size needs to be large enough: If classifier A is statistically significantly better than classifier B, but the AUC difference divided by some expression of variance is very low, then this statistically significant difference is of no practical interest. The lower the power, the higher the chance of committing a type II error; that is, of not rejecting the null hypothesis when it is false. In the context of comparing two classifiers, this means that a low power increases the chances of saying that classifiers A and B perform as well as one another when in fact one of them performs better. Increasing power decreases this chance.

Sample (testing set) size and effect size are related to significance and power as follows: increasing sample size improves the chances of a result being statistically significant, and increasing the significance level increases power. In general, these variables are dependent upon each other (Serdar et al. 2021) and power analysis consists of fleshing out that dependency in the context of the experiment we wish to run and its requirements. As already discussed, power analysis is useful both in designing the experiments (for example, it can help the researcher decide upon the number of samples to use in order to use a desired statistical significance level, effect size, and power) and in deciding whether or not to run one. As machine learning becomes more frequently deployed in consumer goods, and, therefore, requires more and more robust quality assurance tests prior to that deployment, power analysis along with effect sizes and *p*-values will become more and more significant to the testing process as the three quantities impose a check on each other since for results

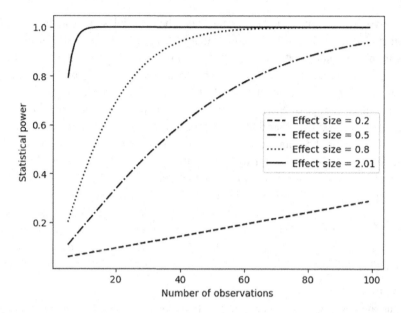

Figure 7.5 A plot showing statistical power as a function of the number of observations. Each curve shows the relationship between these two quantities with respect to the desired effect size(s).

of experiments to be considered good, one requires a low p-value, high power, and large effect size simultaneously.

To illustrate power analysis, we consider the comparison of the decision tree algorithm to SVM on the Labor Relations dataset. For different effect size, we plot the power of the t-test with significance level 0.05 on this comparison, for different numbers of observations in the test set. The plot is shown in Figure 7.5. The plot tells us that if the effect size is high (e.g., 2.01), fewer than 20 observations are sufficient to obtain a power of 1. For an effect size of 0.8, it takes 60 observations to attain a power of 1, and 100 observations are not sufficient to attain a power of 1 if the effect size is 0.5, though with 100 observations, the power is quite close to 1. With effect size 0.2, however, 100 observations allows us to reach only a power of 0.3. There would, therefore, be a high chance that we'd be committing a type II error.

The procedures for building the power analysis figure as well as determining the number of instances needed for a desired power, significance level, and effect sizes are illustrated in the GitHub repository.

7.4 Bayesian Analysis

As discussed in Section 7.1, statistical analysis can be carried out using either frequentist or Bayesian principles. In this section, we now turn our attention to Bayesian analysis, which was recently advocated by a number of scientists. The material we discuss here is based on Benavoli et al. (2017). The authors suggest that instead of using the NHST statistical tests along with the estimation statistics tools discussed in the previous sections, we move away from the frequentist school of thought altogether, and embrace the Bayesian one instead. The advantage of doing so is to bypass the disadvantages of NHST seen in the previous sections. A particular disadvantage of NHST, perhaps not fully expressed in our previous discussion, which focused on specific rather than more general aspects of NHST is that, in NHST, the inference depends on the sampling intention. Since most machine learning researchers do not have sampling intentions prior to running their experiments – the emphasis is often on coming up with novel useful algorithms rather than testing existing ones, and machine learning experts are usually not the scientists tasked with gathering datasets – some argue that it is safer to use a statistical procedure that does not make this kind of assumption.

The type of Bayesian analysis recommended by Benavoli et al. (2017) for machine learning is called Bayesian estimation. The following discusses Bayesian estimation for two different situations:

- Comparison of two classifiers on a single domain;
- Comparison of two classifiers on multiple domains.

The comparison of multiple classifiers on multiple domains will be briefly mentioned at the end of this section as the authors argue that it is similar to the comparison of two classifiers on multiple domains. Furthermore, comparing multiple classifiers on a single domain is similar to the comparison of two classifiers on a single domain.

All the tests discussed in this section will be illustrated in the GitHub repository accompanying this book using the code provided by Benavoli et al. (2017).[21]

7.4.1 Comparison of Two Classifiers on a Single Domain

Benavoli et al. (2017) recommend the use of the Bayesian correlated t-test (Corani et al. 2017) for the purpose of comparing two classifiers on a single domain. This test can be used when analyzing the results obtained through cross-validation on a single dataset. A particular advantage of this test, unlike the traditional frequentist t-test, is that it takes into account the correlation caused by the overlapping nature of the training sets, thus not requiring the corrective actions discussed in Section 7.2.1.

Given a vector $[x_1, x_2, ..., x_k]$ of differences in performance measure between two classifiers A and B, the purpose of the test is to obtain the posterior probability of μ, the estimated difference in accuracy between A and B. This probability depends upon k, the number of cross-validation folds, $\bar{x}$, the mean observed difference in accuracy between A and B across folds, $\hat{\sigma}^2$, the observed variance of that mean, and ρ, the correlation between the cross-validated training sets. Following Nadeau and Bengio (2003), ρ is estimated as

---

[21] See https://github.com/BayesianTestsML/tutorial/.

$\rho = \frac{n_{te}}{n_{tr}+n_{te}}$ with n_{te} and n_{tr} corresponding to the size of the testing and training sets on each fold, respectively. Once the posterior probability of μ is obtained, a number of conclusions can be drawn both visually and mathematically, using the following three analytical and visual concepts:

- The plot of the pdf of the posterior probability of μ;
- The ROPE;
- The HDIs.

The pdf represents the probability distribution function of the difference between the two classifiers. In other words, it shows the likelihood of that quantity taking on different values. The pdf was discussed in greater length in Chapter 2. The ROPE is defined visually and analytically after the user decides how high a difference in performance needs to be for two classifiers to be considered as not being equivalent. In all that follows, and following Benavoli et al. (2017), we considered two classifiers A and B as equivalent if their difference in performance is less than or equal to 1%. In Bayesian estimation, the ROPE is indicated as the region in the interval $[-.01, +.01]$ on the x-axis of the pdf plot and is indicated as two parallel vertical lines on Figure 7.6. An HDI corresponds to the areas of high density on the pdf plot. It shows, for example, the regions on the pdf for which the data covers a given percentage of the entire pdf. We illustrate these three concepts in the plots of Figures 7.6 and 7.7, which are based on the accuracies obtained by the decision tree and SVM on the Labor Relations dataset. The pdf is shown for the difference: $Acc(DT) - Acc(SVM)$. Benavoli et al. (2017) shows a variety of situations obtained on different domains using this approach.

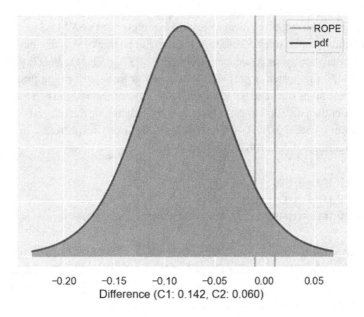

Figure 7.6 Positioning of the ROPE in the Labor Relations dataset.

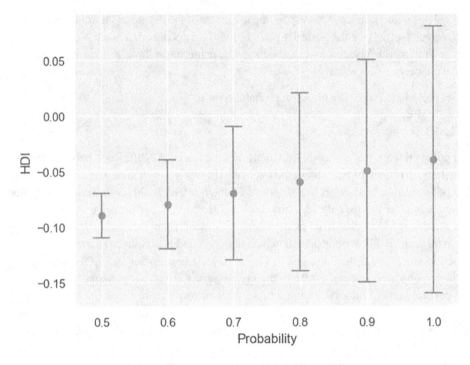

Figure 7.7 HDIs corresponding to Figure 7.6.

In Figure 7.6, we observe that the ROPE is fairly small and that $Acc(DT) - Acc(SVM)$ most often falls on the negative side, suggesting that algorithm's SVM performance is most often superior to decision trees. These conclusions can be drawn visually, but they can also be calculated analytically since we can calculate $P(DT \gtrsim SVM)$, $P(DT \approx SVM)$, and $P(DT \lesssim SVM)$, the posterior probability of decision trees performing practically better than SVM, of decisions trees and SVM being practically equivalent, and of SVM performing practically better than decision trees, respectively, by calculating the integral of the posterior over the intervals $(-\infty, -0.01)$, $[-0.01, 0.01]$, or $(0.01, +\infty)$, respectively. In the particular example of Figure 7.6 these probabilities are

- $P(DT \gtrsim SVM) = 0.92$;
- $P(DT \approx SVM) = 0.038$; and
- $P(DT \lesssim SVM) = 0.039$.

HDI graphs show the intervals in which 50%, 60%, ..., 100% of the data lies. Figure 7.7 Figure 7.7 shows the HDI graph for the pdf of Figure 7.6. Specifically, the graph tells us that 50% of the data is concentrated in the approximate interval $[-0.11, -0.07]$, 60% of it is concentrated in interval $[-0.12, -0.04]$, etc.

We illustrate the code used for plotting the ROPE and HDIs in the GitHub repository that accompanies the book. In particular, we demonstrate its calculation on the comparison of the decision tree and SVM classifiers on the Labor Relations dataset. As previously discussed, the result shows that there is uncertainty as a greater portion of the probability mass is outside the $[-.01,+0.01]$ ROPE, with most of it below -0.01 but some above 0.01. This suggests that SVM is most likely to perform better or as well as decision trees, but it is possible that decision trees are better as well. The HDIs show, among other things, that SVMs beat decision trees by approximately 1% to 12% accuracy with 70% probability.

We now describe the procedure for the Bayesian correlated test in more detail and explain how automatic determination of statistical significance can be made based on it. The procedure for computing the posterior distribution of μ takes four steps:

Step 1 Calculate: $\bar{x} = \frac{\sum_{i=1}^{n} x_i}{n}$ where $x_i, x_2, \ldots$ are the differences in performance measure between two classifiers A and B calculated over the different cross-validation folds on a dataset D.

Step 2 Calculate $\hat{\sigma}^2 = \frac{\sum_{i=1}^{n}(x_i - \bar{x})}{n-1}$.

Step 3 Estimate $\rho = \frac{n_{te}}{n_{tr}+n_{te}}$ with n_{te} and n_{tr} corresponding to the size of the testing and training sets on each fold, respectively, as suggested by Nadeau and Bengio (2003).

Step 4 Compute $St\left(\mu, k-1, \bar{x}, \left(\frac{1}{k} + \frac{\rho}{1-\rho}\right)\hat{\sigma}^2\right)$ where St corresponds to the student distribution. This quantity represents the posterior distribution of μ.

The distribution can then be plotted as in Figure 7.6, with the ROPE represented by two vertical bars added.

If we are involved in too many comparisons for them to be made individually by looking at the graphs, we can automate the process by choosing thresholds on the probability that need to be reached for a conclusion to be drawn. For example, we can decide that A performs significantly better than B if $P(A \gtrsim B) \geq .95$; B performs significantly better than A if $P(B \gtrsim A) > .95$.

7.4.2 Comparison of Two Classifiers on Multiple Domains

Benavoli et al. (2017) propose two approaches for the comparison of two classifiers on multiple domains. The first is a Bayesian version of the sign test and Wilcoxon's signed-rank test, while the second is a hierarchical extension of the Bayesian correlated t-test previously presented. Because of its simplicity and elegance, we present the Bayesian hierarchical correlated t-test here and recommend its use.[22]

---

[22] Note that the accompanying GitHub repository demonstrates the use of both.

The Bayesian hierarchical correlated t-test is an extension of the correlated t-test, which can make inferences jointly on different datasets, keeping into consideration all the information available: the mean, the standard deviation, and the correlation. That is done using a hierarchical model. The hierarchical model has three components. At the basis are the models inferred from the Bayesian correlated t-test on single domains. These models are combined hierarchically and their means are adjusted to account for the fact that they all depend on μ_0, the average difference in performance between two classifiers on all datasets and the quantity of interest in this test. The hierarchical model uses a student distribution with mean μ_0, just discussed, its variance ρ_0, and degree of freedom ν.

The procedure consists of three steps repeated a large number of times (e.g., 4,000 times), which are defined as follows:

Step 1 Sample μ_0, ρ_0, and ν from their posterior probabilities. (Note μ_0 represents the mean difference between learner A and B on all datasets).

Step 2 Use μ_0, ρ_0, and ν, the posterior of the mean difference on the next dataset, N, to estimate μ_{Next}.

Step 3 Calculate the probabilities that A performs better than B on N (θl); B performs better than A on N (θr); and A and B perform approximately equivalently (θe).

After the procedure is repeated 4,000 times, 4,000 triplets ($\theta l, \theta r, \theta e$) are obtained and plotted, yielding visualizations such as the plots of Figure 7.8 where decision trees are compared to SVMs on the 10 real-world domains previously used in Wilcoxon's signed-rank test (breast cancer, liver, balance scale, etc.)

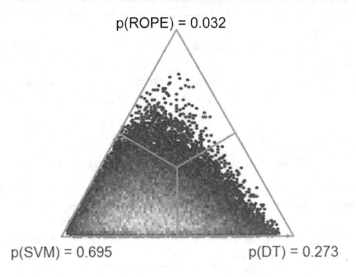

Figure 7.8 Visualizing the result of the Bayesian hierarchical correlated t-test comparing two algorithms (decision trees versus SVMs) over 10 domains. The results show the probabilities where SVM is superior to decision trees (69.5%), where decision trees are superior to SVM (27.3%), and where the two classifiers are equivalent (3.2%).

We illustrate the code used for generating Figure 7.8 using the Bayesian hierarchical correlated *t*-test in the GitHub repository that accompanies the book. The Bayesian sign test described in Benavoli et al. (2017) but whose discussion was omitted from this book is also illustrated in the repository.

7.4.3 Comparison of Multiple Classifiers on Single and Multiple Domains

To extend Bayesian analysis to the case of multiple models on multiple domains, Benavoli et al. (2017) suggest either the use of multilevel analysis (Gelman et al. 2013) or doing nothing in particular; that is, instead, to use the tools presented for the comparison of two classifiers on multiple domains repeatedly. In NHST, a serious worry comes up when multiple comparisons are made. This can be handled through the Bonferroni correction or through the use of specially designed statistical tests such as ANOVA or Friedman, which take these repetitions into consideration. In Bayesian analysis, the use of ROPEs, instead, decreases the chances of making a type I error. This, thus, suggests that the Bayesian correlated *t*-test and the Bayesian hierarchical correlated *t*-test can be used on the comparison of multiple classifiers on a single domain and on the comparison of multiple classifiers on multiple domains, respectively.

7.5 Guidance on Selecting a Statistical Analysis Method

This chapter presented three families of approaches for statistical analysis: NHST, estimation statistics, and Bayesian analysis. NHST and estimation statistics belong to the frequentist school of thought, while Bayesian analysis belongs to the Bayesian school. Although NHST is the best known and by far the most used methodology, it has come under criticism and it is now recommended that instead of being used on its own, it be used in conjunction with estimation statistics. Estimation statistics could be used alone, but it has the disadvantage of issuing answers that are not clear cut and require interpretation, rather than the clear binary answers of NHST (the null hypothesis is either rejected or not). Used together, NHST and estimation statistics offer the possibility for clear-cut answers mitigated by the analysis provided by estimation statistics. Bayesian statistics is convenient in that it answers the statistical questions users ask more directly than either NHST or estimation statistics. More importantly, Bayesian statistics does not make any assumptions about the user's experimental intents the way frequentist approaches do. This is potentially important since the question of intent is commonly ignored when using frequentist tools. On the other hand, Bayesian analysis makes assumptions about the priors used in its calculations and these assumptions may be erroneous. While there are cases where priors are known and Bayesian analysis warranted (e.g., the prevalence of certain types of cancers in the population), it is not clear that priors are known in all cases. Their estimation may, thus, be misleading.

The chapter considered four experimental cases that arise in machine learning. The comparison of:

- two classifiers on a single domain;
- multiple classifiers on a single domain;
- two classifiers on several domains;
- multiple classifiers on several domains.

In each of these cases, it documented how to answer the two essential questions asked by statistics using both frequentist and Bayesian tools:

Question 1 Is the observed result representative of the truth? To what extent? How far from the truth is it?

Question 2 Are the observed results, if credible, of any practical value?

Guidance on what specific tools are available in each case to answer each of the two questions and their sub-parts was given in Section 7.1.5 and subsequently explained in the following sections.

Every tool introduced in this chapter is explained analytically and its practical use in Python is illustrated in the GitHub repository that accompanies the book. All the figures shown are also derived from the code in the repository.

Part III

Evaluation for Other Settings

8

Supervised Settings Other Than Simple Classification

This chapter discusses evaluation strategies for machine learning settings other than simple binary or multi-class classification. In particular, we look at how to evaluate the performance of anomaly or outlier detection, positive-unlabeled learning, ordinal classification, multi-label classification, regression analysis, image segmentation, text generation, time series analysis, data stream mining, lifelong learning, and reinforcement learning. Although some of the paradigms discussed in this chapter touch upon unsupervised learning in certain cases, the bulk of unsupervised learning will be treated seperately in Chapter 9.

8.1 Overview of the Different Machine Learning Settings

Students typically receive their first introduction to the field of machine learning through binary classification or regression. So far this book has focused on binary classification and its extension to multi-class classification. Although references to other modes of learning and their metrics were made in Chapter 4, these topics were only touched upon briefly. This chapter takes a deep dive into the different modes of learning currently practiced or researched, and the ways that have been proposed to evaluate them (with the exception being the subfield of unsupervised learning, which is vast and intricate and is, therefore, discussed on its own in Chapter 9).

Figure 8.1 shows an overview of machine learning settings that differ from simple classification problems. We distinguish between the kind of variation they exhibit from simple classification. In particular, we consider three categories of variations: variations in the label distribution, variations in the format of the output, and variations in the format of the input.

The remainder of this section provides a brief introduction to all the machine learning problems displayed in Figure 8.1. The following sections discuss, in depth, each of these problems in their order of occurrence at the leaves of the tree, along with the evaluation strategies that have been proposed for each of them.

8.1.1 Variations in the Label Distribution

The slightest degree of deviation from simple classification is deviation at the labeling distribution level. Anomaly detection and positive-unlabeled classification both fall in this category. Although they ultimately remain classification problems, there are several reasons

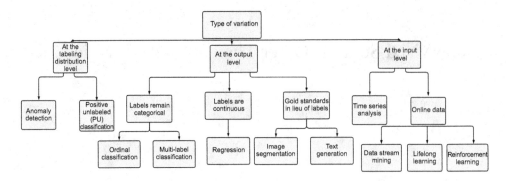

Figure 8.1 Overview of machine learning settings other than classification.

why these problems need to be treated individually: they typically suffer from an extreme class imbalance, they often have very few labeled instances at their disposal, and their goal is different from that of straightforward classification.

As already discussed in Section 5.6, the class imbalance problem makes certain metrics such as accuracy inappropriate. The issue is even more accute when the class imbalance is very pronounced as it often is in the problems considered in this category.

Lack of data labels is another problem when it comes to testing the performance of learning systems. Indeed, what can the results obtained by the learning system be compared to in such cases? In Positive-Unlabeled (PU) problems, where only a handful of positive instances are labeled and none of the negative ones are, two evaluation approaches are followed: the use of engineered datasets; and the use of the unlabeled instances as a proxy for the negative class.

In addition, the purpose of the problem is very important to consider when evaluating learning systems in this category. In anomaly detection, for example, classifying an instance as belonging to the background class (i.e., not an anomaly) is, typically, not that interesting. Detecting anomalies, on the other hand, is the exciting part! Yet, at the same time, the number of background instances wrongly classified as anomalies should also remain small. Similarly, in PU-problems, two questions arise: whether the problem is one of prioritization or one of anomaly detection. In all these cases metrics must be chosen judiciously to address the problem.

8.1.2 *Variations at the Output Level*

The next type of variation considered is deviation at the output level. In one subset of problems, though the labels remain categorical, unlike in classification, they are related to each other or occur together. Ordinal classification, for example, is a type of multi-class classification problem where the classes are related to each other. Multi-label classification, on the other hand, is a case where instead of predicting one label, the classifier must predict multiple ones.

The second subset of problems considered in this category is one where rather than being categorical, the outputs are continuous, as in the case of regression.

Finally, we identified a third class of problems where the output of the learning system is neither categorical nor continuous. Instead, it takes the form of a gold standard such as a shape in image segmentation or written text in text generation. Although we focus on these two particular problems here, there are many more in that category within subfields of computer vision, natural language processing, sound or music processing, and so on, where the goal is to automatically judge the quality of a decision or an output when that output is neither numerical nor categorical.

8.1.3 Variations at the Input Level

The last type of variation considered is deviation at the input level. In this category, we consider time series analysis, on the one hand, and online learning, on the other hand. Time series analysis typically tries to forecast future data based on time-stamped data from the past. In the online category, learning and decision-making take place simultaneously, and thus decision-making keeps on evolving. We distinguish between three different kinds of problems: data stream mining, lifelong learning, and reinforcement learning. When dealing with sequential data of the type just mentioned, it is necessary to design train and test regimen that are necessarily different from those encountered in nonsequential data. These will be discussed, along with metrics used for these tasks.

We now turn to the description of each machine learning problem we introduced together with the way in which their evaluation is typically conducted.

8.2 Anomaly or Outlier Detection

The first problem listed in the hierarchy of Figure 8.1 is the problem of anomaly detection. As per Goldstein and Uchida (2016), anomaly detection, also known as outlier detection, consists of identifying instances that depart from the standard population in the dataset. There are two main reasons for detecting anomalies. The first reason is to remove them from the dataset as they cause shifts in statistical measurements (e.g., the mean) that are detrimental to pattern recognition or machine learning systems. The second is to identify important or suspicious events and, rather than eliminate them, act on them. In the first case, anomalies can be removed or corrected as part of data cleansing since they represent errors in measurements or data entry. In the second case, the anomalies themselves are interesting as they represent instances of computer network intrusion, fraud, medical emergency, and so on, which all need to be further investigated and handled.

Anomaly detection can be performed using supervised, semi-supervised or unsupervised methods (Chandola et al. 2009; Goldstein and Uchida 2016; Pang et al. 2021). Its output can be a label, as in the case of supervised detection or semi-supervised detection outfitted with a threshold, or a score, as in the case of semi-supervised detection used without a threshold, or unsupervised detection. Depending on the kind of output, different metrics are used to evaluate anomaly detection algorithms. Section 8.2.1 overviews the different approaches typically used for anomaly detection, while Section 8.2.2 reviews the metrics that have been proposed to evaluate their outcome.

8.2.1 Approaches to Anomaly Detection

Supervised anomaly detection Supervised anomaly detection corresponds to a task where a fully labeled dataset is used to classify the data as either background (normal) or an anomaly. Typically, the labeled datasets used for anomaly detection are highly imbalanced since there typically are many more instances of the background than of anomalies (Japkowicz and Stephen 2002). To deal with class imbalances, a large number of methods have been proposed to oversample the minority class, undersample the majority class, or modify the cost function of the classifier. SMOTE (Chawla et al. 2002) and its variations (Kovács 2019) are well-known oversampling approaches that have shown a lot of success. More recently, image augmentation (Shorten and Khoshgoftaar 2019) showed a lot of promise for class-imbalanced image data in deep learning. These and other methods are discussed in Branco et al. (2016), Johnson and Khoshgoftaar (2019), and Ghosh et al. (2022).

Semi-supervised anomaly detection Another way of dealing with class imbalances was proposed early on by Japkowicz et al. (1995) and Petsche et al. (1995) who introduced the use of one-class learning for anomaly detection using an autoencoder. Soon thereafter, Schölkopf et al. (1999) and Tax and Duin (2004) adapted support vector machines (SVMs) to one-class learning. Since then, many one-class classification approaches have been devised, as discussed in Chandola et al. (2009), Khan and Madden (2014), Chalapathy and Chawla (2019), Pimentel et al. (2014), and Perera et al. (2021), and the process has become a popular staple in the machine learning, and especially deep-learning, community. One-class learning can be viewed as a form of semi-supervised learning where only one class, the background in this case, is known. One-class classifiers learn to differentiate between the class they know and that (or those) they don't know.[1] If the anomaly detector is to be used as a classifier that distinguishes anomalies from non-anomalies, then a threshold must be set to discriminate between normal instances and anomalies. Once the threshold is set, the system can be treated like a supervised anomaly detector and evaluated as such, as long as labeled data representing both normal and abnormal instances are available.

Unsupervised anomaly detection Unsupervised anomaly detection does not require any labels. It operates under the assumption that background instances are a lot more frequent than anomalies. Chandola et al. (2009) discuss three categories of clustering approaches that have been designed or used for anomaly detection. Each of them relies on a different assumption.

---

[1] Note that the term "semi-supervised" is used a little differently in the subfield of anomaly detection than it is in other areas of machine learning. In other areas it refers to ways in which unlabeled data (of any class) can be integrated to the supervised classification process. In anomaly detection it really refers to the subarea of one-class learning where only instances of the background class need to be labeled.

Assumption 1 Background data belong to a cluster, while anomalies don't.

Assumption 2 Background data can be found close to a cluster centroid while anomalies are far from any.

Assumption 3 Background data lie in relatively large and dense clusters, while anomalies can be found in either small or sparse ones.

Systems relying on the first assumption simply use existing clustering algorithms that do not force every instance into a cluster, such as density-based spatial clustering of applications with noise (DBSCAN). These methods have the disadvantage of using approaches that were not designed for anomaly detection. Systems relying on the second assumption work in two steps. First, clusters are found; and second, the distance of each instance to its closest cluster centroid is calculated. A number of approaches, including self-organizing maps (SOM), expectation-maximization (EM), and others, including some semi-supervised methods, use this technique. A disadvantage of such approaches is that if the anomalies are clustered together, they will be erroneously classified as normal since they will be close to a centroid. Approaches relying on the third assumption classify as anomalies any instances that belong to a small or sparse cluster. Cluster-based local outlier factor (CBLOF) is one approach that follows this technique.

8.2.2 Evaluating Anomaly Detection

We distinguish between three categories of evaluation metrics for anomaly detection: *traditional metrics*, *measures of precision*, and *measures of similarity*. In supervised or thresholded semi-supervised anomaly detection, many of the metrics used in classification are relevant. Of particular interest are precision, recall, precision-recall (PR) curves, and receiver operating characteristic (ROC) curves. In unsupervised or unthresholded semi-supervised anomaly detection, we survey a number of measures of precision that can be used to evaluate the task of anomaly detection. The last category, measures of similarity, is a little different as the measures were designed to compare anomaly detectors in an effort to differentiate between them, in order to subsequently build meaningful ensembles.

Supervised and Semi-Supervised Anomaly Detection

Of particular interest for anomaly detection are precision and recall measures. These metrics are particularly appropriate both because of the light they shine on the results, and the fact that they fare well on imbalanced problems. Specifically, precision gives us a measure of how accurately a detector designates an instance as anomalous (i.e., it indicates the fraction of instances labeled by the system as anomalous that truly are anomalous), and recall indicates the proportion of anomalous instances in the testing set that was accurately discovered by the detector. Both measures are focused on the anomalous class and are, therefore, less sensitive to the class imbalance problem than metrics that evaluate both classes simultaneously such as, for example, accuracy.

Although a threshold is technically available in the cases considered here, it is common for the evaluation method to forgo the threshold and use PR curves and ROC analysis, along with the area under the ROC curve (AUC), in order to assess the strength of the detector. This allows for a more thorough evaluation of the system since it examines the performance at every possible threshold. In addition, it dismisses the fact that "good" detectors could be outfitted with a bad threshold and therefore may perform worse than "bad" detectors outfitted with an appropriate threshold. So results obtained with PR curves or ROC analysis should be viewed as indicative of performance, assuming a good threshold, but not indicative of the performance of a particular detector outfitted with a specific threshold. These practical detectors must be evaluated using classification-appropriate metrics such as precision and recall. Once again, both PR curve and ROC analysis methodologies are very well suited to the anomaly detection problem because they are appropriate in class imbalance cases since the metrics they plot on each axis, in each case, depend on a single class of data. It is important to note, however, that if the classes are extremely imbalanced, or the minority class is very rare, PR curves are actually more appropriate (Davis and Goadrich 2006).[2] Precision, recall, PR curves and ROC analysis were discussed in Section 4.2.2 and in Sections 5.6–5.8, which we refer the reader to.

Although the methods discussed here are most appropriate for supervised anomaly detection where instances of both the background and the anomaly set are available, unsupervised and non-thresholded semi-supervised or one-class learning anomaly detection can also be evaluated using PR curves or ROC analysis if testing instances of both classes are available. Recent examples of such an evaluation in the case of unsupervised and semi-supervised anomaly detection are shown in Goldstein and Uchida (2016), Domingues et al. (2018), and Chalapathy et al. (2018). Garg et al. (2021) goes one step further, presenting an evaluation of semi-supervised and unsupervised anomaly detectors in the context of multivariate time-series analysis. Their work, thus, bridges the topics of anomaly detection evaluation and time series evaluation discussed in Section 8.9.

Semi-Supervised and Unsupervised Anomaly Detection

For unsupervised or unthresholded semi-supervised classification, measures of precision have been designed that rely on the ranking of the data output by the anomaly detector. We describe five different measures of precision metrics as per Campos et al. (2015): precision at n (P@n), R-precision, adjusted precision at n (adjusted P@n), average precision (AP), and adjusted average precision (adjusted AP).

Though an anomaly detector accurately predicting whether an instance is an outlier or not would be the best outcome in anomaly detection, in practice, more often than not, detectors outputting decisions in that format suffer from a huge false positive rate. The practice of not setting a threshold and having the detector output a ranking of all instances provides more flexibility since the user can make a decision based on the detector's output and his or her judgement. Evaluating whether the entire ranking is correct, however, is neither necessary nor adequate to evaluate an anomaly detector. The following metrics have been proposed to address this issue.

---

[2] A practical tutorial on this question is given in https://machinelearningmastery.com/roc-curves-and-precision-recall-curves-for-imbalanced-classification/.

Precision at n (P@n) P@n is based on the premise that the user of an anomaly detector is typically interested in examining a relatively small subset containing the top-ranked instances returned by the detector as potential anomaly candidates. When the number of such top-ranked anomaly candidates is specified in advance as n, we can calculate the proportion of truly anomalous instances in the n top-ranked instances returned by the detector. This corresponds to the precision at n metric, represented by P@n and defined as

$$P@n = \frac{|\{o \in O | rank(o) \leq n\}|}{n},$$

where O represents the number of outliers in the testing set.

R-precision The R-precision is very closely related to the P@n metric. It is based on the fact that how to choose n may not be obvious and suggests using $n = O$ instead of letting the user set its value. R-precision is defined as

$$R\text{-}Precision = \frac{|\{o \in O | rank(o) \leq |O|\}|}{|O|}.$$

Adjusted precision at n (adjusted P@n) There are two problems plaguing the P@n or R-precision metrics. First, these metrics can return very small values that are not representative of the performance of the detector in cases where the testing set contains, relatively speaking, an extremely small number of anomalies. Conversely, if the number of outliers present in the testing set is relatively large, then P@n can return very large values that inflate the worth of the detector. The adjusted precision at n metric intends to correct these issues by adjusting for the class imbalance in the testing set. The adjusted precision at n simply known as adjusted P@n is defined as

$$\text{Adjusted P@}n = \frac{P@n - |O|/N}{1 - |O|/N},$$

where N represents the number of instances in the testing set. For large values of n, the number of outliers, $|O|/n$, must be used instead of 1 in the denominator.

Average precision (AP) The three metrics just described have the disadvantage of depending on the value chosen for n. This means that if instances flagged as outliers in a testing set are ranked toward the top with respect to the total number of testing instances, but that somehow, n is so small that that rank is larger than n, the detector will be viewed as a bad performer even if, in fact, it performs pretty well.

In order to address that issue, the average precision was proposed. The idea is to consider all the ranks assigned by the detector to the instances of the outlier set O and average the value of P@n where n takes all the values of these ranks. In other words, the average precision, also known as AP, is defined as

$$AP = \frac{1}{|O|} \sum_{o \in O} P@rank(o).$$

Adjusted average precision (adjusted AP)   The final measure in this series is the adjusted average precision, which is adjusted in a way similar to the way P@n was adjusted. The adjusted average precision, also known as adjusted AP, is defined as

$$\text{Adjusted AP} = \frac{\text{AP} - |O|/N}{1 - |O|/N},$$

where once again, for large values of n, $|O|/n$ must be used instead of 1 in the denominator.

Other measures of precision   The five measures of precision just discussed assumed that a testing set containing labeled data was available. There may be situations where that is not the case. Goix (2016) discusses two measures of precision for unlabeled testing sets: the excess mass criterion (EM), and the mass volume criterion (MV). He further proposes a method for using these measures in high-dimensional domains where the original metrics usually break. The method consists of using feature subsampling and aggregation. The new methods are pitted against ROC analysis and PR curves and are shown to assess the detectors in a similar way.[3]

Ensemble-Based Anomaly Detection

When constructing ensembles, in addition to assessing the precision of the components used in the ensemble, it is also important to make sure that they are diverse enough to be of use. Schubert et al. (2012) propose a measure of similarity that correlates the scores obtained by the different detectors with no knowledge of their score distribution. The basis of the measure is the Pearson correlation coefficient enhanced by a weighting function meant to lessen the bias toward the normal background class introduced by the severe class imbalance typically present in anomaly detection problems. For more detail about the measure and its use, please see Schubert et al. (2012).

8.3 Positive-Unlabeled (PU) Classifiers

The second problem in our hierarchy is the problem of positive-unlabeled (PU) classification. PU-learning is, in some respects, the opposite of semi-supervised/one-class learning in the context of anomaly detection. As previously discussed, one-class learning, typically learns the background, or negative class, and labels as positive the instances not recognized by the background model. Conversely, PU learning learns from the labeled positive class along with unlabeled data, which may be either positive or negative (Bekker and Davis 2020). The goal of PU classification is the same as that of regular binary classification, but what makes its evaluation different is the lack of negative examples available for testing.

8.3.1 Approaches to PU Classification

Though it is related in some way, PU learning is different from one-class learning because it learns from both labeled and unlabeled data, while one-class learning learns from (only

---

[3] The code for these methods is available at https://github.com/ngoix/EMMV_benchmarks.

one class of) labeled data and no unlabeled ones. In that way, PU learning fits into the traditional category of semi-supervised learning whose goal is to integrate unlabeled data to the learning.[4] A very nice formalization of the problem is provided in Bekker and Davis (2020). The paper also surveys the different categories of methods that have been proposed to address the problem. These fall into three categories: *two-step techniques*, *biased learning*, and *class prior incorporation*. In two-step learning, the system first searches for reliable negative examples, and uses them along with the labeled positive instances in a supervised learning step or a semi-supervised step that uses the reliably labeled as well as the unlabeled dataset. In biased learning, it is assumed that the unlabeled dataset represents the negative class but has a certain amount of class noise. The noise is handled by placing greater misclassification penalties on the positive class than on the negative ones. Many of the approaches devised following this idea are SVM-based. In the third category of methods that incorporate the class prior, the expected proportion of positive to negative examples is used in a preprocessing, postprocessing, or method modification step to modify the training set, the output of the system, or the algorithm, respectively.

8.3.2 Evaluating PU Learning

When evaluating PU learning, two main questions arise whose answers are potentially different from what is done in other subfields of machine learning: "What data to test on?" and "What metric to use?" Saunders and Freitas (2022) considered these questions by reviewing about 50 PU classification papers, studying what evaluation methods were used in the past and concluding with their take on the issue.

Testing Data

Throughout their review of the PU literature, Saunders and Freitas (2022) found that papers used two different types of dataset:

- Engineered PU datasets;
- Genuine datasets abiding by the "selected completely at random" (SCAR) assumption.

In the first type of dataset, fully labeled binary datasets are engineered to hide the labels of all the negative examples used for training and a portion of the positive examples. At testing time, the labels are used to assess the accuracy of the classifier.

In the second type of dataset, it is assumed that the positive data available was selected at random and that, therefore, it is fully representative of both the labeled and unlabeled positive instances.[5] Based on this assumption, metrics, discussed next, can be estimated based on genuine PU datasets. Although these metrics may not be fully robust, they have the advantage of being derived from genuine and non-engineered datasets.

---

[4] As previously mentioned, the term "semi-supervised learning" has a slightly different meaning in the subfield of anomaly detection than it has in the rest of machine learning.
[5] This assumption, by the way, is challenged in Bekker and Davis (2020) who propose alternatives to it.

Saunders and Freitas (2022) suggest that PU classifiers should be tested on a combination of engineered and genuine datasets. For the engineered ones, they suggest that rather than choosing one or a few percentages of positive instances to hide in the training set, researchers should run systematic experiments with different percentages. They provide a repository of datasets for that purpose that varies the percentage of unlabeled positive instances from 5% to 95% in 5% increments. This approach may help standardize research on PU classifiers and provide fairer modes of comparison.

Evaluation Metrics

Saunders and Freitas' survey (2022) found that the three most reported metrics for PU classification research are the F-measure, accuracy, and AUC. The F-measure is an acceptable metric for evaluating PU classification since PU problems typically suffer from high degrees of class imbalances and the F-measure, as discussed before, is not as sensitive to class imbalances as other metrics such as accuracy. On the other hand, the F-measure combines both precision and recall together, which may be detrimental to the task of the classifier. In fact Saunders and Freitas (2022) argue that PU learning can seek to achieve one of two goals: *prioritization* or *anomaly detection*. Depending on what the goal of the problem is, either precision or recall is the more appropriate metric.

Prioritization is useful in contexts such as where the classifier is tasked with finding the instances that are most probably positive using inexpensive computational technology, so that only these most probable instances can be subjected to more expensive laboratory experiments that can only be done on a small scale. For that setting, precision is the metric of greatest interest since one wants to avoid running laboratory experiments that would yield negative results.

In anomaly detection, Saunders and Freitas (2022) argue that recall is more important since one does not want to miss an instance of fraud or computer attack. While that is a good argument, it is also true that if too many false positives occur (which sometimes is the disadvantage of prioritizing recall over precision), that is also problematic for the anomaly detector, which may become overwhelmed with false positives. For this reason, we actually favor the F-measure over recall, to make sure that we keep a balance of both phenomena. As a matter of fact, Saunders and Freitas (2022) recognize the issue as well, and suggest reporting the F-measure along with both recall and precision for all problems, a suggestion we fully endorse.

Saunders and Freitas (2022) do not recommend accuracy as a metric for PU-learning problems due to the imbalanced nature of most PU datasets. AUC, on the other hand, is acceptable, once again, because it is less sensitive to the class imbalance than accuracy. However, it may be slightly less intuitive, and thus, its results more difficult to interpret than those obtained using the F-measure, precision, and recall. It is also a combined metric that does not get decomposed logically the way the F-measure does with respect to precision and recall.

Last but not least, it is important to distinguish how the metrics just discussed are calculated in engineered PU datasets versus how they are calculated in genuine datasets. Their application in engineered datasets is straightforward and exactly the same as in other binary classification problems. It is in the case of genuine datasets that there is a difference. When dealing with a genuine dataset, the classification problem shifts. Rather than predicting the probability

$$Pr(y = 1),$$

where y represents the class of an instance, the classifier predicts the probability of

$$Pr(s = 1),$$

where s represents whether an instance is labeled or not. These are two different problems, which Elkan and Noto (2008) show are related as follows under the SCAR assumption

$$f(x) = \frac{g(x)}{c},$$

where $f(x)$ is a probabilistic classifier that distinguishes between labeled and unlabeled data, $g(x)$ is a probabilistic classifier that distinguishes between positive and negative instances, and c is a constant. In dealing with genuine datasets, researchers use $f(x)$ as a proxy for $g(x)$ and calculate precision, recall, the F-measure, and the AUC using $f(x)$. Elkan and Noto (2008) show that that is not a problem if the SCAR assumption holds and if the only goal of the PU-classifier is to rank instances according to the probability that they belong to the positive class. That is because the difference between $f(x)$ and $g(x)$ appears only as a constant factor. However, if the goal of PU learning is more than ranking and if the SCAR assumption cannot be confirmed, the performance of a classifier on genuine PU datasets cannot be properly estimated.

8.4 Ordinal Classification

Ordinal classification is a mix between a classification and a regression problem. On the one hand, instances need to be categorized into one of several classes, but on the other hand, the classes are not independent of one another, as they are ranked. Examples of such problems include letter grades in a school setting: A+, A, A−, B+, B,..., or product ratings such as star ratings (five stars, four stars, all the way to one or no stars), but there are many more. However, unlike in a regression setting, the classes are discrete so the point of the problem is not to predict a value. Multi-class classification methods can be used for such problems, but they are restrictive in that all the information regarding a class's relation to the other classes is lost. For example, a multi-class evaluation method would penalize assigning an F to an assignment that deserves an A in the same way as it would assigning it an A−. To counter this problem, a number of methods have been designed. They are discussed in Section 8.4.1, followed by a discussion of the evaluation metrics most appropriate for the ordinal classification setting.

8.4.1 Approaches to Ordinal Classification

Gutiérrez et al. (2016) survey the literature on ordinal classification and distinguish between three different categories of methods: *naive methods* that apply existing algorithms, methods based on *ordinal binary decomposition*, and *threshold models*. In the naive category, three approaches are followed. First, the classification labels are assigned real values and regression models are applied; second, the problem is treated as a multi-class classification problem with the relation between the classes lost; third, cost-sensitive classification algorithms are used with larger costs given to errors where the classification and true label are far apart than errors where they are close to one another. In the binary decomposition category, the ordinal problem is turned into a series of binary problems where different categories of problems are considered in parallel. For example, from a problem where students are graded on the A–F scale, problems that distinguish the A students from the others and the A–B students from the others or the F students from the rest, and so on, can be devised and solved either by ensemble methods or multi-label classification methods. In the threshold models category, the idea is to use a two-step method that models a continuous latent variable, followed by a learning method that establishes a set of thresholds that bounds the different ordinal categories. These methods are related to ordinal regression models, except for the fact that the thresholds are not predefined but learned in a subsequent step. They are also related to one-class learning methods, although rather than a single threshold, multiple ones have to be set. In Section 8.4.2, we investigate the methods that have been used to evaluate ordinal classification methods.

8.4.2 Evaluating Ordinal Classification

In Gaudette and Japkowicz (2009), eight evaluation metrics are compared on an ordinal classification task in order to assess which of these metrics are preferable. The metrics considered are some of the metrics used for classification and regression analysis such as accuracy, mean absolute error (MAE), mean squared error (MSE), coefficients of correlation, as well as the specialized metrics *normalized distance performance measure, accuracy within n*, and *accuracy + correlation*. The traditional classification and regression metrics were described in Chapter 5. The regression metrics will be given a deeper coverage in Section 8.6. We now review the specialized metrics used in ordinal classification.

Normalized distance performance measure Normalized distance performance measures (NPDM) measure the number of times the predetermined and systems' rankings are in agreement and disagreement and combine the two measures together. The original metric was described in detail in Yao (1995). Other related metrics were later proposed in Bahari and Hamme (2014). It is important to note that with these metrics, no assumption is made about the magnitude of the error between two classes.

Accuracy within n Accuracy within n allows outputs within a certain range of the correct one to be considered correct. For example, if a system predicted that a student was going to receive an A when in fact the student received an A+, the system is accurate within 1. If the student was predicted to receive an A−, the system is accurate within 2, and so on. With k classes, accuracy within $k-2$ states that all outputs are correct with the exception of the most extreme type of error: mistaking class k (e.g., F) with class 1 (e.g., A+) or class 1 (A+)

Table 8.1. *Multi-label binary classification.*

Instance no.	Movie	Musical	Drama	Family	Fantasy
1	Annie	1	1	1	0
2	Harry Potter	0	0	1	1
3	West Side Story	1	1	0	0
4	The Godfather	0	1	0	0

with class k (e.g., F). Accuracy with n metrics, used in combination can be tuned to give a user the type of information needed to evaluate an ordinal classification problem.

Accuracy + correlation Accuracy + correlation calculates the mean of the accuracy and correlation. It was proposed by Gaudette and Japkowicz (2009).

Comparison of metrics for ordinal classification The experiments in Gaudette and Japkowicz (2009) show that MSE and MAE correlate well with accuracy within n metrics. Correlation does not. Based on these results, MSE and MAE are considered the best metrics for ordinal classification, with preference given to MSE in cases where detecting large errors is very important, and preference given to MAE in cases where tolerance for small errors is lower. Although the study was conducted using a single dataset, its conclusion seems representative as more recent, large comparison efforts in ordinal classification, such as Gutiérrez et al. (2016), reports MAE results.[6]

8.5 Multi-label Classification

Multi-label classification is different from single-label classification for the simple reason that rather than being either right or wrong, a classifier's prediction is more often than not partially correct, and can range from fully inaccurate to fully accurate. We illustrate this issue on a small database of movies (Table 8.1) classified in four different genres, *musical, drama, family,* and *fantasy*. This is a classical multi-label classification setting where belonging to one category does not preclude belonging to another. Indeed, for example, "Harry Potter" is both a fantasy movie and a family movie. Similarly, the movie "Annie" is a musical, a drama, and a family movie, but it does not belong to the fantasy category. Yet, if a classifier predicted that "Harry Potter" was a musical, a family movie, and a fantasy movie, it would not be completely correct nor completely incorrect. Similarly, if the classifier omitted to classify "Annie" as a drama, but classified it as a musical and a family movie, it would also be partially correct and partially incorrect. Some of the multi-label classifier and evaluation metrics attempt to capture this partial accuracy in various ways while others ignore it. We begin by reviewing the methods that have been proposed to handle multi-label classification and then describe existing evaluation metrics for this task.

---

[6] The survey also reports the MZE, a variant of accuracy, despite the fact that important class relation information is lost with its use and that it should be dropped in favor of accuracy within n or MAE metrics.

8.5.1 Approaches to Multi-label Classification

Sorower (2010) presents an extensive overview of the field of multi-label classification. In particular, he presents a variety of solutions including *dataset transformations* and *algorithm adaptations*, as well as *subspace-based, ensemble-based,* and *generative-based methods*. Many solutions to the multi-label classification problem use a dataset transformation approach to turn the problem into one or a series of binary classification tasks. A number of approaches can be considered, including the simple copy transformation method where each instance appears as many times as it has labels (each with a different label). Also popular is the binary relevance method that creates as many datasets as there are labels and trains a different classifier on each dataset, but in doing so assumes label independence. To correct for that issue, the label powerset approach was proposed that gives each combination of labels a new label, thus creating a single dataset. However, while addressing the label independence assumption of the binary relevance approach, it creates a classification problem with many classes and possibly too few instances per class.

In the algorithm adaptation category, the formula being optimized is modified to account for the multiple labels. This is done by modifying the entropy formula in decision trees, the distance function in k-nearest-neighbors techniques, the error function in neural networks, and so on. Shared subspace methods attempt to discover the common subspace shared among the different class labels, while reducing redundancy, as always, but also accounting for label correlations. Such methods use latent semantic indexing, linear discriminant analysis, or other such approaches as feature extraction methods that will be discussed in Chapter 9, and optimize the results using a measure that combines all labels. Ensemble methods have also been proposed that construct label powersets and combine the results together. To decrease the class imbalance problem, some of these methods propose to prune the label powerset that covers only a small number of instances, thus focusing on the most salient labels. Finally, a number of generative modeling approaches have been proposed. The idea is to create a mixture of weights for the different classes and use a parameter estimation method to learn the joint distribution. These methods are, in some cases, similar to the shared subspace methods previously mentioned and will also be discussed in Chapter 9.

8.5.2 Evaluating Multi-label Classification

We now turn to the evaluation of multi-label classification algorithms. Since hard labels may be too strict (e.g., is "Harry Potter" really appropriate for young children?), some classifiers assign soft rather than hard binary labels. We will consider metrics that evaluate systems trained on soft labels, though for most of our discussion, we will assume multiple binary labels as in our film database example. A large number of evaluation schemes have been proposed for this problem, which we discuss one by one using the movie database. In particular, we discuss *example-based metrics* and briefly discuss *label-based* metrics. We raise the question of *nonbinary multiple labels* at the end of the discussion and refer the reader to the literature for discussions of these settings, as well as for information on appropriate data sampling and statistical tests. In all that follows, n represents the number of instances, y_i is the binary vector representing the ground truth of instance i, and $\hat{y}_i$ is the binary

Table 8.2. *Multi-label binary classification: (Left) Ground truth; (Right) predictions.*

Instance no./label	l1	l2	l3	l4
1	1	1	1	0
2	0	0	1	1
3	1	1	0	0
4	0	1	0	0

Instance no./label	l1	l2	l3	l4
1	1	1	1	1
2	0	1	1	0
3	1	1	0	0
4	1	1	0	0

vector representing the classification of instance i. The discussion follows Zhang and Zhou (2014).[7] For illustration purposes, the left-hand side of Table 8.2 reproduces the ground truth of Table 8.1 in a synthesized manner where $l1, l2, l3$, and $l4$ represent the four labels of the database. The right-hand side of Table 8.2 lists the results of a simulated multi-label classifier. As per Zhang and Zhou (2014), evaluation metrics for multi-label classification are categorized as example-based or label-based metrics. Example-based metrics consider each test example and all its labels separately, assign a performance value to them, and calculate the mean of the performance values obtained on the entire testing set. Conversely, label-based metrics treat the testing set as L testing sets, one for each label where L is the total number of labels, use regular classification metrics on each "testing set," and aggregate the results using micro-, macro-, or weighted-average, as previously discussed in Section 4.2.3. Next, we first discuss example-based metrics, then label-based metrics, and finally we discuss the case of nonbinary settings and refer the reader to further readings.

Example-Based Metrics

Exact match ratio and 0/1 loss The exact match ratio (EMR; also known as subset accuracy) calculates the number of times the classification matches the ground truth perfectly. In our example, this happens only once, in the case of "West Side Story," since in all other cases, the results are only partially correct. The value of the EMR will then be 1/4, or .25, since only one of the four instances matches its ground truth perfectly. Formally, the formula for the EMR is

$$EMR = \frac{1}{n} \sum_{i=1}^{n} I(y_i = \hat{y}_i).$$

The opposite of EMR is the 0/1 loss. Its formula is

$$0/1 Loss = 1 - EMR = \frac{1}{n} \sum_{i=1}^{n} I(y_i \neq \hat{y}_i).$$

The 0/1 loss calculates the proportions of instances whose classification does not match the ground truth perfectly. In our example, all the instances except for "West Side Story" do

---

[7] Implementations of the metrics discussed are given in the tutorial found at https://mmuratarat.github.io/2020-01-25/multilabel_classification_metrics.

not have a perfect match with their ground truth. Therefore, the 0/1 loss for our database is 3/4, or .75. It is clear that both these metrics are extremely strict. For example, the classifier classified the movie "Annie" well on three labels, making a mistake only on the fantasy category. Yet the classification was deemed erroneous because of that mistake. Obviously, the more labels, the more likely a classifier is to make at least one mistake on an instance. Yet, one mistake on an instance is all it takes for these two metrics to disqualify the performance of the classifier on that instance. While in certain cases such strictness is warranted (e.g., if the labels correspond to all the tests that need to be performed successfully prior to launching a rocket ship to space), in others, it might not be. Formally, this depends on the error cost of the problem.

Hamming loss The Hamming loss (HL) is a metric that calculates the number of prediction errors (false positives or false negatives) made over all the test instances and labels. The formula for the HL follows

$$HL = \frac{1}{n \times L} \sum_{i=1}^{n} \sum_{j=1}^{L} I\left(y_i^j \neq \hat{y}_i^j\right).$$

In our example database, we have four instances and four labels, so $n \times L = 4 \times 4 = 16$. The first instance has one labeling error (l4 is 1 instead of 0); the second one, two (l2 is 1 instead of 0 and l4 is 0 instead of 1); the third, zero, and the fourth, one (l1 is 1 instead of 0). This amounts to four errors and, therefore, the HL is equal to 4/16 = 1/4 = .25, which is a lot smaller and perhaps fairer in some way than the 0/1 loss. However, the HL comes with problems too. The result tells us that the classifier makes an error one out of four times. One out of four may mean different things, though, and the HL doesn't tell us in what way the error is made. For example, in the current example, one out of four means that, on average, the classifier made one classification error per instance (i.e., one out of the four labels was wrong, on average). However, let us say that three out of 4 instances were perfectly classified (all labels were right) and one instance was completely wrongly classified (all labels were wrong), then the HL would also have given us a value of .25. Note, however, that in this latest case, the 0/1 loss would also have given us a value of .25, so there may be value in using both metrics together, as their combined values may give us a finer grained picture of where the errors are located.

Hamming score (example-based accuracy) The Hamming score (HS) (not the same as the Hamming loss just presented), also known as example-based accuracy, represents the average over all instances of the number of accurately predicted labels over the total number of predicted or actual labels for that instance. The formula is given as

$$HS = \frac{1}{n} \sum_{i=1}^{n} \frac{|y_i \cap \hat{y}_i|}{|y_i \cup \hat{y}_i|}.$$

The HS for our example database is

$$\frac{\frac{3}{4} + \frac{1}{3} + \frac{2}{2} + \frac{1}{2}}{4} = .646.$$

This means that, on average, each example was well classified at 64.6%, or about 2/3 of all the labels for each example were properly predicted. To fully understand this metric, we analyze its result instance by instance. "Annie" received a score of 3/4 because the classifier predicted one extra 1. "Harry Potter" received a score of 1/3 because one of its labels (l3) was properly predicted, but it did not catch l4 and wrongly set l2 to true. "West Side Story" received a perfect score of 1 because it predicted all the labels correctly and "The Godfather" received a score of 1/2 because it predicted l2 correctly but predicted that l1 was true incorrectly. On the one hand, this seems like a good metric in that a human being would agree that "West Side Story" was perfectly classified, that "Annie" received the next best classification, followed by "The Godfather," and that "Harry Potter" was the worst classified of all four instances. So the scores accurately reflect this feeling. On the other hand, it is disturbing that no reward exists for classifiers that correctly refrain from predicting classes as positive. For example, looking at "The Godfather" which got a score of 1/2 and assuming that we are looking at a six-labeled classification problem instead of four and that the classifier correctly assigned a 0 to the extra two labels. Its score would still be 1/2 even though there is more merit in correctly classifying as negative four rather than two labels.

Example-based precision, recall, and the *F*-measure Example-based precision and recall are similar to example-based accuracy (or HS) and given as

$$Precision = \frac{1}{n} \sum_{i=1}^{n} \frac{|y_i \cap \hat{y}_i|}{|y_i|},$$

$$Recall = \frac{1}{n} \sum_{i=1}^{n} \frac{|y_i \cap \hat{y}_i|}{|\hat{y}_i|}.$$

Similarly, the example-based *F*1-measure is given as

$$F1 = \frac{1}{n} \sum_{i=1}^{n} \frac{2 \times |y_i \cap \hat{y}_i|}{|y_i| + |\hat{y}_i|}.$$

For our database, these values amount to

$$Precision = \frac{\frac{3}{3} + \frac{1}{2} + \frac{2}{2} + \frac{1}{1}}{4} = .875,$$

$$Recall = \frac{\frac{3}{4} + \frac{1}{2} + \frac{2}{2} + \frac{1}{2}}{4} = .6875.$$

Looking at these values instance by instance, we see that precision gives top marks to "Annie," "West Side Story," and "The Godfather" because the classifier properly chose positive when it was warranted to do so (even though for the first and last movies, it was too eager to choose positive when it should not have). So precision does not penalize classifiers for being too eager. For recall, there was a penalty every time the classifier was too eager to choose a positive label when the ground truth did not have this label set as positive. Missing a positive label, however, was not penalized. In the second instance, "Harry Potter," the penalty came from the fact that the classifier missed classifying l4 as positive, but the classifier did not get penalized for setting l2 to 1 when it shouldn't have. It was penalized for doing so by precision. Overall, at least on our database, precision is too lenient. Recall seems to the point, penalizing instances 2 and 4 more than instance 1. On the other hand, an overly conservative classifier would be less penalized by recall than it should. For example, if instance 1, "Annie," had only l2 classified as 1 with all other labels being 0 and the ground truth were as it is, the instance would receive a perfect score despite missing l1 and l3. Precision would compensate for that, however, by giving that instance a score of 1/3.

The $F1$-measure for our database is

$$F1 = \frac{1}{4} \times \left(\frac{2 \times 3}{3+4} + \frac{2 \times 1}{2+2} + \frac{2 \times 2}{2+2} + \frac{2 \times 1}{1+2} \right) = .756.$$

According to the $F1$-measure, the first instance received a score of 6/7 (almost perfect), the second one, a score of 1/2, the third, a score of 1, and the last, a score of 2/3. The ranking of the instances from best classified to worst makes intuitive sense. The question of the gaps between the ranks, however, is debatable, although altogether, the $F1$-measure appears reasonable.

Label-Based Metrics

The label-based metrics consist of splitting multi-label problems with L labels into L single-label problems and combining the results of metrics obtained on each single-label problem using a different combination measure: micro-averaging, macro-averaging, or weighted averaging. We will not discuss the classification metrics and combination measures here since these metrics were already discussed in Chapters 4 and 5 along with combination schemes for multi-part metrics in Section 4.2.3. However, we do illustrate label-based metrics here by calculating all the values they obtain on our example database.

In order to calculate the label-based metrics, we begin by creating four confusion matrices, one for each label in our database. The matrices are shown in Figure 8.3. From these confusion matrices, we can calculate the accuracy, precision, recall, and $F1$-measures. Table 8.4 lists the value of these metrics for each label. Macro-, micro-, and weighted-averages are then calculated from these values according to the definitions and illustrations given in Section 4.2.3. Table 8.5 shows the results of these calculations for each metric. The results show that the label-based averages closest to the example-based results are the micro-averages. Both the macro- and weighted- averages yield a higher recall than precision. In addition, for the label-based accuracies, all averages are higher than the HS.

Table 8.3. *Four confusion matrices for labels l1, l2, l3, and l4.*

l1	T	F	l2	T	F	l3	T	F	l4	T	F
Y	2	1	**Y**	3	1	**Y**	2	0	**Y**	0	1
N	0	1	**N**	0	0	**N**	0	2	**N**	1	2

Table 8.4. *Accuracy, precision, recall, and F1-measure for labels l1, l2, l3, and l4.*

Label	Accuracy	Precision	Recall	F1-measure
l1	.75	.67	1	.8
l2	.75	.75	1	.86
l3	1	1	1	1
l4	.5	0	0	0

Table 8.5. *Macro, Micro, and weighted averages for accuracy, precision, recall, and F1-measure for labels l1, l2, l3, and l4.*

Label	Accuracy	Precision	Recall	F1-measure
Macro average	.75	.605	.75	.887
Micro average	.75	.875	.7	.778
Weighted average	.781	.699	.875	.773

Example-Based or Label-Based Metrics?

Altogether, it is difficult to decide whether one should use example-based or label-based metrics. It probably depends on the main focus of the application. If what really matters is optimizing the multi-label classification of the instances, then example-based metrics are recommended. However, it may be useful to know whether some labels are systematically badly predicted. In these kind of diagnostic tasks, a label-based approach may be preferred. Furthermore, in such cases, considering each metric result separately rather than averaging them may be preferable as well.

Metrics for Nonbinary Multi-label Classifiers

For the case where the result of the classifier is not thresholded, Zhang and Zhou (2014) and Gibaja (2014) also list formulae for a number of ranking metrics including macro- and micro-averaged AUC, one-error, coverage, and a few others. Furthermore, Gibaja (2014) discusses the importance of stratification when using one-class classification and refers to specialized stratification methods for the case of multi-labeled data. She also discusses the type of statistical tests that have been used in the case of multi-label classification in the past.

8.6 Regression Analysis

Regression analysis is a cornerstone of statistical analysis that has been studied for many years. Most high school students encounter simple univariate linear regression in their math courses and are thus familiar with the concept of predicting the dependent variable, y, from the independent one, x, by finding the line that best fits a cloud of points relating the two. Multiple regression expands the simple regression case to multiple independent variables being used to predict a single dependent one. Over the years, there have been a large number of approaches designed for multiple-regression stemming from statistical analysis and machine learning. We will start this section by describing a few well-known approaches and then discuss the different metrics that have been proposed to evaluate its results. Some of these metrics were discussed in Section 4.2.4. We review them here in light of more advanced considerations and we also present additional ones.

8.6.1 Approaches to Regression Analysis

There are two important groups of multiple regression analysis methods: linear regression and nonlinear regression.[8] Linear regression techniques stem from statistical analysis while nonlinear regression took root in machine learning, which mixes AI principles together with statistical analysis ones.

In the linear regression category, simple linear regression attempts to fit a line through a cloud of points using an ordinary least square approach. Ridge regression pursues the same goal but uses a ridge estimator, which has a higher bias but lower variance than the ordinary least square estimators, yielding shrinkage in coefficients, a reduction of model complexity, and, thus, in machine learning terms, a reduction in overfitting. LASSO regression is another approach in the same category of regularization approaches that penalizes the sum of absolute values of the coefficients to minimize the prediction error. As a result, some of the variable's regression coefficients shrink to zero. The approach can thus be viewed as performing feature selection while conducting regression analysis.

On the machine learning side, a number of nonlinear classifiers have been adapted for regression analysis as well. In addition to having the capability of learning nonlinear relationships between the independent variables, they have the advantage over purely statistical methods of performing well in the presence of a large number of independent variables. Algorithms in this category of methods include decision tree and random forest approaches, *k*-nearest neighbors, and SVM approaches, along with neural network and deep learning approaches.

8.6.2 Evaluating Regression Analysis

We now turn to the question of how to evaluate the various approaches that have been proposed over the years to perform regression analysis. The discussion in this section is based on (Kapil 2018).[9]

Classical evaluation methods for regression analysis include such metrics as the sum squared error (SSE), the MSE, and the root mean squared error (RMSE), which each, in a slightly different way, calculates the difference between the actual and predicted values.

---

[8] See www.analyticsvidhya.com/blog/2021/01/a-quick-overview-of-regression-algorithms-in-machine-learning/#h2_4 for illustrations of this discussion.

[9] See the model evaluation – regression models part of the blog.

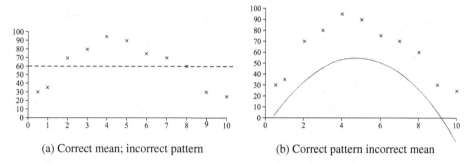

(a) Correct mean; incorrect pattern   (b) Correct pattern incorrect mean

Figure 8.2 Sensitivity to the mean and scale of predictions.

More sophisticated methods, however, have also been designed such as the coefficient of determination, R^2.

Error-Based Metrics

The SSE, MSE, RMSE, and MAE were defined in Section 4.2.4. We use this current section to discuss some of their shortcomings that users should be aware of. One serious problem with the SSE, MSE, and RMSE is their sensitivity to outliers. In particular, it can be shown that a large error in a sample gives similar results to small errors in many samples when using these metrics. The MAE does not square the errors obtained on samples, and thus does not give more weight to large errors. This is helpful in dealing with outliers, although, in certain applications, not penalizing outliers the way SSE, MSE, and RMSE do is detrimental.

Another issue encountered by all four metrics (SSE, MSE, RMSE, MAE) is their sensitivity to the mean and scale of predictions. In other words, a simple model that predicts the mean, or values close to it, will do well according to these metrics despite missing the shape of the distribution as in the extreme case of Figure 8.2(a); whereas a model that correctly captures the pattern but misses the mean will do badly according to these metrics as in the case of Figure 8.2(b).

R^2-Based Metrics

The coefficient of determination, R^2, and adjusted coefficient of determination, adjusted R^2, were defined in Section 4.2.4. In this section, we explain in more depth where the formulae come from and what their strengths and weaknesses are. The coefficient of determination, R^2, indicates the proportion of data samples that fall within the curve formed by the regression model. More formally, R^2 corresponds to the proportion of variance in the predicted value ($\hat{y}$) associated to the variance found in the features ($x_1, x_2, \ldots, x_k$, assuming a k-dimensional problem) of the instance. Now, more informally, R^2 tells us how much of the variance in one variable depends on, or can be explained by, the variance in others. The higher the R^2, the more correlated $\hat{y}$ is to $x_1, x_2, \ldots, x_k$; R^2 can take values between

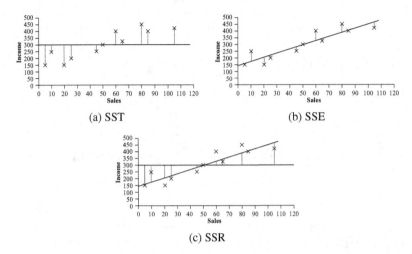

Figure 8.3 An illustration of SST, SSE, and SSR.

0 and 1. High values of R^2 indicate how good a fit the model is to the data. If the regression model fits all samples perfectly, R^2 will have a value of 1. A clear description of how the coefficient of determination for multivariate problems (k-dimensional problems where $k > 1$) can be calculated is given in Abdi (2007) and will not be repeated here; however, Kapil (2018) gives an intuitive description of R^2 for a univariate problem fitted through linear regression. We follow that description.

We calculate R^2 as a combination of three different quantities – the sum of squares totals (SST), The SSE, or residual sum of squares, and the sum of squares regression (SSR). We begin by describing each of these quantities and illustrate them in Figure 8.3.

The *sum of squares totals (SST)* are illustrated in Figure 8.3(a). The solid line represents the mean of the independent variable; that is, x (in a univariate problem where $k = 1$). The SST is calculated by taking the difference of a sample to that mean, squaring that difference, repeating the same operation for every other sample, and adding all the squares together. The SST represents a measure of variance in the data.

The *sum of squares errors (SSE)* are illustrated in Figure 8.3(b). In that graph, the solid line represents the linear regression model that was used to fit the data. The SSE is calculated by taking the distance of a sample to the regression line, squaring that distance, repeating the same operation for every other sample, and adding all the squares together. The SSE represents a measure of deviation between the true and predicted samples. It can also be thought of as the unexplained error because we cannot explain why the regression line does not fit all points perfectly.

The *sum of squares (due to) regression (SSR)* are illustrated in Figure 8.3(c). The two solid lines are those already discussed in the context of SST and SSE. The SSR is calculated by taking the distance between the two lines with respect to each point (i.e., this distance is calculated for each sample), squaring that distance, repeating the same operation for every other sample, and adding all the squares together. The SSR represents the deviation we are able to explain (because we can explain the difference between the average and the regression model).

Now that we have described the SST, SSE, and SSR, we can explain their relationship as well as define R^2. The SST, which represents the total sum of square error, is made up of the explained error (SSR) and the unexplained error (SSE). So we have

$$SST = SSR + SSE,$$

and R^2 is defined as

$$R^2 = \frac{SSR}{SST}.$$

In other words, R^2 represents the proportion with which the total error can be explained. In other words, R^2 represents the percentage of changes in the predicted variable y that can be explained by the independent variable x. The higher this percentage, the better. The advantage of R^2 is that, unlike SSE, MSE, RMSE, and MAE, it is not sensitive to the mean and scale of predictions that was illustrated in Figure 8.2. However, R^2 remains sensitive to outliers and, in cases where the dimensionality of the problem is larger than $k = 1$, it suffers from multicollinearity. This means that if both x_i and x_j are correlated to y, it is possible that x_i and x_j are also correlated. This may optimistically bias R^2.

The adjusted R^2 metric addresses this serious issue of multicollinearity, which is akin to the curse of dimensionality and thus also related to the issue of overfitting, by penalizing R^2 according to the dimensionality of the problem k relative to the number of samples in the dataset. The adjusted R^2 metric is defined as follows:

$$Adjusted\,R^2 = 1 - (1 - R^2) \times \frac{n-1}{n-k-1} = 1 - \frac{SSE}{SST} \times \frac{n-1}{n-k-1},$$

where n is the number of samples in the problem, and k, its dimensionality.

The Adjusted R^2 is such that as k increases, it decreases, thus correcting, somewhat, for the multicollinearity problem.

8.7 Image Segmentation

Image segmentation is the task of finding a specific shape within an image, such as a face, a pedestrian's silhouette, or a bone structure in a medical image. Many approaches have been designed for this task. Section 8.7.1 describes some of these approaches while Section 8.7.2 discusses how they can be evaluated.

8.7.1 Approaches to Image Segmentation

Yuheng and Hao (2017) review a number of techniques that have been proposed to perform image segmentation. These include region-based segmentation and edge detection segmentation. Minaee et al. (2022) focus on the deep learning approaches that have been proposed for the problem. We describe these approaches in turn.

Region-based segmentation uses two basic approaches. The first one is called threshold segmentation, and the second, regional growth segmentation. In threshold segmentation, an image is divided into target and background regions. The search for thresholds can be global, where a region is divided into a target region and a background region, or local, where different thresholds divide the image into several target and background regions simultaneously. Many different criteria for finding thresholds have been used, such as the largest interclass variance method, entropy-based methods, minimum error methods, and so on. In regional growth segmentation, a pixel is chosen as a seed pixel, around which similar pixels are merged. The boundaries of the region are naturally formed when the neighboring pixels are different enough not to be merged into the growing region. Different criteria to determine pixel similarity can be chosen, as can different seed pixels. This can give rise to different results.

The second category of approaches is based on edge detection, which is a search for discontinuous local features in the image. Such changes typically manifest themselves in terms of changes in local brightness, color mutation, texture changes, and so on. Such changes can be detected, most often in a parallel procedure, through first-order differential operators such as the Prewitt, Roberts, or Sobel operators, or second-order ones such as the Laplacian, Kirsch, or Wallis operators.

The third category of methods is based on deep learning. The problem can be construed as a classification problem where either pixels are given semantic labels, or individual objects in the image are to be classified. The first kind of approach is called semantic segmentation while the second is called instance segmentation. A large variety of deep learning methods have been proposed for these problems, including convolutional neural networks, encoder-decoder networks, recurrent networks, attention-based models, generative models, and so on. There are too many methods to describe in this section, but the reader is directed to Minaee et al. (2022) for detailed descriptions.

8.7.2 Evaluating Image Segmentation

We now discuss the issue of how to evaluate image segmentation algorithms. While all the metrics discussed in Chapters 4 and 5, where the classification metrics can be used for image classification were presented, image segmentation requires different metrics. The reason why different metrics are necessary here is because the goal of image segmentation is different from that of classification, or of other tasks discussed so far. Indeed, segmentation consists of dividing an image into semantically meaningful regions. When evaluating whether segmentation was successful or not, the segmented region is pitted against a gold standard region.

The success of the operation is measured by considering the overlap between the segmented and the gold standard regions, which cannot be measured by any of the metrics discussed so far. Instead, we discuss the Jaccard index and the dice coefficient, which are commonly used in this area and are given by the equations

$$J(A, B) = \frac{|A \cap B|}{|A \cup B|},$$

$$D(A, B) = 2 \times \frac{|A \cap B|}{|A| + |B|}.$$

As can be seen from the equations, the Jaccard index calculates the overlap between the predicted shape, *A*, and the true shape, *B*, and divides it by their union. The dice coefficient calculates the overlap between the predicted shape and the true shape times two, and divides it by the sum of the two shapes. The ideal result of both metrics obtained when both shapes match perfectly is a value of 1. The Jaccard index will be revisited in Section 9.1.

Although these two metrics are classical metrics that have been used extensively in the area of image segmentation, a number of other metrics, both supervised and unsupervised, have also been proposed and are surveyed in Zhang (1996) and Zhang et al. (2008).

8.8 Text Generation

Text generation trains a model from a corpus in order to learn the probabilities of potential next words, given a sequence of words that have already occurred. Once the model is trained, it is used as follows: a seed word or phrase is first given to the model, which outputs the next word or token, which is then added to the previous sequence to serve as the next seed. The process continues until it is stopped by the user. Text generation is useful for a number of applications including text summarization and spelling corrections.[10]

In Section 8.8.1, we describe the process in more detail together with the categories of approaches that have previously been proposed to handle the problem. Section 8.8.2 discusses the different methods that have been proposed to evaluate the quality of the generated text. Section 9.4.4 provides more specific detail about generative adversarial network–based text generation and its evaluation.

8.8.1 Approaches to Text Generation

In order to be able to generate text, a language model first needs to be constructed. A language model amounts to a probability distribution defined over a sequence of words. In a language model, for example, the sequence "sleeping beauty" would receive a higher probability than "sleeping artichoke," which, in turn, makes the sequence "sleeping beauty" much more likely to subsequently be generated than "sleeping artichoke." Language models can be constructed using statistical or deep learning principles.

Regardless of the nature of the model, text generation requires two steps. First, a language model must be constructed, and, second, a word selection strategy must be chosen. We discuss different instances of types of language models in the statistical and deep learning traditions, respectively. The statistical models require an explicit word selection step, which is done using a search mechanism over the probabilities learned in the first step. In the deep learning models, the second step is implicit and depends on the weights that were derived in the neural network during training. A survey of text generation models, along with the threats they cause and methods for detecting machine-generated text can be found in Crothers et al. (2023).

---

[10] Some of the concepts discussed in this section are illustrated in www.muratkarakaya.net/2022/11/text-generation-in-deep-learning-with_8.html.

Statistical Language Models

The main statistical approaches proposed for language modeling uses Markov models or conditional random fields. A Markov model models a finite set of states and assigns conditional probabilities to the transitions from one state to another. Conditional random fields are similar but are more flexible.

First-order Markov models A first-order Markov model takes into account a single transition, which means that the probability depends only on the preceding word (or character, if we are generating sequences of characters rather than sequences of words). Such models are effective on short phrases. Such a model would be able to properly model the "sleeping beauty" versus "sleeping artichoke" example above, given a reasonably large and representative corpus, of course.

k-th order Markov models k-th order Markov models extend the dependency of words to more than just the preceding word. It can take into account the two preceding words for $k = 2$ or the three preceding words for $k = 3$. This allows for more accurate language modeling, though it does so at the expense of a more complex model, which requires a larger corpus, more memory, and more computing time.

Hidden Markov Models Hidden Markov Models are similar to first-order Markov Models except that instead of operating on words or characters, they operate on latent (or hidden) variables that represent groupings of words or characters. This allow such models to generate well-formed phrases (e.g., grammatically correct ones). On the other hand, unlike the previous models, they are not sensitive to the particular words or characters seen previously and may, thus, generate text that is structurally correct, but makes no sense semantically.

Conditional Markov models To correct for hidden Markov models' deficiencies, conditional Markov models take into consideration both the state and the word- or character-level preceding input. The produced text is, thus, controlled both at the syntactic and semantic level. In addition, conditional Markov models are such that they can be trained by common machine learning approaches such as multinomial logistic regression, decision trees, or random forests.

Conditional random fields Conditional random fields, like conditional Markov models, consider both the state sequence and the token (word or character sequence) in calculating the probability of the next token. The probabilities assigned to these transitions have the advantage of being more general than those assigned in conditional Markov models, allowing conditional random Fields to, thus, generate more flexible language models.

Deep Learning Models

Several different approaches have been proposed for language modeling in the deep learning realm. These include recurrent neural networks (including LSTM), encoder-decoder networks, also known as sequence-to-sequence models, generative adversarial networks (GANs), and transformer models. Since GANs and their application to text generation are discussed in great detail in Chapter 9, we do not discuss them in this chapter.

Recurrent neural networks Recurrent neural networks combine the current input with the outputs obtained previously through the use of an internal memory. This makes these types of networks appropriate for sequential tasks such as natural language modeling where the current word or character is not standalone but depends on the previous ones. Long short-term memory (LSTM) networks are a specific type of recurrent neural network that perform particularly well on sequential tasks such as text generation. More recent approaches, however, have found a way to combine two recurrent networks to create a scheme known as a sequence-to-sequence model, to obtain even more impressive results.

Sequence-to-sequence models Sequence-to-sequence models (also known as encoder-decoder models) use recurrent neural networks to encode the sequence seen until "now" and to decode it. The recurrent neural network used to encode the sentence takes as input the partial sentence, and creates an embedding that is then decoded by the recurrent neural networks used to decode the embedding and generate text in a foreign language or as an answer to a question, etc. Sequence-to-sequence models are trained by constraining the encoder and decoder to encode a sentence in a source language and decode it into the target language, using methods such as stochastic gradient descent to minimize the cross-entropy loss.

Transformer models Transformer models also use an encoder-decoder strategy, but unlike the sequence-to-sequence models, they do not use recurrent neural networks to encode and decode the data. Instead, they use an "attention mechanism," which emphasizes the important relations in the sentence. This allows ambiguous interpretation of the language, the most complicated issue to deal with when working in natural language processing, to be resolved swiftly. This attention mechanism has allowed transformer models to obtain even better results than the sequence-to-sequence models that preceded them. They are currently the state of the art in natural language processing tasks such as text generation and have recently been brought to the attention of the public through the release of ChatGPT.

8.8.2 Evaluating Text Generation

The main problem with text generation is the open-ended nature of the problem. While in some problems, the right answer is unique (e.g., a single category in classification problems), in text generation, many answers are acceptable (e.g., "cute dog," "adorable canine," "lovely pooch," and so on). Celikyilmaz et al. (2020) identified three different approaches to evaluating computer-generated text: human-centric, quantitative metrics, and machine learning-based approaches. Within each approach, they identified a number of strategies and metrics. We will discuss some of the most important ones here, go into more detail on some others, present a few more in Chapter 9, and refer the reader to Celikyilmaz et al. (2020) for yet additional ones.

Human-Centric Evaluation

Human-centric evaluation is divided into two categories: intrinsic evaluation, where human judges assess the quality of the generated text, and extrinsic evaluation where the quality of the generated text is measured according to how well tasks that depend on that text have been performed. Extrinsic evaluation is more complex to set up, so most of the work relying on human evaluation uses intrinsic evaluation.

Human judges can assess the quality of generated text according to different criteria. These include *adequacy*, or how much of the meaning conveyed by the gold standard is also found in the generated text, *fluency*, or how natural the generated text feels, and *factuality*, whether the facts cited are accurate. Other metrics include *grammaticality, style*, and *formality*.

The choices of human judges is also important in this type of evaluation. The authors of the work or a group of people gathered by the authors (e.g., a cohort of students) could be the people evaluating the quality of the generated text and this work could be done in person, allowing the authors to specify the task better and answer questions that may come up during the evaluation. Alternatively, the evaluation can be conducted online on crowd sourcing platforms such as Amazon Mechanical Turk. Such platforms allow for the recruiting of a greater number of more diverse judges and of a more efficient evaluation. On the other hand, the quality of the evaluation is more difficult to control in such settings.

Because the evaluation of generated text is highly subjective despite the strict directives that may have been given to the judges, it is important to record the measure of agreement between the judges. This can be done by calculating the percent agreement or Cohen's kappa measure of agreement, among others. Such measures were previously discussed in Section 5.4.3.

Quantitative Metrics

Celikyilmaz et al. (2020) identified five categories of quantitative metrics for text generation: *n*-gram overlap metrics, distance-based metrics, diversity metrics, content overlap metrics, and grammatical feature based metrics.

N-gram overlap metrics Metrics in this category compare computer generated text to a ground truth, gold standard text to determine to what extent they match. While the F-score, the dice, and the Jaccard coefficients discussed in Section 8.7.2 can be adapted to this task, other specialized methods such as BLEU, ROUGE discussed in Section 9.4.4, and similar methods have been proposed to deal with the problem. In essence, all the metrics in this category compute the *n*-gram overlap between the generated and the ground-truth texts. Some allow for synonym substitution in order to be more general. The different methods focus on precision, recall, or overlap of the different *n*-grams (or their generalization) considered.

Distance-based metrics These metrics use distance metrics to measure the similarity between the generated text and the ground truth. The approach consists of transforming each text into a vector (by using, for example, term frequency–inverse document frequency (TF–IDF) or different types of embeddings) and computing the distance between these vectors. A small distance corresponds to a higher degree of similarity between the generated and gold-standard text, while a large one corresponds to a greater difference. Distance metrics used for this problem include edit distance and vector similarity–based metrics including the Wasserstein metric, which measures the distance between two probability distributions.

Diversity metrics These metrics compute the span and range of word choice in the generated text. Because it does not focus on text quality, it is usually used in addition to other metrics. It is useful for tasks where the text generation process attempts to write dialogue or stories where accuracy of the statements is less important than the way they read.

Content overlap metrics By contrast, these metrics focus on the content of the generated text. It measures the overlap in semantic and conceptual information between the two texts. Semantic propositional image caption evaluation (SPICE), for example, creates an abstract scene graph representation of the sentences (or images) by encoding the objects considered, their attributes, and their relationships in a graph. This allows for a finer-grained semantic analysis. Other approaches use semantic similarity models such as textual entailment or paraphrase identification, as metrics.

Grammatical feature–based metrics This category of metrics uses part-of-speech tagging information to assess the syntactic similarity of the computer generated text and the gold standard. They do not check the semantic content of the generated text.

Machine Learning-Based Evaluation

The quantitative metrics described in the previous section assume, for the most part, that the words used in the generated text will overlap with the words used in the gold standard. As seen in our earlier example involving "cute dogs," "adorable canines," and so on, this is often not the case and two sentences can be deemed as different when they are, in fact, clearly related. In order to deal with that problem, machine learning-trained evaluation methods can be used. On the one hand, these can take the form of methods that compute sentence embeddings that are able to capture semantic similarity. In particular, a number of recent bidirectional encoder representations from transformers (BERT)-based evaluation methods have been created to take advantage of the information included in the embeddings. On the other hand, if embeddings cannot be used or do not capture the essence of the text-generation problem at hand, the problem of evaluating the generated text has been considered as a supervised regression or classification problem where the human scores obtained on some generated text are used as the metric that the trained model needs to obtain. In other words, machine learning algorithms are used to mimic the judgment of humans on computer-generated text.

8.9 Time Series Analysis

A time series is a dataset in which order and time are fundamental to the data. Time series have been studied for many years, and a large number of methods have been designed for their analyses. Section 8.9.1 will discuss some of the most common approaches that have been designed in the past while Section 8.9.2 discusses their evaluation.

8.9.1 Approaches to Time Series Analysis

Though the goal of time series analysis is typically to forecast the value of the time series at a future time, a number of issues need to be taken into consideration when determining the forecast value. These include whether the time series is stationary, that is, whether its mean and variance remain constant throughout time (this is called the time series trend), whether seasonality is present, that is, whether the time series contains repeating patterns, and whether the values of the time series are auto-correlated, which means that similar values occur at fixed time intervals.[11]

In order to deal with these consideration, the SARIMA approach was conceived; this attempts to determine the signature pattern of the time series once trend, autocorrelation, and seasonality are accounted for. Serious disadvantages of SARIMA and other statistically based time series models are the fact that they are linear regression models and that the dimensionality of the time series they model cannot exceed a few variables. Deep learning methods, on the other hand, are able to deal with these issues and can also output multiple values.[12]

Multi-layer perceptrons, for example, are robust to noise, can handle multivariate input, and are able to output multiple values, thus allowing for multistep forecasting. Furthermore, they are able to model nonlinear relationships. Convolutional neural networks have the same advantages as multi-layer perceptrons but boast a further advantage: the ability to extract the most important features of the time series. In such settings, the time series is treated as a one- or two-dimensional image and features extracted from it. Finally, recurrent neural networks such as long short-term memory networks are another important deep learning paradigm for time series forecasting. That paradigm is aligned with time series analysis since, unlike in multi-layer perceptrons and convolutional neural networks, the model preserves the sequential nature of the data, and is able to map the input to output values with respect to a dynamic context.

8.9.2 Evaluating Time Series Analysis

While the most usual task associated with time series analysis is a task of forecast, where the goal is to predict the real value of a prediction at a future time, based on the time series'

---

[11] Illustrations of these issues can be found at www.cnn.com/2022/07/11/politics/second-covid-19-boosters-all-adults-plan/index.html.

[12] Illustration of deep learning methods for time series analysis are discussed at https://machinelearningmastery.com/deep-learning-for-time-series-forecasting/.

past behavior, it is also possible to attempt to classify time series data (Singh 2022). This would happen, for example, in anomaly detection tasks where the user wants to find out whether a future value should be classified as a normal instance, an outlier (which is still normal but not typical), or an anomaly. When looking at time series from a forecasting perspective, regression-types of metrics are relevant. Scale-dependent metrics such as the RMSE or MAE are commonly used. However, other scale invariant metrics are worth considering when the same method is applied to several time series that each use different units (Hyndman and Athanasopoulos 2013). These will be introduced later in this section. When looking at them from a classification perspective, then the metrics used in classification, and possibly specifically anomaly detection, are of greater relevance.

The issue of which metric to use, however, is only one aspect of time series analysis evaluation. The aspect of time series analysis that really differs from regression or classification in time-independent problems is the fact that, in the case of time-series, as the name suggests, the data is time dependent. This means that the model must be trained on data that occurred prior to any of the events that we want to forecast. In addition, one may be interested in forecasting not only one step ahead, but two, three, or four steps ahead, with the understanding that the larger the number of steps, the less accurate the prediction. It also means that cross-validation cannot take the shape usually assumed in time independent data. We will describe some of the main schemes that have been proposed to deal with the particular presentation of the data in time-series problems (Cerqueira et al. 2020).

Evaluation Metrics

As previously mentioned, all the metrics discussed in the context of regression analysis can be used for forecasting, and similarly, all the metrics discussed for classification or anomaly detection are equally usable.

The metrics used for forecasting that we previously discussed in the context of regression, such as MAE or RMSE, are very popular in forecasting, but they have the disadvantage of being scale dependent. This means that these metrics are not meaningful when used to assess different time series that describe phenomena of different kinds that are measured with different units (e.g., temperatures versus voltage). For such kinds of problems, unit-independent percentage metrics are used. Two such metrics are described below: the mean absolute percentage error (MAPE) and the symmetric mean absolute percentage error (sMAPE); sMAPE was proposed to rectify MAPE's tendency to penalize negative errors more than positive ones. They are defined as

$$MAPE = \frac{\frac{1}{n}\sum_{i=1}^{n} |y_i - \hat{y}_i| \times 100}{|y_i|}$$

and

$$sMAPE = \frac{1}{n}\sum_{i=1}^{n} \frac{|y_i - \hat{y}_i| \times 200}{|y_i| + |\hat{y}_i|}.$$

While these metrics are widely used in time series analysis, they have two disadvantages (Hyndman and Athanasopoulos 2013): if y_i is 0, MAPE is not defined and it goes to infinity if y_i is close to 0. Similarly, in sMAPE, it is likely that if y_i is close to 0, so is $(\hat{y}_i)$. Furthermore, these two metrics assume that the unit has a meaningful 0, which is not always true, such as in the Fahrenheit scale. Alternative non-scaled metrics have been proposed and are discussed in Hyndman and Athanasopoulos (2013).

Estimation Techniques

There currently is no consensus on what sampling paradigm works best to estimate the effectiveness of time series regression methods. Cerqueira et al. (2020) investigated the issue through a large empirical study that considered two categories of methods: cross-validation and holdout. They found that in stationary time series, blocked cross-validation methods are reliable, while in nonstationary settings, holdout repeated in multiple testing periods yielded the best estimates. We now describe the two categories of methods.

Cross-validation Standard cross-validation as described in Chapters 4 and 6 makes the strong assumption that the data is independently and identically distributed. In time series analysis, this is not the case since the data has a time dependency component to it. A number of cross-validation variants have been proposed to address that issue. These include: *blocked cross-validation*, *modifed cross-validation procedure*, and *hv-blocked cross-validation*. In blocked cross-validation, the data is not shuffled prior to being subdivided into folds as it is in regular cross-validation. Instead, the dataset is divided into k blocks of contiguous observations. There is no continuity between the blocks, but within the blocks the data appears in sequential order. In the modified cross-validation procedure, the data is shuffled at the beginning and then divided into k blocks like in normal cross-validation. However, at each fold, instances from the training set that are found to be too correlated to those in the dataset (because too close, temporally, to the data in the test set) are removed. The hv-blocked cross-validation scheme combines the two previous ones. In addition to creating blocks without shuffling the data, first it removes the data that straddles both the training and testing sets. In all cases, like in regular cross-validation, the estimates obtained at each fold are averaged.

Holdout The holdout method is similar to the holdout method used in batch mode. A point is selected that marks the end of the training set and the beginning of the testing set. In order to get a more robust estimate, it is recommended to use a procedure called repeated holdout where the above procedure is repeated several times with different points marking the end of the training set and the beginning of the testing set. The estimates obtained from each repetition are then averaged. One issue to consider, however, is that predicting the next point in the time series is not only the most important test. Sometimes, it is important to predict the value several steps ahead. Holdout methods can easily accommodate these kinds of requirements.

8.10 Data Stream Mining

A data stream is related to, but different from, a time series in that in a time series, it is assumed that all the data from the past is available at the time the model is induced. In other words, it is assumed that data is time-dependent, but that it is all there. In data streams, on the other hand, it is assumed that the data is not all there but will be coming over time. The challenge is to adapt the existing models to the new data while also using the model. That needs to be done within a fixed amount of memory and the examples must be processed quickly as they arrive. In that context, concept drift is a significant challenge encountered in data streams.

8.10.1 Approaches to Data Stream Mining

Bahri et al. (2021) is the most recent survey of data stream mining methods, but previous surveys include Gomes et al. (2019), Krempl et al. (2014), Gaber (2012), and Krawczyk et al. (2017). Data stream mining has been handled by modifying a number of traditional algorithms to allow them to deal with streams. The best known of these is the transformation made to decision trees using Hoeffding bounds, although many variations exist and a number of modifications have also been made to algorithms such as naive Bayes, k-nearest neighbors, ensemble methods, as well as neural networks. Algorithms have also been designed to deal with other learning paradigms in the context of data stream mining, including regression and clustering.

An important area of research in the data stream mining space includes preprocessing, including the extraction of meaningful features, which is particularly challenging given the data stream requirement of working with little memory, dealing with the class imbalance problem in an online fashion, insufficient labeling, and of course, the most challenging problem of all, which is to deal with concept and feature drifts.

8.10.2 Evaluating Data Stream Mining

Data stream mining usually uses the same metrics as those used in classification tasks or those pertaining to any of the other problems the data streaming system is tasked with. Thus, we do not focus on that aspect of evaluation in this section. Instead, we describe some of the main error estimation schemes that have been proposed to deal with the particular presentation of the data in data stream mining problems.

Estimation techniques for data stream mining In data stream evaluation, as discussed in Gama et al. (2013), using the cross-validation or holdout methods used for time series evaluation does not capture the data stream mining exercise. Indeed, data stream mining consists of constantly adapting a learned model to new continuously encountered data. As a result, data stream mining evaluation is interested in capturing two related quantities: the capacity of the model under scrutiny to adapt to new data; and its ability to maintain good enough performance throughout the changes in the data. This is different from the time series evaluation exercise whose goal is to identify the model that is expected to give the best performance when applied to the time series it was trained on where no changes are expected other than those already observed and recorded as seasonality, auto-correlation, and trend.

Two evaluation frameworks are suggested for data stream analysis: the *holdout method* and the *prequential method*. In holdout, the same testing set gets evaluated repeatedly on the different models that are built as time passes and new data is encountered and the results are averaged. This is similar to the holdout method suggested for time series evaluation. In the predictive sequential or prequential method, the idea is to test first and train after. In more detail, the prequential method works by first testing the blocks of data and then using those blocks for training. In the first version of the procedure, the prequential block approach, in the first iteration, one block is used for training and the other for testing. Next the first two blocks are used for training and the third one for testing, and so on. In the prequential blocks sliding windows version, rather than being accumulated, the blocks seen previously are dropped from the training set. The analyzer is always trained on the block just preceding the testing block. This helps when the earlier data becomes irrelevant. Finally, the prequential gap block approach is similar to the prequential block approach except that a gap is created by eliminating one block between the training and testing blocks. Evaluations of these different schemes and those proposed for time series analyses can be found in Cerqueira et al. (2020).

8.11 Lifelong Learning

Lifelong learning, also known as continual, sequential, or incremental learning, extends the current capability of learning systems by allowing them to learn and improve continuously, share knowledge about previous tasks to improve the system's performance on new tasks, and achieve these goals in a computationally efficient way. A major problem in lifelong learning is catastrophic forgetting; that is, the displacement of older knowledge by new knowledge. Most techniques that have been proposed have attempted to deal with that issue. We begin by describing some of the approaches previously proposed for lifelong learning and then discuss methods proposed to evaluate lifelong learning systems.

8.11.1 Approaches to Lifelong Learning

Lange et al. (2022) surveys the different methods that have been proposed to deal with the problem and organizes them into families. In particular, the authors identify three families of methods: replay methods, regularization-based methods, and parameter isolation methods.

The idea of replay methods is to conserve data from the past either in raw format or in the form of a data generator so as to be able to retrain the model from time to time with the older data in order to "refresh" its memory. Another idea is to use constrained optimization, the idea of which is to restrict new task updates so that they do not interfere with older tasks. In regularization-based methods, the idea is to add a regularization term to the loss function that emphasizes the consolidation of old knowledge when learning new things. This can be done in a data-focused or prior-focused way. The data-focused way uses thorough knowledge distillation from a previous model while the prior-focused way estimates the importance of the model parameters and penalizes changes to the most important ones when new tasks are learned. The idea of the parameter isolation method is to reserve a separate set of parameters for each task. This can be done in a static way, where a fixed allocation scheme is used for each task, or in a dynamic way, where the architecture can grow to accommodate new tasks. Despite the similarity between data stream mining and lifelong learning, the two paradigms have traditionally been treated separately. Recent efforts at breaching the gap between both families of methods have been made by Korycki and Krawczyk (2021) and Faber et al. (2023b).

8.11.2 Evaluating Lifelong Learning

While the metrics discussed in the context of classification, regression, and other tasks, are appropriate to evaluate the performance of lifelong learning systems on the specific tasks the system needs to perform, it is also necessary to evaluate how well the system fares as a lifelong learning system. New et al. (2022) propose to use five different metrics to assess lifelong learning performance: *performance maintenance, forward transfer, backward transfer, performance relative to a single task expert (STE)*, and *sample efficiency*. We define each of these metrics in turn with the help of Figures 8.4 and 8.5, which are borrowed from New et al. (2022).

Performance maintenance is a metric that assesses the system's continual learning capability. In particular, it checks the system's robustness to catastrophic forgetting when new tasks or parameters are encountered. A concrete example is whether learning how to play ping-pong after having known how to play tennis hurts a person's tennis performance (catastrophic forgetting), improves it, or leaves it as it was. Performance maintenance is calculated by setting up a scenario where learning blocks and evaluation blocks alternate, and selecting a performance metric appropriate for the tasks at hand. Performance maintenance calculates the difference between the average value obtained on the performance evaluation blocks for that task prior to the last training block and the value obtained on the evaluation block for T, appearing right after the last training block for T. To obtain the performance maintenance during the lifetime, the maintenance value across the lifetime is averaged. If the performance maintenance is negative, it is a sign that the lifelong learning machine system tends to forget what it has previously learned, and that issue needs to be addressed.

Forward transfer measures whether knowledge of a previous task can help in the learning of a new one. A concrete example is whether knowing how to play tennis makes learning ping-pong (from scratch) easier. To compute the forward transfer measure for task 2 (ping-pong) with respect to task 1 (tennis), for example, we can evaluate task 2 (ping-pong) in evaluation block 1 before it has been learned at all, learn task 1 (tennis) in learning block 1, evaluate task 2 (ping-pong) again, in learning block 2 (after task 1 has been learned) and contrast the value obtained on evaluation block 2 to that obtained on evaluation block 1. On Figure 8.4, we want to evaluate the forward transfer from task B to task G. Here, G1 − G0 represents the forward learning that took place on task G. Please note that forward transfer can only be calculated once, before the task to which knowledge is forwarded (ping-pong, task G in this example) has been learned for the first time. For example, G2 (unlabeled on the graph but to the right of B2) cannot be used since learning of task G has already been

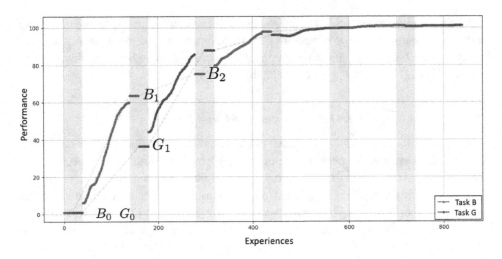

Figure 8.4 An example of lifelong learning on two tasks.

done by the time G is evaluated in evaluation block 2. To obtain an estimate of lifelong forward transfer, we average the forward transfer obtained on each task pair.

Backward transfer measures whether the learning of a new task helps improve performance on an old one. A concrete example is whether knowledge of tennis (after it has previously been learned) improves upon learning how to play ping-pong. Backward transfer is similar to forward transfer, except for the fact that transfer is applied to a task that has previously been learned. To compute the backward transfer measure for task 1 (tennis, task B on the figure), for example, we can learn task 1 (ping-pong, task G on the figure) in learning block 2, evaluate task 2 in evaluation blocks 2 and 3, and contrast their values. On the graph, this consists of calculating B2 − B1. Task B had been learned before, but its performance improved after task G was learned. To obtain an estimate of lifelong backward transfer, we average the backward transfer obtained on each task pair's first calculated backward transfer.

Performance relative to a single task expert This metric is straightforward: it compares the performance of a lifelong learning system to non-lifelong learning single task learners. This is illustrated in Figure 8.5. In Figure 8.5(a), we see that for the task B, the lifelong learning system performs as well as the single task expert on the first training block and slightly better on the second and third. In Figure 8.5(b), we see that the lifelong learning system performs better than the single task expert in all the learning blocks. The performance relative to a single task expert is then computed by calculating the ratio of the performance of the lifelong learning system to the single task expert on the entire experiment.

Sample efficiency measures whether continual or lifelong learning helps the system learn tasks more quickly and efficiently than single task experts. The metric calculates the

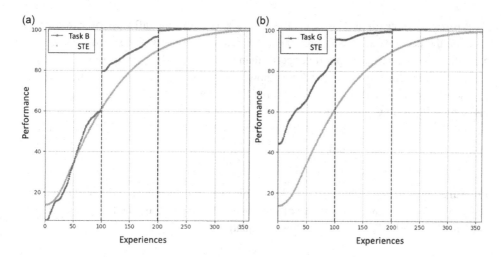

Figure 8.5 An example of learning on two tasks with single task experts shown.

saturation value (maximum it achieves) and the number of learning experiences it took to reach that saturation value. It does so for both the lifelong learning system and the single task expert, as illustrated in Figure 8.5. It then computes two ratios: saturation values of the lifelong learning system and the single task expert, and experience to saturation for the single task expert and the lifelong learning system. The sample efficiency is then calculated by multiplying these two ratios. The lifelong sample efficiency is the average of all the tasks' sample efficiency results.

Other metrics As previously discussed, the metrics discussed here came from New et al. (2022). A number of other people have also proposed lifelong learning metrics. These are discussed in Rodríguez et al. (2018), Farquhar and Gal (2018), and Prokopalo et al. (2020).

Lifelong anomaly detection Emerging problems in lifelong learning include lifelong anomaly detection. Recent works adapted metrics known in lifelong image classification to deal with this problem (Díaz-Rodríguez et al. 2018). Specifically, they consider ROC-AUC as a reference performance metric for a task, and organize single-task results in a matrix $R_{N \times N}$, where $R_{i,j}$ contains results in terms of the ROC-AUC metric obtained on task j after learning task i. This matrix is subsequently used for the evaluation phase (Faber et al. 2023a, 2023b). Based on this definition, the following metrics are devised:

Lifelong ROC–AUC This measures the average anomaly detection performance of the model after learning each task, for all previously learned tasks as well as the current task. It is computed as the average of below-diagonal entries including the main diagonal in R:

$$Lifelong\ ROC - AUC = \frac{\sum_{i \geq j}^{N} R_{i,j}}{\frac{N(N-1)}{2}}. \tag{8.1}$$

Backward transfer for ROC–AUC (BWT) This measures the influence of learning new tasks on the performance on all previously learned tasks. Positive backward transfer indicates that learning new tasks improves performance on previously learned tasks. Conversely, a negative value for backward transfer is known as forgetting. A strongly negative value is also sometimes regarded as catastrophic forgetting. Backward transfer is computed over all tasks, as in the following equation:

$$BWT = \frac{\sum_{i=2}^{N} \sum_{j=1}^{i-1} R_{i,j} - R_{j,j}}{\frac{N(N-1)}{2}}. \tag{8.2}$$

Forward transfer for ROC–AUC (FWT) This measures the overall influence that learning each task has on the performance of tasks learned in the future. The forward transfer is computed over all tasks, as in the following equation:

$$FWT = \frac{\sum_{i<j}^{N} R_{i,j}}{\frac{N(N-1)}{2}}. \tag{8.3}$$

8.12 Reinforcement Learning

Reinforcement learning teaches an agent to perform tasks in an interactive environment.[13] Such environments include video-game worlds or robots in a physical environment. Reinforcement learning is a supervised process in that the agent receives feedback on its actions, but unlike in classical supervised learning, this feedback takes the form of rewards and punishment. It is akin to a person learning to ride a bike and being punished by falling down if too much weight is placed on the right or the left of the bike, but being rewarded by staying on the bike for as long as the person's weight is properly distributed.

Reinforcement learning problems are defined according to five different elements:

Environment the environment in which the agent evolves (e.g., video-game, an interpretation of the physical world);
State the situation of the agents at the current time;
Reward the environment's response to the agents' action;
Policy the policy of the system, or the way in which agents make choices every step of the way;
Values the reward that an agent taking a particular action in a given state would receive.

The goal of a reinforcement-learning agent is to maximize its total cumulative reward. Higher rewards may or may not be available at states not previously explored by the agent. While exploring new states is costly, the chance of a high reward in such a state makes it worthwhile. Yet, if no high reward is found in the new states, then the operation will have been costly. This means that at each step, an agent must decide whether or not to explore new states. This is done following the policy of the system and is known as the exploration

---

[13] The concepts discussed in this section are illustrated in https://towardsdatascience.com/reinforcement-learning-101-e24b50e1d292.

versus exploitation problem. We first dicuss a few approaches that have been proposed for reinforcement learning and then discuss evaluation methods used in the field.

8.12.1 Approaches to Reinforcement Learning

Markov decision processes, defined using the concepts of states, actions, rewards, and probability of transitions, present a typical way of modeling the environment in reinforcement learning. A number of different methods have been proposed for reinforcement learning in the context of Markov decision process modeling. Q-learning and SARSA (state-action-reward-state-action) work by updating the Q-values of the system, which correspond to the value of performing a particular action in a specific state. These two methods use similar exploitation strategies, but different exploration ones. Q-learning and SARSA work well on updating the Q-value of states they have previously seen but cannot estimate the value of unseen states. Deep Q-networks (DQNs), and deep deterministic policy gradient (DDPG) are deep learning methods that address this issue. DQN is more restrictive than DDPG as it can only work in discrete low-dimensional spaces. DDPG, on the other hand, corrects for that problem by working on continuous high-dimensional spaces.

8.12.2 Evaluating Reinforcement Learning

Evaluating a reinforcement learning system is not a simple feat due to the tuning necessary to find the optimal mode of operation of the system and the fact that the same system will run differently in different environments. We discuss the question of evaluation in reinforcement learning, following Poole and Mackworth (2017). The first question is what metric should be reported. A common way to assess the performance of a reinforcement learning system is to report its cumulative reward over time. This can be done by showing the curve of that metric plotted over each of the agent's steps. While such visualizations are useful, it may also be useful to summarize them. This can be done in the following ways

Slope by calculating the slope of the curve once the algorithm is stable;

Minimum by reporting the minimum of the curve which indicates the cost of the exploration/exploitation tradeoff for the particular algorithm under scrutiny;

Step by reporting the time step where the curve crosses the zero reward line, which indicates how fast the algorithm stabilizes after exploration;

Reward by reporting the average reward; that is, the accumulated reward per time step.

Since reinforcement learning algorithms are not deterministic, it is customary to run them in the same environment for a number, N, of times, and calculate the average return from these runs. In terms of testbeds, Arulkumaran et al. (2017) note that the accessibility to large numbers of video games has allowed for a much more robust testing of reinforcement learning algorithms than was previously possible. In order to test algorithms in continuous spaces, physical process simulators have also been used. Many such environments are available on the OpenAI Gym.

While the metrics and estimation procedure just discussed are widely used for evaluating reinforcement learning, in recent years they have been criticized as not being robust enough for realistic environments and practical adoption of the algorithms. Jordan et al. (2020), for example, argue that many results reported using traditional methods have been shown not to be reproducible and propose a novel evaluation method that, they claim, is more reliable. Similarly, Agarwal et al. (2021) argue that the point estimates (means or medians) usually used to report results in reinforcement learning are not reliable and propose statistically more robust methods involving stratified bootstrapped confidence intervals, performance profiles for visual comparisons, and robust aggregate metrics such as the interquartile mean.

8.13 Additional Supervised Learning Paradigms

We now briefly discuss some additional learning paradigms not covered in this section. We acknowledge, however, that despite all our efforts, we may still end up missing important learning settings, and we apologize in advance for our omissions.

Transfer Learning Transfer learning has lately become an important area of research and application in machine learning where a pretrained system is used as a point of departure for learning new related tasks. Though few people are aware of it, transfer learning was being investigated in the early 1990s and culminated in a workshop at NeurIPS (formally known as NIPS).[14] Today, transfer learning has been revived due to the powerful ideas it is based on and the practical fact that very few institutions have the machine power needed to train deep learning systems on large databases of images or text. There have been different approaches to designing transfer learning, including domain adaptation, one-shot learning, zero-shot learning, and a number of studies have been conducted to test different types of approaches (mostly, different types of domain adaptation approaches on specific tasks) (e.g., Ho and Kim 2021; Lee et al. 2020; Ashayeri and Jha 2021). From a more general standpoint, however, Atanov et al. (2022) propose methodological choices for the evaluation of transfer learning including baselines, evaluation practices, and metrics.

Semi-Supervised learning Semi-supervised learning, similarly to transfer learning, has had a new life thanks to the deep learning revolution. Originating in the late 1990s/early 2000s, as one of the many ideas rediscovered and adapted to deep learning today,[15] semi-supervised learning was surveyed in two important studies (Zhu (2005) and van Engelen and Hoos (2019)). Suggestions on how to evaluate semi-supervised approaches are provided in sections 2.3 and 2.4 of van Engelen and Hoos (2019) and a framework for deep semi-supervised learning evaluation is provided in Oliver et al. (2018).

---

[14] See http://socrates.acadiau.ca/courses/comp/dsilver/nips95_ltl/nips95.workshop.pdf.

[15] While the 1990s and 2000s were in some sense a golden age of machine learning where the move to real domains rather than toy datasets (in the same way as today is a golden age for the processing of visual, audio, and text information, allowing us to fill some of the knowledge-acquisition bottleneck that has plagued AI since its inception) allowed the machine learning community to observe and respond to a large number of new phenomena of practical significance in real datasets, it is important to acknowledge that some of the ideas suggested in that period were, sometimes, suggested even further back. For the case of semi-supervised learning, for example, Scudder (1965) published a method for self-training as early as 1965.

Active Learning Active Learning also originated prior to the deep learning revolution. Its purpose is to minimize the amount of labeled data necessary by strategizing the search for instances that need a label. Settles (2009) and Aggarwal et al. (2014) present surveys of traditional active learning, while, more recently, Ren et al. (2020) present a survey of deep active learning. Though none of these surveys discusses the evaluation of deep learning systems, Beck et al. (2021), Munjal et al. (2020), and Li et al. (2022) debate more systematic evaluation protocols in the particular case of image classification.

9

Unsupervised Learning

Unsupervised learning is a branch of machine learning that aims to uncover patterns, structures, and relationships within data without relying on explicit target or labeled examples. Unlike supervised learning, where algorithms learn from labeled data, unsupervised learning solely relies on the inherent structure of the data. Its primary objective is to reveal hidden patterns, gain insights, and extract meaningful information. Unsupervised learning is particularly valuable when working with unlabeled or unstructured datasets, as it allows for the discovery of valuable knowledge and serves as a foundation for further analysis. In this chapter, we will delve into evaluation strategies for clustering and hierarchical clustering, dimensionality reduction, and latent variable modeling as well as generative models.

9.1 Clustering and Hierarchical Clustering

Clustering is a fundamental technique in unsupervised machine learning that aims to group similar data points together. It involves partitioning a dataset into distinct clusters or subgroups based on the underlying patterns or similarities in the data. To illustrate clustering, consider a dataset of customer purchasing behavior in an online store. We want to group customers based on their purchasing patterns to identify segments for targeted marketing. Using the k-means algorithm, we can cluster customers into distinct groups based on factors such as the frequency of purchases, total amount spent, and types of products purchased. Evaluating the quality of clustering can be challenging, especially when dealing with hierarchical clustering. In the case of nonhierarchical (flat) clustering, two general approaches to evaluation exist: intrinsic and extrinsic measures. Intrinsic measures assess the similarity within clusters and dissimilarity between clusters. Various metrics, such as the Davies–Bouldin and Dunn indices, as well as the silhouette coefficient, have been proposed for this purpose. Extrinsic measures, in comparison, utilize available labels from a testing set and employ metrics like F-measure, area under the curve (AUC), purity, or the Rand and Jaccard indices, tailored to clustering tasks. In this chapter, we will focus on the metrics that have not yet been discussed or that were not covered in depth in previous chapters.

Hierarchical clustering is a popular technique in unsupervised machine learning that aims to build a hierarchical structure of clusters. It groups similar data points together based on their distances or similarities, forming a tree-like structure called a dendrogram. Hierarchical clustering does not require a predefined number of clusters and can be visualized at different levels of granularity. There are two main types of hierarchical clustering. The first type is agglomerative hierarchical clustering, which starts by considering each data point as an individual cluster and iteratively merges the closest pairs of clusters based on a distance metric. At each iteration, the two clusters with the smallest dissimilarity are combined until all data points belong to a single cluster. The result is a dendrogram that shows the merging process and the relationships between clusters. The second type is divisive hierarchical clustering. In contrast to agglomerative clustering, divisive hierarchical clustering starts with a single cluster that includes all data points. It recursively divides the cluster into smaller subclusters based on a dissimilarity measure. This process continues until each data point is assigned to its own individual cluster, resulting in a dendrogram that shows the division process. Hierarchical clustering offers advantages such as the ability to visualize the clustering results at different levels of granularity and the absence of a predefined number of clusters. However, it can be computationally expensive for large datasets due to its quadratic time complexity. Additionally, it may not be well suited for datasets with irregular or non-convex shapes.

9.1.1 Evaluating Nonhierarchical (Flat) Clustering

There are two principal types of measures to assess the clustering performance.

Intrinsic measures – these do not require ground truth labels. Some of the clustering performance measures are the silhouette coefficient, the Calinski–Harabasz index, and the Davies–Bouldin index.

Extrinsic measures – these require ground truth labels. Examples include the adjusted Rand index, Fowlkes–Mallows scores, mutual information based scores, homogeneity, completeness, and the V-measure.

Intrinsic Measures

Silhouette coefficient The silhouette coefficient is calculated for each data point using mean intra-cluster distance and mean inter-cluster distance,

$$SC = \frac{b - a}{max(a, b)}, \tag{9.1}$$

where a is the mean intra-cluster distance for the data point. This is the average distance between the data point and all other data points within the same cluster. It measures how close the data point is to the other points in its cluster. The mean inter-cluster distance for the data point is denoted by b. This is the average distance between the data point and all the data points in the nearest neighboring cluster. It measures how far the data point is from the points in the neighboring cluster. The silhouette coefficient ranges from -1 to 1, and a value close to 1 indicates that the data point is well clustered, while a value close to -1 suggests it is likely misclassified. However, a silhouette coefficient of 0 it suggests that the data point is close to the decision boundary between two clusters. Overlapping clusters would typically result in negative silhouette coefficients, but a coefficient of 0 could also indicate that the point is on the border between clusters. By contrast, a value of 1 indicates a dense and well-separated cluster, which is the desired outcome. Therefore, a higher value closer to 1 indicates better clustering quality.

Dunn index The Dunn index is a valuable tool for identifying clusters that exhibit compactness and minimal variance among their members. The formula for the Dunn index is given by

$$DI = \frac{min_{1 \leq i < j \leq c} \delta(x_i, x_j)}{max_{1 \leq k \leq c} \Delta(x_k)}, \tag{9.2}$$

where $\delta(x_i, x_j)$ represents the distance between two different data points x_i and x_j belonging to different clusters, and $\Delta(x_k)$ is the measure of cluster dispersion, often defined as the maximum distance between any two data points within cluster k. The Dunn index calculates the ratio between the smallest inter-cluster distance (i.e., the distance between the two closest data points from different clusters) and the largest intra-cluster distance (i.e., the maximum distance between any two data points within the same cluster) for all clusters in the clustering result. A higher Dunn index value indicates better clustering quality, as it suggests that the clusters are more compact (small inter-cluster distances) and better separated from each other (large intra-cluster distances). Conversely, a lower Dunn index value suggests that the clusters are less compact and/or have less separation, which may indicate suboptimal clustering.

Davies–Bouldin index The Davies–Bouldin index (DBI) was presented and illustrated in Section 4.2.5. We briefly review it here. The DBI can be calculated using the formula

$$DBI = \frac{1}{c} \sum_{i=1}^{c} max_{j \neq i} \frac{\sigma_i + \sigma_j}{d(c_i, c_j)}, \tag{9.3}$$

where c represents the number of clusters, c_i denotes the centroid of the ith cluster, and $d(c_i, c_j)$ represents the distance between the centroids of two clusters. The average distance of all data points in cluster i to c_i is denoted by σ_i. A clustering model that yields low intra-cluster distances and high inter-cluster distances will result in a low Davies–Bouldin index. Hence, a lower Davies–Bouldin index indicates higher clustering quality.

Calinski–Harabasz index The Calinski–Harabasz index (also called the variance ratio criterion) is the ratio between between-cluster dispersion and within-cluster dispersion for all clusters. The Calinski–Harabasz index is given by

$$CHI = \frac{trace(B_c)}{trace(W_c)} \frac{n_E - c}{c - 1}, \tag{9.4}$$

where c is the number of clusters, n_E is the size of the dataset E, $trace(B_c)$ is the trace of the between-cluster (inter-cluster) dispersion matrix, and $trace(W_c)$ is the trace of the within-cluster dispersion matrix. The quantities W_c and B_c are defined as

$$W_c = \sum_{i=1}^{c} \sum_{j=1}^{C_i} (x_j - c_i)(x_j - c_i)^{\top}, \text{ and } B_c = \sum_{i=1}^{c} n_i(c_i - c_E)(c_i - c_E)^{\top}, \tag{9.5}$$

respectively, where C_i represents the set of points in cluster i, c_i denotes the centroid of cluster i, n_i represents the number of data points in cluster i, and c_E is the global centroid of the dataset E. The estimation of the CHI index relies on the distances between data points within a cluster and the cluster centroid, as well as the distances between all cluster centroids and the global centroid. A higher CHI index indicates better clustering quality.

The silhouette coefficient is a popular metric that has the advantage of being bounded between -1 and $+1$. This makes it very convenient for comparing clustering approaches. However, each of the other metrics presents different advantages. Dunn's index, for example, focuses on the clusters' compactness, and the Davies–Bouldin index gives importance to cluster separation. While these metrics rely on distance calculations, the Calinski–Harabasz index relies on the notion of dispersion to calculate similar quantities, possibly yielding different insights.

Extrinsic Measures

Although supervised learning metrics such as accuracy, the AUC, the F-measure, and so on could be used to assess the quality of clustering if labels are known, these metrics may be too focused on the functionality of the problem, and less so on the clustering process itself. The metrics we now introduce assess clustering in a more insightful way.

Purity focuses on the frequency of the most common class into each cluster. To calculate purity, we assign a label to each cluster based on the most frequent class in it. Then the purity becomes the number of correctly matched class and cluster labels divided by the number of total data points. The formula for purity is given by

$$\text{Purity} = \sum_i \frac{|C_i|}{N} \max_j \text{Precision}(C_i, L_j), \tag{9.6}$$

where the precision of a cluster C_i for a given class L_j is defined as

$$\text{Precision}(C_i, L_j) = \frac{C_i \cap L_j}{C_i}. \tag{9.7}$$

Purity serves as a measure to discourage noise within a cluster, but it does not provide any incentives for effectively grouping items belonging to the same class. If a clustering model assigns each observation to its own individual cluster, the purity value becomes one. As a result, purity is unable to strike a balance between the number of clusters and the overall quality of clustering. Moreover, it is evident that purity does not perform well when dealing with imbalanced data.

Normalized mutual information (NMI) NMI is related to information theory since it incorporates the notion of entropy. It gives us the reduction in the entropy of the class labels when we are given the cluster labels. In other words, NMI reveals how much the uncertainty about class labels decreases when the cluster labels are known. The NMI score is given by

$$\text{NMI}(U, V) = \frac{2\text{MI}(U, V)}{H(U) + H(V)}, \tag{9.8}$$

where MI is the mutual information between two label assignments U and V of the same N data points. The entropy of U is defined as the amount of uncertainty for a partition set and the formula is given by

$$H(U) = - \sum_{i=1}^{|U|} P(i) \log(P(i)), \tag{9.9}$$

where $P(i) = |U_i|/N$ is the probability that a data point picked at random from U belongs to class U_i. We similarly define the entropy of V. Therefore, the mutual information between U and V is defined as

$$\text{MI}(U,V) = \sum_{i=1}^{|U|} \sum_{j=1}^{|V|} \frac{|U_i \cap V_j|}{N} \log \left(\frac{N|U_i \cap V_j|}{|U_i||V_j|} \right), \tag{9.10}$$

where $\frac{|U_i \cap V_j|}{N}$ is the probability that a randomly picked data point belongs to the intersection of classes U_i and V_j.

Rand index The Rand index measures the percentage of correct predictions among all predictions given the ground truth class assignments. The equation for the Rand index is given by

$$\text{RI} = \frac{TP + TN}{TP + TN + FP + FN}, \tag{9.11}$$

where TP represents a true positive decision, indicating that two similar observations are correctly assigned to the same cluster. Similarly, TN denotes a true negative decision, which signifies that two dissimilar observations are correctly assigned to different clusters. By contrast, FP represents a false positive decision, where two dissimilar observations are incorrectly assigned to the same cluster, while FN represents a false negative decision, where two similar observations are mistakenly assigned to different clusters. By examining Equation (9.11), we can observe that false positives and false negatives are given equal weight, which may not be desirable in clustering tasks. The Rand index is considered a universal metric as it can be utilized to compare various clustering algorithms.

Adjusted Rand index The adjusted Rand index is the corrected-for-chance version of Equation (9.11). Its formula is given by

$$\text{ARI} = \frac{(\alpha^2 + 1)PR}{\alpha^2 P + R}, \tag{9.12}$$

where $P = \frac{TP}{TP+FP}$, $R = \frac{TP}{TP+FN}$, and α is a user parameter. In the case where $\alpha > 1$, false negatives are penalized more strongly than false positives.

Jaccard index The Jaccard index measures the number of true positive (TP) decisions against the total number (TP, FP, and FN) of decisions. Its formula is given by

$$\text{JI} = \frac{TP}{TP + FP + FN}. \tag{9.13}$$

A higher Jaccard index indicates better performance of the clustering model. However, it is important to note that while the Jaccard index effectively measures similarity between two groups, it may not fully capture the relationship between two clusters. For example, there could be a scenario where one cluster is entirely contained within another cluster, yet they can still be distinctly described as two separate clusters.

9.1.2 Evaluating Hierarchical Clustering

In the context of evaluating hierarchical clustering, using flat clustering evaluation approaches may not always be optimal. This is because errors made at different levels of the hierarchy should not receive the same penalties. It is important to choose the appropriate evaluation measures considering the project goals, the characteristics of the dataset, and the hierarchical structure of the clusters. Hierarchical clustering can be divided into two main approaches: agglomerative clustering and divisive clustering. Both agglomerative and divisive clustering methods create hierarchical structures of clusters, but they differ in their bottom-up (agglomerative) and top-down (divisive) approaches to clustering. Agglomerative clustering is more commonly used, but divisive clustering can be useful in certain scenarios where the data or problem characteristics make a top-down division more appropriate.

Agglomerative Clustering

Agglomerative clustering, also known as bottom-up clustering, is a general approach to hierarchical clustering. It starts with each data point as a separate cluster and iteratively merges similar clusters until a termination condition is met. Agglomerative clustering takes different flavors depending on the similarity measures or linkage measures used (Murtagh and Contreras 2012, 2017; Absalom et al. 2022). The generic algorithm can be summarized as follows:

1. **Initialization** Each data point is initially treated as a separate cluster.
2. **Merge step** The two most similar clusters are successively merged based on a chosen similarity or dissimilarity measure, such as Euclidean distance or linkage methods like single linkage, complete linkage, or average linkage.
3. **Update step** The similarity or dissimilarity between merged clusters is recalculated based on the chosen linkage method.
4. **Termination** The process continues until a desired number of clusters is reached or a termination condition, such as a predefined number of clusters, a threshold distance, or a specified level of hierarchy, is met.

Agglomerative clustering builds a hierarchical structure by gradually merging clusters, starting from individual data points and moving towards a single cluster encompassing all data points. Assessing the quality of agglomerative clustering results is crucial to understand the performance quality and make informed decisions. We now explore various evaluation techniques for assessing agglomerative clustering.

Visual Inspection Visual inspection of agglomerative clustering results can provide valuable insights into the clustering process and the relationships between clusters. The following steps outline the process:

1. To begin, we construct a dendrogram from the agglomerative clustering output. A dendrogram is a tree-like diagram that illustrates the merging process of clusters. The vertical axis represents the dissimilarity or distance between clusters, while the horizontal axis represents the individual data points or clusters. The dendrogram provides a visual representation of the hierarchical structure.
2. Next, we determine a height or distance threshold on the vertical axis of the dendrogram. This threshold will define the desired number of clusters. Cutting the dendrogram at different heights will result in different numbers of clusters.
3. We inspect the dendrogram to identify clusters at different levels based on the chosen height threshold. Moving horizontally from the chosen height threshold towards the bottom of the dendrogram, we can identify the clusters formed. Each vertical line in the dendrogram represents a cluster, and the horizontal lines represent the merging of clusters.
4. Visual inspection allows for interpretation and evaluation of the agglomerative clustering results. By observing the dendrogram and the identified clusters, you can gain insights into the relationships between clusters, the compactness of clusters, and the presence of any outliers. Furthermore, visual inspection can help in determining the appropriate number of clusters. By selecting different height thresholds and examining the resulting clusters, you can assess the impact of cluster merges and identify the level of granularity that best fits the data and the problem at hand.

Stability Analysis Stability analysis can be conducted to evaluate the stability of agglomerative clustering. This involves running the clustering algorithm multiple times with slight variations, such as random perturbations or subsampling of the data, and examining the consistency of the clustering results. If the clusters remain stable across different runs, it indicates robustness and reliability. A step-by-step process for conducting stability analysis in agglomerative clustering is:

1. **Choose a variation strategy** Determine the specific variations to apply to the data or algorithm for each run. Some common strategies include random perturbations, such as adding random noise to the data, or subsampling the data to create different subsets for clustering.
2. **Define the number of runs** Decide how many times to repeat the clustering algorithm with the chosen variation strategy. Running the algorithm multiple times allows for a comparison of the resulting clusters.
3. **Cluster generation** Perform the agglomerative clustering algorithm for each run using the chosen variation strategy. Each run should generate a set of clusters.
4. **Cluster comparison** Compare the clustering results across the different runs. Various metrics can be used to assess the similarity or dissimilarity between the clusters, such as the Jaccard index, the adjusted Rand index, or pairwise cluster agreement. These metrics quantify the consistency of cluster assignments across runs.

5. **Stability assessment** Analyze the consistency of the clustering results. If the clusters exhibit high similarity across the runs, it indicates stability and robustness of the clustering algorithm. Conversely, if the clusters differ significantly between runs, it suggests instability or sensitivity to variations.

6. **Interpretation and decision-making** Based on the stability analysis, interpret the results and make decisions about the reliability of the clusters. If the clusters are stable and consistent across multiple runs, it provides confidence in the clustering solution. However, if the clusters vary greatly, it may indicate limitations or sensitivity of the algorithm.

Domain-specific metrics In certain situations, developing or utilizing domain-specific metrics is necessary to assess the quality of agglomerative clustering. Domain-specific metrics allow you to capture the specific requirements, objectives, or characteristics of the problem you are addressing. By aligning the evaluation metrics with these specific goals, you can more accurately evaluate the clustering results based on the criteria that matter most in your domain. Here, we give a general approach to developing or employing domain-specific metrics for assessing agglomerative clustering:

1. **Identify domain-specific requirements** Determine the unique requirements or objectives of your problem domain. Consider the specific characteristics of your dataset and the goals you aim to achieve through clustering.

2. **Define evaluation criteria** Based on the identified requirements, define evaluation criteria that reflect the specific aspects you want to assess in the clustering results. These criteria could be related to domain-specific attributes, patterns, or relationships that are crucial to your problem.

3. **Develop or adapt metrics** Design or adapt evaluation metrics that quantitatively measure the extent to which the clustering satisfies the defined criteria. These metrics should be tailored to your problem domain and capture the aspects that are most relevant for evaluation. Depending on the nature of the problem, you may need to develop novel metrics or modify existing ones to suit your specific needs.

4. **Calculate and interpret metrics** Apply the developed or adapted metrics to the clustering results. Calculate the metric values and interpret the results to gain insights into the clustering quality based on your domain-specific criteria. These metrics should provide you with a quantitative understanding of how well the clustering aligns with your specific requirements.

5. **Iterative refinement** Continuously refine and iterate upon the evaluation metrics as you gain more insights and refine your understanding of the problem domain. Adjust the metrics based on feedback and new information to ensure they effectively capture the critical aspects of the clustering results.

Divisive Clustering

Divisive clustering, also known as top-down clustering, is another general approach to hierarchical clustering. It takes the opposite approach of agglomerative clustering. Divisive clustering starts with all data points belonging to a single cluster and recursively splits the clusters until the termination condition is satisfied. Depending on the criteria used for the division step, divisive clustering takes different flavors (Absalom et al. 2022). The generic algorithm can be summarized as follows:

1. **Initialization** All data points are initially grouped into a single cluster.
2. **Split step** The algorithm selects a cluster to divide based on a chosen criterion, such as maximizing inter-cluster dissimilarity or minimizing intra-cluster dissimilarity.
3. **Division step** The selected cluster is divided into smaller clusters, typically by selecting a subset of data points or by partitioning based on a chosen clustering algorithm.
4. **Update step** The dissimilarity or similarity between the new clusters is recalculated.
5. **Termination** The process continues recursively until a termination condition is met, such as reaching a desired number of clusters or a specified level of hierarchy.

Divisive and agglomerative clustering can be evaluated using similar techniques, but there are also some differences to consider due to their contrasting approaches to clustering. Both divisive and agglomerative clustering can be assessed using common evaluation measures such as internal validation indices, external validation measures (if ground truth is available), and visual inspection. These techniques provide insights into the quality, structure, and meaningfulness of the obtained clusters. Additionally, both methods can benefit from domain-specific evaluation metrics that capture the specific requirements of the problem domain. However, there are certain differences to consider when evaluating divisive and agglomerative clustering:

1. **Cluster shape and structure** Divisive clustering tends to produce better-separated and distinct clusters, whereas agglomerative clustering can result in more compact and nested clusters due to its bottom-up merging process. Evaluation techniques should consider these differences in cluster shape and structure.
2. **Complexity and scalability** Divisive clustering can be computationally more intensive than agglomerative clustering since it involves recursively splitting clusters. When evaluating divisive clustering, it's important to consider the computational complexity and scalability of the algorithm.
3. **Interpretability** Agglomerative clustering often provides a hierarchical structure of clusters, which can be visually inspected using dendrograms. Divisive clustering, on the other hand, produces a single partition of clusters. Evaluation techniques for divisive clustering may focus more on cluster separation, coherence, or other domain-specific aspects that reflect the desired characteristics of the clusters.
4. **Stability analysis** While stability analysis can be performed for both divisive and agglomerative clustering, the specific approaches may differ. Agglomerative clustering stability analysis typically involves perturbing the dissimilarity matrix or data, while divisive clustering stability analysis may involve randomizing or modifying the divisive process to assess the stability of the obtained clusters.

Quantitative Metrics for Evaluating Hierarchical Clustering

When evaluating hierarchical clustering, using directly flat clustering evaluation approaches may not always be the most appropriate or optimal choice. Hierarchical clustering produces a tree-like structure (dendrogram) that organizes data into a hierarchy of nested clusters. By contrast, flat clustering methods directly partition the data into a specific number of non-overlapping clusters. Using flat clustering evaluation approaches for hierarchical clustering may not be optimal due to the following reasons:

1. **Hierarchical structure** Hierarchical clustering produces a hierarchy of clusters with varying granularities at different levels of the tree. Flat clustering evaluation, which assumes a fixed number of clusters, fails to utilize the hierarchical nature of the results.
2. **Variable number of clusters** Hierarchical clustering does not require prespecifying the number of clusters, unlike most flat clustering algorithms. Evaluating hierarchical clustering with a fixed number of clusters may not fully capture the complexity and structure of the data.
3. **Granularity** Hierarchical clustering allows for different levels of granularity, offering a more detailed view of the data. Flat clustering evaluation, which results in a single partition, may overlook the hierarchical relationships between clusters.
4. **Hierarchical metrics** Hierarchical clustering necessitates specialized evaluation metrics that account for the nested nature of clusters. Using flat clustering evaluation metrics may not adequately capture the hierarchical relationships and clustering quality.

To overcome these limitations, there are specific quantitative evaluation methods designed for hierarchical clustering. Some common approaches include silhouette analysis on the dendrogram, or using information-theoretic metrics like NMI or variation of information (VI). Note that the following evaluation strategies can be used for both divisive and agglomerative hierarchical clustering.

Silhouette analysis on the dendrogram Silhouette analysis is typically used to evaluate flat clustering results, but it can be adapted for hierarchical clustering as well. Instead of using a fixed number of clusters, silhouette analysis involves exploring different levels of granularity in the dendrogram and computing silhouette scores for each cluster at different levels. This analysis helps identify the level at which the clusters have the most meaningful separation and compactness.

NMI and VI NMI measures the mutual information between the true hierarchical clustering and the obtained hierarchical clustering, normalized by the average entropy of the two clusterings. Let X represent the true hierarchical clustering with N data points, and Y represent the obtained hierarchical clustering. The NMI between X and Y is calculated as

$$NMI(X,Y) = \frac{2 \times I(X;Y)}{H(X) + H(Y)},$$ (9.14)

where $I(X;Y)$ is the mutual information between X and Y, which quantifies the amount of shared information between the two clusterings, and $H(X)$ and $H(Y)$ are the entropies of X and Y, respectively, measuring the uncertainty or information content of each clustering.

VI measures the amount of information lost or shared when transitioning from the true hierarchical clustering to the obtained hierarchical clustering, and it is a nonnegative measure. Let X and Y be as defined above. The VI between X and Y is calculated as

$$VI(X,Y) = H(X) + H(Y) - 2 \times I(X;Y), \tag{9.15}$$

where $H(X)$, $H(Y)$, and $I(X;Y)$ are as defined in the NMI formula.

In both formulae, $H(X)$ and $H(Y)$ represent the entropy of the clustering, which measures the degree of uncertainty or information content of the clustering. The mutual information $I(X;Y)$ quantifies the amount of shared information between the two clusterings, indicating how well the obtained hierarchical clustering agrees with the true hierarchical clustering. Higher NMI values and lower VI values indicate better clustering quality, with NMI representing the clustering agreement and VI measuring the information shared or lost between the two hierarchical clusterings.

9.2 Dimensionality Reduction

In numerous practical applications, data often resides in a high-dimensional space. However, it is often observed that the intrinsic dimensionality, which captures most of the relevant information of the data, is significantly lower. This has led to a surge of interest in understanding the lower-dimensional structure associated with datasets across various fields, including computer vision, robotics, medical imaging, natural language processing, and computational neuroscience. A fundamental question arises in this context: How can we evaluate the extent to which a low-dimensional representation estimated by an algorithm accurately captures the underlying data?

To formalize the discussion of evaluating dimensionality reduction techniques, we denote the ith observation as x_i, where $1 \leq i \leq N$. Each x_i represents a real-valued vector in an n-dimensional space. We further represent the projection mapping associated with a dimensionality reduction technique or algorithm as P. Thus, P can be viewed as a transformation that maps an n-dimensional observation to a new space of dimension $q < n$, typically chosen as $q = 2$. There are several common methods that can be used for dimensionality reduction. Here we list some of them:

1. **Principal component analysis (PCA)** PCA is a linear dimensionality reduction technique that seeks to find a set of orthogonal axes, called principal components, which capture the maximum variance in the data. It projects the data onto these components, allowing for dimensionality reduction while preserving as much information as possible.
2. **Linear discriminant analysis (LDA)** LDA is a supervised dimensionality reduction technique that aims to find a linear projection that maximizes the separability between different classes in the data. It is commonly used for feature extraction in classification tasks.
3. **t-distributed stochastic neighbor embedding (t-SNE)** t-SNE is a nonlinear dimensionality reduction technique that emphasizes the preservation of local relationships between

data points. It is particularly effective in visualizing high-dimensional data in a lower-dimensional space while maintaining the clustering structure.

4. **Isomap** Isomap is a manifold learning technique that preserves the geodesic distances between data points. It constructs a low-dimensional embedding by approximating the intrinsic geometry of the data based on their pairwise distances.

5. **Locally linear embedding (LLE)** LLE is a nonlinear dimensionality reduction technique that preserves the local structure of the data. It seeks to find a low-dimensional representation by reconstructing each data point as a linear combination of its neighboring points.

6. **Nonnegative matrix factorization (NMF)** NMF is a dimensionality reduction technique that factorizes a nonnegative matrix into two lower-rank nonnegative matrices. It is commonly used for feature extraction and identifying parts-based representations in data.

These are just a few examples of methods that can be used for dimensionality reduction and there are many other methods available depending on the specific requirements of the data and the problem at hand. It's important to select an appropriate technique based on the characteristics of the data and the objectives of the analysis.

9.2.1 Evaluating Dimensionality Reduction Techniques

Following the classification proposed in Espadoto et al. (2019), metrics are categorized into different groups based on their output dimensionality. We now provide a brief overview of some important quantitative techniques from the literature that have been used to evaluate the quality of dimensionality reduction methods.

Scalar Metrics

Scalar metrics are widely recognized and used for evaluating the results of various dimensionality reduction techniques. These metrics are popular because they produce a single numerical value, making them simple to apply and straightforward to interpret.

Trustworthiness assesses the preservation of local patterns, such as clusters, in a projection by measuring the proportion of original points that remain close to each other after the projection. It provides insights into the reliability of preserving local relationships. The trustworthiness metric, denoted as M_t, is calculated using the formula

$$M_t = 1 - \frac{2}{NK(2n - 3K - 1)} \sum_{i=1}^{N} \sum_{j \in U_i^{(K)}} (r(i, j) - K), \qquad (9.16)$$

where N represents the number of points in the dataset, and $U_i^{(K)}$ denotes the set of points that are among the K nearest neighbors of point i in the projected q-dimensional space but not among the K nearest neighbors of point i in the original n-dimensional space. The index $r(i, j)$ indicates the rank of point j in the ordered set of nearest neighbors of point i in the projected q-dimensional space. The parameter K is chosen by the user and determines the number of nearest neighbors to consider. Trustworthiness ranges between 0 and 1, with 1 indicating the best preservation of local patterns.

Continuity is a metric that measures the proportion of projected q-dimensional points that remain close to each other in the original n-dimensional space. It quantifies the preservation of neighbors in the projection. The continuity metric, denoted M_c, is calculated using the formula

$$M_c = 1 - \frac{2}{NK(2n - 3K - 1)} \sum_{i=1}^{N} \sum_{j \in V_i^{(K)}} (\hat{r}(i, j) - K), \qquad (9.17)$$

where N represents the number of points in the dataset, and $V_i^{(K)}$ denotes the set of points that are among the K nearest neighbors of an n-dimensional point, but not among the K nearest neighbors in the projected q-dimensional space. The index $\hat{r}(i, j)$ indicates the rank of the n-dimensional point j in the ordered set of nearest neighbors of point i in the original n-dimensional space ($\mathbb{R}^n$). Similar to trustworthiness, the continuity metric ranges between 0 and 1, with 1 indicating the best preservation of neighbors.

Normalized stress is a metric that evaluates the preservation of pairwise distances between the original data points and their corresponding projections. Lower stress values indicate more meaningful and accurate projections. The normalized stress metric can be adapted to incorporate labeled data by assigning different weights to distances based on whether the points share the same label. The formula for normalized stress, denoted M_σ, is

$$M_\sigma = \frac{\sum_{ij}(\Delta^n(x_i, x_j) - \Delta^q(P(x_i), P(x_j)))^2}{\sum_{ij} \Delta^n(x_i, x_j)^2}. \qquad (9.18)$$

In this equation, Δ^n and Δ^q represent a distance metric, commonly the Euclidean distance, calculated in different spaces. The numerator calculates the squared differences between the distances in the original n-dimensional space and the distances in the projected q-dimensional space. The denominator normalizes the stress values by summing the squared distances in the original space. The normalized stress metric ranges from 0 to 1, with 0 indicating the best preservation of pairwise distances.

Neighborhood hit measures how well labeled data points are separated in the generated q-dimensional space. This is a useful metric to identify if P is ideal for classification tasks. The formula for neighborhood hit is given by

$$M_{NH} = \sum_{i=1}^{N} \frac{\left| j \in N_i^{(K)} : l_i = L_j \right|}{KN}. \qquad (9.19)$$

Neighborhood hit provides the proportion of the K neighbors $N_i^{(K)}$ of a point in the q-dimensional space that has the same label l as point i, averaged over all points in the resulted q-dimensional space; M_{NH} receives values in $[0, 1]$, with 1 being the optimum value. This metric is useful only if the data is well separable into classes in the original n-dimensional space.

Point-Pair Metrics

While scalar metrics are convenient and often interpretable, relying solely on average distortions to compare dimensionality reduction techniques can be misleading. Averages may hide important details about the preservation of specific distances. Two projections may exhibit similar average distortions but differ in their ability to preserve small distances accurately. To address this issue, point-pair metrics are well suited as they provide a more detailed assessment of distance preservation. Point-pair metrics consider individual pairs of points and evaluate the distortion or discrepancy in their distances between the original high-dimensional space and the projected low-dimensional space. By examining point-pair metrics, it becomes possible to capture variations in distance preservation that may not be apparent from average distortion measures alone. These metrics offer a more nuanced and accurate comparison of dimensionality reduction techniques. By incorporating point-pair metrics into the evaluation process, one can obtain a more comprehensive understanding of the performance of different dimensionality reduction methods, taking into account the preservation of specific distances rather than relying solely on average distortions. This approach allows for a more accurate and informed comparison between techniques.

Shepard diagrams are scatter plots that compare the pairwise Euclidean distances between all points in the projected q-dimensional space with their corresponding distances in the original n-dimensional space. The closer the scatter plot aligns with the main diagonal, the better the overall preservation of distances. To quantitatively assess the Shepard diagram, one can compute its Spearman rank correlation coefficient, denoted M_S. This involves calculating the Spearman rank correlation between the distances in the scatter plot,

$$\text{scatterplot}(||x_i - x_j||, ||P(x_i) - P(x_j)||), \ 1 \leq i \leq N, i \neq j. \tag{9.20}$$

The Spearman rank correlation coefficient ranges from -1 to 1. A value of 1 indicates a perfect correlation between the distances in the original and projected spaces, indicating excellent distance preservation. Additionally, to address the limitation of sample-agnostic metrics, for both scalar and point-pair metrics, local metrics have been proposed. Local metrics aim to capture how projection errors correlate with specific samples or sample groups, providing a more detailed understanding of the quality of dimensionality reduction techniques.

Projection precision scores are metrics used to evaluate the quality of a projection by measuring the normalized distance between two k-dimensional vectors. These vectors are composed of Euclidean distances between a data point y in the resulting q-dimensional space and its K nearest neighbors in the original n-dimensional space. To calculate the projection precision score, one first computes the Euclidean distances between y and its K nearest neighbors in the original n-dimensional space. These distances are then represented as components of a k-dimensional vector. Similarly, the Euclidean distances between y and its K nearest neighbors in the q-dimensional space are computed and represented as the components of the second k-dimensional vector. The projection precision score is obtained by normalizing the distance between these two k-dimensional vectors. The specific normalization method may depend on the context and requirements of the evaluation. The projection precision score provides a measure of how well the distances between a data point and its neighbors are preserved in the projection. A higher score indicates better preservation, while a lower score suggests a larger deviation from the original distances.

Stretching and compression metrics assess the degree of increase (stretching) or decrease (compression) in distances for a specific point y in the resulting q-dimensional space compared to all other points in $\mathbb{R}^q$, relative to the corresponding distances in the original n-dimensional space. These metrics are commonly visualized using a Voronoi-based partitioning of the two-dimensional projection space. To calculate the stretching and compression metrics, the distances between y and all other points in both the original n-dimensional space and the q-dimensional projection space are computed. The ratio of these distances is then used to quantify the stretching or compression effect. The Voronoi-based partitioning of the two-dimensional projection space visualizes the regions of influence for each point, showing how the stretching or compression is distributed across the projection. This visualization helps to interpret and analyze the quality of the dimensionality reduction technique in terms of preserving or distorting distances. By examining the stretching and compression metrics and their corresponding visualizations, one can gain insights into the degree and patterns of stretching or compression in the projection, providing valuable information about the distortions introduced during the dimensionality reduction process.

Average local error metrics provide an assessment of the quality of the placement of each point i in the projection by calculating the average sum $M_\alpha(i)$ of the differences between the normalized distances in both the original n-dimensional space and the q-dimensional projection space to all other points j in the dataset. To compute the average local error, the normalized distances between x_i and x_j in the original n-dimensional space and the distances between $P(x_i)$ and $P(x_j)$ in the q-dimensional projection space are compared. The absolute difference between these normalized distances is computed and summed for all $j \neq i$. The resulting sum is then divided by the total number of points $N - 1$ (excluding the point i itself) to obtain the average local error $M_\alpha(i)$. The values of $M_\alpha(i)$ range from 0 to 1, where smaller values indicate a better placement of point i relative to all other points. A smaller average local error suggests that the distances between the point i and other points are well preserved in the projection. The average local error metric provides a point-wise evaluation of the placement quality in the dimensionality reduction process, allowing for a detailed assessment of individual points and their relationships with other points in the dataset.

9.3 Latent Variable Models

Latent variable modeling is a powerful technique in machine learning that allows us to capture the underlying structure or hidden factors that generate the observed data. It is based on the assumption that the observed variables are influenced by latent variables that are not directly observed. By estimating these latent variables, we can gain insights into the hidden factors that drive the observed data. In latent variable modeling, the observed data is considered to be a result of a generative process involving both observed and latent variables. The goal is to learn the parameters of the model that best explain the relationship between the observed and latent variables. This enables us to represent the data in terms of a lower-dimensional latent space, capturing the essential information while reducing the dimensionality. There are several common latent variable modeling techniques that are widely used in machine learning. Here are some of them:

1. **Factor analysis** Factor analysis is a latent variable modeling technique that assumes the observed variables are linearly related to a set of latent variables. It aims to uncover the underlying factors or common sources of variation that contribute to the observed variables.
2. **Independent component analysis (ICA)** In ICA, the observed data is assumed to be a linear mixture of statistically independent source signals, where the goal is to separate these underlying independent sources from the observed data. The latent variables in ICA represent the independent sources that generate the observed data.
3. **Gaussian mixture models (GMMs)** GMMs are probabilistic latent variable models that assume the observed data is generated by a mixture of Gaussian distributions. Each component in the mixture represents a latent variable, and the mixture weights determine the contribution of each component to the observed data.
4. **Hidden Markov models (HMMs)** HMMs are sequential latent variable models that assume the observed data is generated by a hidden sequence of states. Each state represents a latent variable, and the transitions between states capture the temporal dependencies in the data.
5. **Bayesian networks** Bayesian networks are graphical models that represent the probabilistic relationships between variables using a directed acyclic graph. The nodes in the graph correspond to both observed and latent variables, and the edges represent the conditional dependencies between them.

9.3.1 Evaluating Latent Variable Models

Assessing the efficacy of latent variable models in capturing underlying data structures holds significant importance. Various assessment metrics and methodologies have been devised to evaluate distinct facets of these models. Within this section, we will cover frequently employed evaluation techniques for latent variable models. It is important to recognize that numerous alternative evaluation approaches for such models exist, contingent on the specific application. Here, we describe a few reference examples for interested readers (Bishop and Nasrabadi 2006; Long et al. 2018, 2019; Chang et al. 2009; Lau et al. 2014).

Likelihood-Based Measures

Likelihood-based measures offer valuable insights into the goodness of fit between the model and the observed data. Some commonly used likelihood-based measures for evaluating latent variable models include the following.

Log-likelihood The log-likelihood is an evaluation measure widely used in latent variable modeling. It provides a quantitative assessment of how well a latent variable model captures the observed data. The log-likelihood measures the probability of observing the given data points under the model's parameterization. In the context of latent variable models, the log-likelihood can be seen as a measure of how effectively the model is able to capture the underlying patterns and structures in the data. By maximizing the log-likelihood, the model aims to find the parameter values that best explain the observed data. A higher log-likelihood value indicates a better fit between the model and the data. It suggests that the model is able to generate data points that closely resemble the observed data. Conversely, a lower log-likelihood suggests that the model is less effective at capturing the data distribution. The log-likelihood is often used as an optimization objective during the training phase of latent variable models. The goal is to find the model parameters that maximize the log-likelihood, thereby improving the model's ability to generate realistic and representative data. It is important to note that the log-likelihood alone may not provide a complete picture of model performance. Other evaluation metrics, such as visual inspection, model complexity, and specific task-related measures, should also be considered to gain a comprehensive understanding of the model's capabilities.

Akaike information criterion (AIC) AIC takes into account two important aspects: the quality of the model's fit to the data and the complexity of the model itself. The goal is to find a model that strikes a balance between these two factors. AIC penalizes models with a higher number of parameters, favoring simpler and more parsimonious models. AIC is computed as

$$AIC = -2 \times \text{log-likelihood} + 2 \times \text{number of parameters}.$$

The log-likelihood term measures how well the model fits the observed data. It quantifies the probability of observing the given data points under the model's parameterization. The number of parameters in the model accounts for its complexity and flexibility. By penalizing models with more parameters, AIC encourages the selection of models that explain the data well while avoiding over-fitting. Over-fitting occurs when a model becomes too complex and starts to capture noise or random fluctuations in the data, leading to poor generalization to new, unseen data. Lower AIC values indicate better models. A lower AIC implies a better trade-off between goodness of fit and model complexity. When comparing multiple models, the model with the lowest AIC value is considered the best fit for the given data. AIC is a useful tool for model selection and comparison, as it provides a quantitative criterion for evaluating different models. However, it is important to note that AIC is just one of many evaluation measures, and its interpretation should be considered in conjunction with other metrics and domain-specific knowledge. In summary, the AIC is an evaluation measure that balances the goodness of fit and model complexity. It penalizes models with a higher number of parameters, promoting the selection of simpler and more interpretable models. Lower AIC values indicate better models that provide a good fit to the data while avoiding over-fitting.

Bayesian information criterion (BIC) The BIC is another commonly used evaluation measure that, similar to AIC, balances model fit and complexity. BIC provides a more stringent penalty on model complexity compared to AIC, making it especially useful when selecting models from a large set of alternatives. It is calculated as

$$BIC = -2 \times \text{log-likelihood} + \log(n) \times \text{number of parameters},$$

where log-likelihood represents the value of the log-likelihood function for the given model and data, n is the sample size, and the number of parameters indicates the complexity of the model. The BIC formula includes an additional term, $\log(n) \times$ number of parameters, which penalizes models more heavily for having a larger number of parameters. The penalty term, $\log(n)$, scales with the sample size, n, and helps to address the over-fitting issue by discouraging overly complex models, even more so than AIC. Similar to AIC, lower BIC values indicate better models. The goal is to select the model with the lowest BIC value, as it represents the best trade-off between model fit and complexity. By incorporating the penalty term, BIC tends to favor simpler models that provide a good fit to the data, thus reducing the risk of over-fitting. The choice between using AIC or BIC depends on the specific context and goals of the analysis. BIC is generally preferred when selecting models from a larger set of alternatives or when the sample size is relatively small. In such cases, the more stringent penalty of BIC helps to prevent over-fitting and provides a stronger emphasis on parsimony. BIC places a stronger penalty on model complexity, making it useful for selecting models from a large set of alternatives or when the sample size is small. Lower BIC values indicate better models that provide a good fit to the data while avoiding over-fitting.

Likelihood-ratio test The likelihood-ratio test is a statistical test used to compare the fit of two competing models based on the likelihood of the observed data. It evaluates whether one model fits the data significantly better than the other. This test is particularly useful when comparing nested models, where one model is a special case of the other. To perform the likelihood-ratio test, we start by fitting both models to the data and calculating their respective maximum likelihood estimates. The likelihood ratio is then calculated as the ratio of the likelihoods of the two models,

$$LR = -2 \times (\text{log-likelihood of Model 1} - \text{log-likelihood of Model 2}).$$

The test statistic LR follows a chi-square distribution with degrees of freedom equal to the difference in the number of parameters between the two models. A large LR value indicates a significant difference in fit between the models. To assess the statistical significance of the likelihood ratio, we compute a p-value associated with the observed LR value. This p-value represents the probability of observing a LR value as extreme as or more extreme than the one obtained, assuming that the null hypothesis is true (i.e., the models are equally good fits to the data). If the p-value is below a predetermined significance threshold, typically 0.05, we reject the null hypothesis and conclude that there is a significant difference in fit between the models. The likelihood-ratio test provides a formal statistical framework for model comparison, allowing us to determine whether one model is statistically superior to another based on the observed data. It is widely used in various fields, including statistics, econometrics, and machine learning, to compare models and select the most appropriate one. Note that the likelihood-ratio test assumes that the models being compared are nested, meaning that one model is a special case of the other. Additionally, the test assumes that the data follow certain assumptions, such as independence and identical distribution. Violations of these assumptions can affect the validity of the test results. Therefore, it is recommended that the results of the likelihood-ratio test are interpreted in conjunction with other evaluation measures and that the context and limitations of the specific analysis are considered.

Prediction Accuracy

Prediction accuracy evaluation is a crucial aspect of assessing the effectiveness of latent variable models in accurately predicting unseen or future data. One commonly used technique for evaluating predictive performance is cross-validation, specifically k-fold cross-validation. In k-fold cross-validation, the available data is divided into k subsets of approximately equal size. The model is then trained on $k - 1$ of these subsets and evaluated on the remaining subset. This process is repeated k times, with each subset serving as the evaluation set once. The results from each evaluation can be aggregated to provide an estimate of the model's predictive accuracy. By using cross-validation, we can mitigate the potential bias and variance issues that may arise from evaluating the model on a single split of the data. This technique allows for a more robust assessment of the model's generalization performance by evaluating it on multiple independent subsets of the data. During each fold of the cross-validation process, the latent variable model is trained on the training set, which consists of $k - 1$ subsets. The model learns the underlying patterns and structure from this training data. Subsequently, it is evaluated on the remaining subset, known as the testing set, to measure its predictive accuracy. The evaluation metric used will depend on the specific task and nature of the data, such as accuracy, mean squared error (MSE), or log-likelihood, among others. By employing cross-validation and assessing the predictive accuracy of the latent variable model across multiple folds, we gain valuable insights into its performance in making accurate predictions on unseen or future data. This evaluation method helps in determining the effectiveness and generalizability of the latent variable model beyond the data it was trained on.

Clustering Performance

If the latent variable model is used for clustering or classification tasks, evaluation measures specific to these tasks can be employed. For clustering, measures such as the adjusted Rand index and the NMI can assess the quality of the obtained clusters.

Visualization

Visualization techniques play a crucial role in understanding latent variable models and the representations they learn. These techniques allow us to visually inspect the latent variables or the transformed data in a lower-dimensional space, providing valuable insights into the model's performance and potential issues. One commonly used visualization technique is the scatter plot, which can be used to visualize the latent variables or the transformed data.

By plotting the values of the latent variables or the transformed data points against each other, we can observe patterns, clusters, or any underlying structures in the data. Scatter plots are particularly useful for identifying separability between different classes or groups of data points.

Heatmaps are another visualization tool that can be employed to gain insights into the learned representations. Heatmaps provide a graphical representation of the relationships and similarities between different variables or data points. They can be used to visualize the correlations or patterns in the data, highlighting areas of interest or potential anomalies. A widely used visualization technique for exploring high-dimensional data in a lower-dimensional space is t-SNE. It maps the original high-dimensional data to a two-dimensional or three-dimensional space, while preserving the local structure and similarity relationships between the data points. It can reveal clusters, patterns, or groupings in the data, facilitating the assessment of the latent variable model's ability to capture and represent the data's underlying structure.

Visual inspection of the latent variables or the transformed data through these visualization techniques allows us to qualitatively assess the quality of the learned representations. It can help identify potential issues, such as overlapping clusters, data points that are not well separated, or outliers. Visual inspection also enables the exploration and understanding of the relationships between different variables or features in the transformed space. By utilizing visualization techniques, we can complement quantitative evaluation measures and gain a deeper understanding of the latent variable model's performance. These visual insights can guide further improvements or adjustments to the model and provide a more comprehensive assessment of its capabilities and limitations.

9.4 Generative Models

Generative models are widely used in unsupervised machine learning to model and generate new data samples. Three commonly used generative models are probabilistic PCA (PPCA), Generative adversarial networks (GANs), and variational autoencoders (VAEs).

Probabilistic principal component analysis (PPCA) PPCA is an extension of the classical PCA technique (Tipping and Bishop 1999). PCA aims to find a lower-dimensional representation of high-dimensional data while minimizing the reconstruction error. PPCA builds upon this idea by introducing probabilistic modeling assumptions. In PPCA, it is assumed that the observed data points are generated by a linear transformation of a low-dimensional latent space. The latent variables are assumed to follow a Gaussian distribution. The model learns the transformation matrix and the variance of the Gaussian distribution using the maximum likelihood estimation framework. The goal is to find the optimal projection that maximizes the likelihood of the observed data. One advantage of PPCA is its computational efficiency compared to more complex nonlinear models. The linearity assumption allows for a straightforward optimization process, which makes PPCA particularly suitable for large-scale datasets. The model can be efficiently trained using well-established numerical optimization algorithms. However, PPCA has some limitations. It assumes that the underlying data distribution is Gaussian and linearly related to the latent variables. This restricts its ability to capture complex nonlinear relationships in the data. PPCA may not be suitable for datasets with intricate structures or highly non-Gaussian distributions. Nevertheless, PPCA offers flexibility by allowing the incorporation of prior knowledge about the data. By introducing prior distributions on the latent variables, it is possible to incorporate domain-specific information or constraints into the model. This makes PPCA a versatile tool that can be adapted to various applications and research contexts. In summary, PPCA provides a probabilistic framework for dimensionality reduction by assuming a linear relationship between the observed data and the latent variables. It is computationally efficient and can be extended to incorporate prior knowledge. However, its linear and Gaussian assumptions limit its ability to model complex data distributions.

Generative adversarial networks (GANs) GANs are a class of deep learning models designed to generate synthetic data that closely resembles a given set of training data (Goodfellow et al. 2020). GANs gained significant popularity in various domains, including image generation, music generation, and text generation. By employing a novel adversarial training scheme, GANs have demonstrated the ability to capture complex patterns and generate highly realistic and diverse samples, making them a powerful tool in the field of generative modeling. The basic idea behind GANs is to train two neural networks: a generator network and a discriminator network. The generator network takes random noise as input and generates new data samples, while the discriminator network takes a data sample as input and outputs a probability that the sample is real (i.e., from the training data) rather than fake (i.e., generated by the generator). During training, the generator tries to generate data samples that can fool the discriminator into thinking that they are real, while the discriminator tries to distinguish between real and fake data samples. The generator and discriminator are trained simultaneously in a minimax game, where the generator tries to minimize the probability of the discriminator correctly classifying fake data samples, and the discriminator tries to maximize the probability of correctly classifying real and fake data samples. Once the GAN is trained, the generator can be used to generate new data samples that resemble the training data. This is done by sampling random noise from the same distribution used during training, and feeding the noise through the generator network to generate new data samples.

Variational autoencoders (VAEs) VAEs are a popular class of latent variable models used for unsupervised learning and generative modeling (Kingma and Welling 2013). They consist of two main components: an encoder and a decoder. The encoder takes the input data and maps it to a latent space representation. This mapping is often probabilistic, with the encoder generating a mean and variance for each latent variable, assuming a parametric distribution such as Gaussian. The encoder aims to capture the underlying structure and relevant features of the input data in the latent space. Conversely, the decoder takes a point in the latent space and maps it back to the input space, reconstructing the original data. The decoder is responsible for generating synthetic samples that resemble the input data distribution. During training, VAEs employ a variational approach to learn the model parameters. The objective is to maximize the lower bound of the log-likelihood of the data given the latent variables. This is achieved by minimizing the reconstruction error between the original data and the reconstructed data, as well as regularizing the latent space distribution to follow a prior distribution (often a standard Gaussian). The optimization process typically involves stochastic gradient descent and the use of reparameterization tricks to enable backpropagation. Compared to GANs, VAEs have certain advantages. They are generally easier to train and less prone to mode collapse, which is a phenomenon where the generator produces limited or repetitive samples. VAEs can capture the full data distribution and generate samples that cover a broader range of the data space. However, one limitation of VAEs is that the generated samples can be less diverse compared to GANs. This is because VAEs optimize a reconstruction objective and tend to produce samples that are close to the training data, often resulting in blurry or less varied samples. GANs, on the other hand, optimize a discriminator-based adversarial objective and can generate sharper and more diverse samples. Overall, VAEs offer a trade-off between ease of training and sample diversity. They are particularly useful for tasks such as data compression, feature learning, and semi-supervised learning, where the focus is on capturing the underlying structure of the data rather than generating highly realistic samples.

PPCA, GANs, and VAEs are distinct models with different characteristics and training objectives. While there may be some overlap in the evaluation techniques used for these models, they also have unique evaluation measures tailored to their specific objectives.

9.4.1 Evaluating Probabilistic PPCA

Evaluating the performance of PPCA is important to ensure that the learned representation accurately captures the underlying structure of the data. Here, we describe some evaluation techniques for PPCA.

Reconstruction Error

The reconstruction error in PPCA can be calculated using the MSE between the original input data and the reconstructed data. The formula for the reconstruction error is

$$\text{Reconstruction Error} = \frac{1}{N} \sum_{i=1}^{N} \|x_i - \tilde{x}_i\|^2,$$

where N is the total number of data points, x_i represents the original input data point i, and $\tilde{x}_i$ represents the reconstructed data point i obtained from PPCA.

In PPCA, the reconstructed data points $\tilde{x}_i$ are obtained by encoding the original data points x_i into the latent space using the learned transformation matrix, and then decoding them back to the original input space. The reconstruction error measures the average squared difference between the original input data and their corresponding reconstructed data points. A lower reconstruction error indicates a better reconstruction performance, as it reflects the model's ability to capture the essential information of the data and accurately reproduce it. It is worth noting that the reconstruction error alone may not provide a complete assessment of the PPCA model's performance.

Log-Likelihood

The log-likelihood is a commonly used measure to evaluate the fit of a probabilistic model, including PPCA, to the observed data. In PPCA, the log-likelihood quantifies how well the model captures the underlying patterns and structures in the data.

The formula for the log-likelihood in PPCA is

$$\text{log-likelihood} = -\frac{ND}{2}\log(2\pi) - \frac{N}{2}\log|\mathbf{C}| - \frac{1}{2}\sum_{i=1}^{N}(\mathbf{x}_i - \bar{\mathbf{x}})^T \mathbf{C}^{-1}(\mathbf{x}_i - \bar{\mathbf{x}}),$$

where N is the total number of data points, D is the dimensionality of the data, $\mathbf{x}_i$ represents the original input data point i, $\bar{\mathbf{x}}$ is the mean of the data points, and $\mathbf{C}$ is the covariance matrix of the data.

The log-likelihood measures the probability of observing the given data points under the PPCA model. A higher log-likelihood value indicates a better fit between the model and the data, indicating that the model is able to capture the underlying structure and generate data points that closely match the observed data. To evaluate PPCA, one can compare the log-likelihood values obtained from different models or variations of PPCA. The model with a higher log-likelihood is considered to have a better fit to the data. However, it is important to note that the log-likelihood alone may not provide a complete assessment of the model's performance. Additional evaluation measures and techniques, such as visualization of the latent space or comparison with other models, can be used to gain a comprehensive understanding of the model's effectiveness in capturing the data's underlying structure.

Visualization

Visualization techniques can be used to evaluate the quality of the learned low-dimensional representation. By projecting the data onto the learned low-dimensional space, it is possible to visualize the structure of the learned representation. Clustering algorithms can also be applied to the low-dimensional space to evaluate the quality of the learned representation.

9.4.2 Evaluating Variational Autoencoders

VAEs are generative models used for unsupervised learning. VAEs learn a low-dimensional representation of high-dimensional data that can be used for tasks such as data compression, data reconstruction, and data generation. Here are some evaluation techniques for VAEs. Again there are numerous evaluation strategies for VAEs and the choice of which one to use depends on the application. For instance one could see the work proposed by Liu et al. (2020) and Zhao et al. (2017).

Reconstruction Error

One of the simplest evaluation techniques for VAEs is to measure the reconstruction error of the input data. In VAEs, the reconstruction error is commonly measured using a loss function that quantifies the discrepancy between the input data and the output generated by the VAE's decoder network. The reconstruction error is an important evaluation metric that reflects how well the VAE is able to reconstruct the original input data.

For continuous data (MSE loss),

$$\text{Reconstruction Error} = \frac{1}{N} \sum_{i=1}^{N} \|x_i - \tilde{x}_i\|^2,$$

and for binary data (BCE loss),

$$\text{Reconstruction Error} = -\frac{1}{N} \sum_{i=1}^{N} (x_i \log \tilde{x}_i + (1 - x_i) \log(1 - \tilde{x}_i)),$$

where N is the total number of data points, x_i represents the original input data point i, and $\tilde{x}_i$ represents the reconstructed data point i obtained from the VAE's decoder network.

The reconstruction error measures the discrepancy between the original input data and their corresponding reconstructed data points. A lower reconstruction error indicates better reconstruction performance as it reflects the VAE's ability to capture the essential information of the data and accurately reproduce it. It's important to note that the choice of the loss function may vary depending on the specific task and data type. Other variants of the reconstruction error, such as per-pixel reconstruction error for images or other specialized loss functions, can also be used based on the specific characteristics of the data being reconstructed.

Log-Likelihood

To evaluate VAEs, the log-likelihood is commonly used as a measure of how well the model captures the underlying patterns and structures in the data. The log-likelihood quantifies the probability of observing the given data points under the VAE model. Higher log-likelihood values indicate a better fit between the model and the data. In VAEs, the log-likelihood is often estimated using the evidence lower bound (ELBO) or negative ELBO, which is derived from the variational inference framework. The formula for the negative ELBO is

$$\text{Negative ELBO} = -\frac{1}{N} \sum_{i=1}^{N} \left(\mathbb{E}_{z \sim q_\phi(z|x_i)}[\log p_\theta(x_i|z)] - \text{KL}\left(q_\phi(z|x_i)\|p(z)\right) \right),$$

where N is the total number of data points, x_i represents the original input data point i, $q_\phi(z|x_i)$ is the approximate posterior distribution (encoder) parameterized by ϕ that maps the input data to the latent space, $p_\theta(x_i|z)$ is the generative distribution (decoder) parameterized by θ that reconstructs the input data from the latent space, $p(z)$ is the prior distribution over the latent space, and KL represents the Kullback–Leibler divergence, which measures the difference between the approximate posterior and the prior distributions.

The negative ELBO consists of two components: the expected log-likelihood of reconstructing the data given the latent variable z and the Kullback–Leibler divergence between the approximate posterior and the prior. Maximizing the negative ELBO is equivalent to maximizing the log-likelihood of the data. To evaluate the VAE model, one can compute the negative ELBO for a set of test data points and calculate the average value. A higher negative ELBO, or equivalently, a lower absolute value of the negative ELBO, indicates a better fit between the model and the data.

Interpolation

Interpolation techniques can be used to assess the smoothness of the learned latent space generated by VAEs. By interpolating between two points in the latent space and generating new data points, we can evaluate how effectively the VAE can interpolate and generate data points that smoothly transition between different representations. The interpolation process involves selecting two points in the latent space, typically represented as vectors, and linearly interpolating between them to generate intermediate points. These intermediate points are then decoded by the VAE's decoder network to produce corresponding data points in the original input space. By examining the generated data points along the interpolation path, we can assess the smoothness and continuity of the latent space. Ideally, as we move from one end of the interpolation to the other, the generated data points should exhibit gradual changes and maintain semantic coherence. This implies that the VAE has successfully learned a smooth and meaningful latent space representation. The evaluation of interpolation can be performed qualitatively by visually inspecting the generated data points along the interpolation path. Additionally, quantitative evaluation measures can be used, such as measuring the Euclidean distance or the cosine similarity between adjacent generated data points. Smaller distances or higher similarity scores indicate smoother transitions and better interpolation performance. Interpolation techniques provide valuable insights into the quality of the learned latent space in VAEs.

Here is an interpolation example that can be used to evaluate VAEs. Assuming we have two points in the latent space, z_1 and z_2, we can perform linear interpolation to generate intermediate points z_{interp} between them. The interpolation parameter, denoted t and ranging from 0 to 1, controls the degree of interpolation. The interpolation formula is given by

$$z_{interp} = (1 - t)z_1 + tz_2.$$

Once we have the interpolated points in the latent space, we can decode them using the VAE's decoder network to generate corresponding data points in the original input space. The decoding process is represented by

$$x_{interp} = \text{Decoder}(z_{interp}),$$

where x_{interp} represents the generated data point obtained by decoding the interpolated latent point z_{interp}. To evaluate the interpolation performance, we can visually inspect the generated data points x_{interp} along the interpolation path. Smooth transitions and semantic consistency between adjacent generated data points indicate successful interpolation. Additionally, quantitative evaluation measures can be employed. For example, the Euclidean distance between adjacent generated data points can be calculated using the formula

$$\text{Distance}(x_i, x_{i+1}) = \sqrt{\sum_{j=1}^{D}(x_{i,j} - x_{i+1,j})^2},$$

where $x_{i,j}$ and $x_{i+1,j}$ represent the jth component of the ith and $(i + 1)$th generated data points, respectively. Smaller distances between adjacent points indicate smoother transitions. By combining visual inspection and quantitative evaluation measures, we can assess the smoothness and continuity of the learned latent space in VAEs using interpolation techniques.

9.4.3 Evaluating GANs

In the realm of GANs, numerous metrics have been proposed (Borji 2019). In this section, we concentrate on the most widely used metrics and justify their inclusion in our benchmark. However, we acknowledge the existence of other metrics and briefly mention them without delving into their specifics. For an extensive review of evaluation metrics for GANs, we also refer interested readers to Borji (2019).

Visual Inspection

Visual inspection is a crucial qualitative evaluation method employed in assessing the visual quality of generated images. This evaluation technique involves human judges visually examining and analyzing the generated samples to provide subjective feedback on their realism, fidelity, and overall visual appeal. Unlike quantitative metrics that rely on objective measurements, visual inspection offers a more nuanced and subjective assessment of the generated images. It takes into account human perception, cognitive biases, and the ability to discern intricate details and visual nuances that may not be captured by automated metrics alone.

Human judges, typically experts or individuals with a deep understanding of the domain, carefully examine the generated images and evaluate various aspects such as visual clarity, sharpness, color distribution, texture, object coherence, and overall aesthetic appeal. They compare the generated images with real images to determine how closely they resemble the desired output or the underlying data distribution. One of the main advantages of visual inspection is its ability to capture qualitative aspects that quantitative metrics might miss. Human judges can identify subtle imperfections or artifacts in the generated images that may not be easily quantifiable. They can assess the fidelity of fine details, the realism of textures and shapes, and the overall coherence and believability of the generated scenes. Visual inspection also allows for a comprehensive evaluation of the generated images in the context of the specific application or task. For example, in image synthesis tasks such as generating realistic human faces, judges can examine facial features, expressions, and naturalness of skin tones to determine the success of the generator model. In artistic style transfer tasks, judges can assess how well the style of the generated images matches the desired artistic style. However, visual inspection does have limitations. It is subjective and prone to biases and variations among different judges. The interpretation of visual quality can vary depending on individual preferences and expertise. Additionally, visual inspection is time-consuming and resource-intensive, especially when evaluating a large number of generated samples. Despite these limitations, visual inspection remains a valuable evaluation method. It provides qualitative feedback that complements quantitative metrics and helps assess the perceptual quality and realism of generated images. The combination of objective quantitative metrics and subjective visual inspection allows for a more comprehensive evaluation of the generator model's performance.

Inception Score

The inception score (IS) is a popular evaluation metric used to assess the performance of GANs by measuring the quality and diversity of generated images. The IS evaluates how well the generated images match the distribution of real images. The formula for IS is

$$IS = \exp\left(\mathbb{E}_{x \sim p_{\text{data}}}\left[D_{\text{KL}}(p(y|x)\|p(y))\right]\right),$$

where x represents an image from the real data distribution $p_{\text{data}}(x)$, $p(y|x)$ is the conditional class distribution given the image x, typically estimated using an inception model or a pretrained classifier, $p(y)$ is the marginal class distribution, which can be approximated as the empirical distribution of labels in the training set, and D_{KL} denotes the Kullback–Leibler divergence.

To compute the IS, we first generate a set of images using the GAN. Then, we use an inception model or a pretrained classifier to obtain the conditional class distribution $p(y|x)$ for each generated image. Finally, we calculate the IS by taking the exponential of the average Kullback–Leibler divergence between the conditional class distribution and the marginal class distribution. A higher IS indicates that the generated images are diverse and resemble the distribution of real images more closely. It is important to note that the IS provides a global assessment of the generated images, but it may not capture certain aspects such as local image quality or semantic coherence.

Fréchet Inception Distance

The Fréchet inception distance (FID) is an evaluation metric commonly used to assess the performance of GANs by measuring the quality and diversity of generated images. The FID evaluates both the realism of the generated images and the similarity between their distribution and the distribution of real images.

The formula for the FID is

$$\text{FID} = \|\mu_{\text{real}} - \mu_{\text{fake}}\|^2 + \text{Tr}\left(C_{\text{real}} + C_{\text{fake}} - 2(C_{\text{real}}C_{\text{fake}})^{1/2}\right),$$

where μ_{real} and μ_{fake} represent the mean activation vectors (output of an intermediate layer) of the real and generated images, respectively, C_{real} and C_{fake} are the covariance matrices of the real and generated images, respectively, $\| \cdot \|$ denotes the Euclidean distance, and $\text{Tr}(\cdot)$ represents the trace of a matrix.

To compute the FID, we first extract the activation vectors from a pretrained inception model or a feature extractor for both real and generated images. Then, we calculate the mean (μ) and covariance (C) for each set of activation vectors. Finally, we compute the FID. A lower FID value indicates better performance, indicating that the generated images have a distribution closer to that of real images. The FID metric combines both the mean difference and covariance difference, providing a more comprehensive evaluation of the similarity between the two distributions. It is important to note that computing the FID requires a pretrained inception model or a feature extractor. Additionally, a large number of samples are often used to estimate the mean and covariance accurately. The FID is widely used to assess GAN performance. However, it should be complemented with other evaluation techniques, such as visual inspection, human evaluation, or domain-specific metrics, for a more comprehensive assessment of the generated images' quality and diversity.

Precision and Recall

Precision and recall are fundamental metrics that are commonly employed in image generation evaluation to assess how well the generated images match the real images, particularly in terms of precision and recall. We review these metrics here in the specific case of images.

Precision is a metric that quantifies the accuracy or relevancy of the generated images. It measures the ratio of relevant images among the generated images. In the context of image generation, a relevant image refers to a generated image that closely resembles or aligns with the desired characteristics of real images. A high precision score indicates that a significant proportion of the generated images are relevant and of good quality. By contrast, recall is a metric that gauges the completeness or coverage of the generated images. It measures the ratio of relevant images among the real images. In the context of image generation, a relevant image corresponds to a real image that possesses the desired characteristics or features that the generator aims to replicate. A high recall score suggests that the generator successfully captures the essential aspects of the real images. To compute precision and recall, a comparison is made between the generated images and the real images. Each generated image is evaluated and classified as either relevant or irrelevant, based on its similarity to the real images. Similarly, each real image is classified as relevant or irrelevant, depending on its alignment with the desired characteristics. The ratios of relevant images are then calculated separately for the generated images and the real images, yielding precision and recall scores, respectively.

For example, in the evaluation of a GAN model trained on generating human faces, precision would measure the ratio of generated images that convincingly resemble real human faces among all the generated images. A high precision score indicates that the majority of the generated images closely resemble real human faces. Conversely, recall would measure the ratio of real human faces that are successfully captured and generated by the model among all the real images. A high recall score suggests that the generator successfully reproduces the desired features of human faces.

Coverage

The coverage metric is used to evaluate the diversity and coverage of generated samples by a GAN. It measures how well the generated samples cover the distribution of real samples in the dataset. The formula for coverage is given by

$$\text{Coverage} = \frac{1}{N} \sum_{i=1}^{N} \mathbb{I}(\boldsymbol{x}_i \in G),$$

where N is the total number of real data samples in the dataset, $\boldsymbol{x}_i$ represents a real data sample from the dataset, G is the set of generated samples, and $\mathbb{I}(\boldsymbol{x}_i \in G)$ is an indicator function that returns 1 if the real sample x_i is covered by the generated samples, and 0 otherwise.

To compute the coverage, we need to generate a set of samples using the GAN and compare them to the real data samples. For each real data sample, we check if it is covered by the generated samples. The coverage is then calculated by averaging the coverage indicator values over all real data samples. A higher coverage value indicates that the generated samples cover a larger portion of the distribution of real samples, implying better diversity and coverage. For instance, consider a GAN trained on generating images of animals. The coverage metric would evaluate how well the generated images span the space of different animal species, breeds, poses, and other variations present in the real image dataset. If the generator produces a wide variety of animal images and covers the full range of species and variations found in the real images, it would indicate a high coverage score. The coverage metric provides valuable insights into the ability of the generative model to capture the diversity and distribution of real images. A high coverage score suggests that the generated images effectively span the real image space, indicating a strong and diverse generative performance. Conversely, a low coverage score may indicate limitations in the generative model, such as generating a narrow range of images or failing to capture the full distribution of the real images.

Divergence Metrics

Divergence metrics play a crucial role in evaluating the dissimilarity between the distributions of generated and real images. These metrics, including Kullback–Leibler divergence and Jensen–Shannon divergence, provide valuable insights into the statistical distance or dissimilarity between the two distributions.

Kullback–Leibler divergence is a widely used divergence metric that measures the information lost when one distribution is used to approximate another. In the context of image generation evaluation, Kullback–Leibler divergence quantifies the discrepancy between the distribution of generated images and the distribution of real images. It provides a measure of how much the generated images deviate from the real image distribution in terms of probability density. Jensen–Shannon divergence, by contrast, is a symmetrical and smoothed version of Kullback–Leibler divergence. It calculates the average divergence between the two distributions by considering their joint probability distribution. The formula for Kullback–Leibler divergence between two probability distributions P and Q is

$$KL(P\|Q) = \sum P(x) \cdot \log\left(\frac{P(x)}{Q(x)}\right),$$

where x represents an element or outcome in the support of the probability distributions P and Q. Jensen–Shannon divergence is often preferred over Kullback–Leibler divergence as it overcomes some of its limitations, such as the sensitivity to outliers. By employing these divergence metrics, researchers and practitioners gain insights into the dissimilarity or distance between the distributions of generated and real images. A higher value of Kullback–Leibler divergence or Jensen–Shannon divergence indicates a larger discrepancy or dissimilarity between the two distributions, suggesting that the generated images may not faithfully capture the statistical properties of the real images. The formula for Jensen–Shannon divergence between two distributions P and Q is

$$JS(P||Q) = 0.5 \cdot KL(P||M) + 0.5 \cdot KL(Q||M),$$

where $M = 0.5 \cdot (P + Q)$ is the average distribution.

For example, consider a GAN trained on generating images of natural landscapes. The Kullback–Leibler divergence or Jensen–Shannon divergence can be calculated to evaluate how closely the distribution of the generated landscape images aligns with the distribution of real landscape images. A lower divergence score would suggest that the generated images effectively capture the statistical properties of the real landscapes, indicating a better performance of the generative model. It is important to note that divergence metrics, such as Kullback–Leibler divergence and Jensen–Shannon divergence, provide a quantitative measure of the dissimilarity between distributions. However, they do not capture the visual quality or subjective aspects of the generated images. Therefore, these metrics are often used in conjunction with other evaluation measures to gain a comprehensive understanding of the performance of image generation models.

Wasserstein Distance

The Wasserstein distance is another commonly used metric that can be used to evaluate the performance of GANs. It quantifies the dissimilarity between the generated distribution and the target (real) distribution. The formula for Wasserstein distance is given by

$$W(p_r, p_g) = \inf_{\gamma \in \Gamma(p_r, p_g)} \mathbb{E}_{(x, y) \sim \gamma}[d(x, y)],$$

where p_r represents the target (real) distribution, typically the distribution of real data samples, p_g represents the generated distribution, typically the distribution of samples generated by the GAN, $\Gamma(p_r, p_g)$ is the set of all joint distributions $\gamma(x, y)$ whose marginals are p_r and p_g, respectively, and $d(x, y)$ is a metric or distance function that measures the dissimilarity between two data points x and y.

To compute the Wasserstein distance, we need to find the infimum (minimum) over all joint distributions $\gamma(x, y)$ that align the marginals p_r and p_g. This involves solving an optimization problem to find the optimal transport plan that minimizes the total cost of moving mass from the generated distribution to the target distribution. The cost is typically defined based on the chosen distance function $d(x, y)$. In practice, estimating the exact Wasserstein distance is often infeasible. Instead, an approximation is used. One common approximation is to estimate the Wasserstein distance using samples from the distributions

$$W(p_r, p_g) \approx \frac{1}{K} \sum_{k=1}^{K} d(x_k, y_k),$$

where x_k and y_k are samples drawn from the target and generated distributions, respectively. By calculating the average distance between corresponding samples from the two distributions, we obtain an estimate of the Wasserstein distance. It's important to note that computing the exact Wasserstein distance may require solving complex optimization problems.

Approximations and sampling-based methods are commonly used to estimate it in practice. To assess the performance of GANs using the Wasserstein distance, we need to estimate the distance between the generated distribution and the target distribution. This can be done by sampling from both distributions and calculating the average distance between corresponding samples. By monitoring the Wasserstein distance during GAN training, we can evaluate the convergence and quality of the generated samples. Additionally, the Wasserstein distance can be used as a loss function to guide the GAN training process. As an example, consider a GAN trained to generate images of different types of flowers. The Wasserstein distance can be calculated to assess how closely the distribution of the generated flower images aligns with the distribution of real flower images. A smaller Wasserstein distance implies a more efficient and cost-effective transformation between the two distributions, indicating a higher similarity and better performance of the generative model.

Nearest Neighbor Accuracy

Nearest neighbor accuracy (NNA) measures the ability of the generated samples to resemble the real data by quantifying their similarity to the nearest neighbors in the real data distribution. The formula for NNA is given by

$$\text{NNA} = \frac{1}{N} \sum_{i=1}^{N} \mathbb{I}(x_i \in \text{NN}(\boldsymbol{x}_i, G)),$$

where N is the total number of real data samples, $\boldsymbol{x}_i$ represents an individual real data sample, $\text{NN}(\boldsymbol{x}_i, G)$ denotes the set of nearest neighbors of $\boldsymbol{x}_i$ among the generated samples G, and $\mathbb{I}(\boldsymbol{x}_i \in \text{NN}(\boldsymbol{x}_i, G))$ is an indicator function that returns 1 if the real sample x_i is among its nearest neighbors in the generated samples G, and 0 otherwise.

To compute the NNA, we iterate over each real data sample, find its nearest neighbors among the generated samples, and check if the sample itself is included in the set of nearest neighbors. The NNA is then calculated by averaging the indicator values over all real data samples. A higher NNA value indicates better performance, suggesting that the generated samples are similar to the real data and can be easily mistaken for real samples by nearest neighbor matching. NNA measures the local quality of the generated samples and provides insights into their resemblance to the real data distribution. To use the NNA metric to assess the performance of GANs, we need to generate a sufficient number of samples using the GAN and compare them to the real data samples. By calculating the NNA, we can quantitatively evaluate the similarity between the generated samples and the real data distribution.

Mean Opinion Score

Mean opinion score (MOS) is a well-used subjective evaluation metric to assess the performance of GANs and other generative models. It involves collecting human ratings or opinions on the quality of generated samples. MOS provides a measure of the overall perceived quality or realism of the generated samples. The formula for MOS is straightforward,

$$\text{MOS} = \frac{1}{N} \sum_{i=1}^{N} \text{Rating}_i,$$

where N is the total number of human ratings or opinions collected and Rating$_i$ represents the rating or opinion provided by the ith human evaluator.

To compute the MOS, we collect ratings from multiple human evaluators who are asked to rate the generated samples based on various aspects such as quality, realism, and visual appeal. The ratings are typically provided on a scale, such as a Likert scale, ranging from low to high. The MOS is then calculated by averaging the ratings over all evaluators. A higher MOS indicates better performance, suggesting that the generated samples are perceived as more realistic and of higher quality by human evaluators. MOS provides valuable insights into the subjective assessment of sample quality and can complement other objective evaluation metrics. To use MOS to assess the performance of GANs, we need to design a subjective evaluation study where human evaluators rate the generated samples. This can be done through online surveys, where evaluators are presented with a set of generated samples and asked to provide their ratings. The MOS can then be calculated based on the collected ratings. It is important to note that MOS is a subjective metric and can be influenced by individual preferences and biases. Therefore, it is recommended to collect ratings from a diverse group of evaluators to obtain a more representative and reliable assessment of the generated samples.

9.4.4 GAN-Based Text Generation Evaluation Techniques

Generating text using GANs presents a unique challenge stemming from the non-differentiability of discrete symbol generation. Unlike continuous data, such as images or audio, text is discrete and composed of individual symbols (e.g., words or characters). The nondifferentiability of discrete symbols poses a hurdle in training GANs effectively for text generation tasks. Evaluating the performance of GAN-based text generation models requires careful consideration of the specific challenges associated with discrete symbol generation. To delve deeper into this topic and explore the evaluation methods designed specifically for GAN-based text generation, we recommend referring to Tevet et al. (2018). However, in this section we present some commonly used metrics to evaluate the quality of GAN-based text generation include. Evaluating text generation, in general, was also covered in Chapter 8 where other metrics appropriate for GAN-based text generation can be found. We complement that discussion here.

Perplexity

Perplexity is a commonly used metric to evaluate the performance of language models, including text-based GANs. It measures how well a language model predicts a given sequence of words or text. A lower perplexity value indicates better model performance, suggesting that the model can more accurately predict the next word in a sequence. The formula for perplexity is

$$\text{Perplexity} = \exp\left(-\frac{1}{N}\sum_{i=1}^{N}\log p(x_i)\right),$$

where N is the total number of words or tokens in the test set, x_i represents the ith word or token in the test set, and $p(x_i)$ is the estimated probability assigned by the language model to the word or token x_i.

To calculate perplexity, we need to estimate the probabilities of words or tokens in the test set using the language model. Then, we take the average negative log probability of the words or tokens and exponentiate it.

To assess the performance of text-based GANs using perplexity, we typically follow these steps:

- Train a text-based GAN, such as one with a recurrent generator and discriminator.
- Generate a set of text samples using the trained GAN.
- Split your test dataset into sequences of words or tokens.
- Use the trained GAN to calculate the estimated probabilities for each word or token in the test set.
- Compute the perplexity using the formula.

A lower perplexity score suggests that the GAN has generated text that is more similar to the training data, indicating better performance. It demonstrates that the GAN's language model is more confident in predicting the next word or token in the generated text.

Bilingual Evaluation Understudy (BLEU)

Bilingual evaluation understudy (BLEU) measures the n-gram overlap between the generated text and reference text, providing a score between 0 and 1. Higher BLEU scores indicate better similarity between the generated and reference text. The formula for BLEU is

$$\text{BLEU} = \text{BP} \times \exp\left(\sum_{n=1}^{N} w_n \log \text{precision}_n\right),$$

where BP is the brevity penalty that adjusts the BLEU score based on the length of the generated text compared to the reference text (it penalizes shorter generated text and prevents favoring shorter outputs), w_n is the weight assigned to the n-gram precision (typically, equal weights are used, so $w_n = \frac{1}{N}$, where N is the maximum order of n-gram precision), and precision_n is the n-gram precision, which measures the percentage of n-grams in the generated text that appear in the reference text.

To calculate the BLEU score, you need to perform the following steps:

- Prepare a set of reference texts that serve as the ground truth or target for the generated text.
- Generate text samples using the text-based GAN.
- Compute the n-gram precision for each n (typically from 1 to N), which is the ratio of matching n-grams in the generated text to the reference text.
- Calculate the brevity penalty (BP) to adjust the BLEU score based on the length of the generated text compared to the reference text.
- Calculate the weighted sum the log of n-gram precisions using the weights w_n and exponentiate the result to obtain the BLEU score.

The resulting BLEU score represents the similarity between the generated text and reference text. A higher BLEU score indicates a closer resemblance between the generated text and the target text, reflecting better performance of the text-based GAN.

Recall-Oriented Understudy for Gisting Evaluation (ROUGE)

Recall-oriented understudy for gisting evaluation (ROUGE) is a set of evaluation metrics that can be used to measure the overlap between the generated summary and the reference summary. The ROUGE metrics include ROUGE-N, ROUGE-L, and ROUGE-S. The formula for ROUGE-N is

$$\text{ROUGE-N} = \frac{\sum_{s \in S} \sum_{n \in s} \text{CountMatch}(n)}{\sum_{s \in S} \sum_{n \in s} \text{CountTotal}(n)},$$

where S is the set of sentences in the reference summary, n represents an n-gram (sequence of n consecutive words), CountMatch(n) is the total count of matching n-grams between the generated summary and the reference summary, and CountTotal(n) is the total count of n-grams in the reference summary.

ROUGE-N calculates the precision and recall of the n-grams between the generated and reference summaries. A higher ROUGE-N score indicates better overlap and similarity. Similarly, ROUGE-L measures the longest common subsequence (LCS) between the generated and reference summaries,

$$\text{ROUGE-L} = \frac{\text{LCS}(c,r)}{\text{Length}(r)},$$

where LCS(c,r) is the length of the longest common subsequence between the candidate summary c (generated summary) and the reference summary r, and Length(r) is the total length of the reference summary.

ROUGE-L captures the recall of the longest common subsequence and provides a score between 0 and 1. A higher ROUGE-L score indicates better overlap and similarity. ROUGE-S measures skip-bigram (2-gram with a maximum gap of four words) statistics between the generated and reference summaries. The formula for ROUGE-S is more complex and involves the calculation of recall, precision, and F-score based on skip-bigram matches. To assess the performance of text-based GANs using ROUGE metrics, you typically follow these steps:

- Prepare a set of reference summaries that serve as the ground truth.
- Generate text summaries using the text-based GAN.
- Calculate the ROUGE scores (ROUGE-N, ROUGE-L, ROUGE-S) by comparing the generated summaries to the reference summaries.
- Analyze the ROUGE scores to evaluate the similarity and overlap between the generated and reference summaries.

Higher ROUGE scores indicate better performance, as they indicate higher overlap and similarity between the generated and reference summaries.

Part IV

Evaluation from a Practical Perspective

10

Industrial-Strength Evaluation

Machine learning has matured enough for practitioners to start thinking a bit more carefully about the robust deployment of products that are based on it. Until very recently, machine learning was confined to a few uses in specialized labs or industries. At the time of writing, the situation is very different: machine learning is used in a wide variety of popular products and is considered for inclusion in many others.

In certain products, *robustness* may not appear to matter much. For example, if voice assistant Alexa gets a few commands wrong, the consequences would probably not be that severe. In other products, however, no leniency can be tolerated whatsoever where robustness is concerned because it could have dramatic consequences, such as in self-driving cars, medical robots, and so on. There, errors are unacceptable since they can cost human lives or result in serious damage. While robustness is quite desirable from a business point of view in both situations, it is absolutely necessary in the second. Furthermore, it is important to note that in addition to physical danger, machine learning systems can do a lot of damage to the social texture of society. The Respondus exam-proctering machine learning-based software, for example, made mistakes identifying students of color, unduly shutting them out of exams. Such mistakes are obviously unacceptable.

Lack of robustness in machine learning often comes from the bias inherent to learning algorithms. This bias can be caused by three different factors: the data the algorithm is trained on, the algorithm, and the algorithm's parameters. Another source of problems comes from bugs that can appear in both the platform on which the algorithm is implemented and the implementation itself. All these factors are discussed in this chapter.

While robustness is typically thought of as an engineering problem, issues such as those that came up with the Respondus system touch upon the more philosophical or legalistic side of things as they question whether the system makes *fair* decisions. We think of these issues as belonging to the realm of *responsible* machine learning. Systems that systematically discriminate against certain populations are unacceptable. Addressing such issues by increasing robustness is one way of going about it, but another, complementary, way is to require *explainability* from the system. It is important to note that both fairness and explainability are very hard to achieve. When fairness cannot be guaranteed, explainability becomes of paramount importance as it can indicate whether or not the algorithm made decisions based on fair principles. Explainability is particularly difficult in certain domains such as computer vision and text processing, where the best contenders for a problem are deep neural networks notorious for their opacity. Yet, more often than not, it would be very disturbing, and even unethical, to let a machine make a decision without disclosing to a human being why that decision was made. In addition to the Respondus system's case mentioned above, there is a plethora of situations where explanations are required. For example, a physician would like to understand why an automated system diagnosed a patient in one way or another, to make sure that the decision was made on valid rather than spurious grounds. Similarly, in a credit rating system, it would be completely wrong to let the system determine who is eligible for credit and who isn't. If, for example, the system made decisions based on race, gender, or other such criteria, a human should know about it and mitigate the decision of the system.

There is another problem that falls in the realm of societal issues, that of *privacy*. The data on which the learning system is trained must be anonymized and, very importantly, it should be impossible to reconstruct it from the model alone. That is a very serious problem that must be taken seriously in order to protect the population.

The societal issues just mentioned will be touched upon briefly in this chapter, but Chapter 11 will dive deeply into the questions of responsible machine learning and treat them and others in much greater depth. It is also importat to note that there are more general questions regarding the effect that machine learning-based approaches have on society. This topic, however, is much broader than the scope of this book as it is rooted in ethical, sociological, and psychological questions. Despite their extreme importance and our belief that they must be addressed, they will not be discussed in this book since they are far beyond our sphere of expertise.

To summarize, the purpose of this chapter along with the next one is to explore the issues that are likely to come up when learning models are embedded into practical systems geared toward deployment and distribution. Such issues go beyond the questions considered in the previous chapters and are becoming more and more relevant given the recent success of machine learning approaches and their current popularity. Because the questions considered in this chapter touch upon the area of software engineering that relates to the deployment of computer systems, the chapter starts by reviewing the discipline of software engineering for traditional computer systems and then moves on to the issues that come up in machine learning-based systems.

In more detail, the chapter is organized into nine sections. Section 10.1 begins by reviewing the testing standards previously established by the software engineering community. These standards pertain to deterministic software and, while they seek to discover "doors left open" due to the complexity of the software under scrutiny, they do not consider the non-deterministic cases that occur in machine learning-based solutions. Section 10.2 explains how the uncertainty brought about by machine learning-based solutions affects the testing standards discussed in Section 10.1. Sections 10.3 and 10.4 discuss how these issues can be exacerbated by, on the one hand, imperfections in the datasets being used such as noise, missing data, insufficient labeling, class imbalances, and outliers, and, on the other hand, imperfections and uncertainty in the learning systems used, such as algorithmic bias, extreme degrees of randomness (such as in the many layers of deep learning systems), and lack of transparency in systems, such as deep neural networks, that do not provide explainability features. Section 10.5 discusses additional issues that relate to the platform on which the algorithms are implemented and the implementation itself. While all the issues discussed in Sections 10.3, 10.4, and 10.5 relate to offline issues, it is important to keep in mind that once a system is deployed, new issues that may not have been considered during the offline testing process are likely to arise. Questions about such issues are considered in Section 10.6, which looks into the question of online testing. Section 10.7 goes on to discuss issues related to bias, privacy, and general ethics regarding the use of machine learning-based systems in everyday life. As previously mentioned, this discussion will be expanded upon in Chapter 11. Section 10.8 addresses the current state of the art in moving from laboratory-style machine learning progress to industry-strength software industry settings, and Section 10.9 concludes the chapter with a discussion of what needs to be done to move machine learning safely from an experimental science to a solid industry-strength technology and avoid potential pitfalls.

The chapter is based on the discussion in Zhang et al. (2022). It should be read along with its companion, Chapter 11, which proposes solutions to many of the issues discussed here. In particular, Chapter 11 presents methods for detecting and mitigating bias, improving algorithmic fairness, providing explainability, enhancing privacy and security, and improving robustness through repeatability, reproducibility, and replicability.

10.1 Toward Deployment: Testing Standards in Software Engineering

Starting around the 1980s and 1990s, the art or science of software development turned into a more disciplined engineering practice. In other words, experimental software development became mature enough to spread from universities and research labs to engineering labs, and eventually onto the market. The discipline of software engineering emerged and can be thought of as the systematic application of engineering approaches to the development of software with a view toward the production and deployment of reliable software systems.

Software engineering encompasses different subdisciplines, including *software requirements, software design, software development, software testing,* and *software maintenance.*[1] Software requirements refers to the start of the process where the software engineering team interacts with the client to build a deep understanding of the functionality the software system is required to achieve. Software design refers to the creation of the conceptual architecture of the system, including the description of each component's function and its interaction with the other components. Interface questions are also addressed there. The system is implemented during the software development phase during which basic testing and optimization also take place. Software testing corresponds to the verification that the software system functions as expected. Software testing aims at avoiding bugs and improving performance. It is a thorough and important effort aimed at ensuring that the product is ready for deployment. Finally, software maintenance attempts to anticipate the changes that will be necessary to apply to the system over time and designs realistic solutions to deal with them.

---

[1] See www.computer.org/education/bodies-of-knowledge/software-engineering/v3.

Up to this point in the book, prior to this chapter, all the evaluation questions we considered pertained to what can be thought of as, in software engineering terms, the basic internal assessment of the system and its components during the software design process. Due to the complex nature of a learning system, this kind of assessment is more sophisticated than that needed in other contexts, which is why such a book or other guides to the evaluation of learning systems are needed. However, despite the depth with which the internal validation is carried out during the software development phase, we have not yet touched upon the kinds of issues likely to come up during the software testing phase; that is, the kind of quality assurance necessary to confidently deploy machine learning-based software in real, and not only experimental, situations.

The remainder of this section describes the subfield of software testing. In Section 10.2 we will discuss why the testing standards defined in software engineering and reviewed in this section are difficult to achieve and how they can be adapted to machine learning-based software.

Software testing is the discipline of software engineering that attempts to establish the quality of the software under scrutiny. It tests the following five functionalities: agreement with the system's requirements and expectations from the stakeholders; robustness to a wide variety of inputs; efficiency; user-friendliness; ease of installation and use in a variety of environments. In order to constrain a process that is potentially infinite (in an ideal world, the software system would be tested under all possible conditions), software testing focuses on discovering software bugs; that is, errors, defects, and failures. This falls in the category of functional requirements. However, other nonfunctional requirements such as efficiency, security, usability, and accessibility are also aspects of the system that need to be tested.

With regard to functional requirements, software testing looks for bugs at many different levels including the unit level, the integration level (whether there are issues at the interface level of different units), and the system level. Two main modes of testing are typically used, along with a combination of the two: *white-box testing*, *black-box testing*, and *gray-box testing*. White-box testing is typically used at the unit level. It consists of studying the internal structure of the program and carefully designing input conditions meant to test the areas of vulnerability detected in the code analysis. Black-box testing, by contrast, does not use any knowledge of the code but, instead, focuses on the functionality of the piece of software. It can be applied at the unit, integration, or system level. Gray-box testing mixes the two modes of testing, focusing on functionality but using knowledge of the design to better target the vulnerabilities.

While software testing of deterministic software systems is a complex task that can easily turn into a combinatorial problem impossible to solve, testing machine learning systems that are nondeterministic is even more challenging. Section 10.2 discusses this added level of complexity.

10.2 Adapting Testing Standards to Machine Learning-Based Software

Machine learning software is nondeterministic for a variety of reasons. First and foremost, machine learning systems are subject to the dataset they are trained on, and to the

(a)   (b)

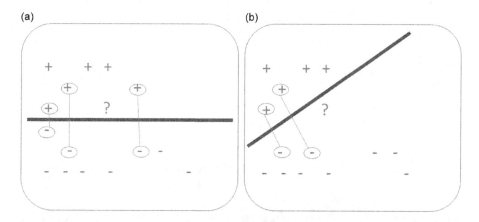

Figure 10.1 (a) The testing point symbolized by a question mark is classified as positive, whereas it is classified as negative in (b) by a simple maximum margin SVM classifier where the support vectors are the circled points.

algorithmic bias of the system. With regard to dataset variability, the same algorithm, say, a linear classifier that maximizes the margin, would learn different discriminators on different datasets, and thus may classify future data in different ways depending on which dataset it was trained on. This can be easily seen in Figure 10.1, where the same query made on the maximum-margin linear classifier in part (a) will return a different output than that output by the discriminator in part (b), where the difference between the training sets in (a) and (b) consists of a positive instance present in (a) and absent in (b) and a negative instance moved slightly downward.

Furthermore, in Figure 10.1, we focus on maximum-margin linear classifiers as the bias of the classifier. However, even staying in the realm of linear classifiers, removing the maximum margin bias would give rise to an infinite number of classifiers with various biases, as in Figure 10.2, each with potentially different outcomes on future data. Since the number of parameters in a linear discriminator applied to a two-dimensional domain is three, this limits the size of the hypothesis space (in its infinity!) Conversely, in nonlinear approaches, the number of parameters involved and/or the reliance of the learner on the data, may be such that the variance of the discriminators is very high. For example, k-nearest neighbors has only one parameter, but it learns local approximations, thus relying strongly on the make-up of the data. Deep neural networks, on the other hand, learn global approximations, but do so with such large numbers of parameters that, in effect, they learn local approximations that depend, to a certain extent, on the random values with which the network was initialized and on the make-up of the data. In summary, no matter what kind of learning algorithm is used, there will be nondeterministic behavior in the resulting software, and this variability will increase as the learner moves from a parametric to a nonparametric format and/or an increase in the number of parameters is involved.

In Zhang et al. (2022), the authors review the question typically asked in software testing exercises in view of the issues just raised. In particular, they focus on three essential questions:

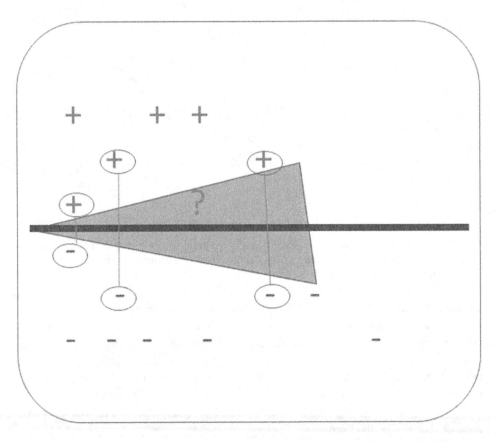

Figure 10.2 After removing the maximum margin constraint, a linear discriminator will be constrained to pass by the tip of the gray slice shown on the figure but can also pass by any other point in that slice. This means that any future points located in this slice or its natural expansion could be classified as positive or negative once a discriminator is chosen.

- **Conditions** What are the conditions that need to be tested in machine learning-based systems?
- **Components** What are the essential components of a machine learning-based system that need to be checked for bugs and vulnerabilities?
- **Methods** What testing methods are most appropriate for machine learning-based systems?

With regard to *conditions*, they identify two categories of requirements: *functional* and *nonfunctional*. The functional requirements include two properties: correctness and model relevance. Correctness refers to the probability of the system outputting the expected result, while model relevance refers to the system's fit to the problem – the model should neither underfit nor overfit the data. The nonfunctional requirements pertain to other conditions such as efficiency, robustness, fairness, security, privacy, and interpretability. Software testing should therefore attempt to establish not only the correctness and model relevance of the system, but also how it adheres to the users' expectations vis-à-vis the nonfunctional requirements.

With regard to the *components* that need to be tested, the authors identify three of them: the *data*, the *learning algorithm*, and the *framework or platform* used for the algorithm. Sections 10.3–10.5 will discuss safety and imperfection issues in each of these components in detail. The kind of issues that will be touched upon are noise or imbalances in the data, dependency upon the tuning of the algorithm or bugs in the code, and bugs or inefficiencies that may occur on various types of platforms, such as scikit, Keras, and so on.

Finally, with regard to the testing method, the authors identify a testing workflow for machine learning-based software organized around two testing phases: *offline testing* and *online testing*. The types of evaluation methods discussed in the book so far are the kind that take place during the offline testing part of the testing process, which also includes more formal software requirement assessments. Online testing has not been considered. Online testing consists of detecting issues once the system is deployed. Online testing can be conducted in different ways, including runtime monitoring, user responses monitoring, and A/B testing. All these methods will be discussed in Section 10.6.

10.3 Safety and Data Imperfection Issues

Many issues that arise in machine learning systems may be related to the data on which the system was trained and tested. This is particularly problematic since while the implementation of a software system can be provided to the team testing the system, it is unusual for the training data on which the system was trained to be available. In particular, providing this data can be impossible since it may be protected by privacy laws (e.g., HIPAA) or NDAs.[2] Even if the data could be and were to be provided, analyzing it is a difficult task in and of itself and is quite different from the tasks typically carried out by software engineers.

Because the data is so central to a machine learning-based software system, taking its properties and potential defects into consideration are necessary during both the offline and the online phases. During the offline phase, four issues come to mind:

1. Does the dataset contain enough samples for the problem at hand to be learned?
2. Is the data correctly represented?
3. Is the data free of noise?
4. Is there overlap in the populations being modeled against one another?

These concerns are just the beginning though! In addition, Mehrabi et al. (2021) surveys the different biases that can creep into the data. They identify a comprehensive list of 23 different biases that can occur in the data due to social or other considerations such as history (e.g., there are many more male CEOs than female ones), representation (a database may contain more instances of facial recognition features from westerners than from people of other backgrounds), omitted variable bias (an important feature may be left out of the feature set). In a Brookings Institute report, Lee et al. (2019) illustrate historical bias with

---

[2] HIPAA stands for the Health Insurance Portability and Accountability Act of 1996; NDA stands for non-disclosure agreement.

practical examples of formerly deployed approaches such as the COMPAS algorithm, or the Amazon recruitment algorithm. In the COMPAS system, since African American men were more likely to be arrested in the past (due to endemic racism), this kind of racism is carried by the data, and an algorithm trained on it would inadvertently continue to carry a tradition that it wishes to eradicate. The same type of issue was seen in the Amazon recruitment algorithm, where female candidates were downgraded due to similar historical prejudice. With regard to representation bias, it is important to realize that many databases underrepresent or overrepresent certain populations. For example, in Buolamwini and Gebru's (2018) facial analysis experiments, since the database contained too few images of dark-skinned individuals relative to the number of white people, the dark-skinned individuals were wrongly classified. For example, dark-skinned women were classified as men. Conversely, in a database with too many representatives of one category (e.g., mugshots of dark-skinned men), that population was more likely to be singled out (Sydell 2016). This, by the way, is not a new problem. Rather, it is one that has been recognized for over 25 years as the *class imbalance problem*. Despite having been known for many years, unfortunately the problem remains extremely challenging today, although a large number of analyses and solutions have been proposed throughout the years (Japkowicz and Stephen 2002; He and Frey 2008; Branco et al. 2016; Johnson and Khoshgoftaar 2019; Ghosh et al. 2022). More recently, the problem has been cast as the long-tailed distribution problem and differs from the class imbalance problem in that it considers multi-class settings where a small number of classes are very well represented, while many have very little representation (Zhang et al. 2023).

While having access to a list of biases that may come up in the data, such as those discussed above, is useful as it can help track down and correct problems, we need a more technical approach for actually pinpointing and resolving problems of representativeness. Roh et al. (2021) do a nice job of surveying the methods that have been used in both the fields of data management that stems from business (data science, data analytics) and machine learning that stems from computer science and statistics, to collect data as thoroughly as possible. Their survey is divided into three areas: data acquisition (e.g., discovery, augmentation, generation), data labeling, and improving existing data. It describes techniques that have been used to deal with the difficulty of collecting data. These include:

- Methods for data sharing and data searching developed by business communities including collaborative initiatives such as DataHub, FusionTables or Kaggle for sharing; and data lakes, Google Data Search (Goods) for searching.
- Methods for data augmentation, where data management techniques used methods such as entity augmentation or data integration to find values for missing items in the data, and where machine learning used latent semantic analysis such as Word2Vec, GloVe or linear discriminant analysis (LDA) to add outside knowledge to the existing data.
- Methods for data generation, which includes crowdsourcing in the data management literature, such as using Amazon Mechanical Turk; and synthetic data generation using methods such as generative adversarial networks and other domain-specific generation methods such as those used in vision problems that include transformations such as rotations, shading, and other such filters.

- Methods for data labeling including, once again, crowdsourcing such as with Mechanical Turk on the data management side; or semi-supervised learning, active learning, and weak supervision (automatically generated labels) in machine learning.
- Methods for data cleaning, using approaches external to the learning model (e.g., cleaning up noisy features, and noisy class labels).
- Methods for making algorithms more robust to defects in the data, including the use of noisy and adversarial examples, as well as transfer learning approaches to deal with tasks with too few instances.

We now turn to the question of safety as it relates to algorithmic imperfections.

10.4 Safety and Algorithmic Imperfection Issues

On top of data-related issues when training learning algorithms, there also are issues related to the algorithms themselves. To begin with, it is important to understand that for any learning to take place, a learning bias needs to be present. If not, the algorithms would only memorize the data and not be able to generalize to new cases (Mitchell 1997). As such, therefore, bias is necessary. However, not every type of bias is acceptable for generalization, and certain kinds lead to unfairness in the decision. This can happen, for example, if the classification relies on features considered sensitive such as gender, age, and race. These, we refer to as *known and controllable biases* and discuss them in Section 10.4.1 as well as in Chapter 11. Another issue has to do with the *unknown and uncontrollable aspects* of the algorithms themselves, and the way in which they process data. This is particularly important in the areas of ensemble learning or deep learning where the decisions made by the algorithms are not understandable. We discuss this issue in Section 10.4.2.

10.4.1 Known and Controllable Bias

Google's English dictionary by Oxford Languages defines the noun "bias" as "prejudice in favor of or against one thing, person, or group compared with another, usually in a way considered to be unfair." Known and controllable biases refer to the biases that a fair and just society attempts to eradicate. Unfortunately, since the databases used in machine learning often contain historical prejudices, often the algorithms trained on them will too. In particular, the data features or descriptors pertaining to those biases will often be chosen by learning algorithms to summarize the data and generalize from it. Such choices, thus, perpetuate the history that led to the database. One approach to counter such bias is to forcibly prevent algorithms from using the features by simply eliminating the information from the data presented to the learning algorithm. In addition to eliminating the obvious information, it is important to think of specific group memberships related to the applications that could help make unfair decisions. For example, as shown in Crothers (2020), a native Russian speaker writing social media posts in English about politics may automatically be flagged as being involved in an online influence campaign. This relates to the discussion in Lee et al. (2019) about *online proxies* for the sensitive attributes. Lee et al. (2019) explains how certain nonsensitive attributes act like proxies for sensitive attributes. This includes zip codes, which can indicate African American and/or nonaffluent neighborhoods, or height and weight, which can account for gender (Barocas and Selbst 2016). On the other hand, Corbett-Davies and Goel (2018) discuss how eliminating sensitive attributes from databases can actually bias the algorithms. They show, for example, that though females are less likely to re-offend than men, and, thus, should be released more often than male offenders, an algorithm that blocks gender would cause females to be released less often than they should be.

This shows that it is important to evaluate the fairness of our machine learning algorithms. To do so, some researchers have already started considering the question. For example, Makhlouf et al. (2021) present different interpretations and measures of fairness based on the traditional kinds of classification metrics. In particular, they define statistical parity where accuracy is the same for each group. This, and many other metrics that implement similar goals, will be discussed in Chapter 11.

10.4.2 *Unknown and Uncontrollable Bias*

Unknown and uncontrollable biases are issues that researchers have been aware of for many years, but are now becoming quite prominent with the advent of deep learning and its use in practical settings. As a result, a strong, concerted effort is being made to consider and handle the problem. The problem we are dealing with here is even more difficult to tackle than the one considered in Section 10.4.1. It relates to the discussion in Section 10.2 that observes that an infinity of functions can be learned from a dataset and that the function that is eventually chosen by the algorithm has been learned because of the algorithmic bias that controls the algorithm. This bias is generally unknown except in some specific cases.

The linear setting is one of the cases where the bias can actually be very well defined. In Fisher's linear discriminant or LDA, naive Bayes or in linear SVMs, for example, the problem is constrained in a way that makes it possible for a user to know ahead of time what the properties of the solution hold. The bias is clearly defined. So amongst the infinity of solutions that could be computed, there is justification for which one is chosen by such methods. Unfortunately, while linear solutions work well on a variety of problems, they are often insufficient for the kind of domains the industry is interested in tackling at this point. For those problems, nonlinear solutions must be used.

There are some nonlinear solutions such as decision trees or rule-based learning whose biases are clear and which, in addition, offer explanations as to why instances are handled the way they are. This allows humans to understand the decisions made by the machine. These classifiers are often quite accurate but do not reach the performance often seen by ensemble methods or deep neural networks, at least on certain kinds of domains such as computer vision and natural language processing. In ensemble methods, the bias is not entirely known because what makes these methods strong is the randomness with which they operate. In deep learning, the random conditions are exacerbated by the huge number of parameters involved. As a result, the bias used by such learning algorithms becomes less clearly defined. Furthermore, the bias is driven by the optimization approach, the system parameters, and/or the random initial conditions, and, in the case of neural networks, the architecture of the network. This complicates the description of the bias and, in practice, means that it is unclear what the algorithm is doing, and why it converged toward a particular solution over another. In practical terms, this means that the models induced by these algorithms are unpredictable. This, obviously, causes serious concerns in the context of machine learning-based software deployment.

We review three approaches that have been proposed to deal with unknown and uncontrollable bias. The first approach seeks to extract *explanations* for why the algorithm made the decision it made on the data it was fed. Another approach is to try to control the algorithm and direct it to behave in a specific way. This is attempted with the introduction of *regularizers* that have a semantically well-defined behavior. The third approach is specifically concerned with deep learning systems. It follows from the observation that deep neural networks learn functions that tend to overfit the data. Instead of decaying gracefully, the compounds of these functions decay abruptly, creating cracks between the different compounds. This causes some data points, *adversarial examples*, to "fall through the cracks" and to be handled or classified incorrectly in very surprising ways. Identifying and avoiding these cracks is another approach that has been proposed to control algorithmic bias. The three approaches are now discussed in more detail.

Explainability The first approach used to tackle unknown and uncontrollable biases has to do with understanding what decisions the algorithms make. It takes the view that interpretability and explainability are an integral part of evaluation. Indeed, while all the discussions, so far, have concentrated on quantitative aspects of evaluation, explainability seeks to verify the correctness of the approach qualitatively. Both aspects are important since an accurate model that is not reasonable is not desirable as it is bound to fail at some point down the line. Conversely, a model that seems to learn correctly but makes many mistakes is not that useful when it comes to deployment. Please see Hansen and Rieger (2019) for details about interpretability and explainability. Neural networks in general, and deep networks in particular, are controlled by large numbers of parameters – the networks' weights – which are trained through optimization methods to learn a function. They do so often better than other learning algorithms, especially in the areas of computer vision and natural language processing. Unfortunately, while other learning processes can give glimpses at what information an induced model uses to make decisions, thus, giving the user some ideas of whether the model used spurious or genuine information, neural networks rely on so many weights distributed amongst so many layers that it is, usually, impossible to reconstruct its computations. Work is underway to extract explanations from neural networks automatically using approaches such as local interpretable model-agnostic explanations (LIME) (Ribeiro et al. 2016) or Shapley additive explanations (SHAP) (Lundberg and Lee 2017), but it is not clear that these approaches are sufficiently advanced to extract the kind of information truly needed. Chapter 11 discusses the important question of explainability in more detail.

Regularization Regularization can be broadly understood as a way to improve generalizability. As discussed in (Kukačka et al. 2017), machine learning researchers and practitioners employ many different types of regularization to achieve better generaliz-ability; that is, higher performance on test data. This takes the form of regularization at the data level, network architecture level, error function level, loss function level, as well as in the optimization procedure. While regularization often involves an intuitive idea of how it can help improve performance, the way in which this intuition transforms into an objective bias is unclear. In addition, since regularization can come from many different places such as subtle data manipulation or the details of an optimization procedure, it is difficult to formulate what the bias of the resulting model is in terms of all the regularization applied to it at many different levels. Once again, the fact that machine learning algorithms can be so subtly influenced causes an issue when it comes to describing the practical bias of an approach. While, as previously discussed, this may not be an issue in certain domains, when deployed in a broad fashion, these kinds of unknowns can yield dangerous situations and societal problems.

Adversarial examples Adversarial examples are input instances that destabilize learning algorithms. Understanding where the fault lines of particular models are located by identi-fying adversarial examples or finding ways to avoid creating models with such fault lines are the two approaches considered by the community within this adversarial category of approaches. As already mentioned, deep learning networks are extremely effective learners that revolutionized machine learning. Indeed, the advent of deep learning gave rise to models capable of classifying images or interpreting text to such a level of accuracy that they became seemingly reliable enough to be considered by industry. Soon after, however, came the observation that deep networks learn discontinuous mappings (Szegedy et al. 2014) that make them susceptible to small disturbances not perceptible by the human eye. While such issues may not be that severe if all images were real and not manipulated, first, it is an Achilles heel that can be exploited by attackers who could, for example, make a self-driving car crash by altering its perception of street signs. For example, an image that clearly depicts a stop sign can be classified as a cow by a deep learning system (while other stop signs and cows were classified properly). Second, it has been shown that real objects can also be altered, rather than just the digital images, to create an adversarial example. In particular, it was shown in Eykholt et al. (2018) that stickers on real objects such as stop signs can make a model designate these objects as something other than what they really are, for example, a speed limit sign. Until a solution is found to deal with this issue, the deployment of machine learning technology in highly sensitive domains such as self-driving cars, medicine, etc., is questionable.

10.5 Safety and Platform and Implementation Imperfection Issues

In addition to the data and algorithmic imperfections discussed in Sections 10.3 and 10.4, two other sources of problems can surface: platform imperfections and implementation errors.

10.5.1 Platform Imperfections

Although not an issue that machine learning researchers and practitioners often think about, platform imperfection is important to consider. In this day and age, the learning algorithms commonly used are so complex that researchers and practitioners do not implement them from scratch anymore, as they did as recently as 20 or so years ago. Instead, they choose an open source platform such as scikit-learn, TensorFlow, Keras, Theano, or Caffe, or a proprietary platform such as Matlab, RapidMiner, IBM Watson Machine Learning, Google Cloud AI Platform, or Azure Machine Learning Studio, and develop their algorithms using the building blocks provided by these platforms. Platforms are typically chosen based on colleagues' recommendations, cost, and personal preferences for particular programming languages or features. Zhang et al. (2022) report that several studies (Xiao et al. 2018; Guo et al. 2018; Sun et al. 2017) have identified vulnerabilities in various frameworks that caused them to crash under certain conditions as well as certain differences in training behavior (though with similarities in the resulting testing accuracies). In addition, many of the frameworks were shown to suffer from low efficiency. Prior to deploying products that use such platforms, it is important to explore any kind of anomaly that could arise from their use.

10.5.2 Implementation Imperfections

While platforms may show different kinds of imperfections, these may not be as detrimental as the many imperfections that creep up in the machine learning algorithms implemented within these frameworks. Roberts (2017) suggests that such problems may be very difficult to trace as they cause subtle, not easily identifiable differences that may, nevertheless, negatively affect the performance of the resulting system. If the programming community were to rely entirely on ChatGPT or other future derivations of such systems to generate code automatically, the problems could even be compounded since it has been found that the code generated by ChatGPT is oftentimes buggy,[3] and that code is probably more difficult to assess and fix since it amounts to correcting someone/something else's code rather than one's own. Typical ways of testing the correctness of programs is through the use of test oracles. Test oracles compare the output of a system on a test case input to the expected result. Oracles, however, are difficult to generate in the machine learning domain due to the probabilistic nature of machine learning algorithms. For that reason, people have suggested the use of metamorphic testing instead (Chen and Kuo 2019). Metamorphic relations are properties that a program is expected to display. In particular, metamorphic relations describe how specific changes in the input change the output of a program. A program that violates such relations is likely to be incorrect. In machine learning, several kinds of metamorphic relations have been proposed such as multiplying all the test inputs or scaling or normalizing test images (Murphy et al. 2007, 2008; Dwarakanath et al. 2018). Such operations are supposed to cause no change to the learning systems' results if the implementation is correct but to cause changes in them if it isn't.

---

[3] See discussion in https://medium.com/geekculture/chatgpt-mistakes-does-it-produces-buggy-code-b32b07730b12.

This concludes our discussion of offline testing issues, which are the first, but insufficient, step toward deployment. The remainder of this section discusses what must come next and how industry-strength testing has been implemented to date.

10.6 Online Testing

While offline testing evaluates machine learning systems on historical data, it is important to realize that such an approach only approximates the behavior of learning systems in real settings and is likely to be overly optimistic. In particular, offline testing focuses on past data and may fail to represent the future. Once offline testing is completed, for companies interested in production another kind of testing is necessary: *online testing*. The purpose of online testing is to identify issues after the system is deployed. It considers issues such as those that can occur at runtime in the real environment, such as missing data or a delay in data production, and through real interactions with users whose behavior may differ from the one expected by the developers (Zhang et al. 2022). There are three major kinds of online testing approaches: *runtime monitoring, monitoring of users' responses,* and *key performance indicator (KPI) tracking.*

Runtime monitoring works by continuously extracting information from the machine learning system at runtime to verify that it fulfills its requirements without violating any runtime properties such as races and deadlocks, among many others.

Monitoring of users' responses is done as a way to find out whether, in certain situations, a new model is preferable to an older one. A popular way to implement this kind of testing is to use *A/B testing*, which is akin to running a randomized experiment. In effect, users get split into two cohorts that each use a different version of the system. The old version can be thought of as the control while the new one corresponds to the treatment. Statistical tests are then used, as in psychology or drug design, to estimate whether the new model improves upon the older one. This approach can also be applied within different application contexts.[4]

KPI tracking consists of defining a number of indicators of interest to the business and tracking these indicators to show that the learning algorithm improves the performance on these key values.

Section 10.8 discusses the current industrial practices associated with the approaches just mentioned, while Section 10.9 discusses how they could be improved in the future.

10.7 Ethics of Machine Learning Deployment

Up to this point, the chapter considered engineering issues and turned to more philosophical questions only insofar as they related to practical concerns. Yet, when evaluating machine learning systems, it is useful to keep a certain number of societal considerations in mind not only because of practical concerns, but also to ensure that the technology we are creating does not damage our society or environment. In addition to how well a learning algorithm

---

[4] More information about A/B testing is available from https://mlinproduction.com/ab-test-ml-models-deployment-series-08/.

performs, one may wonder whether it is necessary or desirable to build such a system. Questions may have to do with whether the resulting product would take away jobs, would not work as well as human beings doing the same job, would hurt human beings using the product (e.g., make them less sociable, less able to perform certain tasks), infringe upon their privacy, and so on. Some of these issues fall beyond the scope of this book and will not be explicitly addressed, but others will be discussed next as well as in Chapter 11.

When considering the broad deployment of machine learning approaches, a lot of care needs to be taken. The interest in machine learning-based products by companies signals an important shift: we are now entering a world, previously only depicted in science fiction works, where machines are asked to make decisions on behalf of and for humans. This is likely to elicit a lot of fear. Some of that fear may not be fully justified since, after all, the machines are programmed to learn from the data in a certain way, and to some extent, we know what they are or are not capable of. Unlike popular beliefs, we can also disable the machine as soon as we are dissatisfied with its performance, though it is clear that in distributed systems that may not be sufficient. Whatever our belief in machine learning's long-term capabilities, a lot of other shorter-term issues remain.

The fear most closely related to the discomfort attached to "machines making decisions on our behalf" is very valid and discussed in Section 10.4.2: while we know that every machine learning system uses a bias to learn, we do not always understand what this bias is, or how it will play out in new instances. Therefore, although the machine is only a collection of electric circuits, it may make decisions that were not foreseen and that a human being might not have made. Therefore, perhaps the popular fear is not fully unjustified after all!

A specific aspect of the fear, which has already been identified, is that of the fairness of the approach. As previously noted, several studies have shown that certain applications worked well on the majority of the population, but fared badly on minorities or misrepresented populations (e.g., bad identification accuracy by machine vision; unfairness in hiring). The algorithms were perceived to "act" in racist or misogynistic ways. Of course, algorithms are neither racist nor misogynistic, but the data they were trained on was not representative of all the segments of the population (as discussed in Section 10.4.1) or the algorithms themselves had biases (as discussed on Section 10.4.2) that ignored the minority populations, as per the class imbalance problem. Eddie Lin's blog[5] discusses another important example of data that is not fully representative of the true situation. In particular, the blog discusses how representative the data collected, cleaned, and stored at the Data@Work Research is, by comparing it to administrative data that is believed to be more reliable, but is more costly and time-consuming to collect. The author of the blog shows the different steps involved in an analysis of representativeness and concludes that in the situation considered in the blog, the Data@Work is only partially representative. The author suggests the addition of more data from the same or a compatible source, if possible, testing for selection bias and duplication, and suggests the use of intelligent stratified resampling techniques. As mentioned before, Mehrabi et al. (2021) presents an excellent survey on bias and fairness.

---

[5] www.dssgfellowship.org/2017/10/06/representativeness_analysis/

In particular, it lists 23 sources of bias in the data and proposes 10 different definitions of fairness organized into three groups: fairness for individuals, for groups, and for subgroups.

Another area of utmost importance when considering the broad deployment of machine learning systems is that of privacy. In Song and Mittal (2021), the authors argue that learning algorithms tend to remember sensitive information that can be intercepted by people trying to breach the system and discover private information. They introduce a privacy risk score that measures the chances of a sample having high privacy risk that could translate into being an open door for attackers seeking to discover private information. Using that score, they perform a thorough analysis of privacy risks in machine learning, which, they conclude, are very much underestimated.

The question of the ethics of machine learning is a vast area that goes well beyond the scope of this book. A good point of departure for this can be found in Bryson (2019), but there are many other discussions as well, including Piano (2020), Müller (2020), and Dubber et al. (2021).

10.8 Current Industry Practice

We now turn to actual current industry practice, surveying the current state of the art in this section, and issuing recommendations in the next.

10.8.1 Deployment Issues

Generally speaking, while there are a number of famous products based on machine learning already available (e.g., Alexa, SIRI, and older voice recognition systems, assisted driving features such as lane departure and speed limit warnings, and others), there seems to be a slow move from lab to deployment.

In his article,[6] Luigi Patruno discusses what deployment means and decries the fact that machine learning and data scientists are not trained to deploy models: they are only trained to generate and test them. Deployment, he suggests, should be conceived of in terms of software engineering. In such terms, when a need is identified, project goals will be defined along with a metric and a code base (available source code from which a software component can be built). A system that meets or even exceeds the desired goals, however, is not a deployed model. That model will be deployed only when the people for whom the model was created have access to the information the model gives them in a format that is convenient to them. In order to deploy a system properly, one needs to understand exactly how the end users will interact with that system. Maurits Kaptein further suggests[7] that while we develop a lot of machine learning models, they are rarely used because they are not deployed properly. This is explained by Eugene Yan[8] who argues that deployment is complicated by the fact that roles are divided among different experts. He suggests that a

---

[6] www.kdnuggets.com/2020/02/deploy-machine-learning-model.html
[7] www.kdnuggets.com/2020/06/stop-training-models-start-deploying.html
[8] www.kdnuggets.com/2020/09/data-scientists-should-be-more-end-to-end.html

data scientist should do all the work from beginning to end, including communication with the client, pipeline building, and so on. In another KDNuggets post,[9] the author explains the AI-driven workflow and states that it includes four stages: data preparation, AI modeling, simulation and testing, and deployment. In the simulation and testing section, the author writes:

To build this level of accuracy and robustness prior to deployment, engineers must ensure that the model will respond the way it is supposed to, no matter the situation.

In particular, the author states that the evaluators should not only worry about the overall accuracy of the model, but also about whether the performance remains as expected in different scenarios and whether the model has considered all edge cases. The author suggests the use of simulation in order to test all possible situations. Though simulation is an important tool to perform evaluation, it is important for practitioners to also keep in mind its limitations. In particular, can we be certain that all edge cases (adversarial examples, outliers) can be found and simulated?

10.8.2 Integration Tests

Another issue that comes up when considering deployment is that the machine learning algorithm needs to be integrated in a pipeline in order to be useful. Prior to deployment, it is therefore important to test the entire pipeline since small changes to a component (say the learning algorithm) can affect the other components and, as a result, the entire outcome. In order to avoid such surprises, it is important to run integration tests in which the entire pipeline is tested when changes are made to the learning algorithm. More detail can be found about this issue in the discussion for machine learning developers found on Google's developer website.[10]

10.8.3 MLOps

In his important KDNuggets post,[11] Henrik Skogstrom introduces the notion of MLOps, the ML equivalent of DevOps, and argues that it is a game changer in the way in which machine learning models are developed. In particular, MLOps recommends that version control, which usually only covers the code, should cover not only the code, but also the data used for training (and more specifically, the code used to collect that data), as well as the parameters used with the algorithm. This kind of documentation will facilitate verification and reproducibility. In particular, the author states that all the procedures used in the machine learning pipeline for collecting the data, testing it, and for model deployment should be included in the code and documented. This way, the model will always follow the same standards no matter how many times it is iterated.

---

[9] www.kdnuggets.com/2020/11/mathworks-ai-four-steps-workflow.html
[10] https://developers.google.com/machine-learning/testing-debugging/pipeline/deploying
[11] www.kdnuggets.com/2020/12/mlops-changing-machine-learning-developed.html

A second recommendation concerns the building of safeguards into the code itself. This is to be done when all processes are automated and documented. This recommendation is meant to address the problem of ad hoc training data and testing procedures. The author suggests that rather than documenting how the training data is collected, cleaned, and tested, for example, on the side in a manual, the procedures should be written into code. This will ensure that the rules followed during development are followed during the production stage as well.

The last point of the post goes back to the importance of the machine learning pipeline already discussed in Section 10.8.2. The model learned by the machine learning system is not sufficient: what really matters is the pipeline. This recognizes that data evolves over time and that machine learning systems need to be retrained to update the model. Without a robust pipeline, that process could be difficult and the resulting model could depart from the previous one. The pipeline, on the other hand, will control the data collection and training of the systems and will ensure a kind of continuity from one model generation to another.

Overall, MLOps attempts to standardize the use of machine learning models and avoid ad hoc decisions that cannot be easily replicated. It is a difficult task, given the volatility of machine learning models, but a highly commendable one if we are to see machine learning used extensively in industry.

10.9 Improving Safe Industrial Deployment of Machine Learning-Based Systems

The approaches for deployment discussed in Section 10.8 suggest that, to date, the industry has not been able to take advantage of the advances made in machine learning because there has not been enough training of machine learning experts in the art of model deployment. MLOps seems to be laying out good standards for model deployment, which, hopefully, will be adopted and followed. However, there could be danger in adopting such standards too quickly as discussed in Section 10.9.1.

10.9.1 Dangers of Fast Deployment

Moving to a culture of fast development could result in the proliferation of machine learning-based products that have not been vetted carefully enough prior to deployment. Indeed, while the posts discussed in Section 10.8 lament the slow pace of deployment, it is not clear that the safety standards that would be used by the industries pushing for a faster pace would be up to the level needed as discussed in this section.

This might not seem necessary in all cases. As previously mentioned several times, the consequences of a badly performing self-driving car or medical system are far worse than those of a natural language understanding system. While this is true, it would be both upsetting and detrimental for the company's public relations if a voice recognition approach worked very badly on a segment of the population presenting a certain type of accent. Therefore, we believe that no matter what the industry is, careful testing both offline and online is extremely important and should not be sacrificed in the name of fast development.

10.9.2 Other Issues

Calibration

While some learning algorithms obtain good accuracy, they may not estimate class probabilities correctly. This could be a problem in practical situations as in the following example: if a model overestimates the risk of patients having a certain condition that requires a particular treatment, then that treatment could be overprescribed (given to patients that don't need it) thus causing unnecessary risks of negative side effects in individuals who didn't need the treatment and burdening the health care systems with unnecessary costs. Calibration was discussed in detail in Section 5.6.2 and is considered in practical clinical settings in Huang et al. (2020).

Looking beyond Software Engineering

Quality assurance and quality control methods Another source of inspiration for robust machine learning evaluation is the area of quality assurance and quality control where, once again, goals are fixed and the product is rigorously tested to see if it fulfills those requirements.[12]

New drug clinical-type of trials for machine learning algorithms Clinical trials[13] are the staple of medical treatment research and are conducted in a very rigorous way. We propose to follow a similar regimen and, in particular, have tests conducted by teams independent from the developer's team to evaluate the robustness of a particular approach and pit it against competing methods. Some survey papers take this approach of comparing different algorithms intended to solve the same problems and issue recommendations to users (e.g., Hulse et al. 2009; Amancio et al. 2014; Rodriguez et al. 2019). Our proposal goes in that direction but formalizes it. It is important to note that such studies are typically looked down upon in the machine learning community, where the creativity involved in designing a new algorithm is what is much admired, even if that algorithm does not always improve the state of the art. This attitude should probably change if a real impact is to be seen by machine learning-based products, and more room should be made for strict algorithm comparisons.

---

[12] https://asq.org/quality-resources/quality-assurance-vs-control
[13] www.roche.com/innovation/process/clinical-trials/about

11

Responsible Machine Learning

Along with the robustness issues discussed in Chapter 10 comes the question of responsibility. Responsible machine learning is an approach to developing and deploying machine learning models that prioritize ethical considerations, fairness, transparency, and accountability. It is a subset of responsible artificial intelligence (AI) (Brundage et al. 2020; Kaur et al. 2022; Li et al. 2023) that focuses specifically on the development and deployment of responsible AI systems. While Chapter 10 raised some of the questions asked in this chapter, it did not provide complete answers to them. The purpose of this current chapter is to review the work that has been done toward answering these questions.

Responsible machine learning involves a number of principles and practices that can be used to guide the development and deployment of machine learning models. Some of these principles are now described.

Data bias detection and mitigation Ensuring that machine learning models are trained on unbiased and representative data, and that potential biases in the data are detected and addressed.

Explainability and interpretability Ensuring that machine learning models are transparent and explainable, and that their decisions and predictions can be understood and evaluated by users.

Model fairness and nondiscrimination Ensuring that machine learning models do not discriminate against individuals or groups based on factors such as race, gender, or religion.

Data privacy and security Respecting the privacy and data protection rights of individuals, and ensuring that personal data is collected, processed, and used in a responsible and ethical manner.

Human-centered design Ensuring that machine learning models are developed with the needs and values of users and society in mind, and that they are developed and deployed in a way that promotes human well-being and dignity.

Reproducible machine learning Ensuring that machine learning models can be replicated and verified by independent parties. It is an essential part of ensuring that AI systems are transparent, and that they can be evaluated and improved over time. Reproducibility is particularly important where machine learning is used to make critical decisions, such as in healthcare, finance, and criminal justice.

Please be aware that while these principles may have some discrepancies and overlaps, we have attempted to present them as distinct entities. Any identification of overlaps will be left to the reader, depending on the specific application they are considering.

Responsible machine learning is crucial because machine learning models are increasingly being used to make important decisions in a wide range of fields, including finance, healthcare, criminal justice, and employment. These models have the potential to transform these fields and improve outcomes for individuals and society as a whole. However, they also pose significant risks and challenges, such as the potential for bias, discrimination, and loss of privacy. By promoting responsible machine learning, we can ensure that these models are developed and used in a way that maximizes their benefits while minimizing their risks and harms. This chapter discusses the above listed principles of responsible machine learning. It is important to highlight that this chapter does not aim to provide an exhaustive review. Instead, its primary focus is on presenting the overarching concepts of the principles listed above, offering readers a solid foundation for practical application.

11.1 Data Bias Detection and Mitigation

Detecting and mitigating data bias in machine learning is important because it improves fairness and decision accuracy, builds user trust, complies with legal and ethical standards, and helps prevent negative consequences for individuals and society. Here are some well-known techniques for data bias detection and mitigation. We also refer readers to Ntoutsi et al. (2020) for a detailed discussion.

11.1.1 Statistical Analysis

Statistical methods provide useful techniques to identify patterns and correlations in the data that may indicate bias. For example, one may use regression analysis to test for the impact of different variables on an outcome. There are several statistical methods that can be used to identify patterns and correlations in the data that may indicate bias such as descriptive statistics, regression analysis, and the use of t-test, ANOVA, and the chi-square test. In particular, descriptive statistics can provide valuable insights into the distribution and characteristics of data, allowing us to identify potential bias or imbalances. Regression analysis can be used to predict the value of one variable based on the value of another variable. It can help to identify relationships between variables and can be used to adjust for confounding variables. The chi-square test can be used to test for independence between two categorical variables. If the test shows a significant association between the two variables, it may indicate bias. A t-test and ANOVA can be used to compare the means of two groups.

Let us present a complete example to demonstrate how different statistical analysis tools can be used to identify data bias in a classification task.

Example

Problem Suppose we have a dataset for a binary classification task where we aim to predict whether a customer will churn[1] ($y = 1$) or not ($y = 0$). The dataset contains several input features x_j for $j = 1, \ldots, p$ and the corresponding target variable y.

Data bias We suspect that the dataset may be biased, meaning that it does not represent the true population distribution fairly. Biased data can lead to inaccurate or unfair predictions, especially for underrepresented groups.

Statistical analysis tools To identify data bias, we can use various statistical analysis tools on the dataset. Here are a few examples:

Class distribution Calculate the proportion of positive ($y = 1$) and negative ($y = 0$) instances in the dataset. If there is a significant imbalance, it may indicate data bias.

Feature distribution Analyze the distribution of input features across different classes. Compare the means, variances, or other summary statistics of each feature for positive and negative instances. Significant differences may suggest bias in feature representation.

Correlation analysis Compute correlations between features and the target variable. Identify any strong correlations or lack thereof. If certain features are strongly correlated with the target variable for one class but not the other, it may indicate bias.

Group comparisons Group the data by relevant demographic attributes, such as gender or race. Compute descriptive statistics within each group and compare them. Significant differences in distributions or summary statistics may indicate bias against certain groups.

Interpreting the results Interpret the results returned by the different statistical analysis tools to assess the presence and extent of data bias. Look for significant disparities, imbalances, or inconsistencies across different metrics and groups.

Addressing data bias If data bias is identified, it is essential to address it to ensure fair and accurate predictions. Possible strategies include:

Collecting more data If possible, collect more data to improve representation and reduce bias in the dataset.

Data augmentation Use techniques such as oversampling or synthetic data generation to balance the dataset and increase representation for underrepresented groups.

Feature engineering Modify or create new features that capture important characteristics for underrepresented groups, thereby reducing bias in feature representation.

Algorithmic modifications Explore fairness-aware algorithms that explicitly incorporate fairness constraints during model training to mitigate bias.

---

[1] The churn rate is the rate at which customers stop doing business with a company over a given period of time.

For a more detailed discussion on various data preprocessing techniques that aim to mitigate discrimination and bias in machine learning classification tasks we recommend Kamiran and Calders (2012).

11.1.2 Blind Testing

Blind testing is a technique used to assess the diversity and inclusiveness of a dataset in machine learning applications. Assessing the diversity and inclusiveness of the dataset, including factors such as race, gender, age, and socioeconomic status, can help researchers identify biases that may be inherent in the data collection process. Blind testing involves evaluating the performance of a trained model on a test dataset where certain attributes or characteristics have been blinded or anonymized. Here, we demonstrate how blind testing can help evaluate and promote diversity and inclusiveness.

Example

Problem Suppose we have a dataset for a classification task where we aim to predict a target variable y based on a set of input features x_j for $j = 1, \ldots, p$. The dataset contains various attributes, including some that might be associated with sensitive information, such as gender, race, or age. To assess the diversity and inclusiveness of the dataset, we can perform blind testing using the following steps:

1. **Identify sensitive attributes** Identify the attributes in the dataset that are associated with sensitive information or protected groups, such as gender or race.
2. **Anonymize or blind the sensitive attributes** Modify or remove the sensitive attributes from the dataset. This can be done by replacing specific values with generic terms or removing the attributes altogether.
3. **Train a model on the blinded dataset** Build a machine learning model using the modified dataset, where the sensitive attributes are anonymized or blinded. Use appropriate evaluation metrics to assess the model's performance on this blinded training dataset.
4. **Perform blind testing** Evaluate the trained model on a separate test dataset, where the sensitive attributes are also anonymized or blinded. Measure the model's performance on this blinded test dataset using the same evaluation metrics.
5. **Compare results** Compare the model's performance on the blinded test dataset with its performance on the original test dataset, where the sensitive attributes are not anonymized or blinded. Significant differences in performance may indicate bias or lack of inclusiveness in the original dataset.

11.1.3 Data Augmentation

Data augmentation is a technique used to increase the size and diversity of a dataset by applying various transformations or modifications to the original data. It can also be used to assess the diversity and inclusiveness of a dataset in machine learning applications. For the same problem setup as we described in Section 11.1.2, we can perform data augmentation using the following steps:

1. **Identify sensitive attributes** Identify the attributes in the dataset that are associated with sensitive information or protected groups, such as gender or race.
2. **Apply data augmentation techniques** Apply data augmentation techniques to create augmented samples from the original dataset. These techniques can include random transformations, noise injection, or perturbations to the sensitive attributes.
3. **Evaluate model performance** Use the trained machine learning model to predict the target variable for both the original samples and the augmented samples. Compare the model's performance and measure any disparities or inconsistencies across different sensitive attributes.
4. **Analyze impact and identify biases** Analyze the impact of the augmented samples on the model's predictions. Identify any biases or disparities in the model's behavior towards different sensitive attributes. Look for cases where the model's predictions differ significantly for augmented samples with different sensitive attribute values.

11.2 Explainable Machine Learning

Explainable machine learning (XML) is a subfield of explainable AI (XAI) and refers to the development and utilization of machine learning models and algorithms that can provide understandable and interpretable explanations for their predictions or decisions.

XML is a rapidly evolving field of AI that seeks to build transparent and interpretable models to improve human understanding of the decision-making process of machine learning algorithms. The goal of XML is to provide human analysts and decision makers with meaningful explanations of how a machine learning system arrives at its conclusions, thereby increasing trust and confidence in the model. This is particularly important in domains where decisions based on machine learning models can have significant real-world consequences, such as healthcare, finance, and autonomous systems.

XML models provide interpretability through a variety of techniques, including model visualization, feature importance ranking, and local explanations, among others. Model visualization allows humans to observe and interpret the decision-making process of a machine learning model by displaying the model's internal structure and the relationships between the input and output data. Feature importance ranking assigns weights to input features based on their contribution to the model's decision-making process, thereby highlighting which features are most critical for a given prediction. Local explanations aim to provide insights into individual model predictions, explaining why the model arrived at a particular decision for a specific input. These approaches enable stakeholders to understand and verify the model's decision-making process, increasing transparency and reducing the potential for unintended bias or discrimination.

It is evident that, currently, the terms interpretability and explainability are often used interchangeably by researchers. Nonetheless, these terms encompass distinct facets related to comprehending machine learning models. Explainability refers to the ability to provide clear and understandable explanations of how a particular process or system works. In the context of machine learning, explainability refers to the ability to understand and interpret the decisions made by machine learning algorithms. It involves providing an explanation of the factors that influence the outcome of a decision, such as which features of the input data are most important, how those features are combined, and why the model arrived at a particular decision. The goal of explainability is to increase transparency and trust in the decision-making process of AI systems.

Interpretability, on the other hand, is the degree to which a human can understand the meaning or significance of a model's input and output. In the context of AI, interpretability is about understanding how a machine learning model processes and transforms the input data to produce its output. It involves understanding the model's internal representations and how they relate to the real-world concepts that the model is trying to learn. The goal of interpretability is to enable humans to understand and interpret the decisions made by AI systems in a way that is consistent with human intuition and knowledge.

In summary, explainability is about explaining the decision-making process of AI systems, while interpretability is about understanding the meaning and significance of the model's input and output. Both are important concepts in the development of transparent and trustworthy AI systems.

11.2.1 A Basic Taxonomy of Explainable Machine Learning

The history of XML (Confalonieri et al. 2021; Linardatos et al. 2020) has been characterized by a progression from interpretable models to complex black-box models, followed by efforts to extract rules, develop visualization techniques, and advance posthoc interpretability methods. The field of XML can be organized according to different criteria that can help researchers, practitioners, and decision-makers better understand and evaluate the different approaches to explainability. Below is a list of criteria for characterizing explainable machine learning:

1. **Model-agnostic vs. model-specific XML** This criterion distinguishes between two broad categories of XML approaches. Model-agnostic XML techniques can be applied to any machine learning model, regardless of its architecture or algorithm. Model-specific XML techniques, on the other hand, are designed to work with specific types of models or algorithms.
2. **Rule-based vs. model-based XML** Rule-based XML techniques use explicit rules or decision trees to generate explanations. These rules can be generated by humans or by automated methods. Model-based XML techniques, on the other hand, use the internal workings of the model itself to generate explanations, such as by highlighting important features or input values.
3. **Posthoc vs. prehoc XML** Posthoc XML techniques generate explanations after the model has made its prediction or decision. These explanations are often generated by analyzing the output of the model, such as the importance of input features or the contribution of different parts of the model to the final decision. Prehoc XML techniques,

on the other hand, generate explanations during the training process, and can be used to ensure that the model is being trained in a transparent and interpretable way.

4. **Local vs. global XML** Local XML techniques generate explanations for individual predictions or decisions, while global XML techniques generate explanations for the entire model. Local XML techniques can be useful for understanding why a particular prediction was made, while global XML techniques can be useful for understanding the overall behavior of the model and its strengths and weaknesses.

5. **Human-centric vs. machine-centric XML** Human-centric XML techniques focus on generating explanations that are understandable and useful for humans, while machine-centric XML techniques focus on generating explanations that are optimized for machine consumption, such as by minimizing the amount of data transmitted or the computational resources required.

6. **Qualitative vs. quantitative XML** Qualitative XML techniques generate explanations in natural language or other forms of human-readable text, while quantitative XML techniques generate explanations in the form of statistical or mathematical measures, such as feature importance scores or decision boundaries.

7. **Interactive vs. static XML** Interactive XML techniques allow users to interact with the model and explore different scenarios or what-if analyses, while static XML techniques generate fixed explanations that cannot be modified or explored further. Interactive XML techniques can be particularly useful for collaborative decision-making and for identifying potential biases or other issues with the model.

These categories are not mutually exclusive, and different XML approaches can be categorized in multiple ways. However, this taxonomy can help provide a structured framework for evaluating and comparing different XML techniques and for identifying their strengths and weaknesses under different machine learning tasks. For a thorough review of explainable AI and machine learning explainability models, we recommend to the reader Linardatos et al. (2020).

11.2.2 Interpretability Methods to Explain Black-Box Models

Interpretability methods for explaining black-box models are techniques used to understand and provide insights into the behavior of complex machine learning models that lack inherent transparency. These methods aim to uncover the internal workings of black-box models and shed light on how they make predictions or decisions. The goal of methods that are used to explain black-box models is to bridge the gap between the complexity of black-box models and the need for human-understandable insights, fostering transparency, trust, and accountability in machine learning systems. We now summarize different methods.

Partial Dependence Plots

Partial dependence plots (PDP), as described in Friedman (2001), provide insights into the relationship between a specific feature and the model's prediction, while controlling for the effects of other features. By averaging the predictions over all possible values of the remaining features, PDP uncovers the average effect of the feature of interest on the prediction. Visualizing the PDP helps in understanding the impact of individual features on the model's decision-making process. Let us break down the idea behind PDP and how to effectively use it in machine learning application tasks.

Background Let X denote the feature space and $x \in X$ represent a specific instance. The prediction function is denoted as $f : X \to Y$, where Y is the set of possible labels.

Partial dependence PDP aims to analyze the relationship between a target feature and the predicted outcome while marginalizing the effects of other features. It provides an estimate of the average effect of a feature on the prediction, considering all possible combinations of the remaining features.

Feature of interest PDP focuses on a specific feature, denoted as x_i, for which the relationship with the prediction is explored.

Marginalization PDP marginalizes the effect of the remaining features, denoted x_{-i}, by averaging the predictions over all possible values of x_{-i}.

PDP computation PDP computes the predictions by fixing the feature of interest at different values while keeping the remaining features constant. The predictions are then averaged to obtain the partial dependence values.

PDP visualization PDP is commonly visualized using line plots, where the feature of interest is plotted on the x-axis, and the corresponding partial dependence values are plotted on the y-axis. Confidence intervals or shaded areas can be added to represent the uncertainty of the estimates.

Local Interpretable Model-Agnostic Explanations (LIME)

LIME (Ribeiro et al. 2016) provides a local and interpretable explanation of a black-box model's predictions by approximating its behavior using a simple and interpretable model. By sampling instances from the neighborhood of interest and training a local model, LIME captures the local relationship between the features and predictions. The explainability weights and measures further highlight the importance of each feature for the black-box model's decision-making process. Below is the description of the mathematical formulation for LIME.

Background Let X denote the input space and $x \in X$ represent a specific instance. The black-box model is denoted as $f : X \to Y$, where Y is the set of possible labels.

Local linearity assumption LIME assumes that the black-box model is locally linear around the instance of interest. A local neighborhood around x is created to approximate the behavior of the model in that region.

Proximity measure LIME uses a similarity measure to define the proximity of instances to the instance of interest. The proximity measure can be based on distance metrics, such as Euclidean distance or cosine similarity.

Local model training LIME generates a local training set by sampling instances from the neighborhood of x according to the proximity measure. The black-box model's predictions are used to obtain the labels for the local training set.

Model-agnostic explanations LIME fits an interpretable model, such as linear regression or decision trees, on the local training set to explain the black-box model's behavior. The interpretable model captures the local relationship between the features and predictions.

Explainability weights LIME assigns importance weights to the local training instances based on their proximity to the instance of interest. The weights reflect the influence of each instance in the interpretable model's fit.

Explainability measure LIME computes the explainability measure, such as feature importance or feature contribution, based on the interpretable model's coefficients or structure. The explainability measure quantifies the impact of each feature on the black-box model's prediction for the instance of interest.

LIME for a natural language processing task In this example we aim to showcase the use of the LIME framework to explain the predictions of a logistic regression classifier in the context of natural language processing (NLP), specifically, for sentiment analysis of movie reviews. For the following example, we use an IMDb dataset containing movie reviews and their associated sentiment labels.[2] A logistic regression classifier is chosen for sentiment analysis. The textual data is converted into numerical features using term frequency-inverse document frequency (TF-IDF) vectorization and the logistic regression model is trained using these features. The accuracy of the model on the training data is evaluated, indicating how well it predicts sentiment labels. LIME offers valuable insights to data scientists and machine learning practitioners, enhancing model transparency and trust. This code underscores the significance of model interpretability, particularly in complex NLP, enabling the understanding of specific predictions in critical real-world applications. In this case, it is essential for understanding why certain movie reviews are classified as positive and how specific words or phrases influence the predictions.

In Figure 11.1, a visual explanation is presented, shedding light on the rationale behind the logistic regression classifier's positive sentiment prediction for a given movie review. This visualization provides valuable insights into the specific words or features within the text that played a pivotal role in driving the positive sentiment classification. Within Figure 11.1, you can observe the prominently highlighted words or features in the review that exerted the most substantial influence on the model's positive sentiment prediction. It is

---

[2] www.kaggle.com/code/lakshmi25npathi/sentiment-analysis-of-imdb-movie-reviews/input

Text with highlighted words

The movie was a true masterpiece, captivating from start to finish with its brilliant storytelling, exceptional performances, and stunning cinematography that left me in awe.

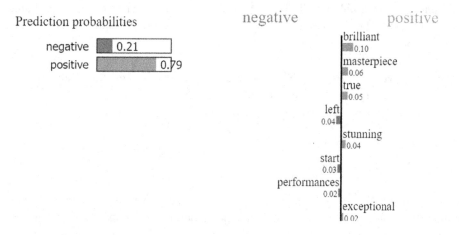

Figure 11.1 LIME's output for a test observation reveals the key terms and their respective influence on the prediction. Note that, for the sake of illustration, we have included the weights for only eight feature words. Nevertheless, it is possible to choose to reveal all of them. The authors artificially simulated this movie review.

important to note that, for the sake of clarity and illustration, we have opted to showcase the weights associated with only eight feature words. However, it is entirely feasible to explore the complete set of these influential features should you wish to do so.

SHapley Additive exPlanations (SHAP)

SHAP (Lundberg and Lee 2017) provides a unified framework for explaining predictions of black-box models by assigning importance values to each feature based on their contributions. The Shapley values capture the average marginal contributions of features across all possible feature combinations, ensuring fairness and consistency in the attribution. The additivity property ensures that the sum of feature importances, along with the baseline value, yields the prediction for a given instance.

Background Let X denote the input space and $x \in X$ represent a specific instance. The black-box model is denoted as $f : X \to Y$, where Y is the set of possible labels.

Feature importance SHAP assigns an importance value to each feature for a given instance. Feature importance, $\phi_i(x)$, represents the contribution of feature i to the prediction for instance x.

Shapley values Shapley values represent the average marginal contribution of a feature across all possible feature combinations. For example, the Shapley value of feature i for instance $\boldsymbol{x}$ is $\phi_i(\boldsymbol{x})$.

Coalitions and marginal contributions A coalition S is a subset of features, excluding feature i. A marginal contribution $\phi_i(\boldsymbol{x}; S)$ measures the additional contribution of feature i when combined with coalition S.

Shapley value computation The Shapley value of feature i is computed as the average marginal contribution over all possible coalitions:

$$\phi_i(\boldsymbol{x}) = \sum_{S \subseteq N \setminus \{i\}} \frac{|S|!\,(|N| - |S| - 1)!}{|N|!} \left[\phi(\boldsymbol{x}; S \cup \{i\}) - \phi(\boldsymbol{x}; S)\right],$$

where N is the set of all features.

Additivity property SHAP exhibits an additivity property, where the sum of feature importances equals the difference between the prediction for an instance and the expected prediction:

$$f(\boldsymbol{x}) = \phi_0 + \sum_{i=1}^{n} \phi_i(\boldsymbol{x}),$$

where ϕ_0 is the baseline value and n is the number of features.

SHAP for an NLP task: In this scenario, we pivot from the LIME framework to explore the use of SHAP to shed light on predictions made by a logistic regression classifier in the context of NLP, specifically concerning sentiment analysis of movie reviews. Previously, we showcased the LIME framework's application to the same task, highlighting its significance for model interpretability. The dataset under examination remains the IMDb dataset, housing movie reviews alongside their corresponding sentiment labels. Our approach for sentiment analysis still relies on a logistic regression classifier. Textual data is still converted into numerical features via TF-IDF vectorization, and the logistic regression model is trained using these features. The training accuracy of the model is assessed to gauge its performance in predicting sentiment labels. SHAP values provide crucial insights into model decision-making. These values quantify the influence of each feature, either positively or negatively. Within the context of sentiment analysis, a large positive SHAP value for a specific word or feature signifies that its presence or prominence strongly contributes to a positive sentiment prediction. Conversely, a large negative SHAP value suggests that the feature impedes the prediction of positive sentiment.

The transition to SHAP from LIME underscores the significance of model interpretability in NLP, allowing us to dissect specific predictions within real-world applications. This interpretability is particularly vital when deciphering why certain movie reviews receive positive classifications and how specific words or phrases affect these predictions. In Figure 11.2, we offer a visual representation of the SHAP-based explanation for the logistic regression

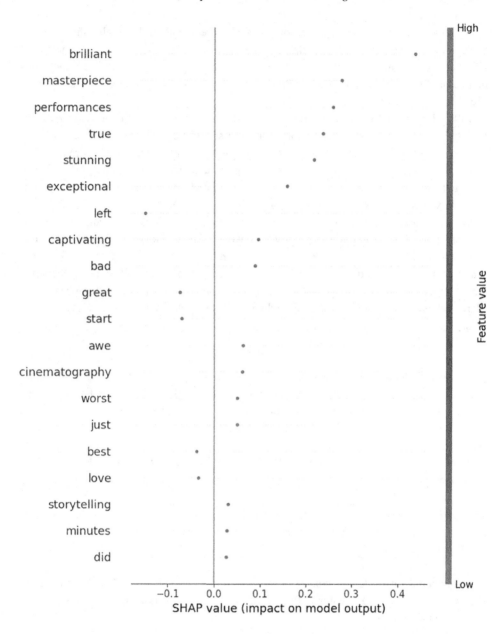

Figure 11.2 SHAP's output for a test observation reveals the pivotal words and their corresponding influence on the prediction. In our analysis, we revisit the same movie review, which reads: "The movie was a true masterpiece, captivating from start to finish with its brilliant storytelling, exceptional performances, and stunning cinematography that left me in awe." The authors artificially simulated this movie review.

classifier's positive sentiment prediction. This visual explanation highlights the words or features within the review that wielded the most influence over the positive sentiment classification. The significance of specific words and their impacts on the prediction becomes clearer in Figure 11.2, making the decision-making process more comprehensible and interpretable as we shift from LIME to SHAP.

Both SHAP and LIME offer similar results when applied to this context. In practice, the choice between these methods hinges on the specific characteristics of the machine learning problem, the complexity of the model, and the interpretability requirements. In some cases, combining both frameworks might provide a more comprehensive understanding of the model's behavior. LIME is a suitable option when dealing with complex or black-box models, where the need is for straightforward, locally valid explanations for individual predictions. It shines when model-agnostic explanations are paramount and can be a practical choice for computationally expensive models, thanks to its surrogate modeling technique. Conversely, SHAP is a more comprehensive choice, providing insight into feature contributions and interactions at both local and global levels. It excels in scenarios where a theoretically sound and robust explanation framework is required. SHAP is particularly valuable for simpler models and when consistency across various model types is a priority.

Heat Maps

Heat maps (Zeiler and Fergus 2014), provide a visual interpretation of convolutional neural networks (CNNs) by highlighting the important regions in the input image. By computing the importance scores based on the gradients of the output class score with respect to the activation maps, heat maps reveal the regions that strongly influence the CNN's decision-making process. This enables better understanding and interpretation of the CNN's behavior, particularly for object recognition and localization tasks. Below is a brief description for heat maps.

Background Let X denote the input space and $x \in X$ represent a specific image instance. A CNN is denoted as $f_\theta : X \to Y$, where θ represents the model parameters and Y is the set of possible labels.

Convolutional layers CNNs consist of multiple convolutional layers that apply filters to the input image to extract features. Each filter performs convolutional operations over the input, producing feature maps.

Activation maps The output of each convolutional layer is a set of activation maps, also known as feature maps. Activation maps capture the presence of specific features or patterns at different spatial locations in the input image.

Global average pooling Global average pooling (GAP) is a downsampling operation that reduces the spatial dimensions of the activation maps. GAP computes the average value of each feature map, resulting in a vector of aggregated features.

Importance score computation Heat maps aim to visualize the importance of different spatial locations in the input image for the CNN's prediction. The importance score for each spatial location is computed based on the gradients of the output with respect to the activation maps.

Gradient-based approaches Gradient-based approaches, such as Grad-CAM (gradient-weighted class activation mapping (CAM)), compute the gradients of the output class score with respect to the activation maps. The gradients are then weighted by the average pooling values to obtain the importance scores for each spatial location.

Heat map visualization The importance scores are used to generate heat maps, where higher scores correspond to more important regions in the input image. Heat maps can be overlaid on the input image to highlight the regions that contribute most to the CNN's prediction.

Example of heat maps for a computer vision task In our illustrative example, we employ CAM techniques to gain insights into the factors that influenced a CNN when making a specific classification decision. CAM visualization is a valuable tool for unraveling the decision-making process of a CNN, particularly in cases involving classification errors and in the broader domain of model interpretability. It enables us to pinpoint specific objects or regions within an image that played a pivotal role in determining the classification outcome. CAM visualization entails the creation of heatmaps that reveal class activation patterns across input images. These heatmaps are 2D grids of scores linked to a particular output class, computed for each location in the input image. They effectively convey the significance of each location with respect to the class in consideration. For example, in the context of distinguishing between "cat" and "dog" images, CAM visualization generates heatmaps for each class, offering insights into how "cat-like" or "dog-like" different parts of the image are perceived.

In this context, we explore the Grad-CAM technique, which helps identify the critical regions in an image that heavily influence a classifier's decision. Grad-CAM works by utilizing the output feature map of a convolutional layer, assigning weights to each channel based on the gradient of the class's output, resulting in a detailed spatial map that shows how strongly the input image activates the target class. We'll demonstrate this method using the pretrained Xception model, aiming to answer two fundamental questions: "Why did the network classify this image as a 'Pembroke' dog?" and "Where, within the image, are the most influential regions for the 'Pembroke' classification?" We begin with image preprocessing, aligning it with the model's specifications. After passing the image through the pretrained network, we decode its prediction vector to reveal human-readable class labels. In our example, the network identifies the image as potentially depicting a "Pembroke" dog out of three possible classification labels: "Pembroke," "Cardigan," and "Basenji." Figure 11.3 plays a pivotal role, displaying an image featuring two happy dogs, one of which falls under the "Pembroke" class. This image seamlessly integrates into our discussion of the Grad-CAM visualization technique, aiding us in uncovering and understanding the specific image regions that have the greatest impact on the "Pembroke" classification.

Figure 11.3 This image depicts two dogs, one of them belonging to the "Pembroke" class. This image is used in the context of our example to demonstrate the Grad-CAM visualization technique and to identify the specific regions of the image that contribute the most to the classification of "Pembroke." Photo by Alvan Nee. https://unsplash.com/photos/pembroke-welsh-corgi-andbrown-dog-running-between-grasses-73flblFUksY.

To visualize which portions of the image are most relevant to the classification of "Pembroke," we establish the Grad-CAM workflow. This involves the creation of two models: one mapping the input image to the activations of the last convolutional layer, and another mapping these activations to the final class predictions. Subsequently, we compute the gradient of the top predicted class concerning the input image in relation to the activations of the last convolutional layer. To derive the class activation heatmap, we apply pooling and importance weighting to the gradient tensor. For visualization purposes, we normalize the heatmap within the range of 0 to 1. Lastly, we generate an image that overlays the original image onto the heatmap, allowing us to visually pinpoint the regions that substantially contributed to the network's classification decision. Figure 11.4 presents the class activation heatmap for the "Pembroke" class superimposed on the test image. In Figure 11.4(a), we also feature the standalone class activation heatmap. Notably, the facial features of the "Pembroke" dog exhibit strong activation, shedding light on how the network distinguishes between the "Pembroke" class and other classes like "Cardigan" or "Basenji."

An important note It is important to acknowledge that while this method proves highly effective in the current context, it is essential to be aware of its potential limitations, especially when considering its applicability in diverse domains. The effectiveness of the Grad-CAM visualization technique can be influenced by various factors, and its performance may not be universally applicable.

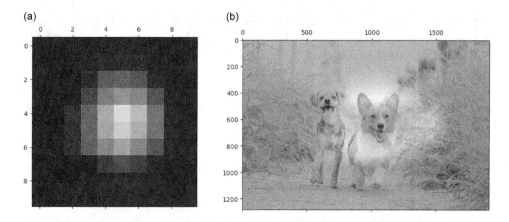

Figure 11.4 (a) Standalone class activation heatmap. (b) Class activation heatmap for the "Pembroke" class superimposed on the test image. (Photo by Alvan Nee. https:// unsplash.com/photos/pembroke-welsh-corgi-andbrown-dog-running-between-grasses-73flblFUksY.)

One notable limitation to consider is the sensitivity to the application domain. The success of Grad-CAM may vary depending on the specific problem being addressed and the nature of the data. Some domains or tasks may require more complex interpretation methods or may involve challenges that make class activation less straightforward. Furthermore, the quality and quantity of data play a significant role in the reliability of this technique. In cases where data is scarce or unrepresentative, the results obtained from Grad-CAM may not be as accurate or informative. Additionally, model architecture and design can impact the effectiveness of Grad-CAM. It may perform differently with different neural network architectures or variations, and some models may not produce as interpretable results.

In summary, while Grad-CAM is a valuable tool for model interpretability, it is important to recognize that its performance can be context-dependent. Careful consideration of its application within the specific domain and data characteristics is essential to make the most of its capabilities and to ensure that the interpretations drawn from it are meaningful and reliable.

11.2.3 Interpretability Methods to Explain Transparent Models

Transparent models are models that are inherently interpretable, meaning that they are designed to be easily understood and analyzed by humans. Some of the interpretability methods used to explain transparent models are now discussed.

Linear Models

Linear models are widely used in machine learning due to their simplicity and interpretability. They offer transparent relationships between input features and the predicted outcome, allowing for better understanding and interpretation of the model's behavior. Let us demonstrate how linear models can lead to interpretable results via a particular example.

Suppose we have a dataset for a regression task, where we aim to predict a target variable Y based on a set of input features X. The goal is to build a linear regression model that provides interpretable insights into the relationship between the features and the target variable.

Interpretable results with linear models To achieve interpretable results with linear models, we can follow these steps:

1. **Feature selection** Select relevant features that are likely to have a direct impact on the target variable. This can be done based on domain knowledge or through feature selection techniques.
2. **Model training** Train a linear regression model using the selected features. The model learns the coefficients (weights) associated with each feature, indicating their contribution to the predicted outcome.
3. **Coefficient interpretation** Interpret the learned coefficients to gain insights into the relationship between the features and the target variable. Positive coefficients indicate a positive influence on the target variable, while negative coefficients indicate a negative influence.
4. **Feature importance** Rank the features based on the magnitude of their coefficients to identify the most important features in predicting the target variable. Higher magnitude coefficients indicate stronger influences on the outcome.
5. **Predictive analysis** Use the trained linear model to make predictions on new data. The simplicity of linear models allows for easy interpretation of how changes in the input features affect the predicted outcome.

Interpreting the results Based on the learned coefficients and feature importance, we can interpret the results to gain insights into the relationship between the features and the target variable. We can identify the most influential features and understand their impact on the predicted outcome. Last, we can analyze the signs and magnitudes of the coefficients to understand the direction and strength of the relationships.

Advantages of interpretability Interpretable results with linear models offer several advantages:

- **Transparency** Linear models provide clear and transparent relationships between features and the target variable, making it easier to understand the model's behavior.
- **Domain insights** Interpretable results allow domain experts to validate and provide insights into the relationship between features and the outcome.
- **Decision-making** The interpretability of linear models enables better decision-making, as the reasoning behind predictions is easily understandable.

By utilizing linear models, we can achieve interpretable results that provide insights into the relationship between input features and the predicted outcome, leading to a better understanding and trust in the machine learning model.

Decision Trees

Decision trees are powerful machine learning models that offer interpretable results (Loh 2011). They provide a clear and intuitive representation of the decision-making processes, making them useful for understanding and explaining the underlying patterns in data. Here, we demonstrate how decision trees can lead to interpretable results. Suppose we have a dataset for a classification task, where we aim to predict a target variable Y based on a set of input features X. The goal is to build a decision tree classifier that provides interpretable insights into the relationship between the features and the predicted outcome.

Interpretable results with decision trees To achieve interpretable results with decision trees, we can follow these steps:

1. **Tree construction** Build a decision tree model using the dataset. The decision tree algorithm recursively partitions the data based on feature values to create a tree structure.
2. **Tree visualization** Visualize the decision tree to understand its structure and decision-making process. Each node represents a decision based on a feature, and each branch represents the outcome of that decision.
3. **Feature Importance** Analyze the decision tree to determine the importance of different features. Features that appear higher in the tree and closer to the root have a higher impact on the predicted outcome.
4. **Interpreting decision rules** Interpret the decision rules of the tree to gain insights into the relationship between the features and the predicted outcome. Each path from the root to a leaf node represents a set of conditions that lead to a specific prediction.
5. **Prediction analysis** Use the trained decision tree to make predictions on new data. By following the decision rules, it is possible to understand why a particular prediction was made.

Example In this example, we explore the concept of decision trees and their role in interpreting classification results. Here, we discuss how decision trees are employed to gain insights into the factors contributing to classification outcomes.

The Iris dataset[3] is a frequently used dataset in the field of machine learning for various classification and data analysis tasks. It is named after the Iris flower species it represents and is often employed for educational and illustrative purposes due to its simplicity and versatility. This dataset contains various features of different iris flower species, making it an ideal candidate for classification exercises. The four different features that we use in our example include sepal length (cm), sepal width (cm), petal length (cm), and petal width (cm). These features correspond to the measurements of the sepal and petal of the iris flowers, and they are used as input features for the classification task. The classification task is to predict the species of iris flowers based on the provided features. The dataset contains samples of three different species of iris flowers: Setosa, Versicolor, and Virginica. The goal of the classification task is to train a model (in this case, a decision tree classifier) to correctly

---

[3] https://scikit-learn.org/stable/auto_examples/datasets/plot_iris_dataset.html

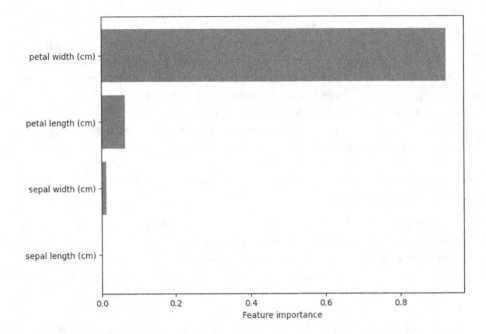

Figure 11.5 Feature importances for the decision tree model: this horizontal bar chart illustrates the relative importance of each feature in the decision-making process of the decision tree classifier. Features with taller bars play a more significant role in classification, offering valuable insights into the model's feature preferences.

classify iris flowers into one of these three species based on their sepal length, sepal width, petal length, and petal width measurements.

We demonstrate the application of a decision tree classifier to the dataset, highlighting how decision trees partition the data into subsets based on the most informative features. Figure 11.5 shows the significance of feature importances in decision tree models. To illustrate this, we provide a visual representation of feature importances using a horizontal bar chart. This plot showcases the relative importance of each feature in making classification decisions. Features with taller bars play a more significant role in classification, offering valuable insights into the model's feature preferences. This interpretation helps users understand which features are most crucial for accurate classification, offering valuable insights into the inner workings of the model.

Bayesian Networks

Bayesian networks are graphical models (Koller and Friedman 2009), that represent probabilistic relationships among variables. They offer interpretable results by providing a clear and intuitive representation of dependencies and causal relationships in data. Here, we demonstrate how Bayesian networks can lead to interpretable results. Suppose we have a dataset with multiple variables, and we want to understand the relationships between these variables and predict a target variable of interest. The goal is to build a Bayesian network that provides interpretable insights into the dependencies and causal relationships among the variables.

Interpretable results with Bayesian networks To achieve interpretable results with Bayesian networks, we can follow these steps:

1. **Variable selection** Select the variables of interest and define their relationships. Consider the causal relationships, dependencies, and conditional probabilities between the variables based on domain knowledge or data analysis.
2. **Network construction** Construct a Bayesian network graph by representing the variables as nodes and the relationships between them as edges. Use directed edges to indicate causal relationships and dependencies.
3. **Probability estimation** Estimate the conditional probabilities associated with each node in the Bayesian network based on the available data. This can be done using statistical methods or domain expertise.
4. **Inference and interpretation** Perform inference on the Bayesian network to make predictions and gain insights into the relationships between variables. Analyze the network structure, conditional probabilities, and the flow of information to interpret the results.

11.3 Restricting Discrimination and Enhancing Fairness in Machine Learning Models

Ensuring fairness and mitigating discrimination are important concerns when building machine learning models. In this section we summarize some popular interpretability methods that can be used to restrict discrimination and enhance fairness in machine learning models. We also refer readers to Ntoutsi et al. (2020) for a detailed discussion.

11.3.1 Fairness Metrics

There are various fairness metrics that can be used to assess and monitor the fairness of machine learning models, such as demographic parity, equalized odds, and equal opportunity. These metrics can be used to identify areas where the model may be biased and to guide model development to improve fairness.

Demographic Parity

Demographic parity (Hardt et al. 2016) is a fairness metric used to assess and promote fairness in machine learning models. It ensures that the predictions made by the model are independent of protected attributes such as gender, race, or age.

Definition Let Y denote the target variable representing the prediction or outcome of interest. Let A denote a protected attribute, such as gender or race, with two possible values: $A = 0$ and $A = 1$. The demographic parity metric compares the probabilities of positive predictions between different values of the protected attribute.

Mathematical formulation Let $P(Y = 1|A = 0)$ denote the probability of a positive prediction given that $A = 0$, and let $P(Y = 1|A = 1)$ denote the probability of a positive prediction given that $A = 1$. Demographic parity is achieved when the probabilities of positive predictions are equal across different values of the protected attribute so that

$$P(Y = 1|A = 0) = P(Y = 1|A = 1).$$

Demographic parity ensures that the model's predictions are not biased based on protected attributes. It promotes fairness by treating individuals from different groups equally, regardless of their protected attributes.

Equalized Odds

Equalized odds (Hardt et al. 2016) ensures that the model's predictions have similar error rates across different values of a protected attribute.

Definition Let Y denote the target variable representing the prediction or outcome of interest. Let A denote a protected attribute, such as gender or race, with two possible values: $A = 0$ and $A = 1$. The equalized odds metric compares the true positive rates (TPR) and false positive rates (FPR) between different values of the protected attribute.

Mathematical formulation Let $TPR(A)$ denote the true positive rate for a given value of the protected attribute A. Let $FPR(A)$ denote the false positive rate for a given value of the protected attribute A. Equalized odds is achieved when the true positive rates and false positive rates are equal across different values of the protected attribute, so that

$$TPR(A = 0) = TPR(A = 1) \quad \text{and} \quad FPR(A = 0) = FPR(A = 1).$$

Equalized odds ensures that the model's predictions are not only unbiased with respect to protected attributes but also have similar error rates across different groups. It promotes fairness by providing equal opportunities for individuals from different groups to have correct predictions while avoiding disproportionate false positives or false negatives.

Equal Opportunity

Equal opportunity (Hardt et al. 2016) ensures that the TPR is equal across different values of a protected attribute, focusing on the prediction performance for positive instances.

Definition Let Y denote the target variable representing the prediction or outcome of interest. Let A denote a protected attribute, such as gender or race, with two possible values: $A = 0$ and $A = 1$. The equal opportunity metric compares the TPR between different values of the protected attribute.

Mathematical formulation Let $TPR(A)$ denote the true positive rate for a given value of the protected attribute A. Equal opportunity is achieved when the true positive rates are equal across different values of the protected attribute, so that

$$TPR(A = 0) = TPR(A = 1).$$

Equal opportunity ensures that the model's predictions are not only unbiased with respect to protected attributes but also provide equal chances for positive instances to be correctly predicted across different groups. It promotes fairness by giving all individuals equal opportunities to benefit from accurate predictions, regardless of their protected attributes.

11.3.2 Fairness Constraints

By incorporating fairness constraints into the model development process, developers can ensure that the model is designed to be fair and unbiased. For example, constraints can be added to ensure that the model treats different groups equally or to limit the impact of sensitive input features on the model's predictions. In the following example, we demonstrate how fairness constraints can be incorporated into a machine learning model to promote fairness and mitigate discrimination.

Problem Suppose we have a binary classification task where we want to predict whether an individual will be approved for a loan ($Y = 1$) or not ($Y = 0$). Our model takes a set of input features X and outputs a prediction $\hat{Y}$.

Fairness constraint We want to ensure that the model's predictions are not biased based on a protected attribute, such as gender. In particular, we aim to achieve demographic parity, which requires that the approval rates for different genders are equal.

Incorporating fairness constraints To incorporate fairness constraints, we modify the standard machine learning objective function to include a fairness penalty term. The objective function becomes

$$\min_{\theta} \mathcal{L}(Y, \hat{Y}) + \lambda \cdot \text{Fairness}(\hat{Y}, A),$$

where θ represents the model parameters, $\mathcal{L}$ is the standard loss function, λ controls the trade-off between accuracy and fairness, $\hat{Y}$ is the predicted outcome, and A is the protected attribute (e.g., gender).

Fairness metric In our case, we define the fairness metric as the absolute difference in approval rates between different genders,

$$\text{Fairness}(\hat{Y}, A) = \left| \frac{\text{Approval Rate}(\hat{Y}, A = 0)}{\text{Total Instances}(A = 0)} - \frac{\text{Approval Rate}(\hat{Y}, A = 1)}{\text{Total Instances}(A = 1)} \right|.$$

Optimization process We optimize the modified objective function using an appropriate optimization algorithm, such as gradient descent or stochastic gradient descent. During the training process, the model learns to balance accuracy and fairness by adjusting the model parameters.

Evaluation and monitoring After training the model, we evaluate its performance using standard metrics such as accuracy, precision, recall, and $F1$ score. Additionally, we monitor the fairness metric to ensure that the model's predictions align with the desired fairness constraints.

11.4 Data Privacy and Security

Data privacy and security are crucial considerations in machine learning projects and vital in responsible machine learning. By employing privacy-preserving techniques, anonymization and de-identification methods, secure data storage and transfer, protecting model privacy, obtaining user consent, implementing auditing and accountability measures, and ensuring secure infrastructure, machine learning practitioners can safeguard sensitive data, maintain user trust, and comply with privacy regulations. Several reputable sources addressing data privacy and security in machine learning are available, including, but not limited to, the following references: Fredrikson et al. (2015); Shokri and Shmatikov (2015); Abadi et al. (2016); Rigaki and Garcia (2020). Please note that the ensuing discussion emphasizes breadth over depth, as we strive to cover many aspects of privacy and security in machine learning.

11.4.1 Privacy-Preserving Techniques

Privacy-preserving techniques are crucial in machine learning to protect sensitive information while allowing for accurate analysis and model development. In this part we attempt to provide an overview of privacy-preserving techniques commonly used in machine learning.

Differential privacy is a mathematical framework that provides strong privacy guarantees. It ensures that the presence or absence of an individual's data does not significantly affect the output or conclusions of a machine learning algorithm. Differential privacy can be achieved through techniques such as adding noise to the data or query responses.

Secure multi-party computation (MPC) allows multiple parties to jointly compute a function on their private inputs without revealing any individual's private data. MPC protocols enable collaborative machine learning without exposing the raw data. The computation is performed in a distributed manner, ensuring privacy.

Federated learning enables model training on decentralized data while preserving privacy. Instead of sending raw data to a central server, local models are trained on individual devices, and only model updates (gradients) are exchanged. This approach keeps the data on the device, reducing the risk of privacy breaches.

Homomorphic encryption allows computations to be performed on encrypted data without decrypting it. This technique enables secure data processing and analysis while keeping the data encrypted. Homomorphic encryption can be used to perform operations on encrypted data in machine learning models.

Secure aggregation techniques allow for the collection and aggregation of sensitive data from multiple parties while preserving privacy. Aggregation can be performed in a way that individual data points are not revealed, ensuring privacy during the data fusion process.

Data perturbation involves adding noise or introducing modifications to the data to protect individual privacy. Randomization techniques, such as randomized response or data sampling with noise, can be used to perturb the data while preserving certain statistical properties.

Privacy-preserving data publishing methods aim to release useful information while protecting individual privacy. Techniques such as data anonymization, generalization, and k-anonymity ensure that individuals cannot be re-identified from the released data.

11.4.2 Data Anonymization and De-identification

To protect individual privacy, data can be anonymized or de-identified. Anonymization techniques, such as k-anonymity and l-diversity, ensure that individuals cannot be re-identified from the released data. De-identification removes or obfuscates personally identifiable information to protect privacy.

Data anonymization involves transforming data in a way that ensures that individuals cannot be re-identified. Anonymization techniques aim to remove or obfuscate personally identifiable information while preserving the utility of the data for analysis. Common anonymization techniques include:

- **Generalization** Generalizing data by replacing specific values with more general or less precise values. For example, replacing exact ages with age ranges.
- **Suppression** Removing or suppressing sensitive attributes or records from the dataset to prevent identification.
- **Perturbation** Introducing noise or randomization to the data to prevent re-identification. This can involve adding random values or perturbing the original data.
- **Data swapping** Exchanging records or attributes among individuals to break the link between data and individuals.

K-anonymity (Sweeney 2002) is a widely used privacy concept that ensures that each record in a dataset is indistinguishable from at least $K-1$ other records with respect to certain attributes. By achieving k-anonymity, the risk of re-identification is reduced as it becomes difficult to identify individuals from the released data.

L-Diversity (Machanavajjhala et al. 2007) extends the concept of k-anonymity by ensuring that each group of records with the same attributes has at least L distinct values for sensitive attributes. This prevents adversaries from linking sensitive attributes to a specific individual.

T-closeness (Li et al. 2006) aims to prevent attribute disclosure by ensuring that the distribution of sensitive attributes in each group of records is not significantly different from the distribution in the overall dataset. This protects against potential inference attacks based on sensitive attributes.

11.4.3 Secure Data Storage and Transfer

Data security measures should be implemented to protect data at rest and in transit. This includes encryption of stored data and secure transmission protocols (e.g., SSL/TLS) when transferring data between systems or over networks. Access controls should be established to restrict unauthorized access.

Encryption is a fundamental technique for secure data storage and transfer. It involves encoding data using cryptographic algorithms, making it unreadable to unauthorized individuals. Two common encryption methods are:

- **Symmetric encryption** In symmetric encryption, the same key is used for both encryption and decryption. It ensures confidentiality but requires securely sharing the encryption key.
- **Asymmetric encryption** Asymmetric encryption uses a pair of keys: a public key for encryption and a private key for decryption. The public key can be freely distributed, while the private key is kept secure. This method provides both confidentiality and authentication.

Secure protocols are essential for transferring data between different entities in a secure manner. Some commonly used secure protocols in machine learning include:

- **Secure socket layer (SSL)/transport layer security (TLS):** SSL/TLS protocols provide secure communication over the internet. They ensure data confidentiality and integrity through encryption and authentication.
- **Secure file transfer protocol (SFTP)** SFTP is a secure version of the file transfer protocol (FTP). It encrypts data during transfer, preventing unauthorized access.
- **Virtual private network (VPN)** A VPN creates a secure and encrypted connection between two or more networks, ensuring the confidentiality and integrity of data transmitted over the network.

Access control mechanisms ensure that only authorized individuals or systems can access the stored data. This includes techniques such as user authentication, role-based access control, and access permissions.

Data integrity is crucial in order to maintain the accuracy and trustworthiness of the stored data. Techniques such as digital signatures, checksums, and hash functions can be used to verify the integrity of data during storage and transfer.

Secure storage infrastructure Choosing a secure storage infrastructure is important to protect data from physical and virtual threats. This includes measures such as data backup, redundancy, secure data centers, and data encryption at rest.

11.4.4 User Consent and Data Usage Policies

Respecting user consent is crucial in machine learning projects. Clear data usage policies should be defined, and user consent should be obtained for collecting, processing, and sharing data. Transparent communication with users fosters trust and ensures compliance with privacy regulations.

User consent refers to obtaining explicit permission from individuals before collecting, storing, and using their data for machine learning purposes.

Data usage policies outline the guidelines and rules governing the collection, storage, and usage of data in machine learning applications. These policies should include:

- **Data purpose limitation** Clearly defining the intended purpose of data usage and ensuring that data is not used beyond the specified purpose without explicit consent.
- **Data minimization** Collecting and retaining only the minimum amount of data necessary to achieve the stated purpose.
- **Data security** Implementing appropriate measures to protect data from unauthorized access, disclosure, alteration, and destruction.
- **Data sharing and third-party access** Clearly stating whether data will be shared with third parties and under what circumstances. If data sharing is involved, obtaining additional consent or implementing data anonymization techniques can be considered.
- **Data retention and deletion** Specifying the duration for which data will be retained and the process for secure data deletion once it is no longer needed.

11.4.5 Secure Infrastructure and System Hardening

Machine learning systems should be built on secure infrastructure. Below we describe a secure infrastructure and system hardening.

Secure infrastructure

- **Network security** Implementing robust network security measures, such as firewalls, intrusion detection systems, and secure network configurations, to protect against unauthorized access and network attacks.
- **Access control** Implementing strong access control mechanisms to ensure that only authorized individuals have access to the infrastructure components and sensitive data. This includes strong password policies, multifactor authentication, and role-based access control.

- **Encryption** Encrypting sensitive data at rest and in transit to protect against data breaches and unauthorized access. This includes utilizing encryption algorithms and secure key management practices.
- **Regular updates and patching** Keeping the infrastructure up to date with the latest security patches and updates to address known vulnerabilities and protect against potential exploits.

System hardening

- **Secure configuration** Implementing secure configurations for all system components, including operating systems, databases, and machine learning frameworks. This involves disabling unnecessary services, enabling secure communication protocols, and enforcing strong security policies.
- **Vulnerability scanning and penetration testing** Conducting regular vulnerability scanning and penetration testing to identify and address potential security vulnerabilities in the system. This helps in proactively identifying and resolving security weaknesses.
- **Logging and monitoring** Implementing robust logging and monitoring mechanisms to detect and respond to security incidents in real-time. This includes monitoring system logs, network traffic, and user activities for any suspicious or unauthorized behavior.
- **Backup and disaster recovery** Implementing regular data backup and disaster recovery strategies to ensure data availability and resilience in case of system failures or security breaches.

11.5 Human-Centered Machine Learning

Ensuring that machine learning models are developed with the needs and values of users and society in mind, and that they are developed and deployed in a way that promotes human well-being and dignity, is a core principle of responsible machine learning. Machine learning models have the potential to affect individuals and society in a variety of ways, from determining credit scores and insurance premiums to making decisions about who is eligible for parole or other forms of release from incarceration. It is therefore important to ensure that these models are developed and used in a way that respects the values and needs of users and society as a whole.

One way to ensure that machine learning models are developed with the needs and values of users and society in mind is to engage in human-centered design. Ensuring human-centered design in machine learning involves a number of practices and principles that can help to ensure that the model is designed with the needs and values of users in mind. The steps that machine learning practitioners can take to ensure a human-centered design are to engage with users and stakeholders throughout the design process to understand their needs, challenges, and goals. This can include conducting user research, surveys, and focus groups to gather feedback and insights. In addition, machine learning practitioners can develop user personas that represent the various types of users who will interact with the model. This can help to ensure that the model is designed to meet the needs of a diverse range of users. Last, they can design the user experience to be intuitive, accessible, and easy to use, incorporate user feedback into the design process, use it to refine and improve the model, and test the model with real users to evaluate its effectiveness, usability, and impact. By following these principles and practices, machine learning designers can ensure that their models are designed with the needs and values of users in mind. One instance of a human-centered machine learning pipeline is showcased in Moroney et al. (2021). In this study, the authors developed a social media dataset and subjected each unreliable tweet to a thorough evaluation for the presence of linguistic attributes that could suggest unreliability. The process involved two stages, resulting in the establishment of a set of linguistic rules. These rules have the potential to hold independent scientific significance. However, more importantly, they serve as a valuable means to evaluate the interpretability of the classification model. By incorporating such linguistic rules, the classification model can be assessed to ensure its usability, effectiveness, and relevance to its intended users. This approach is instrumental in promoting human well-being and dignity within the context of machine learning applications. A comparable study was outlined in Puerto et al. (2022), where the authors engaged a panel of expert chemists to evaluate the trade-off between prediction accuracy and interpretability in topic modeling applied to energetic materials corpora.

Another way to promote human well-being and dignity is to ensure that machine learning models are developed and deployed in an ethical and responsible manner. This includes ensuring that the model is fair and nondiscriminatory, transparent and explainable, and accountable to its users and society as a whole. Finally, promoting human well-being and dignity in machine learning requires an ongoing commitment to evaluation, monitoring, and improvement. This includes continuously monitoring the model's performance, detecting and addressing any biases or errors that may arise, and updating the model as needed to ensure that it remains relevant and effective over time.

By prioritizing human well-being and dignity in the development and deployment of machine learning models, we can help to ensure that these models are developed and used in a way that benefits everyone, not just a privileged few.

11.6 Repeatability, Reproducibility, and Replicability in Machine Learning

Repeatability, reproducibility, and replicability in machine learning are important to validate results, promote transparency, and foster scientific progress by enabling independent verification and comparison of methods and findings. They also facilitate error detection and debugging, ensuring the reliability and accountability of machine learning research and applications. In this section, we provide a comprehensive discussion of reproducibility, replicability, and repeatability in the context of machine learning research and emphasize the importance of clear and detailed reporting of experimental methods, including code, data, and parameter settings, to ensure the reproducibility of results. Several studies such as Drummond 2009, Collberg et al. 2015, Amodei et al. 2016, Adali and Calhoun 2022, and Gundersen et al. 2022 discuss different aspects of repeatability, reproducibility, and replicability in machine learning research. In this section, we aim to present the concepts of repeatability, reproducibility, and replicability in a simple and straightforward manner.

To make these concepts easily understandable for newcomers in the field of machine learning, we provide clear and accessible examples that will help them grasp and apply these aspects effectively.

11.6.1 Repeatability in Machine Learning

Repeatability in machine learning refers to the ability to reproduce the same results when an experiment is conducted multiple times, using the same dataset, model, and experimental setup. It emphasizes the importance of obtaining consistent and reliable outcomes, ensuring that the results are not affected by random variations.

Repeatability plays a crucial role in establishing the reliability and validity of machine learning experiments. It allows for the verification and validation of research findings, fosters reproducibility, and enables the comparison of different approaches or models under the same conditions. Furthermore, repeatability allows researchers to identify potential sources of variability and ensure that any observed differences are due to actual changes in the experimental setup or methodology, rather than random fluctuations.

Example Consider a machine learning experiment where researchers train a CNN for image classification using a publicly available dataset. To ensure repeatability, the following steps can be taken:

1. **Seed initialization** Set the random seed at the beginning of the experiment. This ensures that any random processes involved, such as weight initialization or data shuffling, produce the same outcomes across different runs.
2. **Code versioning** Maintain a version-controlled repository for the codebase used in the experiment. This allows for tracking changes and ensuring that the same code is used for subsequent runs.
3. **Documentation** Keep detailed records of the experimental setup, including hyperparameters, preprocessing steps, and model architecture. This documentation helps in reproducing the experiment accurately.
4. **Hardware and software specifications** Specify the hardware and software configurations used, including the type and version of the machine learning framework, libraries, and dependencies. This information ensures that the experiment can be replicated on different systems.

11.6.2 Reproducibility in Machine Learning

Reproducibility in machine learning refers to the ability to recreate and validate the results of a study or experiment using the same data, code, and methods. It aims to ensure that the findings can be independently verified and that the conclusions are robust and reliable.

Reproducibility plays a crucial role in establishing the credibility and trustworthiness of machine learning research. It allows for the verification and validation of findings, facilitates the comparison of different approaches, and encourages the advancement of the field by building upon existing work. Reproducible research also promotes transparency and fosters collaboration, as it enables others to build upon and extend the reported results.

Example Consider a machine learning study where researchers develop a deep learning model for sentiment analysis on a specific dataset. To ensure reproducibility, the following steps can be taken:

1. **Data availability** Make the dataset used in the study publicly available, or provide detailed information about how to obtain the dataset. This ensures that other researchers can access the same data and reproduce the experiments.
2. **Code sharing** Share the code and scripts used to preprocess the data, train the model, and evaluate the results. Version control tools like Git[4] can be used to maintain a repository that includes the code and its dependencies.
3. **Documentation** Provide comprehensive documentation that describes the experimental setup, including details about hyperparameters, model architecture, and any preprocessing steps. This documentation helps in reproducing the experiments accurately.
4. **Environment description** Specify the software and hardware configurations used in the study, including the version of the machine learning framework, libraries, and dependencies. This information helps in replicating the experiments on different systems.

11.6.3 Replicability in Machine Learning

Replicability in machine learning refers to the ability to reproduce the results of a study or experiment using independent data and methods. It focuses on validating the findings and ensuring that they hold true across different datasets and conditions. Replicability is essential for building a solid foundation of knowledge in machine learning. It allows researchers to validate and verify the reported findings, assess the generalizability of the results, and identify the factors that contribute to the observed outcomes. Replicable research forms the basis for the development of reliable and robust machine learning models and algorithms.

Example Consider a machine learning study where researchers propose a novel algorithm for image classification. To ensure replicability, the following steps can be taken:

1. **Independent data collection** Collect a separate and independent dataset that is different from the one used in the original study. This ensures that the findings can be tested on new data.
2. **Method replication** Replicate the methodology described in the original study, including data preprocessing steps, feature extraction techniques, and model training procedures. Ensure that the implementation details are as close as possible to the original study.

---

[4] Git (https://git-scm.com/) is a distributed version control system primarily used for managing source code during software development. It allows multiple developers to collaborate on projects simultaneously by tracking changes to files and coordinating work among team members. Git enables developers to work on different aspects of a project independently and then merge their changes together seamlessly. It also provides features for branching, merging, and reverting changes, which are essential for maintaining project history and managing codebase evolution.

3. **Comparison and evaluation** Apply the replicated method to the new dataset and compare the obtained results with the original study. Assess the similarity of the outcomes, such as classification accuracy or other relevant performance metrics.

4. **Discussion and interpretation** Discuss the similarities and differences observed between the replicated results and the original findings. Analyze the factors that might have contributed to any discrepancies and provide insights into the generalizability of the proposed algorithm.

11.6.4 Reproducibility Challenges in Machine Learning

Reproducibility is a critical aspect of scientific research, including machine learning. However, several challenges can hinder the reproducibility of machine learning experiments. Understanding and addressing these challenges is crucial for promoting transparency and advancing the field. Some of the challenges are now discussed.

Data availability One of the main challenges in reproducibility is the availability of data. Many machine learning studies use proprietary or restricted datasets, making it difficult for other researchers to access and replicate the experiments. Addressing this challenge involves encouraging open data practices, data sharing platforms, or providing detailed information on how to obtain the dataset.

Code and software dependencies Machine learning experiments often rely on complex codebases and libraries with multiple dependencies. Different versions of software packages or changes in the underlying frameworks can lead to discrepancies and hinder reproducibility. Sharing the code and explicitly specifying the software dependencies can help mitigate this challenge.

Hyperparameter tuning Machine learning models often involve tuning hyperparameters to achieve optimal performance. However, the choice of hyperparameters can significantly impact the results, making it challenging to reproduce the exact findings. Providing clear documentation of the hyperparameters used and their rationale can assist in addressing this challenge.

Hardware and computational resources Machine learning experiments can be computationally demanding and require specific hardware resources. Differences in hardware configurations and computational environments can affect the reproducibility of experiments. Documenting the hardware and computational resources used can aid in replicating the experiments.

Evaluation metrics and baselines Reproducibility also relies on consistent evaluation metrics and appropriate baselines. Differences in the evaluation methodology or the absence of proper baselines can make it challenging to compare and reproduce results. Providing a detailed description of the evaluation metrics and baselines used can help address this challenge.

Experiment documentation Lack of comprehensive documentation can pose a significant challenge to reproducibility. Insufficient details about the experimental setup, preprocessing steps, or model architectures make it difficult to replicate the experiments. Ensuring thorough documentation of the experiment can enhance reproducibility.

11.6.5 Solutions and Tools to Make ML Projects Reproducible

Experiment Tracking and Logging

Experiment tracking and logging play a crucial role in ensuring transparency, reproducibility, and effective management of machine learning projects. These practices help researchers keep track of experiments, record important details, and facilitate collaboration. We provide an overview of experiment tracking and logging in machine learning.

Tracking experiment metadata Experiment tracking involves recording important metadata associated with each experiment. This includes information such as the date and time of the experiment, the machine learning algorithm used, hyperparameters, dataset details, and any preprocessing steps applied. Tracking this metadata helps in understanding and reproducing the experiment's results.

Recording experiment results Experiment logging involves recording the results and metrics obtained from each experiment. This includes metrics like accuracy, precision, recall, $F1$ score, or any other evaluation metric used for assessing the model's performance. Logging these results allows for easy comparison and analysis across different experiments.

Managing code versions Experiment tracking and logging also involve managing code versions. It is essential to keep track of the code used for each experiment, including the specific commit or version. This ensures that the exact code used can be reproduced and traced back to the experiment's results.

Capturing environment details To ensure reproducibility, experiment tracking and logging should capture environment details such as software dependencies, library versions, and hardware configurations. This information helps in replicating the experimental setup in a consistent manner.

Collaboration and documentation Experiment tracking and logging promote collaboration by providing a centralized platform for researchers to document and share their experiments. This allows team members to easily access and reproduce each other's work, enhancing transparency and facilitating knowledge transfer.

Tools for experiment tracking and logging Several tools and frameworks are available for experiment tracking and logging in machine learning. Examples include MLflow, Neptune, Sacred, and TensorBoard. These tools provide features such as experiment versioning, result visualization, and collaboration functionalities.

Artifact Store

In machine learning projects, an artifact store is a dedicated repository or storage system that serves as a central location for storing and managing artifacts produced during the machine learning lifecycle. These artifacts include trained models, datasets, experiment results, code, and other related resources. Below we attempt to provide an overview of an artifact store in machine learning.

Centralized storage An artifact store provides a centralized storage location for all machine learning artifacts. It ensures that all artifacts are organized and easily accessible by team members, facilitating collaboration and knowledge sharing.

Version control Version control is an essential aspect of an artifact store. It allows the tracking and managing of different versions of artifacts, such as models and datasets. This enables reproducibility and ensures that previous versions can be easily retrieved and compared.

Metadata management An artifact store maintains metadata associated with each artifact. This metadata includes information such as the artifact's name, description, author, creation date, and associated experiments. Metadata management enables efficient search, retrieval, and organization of artifacts.

Access control and permissions An artifact store provides access control and permission management functionalities. This ensures that only authorized users or teams can access and modify specific artifacts. Access control helps maintain data security and confidentiality.

Artifact lifecycle management An artifact store facilitates the management of the entire lifecycle of artifacts. It allows tracking the progression of artifacts from initial development to deployment and retirement. This includes recording changes, updates, and dependencies associated with each artifact.

Integration with other tools An artifact store can integrate with other machine learning tools and frameworks. This includes integration with version control systems, continuous integration/continuous deployment (CI/CD) pipelines, experiment tracking tools, and model deployment platforms. Seamless integration enhances workflow efficiency.

Reproducibility and collaboration An artifact store promotes reproducibility and collaboration by providing a central repository for storing and sharing machine learning artifacts. It enables researchers to easily reproduce experiments, share models and datasets, and collaborate with team members.

11.7 The Importance of Responsible Machine Learning

Responsible machine learning is of paramount importance in today's world. It requires a holistic approach that considers ethical considerations, fairness, transparency, accountability, and the potential impact on individuals and society. As machine learning algorithms increasingly influence critical decisions in areas such as healthcare, finance, and criminal justice, it is crucial for machine learning researchers and practitioners to understand the ethical implications of these technologies. Responsible machine learning empowers individuals to critically assess the potential biases, fairness, and social impact of AI systems, enabling them to make informed decisions and advocate for ethical practices. In addition, machine learning researchers and practitioners need to understand how decisions are made by AI algorithms and have access to mechanisms for recourse or redress in case of unjust or harmful outcomes. By demanding transparency and accountability, they can contribute to building a more trustworthy and accountable AI ecosystem. To conclude, responsible machine learning is essential for new generations to navigate the increasingly AI-driven world with awareness, ethics, and a commitment to ensuring that technology benefits society as a whole. By understanding responsible machine learning, they can actively participate in shaping the future of AI, fostering equitable and accountable practices, and mitigating potential harms.

12

Conclusion

We conclude the book with a discussion of how the components of performance evaluation for learning algorithms unify into an overall framework for in-laboratory evaluation, followed by a discussion of how to move from a laboratory setting to a deployment setting. Associated with this deployment, we discuss the particular social consequences of machine learning technology, and their causes. We advocate considering potential social consequences as part of the evaluation framework. The discussion is followed by a few concluding remarks.

12.1 An Evaluation Framework Template for In-Laboratory Evaluation

The raison d'être of the following discussion is to appreciate the breadth and depth of the overall laboratory evaluation process, emphasizing the fact that such evaluation experiments should not be put together in an ad hoc manner, as they are sometimes done now, by merely selecting a random subset of some or all of the components discussed in the book. Indeed, careful consideration is required both of the underlying evaluation requirements and, in this context, of the correlation between the different choices for each component of the evaluation framework.

This section attempts to give a brief snapshot of the different components making up the laboratory evaluation framework, and highlights some of their major dependencies. Moreover, for each component, we also give a template of the various steps necessary to make appropriate choices along with some of the main concerns and interrelations to take into account with respect to both, other steps in a given component, and other evaluation components themselves. Unfortunately, due to the intricate dependencies between the different steps as well as the components, it might seem necessary to make certain choices simultaneously, and check their compatibility afterwards.

The overall evaluation exercise can essentially be broken down into broad components along the lines of the framework of Figure 12.1. As can be seen, each step in the framework corresponds to one of the evaluation components discussed in this book. An implicit assumption made in this framework is that the final aim (though not necessarily the outcome) of the evaluation exercise is known. Given this knowledge, the first step, naturally, is to decide which algorithms to include in the evaluation exercise. Different considerations need to be addressed while making this choice, such as whether a generic or a novel algorithm is to

The Classifier Evaluation Framework

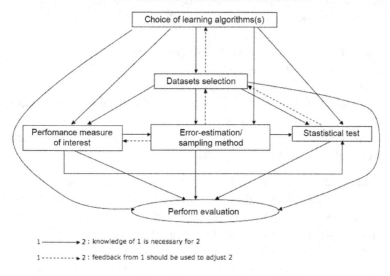

Figure 12.1 Overview of the classifier evaluation procedure.

be evaluated, or whether we are trying to identify an optimal algorithm for a given test bed. The dataset selection component also depends on the experimental question asked. For the generic algorithms case or the testing of a novel approach, the important issues to be addressed may include whether a general characterization of the algorithm is required or some specific criteria of interest need to be tested, whether some specific domain characteristics are desired, and so on. Further, it is important to note that dataset selection is not independent of the other components. In particular, it would affect the error estimation (e.g., due to its size) as well as the performance measure selection (e.g., due to issues such as class imbalance). Similarly, choices made in the statistical significance testing components also depend on choices made in the dataset selection component and the error estimation component. Although the dependency is more subtle, it is worth noting that choices made in the performance measure selection affect the error estimation component and vice versa. For example, if graphical methods such as receiver operating characteristic (ROC) curves that are not effectively averaged are needed, error estimation needs to be parsimonious enough to be able to analyze all the results. If, however, the domain chosen is too small for parsimonious error estimation to be effective, then the choice made in the performance measure selection component may need to be revised.

In addition to the considerations pertaining to the interdependence of the components, each component of the evaluation framework itself requires careful consideration of the available options and their respective assumptions, constraints of application, advantages, and limitations. Before we jump into a discussion of these components, recall that we made the assumption that the aim of evaluation, in this whole exercise, is well understood. The need for evaluation of learning algorithms can arise, broadly, from one of the following broad concerns or situations:

1. comparison of a *new algorithm* to other (maybe generic or application-specific) classifiers on a *specific domain* (e.g., when proposing a novel learning algorithm for a specific
   situation);
2. comparison of a *new generic algorithm* to other generic ones on a set of *benchmark
   domains* (e.g., to demonstrate the general effectiveness of the new approach against other
   approaches);
3. characterization of *generic classifiers* on *benchmarks domains* (e.g., to study the algorithms' behavior on general domains for subsequent use); and
4. comparison of *multiple classifiers* on a *specific domain* (e.g., to find the best algorithm
   for a given application task).

Of course, in some context situations 1 and 2 can be mapped to situations 4 and 3, respectively. However, there will be situations where these cases need to be differentiated.

We now consider, in detail, the different components of the evaluation framework of
Figure 12.1. For each of these components, we again show the dependencies we wish to
highlight in graphical form, unless, as in the case of learning algorithms selection, these
dependencies are largely qualitative and depend not only on the evaluation requirement but
also on the characteristics of the evaluation process itself. The notation used in each of these
graphs is briefly described below.

Notation

Figures 12.2–12.5 display the process and dependencies within each of the components
shown Figure 12.1. In each of the graphs, we use the following conventions. The components are represented by large boxes while arrows between them denote the dependencies
between components. Ovals represent actions. Small boxes within the large boxes represent
the information pertinent to the selection within the corresponding process or step, while
diamonds represent a test or verification necessary to perform successfully prior to taking
an action. The arrows between small boxes or diamonds and ovals represent dependencies between the information contained within the small boxes or diamonds and an action.
Arrows are of two types: solid and dashed. The solid arrows indicate the *requirement* of the
information of the process or components *from which they originate*, to enable the action,
process, or component *to which they point*. Dashed arrows, on the other hand, refer to the
feedback *from the components or process* that they *originate from*. For instance, a dashed
arrow from a diamond box to an oval may signify the feedback of the decision or verification
action that the diamond represents on the possible actions represented by the oval. In this
sense, we should use a bidirectional relationship notation for such feedback, but we use
single dashed arrows, instead, to keep the figures simpler. Note that a small box inside a large
box denotes the information or process that exerts dependencies on the current component,
but is, itself, part of the component denoted by the large box that encloses it.

We now discuss each component in turn.

12.1.1 Selecting Learning Algorithms

Choosing the candidate learning algorithms for the evaluation experiment depends largely (though there are other factors) on the overall goal of the evaluation. Broadly, this boils down to whether one wishes to perform a general evaluation or test a specific algorithm. The objectives of a general evaluation and, accordingly, the subsequent algorithms utilized can be many. For instance, one might be interested in determining a general purpose classifier effective across a variety of tasks. Even for a given specific problem of interest, one might wish to find the most efficient algorithm. However, testing a specific algorithm tends to narrow down the criteria of selecting other learning algorithms against which the effectiveness of the algorithm of interest is to be evaluated. An example can be to evaluate a novel approach in relation to the existing or state-of-the-art approaches. In case the algorithm of interest (possibly, a novel approach) is a generic one, the evaluation would include the most effective generic learning algorithm. On the other hand, if the algorithm of interest is application specific, the evaluation should include the most efficient state of the art approaches for the given application.

The above description makes the algorithm selection process look pretty straightforward. However, this is certainly not the case due to various practical hassles. Not all approaches claimed to be effective and projected as serious candidates for various domains have their implementations available (although, recently, more and more conferences and journals require that the code be provided with the submission).[1] This shifts the onus of developing an implementation from the original inventor of the approach onto the researcher carrying out the evaluation. However, even when making the effort of implementing the claimed approach(es) seems worthwhile or even when the code is available, the issue of the limited familiarity of the researcher carrying out the evaluation to the nitty-gritty aspects of the algorithm or its implementation makes it extremely difficult. In many cases, such details may not be available at all in the public domain. Hence, it turns out that including all possible candidate algorithms in the evaluation may not be feasible. This optimal alternative, then, needs to be traded off in favor of approaches deemed close in performance to the claimed state of the art, even though they are not quite as strong. Such problems are very common in the case of applied research, where the proposed approaches are composed of independent or interdependent components put together in a processing pipeline. Implementing these, then, involves difficulties not only in terms of the availability of the various components, but also in figuring out the exact nature of their relationship to other components of the processing pipeline. If the learning algorithm happens to be only one of the components of such a pipeline, then even more care needs to be taken to make sure that the other components are controlled before making any inference on the performance behavior of the algorithm.

The next natural question in selecting the candidate algorithms is how many algorithms need to be included in the evaluation. Of course, it would be easy to answer this question if there were a universal winner; that is, an algorithm that proved to be better (on the criteria of interest, of course) than all other candidates. Evaluating the algorithm of interest against

---

[1] This does not apply to algorithms developed in industrial settings that remain protected.

this universal winner would possibly be sufficient, at least, as a first step in the evaluation. However, this is almost never the case. As a result, the answer to this question becomes highly subjective. For instance, when a specific application domain is involved, one might want to include state of the art approaches to evaluate the algorithm of interest against. Of course, there can be cases where no (or very few) approaches have been proposed with the chosen application in mind. As a result, even though there may be multiple algorithms that can be applied to the domain, they may not be optimal, at least in their classical form. This may give an unfair advantage to the application-specific approach (optimized with the application of interest in mind). Both the evaluation and interpretation of the subsequent results, at the very least (if optimizing the candidate algorithms is not possible), should bear this caveat in mind. Similarly, if the overall goal of evaluation is to determine the best algorithm for a given domain or a set of domains, then a reasonable first step is to include algorithms with a wide range of learning biases (e.g., linear classifiers, tree-based ensembles, deep learning systems, and so on). Accordingly, evaluating a novel generic algorithm would necessitate testing it against a range of other generic classifiers on a variety of domains.

Other relevant issues concern the characteristics of the domain(s) utilized as well. For instance, an optimal binary classifier may not be the best choice if the goal is multi-class classification, or an algorithm known to be most effective in balanced class scenarios may not be the best choice for domains with highly skewed class distributions. As can be noted, all these considerations also highlight the dependence of the algorithm selection component on other components of the evaluation framework, most notably the dataset selection, which we discuss next.

12.1.2 Selecting Datasets

Figure 12.2 provides an overview of the decision process involved in the dataset selection component of the evaluation framework. As discussed in previous chapters, the choice of the datasets for evaluation depends, in great part, on the purpose of the evaluation. Naturally, evaluating generic learning algorithms would necessitate including a variety of datasets with different characteristics of interest, keeping in mind the purpose and limits of evaluation. On the other hand, an application-specific evaluation would require realistic datasets from the domains of interest.

In the application-specific context, great care should be taken while selecting the datasets as well as other components of the evaluation. Effects such as those of external validity discussed in Chapter 6 should be kept in mind since the learning system selected will most likely not be deployed on the exact same domain. The desired application area can even be broad as in the case of text classification or face recognition, which have specific characteristics, but vary widely depending on the composition of the particular dataset considered. Consequently, the test domains used would need to cover a broad spectrum of the variabilities in data characteristics such as dimensionality, class distributions, noise levels, class overlaps, and so on. In the context of generic learning algorithms, such variabilities also need to be considered in the more general context of various domains. In both cases,

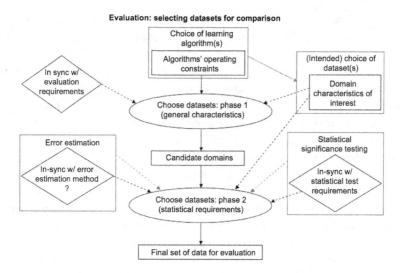

Figure 12.2 Overview of the dataset selection process.

the dependency on the other evaluation framework components, such as the intended performance measures and error estimation method, should also be kept in mind. For instance, measuring accuracy may not bode well with a domain with skewed class distributions. Similarly, the size of the dataset would also affect the error estimation process. Reverse dependencies exist as well. In the case where a leave-one-out error estimation is of interest (say due to concerns over theoretical guarantees) for instance, a very large dataset may not only prove to be computationally prohibitive, but may also result in highly biased estimates. A 10-fold cross-validation method, on the other hand, would require at least a reasonably sized dataset to enable reliable estimates. The choice of the number of datasets can also, in turn, affect the resulting statistical testing. While a large number of domains would help in making more concrete inferences on the broad effectiveness of the approaches, the size and other characteristics of these domains affect the confidence in their performances' statistical differences. A simple two-stage approach, as shown in Figure 12.2, can be effective. While the first stage enables filtering out the domains not relevant to the goals of the evaluation and other compatibility issues based on algorithm selection, the second stage allows for further refinement, based on finer considerations on domain characteristics and their dependency on other components such as error estimation and statistical testing.

Further questions also arise that require some reflection. First comes the obvious question of how many datasets are sufficient for evaluation so that clear inferences can be made about an algorithm's performance. Second, one can ask where the datasets can be obtained from and how to select them from these sources. Finally, one can wonder how the relationship between the domains used for the evaluation can be uncovered. These three questions are closely related and we attempt to answer them as follows. In a generic approach, it is felt that the more varied the datasets are, the better the performance analysis. However, it should be noted that the more varied the datasets are, the greater the chances of obtaining high performance variance by the algorithms, thus jeopardizing sensible interpretation of their comparison. However, conclusions based on too few datasets may be prone to coincidental trends and may not reflect the true difference in the performance of the algorithms. Interestingly, with too many datasets, finding these domains' characteristic trends through a kind of meta-analysis could prove useful. The datasets could then be grouped in clusters representing their most salient common characteristics so as to yield performance estimates with less variance across them. Algorithm behavior could then be studied over these individual groupings. There are three general sources of datasets: application-specific, repository-based, and synthetic. The choice of datasets depends on both the nature of the algorithms and the evaluation requirements and goals. Obviously, if the algorithm under scrutiny was designed for a specific type of application (e.g., DNA-based, face-recognition), then the datasets should be selected from that domain. For more general assessments, repository-based datasets should be fine. Finally, when algorithms were designed to address certain types of domain characteristics, synthetic data embedding these characteristics may be appropriate along with application-specific, repository domains, or both. While there is an advantage of using synthetic datasets to test how learning algorithms respond to particular domain characteristics, it is important to note that such assessments are not sufficient since real domains include many more complexities than synthetically generated ones. A promising new area of research for machine learning evaluation could be the creation of test domains that combine the fields of machine learning and simulation. Perhaps, through these means, we could create realistic datasets that also embed the controlled characteristics we are interested in testing.

The next issue, once the algorithms and the dataset(s) are decided upon, is that of deciding on the yardstick(s) on which the performances of the algorithms are to be measured and subsequently analyzed. Let us then take a peek at the issues involved in choosing the performance measure(s) of interest.

12.1.3 Selecting Performance Measures

The selection of a performance measure is illustrated in Figure 12.3. Once again, we suggest dividing the selection process into two stages: first, a broad filter based on dependencies on other components in the evaluation framework, followed by a second stage of finer filtering based on the synchronization requirements with the error estimation as well as other specific requirements on the chosen measures. Let us discuss these stages in turn.

The first stage of filtering of the candidate performance measures is guided by the previous choices in algorithm selection and dataset selection components, as well as the characteristics of interest in the evaluation, either due to the algorithms' properties or the requirements imposed by the application domain. The choice of learning algorithms can have a crucial effect on the choices that can be made over the performance measures. For instance, this problem occurs when comparing two algorithms with different degrees of reliance on the respective thresholds. Hence, in the event of limited data, an effective threshold-setting procedure would be extremely difficult to optimize.[2] A threshold-sensitive point measure

---

[2] Similar problems will of course be faced in model selection over algorithms.

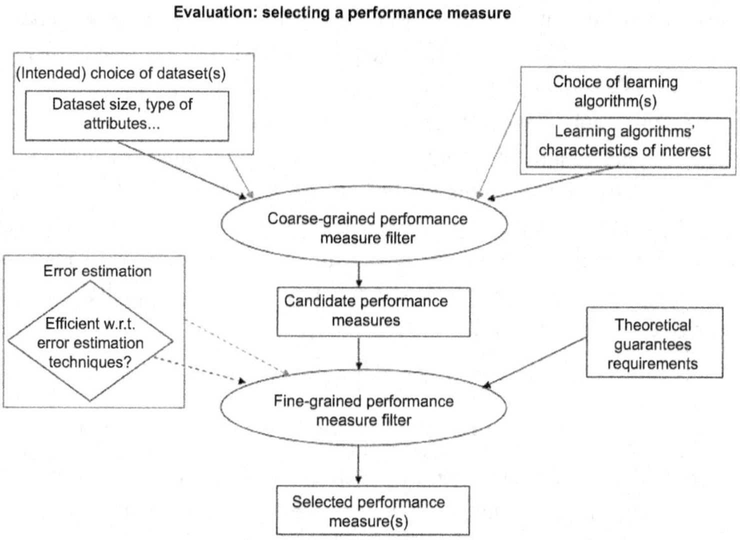

Evaluation: selecting a performance measure

Figure 12.3 Overview of the performance measure selection process.

such as accuracy would be less recommended in such cases against measures such as ROC that can characterize the behavior over the full operating range (of course within the constraint of limited dataset size). The selection of datasets also imposes certain constraints on the possible performance measure choices. We saw the relationship between these two components above too. However, the constraints on the choices of performance measures are also imposed in other ways. If, for example, some of the selected datasets are multi-class domains, it will be impossible to use a one-class focused measure such as precision or recall without collapsing some of the classes together. Such a collapsing action is, of course, not always desirable, and as a result, a measure that applies to multi-class domains, such as accuracy or balanced accuracy, would have to be employed. Similar is the case of hierarchical classification where specialized hierarchical measures must be employed. The characteristic(s) of interest in the evaluation are very important too, for obvious reasons. In medical applications, for example, the sensitivity and specificity of a test matter much more than its overall accuracy. The performance measure will, thus, have to be chosen appropriately.

Once several candidate performance measures have been chosen, a finer-grained filter needs to be applied to ensure that they are in synchronization with our choice of an error estimation technique and that they are associated with appropriate confidence measures or guarantees. The ease and computational complexity of calculating a performance measure will also play a crucial role when assessing its dependence on the error estimation technique. Other guarantees on the performance measures might also be desirable in certain scenarios. Consider, for instance, performance guarantees in the form of either confidence intervals or upper bounds on the generalization performances. Not all performance measures have the means of computing tight confidence intervals associated with them. For example, although point-wise bounds over ROC curves as well confidence bands around the ROCs have been suggested as measures of confidence for ROC analysis, in many cases such bands are not very tight (Elazmeh et al. 2006). Further, subsequent validation (or significance testing) over such measures can affect their choice.

We discussed different viewpoints as well as specific classification performance measures in Chapters 4 and 5, and performance measures for other machine learning settings in Chapter 8. These three chapters discussed the various strengths, limitations, and contexts of application of these measures that would be helpful in making the required choices. Given the performance measures of interest, the next issue will be selecting techniques best suited to obtain their estimate(s) objectively. Hence, we turn our focus to the issue of selecting an appropriate error estimation method.

12.1.4 Selecting an Error Estimation and Sampling Method

Chapter 6 discussed the importance and implications of choosing a proper error estimation method in any given problem context. However, in addition to the general reliance on the error estimation methods to strike a suitable trade-off between the bias–variance behavior of the performance measure, there are other dependencies that need to be taken into account. Figure 12.4 illustrates a template of the decision process involved in choosing an appropriate error estimation method.

The two-stage method of error estimation method selection is a bit different from the two-stage filtering performed in other components of the evaluation framework. At the first stage of the error estimation method, the evaluator must decide which of the basic methods is needed for reliable estimation of the performance measures. At the second stage, the chosen method is fine-tuned (e.g., its parameters are set) based on the requirements of the evaluation

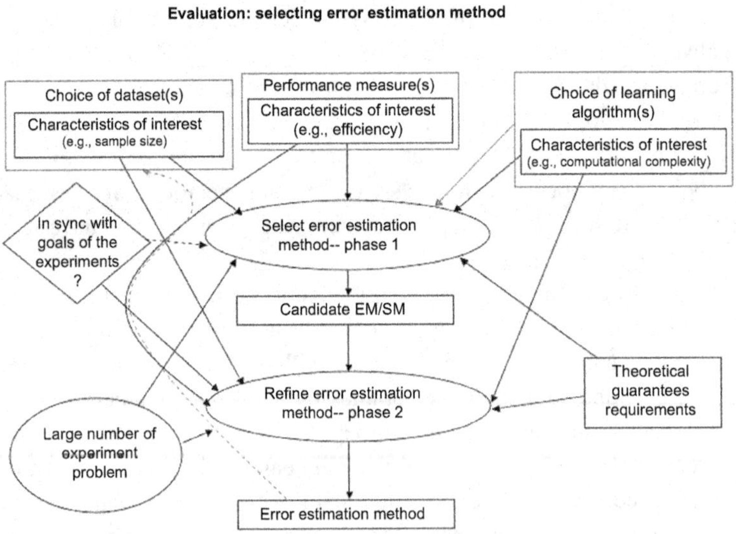

Figure 12.4 Overview of the error estimation selection process.

process. For instance, at the first stage, one can decide that resampling is necessary and that a k-fold cross-validation is the method of choice. At the second stage one can then decide upon the value of k and determine whether stratified cross-validation is needed. However, note that the factors affecting the choice of the error estimation method in the first stage also affects the fine-tuning choices made in the second stage. The main dependence on the error estimation components is exerted from the algorithm selection and dataset selection, as well as the performance measure selection components of the evaluation framework. The choice of the algorithm can affect the error estimation in terms of algorithmic behavior, computational complexity, and so on, in tandem with similar considerations over the error estimation methods themselves. Further, the reliance of the error estimation method on the chosen dataset is easy to note with the most obvious dependency exerted by the size of the dataset. Other properties of the datasets can, further, affect the fine-tuning stage. For instance, stratified resampling may be deemed important in cases where the dataset is imbalanced.

The problem of large numbers of experiments, also known as the multiplicity effect, refers to the fact that if too many experiments are run, then there is a greater chance that the observed results occur by chance. Some of the ways to deal with this problem involve the choice of an error estimation technique. For example, randomization testing may prove to be effective in this case. With regard to performance measures, similar considerations need to be made. Consider, for instance, the need to compute guarantees on the performance measures. As already seen, such computation depends on various aspects. For instance, the holdout risk bound discussed earlier necessitates a separate testing set, which might not be possible if the dataset is already too small, making it impossible for the algorithm to learn reliably. Other performance measure guarantees may be considered in such cases, for instance, training set bounds in cases where a proper learning theoretic characterization of the algorithm can be obtained or is already available. Other considerations also need to be made with respect to statistical significance testing. For example, the statistical guarantees that are derived from bootstrapping have much lower power than those derived from t-tests applied after sampling methods were run. If power is of importance for the particular application, then a sampling error estimation regimen is preferred to a bootstrapping one. In fact, the issues of selecting an error estimation method and associated statistical significance testing are very closely related. We will explore this relationship briefly in the discussion of the next component: selecting statistical tests.

12.1.5 Selecting Statistical Tests

The final component that completes the evaluation framework makes the call on choosing the method best suited to determine the statistical significance of the difference in performance of the learning algorithms in the evaluation study. The process is depicted in Figure 12.5.

Analogous to the previous steps, the process of selecting the best-suited tests for assessing the statistical significance of the performance differences consists of two stages. In the first stage, a subset of candidate statistical tests are chosen, based on the dependencies of other

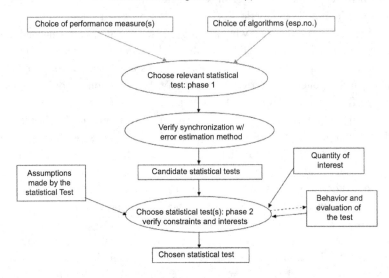

Figure 12.5 Overview of the statistical test selection process.

components, while in the second stage, the tests from this subset that do not meet the more specific criteria of interest or other requirements or constraints of evaluation are filtered out. The first and foremost dependency on the choice of the statistical test comes from the algorithm selection component. For instance, when multiple algorithms are chosen that need to be compared as a group, pairwise tests such as the t-test might not be deemed suitable. Instead, Cochran's Q test or a Bayesian correlated t-test could be used. Similar dependencies exist with other components as well, such as the error estimation (and, by implication, the dataset selection) component as well as the performance measure selection component. Consider, for example, the case of error estimation that yields multiple, relatively independent estimates of performance measurements, in which case a parametric statistical test might be considered. However, if correlated estimates are obtained or the evaluation requires a ranking estimation, nonparametric statistical tests may be more suitable. The first stage of the statistical test selection component takes into consideration such coarse-grained dependencies. Once a number of candidate tests have been selected in the first stage, a second-stage filter is applied to restrict the choice to a single (or a few) tests, taking into account the user's constraints and preferences, as well as procedural constraints. The criteria thus considered might include the evaluation requirement on the quantity (performance measure) of interest with respect to the statistical justification sought. For instance, one might be interested only in determining whether the differences in the performances are statistically significant, or one might require a quantification of the degree of such a statistically significant difference. Other considerations, such as focus on type I or type II errors of the test, may also need to be taken into account. Last but not least, the chosen test will need to be verified with regard to the assumptions and constraints, and their contexts of application. For instance, if the results over the classifiers' performance cannot be approximated relatively well using a normal distribution, the *t*-test may be rendered meaningless.

12.2 From Laboratory Evaluation to Industrial-Strength Evaluation

The evaluation framework outlined in Section 12.1 is robust insofar as laboratory experiments are concerned. Such evaluation, however, is not sufficient when it comes to deployment. In order to move from laboratory to industry, it is useful to look at what other fields have done. But also to recognize that machine learning is different from other disciplines and must design its own evaluation standard. Two particular disciplines lend themselves well as models of what machine learning could aspire to: drug design and software engineering. Machine learning evaluation for deployment, though, also has unique features. These lie in the social consequences such deployment may yield. These will be discussed in Section 12.3.

As a model, drug design is of particular interest because of both the inductive nature of the process and the sensitivity of the outcome. The rigorous process that characterizes the move from laboratory to market with a small-scale phase I process followed by a large-scale phase II process, and so on is very impressive. It is understandable that given the variability of the population and the danger of side-effects that new drugs can cause, such a process should be followed. Though the dangers of machine learning are typically not as clearly defined as those of new drugs, except in rare cases where it is deployed in extremely sensitive applications where lives can be threatened (self-driving cars, computer-assisted surgery, etc.), they are, nonetheless, present and should not be overlooked.

Software engineering is an obvious model for machine learning deployment for the simple reason that machine learning systems are software tools. However, as discussed in Chapter 10, adapting the traditional software engineering practice to machine learning is not straightforward due to the nondeterministic nature of machine learning systems. In traditional software systems, the output space of the algorithm may be too vast for human beings to easily characterize all the possibilities. In machine learning-based software, however, that space is infinite and depends, in a not easily characterizable way, on imperfections in the datasets used to train the algorithms, uncertainties and opaqueness of the algorithms and the parameters they are set with, and the imperfections of the platform on which the algorithms are implemented. Software engineering is concerned with offline testing issues such as those just cited, but also online testing issues, akin to, but not as strictly implemented, the phasic testing of drugs. Additional issues relate to a subset of social issues already identified by the machine learning community such as systematic bias, privacy, and other ethical issues.

While the computer science community has started recognizing the social issues that can be caused by machine learning-based software, the issues identified (e.g., algorithmic bias, data unfairness) and discussed in Chapter 11, while of great importance, only scratch the surface of all the problems such software may cause. Unfortunately, to date these ills have not been as widely acknowledged as one could have hoped, and, most importantly, not satisfactorily addressed. The kind of ills we are referring to are those already mentioned such as historical bias and unfairness in the data, algorithmic bias, issues of privacy, and the more recent but extremely worrisome ills caused by generative technology starting with the generation of fake pictures and followed by generated text. As pointed out in interviews with Gary Marcus[3] and discussed in Crothers et al. (2023), this technology makes it easy for bad actors to spread misinformation and, generally speaking, to reshape the nature of our social fabric by challenging copyright, threatening the education system, and so on. We address some of these concerns in Section 12.3.

12.3 Social Issues Linked to Machine Learning Deployment

Many features surrounding machine learning in particular, and AI in general, lead to political, social, and psychological problems including cybersecurity threats, online influence campaigns, and misinformation. The problems include, but are not limited to, political unrest and foreign interference, the spread of hatred on social media, unemployment, cybercrime, adult, teen, and child depression, suicide, and so on. We attribute this to the following causes and call for more regulation on the kind of software that can be released and its timing. The interesting thing about the subsequent list is that each cause, or almost each cause, starts from a noble and altruistic, albeit perhaps naive, attitude. Unfortunately, in many cases the implications of these attitudes are not fully worked out before the product is deployed. That is not surprising in some sense: the people creating the product are not philosophers, sociologists, psychologists, political scientists, or business experts. Instead, they are mere computer scientists with some notions of these other fields, but no real training in them.

Ease of deployment When compared to other technologies, machine learning software is extremely easy and cheap to deploy. While important technological advances such as the railway engine (or locomotive) needed to be physically built after being designed on paper, a tool as powerful as ChatGPT is just a piece of software; that is, lines of code. They don't cost anything in way of building materials such as steel panels or screws. They don't require teams of builders. True, such software needs to be trained on very powerful computer clusters which, in turn, need to be physically built, but the hardware and software development is independent, and once the hardware, which is multi-purpose, exists, creating a powerful piece of software is relatively easy. True as well, teams of software engineers are needed, but, due to the virtual quality of the product, the lift is not as heavy as it is in other industries, and in fact, new products are easy, fast, and cheap to deploy.

Culture of sharing Machine learning scientists, and in fact, computer scientists as a whole, have advocated a culture where papers, software, and ideas, in general, are exchanged freely and efficiently. Early on, and continuing on today, the discipline favored conferences over journals to accelerate the pace of exchange and, therefore, innovation. The open-source operating system, Linux, and the free language, R, are other instances of the democratization of powerful but expensive tools (Unix, S/Matlab) that otherwise would not be accessible to all. These platforms give anyone the chance to develop new contributions and share them.

---

[3] See, for example, www.youtube.com/watch?v=EoJ6gXGL-zM.

Typically, the best contributions remain while the less useful ones die down (this is very clear with the very popular R packages and those that are rarely used). Today, the collaboration is not centered around a project, but rather platforms have been created to allow for exchanges. GitHub, for software, and ArXiv, for scientific papers, are the two main motors of this sharing culture. Without such a culture, old and new, the progress better appreciated today by lay viewers than in the past when a fair amount of knowledge was needed to understand what was happening with Linux, would not be possible.

Culture of democracy The computer science community, in general, is a strong believer in democracy. People can deploy code, tools, and so on, at will while their ultimate value will be judged by their popularity. Though, in essence, this represents a pure expression of democracy, it does not represent the kind of democratic systems used by the United States or other Western powers, and carries many shortcomings with it. Certain organizations are trying to define governance in cyberspace, but it is not clear as of yet, how that governance can be implemented. By the same token, legal experts are looking at ways to define and enforce rules of cyberspace, but once again, these efforts are at their very beginnings.

Culture of creativity Creativity is highly prized in the machine learning and AI fields. A clever algorithm with potential long-term ramifications ignites much more interest from the machine learning community than a plain algorithm with demonstrated current useful-ness. Though there is nobility in such an attitude, and indeed, benefits for the long run akin to what fundamental science has to offer, little importance is given to more prosaic questions of relevance to today's world and, for that matter, the conduct of convincing evaluation.

Culture of idealism A lot of the tools created by AI and machine learning experts are gen-uinely created with the idea of making the world a better place. Thoughts of connecting like-minded people more easily, providing people with useful resources more easily and cheaply, helping disabled people live a better life, and erasing racism and other kinds of inequities are common motivations for people to enter the field. At the same time, AI researchers and practitioners often are science fiction enthusiasts mesmerized by imagined robots' abilities. Of course, science fiction works usually show the dark side of scientific discoveries, but these negative effects are often those that are easier to grasp, are often exaggerated, and usually do not represent the long-term more subtle consequences of that technology.

Financial benefit Although all the causes mentioned so far started from rather moral and upstanding principles even if, in effect, their social consequences may have been some-what overlooked, this last cause is not rooted in the same good-willing and altruistic space. Instead, financial opportunity may be starting to overtake the selfless sentiments that pre-viously guided machine learning development. Specifically, we may have reached a point where machine learning-based products are released despite the knowledge that they may have negative side effects, just because of the potential for financial gain.

Although the social issues created by new technologies and their potential causes are not topics that normally fall in the purview of evaluation, we believe that in the case of machine learning and, by extension, AI, they should, due to the profound impact that the technology (as well as related ones, such as internet browsers, social media, and so on) has had and will continue to have on society; some of the dangers that are indirectly caused by such technologies; and the ease and, thus, the pace at which the technology is deployed.

The issues raised here relate to an important discussion in the philosophy of science that pits the value-free ideal that considers science in isolation from its impact on society against a system that considers societal concerns. Though the value-free approach may offer a certain kind of objectivity as it shields science from the dangers of politicized science, it may inadvertently create societal harm due to its inattention to any kind of societal concerns (Douglas 2009).[4]

Our suggestions for including an evaluation of the social consequences of machine learning prior to the deployment of tools based on it include the establishment of a regulatory body similar to the CDC or FDA, that would oversee the deployment of AI-based software, a change of culture that could take the form of Institutional Review Board (IRB) certification prior to engaging in AI research and development, and further down the line, the creation of an effective way to govern cyberspace.

12.4 Concluding Remarks

The aim of this book was not only to educate researchers and practitioners who are not familiar with the machine learning evaluation process, its underlying assumptions, and its context of application, but also, more broadly, to help the community realize the importance of the evaluation process itself. We tried to emphasize, by dividing the complete process of evaluation into its basic components, the issues that need to be addressed while making choices at different stages of the exercise. We also attempted to show that these seemingly disparate components are in fact highly correlated. Of course, these dependencies have to be considered together with the more fundamental concerns within each component about the assumptions, constraints, and limitations of the techniques employed, which are not often acknowledged. Moreover, a lack of proper understanding and appreciation of the context in which the different components of the evaluation framework operate may also lead to a misinterpretation of the evaluation outcomes.

Another aim of the book was to cast a broad net over the different machine learning paradigms and discuss the evaluation process within each of them. We also set to move the discussion of the evaluation process from the laboratory setting to the industrial setting, pointing out the challenges necessary to overcome in order to make responsible decisions. We hope that the discussions in this book leave the reader with an increased understanding and appreciation of the process of evaluation. We also hope that it will prompt the community as a whole to reflect upon the consequences of the tools it creates, and to make responsible choices in practical settings.

Finally, following the principle that a scientist should fully understand his or her practices, we tried to shed light on the underlying reasons for these practices.

---

[4] We thank Sabrina Ripsman for pointing out this debate.

We hope that this book succeeds in stringing together the different aspects of evaluation necessary to create robust and responsible machine learning systems and that in doing so, it fills a void in the machine learning, data mining, and data science literature that proves to be a productive step towards meaningful evaluation.

Appendices

Appendix A

Statistical Tables

This appendix presents all the statistical tables necessary for constructing the confidence intervals or for running a hypothesis test of the kind discussed in this book. In particular, we present seven kinds of tables, although, in some cases, the table is broken up into several parts. More specifically, the following eight tables are presented:

1. the Z table
2. the t table
3. the χ^2 table (two subtables)
4. the table of critical values for the signed test
5. the Wilcoxon table
6. the F-ratio table (four subtables)
7. the Friedman table
8. critical values for the Tukey test.

A.1 The Z Table

Table A.1. *Percentage points of the normal distribution.*

P	x(P)	P	x(p)	P	x(P)	P	x(P)	P	x(P)	P	x(P)
50	0.0000	5.0	1.6449	3.0	1.8808	2.0	2.0537	1.0	2.3263	0.10	3.0902
45	0.1257	4.8	1.6646	2.9	1.8957	1.9	2.0749	0.9	2.3656	0.09	3.1214
40	0.2533	4.6	1.6849	2.8	1.9110	1.8	2.0969	0.8	2.4089	0.08	3.1559
35	0.3853	4.4	1.7060	2.7	1.9268	1.7	2.1201	0.7	2.4573	0.07	3.1947
30	0.5244	4.2	1.7279	2.6	1.9431	1.6	2.1444	0.6	2.5121	0.06	3.2389
25	0.6745	4.0	1.7507	2.5	1.9600	1.5	2.1701	0.5	2.5758	0.05	3.2905
20	0.8416	3.8	1.7744	2.4	1.9774	1.4	2.1973	0.4	2.6521	0.01	3.7190
15	1.0364	3.6	1.7991	2.3	1.9954	1.3	2.2262	0.3	2.7478	0.005	3.8906
10	1.2816	3.4	1.8250	2.2	2.0141	1.2	2.2571	0.2	2.8782	0.001	4.2649
5	1.6449	3.2	1.8522	2.1	2.0335	1.1	2.2904	0.1	3.0902	0.0005	4.4172

This table is reproduced from Lindley and Scott (1984). Reproduced with permission of the Licensor through PLSclear.

Statistical Tables

A.2 The *t* Table

Table A.2. *Percentage points of the t distribution.*

P	40	30	25	20	15	10	5	2.5	1	0.5	0.1	0.05
$v = 1$	0.3249	0.7265	1.0000	1.3764	1.963	3.078	6.314	12.71	31.82	63.66	318.3	636.6
2	0.2887	0.6172	0.8165	1.0607	1.386	1.886	2.920	4.303	6.965	9.925	22.33	31.60
3	0.2767	0.5844	0.7649	0.9785	1.250	1.638	2.353	3.182	4.541	5.841	10.21	12.92
4	0.2707	0.5686	0.7407	0.9410	1.190	1.533	2.132	2.776	3.747	4.604	7.173	8.610
5	0.2672	0.5594	0.7267	0.9195	1.156	1.476	2.015	2.571	3.365	4.032	5.893	6.869
6	0.2648	0.5534	0.7176	0.9057	1.134	1.440	1.943	2.447	3.143	3.707	5.208	5.959
7	0.2632	0.5491	0.7111	0.8960	1.119	1.415	1.895	2.365	2.998	3.499	4.785	5.408
8	0.2619	0.5459	0.7064	0.8889	1.108	1.397	1.860	2.306	2.896	3.355	4.501	5.041
9	0.2610	0.5435	0.7027	0.8834	1.100	1.383	1.833	2.262	2.821	3.250	4.297	4.781
10	0.2602	0.5415	0.6998	0.8791	1.093	1.372	1.812	2.228	2.764	3.169	4.144	4.587
11	0.2596	0.5399	0.6974	0.8755	1.088	1.363	1.796	2.201	2.718	3.106	4.025	4.437
12	0.2590	0.5386	0.6955	0.8726	1.083	1.356	1.782	2.179	2.681	3.055	3.930	4.318
13	0.2586	0.5375	0.6938	0.8702	1.079	1.350	1.771	2.160	2.650	2.012	3.852	4.221
14	0.2582	0.5366	0.6924	0.8681	1.076	1.345	1.761	2.145	2.624	2.977	3.787	4.140
15	0.2579	0.5357	0.6912	0.8662	1.074	1.341	1.753	2.131	2.602	2.947	3.733	4.073
16	0.2576	0.5350	0.6901	0.8647	1.071	1.337	1.746	2.120	2.583	2.921	3.686	4.015
17	0.2573	0.5344	0.6892	0.8633	1.069	1.333	1.740	2.110	2.567	2.898	3.646	3.965
18	0.2571	0.5338	0.6884	0.8620	1.067	1.330	1.734	2.101	2.552	2.878	3.610	3.922
19	0.2569	0.5333	0.6876	0.8610	1.066	1.328	1.729	2.093	2.539	2.861	3.579	3.883
20	0.2567	0.5329	0.6870	0.8600	1.064	1.325	1.725	2.086	2.528	2.845	3.552	3.850
21	0.2566	0.5325	0.6864	0.8591	1.063	1.323	1.721	2.080	2.518	2.831	3.527	3.819
22	0.2564	0.5321	0.6858	0.8583	1.061	1.321	1.717	2.074	2.508	2.819	3.505	3.792
23	0.2563	0.5317	0.6853	0.8575	1.060	1.319	1.714	2.069	2.500	2.807	3.485	3.768
24	0.2562	0.5314	0.6848	0.8569	1.059	1.318	1.711	2.064	2.492	2.797	3.467	3.745
25	0.2561	0.5312	0.6844	0.8562	1.058	1.316	1.708	2.060	2.485	2.787	3.450	3.725
26	0.2560	0.5309	0.6840	0.8557	1.058	1.315	1.706	2.056	2.479	2.779	3.435	3.707
27	0.2559	0.5306	0.6837	0.8551	1.057	1.314	1 703	2.052	2.473	2.771	3.421	3.690
28	0.2558	0.5304	0.6834	0.8546	1.056	1.313	1.701	2.048	2.467	2.763	3.408	3.674
29	0.2557	0.5302	0.6830	0.8542	1.055	1.311	1.699	2.045	2.462	2.756	3.396	3.659
30	0.2556	0.5300	0.6828	0.8538	1.055	1.310	1.697	2.042	2.457	2.750	3.385	3.646
32	0.2555	0.5297	0.6822	0.8530	1.054	1.309	1.694	2.037	2.449	2.738	3.365	3.622
34	0.2553	0.5294	0.6818	0.8523	1.052	1.307	1.691	2.032	2.441	2.728	3.348	3.601
36	0.2552	0.5291	0.6814	0.8517	1.052	1.306	1.688	2.028	2.434	2.719	3.333	3.582
38	0.2551	0.5288	0.6810	0.8512	1.051	1.304	1.686	2.024	2.429	2.712	3.319	3.566
40	0.2550	0.5286	0.6807	0.8507	1.050	1.303	1.684	2.021	2.423	2.704	3.307	3.551
50	0.2547	0.5278	0.6794	0.8489	1.047	1.299	1.676	2.009	2.403	2.678	3.261	3.496
60	0.2545	0.5272	0.6786	0.8477	1.045	1 296	1.671	2.000	2.390	2.660	3.232	3.460
120	0.2539	0.5258	0.6765	0.8446	1.041	1.289	1.658	1.980	2.358	2.617	3.160	3.373
∞	0.2533	0.5244	0.6745	0.8416	1.036	1.282	1.645	1.960	2.326	2.576	3.090	3.291

This table is reproduced from Lindley and Scott (1984). Reproduced with permission of the Licensor through PLSclear.

A.3 The χ^2 Table

Table A.3. *Percentage points of the χ^2 distribution.*

P	99.95	99.9	99.5	99	97.5	95	90	80	70	60
$v = 1$	$0.0^6 3927$	$0.0^5 1571$	$0.0^4 3927$	$0.0^3 1571$	$0.0^3 9821$	0.003932	0.01579	0.06418	0.1485	0.2750
2	0.001000	0.002001	0.01003	0.02010	0.05064	0.1026	0.2107	0.4463	0.7133	1.022
3	0.01528	0.02430	0.07172	0.1148	0.2158	0.3518	0.5844	1.005	1.424	1.869
4	0.06392	0.09080	0.2070	0.2971	0.4844	0.7107	1.064	1.649	2.195	2.753
5	0.1581	0.2102	0.4117	0.5543	0.8312	1.145	1.610	2.343	3.000	3.655
6	0.2994	0.3811	0.6757	0.8721	1.237	1.635	2.204	3.070	3.828	4.570
7	0.4849	0.5985	0.9893	1.239	1.690	2.167	2.833	3.822	4.671	5.493
8	0.7104	0.8571	1.344	1.646	2.180	2.733	3.490	4.594	5.527	6.423
9	0.9717	1.152	1.735	2.088	2.700	3.325	4.168	5.380	6.393	7.357
10	1.265	1.479	2.156	2.558	3.247	3.940	4.865	6.179	7.267	8.295
11	1.587	1.834	2.603	3.053	3.816	4.575	5.578	6.989	8.148	9.237
12	1.934	2.214	3.074	3.571	4.404	5.226	6.304	7.807	9.034	10.18
13	2.305	2.617	3.565	4.107	5.009	5.892	7.042	8.634	9.926	11.13
14	2.697	3.041	4.075	4.660	5.629	6.571	7.790	9.467	10.82	12.08
15	3.108	3.483	4.601	5.229	6.262	7.261	8.547	10.31	11.72	13.03
16	3.536	3.942	5.142	5.812	6.908	7.962	9.312	11.15	12.62	13.98
17	3.980	4.416	5.697	6.408	7.564	8.672	10.09	12.00	13.53	14.94
18	4.439	4.905	6.265	7.015	8.231	9.390	10.86	12.86	14.44	15.89
19	4.912	5.407	6.844	7.633	8.907	10.12	11.65	13.72	15.35	16.85
20	5.398	5.921	7.434	8.260	9.591	10.85	12.44	14.58	16.27	17.81
21	5.896	6.447	8.034	8.897	10.28	11.59	13.24	15.44	17.18	18.77
22	6.404	6.983	8.643	9.542	10.98	12.34	14.04	16.31	18.10	19.73
23	6.924	7.529	9.260	10.20	11.69	13.09	14.85	17.19	19.02	20.69
24	7.453	8.085	9.886	10.86	12.40	13.85	15.66	18.06	19.94	21.65
25	7.991	8.649	10.52	11.52	13.12	14.61	16.47	18.94	20.87	22.62
26	8.538	9.222	11.16	12.20	13.84	15.38	17.29	19.82	21.79	23.58
27	9.093	9.803	11.81	12.88	14.57	16.15	18.11	20.70	22.72	24.54
28	9.656	10.39	12.46	13.56	15.31	16.93	18.94	21.59	23.65	25.51
29	10.23	10.99	13.12	14.26	16.05	17.71	19.77	22.48	24.58	26.48
30	10.80	11.59	!3.79	14.95	16.79	18.49	20.60	23.36	25.51	27.44
32	11.98	12.81	15.13	16.36	18.29	20.07	22.27	25.15	27.37	29.38
34	13.18	14.06	16.50	17.79	19.81	21.66	23.95	26.94	29.24	31.31
36	14.40	15.32	17.89	19.23	21.34	23.27	25.64	28.73	31.12	33.25
38	15.64	16.61	19.29	20.69	22.88	24.88	27.34	30.54	32.99	35.19
40	16.91	17.92	20.71	22.16	24.43	26.51	29.05	32.34	34.87	37.13
50	23.46	24.67	27.99	29.71	32.36	34.76	37.69	41.45	44.31	46.86
60	30.34	31.74	35.53	37.48	40.48	43.19	46.46	50.64	53.81	56.62
70	37.47	39.04	43.28	45.44	48.76	51.74	55.33	59.90	63.35	66.40
80	44.79	46.52	51.17	53.54	57.15	60.39	64.28	69.21	72.92	76.19
90	52.28	54.16	59.20	61.75	65.65	69.13	73.29	78.56	82.51	85.99
100	59.90	61.92	67.33	70.06	74.22	77.93	82.36	87.95	92.13	95.81

This table is reproduced from Lindley and Scott (1984). Reproduced with permission of the Licensor through PLSclear.

Statistical Tables

Table A.3. *(Cont.)*

P	50	40	30	20	10	5	2.5	1	0.5	0.1	
V = 1	0.4549	0.7083	1.074	1.642	2.706	3.841	5.024	6.635	7.879	10.83	12.12
2	1.386	1.833	2.408	3.219	4.605	5.991	7.378	9.210	10.60	13.82	15.20
3	2.366	2.946	3.665	4.642	6.251	7.815	9.348	11.34	12.84	16.27	17.73
4	3.357	4.045	4.878	5.989	7.779	9.488	11.14	13.28	14.86	18.47	20.00
5	4.351	5.132	6.064	7.289	9.236	11.07	12.83	15.09	16.75	20.52	22.11
6	5.348	6.211	7.231	8.558	10.64	12.59	14.45	16.81	18.55	22.46	24.10
7	6.346	7.283	8.383	9.803	12.02	14.07	16.01	18.48	20.28	24.32	26.02
8	7.344	8.351	9.524	11.03	13.36	15.51	17.53	20.09	21.95	26.12	27.87
9	8.343	9.414	10.66	12.24	14.68	16.92	19.02	21.67	23.59	27.88	29.67
10	9.342	10.47	11.78	13.44	15.99	18.31	20.48	23.21	25.19	29.59	31.42
11	10.34	11.53	12.90	14.63	17.28	19.68	21.92	24.72	26.76	31.26	33.14
12	11.34	12.58	14.01	15.81	18.55	21.03	23.34	26.22	28.30	32.91	34.82
13	12.34	13.64	15.12	16.98	19.81	22.36	24.74	27.69	29.82	34.53	36.48
14	13.34	14.69	16.22	18.15	21.06	23.68	26.12	29.14	31.32	36.12	38.11
15	14.34	15.73	17.32	19.31	22.31	25.00	27.49	30.58	32.80	37.70	39.72
16	15.34	16.78	18.42	20.47	23.54	26.30	28.85	32.00	34.27	39.25	41.31
17	16.34	17.82	19.51	21.61	24.77	27.59	30.19	33.41	35.72	40.79	42.88
18	17.34	18.87	20.60	22.76	25.99	28.87	31.53	34.81	37.16	42.31	44.43
19	18.34	19.91	21.69	23.90	27.20	30.14	32.85	36.19	38.58	43.82	45.97
20	19.34	20.95	22.77	25.04	28.41	31.41	34.17	37.57	40.00	45.31	47.50
21	20.34	21.99	23.86	26.17	29.62	32.67	35.48	38.93	41.40	46.80	49.01
22	21.34	23.03	24.94	27.30	30.81	33.92	36.78	40.29	42.80	48.27	50.51
23	22.34	24.07	26.02	28.43	32.01	35.17	38.08	41.64	44.18	49.73	52.00
24	23.34	25.11	27.10	29.55	33.20	36.42	39.36	42.98	45.56	51.18	53.48
25	24.34	26.14	28.17	30.68	34.38	37.65	40.65	44.31	46.93	52.62	54.95
26	25.34	27.18	29.25	31.79	35.56	38.89	41.92	45.64	48.29	54.05	56.41
27	26.34	28.21	30.32	32.91	36.74	40.11	43.19	46.96	49.64	55.48	57.86
28	27.34	29.25	31.39	34.03	37.92	41.34	44.46	48.28	50.99	56.89	59.30
29	28.34	30.28	32.46	35.14	39.09	42.56	45.72	49.59	52.34	58.30	60.73
30	29.34	31.32	33.53	36.25	40.26	43.77	46.98	50.89	53.67	59.70	62.16
32	31.34	33.38	35.66	38.47	42.58	46.19	49.48	53.49	56.33	62.49	65.00
34	33.34	35.44	37.80	40.68	44.90	48.60	51.97	56.06	58.96	65.25	67.80
36	35.34	37.50	39.92	42.88	47.21	51.00	54.44	58.62	61.58	67.99	70.59
38	37.34	39.56	42.05	45.08	49.51	53.38	56.90	61.16	64.18	70.70	73.35
40	39.34	41.62	44.16	47.27	51.81	55.76	59.34	63.69	66.77	73.40	76.09
50	49.33	51.89	54.72	58.16	63.17	67.50	71.42	76.15	79.49	86.66	89.56
60	59.33	62.13	65.23	68.97	74.40	79.08	83.30	88.38	91.95	99.61	102.7
70	69.33	72.36	75.69	79.71	85.53	90.33	95.02	100.4	104.2	112.3	115.6
80	79.33	82.57	86.12	90.41	96.58	101.9	106.6	112.3	116.3	124.8	128.3
90	89.33	92.76	96.52	101.1	107.6	113.1	118.1	124.1	128.3	137.2	140.8
100	99.33	102.9	106.9	111.7	118.5	124.3	129.6	135.8	140.2	149.4	153.2

A.4 The Table of Critical Values for the Signed Test

Table A.4. *Critical values of T for the signed test.*

	Level of significance α					Level of significance α			
Two-sided	0.10	0.05	0.02	0.01	Two-sided	0.10	0.05	0.02	0.01
One-sided	0.05	0.025	0.01	0.005	One-sided	0.05	0.025	0.01	0.005
n					n				
1	–	–	–	–	31	11	13	15	17
2	–	–	–	–	32	12	14	16	16
3	–	–	–	–	33	11	13	15	17
4	–	–	–	–	34	12	14	16	16
5	5	–	–	–	35	11	13	15	17
6	6	6	–	–	36	12	14	16	18
7	7	7	7	–	37	11	13	17	17
8	6	8	8	8	38	12	14	16	18
9	7	7	9	9	39	13	15	17	17
10	8	8	10	10	40	12	14	16	18
11	7	9	9	11	45	13	15	17	19
12	8	8	10	10	46	14	16	18	20
13	7	9	11	11	49	13	15	19	19
14	8	10	10	12	50	14	16	18	20
15	9	9	11	11	55	15	17	19	21
16	8	10	12	12	56	14	16	18	20
17	9	9	11	13	59	15	17	19	21
18	8	10	12	12	60	14	18	20	22
19	9	11	11	13	65	15	17	21	23
20	10	10	12	14	66	16	18	20	22
21	9	11	13	13	69	15	19	23	25
22	0	12	12	14	70	16	18	22	24
23	9	11	13	15	75	17	19	23	25
24	10	12	14	14	76	16	20	22	24
25	11	11	13	15	79	17	19	23	25
26	10	12	14	14	80	16	20	22	24
27	11	13	13	15	89	17	21	23	27
28	10	12	14	16	90	18	20	24	26
29	11	13	15	15	99	19	21	25	27
30	10	12	14	16	100	18	22	26	28

This table is reproduced from Lindley and Scott (1984).

A.5 The Wilcoxon Table

Table A.5. *Percentage points of Wilcoxon's signed-rank distribution.*

P	5	2.5	1	0.5	0.1	P	5	2.5	1	0.5	0.1
$n=5$	0	–	–	–	–	$n=45$	371	343	312	291	249
6	2	0	–	–	–	46	389	361	328	307	263
7	3	2	0	–	–	47	407	378	345	322	277
8	5	3	1	0	–	48	426	396	362	339	292
9	8	5	3	1	–	49	446	415	379	355	307
10	10	8	5	3	0	50	466	434	397	373	323
11	13	10	7	5	1	51	486	453	416	390	339
12	17	13	9	7	2	52	507	473	434	408	355
13	21	17	12	9	4	53	529	494	454	427	372
14	25	21	15	12	6	54	550	514	473	445	389
15	30	25	19	15	8	55	573	536	493	465	407
16	35	29	23	19	11	56	595	557	514	484	425
17	41	34	27	23	14	57	618	579	535	504	443
18	47	40	32	27	18	58	642	602	556	525	462
19	53	46	37	32	21	59	666	625	578	546	482
20	60	52	43	37	26	60	690	648	600	567	501
21	67	58	49	42	30	61	715	672	623	589	521
22	75	65	55	48	35	62	741	697	646	611	542
23	83	73	62	54	40	63	767	721	669	634	563
24	91	81	69	61	45	64	793	747	693	657	584
25	100	89	76	68	51	65	820	772	718	681	606
26	110	98	84	75	58	66	847	798	742	705	628
27	119	107	92	83	64	67	875	825	768	729	651
28	130	116	101	91	71	68	903	852	793	754	674
29	140	126	110	100	79	69	931	879	819	779	697
30	151	137	120	109	86	70	960	907	846	805	721
31	163	147	130	118	94	71	990	936	573	831	745
32	175	159	140	128	103	72	1020	964	901	858	770
33	187	170	151	138	112	73	1050	994	928	884	795
34	200	182	162	148	121	74	1081	1023	957	912	821
35	213	195	173	159	131	75	1112	1053	986	940	847
36	227	208	185	171	141	76	1144	1084	1015	968	873
37	241	221	198	182	151	77	1176	1115	1044	997	900
38	256	235	211	194	162	78	1209	1147	1075	1026	927
39	271	249	224	207	173	79	1242	1179	1105	1056	955
40	286	264	238	220	185	80	1276	1211	1136	1086	983
41	302	279	252	233	197	81	1310	1244	1168	1116	1011
42	319	294	266	247	209	82	1345	1277	1200	1147	1040
43	336	310	281	261	222	83	1380	1311	1232	1178	1070
44	353	327	296	276	235	84	1415	1345	1265	1210	1099
45	371	343	312	291	249	85	1451	1380	1298	1242	1130

This table is reproduced from Lindley and Scott (1984). Reproduced with permission of the Licensor through PLSclear.

A.6 The *F*-Ratio Table

Table A.6(a). *10% points of the F distribution.*

$v_1 =$	1	2	3	4	5	6	7	8	10	12	24	∞
$v_2 = 1$	39.86	49.50	53.59	55.83	57.24	58.20	58.91	59.44	60.19	60.71	62.00	63.33
2	8.526	9.000	9.162	9.243	9.293	9.326	9.349	9.367	9.392	9.408	9.450	9.491
3	5.538	5.462	5.391	5.343	5.309	5.285	5.266	5.252	5.230	5.216	5.176	5.134
4	4.545	4.325	4.191	4.107	4.051	4.010	3.979	3.955	3.920	3.896	3.831	3.761
5	4.060	3.780	3.619	3.520	3.453	3.405	3.368	3.339	3.297	3.268	3.191	3.105
6	3.776	3.463	3.289	3.181	3.108	3.055	3.014	2.983	2.937	2.905	2.818	2.722
7	3.589	3.257	3.074	2.961	2.883	2.827	2.785	2.752	2.703	2.668	2.575	2.471
8	3.458	3.113	2.924	2.806	2.726	2.668	2.624	2.589	2.538	2.502	2.404	2.293
9	3.360	3.006	2.813	2.693	2.611	2.551	2.505	2.469	2.416	2.379	2.277	2.159
10	3.285	2.924	2.728	2.605	2.522	2.461	2.414	2.377	2.323	2.284	2.178	2.055
11	3.225	2.860	2.660	2.536	2.451	2.389	2.342	2.304	2.248	2.209	2.100	1.972
12	3.177	2.807	2.606	2.480	2.394	2.331	2.283	2.245	2.188	2.147	2.036	1.904
13	3.136	2.763	2.560	2.434	2.347	2.283	2.234	2.195	2.138	2.097	1.983	1.846
14	3.102	2.726	2.522	2.395	2.307	2.243	2.193	2.154	2.095	2.054	1.938	1.797
15	3.073	2.695	2.490	2.361	2.273	2.208	2.158	2.119	2.059	2.017	1.899	1.755
16	3.048	2.668	2.462	2.333	2.244	2.178	2.128	2.088	2.028	1.985	1.866	1.718
17	3.026	2.645	2.437	2.308	2.218	2.152	2.102	2.061	2.001	1.958	1.836	1.686
18	3.007	2.624	2.416	2.286	2.196	2.130	2.079	2.038	1.977	1.933	1.810	1.657
19	2.990	2.606	2.397	2.266	2.176	2.109	2.058	2.017	1.956	1.912	1.787	1.631
20	2.975	2.589	2.380	2.249	2.158	2.091	2.040	1.999	1.937	1.892	1.767	1.607
21	2.961	2.575	2.365	2.233	2.142	2.075	2.023	1.982	1.920	1.875	1.748	1.586
22	2.949	2.561	2.351	2.219	2.128	2.060	2.008	1.967	1.904	1.859	1.731	1.567
23	2.937	2.549	2.339	2.207	2.115	2.047	1.995	1.953	1.890	1.845	1.716	1.549
24	2.927	2.538	2.327	2.195	2.103	2.035	1.983	1.941	1.877	1.832	1.702	1.533
25	2.918	2.528	2.317	2.184	2.092	2.024	1.971	1.929	1.866	1.820	1.689	1.518
26	2.909	2.519	2.307	2.174	2.082	2.014	1.961	1.919	1.855	1.809	1.677	1.504
27	2.901	2.511	2.299	2.165	2.073	2.005	1.952	1.909	1.845	1.799	1.666	1.491
28	2.894	2.503	2.291	2.157	2.064	1.996	1.943	1.900	1.836	1.790	1.656	1.478
29	2.887	2.495	2.283	2.149	2.057	1.988	1.935	1.892	1.827	1.781	1.647	1.467
30	2.881	2.489	2.276	2.142	2.049	1.980	1.927	1.884	1.819	1.773	1.638	1.456
32	2.869	2.477	2.263	2.129	2.036	1.967	1.913	1.870	1.805	1.758	1.622	1.437
34	2.859	2.466	2.252	2.118	2.024	1.955	1.901	1.858	1.793	1.745	1.608	1.419
36	2.850	2.456	2.243	2.108	2.014	1.945	1.891	1.847	1.781	1.734	1.595	1.404
38	2.842	2.448	2.234	2.099	2.005	1.935	1.881	1.838	1.772	1.724	1.584	1.390
40	2.835	2.440	2.226	2.091	1.997	1.927	1.873	1.829	1.763	1.715	1.574	1.377
60	2.791	2.393	2.177	2.041	1.946	1.875	1.819	1.775	1.707	1.657	1.511	1.291
120	2.748	2.347	2.130	1.992	1.896	1.824	1.767	1.722	1.652	1.601	1.447	1.193
∞	2.706	2.303	2.084	1.945	1.847	1.774	1.717	1.670	1.599	1.546	1.383	1.000

This table is reproduced from Lindley and Scott (1984). Reproduced with permission of the Licensor through PLSclear.

Statistical Tables

Table A.6(b). *5% points of the F distribution.*

$v_1 =$	1	2	3	4	5	6	7	8	10	12	24	∞
$v_2 = 1$	161.4	199.5	215.7	224.6	230.2	234.0	236.8	238.9	241.9	243.9	249.1	254.3
2	18.51	19.00	19.16	19.25	19.30	19.33	19.35	19.37	19.40	19.41	19.45	19.50
3	10.13	9.552	9.277	9.117	9.013	8.941	8.887	8.845	8.786	8.745	8.639	8.526
4	7.709	6.944	6.591	6.388	6.256	6.163	6.094	6.041	5.964	5.912	5.774	5.628
5	6.608	5.786	5.409	5.192	5.050	4.950	4.876	4.818	4.735	4.678	4.527	4.365
6	5.987	5.143	4.757	4.534	4.387	4.284	4.207	4.147	4.060	4.000	3.841	3.669
7	5.591	4.737	4.347	4.120	3.972	3.866	3.787	3.726	3.637	3.575	3.410	3.230
8	5.318	4.459	4.066	3.838	3.687	3.581	3.500	3.438	3.347	3.284	3.115	2.928
9	5.117	4.256	3.863	3.633	3.482	3.374	3.293	3.230	3.137	3.073	2.900	2.707
10	4.965	4.103	3.708	3.478	3.326	3.217	3.135	3.072	2.978	2.913	2.737	2.538
11	4.844	3.982	3.587	3.357	3.204	3.095	3.012	2.948	2.854	2.788	2.609	2.404
12	4.747	3.885	3.490	3.259	3.106	2.996	2.913	2.849	2.753	2.687	2.505	2.296
13	4.667	3.806	3.411	3.179	3.025	2.915	2.832	2.767	2.671	2.604	2.420	2.206
14	4.600	3.739	3.344	3.112	2.958	2.848	2.764	2.699	2.602	2.534	2.349	2.131
15	4.543	3.682	3.287	3.056	2.901	2.790	2.707	2.641	2.544	2.475	2.288	2.066
16	4.494	3.634	3.239	3.007	2.852	2.741	2.657	2.591	2.494	2.425	2.235	2.010
17	4.451	3.592	3.197	2.965	2.810	2.699	2.614	2.548	2.450	2.381	2.190	1.960
18	4.414	3.555	3.160	2.928	2.773	2.661	2.577	2.510	2.412	2.342	2.150	1.917
19	4.381	3.522	3.127	2.895	2.740	2.628	2.544	2.477	2.378	2.308	2.114	1.878
20	4.351	3.493	3.098	2.866	2.711	2.599	2.514	2.447	2.348	2.278	2.082	1.843
21	4.325	3.467	3.072	2.840	2.685	2.573	2.488	2.420	2.321	2.250	2.054	1.812
22	4.301	3.443	3.049	2.817	2.661	2.549	2.464	2.397	2.297	2.226	2.028	1.783
23	4.279	3.422	3.028	2.796	2.640	2.528	2.442	4.375	2.275	2.204	2.005	1.757
24	4.260	3.403	3.009	2.776	2.621	2.508	2.423	2.355	2.255	2.183	1.984	1.733
25	4.242	3.385	2.991	2.759	2.603	2.490	2.405	2.337	2.236	2.165	1.964	1.711
26	4.225	3.369	2.975	2.743	2.587	2.474	2.388	2.321	2.220	2.148	1.946	1.691
27	4.210	3.354	2.960	2.728	2.572	2.459	2.373	2.305	2.204	2.132	1.930	1.672
28	4.196	3.340	2.947	2.714	2.558	2.445	2.359	2.291	2.190	2.118	1.915	1.654
29	4.183	3.328	2.934	2.701	2.545	2.432	2.346	2.278	2.177	2.104	1.901	1.638
30	4.171	3.316	2.922	2.690	2.534	2.421	2.334	2.266	2.165	2.092	1.887	1.622
32	4.149	3.295	2.901	2.668	2.512	2.399	2.313	2.244	2.142	2.070	1.864	1.594
34	4.130	3.276	2.883	2.650	2.494	2.380	2.294	2.225	2.123	2.050	1.843	1.569
36	4.113	3.259	2.866	2.634	2.477	2.364	2.277	2.209	2.106	2.033	1.824	1.547
38	4.098	3.245	2.852	2.619	2.463	2.349	2.262	2.194	2.091	2.017	1.808	1.527
40	4.085	3.232	2.839	2.606	2.449	2.336	2.249	2.180	2.077	2.003	1.793	1.509
60	4.001	3.150	2.758	2.525	2.368	2.254	2.167	2.097	1.993	1.917	1.700	1.389
120	3.920	3.072	2.680	2.447	2.290	2.175	2.087	2.016	1.910	1.834	1.608	1.254
∞	3.841	2.996	2.605	2.372	2.214	2.099	2.010	1.938	1.831	1.752	1.517	1.000

This table is reproduced from Lindley and Scott (1984). Reproduced with permission of the Licensor through PLSclear.

Table A.6(c). *2.5% points of the F distribution.*

$v_1 =$	1	2	3	4	5	6	7	8	10	12	24	∞
$v_2 = 1$	647.8	799.5	864.2	899.6	921.8	937.1	948.2	956.7	968.6	976.7	997.2	1018
2	38.51	39.00	39.17	39.25	39.30	39.33	39.36	39.37	39.40	39.41	39.46	39.50
3	17.44	16.04	15.44	15.10	14.88	14.73	14.62	14.54	14.42	14.34	14.12	13.90
4	12.22	10.65	9.979	9.605	9.364	9.197	9.074	8.980	8.844	8.751	8.511	8.257
5	10.01	8.434	7.764	7.388	7.146	6.978	6.853	6.757	6.619	6.525	6.278	6.015
6	8.813	7.260	6.599	6.227	5.988	5.820	5.695	5.600	5.461	5.366	5.117	4.849
7	8.073	6.542	5.890	5.523	5.285	5.119	4.995	4.899	4.761	4.666	4.415	4.142
8	7.571	6.059	5.416	5.053	4.817	4.652	4.529	4.433	4.295	4.200	3.947	3.670
9	7.209	5.715	5.078	4.718	4.484	4.320	4.197	4.102	3.964	3.868	3.614	3.333
10	6.937	5.456	4.826	4.468	4.236	4.072	3.950	3.855	3.717	3.621	3.365	3.080
11	6.724	5.256	4.630	4.275	4.044	3.881	3.759	3.664	3.526	3.430	3.173	2.883
12	6.554	5.096	4.474	4.121	3.891	3.728	3.607	3.512	3.374	3.277	3.019	2.725
13	6.414	4.965	4.347	3.996	3.767	3.604	3.483	3.388	3.250	3.153	2.893	2.595
14	6.298	4.857	4.242	3.892	3.663	3.501	3.380	3.285	3.147	3.050	2.789	2.487
15	6.200	4.765	4.153	3.804	3.576	3.415	3.293	3.199	3.060	2.963	2.701	2.395
16	6.115	4.687	4.077	3.729	3.502	3.341	3.219	3.125	2.986	2.889	2.625	2.316
17	6.042	4.619	4.011	3.665	3.438	3.277	3.156	3.061	2.922	2.825	2.560	2.247
18	5.978	4.560	3.954	3.608	3.382	3.221	3.100	3.005	2.866	2.769	2.503	2.187
19	5.922	4.508	3.903	3.559	3.333	3.172	3.051	2.956	2.817	2.720	2.452	2.133
20	5.871	4.461	3.859	3.515	3.289	3.128	3.007	2.913	2.774	2.676	2.408	2.085
21	5.827	4.420	3.819	3.475	3.250	3.090	2.969	2.874	2.735	2.637	2.368	2.042
22	5.786	4.383	3.783	3.440	3.215	3.055	2.934	2.839	2.700	2.602	2.331	2.003
23	5.750	4.349	3.750	3.408	3.183	3.023	2.902	2.808	2.668	2.570	2.299	1.968
24	5.717	4.319	3.721	3.379	3.155	2.995	2.874	2.779	2.640	2.541	2.269	1.935
25	5.686	4.291	3.694	3.353	3.129	2.969	2.848	2.753	2.613	2.515	2.242	1.906
26	5.659	4.265	3.670	3.329	3.105	2.945	2.824	2.729	2.590	2.491	2.217	1.878
27	5.633	4.242	3.647	3.307	3.083	2.923	2.802	2.707	2.568	2.469	2.195	1.853
28	5.610	4.221	3.626	3.286	3.063	2.903	2.782	2.687	2.547	2.448	2.174	1.829
29	5.588	4.201	3.607	3.267	3.044	2.884	2.763	2.669	2.529	2.430	2.154	1.807
30	5.568	4.182	3.589	3.250	3.026	2.867	2.746	2.651	2.511	2.412	2.136	1.787
32	5.531	4.149	3.557	3.218	2.995	2.836	2.715	2.620	2.480	2.381	2.103	1.750
34	5.499	4.120	3.529	3.191	2.968	2.808	2.688	2.593	2.453	2.353	2.075	1.717
36	5.471	4.094	3.505	3.167	2.944	2.785	2.664	2.569	2.429	2.329	2.049	1.687
38	5.446	4.071	3.483	3.145	2.923	2.763	2.643	2.548	2.407	2.307	2.027	1.661
40	5.424	4.051	3.463	3.126	2.904	2.744	2.624	2.529	2.388	2.288	2.007	1.637
60	5.286	3.925	3.343	3.008	2.786	2.627	2.507	2.412	2.270	2.169	1.882	1.482
120	5.152	3.805	3.227	2.894	2.674	2.515	2.395	2.299	2.157	2.055	1.760	1.310
∞	5.024	3.689	3.116	2.786	2.567	2.408	2.288	2.192	2.048	1.945	1.640	1.000

Table A.6(d). *1% points of the F distribution.*

$v_1 =$	1	2	3	4	5	6	7	8	10	12	24	∞
$v_2 = 1$	4052	4999	5403	5625	5764	5859	5928	5981	6056	6106	6235	6366
2	98.50	99.00	99.17	99.25	99.30	99.33	99.36	99.37	99.40	99.42	99.46	99.50
3	34.12	30.82	29.46	28.71	28.24	27.91	27.67	27.49	27.23	27.05	26.60	26.13
4	21.20	18.00	16.69	15.98	15.52	15.21	14.98	14.80	14.55	14.37	13.93	13.46
5	16.26	13.27	12.06	11.39	10.97	10.67	10.46	10.29	10.05	9.888	9.466	9.020
6	13.75	10.92	9.780	9.148	8.746	8.466	8.260	8.102	7.874	7.718	7.313	6.880
7	12.25	9.547	8.451	7.847	7.460	7.191	6.993	6.840	6.620	6.469	6.074	5.650
8	11.26	8.649	7.591	7.006	6.632	6.371	6.178	6.029	5.814	5.667	5.279	4.859
9	10.56	8.022	6.992	6.422	6.057	5.802	5.613	5.467	5.257	5.111	4.729	4.311
10	10.04	7.559	6.552	5.994	5.636	5.386	5.200	5.057	4.849	4.706	4.327	3.909
11	9.646	7.206	6.217	5.668	5.316	5.069	4.886	4.744	4.539	4.397	4.021	3.602
12	9.330	6.927	5.953	5.412	5.064	4.821	4.640	4.499	4.296	4.155	3.780	3.361
13	9.074	6.701	5.739	5.205	4.862	4.620	4.441	4.302	4.100	3.960	3.587	3.165
14	8.862	6.515	5.564	5.035	4.695	4.456	4.278	4.140	3.939	3.800	3.427	3.004
15	8.683	6.359	5.417	4.893	4.556	4.318	4.142	4.004	3.805	3.666	3.294	2.868
16	8.531	6.226	5.292	4.773	4.437	4.202	4.026	3.890	3.691	3.553	3.181	2.753
17	8.400	6.112	5.185	4.669	4.336	4.102	3.927	3.791	3.593	3.455	3.084	2.653
18	8.285	6.013	5.092	4.579	4.248	4.015	3.841	3.705	3.508	3.371	2.999	2.566
19	8.185	5.926	5.010	4.500	4.171	3.939	3.765	3.631	3.434	3.297	2.925	2.489
20	8.096	5.849	4.938	4.431	4.103	3.871	3.699	3.564	3.368	3.231	2.859	2.421
21	8.017	5.780	4.874	4.369	4.042	3.812	3.640	3.506	3.310	3.173	2.801	2.360
22	7.945	5.719	4.817	4.313	3.988	3.758	3.587	3.453	3.258	3.121	2.749	2.305
23	7.881	5.664	4.765	4.264	3.939	3.710	3.539	3.406	3.211	3.074	2.702	2.256
24	7.823	5.614	4.718	4.218	3.895	3.667	3.496	3.363	3.168	3.032	2.659	2.211
25	7.770	5.568	4.675	4.177	3.855	3.627	3.457	3.324	3.129	2.993	2.620	2.169
26	7.721	5.526	4.637	4.140	3.818	3.591	3.421	3.288	3.094	2.958	2.585	2.131
27	7.677	5.488	4.601	4.106	3.785	3.558	3.388	3.256	3.062	2.926	2.552	2.097
28	7.636	5.453	4.568	4.074	3.754	3.528	3.358	3.226	3.032	2.896	2.522	2.064
29	7.598	5.420	4.538	4.045	3.725	3.499	3.330	3.198	3.005	2.868	2.495	2.034
30	7.562	5.390	4.510	4.018	3.699	3.473	3.304	3.173	2.979	2.843	2.469	2.006
32	7.499	5.336	4.459	3.969	3.652	3.427	3.258	3.127	2.934	2.798	2.423	1.956
34	7.444	5.289	4.416	3.927	3.611	3.386	3.218	3.087	2.894	2.758	2.383	1.911
36	7.396	5.248	4.377	3.890	3.574	3.351	3.183	3.052	2.859	2.723	2.347	1.872
38	7.353	5.211	4.343	3.858	3.542	3.319	3.152	3.021	2.828	2.692	2.316	1.837
40	7.314	5.179	4.313	3.828	3.514	3.291	3.124	2.993	2.801	2.665	2.288	1.805
60	7.077	4.977	4.126	3.649	3.339	3.119	3.953	2.823	2.632	2.496	2.115	1.601
120	6.851	4.787	3.949	3.480	3.174	2.956	2.792	2.663	2.472	2.336	1.950	1.381
∞	6.635	4.605	3.782	3.319	3.017	2.802	2.639	2.511	2.321	2.185	1.791	1.000

This table is reproduced from Lindley and Scott (1984). Reproduced with permission of the Licensor through PLSclear.

A.7 The Friedman Table

Table A.7. *Upper percentage points of Friedman's distribution.*

k = 3

P	10	5	2.5	1	0.1
n = 3	6.000	6.000	–	–	–
4	6.000	6.500	8.000	8.000	–
5	5.200	6.400	7.600	8.400	10.00
6	5.333	7.000	8.333	9.000	12.00
7	5.429	7.143	7.714	8.857	12.29
8	5.250	6.250	7.750	9.000	12.25
9	5.556	6.222	8.000	9.556	12.67
10	5.000	6.200	7.800	9.600	12.60
11	5.091	6.545	7.818	9.455	13.27
12	5.167	6.500	8.000	9.500	12.67
13	4.769	6.615	7.538	9.385	12.46
14	5.143	6.143	7.429	9.143	13.29
15	4.933	6.400	7.600	8.933	12.93
16	4.875	6.500	7.625	9.375	13.50
17	5.059	6.118	7.412	9.294	13.06
18	4.778	6.333	7.444	9.000	13.00
19	5.053	6.421	7.684	9.579	13.37
20	4.900	6.300	7.500	9.300	13.30
21	4.952	6.095	7.524	9.238	13.24
22	4.727	6.091	7.364	9.091	13.45
23	4.957	6.348	7.913	9.391	13.13
24	5.083	6.250	7.750	9.250	13.08
25	4.880	6.080	7.440	8.960	13.52
26	4.846	6.077	7.462	9.308	13.23
27	4.741	6.000	7.407	9.407	13.41
28	4.571	6.500	7.714	9.214	13.50
29	5.034	6.276	7.517	9.172	13.52
30	4.867	6.200	7.400	9.267	13.40
31	4'839	6.000	7.548	9.290	13.42
32	4.750	6.063	7.563	9.250	13.69
33	4.788	6.061	7.515	9.152	13.52
34	4.765	6.059	7.471	9.176	13.41
∞	4.605	5.99I	7.378	9.210	13.82

k = 4

P	10	5	2.5	1	0.1
n = 3	6.600	7.400	8.200	9.000	–
4	6.300	7.800	8.400	9.600	11.10
5	6.360	7.800	8.760	9.960	12.60
6	6.400	7.600	8.800	10.20	12.80
7	6.429	7.800	9.000	10.54	13.46
8	6.300	7.650	9.000	10.50	13.80
9	6.200	7.667	8.867	10.73	14.07
10	6.360	7.680	9.000	10.68	14.52
11	6.273	7.691	9.000	10.75	14.56
12	6.300	7.700	9.100	10.80	14.80
13	6.138	7.800	9.092	10.85	14.91
14	6.343	7.714	9.086	10.89	15.09
15	6.280	7.720	9.160	10.92	15.08
16	6.300	7.800	9.150	10.95	15.15
17	6.318	7.800	9.212	11.05	15.28
18	6.333	7.733	9.200	10.93	15.27
19	6.347	7.863	9.253	11.02	15.44
20	6.240	7.800	9.240	11.10	15.36
∞	6.251	7.815	9.348	11.34	16.27

k = 5

P	10	5	2.5	1	0.1
n = 3	7.467	8.533	9.600	10.13	11.47
4	7.600	8.800	9.800	11.20	13.20
5	7.680	8.960	10.24	11.68	14.40
6	7.733	9.067	10.40	11.87	15.20
7	7.771	9.143	10.51	12.11	15.66
8	7.700	9.200	10.60	12.30	16.00
9	7.733	9.244	10.67	12.44	16.36
∞	7.779	9.488	11.14	13.28	18.47

k = 6

P	10	5	2.5	1	0.1
n = 3	8.714	9.857	10.81	11.76	13.29
4	9.000	10.29	11.43	12.71	15.29
5	9.000	10.49	11.74	13.23	16.43
6	9.048	10.57	12.00	13.62	17.05
∞	9.236	11.07	12.83	15.09	20.52

A.8 The Table of Critical Values for the Tukey Test

Table A.8. *Critical values of the studentized range statistic[1] for use with Tukey test.*

		Number of groups								
df$_{wG}$	α	2	3	4	5	6	7	8	9	10
5	.05	3.64	4.60	5.22	5.67	6.03	6.33	6.58	6.80	6.99
	.01	5.70	6.98	7.80	8.42	8.91	9.32	9.67	9.97	10.24
6	.05	3.46	4.34	4.90	5.30	5.63	5.90	6.12	6.32	6.49
	.01	5.24	6.33	7.03	7.56	7.97	8.32	8.61	8.87	9.10
7	.05	3.34	4.16	4.68	5.06	5.36	5.61	5.82	6.00	6.16
	.01	4.95	5.92	6.54	7.01	7.37	7.68	7.94	8.17	8.37
8	.05	3.26	4.04	4.53	4.89	5.17	5.40	5.60	5.77	5.92
	.01	4.75	5.64	6.20	6.62	6.96	7.24	7.47	7.68	7.86
9	.05	3.20	3.95	4.41	4.76	5.02	5.24	5.43	5.59	5.74
	.01	4.60	5.43	5.96	6.35	6.66	6.91	7.13	7.33	7.49
10	.05	3.15	3.88	4.33	4.65	4.91	5.12	5.30	5.46	5.60
	.01	4.48	5.27	5.77	6.14	6.43	6.67	6.87	7.05	7.21
11	.05	3.11	3.82	4.26	4.57	4.82	5.03	5.20	5.35	5.49
	.01	4.39	5.15	5.62	5.97	6.25	6.48	6.67	6.84	6.99
12	.05	3.08	3.77	4.20	4.51	4.75	4.95	5.12	5.27	5.39
	.01	4.32	5.05	5.50	5.84	6.10	6.32	6.51	6.67	6.81
13	.05	3.06	3.73	4.15	4.45	4.69	4.88	5.05	5.19	5.32
	.01	4.26	4.96	5.40	5.73	5.98	6.19	6.37	6.53	6.67
14	.05	3.03	3.70	4.11	4.41	4.64	4.83	4.99	5.13	5.25
	.01	4.21	4.89	5.32	5.63	5.88	6.08	6.26	6.41	6.54
15	.05	3.01	3.67	4.08	4.37	4.59	4.78	4.94	5.08	5.20
	.01	4.17	4.84	5.25	5.56	5.80	5.99	6.16	6.31	6.44
16	.05	3.00	3.65	4.05	4.33	4.56	4.74	4.90	5.03	5.15
	.01	4.13	4.79	5.19	5.49	5.72	5.92	6.08	6.22	6.35
17	.05	2.98	3.63	4.02	4.30	4.52	4.70	4.86	4.99	5.11
	.01	4.10	4.74	5.14	5.43	5.66	5.85	6.01	6.15	6.27
18	.05	2.97	3.61	4.00	4.28	4.49	4.67	4.82	4.96	5.07
	.01	4.07	4.70	5.09	5.38	5.60	5.79	5.94	6.08	6.20
19	.05	2.96	3.59	3.98	4.25	4.47	4.65	4.79	4.92	5.04
	.01	4.05	4.67	5.05	5.33	5.55	5.73	5.89	6.02	6.14
20	.05	2.95	3.58	3.96	4.23	4.45	4.62	4.77	4.90	5.01
	.01	4.02	4.64	5.02	5.29	5.51	5.69	5.84	5.97	6.09
24	.05	2.92	3.53	3.90	4.17	4.37	4.54	4.68	4.81	4.92
	.01	3.96	4.55	4.91	5.17	5.37	5.54	5.69	5.81	5.92
30	.05	2.89	3.49	3.85	4.10	4.30	4.46	4.60	4.72	4.82
	.01	3.89	4.45	4.80	5.05	5.24	5.40	5.54	5.65	5.76
40	.05	2.86	3.44	3.79	4.04	4.23	4.39	4.52	4.63	4.73
	.01	3.82	4.37	4.70	4.93	5.11	5.26	5.39	5.50	5.60
60	.05	2.83	3.40	3.74	3.98	4.16	4.31	4.44	4.55	4.65
	.01	3.76	4.28	4.59	4.82	4.99	5.13	5.25	5.36	5.45
120	.05	2.80	3.36	3.68	3.92	4.10	4.24	4.36	4.47	4.56
	.01	3.70	4.20	4.50	4.71	4.87	5.01	5.12	5.21	5.30
∞	.05	2.77	3.31	3.63	3.86	4.03	4.17	4.29	4.39	4.47
	.01	3.64	4.12	4.40	4.60	4.76	4.88	4.99	5.08	5.16

[1] This table is abridged from Table 29 in Pearson and Hartley (1970).

Appendix B

Advanced Topics in Classification Metrics

Performance metrics for classification represent a very large area of investigation. While Chapter 5 presented the principal elements of this vast field, this appendix is devoted to a number of more advanced topics that have been left out of the main discussion for clarity's sake. We first discuss further work that has been done on both quantitative and qualitative metrics and touch upon more recent considerations related to how to evaluate machine learning-based systems ahead of deployment. We then discuss both theoretical and experimental frameworks that have been proposed for evaluation, survey a number of methods that have been proposed to combine different metrics beyond those already discussed such as the F-Measure, G-Mean, etc., and conclude the appendix with insights from machine learning theory. Most of the information conveyed in this appendix first appeared in Japkowicz and Shah (2011). The appendix can be skipped without consequences for the rest of the book.

B.1 Performance Metrics

We survey two different types of advances that have been made in the study and design of performance metrics. The first ones continue to address the traditional performance criteria already discussed in Chapters 3 and 4, while the second moves beyond these criteria to include qualitative considerations. Let us discuss these advances in turn.

B.1.1 Quantitative Metrics

Various attempts have been made to study the characteristics of individual performance metrics and to identify their limitations. In addition, attempts have also been made to study the interrelation between pairs of performance metrics in the hope of studying their suitability in various scenarios and applications. The measure that traditionally received the most attention is accuracy (and hence, indirectly, the misclassification error), since it has long been the metric of choice for reporting the empirical performance of classifiers. This, then, is followed by studies on the area under the receiver operating characteristic (ROC) curve (AUC), which subsequently replaced accuracy as the preferred metric for reporting results on scoring classifiers due to its ability to summarize the performance of algorithms over different cost ratios. Inevitably, this led to studies that focused on investigating the comparative behavior of the two metrics, yielding some interesting insights. These include Provost and Domingos (2003); Ferri et al. (2003); Cortes and Mohri (2004). An interesting insight was also obtained by Rosset (2004), who experimentally showed how optimizing AUC on a validation set yields better accuracy on the test set. This was an interesting finding in terms of the interrelation between the performance metrics and their potential agreement. Other studies have focussed on alternate metric pairs for comparison (e.g., Davis and Goadrich (2006) and Saito and Rehmsmeier (2015) compare ROC and precision-recall curves, also known as PR-curves). Efforts at studying the statistical characteristics of some extensions to AUC in specific settings have also been made (see, for instance, He and Frey (2008) and references therein for medical imaging application). Performance guarantees over the AUC and ROC curves, in general, have also been studied in terms of confidence bounds (see, for instance, Cortes and Mohri (2005) for confidence bounds on AUC, Macskassy et al. (2005) for pointwise confidence bounds on ROC, and references therein for more general confidence bands around ROCs, as well as Cho et al. (2019) and Yousef et al. (2005) on another approach to studying the uncertainty of the mean AUC). Yousef et al. (2006) also use AUC and its statistical properties to assess classifiers.

These and other efforts have also enabled a better understanding of measures such as the AUC and identifying their limitations. The limitations of AUC, in particular, have been studied in Vanderlooy and Hüllermeier (2008), Hand (2006), and Halligan et al. (2014), among others. These are, indeed, clearly articulated by Hand (2009), who also proposes an alternative summary statistic called the H measure to alleviate these limitations. This measure depends on the class priors, unlike the AUC, and addresses one of the main concerns of the AUC - that of treating the cost considerations as a classifier-specific problem. This, indeed, should not be the case since relative costs should be the property of the problem domain, independently of the learning algorithm applied.

Other novel metrics have also been proposed such as the scored AUC (abbreviated to SAUC) (Wu et al. 2007), which aims to address the dependency of AUC on score imbalances (less positive scores than negative for instance), implicitly mitigating the effects of class imbalance. In a similar context, Klement et al. (2011) show how to build a more precise scored ROC curve and calculate a scored AUC from it. In a different vein, an extension of the AUC to multiple classes was proposed by Kleiman and Page (2019), while Santos-Rodríguez et al. (2009) investigate the utility of the adjusted Rand index, a commonly used measure in unsupervised learning, for performance assessment as well as model selection in classification, and Chicco and Jurman (2020) compare Matthews' correlation coefficient to accuracy and the $F1$-measure for binary classification. While these and other novel metrics open the way for new evaluation methods, it is important to note that they have yet to be rigorously studied and validated against current measures before they become mainstream.

The issue of asymmetric cost, where the cost of misclassifying an instance of one class differs from that of other class(es), has also received considerable attention, albeit in the context of specific metrics. The inherent difficulty in obtaining specific costs has long been appreciated by the machine learning community, leading, in part, to cost- or skew-ratio approaches such as ROC analysis, based on the premise that even though quantifying specific misclassification costs might be difficult, it might be possible to provide relative costs. Other efforts have also been made with regard to cost-sensitive learning, as it is quite often referred to. See, for instance, Santos-Rodríguez et al. (2009) with regard to using Bregman divergences for this purpose, Zadrozny and Elkan (2002), Lachiche and Flach (2003), and O'Brien et al. (2008) for cost-sensitive learning using Bayesian theory, Zadrozny et al. (2003) and Liu and Zhou (2006) for approaches based on training instance weighting, and Landgrebe et al. (2004) for examples of such attempts in experimental settings. Previous attempts to perform cost-sensitive learning with regard to individual classifiers include those of Bradford et al. (1998), Kukar and Kononenko (1998), and Fan et al. (1999).

Other proposed metrics include extensions to existing metrics and new measures for ensemble classifiers. Various approaches with regard to combination of classifiers and their subsequent evaluation have been proposed. Some specific works include Kuncheva et al. (2003) and Melnik et al. (2004) on analyzing accuracy-based measures, while Lebanon and Lafferty (2002), Freund et al. (2003), and Cortes and Mohri (2004) focus on alternate measures in such scenarios. Theoretical guarantees and analysis have also been proposed with regard to these measures. See, for instance Narasimhamurthy (2005) for theoretical bounds over the performance of ensemble classifiers, and Murua (2002) for bounds on error rates for linear combinations of classifiers.

The relationship between performance metrics and their use for model selection has also been investigated. In addition to the work done on ROC curves for this purpose, probabilistic measures have been investigated by Zadrozny and Elkan (2002). See also Yan et al. (2003) for the use of the Wilcoxon–Mann–Whitney statistic for model selection and Gardner et al. (2018) for evaluating probabilistic models outputs. Learning theoretic attempts have also been made to assess classifier performance using risk bounds and using these to subsequently guide the learning process (see, for instance, Shah (2006) and Laviolette et al. (2010)).

Our overview of approaches for designing, analyzing, comparing, and characterizing performance metrics in various settings is not meant to be comprehensive, but to be representative of the work that has been pursued in this area. Constant advances are being made and we have, inevitably, missed some complementary approaches, not to mention approaches related to reinforcement learning, active learning, online learning, unsupervised learning, and so on, where performance assessments take on different meanings with regard to the assessment criteria of interest. Such methods are discussed in Chapter 8, although again, we cannot guarantee complete coverage of all the proposed approaches.

B.1.2 Qualitative Metrics

The performance criteria studied so far aim at evaluating the algorithms empirically on various kinds of data. This, however, does not provide the means for performing any kind of qualitative evaluation. Drummond (2006) emphasized the need to look at criteria of importance that cannot be easily assessed because of their qualitative nature, in conjunction with the traditional empirical performance criteria, in order to assess and compare learning algorithms properly. These criteria include, for example, understandability, usability, novelty, interestingness of the discovered rules, and so on. Such concerns with regard to qualitative evaluation have, in fact, been raised before. Nakhaeizadeh and Schnabl (1998), for instance, looked at the issue of qualitative criteria earlier and broadly categorized these as nominal or ordinal. While the nominal criteria, those that assign a category to the performance, are not directly comparable, the ordinal criteria, those that can be ordered (and, hence, ranked), can be used to quantify the differences. Criteria such as understandability or usability can belong to the latter category, even if the scale used in judging the quality is human-based and subjective, as opposed to the objective nature of quantitative criteria. For instance, the user can rate the understandability of a classifier on a scale from 1 to 5, 1 being the worst and 5 the best. More sophisticated classifiers, such as neural networks, can be rated as 1 on the scale while simple decision rules as 5. However, the relationships between different scale values may not be easy to interpret. For example, what about a rule learning system, which is often more understandable than a neural network? Should it be given a 5? Should both the decision tree and the rule learner be given 5 or should the decision tree be demoted to 4? How about naive Bayes? Does it belong at 3, perhaps? If so, is the difference between 4 (the decision tree) and 5 (the rule-based learner) the same as the difference between 3 (naive Bayes) and 4 (the decision tree)? Probably not. Decision trees and rule-based learners may seem closer in understandability than naive Bayes and decision trees, which, again, is a subjective opinion. Consequently the representation of the scale itself for such criteria is important. For instance, Nakhaeizadeh and Schnabl (1998) suggest the following raw scale for understandability:

```
0   0   1   ==> Low understandability
0   1   1   ==> middle understandability
1   1   1   ==> high understandability
```

While the scale can be simplified to the first two bits, the third bit can be used to denote finer scale values. Increasing the number of bits can result in a finer resolution, but the approach can become impractical with too many ordinal values. Alternatively, a single output taking natural number values can be used, but again, this representation remains arbitrary (since the differences between 1 and 2, and 3 and 4 are not necessarily equal, even though they are in this representation) and is not robust (if someone arranged the scale from 0 to 4 rather than 1 to 5, the values would not be correct anymore).

With the simultaneous explosion of deep learning methods and the use of machine learning tools in practical settings, the question of understandability, also known as explainability, has recently become a major question in the evaluation of machine learning systems. Indeed, how can we allow software systems based on machine learning principles to make decisions that can be vital without understanding why the system made a particular decision. Zhou et al. (2021) look at the question of how to evaluate the explainability of machine learning methods, and Chapter 11 develops the topic more fully.

Taking into account qualitative criteria along with the empirical performance-based assessment of classifier performance can, indeed, be more insightful. However, striking a proper balance between their trade-off, which is inevitable, has not been properly formalized yet. Some attempts have been made at combining such criteria, as we will briefly see in

Section B.3.2. For now, however, we shift our focus and attempt to study the performance measures in a unified manner, exploring their interrelationships both theoretically and experimentally.

B.2 Frameworks for Performance Metrics

Various frameworks, both theoretical and empirical, have been explored to analyze the behavior of the different metrics in assessing the classifier performance as well as study their interrelationships. Some frameworks have also been designed to unify the metrics under a common paradigm and use the insights from this exercise to come up with more informed or finer measures.

B.2.1 Theoretical Frameworks

On the theoretical front, the studies of Huang and Ling (2007), Flach (2003), and Buja et al. (2005) are three examples that have aimed to perform such an analysis, each within a different framework. While the first tries to develop a general framework that can encompass not just the quantification of the evaluation measures, but also some qualitative aspects, the second and third studies are purely quantitative.

Ling et al. (2003) and Huang and Ling's (2007) approach of coming up with a framework for comparing different metrics aims to characterize the metrics while taking into account their qualitative "goodness." In order to quantify this, two criteria called the *consistency* and the *discriminancy* of the measures are defined.

Definition B.1 *Consistency.* For two measures pm_1 and pm_2 on domain S, pm_1 and pm_2 are strictly consistent if there exist no two points $a, b \in S$ such that $pm_1(a) > pm_1(b)$ and $pm_2(a) < pm_2(b)$.

Definition B.2 *Discriminancy.* For two measures, pm_1 is strictly more discriminating than pm_2 if there exist two points on domain S, $a, b \in S$, such that $pm_1(a) > pm_1(b)$ and $pm_2(a) = pm_2(b)$, and there exist no two points $a, b \in S$ such that $pm_2(a) > pm_2(b)$ and $pm_1(a) = pm_1(b)$.

Given these, the degrees of consistency and discriminancy are defined.

Definition B.3 *Degree of consistency.* For two measures pm_1 and pm_2 on domain S, let

$$C_R = \{(a,b)|a,b \in S, pm_1(a) > pm_1(b);\ pm_2(a) > pm_2(b)\},$$

and let

$$C_S = \{(a,b)|a,b \in S, pm_1(a) > pm_1(b);\ pm_2(a) < pm_2(b)\}.$$

Then, the degree of consistency of pm_1 and pm_2 is Con, where

$$Con = \frac{|C_R|}{|C_R| + |C_S|}.$$

Definition B.4 *Degree of Discriminancy.* For two measures pm_1 and pm_2 on domain S, let

$$D_P = \{(a,b)|a,b \in S, pm_1(a) > pm_1(b);\ pm_2(a) = pm_2(b)\},$$

and let

$$D_Q = \{(a,b)|a,b \in S, pm_2(a) > pm_2(b);\ pm_1(a) = pm_1(b)\}.$$

The degree of Discriminancy for pm_1 over pm_2 is Dis, where

$$Dis = \frac{|D_P|}{|D_Q|}.$$

Based on these quantities, the goodness of a measure can then be characterized.

Definition B.5 *Goodness of a Measure.* A measure pm_1 is statistically consistent and more discriminating than pm_2 if and only if $Con > 0.5$ and $Dis > 1$. In such cases, we say that pm_1 is a better measure than pm_2.

They define two versions of their concepts of consistency and discriminancy. The first one is a strict Boolean definition, which looks for perfect instances of these concepts, while the second version relaxes the strict definition by adding a probabilistic component to it. Informally, two measures, pm_1 and pm_2, are *consistent* with each other if whenever pm_1 decides that A is a strictly better algorithm than B, then pm_2 does not stipulate that B is better than A. We think of pm_1 as being more discriminating than pm_2 if pm_1 can sometimes tell that there is a difference between algorithms A and B, whereas pm_2 cannot. The study, in keeping with the more general tradition of comparing AUC with accuracy, does just that, and showed that AUC is statistically consistent and more discriminating than accuracy. From a practical point of view, they use the finer metric AUC to optimize a model and show that the resulting model performs better on accuracy than the model optimized using accuracy. Notice that this is in line with the finding of Rosset (2004). However, in a followup, Huang et al. (2008) suggest that this result is not statistically significant and that, in fact, one is better off optimizing a model using the metric that is to be used in the deployed system.

Another interesting analysis for studying the interrelationship between performance measures was done by Flach (2003), who focuses on the ROC space and its role in characterizing various performance metrics. By considering the generalised three-dimensional ROC space, Flach (2003) and then Fuernkranz and Flach (2005) study various metrics such as AUC, accuracy, F-measure, and so on, in this space.

Buja et al. (2005) considered a Fisher-consistency of the performance metrics and verifies whether they can be characterized as proper scoring rules. The focus of the study was on scoring rules that can yield probability estimates on the data in a Fisher-consistent manner. The analysis is beyond the scope of this book and we refer interested readers to the original study.

In recent work, Canbek et al. (2022) proposes an interesting theoretical framework summarized in a clever information table, called the periodic table of performance instruments, mapped on the periodic table of elements, to describe the relationship of 57 binary classification metrics. The table is derived from three research questions that seek to differentiate between metrics semantically and formally, identify properties of the metrics relating to their similarities, redundancies, and dependencies, and help select the most appropriate metrics for research and applications.

B.2.2 Experimental Frameworks

On the experimental front, various attempts have been made at analyzing the relationship between two or more performance metrics. Two independent large-scale experimental evaluation studies are especially worth noting.

Caruana and Niculescu-Mizil (2004) studied nine different performance metrics for binary classification, using two different tools: a visual tool (or projection approach), *multi-dimensional scaling (MDS)*, and a statistical tool, *correlation analysis*. The metrics were compared according to the results they obtained on seven learning models and seven different domains from the UCI repository and other sources. The study was, thus, quite extensive. The metrics were organized into three families:

1. **Threshold metrics** These are metrics, such as accuracy, for which a threshold is set ahead of time within the classifier and for which the distance from the threshold does not matter. All that matters is whether the classifier issues a value above or below the threshold.
2. **Ordering/rank metrics** These are metrics, such as AUC, for which the test examples are assumed to be ordered according to the predicted values output by the classifier. These metrics measure to what extent the classifiers ranked positive instances above the negative ones. Another way to interpret such measures is to think of them as summaries of the classifiers' performance over all possible thresholds.
3. **Probability metrics** These are metrics, such as root mean square error (RMSE), which compute how far the truth lies from the predicted values output by the classifiers. They do not directly compare results to a threshold, like the threshold metrics, nor do they directly compare the instances' ranks from one another, the way ordering metrics do it. However, they could be thought of as performing these two tasks indirectly.

The MDS and correlation analysis showed that all the ordering metrics cluster close to one another in metric space and are highly correlated. Accuracy, on the other hand, did not seem to correlate with the other threshold metrics. Instead, it was often closely related to RMSE, a probability metric. An important observation was made that RMSE is a very robust metric, well correlated to all the others. Caruana and Niculescu-Mizil (2004) recommended it for general-purpose experiments where no specific practical outcome is sought. In fact, a new combination metric, discussed in Section B.3.1, was also proposed but was found to be highly correlated with RMSE.

Another large-scale experimental framework was developed in Ferri et al. (2009), which is similar to Caruana and Niculescu-Mizil (2004) in some respects but which expanded the latter to the multi-class case and studied the sensitivity of metrics to different domain characteristics, in particular, misclassification noise (changes in class threshold), probability noise (change in calibration with no effect to the ranking), ranking noise (change in ranks that do not affect the classification) and changes in class frequency. While retaining the categorization of metrics in the three categories as done by Caruana and Niculescu-Mizil (2004), the framework considered a total of 18 metrics, doubling the number from the previous study, including the variations of common metrics especially in multi-class setting. The 30 small- and medium-sized test domains from the UCI repository consisted of a balanced set of binary and multi-class as well as balanced and imbalanced domains. Groupwise correlation analysis was subsequently performed.

The findings show the various ranking measures to be similar, while the classification and reliability measures were found to be more correlated. The two sets, ranking measures on the one hand and the classification and reliability measures on the other, were found to be farther apart in their groupwise behavior. This, then, justified the use of AUC as a different view on the problem. One difference of note with the study of Caruana and Niculescu-Mizil (2004) was the relatively lower correlation of RMSE in the multi-class setting (as opposed to the binary setting considered earlier). While in binary domains RMSE is more closely correlated to the ranking metrics than it is to the classification metrics, this relationship is reversed in the multi-class setting.

The results obtained on balanced versus imbalanced domains supported very well the intuitive notion that the choice of metrics is important in imbalanced datasets. Indeed, we see that the classification metrics behave fairly similarly in the balanced case, while they behave quite differently in the imbalanced case. This is true for all the other categories and across categories as well. With respect to small versus large domains, the correlation results show that classification and ranking metrics are closer to each other than to the reliability metrics in the small domain case, but that in the case of large domains, ranking metrics are quite separated from classification and reliability metrics, which are more closely related.

The classification measures are found to be relatively better behaved than the ranking and reliability measures in the presence of class noise. If probability noise is present, then classification metrics are not reliable. By contrast, ranking metrics seem quite robust to this kind of distortion. The reliability measures' performance in this scenario falls midway between those of the classification and ranking metrics. When ranking noise is present, once again the classification metrics are the ones that are most affected, while ranking and reliability metrics are more robust. Finally, ranking metrics are found to be more sensitive to variations in class frequency and seem to be unreliable when a particular class is represented by only very rare cases. However, as long as these measures take into consideration the proportion of examples in each class, the classification and reliability metrics seem well behaved. Some of these results could have been expected from the characterization of the performance metrics that we outlined in Chapter 4 and 5 and, in fact, place these insights into a practical perspective.

More recently, Hossin and Sulaiman (2015) reviewed a number of performance metrics and contrasted them in terms of distinctiveness, discriminability, informativeness, and bias. They discuss different issues that have affected classification metrics: the fact that most were designed for binary classification problems and may not adapt well to multiclass ones, the issue encountered due to class imbalances, and the computational cost of some of the metrics.

Luque et al. (2019) reviewed metrics in the specific context of class imbalances and derived important results about the G-Mean, a metric called bookmaker informedness, and Matthews correlation error coefficient, and they propose class balance metrics to extend the idea of class-balanced accuracy to other metrics. Similarly, Brzezinski et al. (2020) proposed a graphical histogram-based method that allows for a probabilistic interpretation of performance measures in the context of class imbalances.

B.2.3 Do More Informed Metrics Yield Better Information?

The question that may be asked after considering the wealth of evaluation metrics available is how useful the more sophisticated metrics are in algorithmic evaluation. A simple strategy for selecting measures could be to use classification measures when the goal of the exercise is pure classification, a ranking measure when ranking is necessary and, possibly, a probabilistic measure when building classifier ensemble methods. Nonetheless, metrics have been assessed across domains. In particular, based on the observation that ROC-based methods are not sensitive to prior class distributions the way accuracy is, AUC, a measure that summarizes the results of ROC analysis, is often used in place of accuracy, especially in class imbalanced problems, but recently, even as a general measure. As a matter of fact, there is merit in crossing such boundaries: the more information we can gather about the classifiers, the better off we are. The only problem, however, is that it is not entirely clear how to interpret this information. Intuitively, it would seem that the more informed metrics should give us better insights about the behavior of the classifiers on future data, but very few studies to date have asked this question. As already discussed, Rosset (2004) and Huang and Ling (2007) have looked at the relation of using one measure (AUC) to train the algorithm and its effect on measuring the effectiveness of the algorithm in test domains using another measure (accuracy). Reliability metrics, such as RMSE and Kononenko and Bratko's (2024) information score metrics, while generally slightly less appropriate than accuracy on binary classification tasks, sometimes fare slightly better in multi-class or imbalanced domains.

The attempts to analyze the performance metrics in a unified manner under the constraints of a framework have not only resulted in the characterization of their behavior, but have also provided some understanding as to how these can either be improved or combined so as to obtain finer measures of performance. We now move on to the attempts that have been made to obtain metrics by combining the existing ones.

B.3 Combining Metrics

The attempts to combine metrics can be categorized into three main groups. The first stems from the evaluation frameworks discussed in Section B.2. The second group consists of measures that aim to combine the qualitative considerations with the quantitative measures of performance. These approaches are commonly known as multi-criteria metrics. The final group consists of approaches inspired from visualization by the way of projection of metrics on a common space.

B.3.1 Framework-Based Combination Metrics

Evaluation frameworks such as those of Ling et al. (2003) or Flach (2003) can give important insights into the conceptually different but complementary nature of the performance measures in their respective settings. A natural extension to such an analysis would, then, be to investigate whether combining measures or coming up with more sophisticated measures can result in better assessments of classifier performance. Not surprisingly then, attempts have been made to this effect. Consider, for instance the, SAR metric derived from the experimental framework of Caruana and Niculescu-Mizil (2004), which linearly combines the most prominent member of each of the categories they devised, namely, accuracy, AUC, and the RMSE, in an attempt to obtain a more informative measure. Their measure takes the following form:

$$SAR = \frac{(Accuracy + AUC + (1 - RMSE))}{3}.$$

Similarly, a combined metric was also proposed as a consequence of derivation from the framework of Ling et al. (2003) in the form of AUC:accuracy which is an instance of the general two-level framework discussed in Huang and Ling (2007). The basic idea is that when comparing two algorithms, AUC is the first measure used. If a tie is observed when using AUC, then the comparison is done using accuracy instead. This is different from the linear combination proposed by Caruana and Niculescu-Mizil (2004). It also applies more generally with AUC and accuracy being replaced by any other two performance metrics. In general, Huang and Ling (2007) show that the two-level measure is consistent with, and finer than, the two measures it is based on. When used with AUC and accuracy, it is also shown to correlate with RMSE better than either AUC or accuracy. More recently, Choudhury and Daly (2019) proposed combining quality metrics on the particular task of image quality assessment using a machine learning method. In particular, they combined high dynamic range, standard dynamic range, and color difference measures, specific image quality metrics, and tested several classifiers use as meta-learners to select the metric combinations that yielded the best results.

These combined metrics, however, are yet to be extensively evaluated and studied for their adherence to their expected behavior. For instance, SAR, although apparently more powerful than individual metrics, was found not to present much advantage over the simple RMSE, which correlates very well with it.

B.3.2 Multi-criteria Metrics

Considerable effort has been devoted to investigating metrics that can, in addition to measuring the performance of classifiers under the criterion of interest, weigh it against the gains in other complementary, and even qualitative criteria. The best algorithm under this setting would then be the one that achieves an optimal trade-off of the assessment criteria of interest. We will explain, in some detail, the main measures proposed along these lines. Four main approaches of multi-criteria evaluation have been proposed: the efficiency method, the simple and intuitive measure, the measure-based method, and the accurate multi-criteria decision-making methodology. An attempt to synthesize the first of these three approaches lead to the candidate evaluation function. We briefly discuss each of these in turn. These approaches should not be confused with the combination metrics such as SAR and AUC:accuracy, discussed in Section B.3.1, which do not generalize to take qualitative criteria into account. In the current settings, we consider all performance metrics to be normalized in a specific interval, typically [0, 1] with necessary sign adjustments so that higher values are better.

The Efficiency Method

Motivated from the operations research concept of data envelopment analysis (DEA), the efficiency method introduced by Nakhaeizadeh and Schnabl (1997) aims to weight the positive metrics (whose higher values are desirable) against the negative metrics (whose lower values are desirable). The positive metrics can be the ones such as accuracy, while the negative ones can be characteristics such as computational complexity or execution time. Even qualitative metrics such as the *interestingness* of an algorithm can be included. On a given dataset S, the efficiency of a classifier f, denoted $\mathcal{E}_S(f)$, is given by

$$\mathcal{E}_S(f) = \frac{\sum_i w_i \, pm_i^+(f)}{\sum_j w_j \, pm_j^-(f)},$$

where the index i runs through positive metrics while j runs through negative metrics.

As can be easily seen here, assigning w_i's is, unfortunately, nontrivial. Nakhaeizadeh and Schnabl (1997) propose to set them by optimizing the efficiency of all the algorithms simultaneously. These efficiencies should be as close as 100% as possible and none should exceed 100%. This optimization problem can, then, be solved using linear programming techniques. In addition to this general idea, Nakhaeizadeh and Schnabl (1998) go on to discuss how the approach deals with subjective judgements of how the different criteria are assessed. This is implemented by applying restrictions on the automatic weight computations that correspond to the user's preferences.

The Simple and Intuitive Measure (SIM)

The simple and intuitive measure (SIM) proposed by Soares et al. (2000) considers the combined effect of the distance between an evaluated algorithm's performance measure and the optimally obtainable result on that measure. The combination, in the form of a product, is typically unweighted. Let $\mathcal{I}$ denote the set of different performance metrics. Then SIM is defined as

$$\mathcal{S}_S(f) = \prod_{i \in \mathcal{I}} |pm_i(f) - pm_i^o|,$$

where pm_i^o denotes the optimal value of performance measure pm_i.

Obviously, it is desirable that the distance measures reflect the possiblity of discrepancy in case the results on one or more measures are unacceptable. The distance for those measures should then go out of bounds, and so does the result of the combination, thus signaling a bad algorithm. The following bounded version of the measure aims to achieve this, where each performance measure $pm_i(f)$ is expected to lie in a respective interval:

$$
\mathcal{S}_S^B(f) = \begin{cases} \mathcal{S}_S(f) & \text{if } \forall\, i(pm_i(f) \in [pm_i^l, pm_i^u]), \\ \infty & \text{otherwise.} \end{cases}
$$

Finally, in a comparative setting the result can be normalized to generate a score for the algorithm as

$$
\mathcal{S}_S^{NB}(f) = \frac{\mathcal{S}_S^B(f)}{\prod_i |pm_i^u - pm_i^l|}.
$$

SIM can also be used in an exploratory way as it can be represented graphically so that the user may interact with it on the fly, trying different settings. The advantage of this approach over the efficiency method of Nakhaeizadeh and Schnabl (1997) is that it uses no weights, which are typically difficult to set. Instead, it combines quantities that the user knows should not exceed certain bounds. The different criteria on which the evaluation is based are assumed to have the same weight; that is, they are considered to be equally important. As a result, SIM is able to handle uncertainty in the estimates of the criteria that the efficiency approach could not account for. Nonetheless, by the same argument, the efficiency approach has the advantage of being more precise as it allows certain criteria to be considered more important than others.

The Measure-Based Method

The measure-based method proposed by Andersson et al. (1999) attempts to define measure functions denoting the algorithm-neutral aspects of the problem that we want to optimize. These measure functions get evaluated on algorithm-application pairs, and their results are combined in a weighted linear fashion. Again, let $\mathcal{I}$ denote the set of different performance metrics. The measure function, denoted as $\mathcal{M}_S(f)$ of a classifier f over dataset S, is defined as

$$
\mathcal{M}_S(f) = \sum_{i \in \mathcal{I}} w_i \cdot pm_i(f).
$$

The measure-based method decomposes the evaluation problem into simpler components of the evaluation, such as whether the training instances are classified correctly, whether similar examples are classified similarly, and how simple the partition learned by the algorithm is. Each component is evaluated separately, and these components are then combined linearly by the user, who can choose to weigh some components more than others, at will. Accordingly, the pm_i's in this measure need not concern themselves only with standard performance measures as before, but rather refer to the components under consideration. This method presents some similarity with the efficiency method of Nakhaeizadeh and

Schnabl (1997), but it focuses on the learned model rather than the learning algorithm and is more concerned with generalizing issues than with qualitative ones.

The Candidate Evaluation Function

The candidate evaluation function proposed by Lavesson and Davidsson (2008a) (also see Lavesson and Davidsson (2008b)) extends the measure-based method by incorporating elements of the simple and intuitive measure, namely, its bounds to yield

$$
\mathcal{C}_S(f) = \begin{cases} \sum_i w_i \, pm_i(f) & \text{if } \forall \, i (pm_i(f) \in [pm_i^l, 1]), \\ 0 & \text{otherwise} \end{cases}
$$

such that $\sum_{i \in I} w_i = 1$ assuring boundedness of $\mathcal{C}_S(f)$; that is, $\mathcal{C}_S(f) \in [0, 1]$. The aim of the approach is to verify that the application domain constraints are not violated (as ascertained by SIM), while at the same time being able to perform the component-wise evaluation as the measure-based method. SIM's normalization is also adopted to ensure that all the combined measures are in the same range, since this is a necessary prerequisite to meaningful weighting. Lavesson and Davidsson (2008b) suggest the use of a taxonomy of performance quality attributes that could be subdivided into time, space, and accuracy components. Further quality attributes such as comprehensibility, complexity, and interestingness can also be included. However, operationalizing these ideas is difficult for the same reason that quantifying a qualitative measure of interest is nontrivial.

The Accurate Multi-criteria Decision-Making Methodology

Ali et al. (2017) propose a method for combining large numbers of metrics pertaining to a number of different qualitative criteria: the correctness of the classification, its complexity, both in time and memory space, the responsiveness of the algorithm, the consistency of the results, the comprehensibility of the algorithm, its reliability, its robustness, and its separability. In addition, the combination method incorporates implicit as well as explicit constraints from the user, such as that training time should be minimized and accuracy maximized simultaneously, and other such constraints. The method then ranks the combinations it produces so that the user can then select his or her preferred combination given the problem at hand.

B.3.3 Visualization-Based Combination Metrics

The argument behind the visualization approach proposed by Alaiz-Rodríguez et al. (2008) is that in conventional methods of combining metrics, the information is lost at two stages: first when scaling the individual metrics and then when these scaled metrics are combined. The metrics combination issue in this approach is addressed by means of a graphical projection and has the advantage over other combination methods to provide a component-wise comparison of different classifiers applied to different domains and evaluated by different metrics.

The approach works by recording all the results associated with a single classifier on the various domains considered and with all the performance metrics selected by the user, into a single vector. Every classifier compared in the study is, thus, represented by a vector whose entries comprise the values of the performance measures used. This organization in vector form guarantees that there is a pairwise correspondence of each vector component from one classifier to the next. Using a distance measure (the Euclidean distance) and a projection method (MDS), the vectors are then projected into a two-dimensional space.

As opposed to aggregating the performance measures and then comparing these across classifiers, the visualization approach preserves these in their original form, simply concatenated into a vector. The transformation is delayed until the projection is applied. This means that in the visualization approach, information is lost only once, in the projection phase. In the traditional approach, information is lost with every such aggregation. The resulting projections can then be visualized and their relationship over classifiers studied in this projected space.

Note, however, the dependency of the approach on the distance measure (Euclidean distance) as well as the projection method. Wildly varying measures can adversely affect the distances in such cases since the resulting distances can be skewed. Similarly, the relationship would also depend on how well behaved the projections are in preserving the relationship of different classifier performances. These points were considered by Japkowicz et al. (2008), who compared the results of two projection methods, including a distance-preserving projection, and two distance measures. However, more research is needed to gain a better understanding of this approach.

References

Abadi, M., Chu, A., Goodfellow, I. et al. (2016). Deep learning with differential privacy. In C. Kruegel, A. Myers, and S. Halevi (eds.) *Proceedings of the 2016 ACM SIGSAC Conference on Computer and Communications Security*, 308–318. Association for Computer Machinery.

Abdi, H. (2007). Multiple correlation coefficient. In N. J. Salkind (ed.) *Encyclopedia of Measurement and Statistics*, *648*, 651. SAGE Publications.

Absalom, E. E., Ikotun, A. M., Oyelade, O. N. et al. (2022). A comprehensive survey of clustering algorithms: state-of-the-art machine learning applications, taxonomy, challenges, and future research prospects. *Engineering Applications of Artificial Intelligence*, *110*, 104743. https://doi.org/10.1016/j.engappai.2022.104743

Adali, T., Anderson, M., and Fu, G.-S. (2014). Diversity in independent component and vector analyses: identifiability, algorithms, and applications in medical imaging. *IEEE Signal Processing Magazine*, *31*(3), 18–33.

Adali, T., and Calhoun, V. D. (2022). Reproducibility and replicability in neuroimaging data analysis. *Current Opinion in Neurology*, *35*(4), 475–481.

Agarwal, R., Schwarzer, M., Castro, P. S., Courville, A. C., and Bellemare, M. G. (2021). Deep reinforcement learning at the edge of the statistical precipice. *Advances in Neural Information Processing Systems*, *34*, 29304–29320.

Aggarwal, C. C., Kong, X., Gu, Q., Han, J., and Yu, P. S. (2014). Active learning: a survey. In C. C. Aggarwal (ed.) *Data Classification: Algorithms and Applications*, 599–634. Chapman and Hall.

Alaiz-Rodríguez, R., Japkowicz, N., and Tischer, P. (2008). Visualizing classifier performance on different domains. In *Proceedings of the 20th IEEE International Conference on Tools with Artificial Intelligence*, 3–10. IEEE Computer Society.

Ali, R., Lee, S., and Chung, T. C. (2017). Accurate multi-criteria decision making methodology for recommending machine learning algorithm. *Expert Systems with Applications*, *71*, 257–278.

Alpaydn, E. (1999). Combined 5×2 cv F test for comparing supervised classification learning algorithms. *Neural Computation*, *11*, 1885–1892.

Amancio, D. R., Comin, C. H., Casanova, D. et al. (2014). A systematic comparison of supervised classifiers. *PLoS ONE*, *9*(4), e94137.

Amodei, D., Olah, C., Steinhardt, J. et al. (2016). Concrete problems in AI safety. arXiv:1606.06565.

Andersson, A., Davidsson, P., and Linden, J. (1999). Measure-based classifier performance evaluation. *Pattern Recognition Letters*, *20*(11–13), 1165–1173.

Armstrong, J. S. (2007). Significance tests harm progress in forecasting. *International Journal of Forecasting*, *23*, 321–327.

Arulkumaran, K., Deisenroth, M. P., Brundage, M., and Bharath, A. A. (2017). A brief survey of deep reinforcement learning. arXiv:1708.05866.

Ashayeri, C., and Jha, B. (2021). Evaluation of transfer learning in data-driven methods in the assessment of unconventional resources. *Journal of Petroleum Science and Engineering*, *207*, 109178.

Atanov, A., Xu, S., Beker, O., Filatov, A., and Zamir, A. (2022). Simple control baselines for evaluating transfer learning. arXiv:2202.03365.

Bahari, M. H., and Hamme, H. V. (2014). Normalized ordinal distance; a performance metric for ordinal, probabilistic-ordinal or partial-ordinal classification problems. In B. Issac and N. Israr (eds.) *Case Studies in Intelligent Computing: Achievements and Trends*, 285–302. CRC Press.

Bahri, M., Bifet, A., Gama, J., Gomes, H. M., and Maniu, S. (2021). Data stream analysis: foundations, major tasks and tools. *Wiley Interdisciplinary Reviews: Data Mining and Knowledge Discovery*, *11*(3), e1405.

Barocas, S., and Selbst, A. D. (2016). Big data's disparate impact. *California Law Review*, *104*, 671–732.

Beck, N., Sivasubramanian, D., Dani, A., Ramakrishnan, G., and Iyer, R. K. (2021). Effective evaluation of deep active learning on image classification tasks. arXiv:2106.15324.

Bekker, J., and Davis, J. (2020). Learning from positive and unlabeled data: a survey. *Machine Learning*, *109*, 719–760.

Bellinger, C., Corizzo, R., and Japkowicz, N. (to appear). Performance estimation bias in class imbalance with minority subconcepts. In N. Moniz, P. Branco, N. Japkowicz, M. Woźniak, and S. Wang (eds.) *Proceedings of Machine Learning Research*.

Benavoli, A., Corani, G., Demšar, J., and Zaffalon, M. (2017). Time for a change: a tutorial for comparing multiple classifiers through Bayesian analysis. *Journal of Machine Learning Research*, *18*(1), 2653–2688.

Berrar, D. P. (2016). Confidence curves: an alternative to null hypothesis significance testing for the comparison of classifiers. *Machine Learning*, *106*, 911–949.

Berrar, D. P., and Lozano, J. A. (2013). Significance tests or confidence intervals: Which are preferable for the comparison of classifiers? *Journal of Experimental & Theoretical Artificial Intelligence*, *25*, 189–206.

Bishop, C. M., and Nasrabadi, N. M. (2006). *Pattern recognition and machine learning*. Springer.

Borji, A. (2019). Pros and cons of GAN evaluation measures. *Computer Vision and Image Understanding*, *179*, 41–65.

Bouckaert, R. R. (2003). Choosing between two learning algorithms based on calibrated tests. In T. Fawcett, and N. Mishra (eds.) *Proceedings of the Twentieth International Conference on Machine Learning*, 51–58. AAAI Press.

Bouckaert, R. R. (2004). Estimating replicability of classifier learning experiments. In C. Brodley (ed.) *Proceedings of the Twenty-First International Conference on Machine Learning*, paper 15. AAAI Press.

Bousquet, O., Boucheron, S., and Lugosi, G. (2004). Introduction to statistical learning theory. In *Advanced Lectures on Machine Learning*, vol. 3176 of Lecture Notes in Artificial Intelligence, 169–207. Springer Verlag.

Bradford, J. P., Kunz, C., Kohavi, R., Brunk, C., and Brodley, C. E. (1998). Pruning decision trees with misclassification costs. In *Proceedings of the European Conference on Machine Learning*, 131–136. Springer.

Branco, P., Torgo, L., and Ribeiro, R. P. (2016). A survey of predictive modeling on imbalanced domains. *ACM Computing Surveys*, *49*, 1–50.

Branco, P., Torgo, L., and Ribeiro, R. P. (2017). Relevance-based evaluation metrics for multi-class imbalanced domains. In J. Kim, K. Shim, L. Cao, J.-G. Lee, X. Lin, and Y.-S. Moon (eds.) *Pacific-Asia Conference on Knowledge Discovery and Data Mining*, 698–710. Springer International Publishing.

Brownlee, J. (2016). Statistical methods for machine learning. Discover how to transform data into knowledge with Python. Jason Brownlee https://machinelearningmastery.com/statistics_for_machine_learning

Brundage, M., Avin, S., Wang, J. et al. (2020). Toward trustworthy AI development: mechanisms for supporting verifiable claims. arXiv:2004.07213.

Bryson, J. J. (2019). The past decade and future of AI's impact on society. www.bbvaopenmind.com/en/articles/the-past-decade-and-future-of-ais-impact-on-society/

Brzezinski, D. W., Stefanowski, J., Susmaga, R., and Szczech, I. (2020). On the dynamics of classification measures for imbalanced and streaming data. *IEEE Transactions on Neural Networks and Learning Systems*, *31*, 2868–2878.

Buja, A., Stuetzle, W., and Shen, Y. (2005). Loss functions for binary class probability estimation: structure and applications. www-stat.wharton.upenn.edu/~buja/PAPERS/paper-proper-scoring.pdf

Buolamwini, J., and Gebru, T. (2018). Gender shades: intersectional accuracy disparities in commercial gender classification. In *Conference on Fairness, Accountability, and Transparency*, 77–91. Proceedings of Machine Learning Research.

Campos, G. O., Zimek, A., Sander, J. et al. (2015). On the evaluation of unsupervised outlier detection: measures, datasets, and an empirical study. *Data Mining and Knowledge Discovery*, *30*, 891–927.

Canbek, G., Temizel, T. T., and Sağiroğlu, S. (2022). PToPI: a comprehensive review, analysis, and knowledge representation of binary classification performance measures/metrics. *SN Computer Science*, *4*(1), 13.

Caruana, R., and Niculescu-Mizil, A. (2004). Data mining in metric space: an empirical analysis of supervised learning performance criteria. In J. Gehrke and W. DuMouchel (eds.) *Proceedings of the 10th International Conference on Knowledge Discovery and Data Mining*, 69–78. Association for Computing Machinery.

Caruana, R., and Niculescu-Mizil, A. (2006). An empirical comparison of supervised learning algorithms. In W. Cohen and A. Moore (eds.) *Proceedings of the 23rd International Conference on Machine Learning*, 161–168. Association for Computing Machinery.

Celikyilmaz, A., Clark, E., and Gao, J. (2020). Evaluation of text generation: a survey. arXiv:2006.14799.

Cerqueira, V., Torgo, L., and Mozetic, I. (2020). Evaluating time series forecasting models: an empirical study on performance estimation methods. *Machine Learning*, *109*, 1997–2028.

Chalapathy, R., and Chawla, S. (2019). Deep learning for anomaly detection: a survey. arXiv:abs/1901.03407.

Chalapathy, R., Menon, A. K., and Chawla, S. (2018). Anomaly detection using one-class neural networks. arXiv:1802.06360.

Chandola, V., Banerjee, A., and Kumar, V. (2009). Anomaly detection: a survey. *ACM Comput. Surv.*, *41*, 15:1–15:58.

Chang, J., Gerrish, S., Wang, C., Boyd-Graber, J., and Blei, D. (2009). Reading tea leaves: how humans interpret topic models. In *Proceedings of the 22nd International Conference on Neural Information Processing Systems*, 288–296. Curran Associates Inc.

Chawla, N., Bowyer, K., Hall, L. O., and Kegelmeyer, W. P. (2002). SMOTE: synthetic minority over-sampling technique. *Journal of Artificial Intelligence Research*, *16*, 321–357.

Chen, T. Y., Kuo, F.-C., Liu, H. et al. (2019). Metamorphic testing: a review of challenges and opportunities. *ACM Computing Surveys*, *51*(1), 4.

Chernik, M. R. (2007). *Bootstrap methods: a guide for practitioners and researchers*. 2nd ed. Wiley.

Chicco, D., and Jurman, G. (2020). The advantages of the Matthews correlation coefficient (MCC) over F1 score and accuracy in binary classification evaluation. *BMC Genomics*, *21*(1), 1–13.

Cho, H., Matthews, G. J., and Harel, O. (2019). Confidence intervals for the area under the receiver operating characteristic curve in the presence of ignorable missing data. *International Statistical Review*, *87*, 152–177.

Choudhury, A., and Daly, S. J. (2019). Combining quality metrics using machine learning for improved and robust HDR image quality assessment. *Electronic Imaging*, *31*, 1–7.

Cohen, J. (1960). A coefficient of agreement for nominal scales. *Educational and Psychological Measurements*, *20*, 37–46.

Cohen, J. (1992). A power primer. *Psychological Bulletin*, *112*(1), 155.

Collberg, C., Proebsting, T., and Warren, A. M. (2015). Repeatability and benefaction in computer systems research. Technical Report. *14*(4). University of Arizona.

Confalonieri, R., Coba, L., Wagner, B., and Besold, T. R. (2021). A historical perspective of explainable artificial intelligence. *Wiley Interdisciplinary Reviews: Data Mining and Knowledge Discovery*, *11*(1), e1391.

Corani, G., Benavoli, A., Demšar, J., Mangili, F., and Zaffalon, M. (2017). Statistical comparison of classifiers through Bayesian hierarchical modelling. *Machine Learning*, *106*(11), 1817–1837.

Corbett-Davies, S., and Goel, S. (2018). The measure and mismeasure of fairness: a critical review of fair machine learning. arXiv:1808.00023.

Cortes, C., and Mohri, M. (2004). AUC optimization vs. error rate minimization. In S. Thrun, L. K. Saul, and B. Schölkopf (eds.) *Proceedings of the 16th International Conference on Neural Information Processing Systems*, *16*, 313–320. MIT Press.

Cortes, C., and Mohri, M. (2005). Confidence intervals for the area under the ROC curve. In L. Saul, Y. Weiss, and L. Bottou (eds.) *Proceedings of the 17th International Conference on Advances in Neural Information Processing Systems*, *17*, 305–312. MIT Press.

Crothers, E. (2020). Ethical detection of online influence campaigns using transformer language models. Masters thesis, University of Ottawa, Canada.

Crothers, E., Japkowicz, N., and Viktor, H. L. (2023). Machine-generated text: a comprehensive survey of threat models and detection methods. *IEEE Access*, *11*, 70977–71002.

Cumming, G. (2013). *Understanding the new statistics: effect sizes, confidence intervals, and meta-analysis*. Routledge.

Damasceno, L. P., Cavalcante, C. C., Adalı, T., and Boukouvalas, Z. (2021). Independent vector analysis using semi-parametric density estimation via multivariate entropy maximization. In *ICASSP 2021–2021 IEEE International Conference on Acoustics, Speech and Signal Processing*, 3715–3719. IEEE.

Davis, J., and Goadrich, M. H. (2006). The relationship between precision-recall and ROC curves. In W. Cohen and A. Moore (eds.) *Proceedings of the 23rd International Conference on Machine Learning*, 233–240. Association for Computing Machinery.

Deeks, J. J., and Altman, D. G. (2004). Diagnostic tests 4: likelihood ratios. *British Medical Journal*, *329*, 168–169.

Dembla, G. (2020). Intuition behind log-loss score. *Medium, Blog.* https://towards datascience.com/intuition-behind-log-loss-score-4e0c9979680a

Demšar, J. (2006). Statistical comparisons of classifiers over multiple data sets. *Journal of Machine Learning Research, 7,* 1–30.

Demšar, J. (2008). On the appropriateness of statistical tests in machine learning. In *Workshop on Evaluation Methods for Machine Learning in Conjunction with ICML,* 65. Citeseer.

Díaz-Rodríguez, N., Lomonaco, V., Filliat, D., and Maltoni, D. (2018). Don't forget, there is more than forgetting: new metrics for continual learning. arXiv:1810.13166.

Dietterich, T. G. (1998). Approximate statistical tests for comparing supervised classification learning algorithms. *Neural Computation, 10*(7), 1895–1923.

Domingos, P. (2000). A unified bias–variance decomposition and its applications. In *Proceedings of the 17th International Conference on Machine Learning,* 231–238. Morgan Kaufmann.

Domingues, R., Filippone, M., Michiardi, P., and Zouaoui, J. (2018). A comparative evaluation of outlier detection algorithms: experiments and analyses. *Pattern Recognition, 74,* 406–421.

Douglas, H. (2009). Science, policy, and the value-free ideal. University of Pittsburgh Press.

Drummond, C. (2006). Machine learning as an experimental science (revisited). In C. Drummond, W. Elazmeh, and N. Japkowicz (eds.) *Proceedings of the AAAI'06 Workshop on Evaluation Methods for Machine Learning.* AAAI Press.

Drummond, C. (2009). Replicability is not reproducibility: nor is it good science. In *Proceedings of the Evaluation Methods for Machine Learning Workshop at the 26th ICML.* www.site.uottawa.ca/~cdrummon/pubs/ICMLws09.pdf

Dubber, M., Pasquale, F., and Das, S. (2021). The Oxford handbook of ethics of AI. Oxford University Press.

Dwarakanath, A., Ahuja, M., Sikand, S. et al. (2018). Identifying implementation bugs in machine learning based image classifiers using metamorphic testing. In E. Bodden (ed.) *Proceedings of the 27th ACM SIGSOFT International Symposium on Software Testing and Analysis,* 118–128. Association for Computing Machinery.

Efron, B., and Tibshirani, R. (1993). An introduction to the bootstrap. Chapman and Hall.

Elazmeh, W., Japkowicz, N., and Matwin, S. (2006). A framework for measuring classification difference with imbalance. In J. Fürnkranz, T. Scheffer, and M. Spiliopoulou (eds.) *Proceedings of the 2006 European Conference on Machine Learning,* 126–137. Springer-Verlag.

Elkan, C. P., and Noto, K. (2008). Learning classifiers from only positive and unlabeled data. In *Proceedings of the 14th ACM SIGKDD International Conference on Knowledge Discovery and Data Mining,* 213–220. Association for Computing Machinery.

Espadoto, M., Martins, R. M., Kerren, A., Hirata, N. S., and Telea, A. C. (2019). Toward a quantitative survey of dimension reduction techniques. In *IEEE Transactions on Visualization and Computer Graphics, 27*(3), 2153–2173.

Eykholt, K., Ivan E., Earlence F. et al. (2018). Robust physical-world attacks on deep learning visual classification. In *Proceedings of the IEEE Conference on Computer Vision and Pattern Recognition,* 1625–1634. IEEE.

Faber, K., Corizzo, R., Sniezynski, B., and Japkowicz, N. (2022a). Active lifelong anomaly detection with experience replay. In *IEEE 9th International Conference on Data Science and Advanced Analytics,* 1–10. IEEE.

Faber, K., Corizzo, R., Sniezynski, B., and Japkowicz, N. (2023a). Lifelong learning for anomaly detection: new challenges, perspectives, and insights. arXiv:2303.07557.

Faber, K., Corizzo, R., Sniezynsky, B., and Japkowicz, N. (2023b). Vlad: task-agnostic VAE-based lifelong anomaly detection. *Neural Networks, 165*, 248–273.

Fan, W., Stolfo, S. J., Zhang, J., and Chan, P. K. (1999). AdaCost: misclassification cost-sensitive boosting. In *Proceedings of the 16th International Conference on Machine Learning*, 97–105. Morgan Kaufmann.

Farquhar, S., and Gal, Y. (2018). Towards robust evaluations of continual learning. arXiv:abs/1805.09733.

Fawcett, T. (2004). ROC graphs: notes and practical considerations for data mining researchers. *Machine Learning, 31*(1), 1–38.

Fawcett, T. (2006). An introduction to ROC analysis. *Pattern Recognition Letters, 27*, 861–874.

Fawcett, T., and Niculescu-Mizil, A. (2007a). PAV and the ROC convex hull. *Machine Learning, 68*(1), 97–106.

Ferri, C., Flach, P. A., and Hernandez-Orallo, J. (2003). Improving the AUC of probabilistic estimation trees. In *Proceedings of the 14th European Conference on Machine Learning*, 121–132. Springer.

Ferri, C., Hernandez-Orallo, J., and Modroiu, R. (2009). An experimental comparison of performance measures for classification. *Pattern Recognition Letters, 30*, 27–38.

Fisher, R. A. (1925). *Statistical methods for research workers*. Oliver and Boyd.

Flach, P. A. (2003). The geometry of ROC space: understanding machine learning metrics through ROC isometrics. In *Proceedings of the Twentieth International Conference on Machine Learning*, 194–201. AAAI Press.

Fleiss, J. L. (1971). Measuring nominal scale agreement among many raters. *Psychological Bulletin, 76*(5), 378–382.

Fredrikson, M., Jha, S., and Ristenpart, T. (2015). Model inversion attacks that exploit confidence information and basic countermeasures. In *Proceedings of the 22nd ACM SIGSAC Conference on Computer and Communications Security*, 1322–1333. Association for Computing Machinery.

Freund, Y., Iyer, R., Schapire, R. E., and Singer, Y. (2003). An efficient boosting algorithm for combining preferences. *Journal of Machine Learning Research, 4*, 933–969.

Friedman, J. H. (2001). Greedy function approximation: a gradient boosting machine. *Annals of Statistics, 29*(5), 1189–1232.

Fuernkranz, J., and Flach, P. A. (2005). Roc 'n' rule learning – towards a better understanding of covering algorithms. *Machine Learning, 58*(1), 39–77.

Gaber, M. M. (2012). Advances in data stream mining. *Wiley Interdisciplinary Reviews: Data Mining and Knowledge Discovery, 2*(1), 79–85.

Gama, J., Sebastião, R., and Rodrigues, P. P. (2013). On evaluating stream learning algorithms. *Machine Learning, 90*, 317–346.

García, S., and Herrera, F. (2008). An extension on "statistical comparisons of classifiers over multiple data sets" for all pairwise comparisons. *Journal of Machine Learning Research, 9*, 2677–2694.

Gardner, P., Lord, C., and Barthorpe, R. J. (2018). An evaluation of validation metrics for probabilistic model outputs. In *Proceedings of the ASME 2018 Verification and Validation Symposium*, VVS2018–9327. IEEE.

Garg, A., Zhang, W., Samaran, J., Savitha, R., and Foo, C.-S. (2021). An evaluation of anomaly detection and diagnosis in multivariate time series. *IEEE Transactions on Neural Networks and Learning Systems, 33*(6), 2508–2517.

Gaudette, L., and Japkowicz, N. (2009). Evaluation methods for ordinal classification. In *Proceedings of the 2009 Canadian Conference on Artificial Intelligence*, 207–210. Springer-Verlag.

Gautret, P., Lagier, J.-C., Parola, P. et al. (2020). Hydroxychloroquine and azithromycin as a treatment of COVID-19: results of an open-label non-randomized clinical trial. *International Journal of Antimicrobial Agents*, 56, 105949–105949.

Gelman, A., Carlin, J. B., Stern, H. S. et al. (2013). *Bayesian data analysis*. Chapman and Hall.

Ghosh, K., Bellinger, C., Corizzo, R. et al. (2022). The class imbalance problem in deep learning. *Machine Learning*, 1–57. https://doi.org/10.1007/s10994-022-06268-8

Gibaja, E. L., and Ventura, S. (2014). A tutorial on multi-label learning. *ACM Computing Surveys, 47*(3), 1–38.

Gill, J., and Meir, K. (1999). The insignificance of null hypothesis significance testing. *Political Research Quarterly, 52*, 647–674.

Goix, N. (2016). How to evaluate the quality of unsupervised anomaly detection algorithms? arXiv:abs/1607.01152.

Goldstein, M., and Uchida, S. (2016). A comparative evaluation of unsupervised anomaly detection algorithms for multivariate data. *PLoS ONE, 11*(4), e0152173.

Golub, T. R., Slonim, D. K., Tamayo, P. et al. (1999). Molecular classification of cancer: class discovery and class prediction by gene expression monitoring. *Science, 286*(5439), 531–537.

Gomes, H. M., Read, J., Bifet, A., Barddal, J. P., and Gama, J. (2019). Machine learning for streaming data: state of the art, challenges, and opportunities. *ACM SIGKDD Explorations Newsletter, 21*, 6–22.

Goodfellow, I., Pouget-Abadie, J., Mirza, M. et al. (2020). Generative adversarial networks. *Communications of the ACM, 63*(11), 139–144.

Gundersen, O. E., Shamsaliei, S., and Isdahl, R. J. (2022). Do machine learning platforms provide out-of-the-box reproducibility? *Future Generation Computer Systems, 126*, 34–47.

Guo, Q., Xie, X., Ma, L. et al. (2018). An orchestrated empirical study on deep learning frameworks and platforms. arXiv:abs/1811.05187.

Gutiérrez, P. A., Pérez-Ortiz, M., Sánchez-Monedero, J., Fernández-Navarro, F., and Hervás-Martínez, C. (2016). Ordinal regression methods: survey and experimental study. *IEEE Transactions on Knowledge and Data Engineering, 28*, 127–146.

Hackenberger, B. K. (2019). Bayes or not Bayes, is this the question? *Croatian Medical Journal, 60*(1), 50–52.

Halligan, S., Altman, D. G., and Mallett, S. (2014). Disadvantages of using the area under the receiver operating characteristic curve to assess imaging tests: a discussion and proposal for an alternative approach. *European Radiology, 25*, 932–939.

Hand, D. J. (2006). Classifier technology and the illusion of progress. *Statistical Science, 21*(1), 1–15.

Hand, D. J. (2009). Measuring classifier performance: a coherent alternative to the area under the ROC curve. *Machine Learning, 77*(1), 103–123.

Hand, D. J., and Till, R. J. (2001). A simple generalisation of the area under the ROC curve for multiple class classification problems. *Machine Learning, 45*, 171–186.

Hansen, L. K., and Rieger, L. (2019). Interpretability in intelligent systems - a new concept? In W. Samek, G. Montavon, A. Vedaldi, L. K. Hansen, and K.-R. Müller (eds.) *Explainable AI: Interpreting, Explaining and Visualizing Deep Learning*, 41–49. Springer.

Hardt, M., Price, E., and Srebro, N. (2016). Equality of opportunity in supervised learning. In D. D. Lee, U. von Luxburg, R. Garnett, M. Sugiyama, and I. Guyon (eds.) *Proceedings of the 30th International Conference on Neural Information Processing Systems*, 47. Curran Associates Inc.

Hastie, T., Tibshirani, R., and Friedman, J. (2001). *The elements of statistical learning: data mining, inference and prediction*. Springer-Verlag.

He, X., and Frey, E. C. (2008). The meaning and use of the volume under a three-class ROC surface (VUS). *IEEE Transactions in Medical Imaging, 27*(5), 577–588.

Herbrich, R. (2002). *Learning kernel classifiers*. MIT Press.

Hinton, P. (1995). *Statistics explained*. Routledge.

Ho, N., and Kim, Y.-C. (2021). Evaluation of transfer learning in deep convolutional neural network models for cardiac short axis slice classification. *Scientific Reports, 11*, 1839.

Hossin, M., and Sulaiman, M. N. (2015). A review on evaluation metrics for data classification evaluations. *International Journal of Data Mining & Knowledge Management Process, 5*, 1–11.

Howell, D. C. (2020). *Statistical methods for psychology*. 5th ed. Wadsworth Press.

Huang, J., and Ling, C. X. (2007). Constructing new and better evaluation measures for machine learning. In *Proceedings of the 20th International Joint Conference on Artifical Intelligence*, 859–864. Morgan Kaufmann.

Huang, J., Ling, C. X., Zhang, H., and Matwin, S. (2008). Proper model selection with significance test. In *Proceedings of the European Conference on Machine Learning*, 536–547.

Huang, Y., Li, W., Macheret, F., Gabriel, R. A., and Ohno-Machado, L. (2020). A tutorial on calibration measurements and calibration models for clinical prediction models. *Journal of the American Medical Informatics Association, 27*, 621–633.

Hulse, J. V., Khoshgoftaar, T. M., and Napolitano, A. (2009). An empirical comparison of repetitive undersampling techniques. In *2009 IEEE International Conference on Information Reuse & Integration*, 29–34. IEEE.

Hyndman, R. J., and Athanasopoulos, G. (2013). *Forecasting: principles and practice*. 3rd ed. OTexts. https://otexts.com/fpp3/

Japkowicz, N., Myers, C. E., and Gluck, M. A. (1995). A novelty detection approach to classification. In *Proceedings of the 14th International Joint Conference on Artificial Intelligence*, 518–523. IJCAI.

Japkowicz, N., Sanghi, P., and Tischer, P. (2008). A projection-based framework for classifier performance evaluation. In *Proceedings of the 2008 European Conference on Machine Learning and Knowledge Discovery in Databases – Part I*, 548–563. Springer-Verlag.

Japkowicz, N., and Shah, M. (2011). *Evaluating learning algorithms: a classification perspective*. Cambridge University Press.

Japkowicz, N., and Stephen, S. (2002). The class imbalance problem: a systematic study. *Intelligent Data Analysis, 6*(5), 429–450.

Johnson, J. M., and Khoshgoftaar, T. M. (2019). Survey on deep learning with class imbalance. *Journal of Big Data, 6*, 1–54.

Johnson, S. C. (1967). Hierarchical clustering schemes. *Psychometrika, 32*(3), 241–254.

Jordan, S. M., Chandak, Y., Cohen, D., Zhang, M., and Thomas, P. S. (2020). Evaluating the performance of reinforcement learning algorithms. arXiv:abs/2006.16958.

Kamiran, F., and Calders, T. (2012). Data preprocessing techniques for classification without discrimination. *Knowledge and Information Systems, 33*(1), 1–33.

Kapil, A. R. (2018). *Data vedas: an introduction to data science*. Archish Rai Kapil.

Kaur, D., Uslu, S., Rittichier, K. J., and Durresi, A. (2022). Trustworthy artificial intelligence: a review. *ACM Computing Surveys, 55*(2), 1–38.

Khan, S. S., and Madden, M. G. (2014). One-class classification: taxonomy of study and review of techniques. *The Knowledge Engineering Review, 29*, 345–374.

Kim, T., Eltoft, T., and Lee, T.-W. (2006). Independent vector analysis: an extension of ICA to multivariate components. In *International Conference on Independent Component Analysis and Signal Separation*, 165–172. Springer.

Kingma, D. P., and Welling, M. (2013). Auto-encoding variational Bayes. arXiv:1312.6114.

Kleiman, R., and Page, D. (2019). AUCμ: a performance metric for multi-class machine learning models. In *International Conference on Machine Learning*, 3439–3447. Proceedings of Machine Learning Research.

Klement, W., Flach, P. A., Japkowicz, N., and Matwin, S. (2011). Smooth receiver operating characteristics (smROC) curves. In *Proceedings of Machine Learning and Knowledge Discovery in Databases: European Conference*, Part II, 193–208. Springer.

Kohavi, R. (1995). A study of cross-validation and bootstrap for accuracy estimation and model selection. In *Proceedings of the 14th International Joint Conference on Artificial Intelligence*, 1137–1143. Morgan Kaufmann.

Koller, D., and Friedman, N. (2009). *Probabilistic graphical models: principles and techniques*. MIT Press.

Kononenko, I., and Bratko, I. (2004). Information-based evaluation criterion for classifier's performance. *Machine Learning, 6*: 67–80.

Korycki, Ł., and Krawczyk, B. (2021). Streaming decision trees for lifelong learning. In *Proceedings of Machine Learning and Knowledge Discovery in Databases. Research Track: European Conference*, Part I, 502–518. Springer.

Kovács, G. (2019). Smote-variants: a Python implementation of 85 minority oversampling techniques. *Neurocomputing, 366*, 352–354.

Krawczyk, B., Minku, L. L., Gama, J., Stefanowski, J., and Wozniak, M. (2017). Ensemble learning for data stream analysis: a survey. *Information Fusion, 37*, 132–156.

Krempl, G., Žliobaitė, I., Brzezinski, D. W. et al. (2014). Open challenges for data stream mining research. *ACM SIGKDD Explorations Newsletter, 16*, 1–10.

Kubat, M., Holte, R. C., and Matwin, S. (1998). Machine learning for the detection of oil spills in satellite radar images. *Machine Learning, 30*, 195–215.

Kukačka, J., Golkov, V., and Cremers, D. (2017). Regularization for deep learning: a taxonomy. arXiv:1710.10686.

Kukar, M., Kononenko, I., and Ljubljana, S. (2002). Reliable classifications with machine learning. In *Proceedings of the 13th European Conference on Machine Learning*, 219–231. Springer.

Kukar, M. Z., and Kononenko, I. (1998). Cost-sensitive learning with neural networks. In *Proceedings of the 13th European Conference on Artificial Intelligence*, 445–449. Wiley.

Kuncheva, L. I. (2014). *Combining pattern classifiers: methods and algorithms*, 2nd ed. Wiley.

Kuncheva, L. I., Whitaker, C. J., Shipp, C. A., and Duin, R. P. W. (2003). Limits on the majority vote accuracy in classifier fusion. *Pattern Analysis and Applications, 6*, 22–31.

Lachiche, N., and Flach, P. (2003). Improving accuracy and cost of two-class and multi-class probabilistic classifiers using ROC curves. In *Proceedings of the 20th International Conference on Machine Learning*, 416–423. AAAI Press.

Landgrebe, T., Pacl'ik, P., Tax, D. J. M., Verzakov, S., and Duin, R. P. W. (2004). Cost-based classifier evaluation for imbalanced problems. In *Proceedings of the 10th International Workshop on Structural and Syntactic Pattern Recognition and 5th International Workshop on Statistical Techniques in Pattern Recognition*, 762–770, vol. 3138 of Lecture Notes in Computer Science. Springer Verlag.

Lange, M. D., Aljundi, R., Masana, M. et al. (2022). A continual learning survey: defying forgetting in classification tasks. *IEEE Transactions on Pattern Analysis and Machine Intelligence*, 44, 3366–3385.

Lau, J. H., Newman, D., and Baldwin, T. (2014). Machine reading tea leaves: automatically evaluating topic coherence and topic model quality. In *Proceedings of the 14th Conference of the European Chapter of the Association for Computational Linguistics*, 530–539. Association for Computational Linguistics.

Lavesson, N., and Davidsson, P. (2008a). Generic methods for multi-criteria evaluation. In *Proceedings of the 8th SIAM International Conference on Data Mining*, 541–546. SIAM.

Lavesson, N., and Davidsson, P. (2008b). Towards application-specific evaluation metrics. In *Proceedings of the 3rd Workshop on Evaluation Methods for Machine Learning*. ICML.

Laviolette, F., Marchand, M., Shah, M., and Shanian, S. (2010). Learning the set covering machine by bound minimization and margin-sparsity trade-off. *Machine Learning*, 78(1–2), 275–301.

Lebanon, G., and Lafferty, J. D. (2002). Cranking: combining rankings using conditional probability models on permutations. In *Proceedings of the 19th International Conference on Machine Learning*, 363–370. Morgan Kaufmann.

Lee, K.-S., Jung, S.-K., Ryu, J.-J., Shin, S., and Choi, J. (2020). Evaluation of transfer learning with deep convolutional neural networks for screening osteoporosis in dental panoramic radiographs. *Journal of Clinical Medicine*, 9(2), 392.

Lee, N. T., Resnick, P., and Barton, G. (2019). Algorithmic bias detection and mitigation: best practices and policies to reduce consumer harms. *Brookings Institute Reports*. www.brookings.edu/articles/algorithmic-bias-detection-and-mitigation-best-practices-and-policies-to-reduce-consumer-harms/

Li, B., Qi, P., Liu, B. et al. (2023). Trustworthy AI: from principles to practices. *ACM Computing Surveys*, 55(9), 1–46.

Li, M., and Vitanyi, P. (1997). *An introduction to Kolmogorov complexity and its applications*. 2nd ed. Springer-Verlag.

Li, N., Li, T., and Venkatasubramanian, S. (2006). t-Closeness: privacy beyond k-anonymity and ℓ-diversity. In *23rd International Conference on Data Engineering*, 106–115. IEEE.

Li, Y., Chen, M.-H., Liu, Y., He, D., and Xu, Q. (2022). An empirical study on the efficacy of deep active learning for image classification. arXiv:abs/2212.03088.

Linardatos, P., Papastefanopoulos, V., and Kotsiantis, S. (2020). Explainable AI: a review of machine learning interpretability methods. *Entropy*, 23(1), 18.

Lindley, D., and Scott, W. (1984). *New Cambridge statistical tables*, 2nd ed. Cambridge University Press.

Lindquist, E. F. (1940). *Statistical analysis in educational research*. Houghton Mifflin.

Ling, C. X., Huang, J., and Zhang, H. (2003). AUC: a statistically consistent and more discriminating measure than accuracy. In *Proceedings of the 18th International Joint Conference on Artificial Intelligence*, 519–526. IJCAI.

Liu, W., Li, R., Zheng, M. et al. (2020). Towards visually explaining variational autoencoders. In *Proceedings of the IEEE/CVF Conference on Computer Vision and Pattern Recognition*, 8642–8651. IEEE.

Liu, X. Y., and Zhou, Z. H. (2006). Training cost-sensitive neural networks with methods addressing the class imbalance problem. *IEEE Transactions on Knowledge and Data Engineering*, *18*(1), 63–77. IEEE.

Loh, W.-Y. (2011). Classification and regression trees. *Wiley Interdisciplinary Reviews: Data Mining and Knowledge Discovery*, *1*(1), 14–23.

Long, Q., Bhinge, S., Levin-Schwartz, Y. et al. (2019). The role of diversity in data-driven analysis of multi-subject fMRI data: comparison of approaches based on independence and sparsity using global performance metrics. *Human Brain Mapping*, *40*(2), 489–504.

Long, Q., Jia, C., Boukouvalas, Z. et al. (2018). Consistent run selection for independent component analysis: application to fMRI analysis. In *IEEE International Conference on Acoustics, Speech and Signal Processing*, 2581–2585. IEEE.

Lundberg, S. M., and Lee, S.-I. (2017). A unified approach to interpreting model predictions. In *Proceedings of the 31st Conference on Neural Information Processing Systems*. Curran Associates. https://proceedings.neurips.cc/paper_files/paper/2017/file/8a20a8621978632d76c43dfd28b67767-Paper.pdf

Luque, A., Carrasco, A., Martín, A., and de las Heras, A. (2019). The impact of class imbalance in classification performance metrics based on the binary confusion matrix. *Pattern Recognition*, *91*, 216–231.

Lydersen, S. (2019). Statistical power: before, but not after! *Tidsskr Nor Laegeforen*, 139 (2), 10.4045/tidsskr.18.0847. doi:10.4045/tidsskr.18.0847.

Machanavajjhala, A., Kifer, D., Gehrke, J., and Venkitasubramaniam, M. (2007). ℓ-diversity: privacy beyond k-anonymity. *ACM Transactions on Knowledge Discovery from Data (TKDD)*, *1*(1), 3–es.

MacQueen, J. (1967). Classification and analysis of multivariate observations. In *5th Berkeley Symposium of Mathematics, Statistics, and Probability*, 281–297. De Gruyter.

Macskassy, S. A., Provost, F., and Rosset, S. (2005). Pointwise ROC confidence bounds: an empirical evaluation. In *Proceedings of the Workshop on ROC Analysis in Machine Learning*, 537–544. Association for Computing Machinery.

Makhlouf, K., Zhioua, S., and Palamidessi, C. (2021). Machine learning fairness notions: bridging the gap with real-world applications. *Information Processing & Management*, *58*, 102642.

Marchand, M., and Shawe-Taylor, J. (2002). The set covering machine. *Journal of Machine Learning Research*, *3*, 723–746.

Mehrabi, N., Morstatter, F., Saxena, N. A., Lerman, K., and Galstyan, A. G. (2021). A survey on bias and fairness in machine learning. *ACM Computing Surveys*, *54*, 1–35.

Melnik, O., Vardi, Y., and Zhang, C. (2004). Mixed group ranks: preference and confidence in classifier combination. *IEEE Transactions on Pattern Analysis and Machine Intelligence*, *26*, 973–981. IEEE.

Merkle, E. C., and Steyvers, M. (2013). Choosing a strictly proper scoring rule. *Decision Analysis*, *10*, 292–304.

Midway, S. R., Robertson, M., Flinn, S., and Kaller, M. D. (2020). Comparing multiple comparisons: practical guidance for choosing the best multiple comparisons test. *PeerJ*, *8*, e10387.

Minaee, S., Boykov, Y., Porikli, F. M. et al. (2022). Image segmentation using deep learning: a survey. *IEEE Transactions on Pattern Analysis and Machine Intelligence*, *44*, 3523–3542. IEEE.

Mitchell, T. M. (1997). *Machine learning*. McGraw-Hill.

Moroney, C., Crothers, E., Mittal, S. et al. (2021). The case for latent variable vs deep learning methods in misinformation detection: an application to COVID-19. In *24th International Conference on Discovery Science*, 422–432. Springer.

Müller, V. C. (2020). Ethics of artificial intelligence and robotics. In E. N. Zalta and U. Nodelman (eds.) *The Stanford Encyclopedia of Philosophy*. Fall 2023 ed. Stanford University.

Munjal, P., Hayat, N., Hayat, M., Sourati, J., and Khan, S. (2020). Towards robust and reproducible active learning using neural networks. In *IEEE/CVF Conference on Computer Vision and Pattern Recognition*, 223–232. IEEE.

Murphy, C., Kaiser, G. E., and Arias, M. (2007). An approach to software testing of machine learning applications. In *Proceedings of the International Conference on Software Engineering and Knowledge Engineering*, 167. Knowledge Systems Institute Graduate School.

Murphy, C., Kaiser, G. E., Hu, L., and Wu, L. L. (2008). Properties of machine learning applications for use in metamorphic testing. In *Proceedings of the International Conference on Software Engineering and Knowledge Engineering*, 867–872. Knowledge Systems Institute Graduate School.

Murtagh, F., and Contreras, P. (2012). Algorithms for hierarchical clustering: an overview. *Wiley Interdisciplinary Reviews: Data Mining and Knowledge Discovery*, 2. https://api .semanticscholar.org/CorpusID:18990050

Murtagh, F., and Contreras, P. (2017). Algorithms for hierarchical clustering: an overview, II. *Wiley Interdisciplinary Reviews: Data Mining and Knowledge Discovery*, 7. https:// api.semanticscholar.org/CorpusID:38660367

Murua, A. (2002). Upper bounds for error rates of linear combinations of classifiers. *IEEE Transactions on Pattern Analysis and Machine Intelligence*, 24(5), 591–602.

Nadeau, C., and Bengio, Y. (2003). Inference for the generalization error. *Machine Learning*, 52(3), 239–281.

Nakhaeizadeh, G., and Schnabl, A. (1997). Development of multi-criteria metrics for evaluation of data mining algorithms. In *Proceedings of KDD97 Conference*, 37–42. AAAI Press.

Nakhaeizadeh, G., and Schnabl, A. (1998). Towards the personalization of algorithms evaluation in data mining. In *Proceedings of KDD98 Conference*, 289–293. AAAI Press.

Narasimhamurthy, A. M. (2005). Theoretical bounds of majority voting performance for a binary classification problem. *IEEE Transactions on Pattern Analysis and Machine Intelligence*, 27(12), 1988–1995.

New, A., Baker, M. M., Nguyen, E. Q., and Vallabha, G. (2022). Lifelong learning metrics. arXiv:abs/2201.08278.

Neyman, J., and Pearson, E. S. (1928). On the use and interpretation of certain test criteria for purposes of statistical inference. Part I. *Biometrika 20A* (1/2), 175–240.

Niculescu-Mizil, A., and Caruana, R. (2005). Predicting good probabilities with supervised learning. In *Proceedings of the 22nd International Conference on Machine Learning*, 625–632. Association for Computing Machinery.

Nixon, J., Dusenberry, M. W., Zhang, L., Jerfel, G., and Tran, D. (2019). Measuring calibration in deep learning. arXiv:abs/1904.01685.

Ntoutsi, E., Fafalios, P., Gadiraju, U. et al. (2020). Bias in data-driven artificial intelligence systems—an introductory survey. *Wiley Interdisciplinary Reviews: Data Mining and Knowledge Discovery*, 10(3), e1356.

Nuzzo, R. (2014). Statistical errors. *Nature*, 506(7487), 150.

O'Brien, D. B., Gupta, M. R., and Gray, R. M. (2008). Cost-sensitive multi-class classification from probability estimates. In *Proceedings of the 25th International Conference on Machine Learning*, 712–719. Association for Computing Machinery.

Oliver, A., Odena, A., Raffel, C., Cubuk, E. D., and Goodfellow, I. J. (2018). Realistic evaluation of deep semi-supervised learning algorithms. In *Proceedings of the 32nd Conference on Neural Information Processing Systems*. Curran Associates.

Pang, G., Shen, C., Cao, L., and van den Hengel, A. (2021). Deep learning for anomaly detection. *ACM Computing Surveys*, *54*, 1–38.

Pearson, E. S., and Hartley, H.O., eds. (1970). *Biometrika tables for statisticians*. Vol 1. 3rd ed. Cambridge University Press.

Perera, P., Oza, P., and Patel, V. M. (2021). One-class classification: a survey. arXiv:abs/2101.03064.

Perezgonzalez, J. D. (2015). Fisher, Neyman–Pearson or NHST? A tutorial for teaching data testing. *Frontiers in Psychology*, *6*, 233.

Petsche, T., Marcantonio, A., Darken, C. J. et al. (1995). A neural network autoassociator for induction motor failure prediction. In *Proceedings of NIPS Advances in Neural Information Processing Systems*. MIT Press.

Piano, S. L. (2020). Ethical principles in machine learning and artificial intelligence: cases from the field and possible ways forward. *Humanities and Social Sciences Communications*, *7*, 1–7.

Pimentel, M. A. F., Clifton, D. A., Clifton, L. A., and Tarassenko, L. (2014). A review of novelty detection. *Signal Processing*, *99*, 215–249.

Platt, J. (1999). Probabilistic outputs for support vector machines and comparisons to regularized likelihood methods. *Advances in Large Margin Classifiers*, *10*(3), 61–74.

Poole, D. L., and Mackworth, A. K. (2017). *Artificial intelligence – foundations of computational agents*. 2nd ed. Cambridge University Press.

Prokopalo, Y., Meignier, S., Galibert, O., Barrault, L., and Larcher, A. (2020). Evaluation of lifelong learning systems. In *Proceedings of the Twelfth Language Resources and Evaluation Conference*, 1833–1841. European Language Resources Association.

Provost, F., and Domingos, P. (2003). Tree induction for probability-based ranking. *Machine Learning*, *52*(3), 199–215.

Puerto, M., Kellett, M., Nikopoulou, R. et al. (2022). Assessing the trade-off between prediction accuracy and interpretability for topic modeling on energetic materials corpora. arXiv:2206.00773.

Rashka, S. (2014). cochrans$_q$: Cochran's Q test for comparing multiple classifiers. https://rasbt.github.io/mlxtend/user_guide/evaluate/cochrans_q/

Reich, Y., and Barai, S. V. (1999). Evaluating machine learning models for engineering problems. *Artificial Intelligence in Engineering*, *13*(3), 257–272.

Ren, P., Xiao, Y., Chang, X. et al. (2020). A survey of deep active learning. *ACM Computing Surveys*, *54*, 1–40.

Ribeiro, M. T., Singh, S., and Guestrin, C. (2016). "Why should I trust you?" explaining the predictions of any classifier. In *Proceedings of the 22nd ACM SIGKDD International Conference on Knowledge Discovery and Data Mining*, 1135–1144. Association for Computing Machinery.

Rigaki, M., and Garcia, S. (2020). A survey of privacy attacks in machine learning. arXiv:2007.07646.

Roberts, C. (2017). How to unit test machine learning code. *Medium, Blog*. https://thenerdstation.medium.com/how-to-unit-test-machine-learning-code-57cf6fd81765

Rodriguez, M. Z., Comin, C. H., Casanova, D. et al. (2019). Clustering algorithms: a comparative approach. *PLoS ONE*, *14*(1): e0210236.

Rodríguez, N. D., Lomonaco, V., Filliat, D., and Maltoni, D. (2018). Don't forget, there is more than forgetting: new metrics for continual learning. arXiv, abs/1810.13166.

Roh, Y., Heo, G., and Whang, S. E. (2021). A survey on data collection for machine learning: a big data - AI integration perspective. *IEEE Transactions on Knowledge and Data Engineering*, *33*, 1328–1347.

Rosset, S. (2004). Model selection via the AUC. In *Proceedings of the Twenty-First International Conference on Machine Learning*, 89. Association for Computing Machinery.

Saito, T., and Rehmsmeier, M. (2015). The precision-recall plot is more informative than the ROC plot when evaluating binary classifiers on imbalanced datasets. *PLoS ONE*, *10*(3): e0118432.

Salzberg, S. L. (1997). On comparing classifiers: pitfalls to avoid and a recommeded approach. *Data Mining and Knowledge Discovery*, *1*, 317–327.

Santos-Rodríguez, R., Guerrero-Curieses, A., Alaiz-Rodríguez, R., and Cid-Sueiro, J. (2009). Cost-sensitive learning based on Bregman divergences. *Machine Learning*, *76*(2–3), 271–285.

Saunders, J. D., and Freitas, A. A. (2022). Evaluating the predictive performance of positive-unlabelled classifiers: a brief critical review and practical recommendations for improvement. arXiv:abs/2206.02423.

Schölkopf, B., Williamson, R. C., Smola, A., Shawe-Taylor, J., and Platt, J. C. (1999). Support vector method for novelty detection. In *Proceedings of NIPS Advances in Neural Information Processing Systems*. MIT Press.

Schubert, E., Wojdanowski, R., Zimek, A., and Kriegel, H.-P. (2012). On evaluation of outlier rankings and outlier scores. In *Proceedings of the 2012 SIAM International Conference on Data Mining*, 1047–1058. SIAM.

Scott, W. A. (1955). Reliability of content analysis: the case of nominal scale coding. *Public Opinion Q*, *19*, 321–325.

Scudder, H. J. (1965). Probability of error of some adaptive pattern-recognition machines. *IEEE Transactions in Information Theory*, *11*, 363–371.

Serdar, C. C., Cihan, M., Yücel, D., and Serdar, M. A. (2021). Sample size, power and effect size revisited: simplified and practical approaches in pre-clinical, clinical and laboratory studies. *Biochemia Medica*, *31*(1), 27–53.

Settles, B. (2009). Active learning literature survey. Technical Report. University of Wisconsin.

Shah, M. (2006). Sample compression, margins and generalization: extensions to the set covering machine. Ph.D. thesis. University of Ottawa, Canada.

Shokri, R., and Shmatikov, V. (2015). Privacy-preserving deep learning. In *Proceedings of the 22nd ACM SIGSAC Conference on Computer and Communications Security*, 1310–1321. Association for Computing Machinery.

Shorten, C., and Khoshgoftaar, T. M. (2019). A survey on image data augmentation for deep learning. *Journal of Big Data*, *6*, 1–48.

Singh, A. (2022). A hands-on introduction to time series classification (with Python code). *Analytics Vidhya*. www.analyticsvidhya.com/blog/2019/01/introduction-time-series-classification/

Soares, C., Costa, J., and Bradzil, P. (2000). A simple and intuitive measure for multicriteria evaluation of classification algorithms. In *Proceedings of the ECML'2000 Workshop on Meta-Learning: Building Automatic Advice Strategies for Model Selection and Method Combination*, 87–96.

Sokolova, M., Japkowicz, N., and Szpakowicz, S. (2006). Beyond accuracy, F-score and ROC: a family of discriminant measures for performance evaluation. In *Proceedings of the 2006 Australian Conference on Artificial Intelligence*, 1015–1021. Springer.

Sokolova, M., and Lapalme, G. (2009). A systematic analysis of performance measures for classification tasks. *Information Processing & Management*, *45*(4), 427–437.

Song, L., and Mittal, P. (2021). Systematic evaluation of privacy risks of machine learning models. arXiv:2003.10595.

Sorower, M. S. (2010). A literature survey on algorithms for multi-label learning. *Oregon State University, Corvallis*, *18*(1), 25.

Stapor, K., Ksieniewicz, P., García, S., and Wozniak, M. (2021). How to design the fair experimental classifier evaluation. *Applied Soft Computing*, *104*, 107219.

StatSoft (2006). *Electronic Statistics Textbook.* www.researchgate.net/publication/ 50927580_The_Electronic_Statistics_Textbook

Sun, X., Zhou, T., Li, G. et al. (2017). An empirical study on real bugs for machine learning programs. In *24th Asia-Pacific Software Engineering Conference*, 348–357. IEEE.

Sweeney, L. (2002). *k*-Anonymity: a model for protecting privacy. *International Journal of Uncertainty, Fuzziness and Knowledge-Based Systems*, *10*(05), 557–570.

Sydell, L. (2016). It ain't me, babe: researchers find flaws in police facial recognition technology. NPR. www.npr.org/sections/alltechconsidered/2016/10/25/499176469/it-aint-me-babe-researchers-find-flaws-in-police-facial-recognition

Szegedy, C., Zaremba, W., Sutskever, I. et al. (2014). Intriguing properties of neural networks. arXiv: 1312.6199.

Tax, D. M. J., and Duin, R. P. W. (2004). Support vector data description. *Machine Learning*, *54*, 45–66.

Tevet, G., Habib, G., Shwartz, V., and Berant, J. (2018). Evaluating text GANs as language models. arXiv:1810.12686.

Tipping, M. E., and Bishop, C. M. (1999). Probabilistic principal component analysis. *Journal of the Royal Statistical Society: Series B*, *61*(3), 611–622.

Tomczak, M., and Tomczak, E. (2014). The need to report effect size estimates revisited. An overview of some recommended measures of effect size. *Trends in Sport Sciences*, *1*(21), 19–25.

Vaicenavicius, J., Widmann, D., Andersson, C. R. et al. (2019). Evaluating model calibration in classification. In *Proceedings of the 22nd International Conference on Artificial Intelligence and Statistics*, 3459–3467. Proceedings of Machine Learning Research.

van Engelen, J. E., and Hoos, H. H. (2019). A survey on semi-supervised learning. *Machine Learning*, *109*, 373–440.

Vanderlooy, S., and Hüllermeier, E. (2008). A critical analysis of variants of the AUC. *Machine Learning*, *72*(3), 247–262.

Weiss, S. M., and Kulikowski, C. A. (1991). *Computer systems that learn: classification and prediction methods from statistics, neural nets, machine learning and expert systems*. Morgan Kaufmann.

Wood, M. (2005). Bootstrapped confidence intervals as an approach to statistical inference. *Organizational Research Methods*, *8*, 454–470.

Wu, S., Flach, P. A., and Ferri, C. (2007). An improved model selection heuristic for AUC. In *18th European Conference on Machine Learning*, vol. 4701, 478–487. Springer.

Xiao, Q., Li, K., Zhang, D., and Xu, W. (2018). Security risks in deep learning implementations. In *2018 IEEE Security and Privacy Workshops*, 123–128. IEEE.

Yan, L., Dodier, R., Mozer, M. C., and Wolniewicz, R. (2003). Optimizing classifier performance via the Wilcoxon–Mann–Whitney statistic. In *Proceedings of the International Conference on Machine Learning*, 848–855. AAAI Press.

Yao, Y. (1995). Measuring retrieval effectiveness based on user preference of documents. *Journal of the American Society for Information Science*, *46*(2), 133–145.

Yousef, W. A., Wagner, R. F., and Loew, M. H. (2005). Estimating the uncertainty in the estimated mean area under the ROC curve of a classifier. *Pattern Recognition Letters*, *26*, 2600–2610.

Yousef, W. A., Wagner, R. F., and Loew, M. H. (2006). Assessing classifiers from two independent data sets using ROC analysis: a nonparametric approach. *IEEE Transactions on Pattern Analysis and Machine Intelligence*, *28*(11), 1809–1817.

Yuheng, S., and Hao, Y. (2017). Image segmentation algorithms overview. arXiv:abs/1707.02051.

Zadrozny, B., and Elkan, C. (2001). Obtaining calibrated probability estimates from decision trees and naive Bayesian classifiers. In *Proceedings of the 18th International Conference on Machine Learning*, 609–616. Morgan Kaufmann.

Zadrozny, B., and Elkan, C. (2002). Transforming classifier scores into accurate multiclass probability estimates. In *Proceedings of the 8th ACM SIGKDD International Conference on Knowledge Discovery and Data Mining*, 694–699. Association for Computing Machinery.

Zadrozny, B., Langford, J., and Abe, N. (2003). Cost-sensitive learning by cost-proportionate example weighting. In *Proceedings of the 3rd IEEE International Conference on Data Mining*, p. 435–442. IEEE.

Zaiontz, C. (2023). Real statistics using Excel. https://real-statistics.com/

Zeiler, M. D., and Fergus, R. (2014). Visualizing and understanding convolutional networks. In D. Fleet, T. Pajdla, B. Schiele, and T. Tuytelaars (eds.) *Computer Vision. ECCV 2014*, vol. 8689 of Lecture Notes in Computer Science, 818–833. Springer.

Zhang, Y.-J. (1996). A survey on evaluation methods for image segmentation. *Pattern Recognition, 29*(8), 1335–1346.

Zhang, H., Fritts, J. E., and Goldman, S. A. (2008). Image segmentation evaluation: a survey of unsupervised methods. *Computer Vision and Image Understanding, 110*(2), 260–280.

Zhang, J., Harman, M., Ma, L., and Liu, Y. (2022). Machine learning testing: survey, landscapes and horizons. *IEEE Transactions on Software Engineering*, *48*, 1–36.

Zhang, M.-L., and Zhou, Z.-H. (2014). A review on multi-label learning algorithms. *IEEE Transactions on Knowledge and Data Engineering*, *26*, 1819–1837.

Zhang, Y., Kang, B., Hooi, B., Yan, S., and Feng, J. (2023). Deep long-tailed learning: a survey. *IEEE Transactions on Pattern Analysis and Machine Intelligence, 45*(9), 10795–10816.

Zhao, S., Song, J., and Ermon, S. (2017). InfoVAE: information maximizing variational autoencoders. arXiv:1706.02262.

Zhou, J., Gandomi, A. H., Chen, F., and Holzinger, A. (2021). Evaluating the quality of machine learning explanations: a survey on methods and metrics. *Electronics*, *10*(5), 1–19.

Zhu, X. (2005). Semi-supervised learning literature survey. Technical Report 1530. University of Wisconsin, Madison.

Index

error bounds, 50, 152
generated
  images, 277–281
  samples, 273, 277, 279–280, 282–283
  text, 235, 238–239, 284–285, 354
generator, 43, 272–273, 279–280
geometric mean (*G*-Mean), 80, 98, 104–106, 127, 373, 381
Grad-CAM visualization technique, 321–322

Hamming loss (HL), 226
Hamming score (HS), 226–228
Harabasz index, 253–255
HDIs, 165, 203–205
  HDI graphs, 204
heatmaps, 271, 321–322
holdout, 6, 128, 141–143, 242–243
  estimate, 132–133
  method, 72, 74, 128–131, 134, 136, 142, 177, 242–244
human-centric
  evaluation, 238
  machine learning, 7, 334
human-centric evaluation, 238
hypothesis, 6, 8, 21, 25–28, 75, 143, 149, 160–161, 175, 179–180, 183
hypothesis test, 25, 27–29, 31, 172, 361
  multiple, 184–186
  statistical, 22–28, 169

image
  classification, 234, 251, 336–337
  generation, 272, 279
  segmentation, 5, 7, 41, 79, 211, 213, 233–235
industrial strength evaluation, 5, 79, 290–306, 353
information, mutual, 253, 256, 261–262
interpolation, 276
interpretability and explainability, 85, 260, 294, 299, 308, 312–313, 318, 323–324, 335
  interpretable results, 323–327
  interpretation, 22, 25, 123, 194, 197, 258–259, 320, 323–324, 326–327, 338, 346
  interpretations and measures of fairness, 298
isomap, 42, 263
isometrics, 121

Jaccard index, 234–235, 256–258

Kendall's W test value, 168
k-fold cross-validation, 6, 72–73, 122, 128, 137–143, 148, 151–152, 170–171, 175–176, 270, 351
  classical, 141

label-based metrics, 225, 228–229
label generation process, 12, 94–95

language models, 235, 283–284
latent variable modeling, 6–7, 33, 41–42, 252, 266–270, 272
  latent variables, 42–43, 267, 270–273, 275
leave-one-out, 73–74, 128–129, 137–139, 141–142, 151
lifelong learning, 7, 80, 211–213, 244–247
  metrics, 247
  systems, 244–247
lift charts, 125
likelihood, 24, 109, 203, 269, 271
  likelihood-based measures, 267
  likelihood ratios, 98, 106–109, 111, 269
  likelihood-ratio test, 269–270
linear models, 42, 323–324
local interpretable model-agnostic explanations (LIME), 299, 315–316, 318, 320
log-likelihood, 268–270, 272, 274–275
log loss, 87, 110, 114–116
longest common subsequence (LCS), 285
long tail distributions, 110
loss, zero-one, 37, 47–48, 83, 130, 135
loss function, 6, 15, 33, 36–38, 44–47, 49, 134, 153, 244, 274–275, 282
  arbitrary, 44–46

machine learning deployment, xvi, 302–303, 353–355
macro-average, 65–66
McNemar's test, 168–169, 171, 177–180
mean absolute error (MAE), 66–68, 222–223, 231, 233, 241
mean absolute percentage error (MAPE), 241
mean opinion score (MOS), 282–283
mean squared error (MSE), 67–68, 75, 115, 222–223, 230–231, 233, 270, 273
micro, 6, 225, 228–229
misclassification costs, 91, 93, 97, 110–112, 374
  incorporating, 112
  unequal, 91
mitigating data bias, 309
MLOps, 305–306
model
  deployment, 305–306
  interpretable, 268, 312–313, 315–316
  selection, 38–39, 48–50, 63, 130, 135–136, 142–143, 152, 268, 374–375
  selection criterion, 39, 50
  selection process, 50, 134, 136
  visualization, 312
multi-class classification, 51, 65–66, 85, 92, 115, 122, 124, 140, 211, 346
multi-class focus, 85–86, 90–91, 93, 95, 97
multi-criteria
  evaluation, 383
  metrics, 87, 381–382
multi-label classification, 211–212, 223–225, 227, 229
multiple resampling, 128, 144–145, 147, 149–150

Printed in the United States
by Baker & Taylor Publisher Services